Sexual Revolution in Early America

Gender Relations in the American Experience
Joan E. Cashin and Ronald G. Walters, Series Editors

Sexual Revolution in Early America

RICHARD GODBEER

The Johns Hopkins University Press
Baltimore and London

© 2002 The Johns Hopkins University Press
All rights reserved. Published 2002
Printed in the United States of America on acid-free paper
2 4 6 8 9 7 5 3 1

The Johns Hopkins University Press
2715 North Charles Street
Baltimore, Maryland 21218-4363
www.press.jhu.edu

Library of Congress Cataloging-in-Publication Data
Godbeer, Richard.
Sexual revolution in early America / Richard Godbeer.
p. cm.—(Gender relations in the American experience)
Includes bibliographical references (p.) and index.
ISBN 0-8018-6800-9 (hardcover : alk. paper)
1. Sex customs—United States—History.   2. United States—
Social life and customs—To 1775.   3. Sex role—United States—History.
4. Sex customs—North America—History.   I. Title.
HQ18.U5 G585   2002
306.7′0973—dc21
2001002304

A catalog record for this book is available from the British Library.

For
Ann Coghlan
Jean Hood
and
Elfrida Green

Contents

CONTENTS

Acknowledgments

It might be tempting to envisage working on a book like this as a solitary enterprise, yet nothing could be further from the truth. My visits to archival collections have left me indebted to many curators and librarians whose expertise and good cheer ensured that my research was both productive and pleasant. I am grateful to the staff of the Massachusetts Historical Society; the Massachusetts State Archives; the American Antiquarian Society; the New England Historical and Genealogical Society; the Boston Public Library; the Essex Institute; the Andover Historical Society; the Andover-Newton Theological School; the Connecticut State Library; the Pennsylvania State Archives; the Historical Society of Pennsylvania; the City and County Archives of Philadelphia; the Library Company of Philadelphia; the American Philosophical Society; the Virginia State Library; Alderman Library at the University of Virginia; the Research Department of the Colonial Williamsburg Foundation; the Hall of Records in Annapolis, Maryland; the North Carolina State Archives; the Southern Historical Collection at the University of North Carolina, Chapel Hill; the Special Collections Library at Duke University; the Friends Historical Collection at Guilford College; the South Carolina Historical Society; the South Carolina State Archives; the South Caroliniana Library; the Huntington Library; the James Ford Bell Library at the University of Minnesota; the Public Records Office in London; Rhodes House Library in Oxford; and the Lincoln County Record Office for their kind assistance. My thanks go to Patricia Bonomi, Trevor Burnard, Cornelia Hughes Dayton, Gregory Dowd, Mary Fissell, Christine Heyrman, Susan Juster, Jeffrey Kahan, Alan Karras, Annette Laing, James LeShana, Kenneth Lockridge, Debra O'Neal, Christopher Ontiveros, Ann Plane, Elizabeth Reis, Erik Seeman, William Schmechel, Todd Shacklett, and Alfred Young for their generosity in sharing material and providing numerous citations. I am especially indebted to my research assistant, Keith Pacholl, who shared the onerous task of reading eighteenth-century newspapers and magazines, and to the Interlibrary

Loan staff of Tomas Rivera Library at the University of California, Riverside, for the enthusiasm and speed with which they tracked down many of the printed sources used in this book.

My research was made possible by a National Endowment for the Humanities Travel to Collections Grant, two research grants from the American Philosophical Society, an Archie K. Davis Fellowship from the North Caroliniana Society, an Andrew W. Mellon Foundation Fellowship from the Huntington Library, and funding from the Academic Senate at the University of California, Riverside, over a period of several years. A Resident Faculty Fellowship at UCR's Center for Ideas and Society provided time and a stimulating intellectual environment in which to work on portions of a first draft. A University of California President's Research Fellowship in the Humanities gave me an invaluable year of leave, during which I finished the manuscript.

I am grateful for permission to include in this book passages from previously published essays, now much revised. Material included in chapters 1, 2, and 3 first appeared in "The Cry of Sodom: Discourse, Intercourse, and Desire in Colonial New England," *William and Mary Quarterly*, 3d ser., 52 (1995): 259–86; and in "Love Raptures: Marital, Romantic, and Erotic Images of Jesus Christ in Puritan New England, 1670–1730," *New England Quarterly* 68 (1995): 355–84. Chapters 5 and 6 incorporate reworked portions of "Eroticizing the Middle Ground: Anglo-Indian Sexual Relations along the Eighteenth-Century Frontier," published in Martha Hodes, ed., *Sex, Love, Race: Crossing Boundaries in North American History* (New York, 1999), 91–111; and "William Byrd's 'Flourish': The Sexual Cosmos of a Southern Planter," published in Merril D. Smith, ed., *Sex and Sexuality in Early America* (New York, 1998), 135–62.

I count myself fortunate in having been able to draw on an impressive new body of scholarship that examines family life, gender relations, and sexual mores in early America. That growing literature has inspired and undergirded this book. I am especially indebted to sophisticated and provocative studies by Kathleen M. Brown, Cornelia Hughes Dayton, Mary Beth Norton, and Laurel Thatcher Ulrich that analyze sexual relations in the context of gendered hierarchies. Recent essay collections and many other articles cited in the endnotes to this book, Roger Thompson's pioneering study of Essex County, Massachusetts, and outstanding dissertations by emerging scholars such as Sharon Block, Kirsten Fischer, Thomas Foster, and Clare Lyons have provided a stimulating and ever-expanding context for my own work. More than fifty years ago, Edmund Morgan showed how enlightening it can be to examine the links, constructive as well as constricting, between sex and religious faith; those of us who follow in his footsteps can only hope to emulate the insightful humanity of his work.

I appreciate having had the opportunity to give papers relating to this project at conferences, seminars, and workshops where commentators and audience members asked supportive and yet challenging questions that have spurred me onward. In particular, I would like to thank participants in discussions sponsored by the Johns Hopkins University; the Columbia Seminar in New York; the Bay Area Seminar in Early American History and Culture; the Early America Seminar at the University of California, Santa Barbara; the Early American Seminar at the Huntington Library; and sessions at annual meetings of the Organization of American Historians and the American Studies Association. I owe a special debt of thanks to my fellow fellows at the Center for Ideas and Society—Carole Fabricant, Lora Geriguis, George Haggerty, Stephanie Hammer, John Jordan, Ashley Stockstill, and Linda Tomko—for a series of lively, often hilarious, and always constructive conversations that helped me to think about my material in new ways. At Johns Hopkins University Press, Bob Brugger's steadfast faith in this project over the past several years has been much appreciated; copy editor Lois Crum and the production team at the press have steered the book toward publication with tact and cheerful efficiency.

A long list of colleagues and friends have read and commented on portions of the book at various stages of its development. I am especially grateful to Gene Anderson, Myra Appel, Patricia Bonomi, Francis Bremer, B. R. Burg, Andrew Cooper, Emory Elliott, Joan Gunderson, Bert Hansen, Jennifer Hildebrand, Martha Hodes, Susan Juster, Jane Kamensky, Alan Karras, Michael McGiffert, John Murrin, Christopher Ontiveros, Keith Pacholl, Linda Smith Rhoads, Merril Smith, Alan Taylor, and Roger Thompson for their many suggestions and encouragement. Several stalwart friends read the entire manuscript. Thomas Foster and Wendy Lucas provided invaluable comments and helped to clarify many of my arguments. Ann Plane and Alfred Young not only offered innumerable specific insights that reflected their careful and astute reading of the manuscript but also proved instrumental in the evolution of the book's overarching thesis and structure. Whatever its remaining weaknesses, this volume is immeasurably stronger than it would have been without their wise and generous counsel. But my greatest debt is to Christine Heyrman, my erstwhile dissertation adviser. Over the past decade, she has engineered a graceful transition through which she has become a treasured colleague and close friend while remaining a sage and trusted mentor. Her incisive wit, unerring judgment, and sensitivity to the nuances of human motivation have sustained and enriched this project in countless ways. Christine's friendship and support are extraordinary gifts; I can only hope that she realizes how much they mean to me.

As I reach the end of this project, it is a genuine pleasure to thank those many other friends and colleagues who have supported me throughout, listening with patience and good humor as I recounted my latest finds and reminding me (for the most part, tactfully) of a world beyond that evoked in this book. Piotr, Andrew, Sonya, Mary, and Christopher have, in particular, sustained me with a generous love that I find truly humbling. And my family has, as always, provided an emotional bedrock that I hope I will never take for granted.

Finally, I would like to acknowledge three remarkable women who are without any doubt responsible for my having become a cultural historian. Each taught me for several years at my high school in Cirencester, a little town at the heart of the English Cotswolds. Ann Coghlan took my interest in history and turned it into a lifelong passion. Jean Hood, my Latin teacher, reinforced that passion, encouraged me to start thinking about the meaning of culture, and provided an unforgettable model of irreverence. As did Elfrida Green, my English literature teacher, who also inspired my interest in the ways that we use language to communicate our assumptions and values. Elfrida later became a close and dear friend who could always be relied upon as a source of encouragement, wide-ranging conversation, and much hilarity. As the years pass by, I realize ever more clearly how much I owe to these three formative figures. It is with profound gratitude that I dedicate this book to them.

Sexual Revolution in Early America

Introduction

Sex, Marriage, and Moral Order
in Early America

THE YEAR IS 1604, and England is about to establish a colonial presence in North America. Three years from now, the Virginia Company
will found Jamestown, the first permanent English settlement across the
Atlantic. In 1620 the Mayflower will disgorge its cargo of Puritans onto
the shore at Plymouth Plantation. For each of England's North American
colonies, sexual morality will become a conspicuous and controversial
issue. This is hardly surprising in that sex has recently been the subject
of lively debate back in England. Consider a new play that has opened
in London, entitled *Measure for Measure* and written by one of the city's
most popular dramatists, William Shakespeare.[1]

The play unfolds in a dissolute city where the laws against immorality
have long since fallen into disuse. Brothels, bawds, and pimps thrive while
the city's more debauched inhabitants wallow in the pleasures of the flesh
without fear of reprisal. The duke who rules the city has come to regret that the laws against fornication are "drowsy and neglected," but he
values his popularity and so is reluctant to take on the thankless task of
sexual reform. The duke decides to absent himself from government and
the city, appointing a deputy named Angelo to rule in his place, free "to
enforce or qualify the laws as to [his] soul seems good." Given that Angelo
is deeply religious, "a man of stricture" who believes in "firm abstinence,"
there can be little doubt where his conscience will lead him. Sure enough,
the deputy orders a swift and ruthless cleanup of the city. Bawds such
as Mistress Overdone and their lewd hangers-on are swept off the streets
and into prison to await the execution of justice.[2]

Angelo targets not only the city's seamy underworld but also those
citizens whose behavior is unimpeachable save in one regard: they have

I

broken the law against premarital sex. Claudio, a young gentleman, is engaged to marry Juliet; since their betrothal, he has "got possession of Juliet's bed," and she is now visibly pregnant. Angelo decides to make an example of Claudio, so the expectant father is arrested and condemned to death. The deputy's purge of the city leaves its inhabitants aghast. "Does your lordship mean," asks an imprisoned pimp, "to geld and splay all the youth of the city?" Angelo's determined campaign against what he describes as "filthy vices" is eventually thwarted by his own tormented lust, which he has previously kept firmly under control. When Isabella, Claudio's devout and chaste sister, comes to beg for her brother's life, Angelo is overwhelmed by desire. The "outward-sainted deputy" offers to pardon Claudio in return for a tryst with Isabella. This proposed exchange of Claudio's life for Isabella's maidenhead leads to the downfall of Angelo's regime.[3]

Measure for Measure was one of Shakespeare's most overtly topical and courageous plays. Zealous Protestant reformers had been agitating throughout Elizabeth I's reign for more stringent moral regulation. In addition to doctrinal and liturgical changes, these "Precisionists" or "Puritans" (as unappreciative contemporaries branded them) wanted a thoroughgoing "reformation of manners" that would cleanse society of dissipation and debauchery. They called for the suppression of maypoles, alehouses, theaters, and brothels; they denounced those who made merry on the Sabbath; and they wanted a crackdown on all nonmarital sex. Taken together, these austere proposals amounted to nothing less than a moral revolution. Not surprisingly, they failed to attract broad popular support. Elizabeth's government was well aware of that fact and had no intention of provoking unrest by endorsing a wholesale attack on activities that most people saw as relatively harmless. Though supportive in principle of moral reformation, her regime offered little more than vague assurances of goodwill to those who called for strict measures. Without vigorous official support, the Puritans had to fight an uphill struggle against the "licentiousness" that they perceived all around them. But Elizabeth, who had elevated prevarication to a fine art, was now dead. In 1603 a new king had ascended to the throne, and there was much uncertainty as to the direction his government would take. It was at this crucial juncture that Shakespeare penned his dark and provocative study of sexual politics.[4]

The campaign for moral reform that Shakespeare scrutinized in his play took aim not only at casual promiscuity but also at longstanding popular assumptions about when sex became legitimate within a committed relationship. Claudio and Juliet fully intended to become husband and wife; once betrothed, they considered themselves married in all but "outward order" and so saw nothing wrong with having sex.[5] That attitude was not unusual in early modern England. Indeed, roughly one-fifth of English brides in the late sixteenth and early seventeenth centuries were already pregnant by the time they formally married. Widespread premarital intercourse did not represent a wanton rejection of moral propriety by ordinary people. Instead, it arose from a common belief that the boundary between illicit and licit sex was crossed once a couple became committed to each other.

The Church of England, however, insisted that couples should remain abstinent until they were formally wed. Premarital intimacy had political as well as moral implications since it brought into question the authority of local clergymen—and, by extension, the church as a whole—to control the moment at which a man and a woman became a couple. Church officials fought with increasing resolve during Elizabeth's reign to establish formal marriage as the point at which sex became licit, berating those with alternative points of view and punishing couples who conceived before they married. Given the reliance of ecclesiastical courts upon local informers, the growing number of disciplinary cases involving premarital sex by the early seventeenth century suggests that more and more people agreed with reformers that sex before marriage was unacceptable. But these cases also testify to the persistence of popular belief in the legitimacy of sex once a couple was betrothed. Though reformers saw themselves as fighting moral laxity, prosecutions for premarital sex are better understood as a clash between different perspectives on sexual propriety.[6]

Sexual morality and its implications for the larger well-being of society had become a matter of heated debate in England during the period of New World exploration. Sex figured in these public discussions both as an issue in its own right and as a symbol of manifold dangers facing the nation. In a period beset by political, economic, and religious uncertainty, commentators often framed anxieties about the future in terms of encroaching disorder and immorality. Nonmarital sex handily exemplified both of these threats and became a primary target of those who sought to protect English society from sin and chaos. That campaign for moral reformation would extend across the Atlantic to the colonies of North America, as religious and secular authorities sought with varying degrees of success to impose their blueprint for an orderly and virtuous society. Sexual mores took on additional significance in a colonial setting: imposing moral order was rendered both more urgent and more far-fetched by the primitive surroundings in which colonists found themselves, "a desolate wilderness" located "at the end of the world." Such an environment seemed to encourage debased, even barbaric, tendencies among those who migrated to North America, raising the grim prospect of cultural degeneration. That danger was compounded in the eyes of many contemporaries by the presence of apparently savage Indians and Africans, who threatened to contaminate the colonists and further compromise their civility.[7]

English descriptions of the New World were rich in sexual imagery. They envisaged the lush and fertile landscape of North America as a "maidenhead" waiting to be taken, its "fruitful womb" soon to be fertilized by English "art and industry." Just as the land itself resembled "a fair virgin, longing to be sped and meet her lover in a nuptual bed," so its native inhabitants were apparently eager to share their favors with the colonists. According to Captain Seagull, a character in the 1605 play *Eastward Ho*, English adventurers had already "married with the Indians, and make 'em bring forth as beautiful faces as any we have in England; and therefore the Indians are so in love with 'em, that all the treasure they have, they lay at their feet." Fantasies of sexual cornucopia in far-flung, exotic locations inspired a short seventeenth-century novel entitled *The Isle of Pines*, in which a young man named George Pine is shipwrecked on a luxuriant island with four women: the fourteen-year-old daughter of a mercantile agent with whom he had been traveling as a bookkeeper to the East Indies, two servants, and a "negro female slave." After living in "idleness" for several months, George becomes eager to "enjoy" the women with whom he has been marooned. He accordingly persuades the two servants, Mary and Elizabeth, to let him "lie with them, which I did at first in private; but after, custom taking away shame, there being none but us, we did it more openly, as our lust gave us liberty." Sarah, his master's daughter, joins in soon thereafter, followed by the "negro" slave, whose name is Philippa. George proceeds to sire 47 children, who are themselves equally fecund: in his sixtieth year, George has 545 children, grandchildren, and great-grandchildren; by his eightieth year, the number has grown to 1,789. He and his prolific family have truly been blessed "with the dew of heaven and the fat of the earth."[8]

Although the island in this novel has no native inhabitants, Philippa's presence injects a racial element into the story. As George Pine sets aside his inhibitions to indulge in the sexual possibilities afforded by this remote and unregulated setting, his one persistent reservation about such behavior pertains to racial difference. Philippa is initially excluded from young Pine's sexual ménage, but one night she approaches him while he is sleeping, "thinking in the dark to beguile me." George realizes who it is, "yet willing to try the difference" between Philippa and the other three, he gives way to her advances. They subsequently become regular bedfellows, and Philippa bears twelve of his children. But whereas George has sex with the three white women at all hours of the day, he lies with Philippa "at night and not else": he cannot "stomach" her unless it is dark, even though she is "one of the handsomest blacks" he has seen. And whereas he refers to his other companions as wives, Philippa remains a distinct member of the family ("my negro").

The ambiguity intrinsic to this relationship exemplifies English attitudes toward miscegenation during this period. Physical attraction toward African and Indian women was offset by distaste for "black" and "tawney" skin color, which Englishmen associated with dirt, sin, and savagery.[9] Explorers and colonists were equally ambivalent about the sexual customs of Indian and African peoples, which struck them as both enticingly and disturbingly licentious. Ironically, the physical and cultural traits that marked "savages" as inferior in English eyes also rendered them beguiling. As we will see, Englishmen living in North America often allowed their lust for nonwhite women to prevail over cultural inhibitions. The circumstances in which these unions took place ranged from violent rape to long-lasting and loving relationships. But even the latter were often blighted by an overarching context of racial subordination and persistent uneasiness regarding cultural allegiance. The grim realities of conquest and enslavement overshadowed interracial relations in North America: assertions of superiority over Indians and Africans worked in deadly symbiosis with mistreatment of nonwhite men and women to complicate unions that crossed racial boundaries. The possibility of constructive relations, sexual and otherwise, between white and nonwhite residents of North America was further compromised by English anxieties about the preservation of civility in a colonial setting.

On both sides of the Atlantic, perceptions of racial difference were self-referential, reaffirming English claims to virtue and cultural propriety. As proponents of moral reformation back in England challenged their fellow countrymen to confront and quell their depravity, encounters (whether in person or through secondhand accounts) with Indian and African peoples enabled Englishmen to contrast the apparent savagery of nonwhite peoples with their own relative civility. And as colonists in North America struggled to sustain a sense of themselves as civilized Englishmen, comparison of their own efforts with those who seemed more evidently lacking provided welcome reassurance. Miscegenation undercut that enterprise: critics of interracial sex argued that such unions brought about literal and figurative pollution as Englishmen allowed their civilized instincts to be overwhelmed by lust. Anglo-Americans did not believe that racial identity was fixed: "savages" could undergo physical and cultural "improvement" as a result of interacting, sexually and otherwise, with more "civilized" people. But racial mutability could operate in both directions, so that English men and women might degenerate through contact with Indians and Africans. Instead of "blanching" their partners, the English might themselves become "blackened." [10]

The prospect of sexual contact between white women and African or Indian men aroused particularly vehement anxiety. Although contemporaries did worry that English men might become contaminated by nonwhite lovers, the assumption that male colonists who had sex with Indian and African women took a dominant position in any such union did at least fit with English notions of racial and gendered hierarchy. But a scenario in which nonwhite men assaulted or had consensual relations with English women challenged the dominion of English men over both their womenfolk and nonwhite males. English women who conceived children by Indian or African men introduced nonwhite blood into English families and quite possibly their lines of inheritance. Shakespeare engages these anxieties in *The Tempest* through his portrayal of Caliban, a native to the island on which Prospero and his daughter Miranda settle. Caliban is described by Prospero and other Europeans who arrive during the course of the play as a deformed "monster" that was sired "by the devil himself" upon a "foul witch" named Sycorax. He has grown up considering the island his own, but he is enslaved by Prospero and banished from the interlopers' shelter after he tries "to violate" Miranda. Caliban understands quite clearly what Prospero fears and declares mockingly that had not his master prevented him, he "had peopled else this isle with Calibans." For George Pine to populate his island through sexual relations with Philippa is sufficiently problematic, but for Caliban to do so with Miranda is intolerable. Such unions would, at least from Prospero's perspective, undercut his own authority and debase his kingdom in the New World. [11]

If alleged savages posed a threat to English virtue and civility, so too did the mundane challenges of the North American "wilderness" itself. Establishing and sustaining a regulatory infrastructure that would enforce authorized sexual values would prove a daunting enterprise in fledgling and often scattered settlements. Colonial governments, clergymen, and other proponents of a conventional moral order worried about the ease with which colonists became debased of their own accord if left unsupervised, wallowing in "loose embraces," as one official put it, and raising their children with as little attention to decency as if they were "a litter of pigs." To the emissaries of church and state, settlers who lived in the backcountry, far removed from established colonial communities and their supposedly civilizing influence, appeared downright brutish, having "degenerated into a state of ignorance and barbarism not much superior to the native Americans."[12]

We should, of course, beware of taking at face value outraged denunciations by contemporary critics. Some of the unions that these would-be reformers condemned were in fact committed, though informal, relationships that many settlers considered quite legitimate. According to English law, a man and a woman could become married without a public ceremony, without the exchange of specific vows, and even without witnesses: couples could declare themselves husband and wife in private and henceforth consider their unions legally valid. Indeed, this was the basis for widespread popular acceptance of premarital sex: mutual commitment, however private, legitimated sexual union. By the late sixteenth century, church marriage had become the norm in England.[13] But across the Atlantic, informal marriage underwent a major revival, especially in those regions of British America where ministers and magistrates were in short supply.

Colonial governments tried to impose their version of marital and sexual propriety upon the population, passing laws that required public marriage and denouncing any other form of sexual relationship. Yet in addition to the problem that representatives of church or state were scarce in areas of sparse settlement, many residents saw no urgent need to formalize their unions: what mattered to them was that they and their neighbors understood and respected the nature of their relationships. It was, furthermore, not unusual for settlers to have several domestic partners during their adult lives, despite official emphasis upon the sanctity and permanence of marriage. In passing from one union to the next, these colonists often paid little or no regard to legal formalities. Men and women who did marry in a legal ceremony, subsequently split up, and then entered relationships with other people were officially guilty of either bigamy or adultery, depending on whether they remarried or not. The unavailability in many areas of officials licensed to marry, the lack of investment on the part of many colonists in marital formalities, and widespread serial monogamy created complex, at times labyrinthine, personal histories that horrified proponents of a more legalistic sexual and marital protocol.

Among such proponents was John Miller, a clergyman who traveled through the province of New York in 1695. Miller was appalled to observe that "many couples live[d] together without ever being married in any manner of way." It was not uncommon, he reported, for such couples to separate after several years of living together, whereupon both would "take unto themselves, either in New York or some other province, new companions." Those who did "intend to be married together" often engaged in "ante-nuptual fornication," which was "not looked upon as any scandal or sin." Because of a lack of ministers, most of those who did wed were joined together by magistrates. Some of these officials were sufficiently ill-informed or unprincipled that they could be "prevailed upon to marry a couple together" even though "either one or both of them" were already "engaged or married to other persons." Even New Yorkers who were legally married thought it "no great matter to divorce themselves, as they term it, and marry to others where they can best, and according to their own liking." Miller condemned these settlers as "debauched" and "wandering libertines." They, of course, may well have perceived the situation rather differently.[14]

The attitudes and practices that so shocked this punctilious cleric proved to be remarkably resilient, surviving in some parts of British America throughout the seventeenth and eighteenth centuries. Most colonists considered marriage and the family household to be basic social building blocks, yet there was no consensus among settlers as to what constituted a licit marriage and thus a legitimate sexual relationship. Given that matrimony provided the only officially authorized context for a sexual union, controversy over marital formation and dissolution had profound implications for sexual politics, in local communities as well as in county courts and legislative assemblies. Some men and women rejected altogether the need for any moral code; as we will see, there were profligates aplenty in the British colonies of North America. Far more significant in their

8

numbers, however, were those who relied on pragmatic criteria rooted in popular tradition instead of official standards in determining whether a union was licit. Even in New England, where Puritan leaders were determined to transform their stringent ideals into what John Winthrop described as "familiar and constant practice," enforcing sexual norms proved an uphill struggle.[15] Though hardly a sink of depravity, New England was a good deal less orderly in sexual as in other regards than its leaders would have liked. Their agenda was thwarted in part by the presence of "profane" settlers whose investment in moral rectitude was minimal and in part by the practical obstacles to thoroughgoing regulation posed by the mobility and elusive personal histories of a colonial population. But equally significant was the persistence of alternative moral values among those colonists who considered themselves decent and devout. For example, even church members proved resistant to the official position that premarital sex was unacceptable.

The campaigns waged in British America by those who sought moral reformation amounted to a culture war, pitting different conceptions of sexual and marital etiquette against each other. Popular customs and attitudes persisted throughout the seventeenth and eighteenth centuries, despite attempts by church and state to impose quite different ideals. Though not intrinsically subversive, popular beliefs and practices became oppositional once the authorities labeled them as immoral, disorderly, and dangerous. The imposition of a value-laden vocabulary was crucial to that campaign for sexual reformation. When magistrates and ministers used the word *fornication* (by which they meant unmarried and therefore illicit sex) to describe intercourse between a man and woman who had already committed to marry but were not yet formally wed, they sought to de-legitimate and criminalize acts that ordinary folk often considered unexceptionable. Words such as *marriage* meant different things to different people: whereas clergymen understood marriage to involve a public ceremony in the presence of an authorized official, some settlers saw neither public ritual nor official validation as a prerequisite for marital respectability. Colonists sometimes resisted the imposition of specific definitions and the values that came with them. In 1652, when a Maryland couple was prosecuted for unmarried cohabitation, a neighbor declared defiantly that the defendants were indeed married "but only for the ceremony." As early Americans talked about sex, terminology became a battlefield in its own right.[16]

Settlers who followed sexual and marital codes that diverged from legal and theological guidelines became, often unwittingly, cultural rebels. We should beware of creating a false dichotomy between officials and other colonists. Many of the former were themselves local settlers, and by no means all those invested with formal authority held to or enforced the standards that they were supposed to protect and impose. Neither official nor popular values were monolithic: each included a range of positions, priorities, and motivations. But in broad strokes it is helpful to distinguish between two approaches to sexual morality during the colonial period: one more rigorously tied to ideology and exclusivist in its demands for allegiance; the other more expansive and pragmatic in its combination of officially authorized values, customary assumptions, and practicality.[17]

This book examines the attitudes, reformative agendas, and social dynamics that shaped sexual culture in early America. It reconstructs the various traditions and sensibilities, some complementary and others antagonistic, that underlay sexual behavior. It describes the battles fought by those invested with political, legal, and religious authority as they sought to reform the sexual mores of settlers whose values and priorities often diverged from official standards and goals. It considers the often insidious interplay of lust, love, and social prerogative in sexual encounters and intimate relationships between men and women of differing status. It places particular emphasis upon the ways in which issues of race interwove with those of civility and morality in colonial minds as diverse peoples tried (some harder than others) to coexist in the settlements of British America. And it shows a fundamental shift in sexual culture during the eighteenth century away from an ethos rooted in organic conceptions of society and toward a more individualistic marketplace of sexual desire and fulfillment, much to the horror of those who feared that greater personal freedom brought with it greater individual vulnerability. The pages that follow blend intellectual, cultural, and social history as they examine the impact of ideas and assumptions about sex upon people's lives. In writing a book that focuses attention upon sexual mores and the debates to which they gave rise, I do not mean to suggest that colonists spent all or even most of their time thinking about such matters. But early Americans did consider sex to be important as a social, economic, political, legal, moral, and religious issue. Sexual values and behavior mattered to settlers in their own right and also as emblems of where colonial society (and later the United States) was heading as a cultural entity. Early Americans worried about sex because they believed that it embodied, quite literally, their identity and worth, individually and collectively.

IN THIS BOOK I seek to reconstruct the meanings and values that early Americans attached to sex—that is, erotically charged interactions tending toward though not necessarily including genital orgasm. People never simply engage in sex: at some level of consciousness, they interpret their physical desires and ascribe significance to their behavior. Sex is always "scripted" in that cultural norms and personal attitudes influence how we understand sexual impulses and the circumstances under which we enact them. The meanings attributed to sex vary from one culture to another, from one time and place to another, and from one individual to another. Sex may be universal, but sexual categories are not. Many modern westerners define themselves and each other in terms of *sexuality* and *sexual orientation:* they presuppose a distinct causal agency within each man and woman that drives sexual attraction, impels us toward members of the same or the opposite sex, and even shapes overall personality. Yet the very notion of sexuality is a modern invention. If we are to understand the ways in which early Americans (and other premodern societies) understood sexual desire and experience, we must set aside the assumptions that underlie modern taxonomy. The latter, writes classical scholar David Halperin, pose "a significant obstacle to understanding the distinctive features of sexual life in non-Western and pre-modern cultures." [18]

People living in the seventeenth and eighteenth centuries did not think about their sexual feelings and behavior as a distinct realm of identity. They viewed sex not as a product of sexuality but as a component of spirituality, cultural identity, and social status. William Byrd, an eighteenth-century southern planter, described intercourse with his wife as a courtly "flourish" and bemoaned as a form of spiritual "pollution" his masturbatory tendencies. In so doing, he incorporated sexual acts into his sense of himself as a gentleman and as a Christian: he understood sex in terms of categories that were not themselves intrinsically sexual. [19] This has dramatic implications for how we reconstruct attitudes toward sex in the past. There were, for example, men living in British America who found themselves attracted to other men, but early Americans did not conceive of same-sex desire as we might today in terms of homosexuality. Though some colonists recognized in themselves or their neighbors an ongoing attraction toward members of the same sex, the modern paradigm of sexual orientation would have made little sense to them. They used a range of different assumptions and conceptual frameworks to understand "sod-omitical actings." Strictly speaking, men who practiced sodomy during this period did not engage in homosexual acts any more than men who had sex with women engaged in heterosexual acts. Even the word *sexuality* can obscure more than it illuminates when applied to a premodern context, and therefore I avoid it in the pages that follow.[20]

Gaining access to the sexual lives and attitudes of people who lived in British America is no easy matter, especially once one ventures outside the social elite. Reconstructing official ideologies and moral norms is a relatively straightforward task: these can be ascertained from sermons, theological treatises, governmental decrees, laws, judicial decisions, and didactic literature. Figuring out what people actually thought about sexual issues is much more challenging, though by no means impossible. Elite white males left behind them private journals, diaries, and correspondence in which they sometimes gave voice to erotic feelings and recorded their sexual behavior. Because poorer men and women were much less likely to acquire writing skills, their attitudes are more elusive.[21] Fortunately for us, depositions from sex-related court cases do preserve the words of townsfolk and villagers who often could not write for themselves and yet were eager to comment on the sexual activities going on around them. Legal transcripts provide an indirect but invaluable link to what ordinary men and women had to say about sex. Deponents were rarely as expansive and discursive as we might like, but the comments and allusions made in court testimony are nonetheless revealing; the content and tone of these depositions were often far removed from the values that officials espoused. Eighteenth-century newspapers, magazines, and almanacs combine the perspectives voiced in normative pronouncements, private writings, and legal records. Ephemeral print provided a channel for the circulation of sexual and moral norms, yet it also gave voice to alternative points of view, ribald humor, and at times vicious satire. As these publications reported sexual scandals and criminality, they often divulged information about unauthorized behavior inside and outside the elite that can now prove valuable to historians of sexual culture.

When I started work on this project almost a decade ago, a close friend urged me to abandon the enterprise on the grounds that I would not find sufficient evidence to piece together the puzzle I had in mind. I decided to ignore this advice and have never regretted doing so. I have been astonished by the richness of the material that survives on this subject. That material is admittedly uneven and will not yield answers to all the questions that we may want to ask. Yet it does enable the reconstruction of sexual attitudes not only within the colonial elite but also among less privileged settlers, revealing a complex and conflict-ridden sexual culture in which little could be taken for granted. The ways people expressed themselves in public print, court testimony, and more private forms of communication repay close attention. Given the power of language to reflect and shape our mental worlds, the vocabulary and imagery marshaled by early Americans talking and writing about sex provide rich clues as to how colonists made sense of their feelings and behavior. "We must never mistake texts for people," cautions historian Roy Porter, "but texts, properly read, can illuminate."[22]

THE NINE CHAPTERS of this book are divided into three parts, each examining a different context in which sex became controversial among early Americans. They encompass two centuries and a vast territory of British settlement that stretched from New England down to the southern colonies and outward to the West Indies. I make no claim to comprehensive coverage of that territory. Rather than providing a survey of sexual values and behavior, I have chosen to focus on a selection of situations and debates that illuminate three central themes in the sexual history of early America: an ongoing struggle among different versions of sexual morality; the role of sex in fostering and combating a profound fear of cultural debasement in the New World; and the interplay of sexual with political revolution in the late eighteenth century. This study extends beyond the colonial era and into the first few decades of the republic in order to show how changes taking place in sexual culture on the eve of Independence were intensified and reframed by the dynamics of the American Revolution. It examines, then, the place that sex occupied in the moral and cultural architecture of early American society, along with the ways in which sexual controversy became interwoven with the evolution of colonial and then republican identities.

Part I, "Passionate Pilgrims," focuses on seventeenth-century New England, where Puritan leaders sought to impose sexual revolution upon the colonial population. New England was not the first region of North America to be settled by the English; nor was it typical in terms of its religious character or social composition. Yet New England Puritans have long dominated stereotypes of early America, which in turn often focus on repressed and repressive sexual attitudes. I have chosen to begin with New England partly in order to highlight how diverse and contested sexual values were even there. The sexual revolution that Puritan architects had in mind was achieved only in part as the invocation of religious ideals clashed with the limitations of popular support and the practical challenges of sexual regulation. Thoroughgoing Puritans were themselves much more permissive in some respects than popular mythology and some academics would allow: New England pastors encouraged an active sexual relationship within marriage, as an expression of sensual love between husband and wife as well as for purposes of procreation; they also sought to eroticize their spiritual relations, embracing their savior with ardent and sometimes downright erotic passion. Though deeply hostile to what they perceived as illicit sex, Puritans had no intention of desexualizing their lives.

Sexual regulation also emerged as a vital issue in the southern regions of British America, though for somewhat different reasons. Sex figured as a prominent part of southern campaigns to reassert order and civility in an environment that appeared both chaotic and barbarous to some contemporaries. The demonstration of civility became especially important to those members of the southern gentry who aspired, despite their colonial status, to membership within a transatlantic genteel elite. Part 2, "Sex and Civility," explores two contexts in which the sexual behavior of colonists gave rise to fears that they might be forsaking their identity as civilized Englishmen and degenerating into savagery: a revolution of cultural debasement. It first examines the prolonged struggle to suppress informal marriage and serial monogamy among poorer white southerners. To moral critics, this seemingly licentious behavior was disturbingly like that of "savage" Indians. Even more worrisome were interracial unions, in which white southerners of all social ranks were implicated. Some residents feared that miscegenation between planters and slaves would defile white society and undermine the region's claim to civility. The evolution of southern colonies into slave societies had profound implications for sexual culture in the region as emerging ideals of racial purity clashed with the widespread occurrence of interracial sex, made manifest in a large mulatto population. Emphasis upon the need for women in particular to eschew interracial unions deflected attention away from liaisons involving white planters as their wives and daughters became the principal repositories of racial purity. Yet even so, the evident prevalence of miscegenation and concern about the fragility of racial as well as cultural identity intertwined with insecurities about colonial respectability to create an ambiguous and unsettled sexual climate.

Meanwhile, a gradual transformation in sexual practices and attitudes within the white population of British America gave rise to new forms of anxiety about sexual ethics and their broader social significance. Part 3, "The Sexual Revolution," turns our attention to that transformation and its ambiguous relationship with the political revolution that brought about an independent United States. It investigates the erosion of restraints upon sexual behavior in rural and urban settings during the course of the eighteenth century. It focuses in particular upon growing anxiety about the implications of greater sexual freedom, especially for young women who became sexually active prior to marriage and who might be abandoned to single motherhood by unscrupulous male lovers. These developments correlated with the American Revolution in two distinct ways. On the one hand, young adults appropriated revolutionary rhetoric and its invocation of liberty to justify their insistence upon sexual independence. On the other, republican ideology stressed the need for moral virtue as the lifeblood of free institutions; that emphasis in polemical writings played a crucial role in shaping contemporary responses to increasing personal freedom.

Chapter 7 examines the sexual revolution that occurred in northern rural communities and the pragmatic ways in which New Englanders reacted to the dangers facing young women in a more permissive sexual climate. Chapter 8 focuses on literary discussion of courtship in the late eighteenth century as authors responded to a climate of greater sexual freedom and its potential dangers by reassessing the moral character of men and women: whereas earlier writings had often emphasized the untrustworthiness of women, didactic literature now portrayed them as the natural guardians of virtue and depicted men as morally depraved. That regendering of virtue had insidious implications since it made women responsible for their own safety and provided an alibi of sorts for male irresponsibility. Chapter 9 investigates the distinct sexual culture that emerged in cities on the eastern seaboard during the second half of that century. It considers the practical and ideological dangers that contemporaries identified as they observed and experienced the unbridled atmosphere prevailing in seaports such as Philadelphia, the nation's capital until 1800. Citizens of the fledgling republic now pondered in a new context the interdependence of sexual, moral, and cultural identity.

I

Passionate Pilgrims

I

"Chambering and Wantonising"
Popular Sexual Mores in Seventeenth-Century New England

THERE WERE MANY REASONS that Puritan evangelists became controversial figures in late-sixteenth-century and early-seventeenth-century England, but not least among these was their uncompromising demand for
sexual reform. The vehemence with which Puritans condemned those
who failed to meet their exacting standards provoked widespread resentment, particularly since they lambasted not only outright promiscuity but
also behavior that many upstanding citizens were willing to overlook,
including sexual intimacy between betrothed but as yet unwed couples.
Shakespeare's portrayal of the "precise" Angelo and his sexual crusade
in *Measure for Measure,* the hostility that his regime aroused, and the
humiliation that Angelo suffered once his own misdemeanors came to
light must have resonated powerfully with audiences in 1604 as Puritans
and their message continued to provoke debate. Accusations of hypoc-
risy were a favorite countercharge against the likes of Angelo: thus sanctimonious spokesmen for the self-styled moral minority could be tarred
as egregious sinners in their own right.[1]

New England Puritans were not exempt from such attacks. A seventeenth-century English broadside entitled "The Summons to New England" claimed that the supposedly "unspotted" and "pure" church established there had used the notion of religious freedom to justify sexual
libertinism:

> Loe in this Church all shall be free
> To enjoy their Christian liberty;
> All things made common, t'[a]voide strife,
> Each man may take another's wife,

And keep a handmaid too, if need,
To multiply, increase, and breed.[2]

Though the New England authorities were never actually so accommo-
dating as to sanction such practices, they did acknowledge that the moral
tone of their new society was not all that they had hoped for. The un-
disputed occurrence of sexual offenses among the saints provided anti-
Puritans with a golden opportunity. According to the "Letter from New-
England" published by a London press in 1682, the frequent appearance
in court of sexual transgressors showed that the settlers' moral laws were
mere "scarecrows, or for fashion's sake": "In their practice they outgo the
most notorious of offenders; Messalina was chaste in comparison of their
lewd and repeated fornications and adulteries . . . there hardly passes a
court day but four or five are convened for fornication or adultery; and
convictions in this nature are very frequent . . . Now most certainly if
justice finds out so many transgressors in this kind, how many must the
private ones amount to?" Another passage recounted the search for the
mother of a murdered infant that had been found drowned in the Boston
docks: officials did not succeed in identifying the "murderess," but during the search they discovered several young women in godly households
"that went under the denomination of maids" and yet were found to be
pregnant. The "sweet sin of lechery" was clearly "agreeable" to those "apt
to say, 'Stand off, for I am more holy than thou.' "[3]

That anecdote may well have been apocryphal, yet it does not seem far-
fetched, given the scores of women, some of them church members, who
were prosecuted in seventeenth-century New England courts for bearing
children outside wedlock. More than a hundred women were convicted
for that offense in Essex County between 1640 and 1685. Several thousand seventeenth-century New Englanders appeared before church congregations and in court charged with lewd speech, fornication, adultery,
bigamy, rape, incest, sodomy, and bestiality. John Winthrop, the first governor of Massachusetts, noted in journal passages throughout the 1630s
and early 1640s that the church and civil authorities had frequent cause
to act against "lewdness" and "incontinency." William Bradford, who
served as Plymouth Colony's governor for many years, also acknowledged
"the breaking out of sundry notorious sins," including and especially "uncleanness," even though this was "so much witnessed against and so narrowly looked into." The Suffolk County Court in Massachusetts dealt
with just over two hundred cases involving illicit sex during the 1670s

alone. And in New Haven, sexual offenses outnumbered all other categories of criminality handled by the county court.[4]

This is not to suggest that a majority of New Englanders were engaged in some form of illicit sex, but both friends and foes of New England considered the frequency with which such offenses came to light deeply embarrassing for the Puritan cause. Colonial leaders such as William Bradford insisted rather defensively that New Englanders were not committing more sexual offenses than were committed elsewhere, indeed "nothing near so many by proportion as in other places." Bradford contended that the abundance of sex cases testified not to the community's failure in establishing a godly society but to its determined campaign against the corrupt impulses present in all men and women, "so hardly bridled, subdued, and mortified." Because "the churches look[ed] narrowly to their members, and the magistrates over all," such offenses were more likely to be "discovered and seen and made public." Ironically, the very success of community surveillance raised the specter of failure in Puritan as well as others' eyes. According to Bradford, no amount of policing, admonishing, fining, or flogging could do away with human depravity. One way or another, it would find a way to express itself:

> it may be in this case as it is with waters when their streams are stopped
> or damned up. When they get passage they flow with more violence and
> make more noise and disturbance than when they are suffered to run
> quietly in their own channels; so wickedness being here more stopped
> by strict laws, and the same more nearly looked unto so as it cannot
> run in a common road of liberty as it would and is inclined, it searches
> everywhere and at last breaks out where it gets vent.

The Devil, Bradford insisted, should also take his share of the blame for New England's iniquity. Because the settlers had determined "to preserve holiness and purity," Satan was determined to "cast a blemish and stain upon them in the eyes of the world" by tempting colonists into sin.[5]

Yet Bradford was a practical man and recognized that there were mundane reasons for "the breaking out" of illicit sex in the northern colonies. Having given due weight to theology and the ironic consequences of Puritan vigilance against sin, he proceeded to consider the actual demographics of migration and its implications for the moral tone of life in New England. By no means did all settlers identify with the spiritual goals espoused by leading colonists. The New England population was, Bradford bemoaned, "a mixed multitude." The need for "labor and service" in "building and planting" had, he wrote, necessitated the admission of "untoward" settlers whose skills made them indispensable, however dubious their spiritual qualifications. These laborers and craftsmen, many of them non-Puritans (or, in Bradford's words, "wicked persons and profane people"), changed the atmosphere of the northern colonies in ways deplored by those who "came for religion's sake." Other colonists with "untoward" pasts or who violated official codes once in New England might elude detection or punishment because of their mobility. As Bradford and his fellow magistrates would discover, movement within the Americas as well as across the Atlantic posed a serious obstacle to the effective regulation of sexual behavior.[6]

The intermingling of people with divergent values and priorities did make for an ambiguous, sometimes volatile, sexual culture. But it would be misleading to suggest that non-Puritans were primarily responsible for the sexual crimes committed in seventeenth-century New England. Nor will it suffice to concede that some offenders were devout men and women who gave way to temptation. Puritan orthodoxy had to contend with alternate beliefs and standards even among those who considered themselves respectable, God-fearing men and women: the covenanted community itself proved to be a hybrid culture. Many young couples who aspired to church membership or were already members, for example, saw no reason to wait until they were formally married before becoming sexually intimate. Longstanding popular tradition condoned premarital sex and proved more potent than official proscription in shaping the sexual histories of these New Englanders. Colonists tended, moreover, to respond pragmatically when dealing with sexual transgressors in their midst: they often placed personal loyalties and the needs of the local community before the imperative to enforce moral absolutes. Puritan leaders had hoped to bring about a fundamental reformation of sexual mores in the northern colonies, but the demographic, cultural, and social dynamics that shaped New England resulted in a compromised and contested moral regimen.

BRADFORD WAS QUITE CORRECT in stating that the fledgling colonies' need for workers with specific skills necessitated the presence of people whose behavior flew in the face of Puritan ideals. Most notorious were the inhabitants of seaports, crucial economic hubs and yet abhorrent to the guardians of spiritual purity as a breeding ground for all manner of dissipation and disorder.[7] Charlestown, Massachusetts, was a notoriously bawdy place, despite efforts by the town government to impose order and

clean up the port's image. Sailors staying in town while their ships un-
loaded and prepared for the next voyage were eager to pleasure themselves, and the wives of absent seamen were often happy to oblige. Elizabeth Martin, who was married to the captain of *The Blossom*, frequently
entertained mariners while her husband was away at sea. She and her
daughters held parties that lasted well into the night and featured heavy
drinking, "uncivil songs," "chambering and wantonising." The Martin
women cheerily shared their sexual partners with each other: Elizabeth
Martin apparently "played the whore" with a privateer "upon the stair-
case" and then rearranged the sleeping arrangements in the house so that
he and daughter Betty could "lie" together. A more punctilious young
woman living in their house became upset when a drunk but not yet sexually satiated neighbor who had joined the Martins for an evening of fun
"kept pleading with [her] to come to him for he said he had had a bout
with the other three and [she] must have a bout with him too."[8]

The "rout and disturbance" that took place in the Martin household
was far from anomalous in Charlestown. Susannah Cross, wife of another
mariner, also kept "a disorderly house" in her husband's absence, engaging in "lascivious and wanton practices."[9] Elsewhere in town, Sarah
Smith, whose husband had left on a trip to Barbados, was discovered
entertaining sailor John Chattendon and Mary Harris, a recently arrived
woman of dubious reputation, "in a very unhandsome and lascivious
manner, all embraced in said Chattendon's lap." Smith had apparently
had sex with Chattendon on several occasions.[10] The Martins, Cross, and
Smith were all prosecuted for their misbehavior, but the authorities were
fighting a losing battle against "wanton practices" in the seaport. In 1687
a maypole was set up, symbol of carefree frolicking and a red flag to Puritans; when the town watch tore it down, determined revelers erected an
even bigger one in its place, this time decorated with a garland.[11]

Nor were inland communities exempt from the disruptive behavior
of migrants whose occupations made them economically valuable even
as their general deportment offended the godly. Consider the Leonards,
a family of ironworkers that became embroiled in a string of prosecutions for debt, robbery, arson, assault, profanity, and "indecent" behavior.
Ironworkers were notorious on both sides of the Atlantic for their lewd,
rowdy, and irreligious behavior. But the Bay colonists' eagerness to minimize their dependence on imported goods drove them to court laborers,
however undesirable, for local ironworks. So eager were the authorities to
accommodate those involved in the fledgling enterprise that the conces-

sions granted in 1645 to the company building an ironworks at Lynn included exemption from church attendance. They hoped that ironworkers would be "cured of their distempers" by "good example and discipline," but this proved rather quixotic.[12]

The brash and indecorous behavior of Leonard family members appalled their more fastidious neighbors. Mary Leonard, who was accused of "dressing [when] there were several men in the room" and of "us[ing] bad language and sing[ing] indecent songs," had sat by the Rowley Village pond "when her sons and other men were swimming and washing themselves, and some of the men who were more modest than the rest were forced to creep up into the bushes and others put on their shirts in the water, letting them fall down by degrees as they came out." Several of the Leonard menfolk "came out of the water naked and ran races." The Leonard boys had a reputation for making unwanted sexual advances toward women in the neighborhood and were put on trial for attempted rape in 1674.[13] Although the Leonards had found themselves in court due to various conflicts with neighbors from the late 1640s onward, it was only in the early 1670s, when Henry Leonard leased the Rowley ironworks and failed to make a success of the enterprise, that locals expressed their hostility toward the family in a rapid proliferation of criminal as well as civil cases. Once the Leonards' value as ironworkers was undercut by their failure in managing the Rowley operation, they became fair game. Their previous reputation as indispensable to the colony's plans for ironmaking ("Where you find ironworks, there you will find a Leonard") had protected them somewhat from public censure.[14]

In addition to uncouth laborers who were tolerated, albeit grudgingly, because of the skills they possessed and the services they performed, godly settlers also had to deal with "profane" migrants who managed to reach New England because of flaws in the vetting process on the other side of the Atlantic. Bradford complained that those in the business of shipping colonists and their goods to North America were anxious to fill their vessels and "cared not who the persons were, so they had money to pay them." Some individuals with shady pasts were shipped across to the new colonies by "friends" who either hoped that they would "be made better" in the company of the godly or simply wanted to get rid of them and the "shame" that "necessarily follow[ed] their dissolute courses." If it became clear during the lengthy voyage across the Atlantic that particular migrants did not meet the moral standards expected of them, they could find themselves returned to England with documentation of their failings.

The Reverend Francis Higginson recorded in his journal that aboard the *Talbot* in 1629, he and other prominent members of the Bay Company "examined five beastly sodomitical boys, wh[o] confessed their wickedness not to be named." So "foul" did Higginson and his colleagues consider the boys' crime that they "reserved them to be punished by the governor when we came to New England." The General Court, however, decided to send them back across the Atlantic to London, where it would be determined "what punishment may be inflicted upon them, and how the Company may be legally discharged of them." In 1672 Sarah Blacklock confessed mid-Atlantic that back in England she had become pregnant by her "sweetheart," a Dutch man named Henry Saffery, and then miscarried after four months; her father's maidservant had buried the fetus "privately" in the garden. If Blacklock hoped to unburden her conscience and then start a new life, she was sorely disappointed: once she reached Massachusetts, the Suffolk County Court heard of her confession, summoned her, and, after she "owned the sin," had her sent back to England along with "the records of the court concerning her."[15]

The New England authorities had rid themselves of the "sodomitical boys" and Sarah Blacklock, but many other undesirables remained, each of them a thorn in the side of Puritan magistracy and the cause of much outrage among godly settlers. One gets the distinct impression that earthier colonists sometimes set out quite deliberately to embarrass or shock more pious neighbors. Mary Leonard, for example, must have realized that her presence on the bank of the Rowley pond would mortify those bathers "who were more modest." In 1679 Moses Parker was convicted of "obscene carriages" after "drawing out his yard in the presence of many persons" at the Roxbury tavern. Whether he did so with the encouragement of his drinking companions or in order to shock them, and whether or not he was drunk, Parker must have realized at some level of consciousness that "drawing out his yard" in a Puritan-licensed tavern was highly provocative. In another case of indecent exposure, Samuel Terry of Springfield was seen on the Sabbath "standing with his face to the meetinghouse wall near the corner of the meetinghouse next [to] the street chafing his yard to provoke lust, even in sermon time." Whether or not Terry's masturbatory activity was intended as a pun on the devotions within (contemporaries did, after all, describe both seminal emission and prayer as ejaculation), it seems clear that his behavior was deliberately blasphemous. Indeed, Terry had a propensity toward subversive performance. In 1673 he was one of several locals punished by the Springfield court for staging a play that included "uncivil, immodest, and beastly acting."[16]

The "profane people" who gained admittance to New England horrified godly folk not only by cavorting naked around village ponds, exposing their privates, and engaging in other forms of "immodest" or "bawdy" behavior, but also by talking openly and crassly about sexual matters. The guardians of Puritan morality held that "filthy" words—whether spoken, written, or sung—had as much power to disrupt and pollute as did "unclean" acts. The content and tone of speech expressed moral character just as powerfully as did one's actions, so that "government of the tongue" was as crucial to the individual and collective welfare as was regulation of behavior. Those who refused to abide by "rules of right speaking" were to be held accountable in court.[17] Joseph King was "sharply reprehended" in 1641 for "uncomely and obscene speeches." Giles Black, accused by his master of embezzling goods in 1665, was also presented for "lascivious and corrupt speeches," having "spoken many things of making maids loving of him and kissing him in the stocks." Goodwife Bailey of New Haven found herself in trouble as a result of her "filthy and unclean speeches." When the Baileys' dog had tried to "copulate" with a sow, neighbor John Moss told Goodman Bailey that he should kill the animal, to which Bailey replied that "he would, or geld him." But Goody Bailey declared afterward to neighbor Goody Barnes, "What would you have the poor creature do, if he had not a bitch he must have something." In a similar vein, when gossiping about George Larremore's alleged adultery, she said, "Alas, what would you have the man do, if his own wife was weak, he must have somebody." Bailey may have thought that she was giving voice to common sense, but others found such talk diabolical. The court declared that she had "acted as one possessed with the very devil," and she was charged that same year with witchcraft.[18]

These cases, ostensibly a testimonial to the Puritans' bridling of unruly tongues, reveal in equal measure the ribald tone of everyday conversation among at least some New Englanders. Ironically, the exposure of "uncomely" speech or behavior necessitated its recapitulation in court: the cleansing of the community required that magistrates permit dirty talk. But reporting obscene remarks or bawdy behavior, even if in lurid detail, was quite different in Puritan eyes from engaging in gratuitously smutty conversation outside the courtroom. Salacious speech posed a threat not only to the general tone of community life but also to specific individuals whose reputations could be damaged by gossip that may or may not have been accurate. Rebecca Bishop of Newbury, angry with Thomas Silver for reporting that her daughter Mary Rolfe "entertained" male visitors while her husband was away, said that he might as well have "taken an axe and knocked one of her cows on the head as to take away her daughter's good name."[19]

The plethora of cases involving sexual slander that passed through the courts testifies both to the importance that at least some settlers attached to sexual reputation and to the pervasiveness of sexual gossip, some of it pruriently sanctimonious. The latter could serve as an informal instrument of social control, exposing those who engaged in dubious behavior and shaming them. Gossip could also be used as a weapon to blacken the names of personal enemies.[20] But not all tittle-tattle was so purposeful. Although some sexual slander cases arose from deliberate attempts to taint reputations or expose malefactors, other remarks judged defamatory by reputation-conscious folk may well have originated as casually bawdy gossip that seemed harmless enough to neighbors who had different values and thicker skins.

Some of those who engaged in "obscene conversation" clearly intended to establish a reputation for sexual experience and prowess. Forty-six-year-old Thomas Langhorn, a resident of Cambridge who was married with five children, evidently hoped that bawdy talk would facilitate bawdy deeds. When he set out to seduce nineteen-year-old Elizabeth Holmes, he regaled her with what Elizabeth described as "filthy" speeches about his own sexual abilities as well as sexual intercourse in general. The following extract from her lengthy 1663 complaint against Langhorn will give readers a sense of his posturing as a man well equipped in more ways than one to educate young women in the pleasures of the flesh:

> He said he would lie with his wife three or four times in the night and when he had done it would be as limber as a rag and that it would be two hours in filling and there was vessels in the man's back that the seed emptied from vessel to vessel till the member was full again, also that his member entered three handfulls into his wife's body, and [he] measured a stick and showed it me as it grew bigger and longer in the acting of it. Also he told me he would teach me how to lie with my husband that it should not hurt me and that I must pull up my legs, and he said that he had taught a maid so and after she was married she thanked him for it.

Langhorn claimed that his knowledge of matters sexual came not only from his own experiences but also from "Aristotle and from honest men and women." Many early modern midwifery texts claimed to be based on Aristotle's teachings (though their debts to the Greek philosopher were actually few and far between). These manuals, which contained information and advice about sexual relations as well as gynecological material, were apparently circulating in Cambridge. Elizabeth Holmes told magistrate Thomas Danforth "that some girls in the town had books that learned them pretty things."[21]

As well as engaging in bawdy conversation, some colonists drew pictures, wrote, and sung in ways that offended godly sensibilities. Ralph Earle of Plymouth Colony was presented in 1663 "for drawing his wife in an uncivil manner in the snow." Joseph Turner, also a Plymouth man, was punished in 1668 for "making and publishing a scurrilous and infamous writing, wherein is contained many lascivious and filthy verses." Samuel Greenfield got himself in trouble with the Essex County Court for "singing a lascivious song and using unseemly gestures therewith." And Thomas Langden of New Haven was "complained of for disorderly entertaining of young men in his house at unseasonable times in the night to drink wine, strong water, and take tobacco," during which gatherings he had "been heard to sing filthy corrupting songs." Langden had apparently said that "he saw no harm in such songs" and that "if they were in Old England they could sing and be merry." His wife, however, had "blamed him" for singing the lewd ditties: she may have disapproved on principle, or she may simply have feared that his behavior would land him in trouble.[22]

It seemed to New England's ministers and magistrates that the offenses committed by lewd tongues and other licentious members became more numerous with each passing decade. In 1699 clergyman John Williams remarked that "uncleanness" was widely "thought to be a prevailing, growing evil."[23] The fear of moral decay that ministers voiced throughout the second half of the century was echoed in legislative statements and substantiated by a rising tide of prosecutions that outstripped the growth in population. In 1665 the Massachusetts General Court complained that fornication was "much increasing among us" and ordered that henceforth freemen convicted of the crime should be disfranchised. In 1672 it again lamented the "too obvious" fact that "the sin of whoredom and uncleanness grows amongst us, notwithstanding all the wholesome laws made for the punishing and suppressing such land-defiling evils." This latter denunciation was prompted by the discovery in Boston of a brothel run by widow Alice Thomas.[24] But the increase in fornication cases during these years could not be blamed solely on the expansion of seaports such as Boston with their more diverse population and disproportionate tendency toward dissipation. Sexual misdemeanors were on the rise even in more homogeneous inland communities, and those who disregarded Puritan norms found allies aplenty within Puritan households.

The distinction between godly and ungodly families became hazier with each passing decade as the children of New England's settlers reached sexual maturity. Whereas many of the northern colonists had crossed the Atlantic specifically to become part of a covenanted community, their children were not self-selecting. Puritan householders found that their offspring were just as likely to engage in illicit behavior as were those of neighboring non-Puritans. Some young people had no interest in following their parents' example of sexual continence; others would do so in time but meanwhile were neither able nor willing to restrain what pastors referred to as "youthful lusts." Almost half of the convictions for fornication in Middlesex County during the second half of the seventeenth century involved at least one church member or child of a church member. Even ministers had serious problems with sexually promiscuous offspring. Unlike the younger Leonards, who engaged in lewd behavior quite openly and whose parents did likewise, the sons and daughters of godly settlers found illicit pleasures in secret liaisons. Finding opportunities to do so was not as difficult as Puritan leaders would have liked, though the circumstances under which young people came together to explore forbidden topics and cravings were always precarious.[25]

It was by no means impossible for young lovers to elude the watchful eyes of parents, masters, and neighbors. Sarah Doolittle, a New Haven servant who was prosecuted for "many filthy and unclean practices," confessed to having had sex on three separate occasions with Joseph Preston in her master's house: in the kitchen, in the wood yard, and "in the chamber upon her bed when all in the house were in bed." Such trysts were risky: Michael Todd, another servant, heard Preston "come up into the chamber" and then listened as the lovers "whisper[ed] together." Doolittle also confessed that she and John Thomas Jr. tried to have sex in the house "when the rest of the company were gone out of doors," but although "they lay down and he upon her naked body and attempted to penetrate her body," he "could not, saying he was afraid."[26] Young

Thomas was not alone in worrying about the possibility of discovery: in November 1665 cooper William Clark was entwined with servant Hannah Green in an outbuilding when "a noise affrighted him and made him run away and he then carried away in haste her petticoat instead of his britches."[27] But there were ways of minimizing the risk. Servants who were left alone and unsupervised during church meetings, court sessions, and militia training could and did use the opportunity for lovemaking.[28] Most trysts appear to have taken place at night, when parents and masters were least likely to be vigilant. Elizabeth Pierce, who lived with her daughter and son-in-law, "often heard somebody moving in the house late at night and doors opening." She told her son-in-law, "but he was weary and careless." Isaac Melyen of New Haven had visited Hester Clark, a maid in the Reverend John Davenport's house, "after they was all in bed, and went into her bedchamber," with the active collusion of another servant, Samuel Hall. Questioned as to whether he had climbed in at the window, he replied that the door was "only latched."[29] Richard Matticks and Mary Hitchcock, two servants living in the same household, managed to have sex on several occasions before the arrival of another maidservant cramped their style. Hitchcock and Matticks sometimes stayed downstairs in the kitchen "later than her master and mistress was willing to" and Mary "made choice to lie in the garret when her mistress rather desired that she should lodge in a room with them."[30]

Under cover of night, young people gathered for "junkets," merrymaking excursions that sometimes included sexual gossip and horseplay. William Harding of New Haven was whipped and fined in 1642 for "base carriage and filthy dalliances with divers young girls" at "night meetings and junketting." This was evidently not an isolated incident: in 1660 the New Haven General Court railed against young people who "mispend and waste" their time at "night meetings," debauching themselves in "corrupt songs, and foolish jesting, or such like discourses, wanton and lascivious carriage, [and] mixed dancing."[31] Young people were also adept at appropriating authorized activities for their own ends. The New Haven court became sufficiently worried about illicit goings-on "at times of husking Indian corn" that it forbade single persons to meet "upon pretense of husking" after nine at night unless accompanied by a parent or master so as "to prevent disorder at such times." Some junkets took place in broad daylight and even on the Sabbath. In 1675 the Massachusetts General Court condemned young people who rode from town to town together "upon pretense of going to lecture" but actually "drink[ing] and revel[ling] in ordinaries and taverns." The court declared this subterfuge to be "in itself scandalous" and also "a notable means to debauch our youth and hazard the chastity of such as are drawn forth thereunto."[32]

The measure of independence afforded by residence at Harvard College in Cambridge facilitated illicit gatherings to which students invited young people from outside the college. In 1660 Sarah Boatson admitted that she had been "in a room" at the college that belonged to "one of the scholars [whom] she knew not." There was apparently quite a crowd and she saw "some of the young men kissing the maids." Boatson herself had sat on twenty-two-year-old Samuel Stearns's lap and kissed him. Eighteen-year-old John Fleming, she added, "did kiss and dally" with Evan Thomas's stepdaughter Mary. Earlier that day, Fleming had been seen at a militia training with Mary, "in a very uncivil manner walking up and down." According to shocked observers, he had "salute[d] the said wench by kissing her sundry times, the which was matter of great offence to them and several others." Stearns, Fleming, and nine young women were later charged with "suspicion of uncivil carriages and disorderly conduct." It would appear that "disorderly" behavior on the fringe of the militia meeting and in Belcher's tavern had continued at the college itself in a junket that included both students and nonstudents.[33] No wonder, then, that minister Thomas Shepard warned his son, as he enrolled at Harvard in 1672, of "youthful lusts, speculative wantonness, and secret filthiness . . . Look that you lose not your precious time by falling in with idle companions, or by growing weary of your studies, or by love of any filthy lust . . . there are and will be such in every scholastic society for the most part, as will teach you how to be filthy."[34]

But not all adults shared Shepard's concern, and the disciplining of young people for junketing could prove controversial. In the winter of 1676–77, a group of young people living in the Cambridge vicinity gathered regularly at night to eat, drink, sing, and dance. One night in January they became so rowdy that their ongoing revelry was exposed. Magistrate Thomas Danforth admonished four women and nine men for "meeting at unseasonable times, and night walking, and companying together contrary to civility and good nurture to vitiate one another." Yet fifty-five-year-old Abraham Arrington commented that "it was a pitiful thing that a young man and maid could not be together but such reports must come of it, and he did believe ere long the young men must pass by the maids like Quakers and take no notice of them . . . let them [the authorities] do all they could, a young man could never be made an old man."[35]

Some householders became furious if they discovered that young people were meeting secretly on their premises. When Robert Wing, a tavernkeeper in Boston, found out that Mary Atherton and Richard Deacon were alone together upstairs in his house behind a locked door, he and two friends broke down the door with an axe and "threw them down the stairs." "Come down," cried Wing, "you shan't play the whore in our house." But other townsfolk who saw no harm in youthful trysts knowingly hosted such get-togethers. One New Haven couple was fined in 1663 for allowing young people to gather at their house "unseasonably, contrary to both the knowledge and consent of their parents and masters." Their guests spent the evening after Sabbath "playing at cards and singing and dancing." Another couple was summoned for "disorderly inviting Mr. Crane's maid in the night," ostensibly "to eat a sack posset," but actually so that she could meet a young man there in secret. Mariah Melyen, also of New Haven, had allowed Sarah Tuttle to spend "almost half an hour" sitting "in the presence of others" with Mariah's brother Jacob Melyen, "his arm being about her, and her arm upon his shoulder or about his neck, and he kissed her, and she him." The court told Mariah that she "should have showed her indignation" toward Jacob and Sarah. Mariah may not have cared about Jacob and Sarah's kissing and cuddling; or perhaps she felt that allowing them to do so in the company of older adults was safer than restraining them and so prompting them to find more private opportunities for intimacy. What the court condemned as permissiveness may have been pragmatism on her part.[36]

Protecting young people from "bawdy, unclean exorbitances" became ever more challenging toward the end of the seventeenth century, especially in larger towns.[37] Puritan worthies in Boston agonized about the temptations to which young people were subjected in an increasingly worldly and cosmopolitan environment. The growing popularity of dancing was particularly worrisome to some observers because of its sexual connotations. Increase Mather warned that "the very motion of the body which is used in dancing" had "a palpable tendency to that which is evil." He condemned "mixed or promiscuous dancing, viz. of men and women" as "utterly unlawful," "a scandalous immorality," "a recreation fitter for pagans and whores and drunkards than for Christians."[38] The sermon in which Mather voiced his disapproval, "An Arrow against Profane and Promiscuous Dancing," was delivered and soon afterward published in response to the arrival in Boston of Francis Stepney, a dancing master, in 1685. A group of ministers, including Mather, visited the General Court to protest Stepney's plans for a dancing school. He had apparently announced that classes would take place on the Sabbath. The magistrates, having listened attentively, forbade Stepney "to keep a dancing school" on penalty of being "taken in contempt" and "proceeded with accordingly." But even some church members had encouraged Stepney in his planned venture, and Puritan leaders could not insulate their community indefinitely from the fashionable pastimes of transatlantic polite society. Different versions of social respectability as well as generational conflict now hampered their moral agenda. Increase Mather noted in a diary entry for 1704 that "a profane dancing school" had now been established in Boston, a fitting testimony to "these sad times."[39]

THROUGHOUT THE SEVENTEENTH CENTURY, the guardians of sexual orthodoxy had faced another significant obstacle to the realization of their ideals. Values and beliefs that ministers and magistrates considered antithetical to moral order had proved extremely resilient even among New Englanders who espoused the Puritan cause. Many avowedly devout men and women clung to notions that were familiar or convenient even when those notions contradicted the ideals to which they subscribed: ordinary folk were often much less invested in rigorous consistency than those who sought to guide them; they compartmentalized, switching back and forth as seemed appropriate between the mandates of their faith and inherited cultural assumptions. Ministers were horrified to find, for example, that church members turned to divination, healing charms, and countermagic despite condemnation of such practices by Puritan theology.[40] A similar pattern characterized popular attitudes toward premarital sex: even godly colonists sometimes ignored the official precept that a sexual relationship should occur only after a publicly constituted marriage had taken place. These men and women did not condone casual sex, but they believed that sexual intercourse became licit once a couple had committed to marry. In taking that view, they followed longstanding popular tradition.

On neither side of the Atlantic was there general agreement as to when a couple might justifiably become sexually intimate. The Church of England taught that couples should wait until after they were formally wed in an ecclesiastical ceremony. Yet many Englishmen considered unmarried sex to be unexceptionable if the parties had engaged with each other to marry. During the Elizabethan period, church courts had mounted a campaign to discipline couples who conceived children prior to marriage in an attempt to quash popular assumptions regarding the acceptability of premarital sex. Puritan leaders diverged from the orthodox Anglican position in arguing that marriage was "a civil thing" and so should not take the form of a religious ceremony.[41] New England couples planning to become husband and wife had to give public notice of their intentions and then formalize their union in the presence of a government official who was licensed to marry; only at the end of the seventeenth century did clergymen begin to officiate at weddings.[42] But the New England authorities were at least as concerned as the English church courts to ensure that couples remained celibate until the marriage ceremony had been performed.

·Yet many New England settlers, including church members, persisted in treating a mutual commitment to marry as the crucial step after which sexual intimacy could be justified. Colonists who acted on that presumption ran the risk of being disciplined by their church congregations or punished in court for "knowing each other carnally before they were married legally." More than 150 couples living in Essex County were convicted of premarital sex between 1640 and 1685. Others may well have been guilty of the misdemeanor but did not conceive and so were not detected.[43] Elizabeth Denham, a member of Boston's Second Church, was presented in 1692 for "having an infant born within too few weeks after she was married." And Stephen Johnson, who belonged to the same congregation, was disciplined in 1701 for having "sinfully conversed with her who was now his wife, before she were so."[44] The greatest challenge facing magistrates and ministers was not blatantly immoral or amoral colonists, but rather those who identified as Puritans and yet either did not understand or quietly ignored official condemnation of premarital sex. Some of these couples may have intended to wait but were unable to restrain themselves. Others saw no reason to wait.[45]

Most of those who found themselves in court or a church disciplinary meeting charged with this offense were already married; they had been exposed by their first child's date of birth. But couples who engaged in premarital sex were occasionally discovered before their marriage took place. One such couple, Samuel Hoskins and Elizabeth Cleverly, told the New Haven court in 1642 that they had "entered into contract" with their parents' consent before their "unclean passages." Cleverly and Hoskins clearly saw their having "entered into contract" before becoming sexually intimate as a significant mitigating factor. Indeed, Plymouth Colony's legal code punished fornication "after contract and before marriage" less severely than fornication "before or without legal contract." But neither New Haven nor the other New England colonies made any such distinction in their laws. Hoskins and Cleverly were duly whipped for "their filthy dalliances together." Although they failed "to make proof of their parents' consent," the court gave them permission to marry, partly on the grounds that they had "made themselves unfit for any other."[46]

Magistrates sought to use premarital sex prosecutions as a tool of cultural conversion. Not only were the public floggings and fines imposed for this offense intended to deter other young couples from similar behavior, but in addition the judgments given out were sometimes clearly designed to persuade people that they should abstain from premarital sex on principle. It was hoped that such homilies would be disseminated by those present at the trial among their relatives, neighbors, and acquaintances. In 1648 the New Haven court fined a couple for having had sex before marriage and ordered that "they be brought forth to the place of correction that they may be ashamed." The magistrates also took the opportunity to emphasize the heinous nature of the offense, "a sin which lays them open to shame and punishment in this court. It is that which the Holy Ghost brands with the name of folly, it is wherein men show their brutishness, therefore as a whip is for the horse and asse, so a rod is for the fool's back." Yet persuading even the defendants that they had acted wrongly could be extremely difficult. Benjamin Graves did not see himself as blameworthy in having slept with Ruth Briggs after they agreed to marry. Briggs later informed Graves that she would not wed him after all, but the young man had considered himself betrothed at the time of their sexual intimacy. The court "laboured much with him, to bring him to a sight of his sin, but little prevailed." Graves was well aware, however, that not everyone shared his views on the subject: when he asked John Luddington, who had also been espoused to Briggs, if he had "carnal knowledge of her," Luddington responded "that he scorned to do that before marriage."[47]

Given the coexistence of different perspectives on premarital sex as well as the tension between ethical principles and lust, it would not be surprising if some young couples felt ambivalent or conflicted about this issue. In some cases, one partner may have had more scruples than the other. When Jacob Melyen suggested to his future wife, Hannah Hubbard, that they become sexually intimate, she cited "the speech of Christ to the woman taken in adultery" as reason for abstaining until they were married. He, however, persuaded her that the passage in question referred only to "a married woman": "it was," he assured her, "no sin in single persons." Hannah was convinced and yielded.[48] In one of those fortuities that gladden the hearts of historians, there survives a detailed account of one young couple's conversation about whether or not to have premarital sex. In 1662 William Payne of New Haven lodged a complaint against John Frost, a farm worker, for seducing his daughter. Mercy, Payne's daughter, told the court that Frost had repeatedly propositioned her over a period of several months; he had coupled these sexual advances with initially vague but increasingly specific allusions to the possibility of their marrying. Mercy insisted that she was far too young to marry and that in any case her parents would not approve.

One day when they were spreading dung together, John persuaded Mercy to sit down for a rest and set about assuring her that sex before marriage was an acceptable and sensible trial of their compatibility. Mercy reconstructed their conversation as follows:

> Then he said to her: Come, let us see if we be fit to marry together.
> But she said: No, John, then she should be a whore.
> He said: No, she would not except she be with child.
> She said: Then I shall be hanged.
> He replied: He wondered she talked so sillily, she would neither be
>   hanged nor whipped, what if they be whipped, that was nothing.
> Then she said: It was a grievous sin.
> He said: No, everyone does so and must do so before they are married.
> She said: She would not believe it.
> He said: Indeed they do.
> She said: No, it is a grievous sin.
> But he said: He would do it.
> She said: What if any[one] should see them?
> He said: No, they would not.
> She said: One above would.
> But he said, Come let us, and would whether she would or no, and said,
>   If any should see them, he would have them to the court and fined
>   a great deal for he was of good esteem in the town.

The young man's combination of reassurance, bravado, and pressure had eventually prevailed over Mercy's spiritual concerns and fear of discovery and punishment. There followed the first of several sexual encounters in which Mercy now claimed to be a reluctant participant. John denied "sinful actings with her," but the court refused to believe him. Both were

36

sentenced to be whipped, though Mercy's sentence was reduced to a fine because she was unwell. She and John married within a few years of the trial.[49]

Men sometimes promised marriage as part of a sexual advance without any intention of keeping their word, thus seducing women who would not otherwise have agreed to have intercourse by exploiting their belief that betrothal legitimized sexual intimacy. John Frost may have been sincere in committing himself to marry Mercy Payne. But the smooth-tongued Christopher Grant seems a more dubious character. In 1669 Sarah Crouch named Grant as the father of her illegitimate child. She told the Middlesex County Court that she had demurred when he first made sexual overtures, but Grant "promised her no hurt should come of it: if there did he would marry her or else he were a rogue in his heart . . . If she was not good enough to make his wife, she was not good enough to make his whore." He added reassuringly that "it would not be known if he married her soon after." Subsequently they had sex on at least three separate occasions. When Crouch later told him that she was pregnant, Grant "said he would marry me if I would make away with the child." Perhaps Grant wanted them to be able to pose as "chaste" at the time of their marriage; or perhaps this was a devious attempt to persuade her to abort the pregnancy so that he would not have to take responsibility for the child. In any case, she had the baby. He then denied having had sex with her at all, but the court nonetheless named him the father.[50] Sarah Crouch was by no means the only New England woman who fell prey to a duplicitous suitor. John Lee was whipped and fined for, among other things, "abusing a maid" by "pretending love in the way of marriage, when himself professes he intended none," and "enticing her to go with him into the cornfield." Sarah Wood became sexually intimate with Zechariah Maynard because she thought they were committed to each other: "he often showed much love to me and promised to marry me." She was subsequently shocked to find herself a single mother: "I did not think that he would have run away and le[ft] me in this condition."[51]

Women who put their faith in a distinction between sex involving single persons and that involving a couple committed to wed could not take for granted that neighbors would share their perspective. Since other settlers subscribed to the official teachings on this subject, any form of premarital intimacy could prove controversial and legally risky. Thirty-five-year-old widow Sarah Stickney determined to extract a promise of marriage from sailor Samuel Lowell because she was worried that neighbors had seen her "merry in discourse" with him and "wondered at their familiarity." Stickney hoped that her neighbors would be more inclined to condone her "familiarity" with Lowell if they knew she was going to marry him and so asked Lowell "to write a publishment of the intentions." Lowell, reported a neighbor who was present that evening, "did so to satisfy her," but she "was more earnest about it than he was" and "it was not a legal publishment." Stickney was right to be concerned about the consequences of her "merry" behavior but wrong in thinking that a promise of marriage would mollify all potential critics. When Lowell began turning up at her house late at night, demanding admittance and threatening to force his way in, her brother persuaded her to lodge a complaint. But witnesses came forward to testify that she had carried herself "lightly." John Mighill had seen her with Lowell and other sailors, "very jocund and merry, sitting in their laps," which he "thought was just cause for complaint to authority." Instead of securing Lowell's punishment for what she and her brother evidently saw as threatening behavior, she ended up being fined with him "for committing fornication."[52]

JUST AS THERE WAS NO consensus among New Englanders on the issue of premarital sex, so too different attitudes toward marriage formation and dissolution gave rise to confusion and controversy. Whereas English law allowed couples to declare themselves married informally, in private, and even without witnesses, New England legislators insisted that marriage should take the form of a public ceremony with an appointed official on hand to conduct the proceedings. Colonists living farther south in British America often married informally, sometimes because they did not have ready access to a minister or public official and sometimes because they saw no need for a formal ceremony. Informal marriages were less common in New England than elsewhere in the British colonies, partly because a larger proportion of the settlers were punctilious about such matters and partly because official regulation was more effective. But not all New Englanders cared about marriage protocol. In *An Abstract of Some of the Printed Laws of New England,* published in 1689, a memorandum following the Massachusetts Marriage Act of 1646 claimed that "many thousands not agreeing to the reasonableness of it live together unmarried."[53] The reference to "many thousands" was presumably hyperbolic, but self-marriage was far from unheard of in New England. Officials in Essex County received a report in 1680 that Thomas Stevens and Rebecca Harris "had lived together as man and wife for some months past and [that] they had often said they were married." No public ceremony had marked the beginning of this cohabitational relationship, and so the arrangement was illegal; yet Stevens and Harris may well have considered themselves a married couple.[54] As with prosecutions for premarital sex, what struck the authorities as immoral and disorderly behavior could seem quite unproblematic from the perspective of colonists less invested in marital formalities.

That disjunction between official and popular attitudes became all too clear in a case heard by the General Court of Rhode Island in 1665. Magistrates discovered that Horod Long had been living with George Gardiner for "eighteen or twenty years together . . . under the covert of pretended marriage." Long had been married previously to John Hicks and was apparently still his wife (she claimed that a Rhode Island court had granted her a formal separation from him, but no record of this survives, and her assertion does not appear to have been substantiated during the subsequent proceedings). She and Hicks had migrated to New England in 1637, settling first in Massachusetts and then moving to Rhode Island in 1640. Five years later, Hicks left Long and resettled on Long Island: he claimed that she had committed adultery, she that he had abandoned her without cause. Long told the court in 1665 that she had found herself in desperate straits following the separation and so entered into a relationship with Gardiner. Be that as it may, she was not formally married to Gardiner and so, from a legal and theological perspective, had lived "all this time in that abominable lust of fornication."[55]

The court noted, however, that such an interpretation was "contrary to the general apprehension of her neighbors, she having had by the aforesaid Gardiner many children." In other words, the local community assumed that they were married *because* they were living in a stable domestic relationship and were raising a family together. When asked if "ever he were according to the manner and custom of the place married," Gardiner replied "that he cannot say that ever he went on purpose before any magistrate to declare themselves, or to take each other as man and wife, or to have their approbation as to the premises." But although Gardiner and Long had never become publicly and legally married, they had apparently committed themselves in a private ceremony. Robert Stanton testified that "one night being at his house both of them did say before him and his wife that they did take one the other as man and wife." Long clearly understood that self-marriage was illegal in New England and, now that her relationship with Gardiner had collapsed, sought to exploit that fact: it was she who provoked the investigation of her marital history by asking for a formal separation from Gardiner on the grounds that they had never been legally married in the first place. Having chosen self-marriage over legal marriage, she now sought to capitalize on that decision. The court did judge their union to be invalid, and so Long achieved her objective, but at a price: she and Gardiner were fined twenty pounds each.[56]

The General Assembly was evidently embarrassed by the Long case, "brought to light and most shamefully exposed to the public view, to the extreme reproach and scandal of this jurisdiction." It issued a general statement regarding marriage formation, demanding that the 1647 law requiring public marriage be "more duly minded and observed." That law had declared that "no contract or agreement between a man and a woman to own each other as man and wife" would "be owned from henceforth throughout the entire colony as a lawful marriage" unless duly published and then formalized by a licensed official. But the court order exempted from punishment all those who had commenced living together "as man and wife by the common observation or account of their neighbors" before the 1647 act had passed, even though they had not observed all "the rules and directions" laid down in the act. The children from such relationships were not to be "reputed illegitimate." However, such couples could not "take any advantage" of the way they had married "to leave either such wife or such husband." Such marriages were "deemed to be good, firm, and authentic."[57]

This announcement conceded implicitly that informal marriages were not uncommon and offered an amnesty to what sounds like a significant number of couples, even as it sought to bring marriage formation more firmly under public control for the future. Any couples living together without having legally married would henceforth "be proceeded against and punished as for fornication, and that from time to time, or from one General Court of Trials to another, until they shall either live apart or observe the rule premised and prescribed in the aforesaid law and orders." The General Court sought to engineer a transition away from a situation in which formal and public marriage coexisted alongside informal self-marriage; it did so through a combination of pragmatism regarding what had already transpired and tough-mindedness with regard to the future. The court focused quite explicitly on the issue of sex: its ultimate objective was to transform "fornication" into "lawful marriage." The court made clear its determination to take action against couples not covered by its amnesty the following year when it fined William Long and Ann

Brownell "for owning one another [as] man and wife, notwithstanding the magistrates' prohibition."[58]

Other colonists were less than punctilious about abiding by the legal requirement that they formally dissolve one marriage before entering into another relationship. It was not unusual for early Americans to pass from one cohabitational relationship to the next with scant regard for the formalities of divorce and remarriage. If an individual married in public, then separated informally and subsequently remarried, the new relationship would be bigamous from a legal and ecclesiastical perspective; those who chose instead to live informally with a new partner were guilty, at least officially, of adulterous cohabitation. But those concerned did not necessarily see their unions in this light. Here again the challenge to official standards and requirements was much less serious in New England than farther south in the early Chesapeake and the eighteenth-century Carolinas, but by no means all New Englanders who wanted to end their relationships sought official approval. In some cases they doubtless realized that a petition would fail, and in others they must have known that the circumstances would get them in trouble: simply declaring that one's marriage no longer worked did not constitute grounds for divorce in a New England court; if one party claimed or confessed malfeasance such as adultery, magistrates might accede to the petition, but then the guilty party would be punished.

Some individuals did see fit to mark the end of a marriage but preferred an informal renunciation. When Robert Jarrad left his wife Elizabeth, he "affirmed before Mr. Richard Smith that he would have nothing more to do with her and wished her to take her course." He apparently promised to apply for a formal divorce, but he failed to do so.[59] Magistrates occasionally came close to recognizing the validity of informal divorce. One local court gave Sarah Pickering permission to live apart from her husband after she produced letters from him "renounc[ing] her as a wife." And another decided that Mary Bidgood would not have to return to her husband in England because he "by his letters had left her to herself and her friends here."[60] But these were exceptional judgments from a system that generally demanded public and formal indications of marital status. John Smith, who lived in Medfield, Massachusetts, was presented to the Suffolk County Court for "going away from his wife and accompanying with Patience Rawlins, and declaring that she was his wife." Smith did not necessarily desert his wife: the couple may have agreed to separate and henceforth considered themselves free to enter other relationships.

Smith and Rawlins may well have been quite sincere when they described themselves as married, but they had not formally wed and so in the eyes of the court were guilty of adulterous cohabitation.[61]

Regulating the formation and dissolution of marriages was made much more difficult by mobility within North America as well as across the Atlantic. It was sometimes extremely difficult to tell whether couples who claimed to have formalized their relationships elsewhere were indeed legally married. The Connecticut Court of Assistants called Josiah Clark and Mary Crow to account in 1681 for "their clandestine removing hence, and returning and carrying towards each other as man and wife, and not being able to give in testimony of their being lawfully married to each other." Clark and Crow's motive for "removing" to marry (if indeed they did so) is irrecoverable, but some couples did shift from one place to another so as to pass themselves off as married, thus camouflaging a self-consciously illicit relationship. In 1685 Elizabeth Gilligan, a married woman, departed Marblehead to visit relatives at Pascataqua in the company of John Hunniwell, who had a wife and six children back in England. She went with him ostensibly because it was "bad for a woman to go alone through the woods." Her husband, Alexander, had given his permission because Hunniwell was heading in the same direction, allegedly to visit relatives of his own. But during their stay at Pascataqua, they "lived as man and wife." Hunniwell claimed when questioned about their relationship "that she was his wife and [he] had been married to her about five or six weeks."[62]

Given the expense and difficulty of securing a legal divorce in England, transatlantic migration may well have seemed an attractive option to individuals who wanted to escape unhappy marriages and establish new relationships elsewhere. We cannot assume that such individuals saw their new relationships as illicit, but at least some of them became only too aware that the New England authorities did. Because of the constant flow of correspondence across the Atlantic and the frequency of return visits by settlers, the preexisting marital commitments of colonists sometimes came to light. In 1639 James Luxford was "presented for having two wives" and sent back to his first wife in England; his second marriage in Massachusetts was declared void and all his assets in the colony "appointed to her whom he last married." Five years later, John Richardson's marriage to Elizabeth Frier was declared bigamous after the General Court of Massachusetts received information that Richardson had another wife still alive in England.[63]

Massachusetts and Connecticut law required that settlers whose spouses still lived in England or elsewhere be sent back "by the first opportunity" unless they could show "just cause to the contrary." The law pointed out that such individuals had often proved themselves a moral threat: "they live under great temptations, and some of them commit lewdness and filthiness here amongst us, and others make love to women, and attempt marriage, and have attained it."[64] The Essex County Court suspected that Philip Cromwell, who had been "living from his wife seven or eight years," intended "overmuch familiarity" and "filthiness" in keeping company with women when their husbands were absent, "to the disturbance of the neighbors" and "giving grounds for jealousy." He was ordered not to "keep company" with married women "unseasonably or unnecessarily" and "to go over to England to his wife," bringing her with him if he chose to return.[65]

New Englanders of both sexes found themselves deserted by spouses who left to establish new lives and relationships elsewhere in the Americas. James Skiffe of Plymouth Colony secured a divorce in 1670 on the grounds that his wife had "forsaken" him, removed to Roanoke in Virginia, and there had "taken another man for to be her husband." Phoebe Cook of Rhode Island petitioned for a divorce from her husband, John, in 1684 after he left her and remarried, "or at least liveth with another woman, owning her to be his wife," on New Providence, one of the Bahama Islands. The court record added that he had "lived a debauched life in this colony," had "denied his said wife Phoebe," and had "twice endevoured to be married to others." It is possible that Cook "denied" his wife in order to signify his termination of their relationship, paving the way for remarriage. But Thomas Stevens was clearly a blackguard. Elizabeth Wade of Plymouth married Stevens only to discover afterward that he already had three other wives, one in Boston, another with children in England, and a third in Barbados. The court dissolved their marriage, freeing Elizabeth to remarry and sentencing Thomas to be "severely whipped at the post" for his "abominable wickedness."[66]

When a spouse simply disappeared, the person who had been abandoned was expected to wait patiently for information about the missing husband or wife before becoming involved with someone else. In 1696 Hannah Bishop found herself in trouble with the Second Church in Boston because she had "made overtures and promises of marriage" to Daniel Hodgson, although her husband "had not been gone a twelvemonth to sea, nor was there any advice come of his death, one way or another." The church pointed out that if she had "consummated" the promised marriage, "her offence had by the law of this province been capital." In other words, she would have committed adultery, the penalty for which was death.[67] Yet the authorities recognized that it was in the moral interests of the abandoned individual and the community as a whole to allow remarriage after a reasonable space of time had passed, usually seven years.[68] In 1674 the colony's General Court granted Elizabeth Jarrad a divorce in part to free her "from such temptation as ha[d] occasioned her gross and scandalous fall into the sin of uncleanness" after the departure of her husband. Jarrad had evidently not been sexually abstinent since that separation; remarriage would protect her from further temptation to sin.[69]

That New England courts were determined to engineer orderly transitions from one publicly sanctioned marriage to the next is hardly surprising, given their general insistence upon social and moral decorum. But one kind of disorder recurs as a matter of stated concern throughout these cases, namely, illicit sex. Puritan magistrates cared about marital formation and dissolution largely in terms of preventing what they perceived to be illegitimate sexual relationships. Yet the authorities had to reckon with those who defined sexual propriety quite differently, as well as those who did not care. Establishing and maintaining control over sexual ideology and practice was made more difficult by the mobility and elusiveness of a colonizing population, as men and women uprooted to shift not only across the Atlantic but also from one colony to another in the New World. The very nature of the colonial enterprise frustrated, at least to some degree, the vision of moral order that had motivated New England settlement in the first place.

IN SEXUAL AS IN other matters, some New Englanders turned out to be a good deal more independent-minded than their leaders expected or desired. They were also willing for practical reasons to tolerate in their midst behavior that official ideology held to be intolerable and that they themselves may have considered to be less than desirable. This becomes very clear when we examine how townsfolk and villagers responded to sodomy. Not all New Englanders shared the virulent horror of sodomitical acts expressed in official statements. And even those who did disapprove seem to have been loath to invoke legal sanctions against neighbors who committed sodomy. Colonists were generally pragmatic in their response to such individuals, focusing on the mundane interests of the local community rather than moral absolutes. Much of the time, they appear

44

to have found nonsexual aspects of a person's behavior more significant in determining his or her social worth.

Consider the experience of Nicholas Sension, who settled in Windsor, Connecticut, around 1640, married in 1645, and became a prosperous member of his community during the ensuing years. Sension's marriage was childless, but his life appears to have been otherwise unexceptional save in one regard: in 1677 he appeared before the colony's General Court, charged with sodomy.[70] Sension had been making sexual overtures toward men in and around Windsor since the 1640s. These advances, deponents claimed, had often taken the form of attempted assault:

I was in the mill house . . . and Nicholas Sension was with me, and he took me and threw me on the chest, and took hold of my privy parts. [ca. 1648]

I went out upon the bank to dry myself [after swimming], and the said Sension came to me with his yard or member erected in his hands, and desired me to lie on my belly, and strove with me, but I went away from him. [ca. 1658]

On other occasions Sension had offered to pay for sex: "He told me," claimed Peter Buoll, "if I would let him have one bloo [blow] at my breech he would give me a charge of powder."[71] Sension had approached a number of men repeatedly, but the young fellow on whom he fixed his attentions most assiduously was Nathaniel Pond, a servant in the Sension household. Pond had complained to his brother Isaac about his master's "grossly lascivious carriages toward him, who did often in an unseemly manner make attempts tending to sodomy."[72] Several witnesses claimed to have seen Sension attempt sodomy with Pond, mostly in the sleeping quarters at Sension's house, where the master seems to have prowled at night, a sexual predator among his servants.

Sension's predilections were apparently well known. Whether or not he found willing partners in and around Windsor, Sension had a reputation for being sexually aggressive that made at least some of his neighbors and acquaintances nervous. When Thomas Barber, another man's servant, found that he was expected to sleep with Sension "in a trundel bed" during a stay in Hartford, he was "unwilling and afraid" to do so "because of some reports he had heard formerly concerning him." Barber overcame his apprehension, partly because he was reluctant to make "disturbance in a strange house" and partly because members of the General Court "lay in the chamber" and so "he hoped no hurt would come of it." But not long after Barber got into bed, Sension "strove to turn [Barber's] back parts upwards and attempted with his yard to enter his body." Barber now found himself "in a great strait," on the one hand "fearing to disturb the courtiers in the other bed" and on the other "fearing he should be wronged." The anxious servant "turned his elbow back to Sension's belly with several blows which caused him to desist for that time." Barber "slept in fear all night, and in [the] morning told his master . . . that he would lie no more with Goodman Sension."[73]

Sension was well aware of the legal dangers that faced him. He described his persistent advances toward Pond as "foolish," and John Enno, who had witnessed several incriminating incidents, told the court that Sension had begged him "to say nothing of these things." Far from being brazen about his attempts at sex with the young men who slept in his house, he was clearly scared and did his best to dissimulate when caught in the act. Samuel Wilson testified that one night in 1671 he "lay back to back" with Nathaniel Pond when Sension came to the bed and started to fondle Pond's "breech," whereupon Wilson "turned about." Sension immediately pulled his hand "out of the bed and said he had come for some tobacco."[74] Sension was also clearly tormented by his sexual proclivities and worried about his fate in the next world as well as this one. Enno deposed at the trial that one night he saw Sension slip into bed with one of his servants, masturbate against him, and then go into the adjoining room, where Enno "heard Sension pray God to turn him from this sin he had so long lived in."[75] But neither fear of legal proceedings, nor repeated rejection, nor spiritual misgivings could deflect Sension from his "sodomitical actings."

And yet Sension's neighbors were remarkably slow to bring charges against him. His persistence in pursuing young men, despite his notoriety and the danger in which that placed him, may have been encouraged by the live-and-let-live attitude adopted by the worthies of Windsor. Town elders investigated Sension's behavior and reprimanded him informally on two occasions, first in the late 1640s and again in the late 1660s. Both investigations were prompted by complaints from relatives of young men who had been approached by Sension. On the former occasion, William Phelps prompted the town elders to reprimand Sension after discovering that Sension had made advances to his brothers and other young men in the neighborhood. Twenty years later, Isaac Pond initiated a second investigation after his brother Nathaniel complained to Isaac about his master's attempts to sodomize him. Yet no formal action was taken against Sension until 1677. After investigating his sexual aggression toward Pond, town elders insisted only that Sension shorten the young man's indenture by one year and pay him forty shillings "for his abuse." The primary concern seems to have been to compensate Pond, not to punish Sension. It is striking that community leaders allowed Pond to stay in the Sension household and, in general, that Sension was able to continue his pursuit of men for over three decades before being brought to trial.[76]

There were those in and near Windsor who had long condemned Sension's interest in men and feared that others might be seduced into similar behavior. It was, William Phelps claimed, the "hazard" of Sension's "infecting the rising generation" that drove him to initiate the first informal inquiry into Sension's "actings." Barber was not the only young man who was displeased by his attentions. When Sension got into bed with Daniel Saxton and tried to mount him, Saxton "thrust him off" and declared, "You'll never leave this devilish sin till you are hanged." Saxton left his master before his indenture was completed and told several acquaintances that he did so because of Sension's attempts to have sex with him. Yet the town as a whole seems to have been remarkably tolerant of Sension's behavior. There was no consensus as to how, or whether, to respond.[77]

Sension's popularity among his neighbors and acquaintances doubtless worked in his favor. The court depositions are remarkable for their lack of hostility to the accused, save in regard to his sexual behavior. Sension's evident attraction to men did not undermine the general esteem in which he was held. Thomas Barber, whom Sension had tried to sodomize in Hartford, declared that he was "much beholden" to the accused for "entertainment in his house" and "therefore [was] much troubled that he should be any instrument to testify against him in the least measure." Similar feelings on the part of other Windsor citizens may have long delayed legal proceedings against him.[78] Nathaniel Pond's feelings toward Sension were clearly ambivalent. On the one hand, he resented his master's advances and complained about them to his brother. On the other, when Sension responded to a local investigation of his behavior by offering to release Pond from his indenture, the young man refused, claiming that "he was loathe to leave him who had the trouble of his education in his minority." Sension's interest in Pond does not appear to have been purely physical. In conversation with neighbor Joshua Holcombe, he spoke of the "fond affections which he had toward" the young man.

Nathaniel, who referred to his master as "Uncle Sension," may well have felt a loyalty and attachment to Sension that Sension misinterpreted as an invitation to physical intimacy.[79]

Reluctance to tear the fabric of community life by taking formal action against an established citizen and employer may also have counterbalanced disapproval of Sension's sexual proclivities. And the status accorded him as one of the wealthiest householders in town probably shielded him to some degree. Why, then, the community's change of heart in the late 1670s? The key event seems to have been the death of Nathaniel Pond in 1675, after which Sension's approaches to other young men became more frequent. This would have provided his enemies with ammunition to secure the support, however grudging, of formerly loyal neighbors such as Barber. There is no evidence from the preceding decades to suggest that any of Sension's neighbors actually condoned his behavior, but neither does it appear that many people in Windsor, apart from the targets of Sension's lust and their relatives, cared sufficiently about his sexual tastes to advocate a strong community response. Legal prosecution became possible only when the social disruption brought about by Sension's advances seemed to outweigh his worth as a citizen. Fortunately for the defendant, only one witness at the trial claimed to have seen Sension engage in actual intercourse with another man. Because this was a capital crime that required two witnesses for a conviction, Sension could be found guilty only of attempted sodomy. He was sentenced to a severe whipping, public shaming by "stand[ing] upon a ladder by the gallows with a rope about his neck," and disfranchisement. His entire estate was placed in bond for his good behavior. Sension died twelve years later. No information survives to indicate whether he changed his ways as a result of the prosecution.

The extent to which Sension pursued his sexual inclinations with impunity suggests an attitude on the part of his neighbors that was far removed from the spirit of official pronouncements on the subject. We should not downplay too much the effectiveness of such pronouncements: they may well have deterred some individuals from experimenting with sodomy and doubtless incited condemnation of those who committed it. Sension did, after all, end up in court and in danger of losing his life. Some townsfolk may have neglected to act against sodomitical behavior because they were slow to recognize or label it as such. Sension's interest in sodomizing men was articulated, for the most part, in the context of established hierarchical relationships. Most of the men whom he approached were, like Nathaniel Pond, in their teens or early twenties. Some of them were his own servants. Sension appears to have been interested in penetrating men whose age and status placed them in a position subordinate to himself.[80] For most sodomy prosecutions in early New England, there survives only a brief record of the charge and the outcome; in some cases, we do not even know the names of those involved, let alone their age or status relative to each other. But the social context that emerges from the transcripts for Sension's trial does at least suggest that for men attracted to members of the same sex in New England, as elsewhere in early modern English culture, intercourse, hierarchy, and power were closely intertwined. Just as sexually predatory behavior toward a female servant might not always be perceived as a distinct issue of assault because it seemed to fall within the parameters of a master's prerogative, so sexual advances made by a master toward a male servant could also be understood in terms of the power dynamic between the two individuals; there was no compelling need to treat the sexual act as distinct from the broader relationship or to label it explicitly as sodomy. Some townsfolk may have been disturbed by what they saw but were unable to respond because the behavior was undefined and bound up with the expression of conventional social power.[81]

New Englanders who did identify and condemn sodomy might choose for any number of practical reasons to hold back from initiating formal action against offenders. The rigorous demands of the legal system constituted a powerful deterrent. It may be that hostile neighbors and acquaintances delayed until they had accumulated enough evidence to mount a credible prosecution. Informal measures may well have seemed an attractive alternative to the expensive and often intractable legal system. Addressing the situation through nonjuridical channels was, moreover, less dire than invoking capital law and so would have appealed to those who wanted to proceed against offenders but did not want the accused to hang. If the local standing of the offender was also an element, as in the Sension case, an informal investigation would provide a more discreet way of addressing the situation. And finally, the positive attributes of men such as Sension might counterbalance disapproval of their sexual propensities. Risking the loss of a good neighbor and the disruption of social and economic relations in the local community may have struck the practical-minded as too high a price to pay for the expunging of the unclean.

But we cannot assume that a majority of New Englanders took their leaders' strictures against sodomy all that seriously.[82] Some incidents relating to sodomy may never have reached court records because too few people were upset for prosecution to be worthwhile. In the Sension case, formal action was taken only when illicit behavior became socially disruptive. Responses to sodomy seem to have ranged from outright condemnation to a live-and-let-live attitude that did not go so far as to condone such behavior but that did enable peaceful cohabitation, especially if the individual concerned was an otherwise valued member of the local community. Those who favored legal action could face a considerable challenge in persuading their neighbors to join them in pressing charges, even against notorious individuals. The weight of opinion does not appear to have rested with those actively hostile toward sodomy. Thus, the citizens of Windsor allowed Nicholas Sension to avoid prosecution for over thirty years and to live as a respected member of his community, despite his "sodomitical actings."

THE COMBINATION OF practicality and forbearance that we have seen at work in Windsor, Connecticut, was hardly in step with the official injunction that New Englanders "walk not only sincerely but exactly."[83] Indeed, the obstacles to bringing about the kind of sexual culture envisaged by Puritan leaders were multifarious. Practical exigency dictated that non-Puritans be admitted as settlers in the fledgling colonies; and there was no way to ensure that the children of even godly colonists would emulate the sexual values of their parents once they reached adolescence and adulthood. Community surveillance, however zealous, was often no match for those determined to act in violation of sexual norms. Even God-fearing colonists sometimes held views on sexual matters that diverged significantly from official statements. New England settlers tended to be much more restrained and pragmatic in responding to illicit behavior in their midst than clergymen or magistrates would have advocated. They had their own priorities and their own beliefs: some they shared with or learned from their leaders; others they clung to despite official teachings to the contrary, valuing tradition and convenience over religious orthodoxy.

The social and cultural dynamics at work in seventeenth-century New England communities by no means automatically favored those who wanted a fundamental reformation of sexual mores. Back in England, reformers had to fight long and hard against traditional popular beliefs regarding sexual and marital protocol. That struggle continued in New England, despite the political ascendency of uncompromising reformists and a preponderance of colonists who identified with the Puritan errand. The version of sexual morality that Puritan ministers and magistrates sought to enforce in the northern colonies presented a stark challenge not only to the earthy and often ribald sexual culture that non-Puritans embraced but also to the hybrid values of many church members. It is to that alternative and radical vision of sexual ethics contained within Puritan theology that we now turn our attention.

2

"A Complete Body of Divinity"
The Puritans and Sex

EDWARD TAYLOR, the young pastor at Westfield, Massachusetts, was about to be married. In September 1674, two months before his wedding to Elizabeth Fitch, Taylor sent his prospective wife a passionate love letter: "I know not how," he wrote, "to use a fitter comparison to set out my love by, than to compare it unto a golden ball of pure fire rolling up and down my breast, from which there flies, now and then a spark like a glorious beam from the body of the flaming sun." Taylor urged Fitch not to dismiss these words as "love's hyperboles" or "the lavish language of a lover's pen." Even "sparkling metaphors" such as he was using could not express the intensity of his fervor. "My love within my breast," he assured her, "is so large that my heart is not sufficient to contain it." Taylor rejoiced in his "conjugal love" as "sanctified" by God. In a diagrammatic poem that he enclosed with his letter, Taylor illustrated his conviction that ardent passion between a devout husband and wife was consecrated by their faith and redounded "to the glory of God." The text of the poem was arranged around an image of "love's swelt'ring heart" within a "ring of love," itself "confin'd within the trinitie" (see fig. 1).[1]

But Elizabeth Fitch was not the only love on Edward Taylor's mind, as the young man openly confessed. He assured her that his heart had not "taken up its lodging" in any human "bosom" other than her own. But "conjugal love," however sincere and intense, must always be "limited and subordinate" to the "boundless and transcendent" love "betwixt Christ and his church."[2] The reference to "church" might sound impersonal, but for Taylor the spiritual marriage between redeemed souls and their heavenly bridegroom was anything but that. The love that he expressed toward his savior was intimate, romantic, sensual, and often explicitly erotic. In

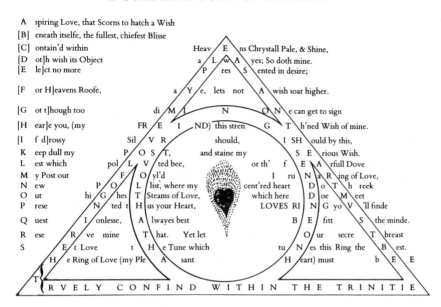

A spiring Love, that Scorns to hatch a Wish
[B] eneath itselfe, the fullest, chiefest Blisse
[C] ontain'd within   Heav E ns Chrystall Pale, & Shine,
[D ot]h wish its Object   a L w A yes; So doth mine.
[E le]ct no more   P res S ented in desire;

[F or H]eavens Roofe,   a Y e, lets not A wish soar higher.

[G ot t]hough too   di M N O N e can get to sign
[H ear]e you, (my   FR E I ND) this stren G T h'ned Wish of mine.
[I f d]rossy   Sil V R should, I SH ould by this,
K eep dull my   P O S T, and staine my S E rious Wish.
L est which   pol L V ted bee, or th' f E A rfull Dove
M y Post out   F O yl'd I ru N a R ing of Love,
N ew   P O L list', where my cent'red heart D o T h reek
O ut   hi G hes T Steams of Love, which here D oe M eet
P rese   N ted t H us your Heart, LOVES RI N G yo V 'll finde
Q uest   I onlesse, A lwayes best B E fitt S the minde.
R ese   R ve mine T hat. Yet let O ur secre T breast
S   E t Love t H e Tune which tu N es this Ring the B est.
    H e Ring of Love (my Ple A sant H eart) must b E E
T
   R V E L Y   C O N F I N D   W I T H I N   T H E   T R I N I T I E

V { pon your Hearte (I pray you) put Loves Ring
    nerringly; Loves Swelt[ring] Hearte herein
W { earing a True-Loves-Knot at Centre's set.
    here with I sent to you an Alphabet
X { enodick whence all Syllables compleat,
    tracted are to spell what Love can speake.
Y   ea, See, then what I send: yet I design,
Z   ion my Ring shall Licen[c]e with her Trine.

FIG. 1. *Edward Taylor's love poem to Elizabeth Fitch, September 1674, as transcribed in Thomas M. Davis and Virginia L. Davis, eds.,* The Unpublished Writings of Edward Taylor, *3 vols. (Boston, 1981), 3:40–41. Read from extreme left to right. The text in the triangle reads: "The ring of love my pleasant heart must be truely confin[e]d within the Trinitie." The text in the circle reads: "Lov[e']s ring I send that hath no end."*

poetry written between the 1680s and 1720s, Taylor envisaged Christ as "a spotless male in prime" and addressed his savior in language of utter infatuation:

> Thou art the loveli'st object over spread
> With brightest beauty object ever wore
> Of purest flushes of pure white and red
> That ever did or could the love allure.
> Lord make my love and thee its object meet
> And me in folds of such love raptures keep.

Faith would prepare Taylor's heart as a "feather-bed . . . with gospel pillows, sheets, and sweet perfumes" to welcome Christ the lover. The pastor yearned for divine arousal of his spiritual "fancy" in vividly sexual terms: "Yea, with thy holy oil make thou it slick till like a flash of lightning it grow quick." Indeed, the poems leave no room for doubt that he anticipated union with Christ through the ecstatic experience of orgasm and penetration:

> O let thy lovely streams of love distill
> Upon myself and spout their spirits pure
> Into my viall, and my vessel fill
> With liveliness . . .

According to Taylor, the soul was "the womb," Christ "the spermadote," and "saving grace the seed cast thereinto." Once "impregnate[d]" by Christ, the soul was "with child" and in due course would produce "the babe of grace." That infant, Taylor's poems make abundantly clear, was the fruit of matchless passion, conceived "in folds of such love raptures" as only Christ could provide.[3]

Edward Taylor's dual passion for Elizabeth Fitch and his heavenly bridegroom was neither unique nor unorthodox. Yet such sentiments are far removed from the persistent stereotype of Puritan New Englanders as sour, repressed, and joyless. The strength of that stereotype is due in no small part to the influence of Nathaniel Hawthorne, whose fictional works have cast a powerful spell over many generations of readers. The Puritans who stalk the pages of his novels and short stories are blinkered, judgmental, repressive, and tormented. Characters such as Arthur Dimmesdale embody and sustain the image of Puritans as bedeviled by sexual frustration and "the haunting, haunting fear that somewhere, someone may be happy."[4] That impression is not entirely inaccurate. Some of the New Englanders who appear in the pages that follow might seem upon first acquaintance quite compatible with the harsh and brooding figures of Hawthorne's imagination. But the Puritans who lived and loved in the seventeenth-century northern colonies were in fact much more complicated and interesting than these persistent caricatures would allow.

Historians have disagreed as to how sexually repressed and repressive the godly really were.[5] The truth is that Puritans celebrated sexual passion in certain contexts and denounced it in others. Puritan teachers lauded marital sex as an expression of love and fellowship between husband and wife; but they condemned sex outside marriage, including premarital sex, as "unclean" and "disorderly." They also warned that even marital sex could become illicit if a husband and wife allowed their desire for each other to eclipse their love of God; the corrupt tendencies inherited from Adam and Eve could taint even sanctioned intercourse. Such ambiguities combined with the uncompromising tone in which the clergy denounced "filthy lusts" to earn Puritans a reputation for hostility toward sex in general. Yet when it came to sexual relations, Puritans were both exuberantly permissive and vehemently restrictive. In this chapter I seek to convey the joy and fear that pervaded in equal measure Puritan attitudes toward sex. Those attitudes are best understood on their own terms as a distinct, coherent sensibility that conjoined earthly and spiritual passion. Thomas Hooker used a gardening metaphor (he was, after all, an Englishman) to capture the essence of that sensibility: "I know there is wild love and joy enough in the world, as there is wild thyme and other herbs, but we would have garden love and garden joy, of God's own planting." Puritans sought not to repress their sexual instincts but to keep them within ordained borders. Although determined to root out "wild love" as unruly and pernicious, they extolled love "of God's own planting" as one of humanity's greatest blessings. Even marital sex had the potential to become "wild" if not appropriately managed: all human affections must serve and remain subordinate to spiritual ardor. But a symbiotic passion for one's earthly spouse and heavenly bridegroom was truly a "garden love and garden joy."[6]

Perhaps the most remarkable aspect of Puritan sexuality was not its spiritualization of the erotic but its eroticization of the spiritual. Scripture invites believers, male and female, to conceive of Christ as a husband and to envisage union with him in vividly sensual, even sexual, terms. The challenge that biblical images of Christ as bridegroom and lover pose to what we might term male heterosexuality has been met in various ways by different Christian cultures. Modern westerners have, for the most part, ignored biblical passages that contain this imagery. But previous Christian traditions have chosen options other than the suppression and bowdlerization of biblical text.[7] New England Puritans welcomed and celebrated the sensual possibilities embedded within the Scripture from which they drew inspiration. Their ability to do so was due in large part to remarkably fluid conceptions of gender within Puritan culture. As a result, in this world and the next, through both human marriage and espousal to the savior, Puritans could find sensual and sexual fulfillment within the Lord's garden.

Clerical references to Christ as a husband and lover became more frequent and more vividly detailed in the late seventeenth century, during the period when ministers were also voicing concern about a rising tide of immorality, especially among the young. This was surely no coincidence. Faced with the maturation of men and women who had not chosen to live in a godly commonwealth and who had to be persuaded to embrace orthodoxy, pastors responded in two ways. On the one hand, they warned against the dangers of "youthful lust" and sought to convince their flocks that even seemingly harmless sexual experimentation had a corrupting and cumulative impact that could lead to spiritual catastrophe. On the other, they sought to seduce the youth of New England into the covenanted community by stressing the voluptuous pleasures that awaited them in the form of a devastatingly handsome and loving savior. Only by eschewing illicit pleasures of the flesh could they hope to gain access to the "love raptures" of which Taylor wrote in his poetry.

PURITAN PASTORS ON BOTH SIDES of the Atlantic taught that a loving friendship and its expression through sexual union was essential to marriage. "Love," they insisted, was "the life and soul of marriage, without which it differs as much from itself as a rotten apple from a sound, and as a carcass from a living body." Just as a well-tuned instrument made "sweet music whose harmony doth enravish the ear," so "when the golden strings of true affection" were modulated as befits "right conjugal love, thus sweetly doth this state then harmonize to the comfort of each other." "Conjugal love," declared Samuel Willard, a leading minister in Boston at the end of the seventeenth century, should be demonstrated through "conjugal union, by which [husband and wife] become one flesh." This oneness was "the nearest relative conjunction in the world . . . follow[ing] from a preference that these have of each other in their hearts, above all the world." Thomas Thatcher, who served as pastor at Boston's South Church, characterized a successful marriage in terms of "dear affection, singular contentment, delight in each other," and "the mutual acknowledgement of each other's power [over] each other's body in conjugal communion."[8]

The private correspondence, diaries, and poetry that Puritans left behind them testify to the physical passion that married couples shared with each other. John Winthrop wrote dozens of letters to his wife Margaret in which he expressed ardent yearning for his "sweet spouse and only beloved." Sample the loving and longing words with which he sought to bridge the miles between them:

> It is now bed time; but I must lie alone; therefore, I make less haste. Yet I must kiss my sweet wife.

> Oh, how loathe am I to bid thee farewell! But since it must be, farewell, my sweet love, farewell.

> Come, my dear, take him and let him rest in thine arms who will ever remain thy faithful husband.

> I kiss and embrace thee, my dear wife.

During their betrothal in 1618, John had written to Margaret that he was "filled with the joy of thy love and wanting opportunity of more familiar communion with thee, which my heart fervently desires." Once married, he found his absences "harsh and grievous," a sentiment that Margaret evidently shared as she wrote, "I shall long for that happy hour when I shall see you and enjoy my sweet and dear husband." When Winthrop left for New England in 1630, he and Margaret decided to "ease" their temporary separation by committing themselves to "meet in spirit till we meet in person" on Mondays and Fridays "at five of the clock at night." "Oh, how it refresheth my heart," he wrote, "that I shall yet again see thy sweet face in the land of the living."[9]

The Winthrops were not anomalous. Just before his marriage to Dorothy Bradstreet, Seaborn Cotton envisioned his impending union with a metaphor that combined clear sexual connotations with quiet romantic assurance. "Women [are] the centre and lines are men," he wrote. "Circles draw many lines unto the centre, but love gives leave to only one to enter."[10] Other Puritans used more extravagant language to express the erotic component of "conjugal love." Anne Bradstreet wrote for her "dear and loving husband" a poem unabashedly sensual and sexual in its imagery:

> I prize thy love more than whole mines of gold
> Or all the riches that the East doth hold.
> My love is such that rivers cannot quench,
> Nor ought but love from thee, give recompence.

Other poems that Bradstreet addressed to her husband, "absent upon public employment," were just as passionate, the physicality of their love utterly transparent. Anne likened Simon to the sun, "Whom whilst I [en]joyed, nor storms, nor frosts I felt,/His warmth such frigid colds did cause to melt." She urged her husband to return in haste to "view those fruits which through thy heat I bore." Meanwhile, as long as he could not "treat by loving mouth," at least his "rayes afar" could "salute her from the south." She hoped that her sun-lover would "never set, but burn within the cancer of my glowing breast, the welcome house of him my dearest guest." [11]

Puritans acknowledged that God had ordained sex between husband and wife in part for purposes of procreation, but "conjugal union" also embodied the love that should unite a married couple. William Gouge, an English minister whose guide to domestic relations was read by New Englanders, characterized marital sex as "due benevolence," a telling phrase that emphasized its loving nature and indispensability. Although sex within marriage was a duty, it "must be performed with good will and delight, willingly, readily, and cheerfully." Gouge argued that a "barren" man could still fulfill his sexual responsibilities as a husband, whereas an "impotent" man could not; in other words, what mattered was his ability to sustain an erection and copulate, not his capacity to sire offspring. Procreation was "one end of marriage," he wrote, but "not the only end." [12]

New England's theologians rejected scornfully the Catholic veneration of sexual abstinence, along with the official "Romish" position that marital sex constituted a necessary evil. John Cotton, one of the most influential of the first-generation New England ministers, wrote that "God was of another mind" than to believe in "the excellence of virginity." He condemned the notion of "Platonic love" within marriage as "an effort of blind zeal," contrary to "that holy spirit, which saith, 'It is not good that man should be alone.'" Ministers pointed out that the Old Testament provided ample justification for their enthusiastic validation of "conjugal communion": Isaac, for example, "sported with Rebecca his wife," Solomon bid "the husband be always ravished with her beauty," and "Ezekiel's wife was called the desire of his eyes." According to Edward Taylor, "the use of the marriage bed" was "founded in man's nature." Samuel Willard pointed out that God himself had authored "the natural inclinations of men." [13]

According to Puritan teachers, marital sex should be extolled as a necessary good, not conceded as a necessary evil. But ministers did not abandon the ideal of chastity. Instead, they redefined it. Willard characterized chastity not as sexual abstinence but as "a moderation, whereby we are to keep ourselves in due bounds, in whatsoever hath any respect to natural generation." Unmarried persons, he emphasized, must maintain celibacy: bachelors and spinsters, along with the widowed, should comport themselves "with great sobriety" until "the time when God shall call them to change their condition." But within the context of marriage, chastity meant fidelity to one's spouse (which was, of course, quite compatible with an active sex life). Thus, Puritans could sanctify sex between husband and wife and at the same time demand "chastity in every condition." "Ye Popish dogs, at marriage bark no more," declared Nicholas Noyes, the minister at Salem Town. "Marriage, that honorable chastity, let none but [the] filthy Antichrist decry." [14]

So essential was sex to the Puritans' notion of a healthy marriage that refusal to engage in relations with one's spouse could lead to a disciplinary hearing at the local church or judicial prosecution. James Mattock, a cooper, was excommunicated by the Boston congregation in 1640 for having, among other things, "denied conjugal fellowship unto his wife for the space of two years together." John Williams of Plymouth Colony was summoned to court in 1665 to answer for "abusive carriages" toward his wife, "in special his sequestration of himself from the marriage bed" and "refusing to perform marriage duty towards her according to the law of God and man." Refusal to provide sexual companionship had serious consequences for a man's reputation. In 1666 recently widowed Edward Pinson complained to the Middlesex County Court about "false reports that he broke his deceased wife's heart with grief that he would be absent from her three weeks together when he was at home and would never come near her and such like." [15]

In common with other seventeenth-century Englishmen, Puritans held that both sexes should experience "delight" during sexual intercourse. According to early modern English medical and marital advice literature, both men and women produced seed that had to mix in order for conception to occur. That could not happen without female orgasm, which required that the woman become sexually aroused. As one manual put it, the womb, "skipping as it were for joy," produced seed "in that pang of pleasure." [16] In 1654, when Martha Richardson of New Haven claimed that she had been impregnated while in "a fit of swooning," the magistrates responded that "no woman can be gotten with child without some knowledge, consent, and delight in the acting thereof." [17] Advice literature held that it was the man's responsibility to stimulate his sexual partner. "When the husband cometh into the wife's chamber," declared a popular guide to sexual relations and midwifery, "he must entertain her with all kind of dalliance, wanton behavior, and allurements to venery." New England courts upheld the view that women had a right to expect "content and satisfaction" in bed; he who failed to provide it was judged "deficient in performing the duty of a husband."[18]

Male inability to provide sexual satisfaction constituted grounds for divorce. That women availed themselves of this option testifies to their conviction that sex was vital to a marriage and that they had a right to demand sexual fulfillment. When New England wives sued for divorce on the grounds that their husbands were impotent, they did so only in part because this prevented them from having children. New Haven's divorce statute, contained in a book of laws that was given to every family in the colony, followed Gouge in describing marital sex as "due benevolence." It allowed a wife to divorce her husband if he proved unable "to perform or afford the same," regardless of whether she was "fit to bear children." A man who proved incapable of providing "that corporal communion which is reciprocally due between husband and wife" was considered nothing more than a "pretended husband." Mary Drury described her spouse in these terms (he was, she declared, but an "outward husband") when explaining to the court in Suffolk County, Massachusetts, why she refused to live with him. Significantly, Drury was fifty-four years old, well past her childbearing years; the issue was clearly not whether she and Hugh Drury would be producing children. According to witnesses for Hugh, Mary had said that she received "full content and satisfaction" from their sexual relationship; these deponents also understood pleasure to be a prime purpose of marital relations.[19]

In addition to lauding and requiring sex as the "due" expression of "conjugal amity," Puritans recommended an active sexual relationship between husband and wife for pragmatic reasons. Not only was reproduction crucial in order to populate New England, but Puritans also believed that abundant marital sex was the key to preventing illicit, non-marital unions: it promoted what Willard called "due continency." God had created sexual desire and included these "natural inclinations" as a part of "innocent nature." The "apostacy" of Adam and Eve, however, had unleashed "inclinations" that were far from "orderly and laudable": "in nothing doth the raging power of original sin more discover itself," Willard reminded his congregation, "than in the ungoverned exorbitancy of fleshly lusts." Ministers hoped that a lively sexual relationship within marriage would dull the allure of illicit passion. "To avoid fornication," advised Gouge, "render due benevolence." In 1674 the Connecticut Court of Assistants granted Elizabeth Jarrad a divorce. The magistrates learned that her husband Robert had "deserted her for several years" and that she had not been celibate throughout that period. Given that Jarrad was still formally married, such behavior was adulterous, but the court sympathized with her plight and assumed that she had erred because her husband had left her and so consigned her to sexual frustration. If she could remarry, she would once again have access to licit sex and so "be freed from such temptation as hath occasioned her gross and scandalous fall into the sin of uncleanness." Few of Adam and Eve's progeny, opined Willard, could "live chastely" without entering into the "conjugal relation." Had it not been for marriage, "mankind must have lived promiscuously like beasts, which would have subverted all order, and been a foundation of confusion." Abstention from marital sex, wrote Edward Taylor, "denie[d] all relief in wedlock unto human necessity" and would tempt those who lacked "the gift of continency" to engage in illicit unions. Conjugal intercourse, then, constituted a bulwark against sexual sin and chaos.[20]

But even marital sex had its seamy side. Ambiguity that at times verged on contradiction figured in Puritan conceptions of sex as in so many other aspects of their faith. Their celebration of "conjugal union" as the expression of "conjugal love" was limited and partly undercut by their belief that original sin was transmitted through sex. The act of generation was tainted, they believed, by its association with the curse placed on Adam and Eve; this contaminated intercourse itself and the children that resulted from it. As clergyman John Williams, paraphrasing Psalm 51:5, put it, "you were shapen in iniquity, and in sin did your mother conceive you." Anne Bradstreet lamented that men and women were "conceived in sin and born with sorrow"; schoolteacher Joseph Green also wrote that he was "brought forth in iniquity." Cotton Mather, a prominent minister in Boston, confessed to his diary in 1711 that he was "continually crying to God" on his children's behalf, lamenting the "inexpressible circumstances of meanness relating to their origin, their production and conception." Significantly, their pardon would come "through the blood of that holy thing which was born of the virgin." As Willard explained, Mary herself was sinful because born of a man and woman, but Christ was conceived "by the power of the Holy Ghost," not "in the natural way of generation," and so was born "without sin." Despite their rejection of celibacy and insistence that marital sex was blessed by God, Puritans continued to see sexual intercourse as a channel for sin. Their rehabilitation of "conjugal union" was sincere but not unequivocal: marital sex was ordained and beautiful but also human and thus flawed.[21]

Pastors warned that earthly love ceased to be sanctified once it distracted husbands and wives from spiritual devotion. John Cotton condemned couples "so transported with affection" that they conceived of "no higher end than marriage itself" and urged them to think of their relationships as ordained "not for their own ends, but to be better fitted for God's service." Thomas Shepard warned that "doting upon and loving the creature more than the Creator" amounted to "horrible idolatry." And Winthrop sometimes worried that his passion for his wife might distance him from Christ: "the love of this present world, how it bewitcheth us and steals away our hearts from him who is our only life and felicity." Such fears echoed throughout the seventeenth century and beyond. Cotton Mather hoped that his earthly marriage could "exhibit in it a conformity to the good one, and a pattern to all observers," yet he feared "inordinate affection as may grieve the holy spirit of God." In a 1718 diary entry, Mather committed himself to being "temperate" in his "conversation" with his wife. "Heaven," he consoled himself, "does not require me utterly to lay aside my fondness for my lovely consort." However, he continued, "I must always purpose a good and an high end in it; something that may be an expression or an evidence of my obedience to God."[22]

THE PURITANS' QUEST TO ENSURE "due continence" within themselves and others was bound up with their conception of the body and its role in the drama of redemption. The physical body, ministers taught, could serve both virtuous and sinful purposes. It was "set up to be an house for the soul to dwell and act in," Jonathan Mitchell explained, and so men and women should strive to "improve and employ [their] bodies for the Lord," taking care not to "abuse th[e] body or the members thereof unto sin." According to Willard, the temptations of "concupiscence" threatened constantly to subvert and taint "bodily members": "lust endeavors to keep them in its service and slavery, to do its drudgery, but grace obligeth them to be the servants of righteousness, and employed in the glorifying of God." It was each man and woman's responsibility to ensure that the body became a monument to the Lord and not to the Devil. Cotton Mather declared that the body, "being brought under a due consecration unto the glorious God," became "a living temple" that could also "do the part of a priest, and as a priest offer itself unto God." The godly should react to "unchaste" thoughts "as at a swine got upon the gates of the temple."[23]

That image of the body as a temple that should be consecrated to God and kept safe from the pollution of sin was a staple of Puritan sermons on sex. Since God's law was "holy and pure," all sin was "filth and uncleanness." Yet sexual sin "by particular use" bore "the name of uncleanness" since it was through illicit sex that women and men most literally perverted and polluted their own bodies. Nonmarital sex constituted "a sin against a man's own body . . . a defiling of that which should be the temple of God." Pastors illustrated that argument with vivid images of desecration: "What a reproach is this, that the sons of God are become flesh, carnal, sensual, debauched; that the members of Christ are made the members of a harlot, yea the members of a beast; that the temple of the holy ghost is become a stews and brothel-house, yea a cage of unclean birds, yea a very hog-sty! What horrid profaneness, what hellish sacrilege is this!"[24] When Puritans referred to unauthorized sex as "unclean," "filthy," "defiling," "vile," and "polluting," they framed the subject, then, in terms of their responsibility to protect their bodies from contamination for the sake of their souls. Ministers sought to prevent New Englanders from using their "members" (a word that signified not only limbs in general but also the penis in particular) as "weapons of unrighteousness." In his diary, Cotton Mather committed himself to "anatomically and particularly consider every part of my body, and, with as explicit an ingenuity as may be, consider the several actions and uses thereof, and then go on to consider on what methods I may serve the glorious God with them," praying that God would preserve him "from ever perverting my body unto any employments forbidden by him."[25]

The godly must beware lest they prize physical beauty for its own sake, particularly since it might seduce them into sexual sin and so lead them to defile the very bodies of which they were enamored. A virtuous woman should take care, Mather warned, that her "good proportion and symmetry of the parts," "skin well favoured," "handsome carriage," and "graceful motions" not "deceive unwary men into those amours which bewitching looks and smiles do often betray the children of men." Men should also exert themselves to resist becoming preoccupied with women's physical beauty. In March 1710 Jeremiah Dummer, who was residing in London as an agent for the Massachusetts Colony, went to the House of Lords to hear a trial and "was entertained with a sight of all the great female beauties of the court, which pleased me to that degree that I could have gazed on them forever." Later that day, he castigated himself for what "seem[ed] a great fault and weakness in [his] mind."

> I consider beauty is extremely superficial, but skin deep; if you take the finest woman in the world and strip off the epidermis, you'll see that the horror of her aspect will fright away the beholder faster than her charms attracted [th]em before. And it's very fading: a short fit of sickness will draw a veil over all its glories. Or if by a rare example that should not happen, yet time and age will certainly lay it all in ruins.

Dummer committed himself to pursue instead "the beauty and lustre of a virtuous mind," which would prove more "durable" and improve instead of degenerating with age. "Oh my God," he wrote, "let me be in love only with virtue, and let my heart be ravished with its beauties! Let me court it with the greatest assiduity, and never rest [un]til I am possessed of it."[26]

Yet an appropriate recognition of earthly transience should not lead the godly to disregard the body as a vessel of redemption. In December 1709 Dummer attended an anatomical lecture that included a dissection of a dead man. Much "affected" by the experience, Dummer "determined, by divine grace, to be more careless about my body for the future than ever I have yet been." Why, he asked himself, should he "pamper and adorn this body, which in a short time will be so foul and ghastly that my nearest friends will start when they behold it[?]" However, Dummer then reminded himself that his savior "took on him this human nature" and that his body must "one day rise from the corruption of the grave." Consequently, there was "a reverence due to it so far, that I should possess this earthern vessel in sanctification and honor, and that I ought not at any time to abuse the members of it to uncleanness or unrighteousness."[27]

Puritan theology judged sexual thoughts and acts according to their impact upon the ongoing struggle between depraved and redemptive urges that raged within each man and woman. That incorporation of sex and the body into a larger moral drama also conditioned the ways in which New England ministers explained sexual impulses. They evoked neither sexuality as an independent force that gave rise to erotic desire nor sexual orientation as a determinant of who was attracted to whom. They explained masturbation, sex involving an unmarried couple, adultery, sodomy, and bestiality just as they did any other sin, such as drunkenness or falling asleep during a sermon: they were all driven by the innate corruption of fallen humanity, and all embodied disobedience to God's will. Puritan leaders divided illicit sexual acts into categories and clearly saw some as more egregiously sinful than others, but they made no distinction among them when accounting for their incidence. They all derived, in William Bradford's words, from "our corrupt natures, which are so hardly bridled, subdued and mortified."[28] Official teaching did not, then, conceive of sexual sin as distinct from any other manifestation of human depravity. The basic issue was moral rather than sexual orientation. Sexual sin could be traced to a particular frame of mind, but that mental state was not specific to any one category of offense, nor was it even specifically sexual.

Sexual lust figured in the clergy's moral universe as one of many sins that fed on each other. Just as pride, gluttony, drunkenness, sloth, disobedience to parents and masters, "evil company," and "irreligion" constituted "the very fodder and fuel of the sin of uncleanness," so unclean acts would in turn encourage all manner of sin by "pollut[ing] the noble faculties of the soul, the mind, and the conscience." The Essex County Court saw fit to note in 1642 that Elizabeth Johnson, who was accused of "unseemly practices" with "another maid," also covered "her ears with her hands when the Word of God was read"; Governor Winthrop noted that William Plaine, convicted of various sexual crimes in 1646, "did insinuate seeds of atheism, questioning whether there was a God." When Samuel Danforth delivered the execution sermon for Benjamin Goad, a young man convicted of bestiality in 1673, he emphasized Goad's disobedience to his parents, lying, stealing, Sabbath breaking, avoidance of catechism, and idleness ("a great breeder and cherisher of uncleanness") as inextricably connected to his sexual degeneracy.[29]

Puritans used the words *uncleanness, lust, carnality,* and *concupiscence* to indicate sinfulness in general as well as sexual offenses in particular. Thomas Shepard condemned the use of improper religious practices as disregarding "that spiritual chastity and virgin spirit which . . . ought to be in all the true followers of the Lamb" and denounced its advocates as "adulterous." Regardless of the sin in question, New England pastors tended to couch their discussions in erotic terms. Temptation itself became a potent sexual force in Samuel Willard's sermonic prose. Willard portrayed the intrusion of sinful thoughts as tantamount to sexual assault: "if they offer to ravish our hearts, we must cry out as the seized virgin, and call in help from heaven, to rescue us from the rape they offer to us."[30] That words such as *lust* had a sexual connotation and yet denoted a much broader range of sinful impulses was doubly significant. On the one hand, the deployment of a highly sexualized language in discussing sin underlined clerical conviction that unauthorized sex was the quintessential expression of human depravity: "there is nothing," declared Willard, "wherein the lusts of the flesh are more apt to vent themselves." Even pride, the fount of all sin in Puritan eyes, had an erotic charge: in early modern English, one of the word's meanings was sexual heat or arousal. On the other hand, sexual offenses made little sense to Puritans unless placed in a larger context. Ministers reminded their congregations of the fate suffered by the citizens of Sodom in order to warn against "all the sins" in which the Sodomites had engaged, not specifically their sexual offenses. When Jonathan Mitchell referred in a sermon to "the Apple of Sodom," he combined two potent images to invoke not any particular sin, but general depravity and its fruits.[31]

Sexual sin, pastors taught, should be understood in tandem with, not in isolation from, other forms of sin. Yet official condemnation of illicit sex was far from indiscriminate: pastors addressing their flocks on the subject distinguished carefully between different kinds and degrees of offense. Samuel Danforth, the minister at Roxbury, Massachusetts, argued that "uncleanness" could be "expressed by and comprehended under these two terms, *fornication,* and *going after strange flesh.*" He explained that "*fornication*" was to be "taken in a large sense" to include four offenses: sex between two unmarried persons ("whoredom" or "the vitiating of a single woman"), adultery, incest, and masturbation ("self-pollution"). The second category, "*going after strange flesh,*" incorporated sodomy ("filthiness committed by parties of the same sex") and bestiality ("when any prostitute themselves to a beast"). Willard used different terminology to make a similar distinction. He told his congregation that "unlawful and prohibited mixtures" could be "ranked under two heads": "natural" and "unnatural." Bestiality and sodomy, he claimed, were "unnatural" because of "the species and sexes" involved, whereas "fornication" (sex "between persons who are single"), adultery, polygamy, and incest were "(in some sense) more natural" because they came "within the compass of the species and sexes."[32]

Danforth and Willard classified sexual acts in terms of those involved and their relationships to each other: their marital status, sex, and species. They and other commentators made a clear distinction between illicit sex performed by a man and woman and that between either two persons of the same sex or a human being and an animal. William Bradford, condemning a "breaking out of sundry notorious sins" in Plymouth during the early 1640s, differentiated between "incontinency" involving married or unmarried persons of the opposite sex and "that which is worse, even sodomy and buggery (things fearful to name)." In 1654 Jonathan Mitchell distinguished between "wantonness and unnatural pollutions," terms equivalent to Danforth's "fornication" and "going after strange flesh." According to New England's spiritual teachers, sodomy and bestiality crossed scripturally ordained boundaries between sexes and species. They were thus more clearly sinful and disorderly than was "uncleanness" between a man and a woman.[33]

Clerical denunciations of those who pursued "strange flesh" were harsh and unequivocal. New England, Charles Chauncy wrote, was "defiled by such sins." They should be punished, declared Cotton Mather, "with death, without mercy."[34] Bestiality struck ministers as especially horrifying. All sin revealed the "brutishness" that lurked within humanity and that threatened constantly to usurp the sway of reason.[35] But this offense in particular showed how fragile was the distinction between human beings and animals. Bestiality, railed Danforth, was "a horrid and prodigious sin," an "abominable confusion in the sight of God," a "monstrous" act that "turne[d] a man into a brute beast" and "pollute[d] the very beast," making it "more unclean and beastly than it was, and unworthy to live among beasts." Indeed, Danforth avowed, Scripture had "appointed the beast itself to be slain" as well as the human malefactor. Such language, though deployed by commentators on both sides of the Atlantic, would have had a particular resonance for early American colonists, given their characterization of the land around them as a wilderness and of Indians as savage beasts. In light of the Puritans' quest to tame their surroundings and its apparently bestial native inhabitants, it would be particularly disturbing if they could not quell such egregious manifestations of "brutishness" within themselves. Not surprisingly, ministers portrayed the inner savage, like the savages abroad, as diabolical and possessed. Referring to a New Haven man who had been seen "confounding himself with a bitch" and "hideously conversing with a sow," Cotton Mather denounced the malefactor as a "hell hound" and a "bewitch'd beast."[36]

Pastors felt it necessary to provide their flocks with a comprehensive anatomy of unauthorized sex in part because they believed that all of its variants were founded in universal corruption, which, as the term implied, afflicted everyone. The sensibility that Puritan ministers brought to bear upon sexual matters was remarkably open-ended in its refusal to see particular men or women as constitutionally inclined or limited to any one form of sexual offense. John Rogers reminded his flock that "every child of Adam" was "a lump of uncleanness . . . pregnant with the seeds of all sin, though all do not shoot forth together, or in every individual." Shepard assured members of his congregation that even those who avoided actual sin entertained sinful thoughts: they were, each and every one of them, guilty of "heart whoredom," "heart sodomy," and "heart buggery" (as well as "heart blasphemy," "heart drunkenness," and "heart idolatry").[37]

According to ministers, sexual sins fitted into a single developmental framework. In a 1693 sermon entitled "An Holy Rebuke to the Unclean Spirit," marking the execution of two women "for murdering of their bastard children," Cotton Mather laid out the steps by which those given over to their "lusts" proceeded on a downward path into a "pit of uncleanness." First came masturbation ("cursed self-pollution"), followed by "odious fornication . . . wherein unwedded persons of both sexes do prostitute themselves." Once married, "the unclean spirit" would "haunt" those who had committed these youthful offenses, leading them into "inordinate affection" (desiring each other as an end in itself rather than as a means to glorify God) or perhaps adultery. Some would be drawn into incest, "invad[ing] that comfortable and profitable order which God has established in human society." Those whose hearts were most corrupted by "hellish fires" sank into the "unutterable abominations and confusions" of sodomy and bestiality. With each step, "sinful creatures" became more wedded to their "diabolical pranks" until, like Benjamin Goad, "grown old in wickedness, and ripe for vengeance."[38]

Young people, ministers agreed, were "in a peculiar manner addicted" to "sensual pleasures" and so required especial attention. Thomas Foxcroft argued that "sensuality" and "pride" (a word that, as already noted, had sexual connotations) "dogg[ed] that season of life more than any other." The young were apparently prone to all manner of sexual temptation, but one particular sin stood out in clerical minds: masturbation was "commonly the young man's sin." Because "self-pollution" was usually "the first pit of uncleanness" into which young people fell, ministers took care to highlight the "abominable" nature of that sin. There was especial cause for concern in that many who "would be loathe to commit other kinds of uncleanness" saw masturbation as a "little, venial, easy peccadillo" and so gave in to temptation, only to be drawn onward into "other

kinds of uncleanness." Discussions of "self-pollution" repay close attention since they illuminate in vivid, even lurid, colors the concerns that
underlay attacks on illicit sex.[39]

Masturbators defiled themselves, Puritans claimed, because ejaculation was intended for procreative intercourse between husband and wife.
As we have already seen, reproduction was not the only goal of marital
sex, but to engage in behavior that involved ejaculation and yet deliberately avoided the possibility of conception seemed perverse and sacrile-
gious to Puritans. It "tended to the frustrating of the ordinance of marriage and the hindering the generation of mankind."[40] Cotton Mather
condemned masturbation as "the cursed way of producing a discharge,
which the God of nature has ordered only to be made in a way which a
lawful marriage leads unto." According to Samuel Danforth, a man who
"practise[d] uncleanness with his own body alone" became "both bawd,
and whore, and whoremaster."[41]

"Self-pollution," declared its critics, had devastating consequences for
body and soul. Cotton Mather described masturbation as a form of "self-
murder" and warned that by "vengeance of God" it "cruelly waste[d] the
bodies of those that are addicted thereunto." According to an English
tract that was reprinted in New England, female masturbation could lead
to incontinence, "a whole legion of diseases" associated with the womb,
a pallid complexion, hysteria, consumption, and barrenness. Some
female masturbators "actually deflower[ed] themselves" and so "foolishly
part[ed] with that valuable badge of their chastity and innocence, which
when once lost, is never to be retrieved." Male masturbation led to "para-
phymosis" (genital inflammation), which in turn could result in ulcers or
"other worse symptoms." It caused "stranguries" (the slow and painful
emission of urine), either "priapisms" (persistent erection) or "a weakness in the penis and loss of erection," premature ejaculation, and "gonorrhea." In the early modern period, gonorrhea referred not only to sexually transmitted disease but also to uncontrollable discharges that were
believed to result from masturbatory excesses. The latter could also cause
stunted growth, fainting fits, epilepsy, and consumption.[42]

Cotton Mather provided a particularly gruesome image of the physio-
logical damage that masturbators apparently inflicted upon themselves.
A physician at Bologna, he wrote, had published "the picture of a wretch
putrifying and emaciated under the arrest of that foul disease." Mather
thought this an excellent "advertisement" for anyone who had committed
the "foul" sin, or was tempted to do so:

Verily, if you should but see the picture of a young man by this impiety reduced unto a woeful consumption; his visage pale and lean, and stomach depraved, and his depauperated blood filled with acid and acrid particles, which do at the same time further provoke the venereal appetites, and also bring all the loathsome accidents of a filthy dreamer upon him; one would think it would be an infallible preservative; and that it would be hardly possible for you to go on, and give your years unto the cruel destroyer.

Mather also laid great stress on the "various and lasting mischiefs" that "self-pollution" wrought in later life. Reaffirming the importance of a lively physical relationship within Puritan marriage, he lamented that masturbating men would not be able to satisfy their wives sexually. "They strangely disable themselves for things expected by them, and from them," he wrote, "and they render themselves unacceptable, where they would much desire to be otherwise."[43]

But the most grievous harm inflicted by "self-pollution" was spiritual. If the purpose of ejaculation was to fulfill the will of God through reproduction, those who engaged in masturbatory ejaculation "sacrifice[d] their seed unto the Devil." Charles Morton, the pastor at Charlestown, Massachusetts, argued in his *Compendium Physicae* (a textbook for the natural sciences adopted by Harvard College in the late 1680s) that semen was "a matter of much higher concoction and preparation than blood," containing "much spirit, and little gross matter." For that reason, "the abuse of it in any wicked way" was "consecrating the best of our bodies to the Devil."[44] Even taken in isolation, warned Danforth, this was an "impious, loathsome, and detestable sin." But masturbation inclined the perpetrator to other sexual offenses and thus "eternal obduration": those who "wallowed in the nasty vices and puddles of unchastity" would become addicted to every kind of impiety.[45]

Ministers labored to impress upon their flocks the ghastly fate that awaited those who desecrated their bodies by engaging in illicit sex. Danforth warned that "abusers of themselves" had "no inheritance in the kingdom of God, but [were] shut out among the dogs, and cast into the lake which burneth with fire and brimstone, which is the second death." But grim warnings and threats were not the only instruments in the clerical armory. More crucially, pastors sought to focus the attention of potential sinners upon the delights of marital union and the compassionate, self-sacrificing love of their savior. In particular, they set about "wooing

. . . young souls" on behalf of their "glorious master, the Prince of Life," so as to ensure an "early religion" that would shield them against temptation.[46] As John Cotton had pointed out, young men "troubled with lust after women" would find that their problem dissipated once they focused their attention on Christ, "the fairest of ten thousand." Declared Cotton Mather, "Such thoughts as these leisurely and thoroughly prosecuted will nail thy lust unto the cross of the Lord Jesus Christ; and let me tell thee, there is no way to mortify a lust, but by hanging it on that blessed cross." This sounds like a classic ascetic strategy. But in "nail[ing]" their "lust" on Christ's cross, believers were not "mortify[ing]" all sensual cravings for the sake of their souls: they were instead exchanging illicit lust for the ultimate in romantic passion, an eternal love affair with Jesus Christ.[47]

ON 19 OCTOBER 1717, Samuel Sewall's first wife, Hannah Hull, died at the age of fifty-nine. God, Sewall wrote in his diary, would now teach him "a new lesson; to live a widower's life." By February 1718, though, Sewall was already contemplating another loving union. But the prospective spouse about whom he enthused to his diary was not one of the Boston widows before whom he would later lay his suit. "I had a sweet and very affectionate meditation concerning the Lord Jesus; nothing was to be objected against his person, parentage, relations, estate, house, home! Why did I not resolutely, presently close with him! And I cried mightily to God that he would help me so to do." That April, Sewall officiated at a marriage and then wrote, "Oh! that they and I might be married to CHRIST; and that our marriage might be known to ourselves, and others!" During the same year in which Sewall was contemplating Christ's unimpeachable qualifications as a spouse, Increase Mather published his *Practical Truths Plainly Delivered,* wherein he described a "marriage" with Christ as "the most desirable one that ever was or that possibly can be." No "greater dignity" was imaginable than marrying "the only son of the King of Heaven," no "greater felicity" than to have as a husband "the wisest and richest that can be thought of." The bride of such a groom would be "made happy for ever." That June, Mather's son Cotton preached "to the flock on [how] the marriage of our saviour unto his people may be attended with many happy consequences," a sermon he published in 1719 under the title *A Glorious Espousal.*[48]

When Puritans evoked scriptural images of Christ as bridegroom and lover, they drew upon a tradition well established in Christian devotional literature, both Catholic and Protestant. Yet such imagery took on new meaning in the context of Puritan attitudes toward marriage. Medieval mystics had described union with Christ in terms of feelings and relationships that they shunned in an earthly setting. Members of the religious orders yearned for marriage with their savior and yet committed themselves to celibacy as a prerequisite for sanctity. The joyful anticipation of ecstatic union with Christ by men and women who had taken vows of chastity affirmed their opposition of physical and spiritual realms as well as their belief that devotion necessarily involved transcendence of the body.[49] The Reformation's emphasis on a believer's personal relationship with God gave new significance to marital imagery among Protestants in general. But Puritans went further: their spirited affirmation of marriage, and of sex within it, transformed their notion of espousal to the savior.[50]

Instead of depicting union with Christ in mystical terms that eschewed the impurities of physical desire, Puritans used concrete, earthy language to draw direct parallels between human marriage and the soul's espousal.[51] Christ's marriage to believers now provided a model for husband and wife as they sought to build and sustain their relationship. "The ground and pattern of our love," wrote John Winthrop to Margaret Tyndal just before their marriage in 1618, "is no other but that between Christ and his dear spouse." When Benjamin Colman urged husbands to give virtuous wives "a singular respect, and the most honourable treatment in the world," he drew their attention to the example set by Christ the bridegroom: "The expressions of the love of Christ to his church in the Book of Canticles is the best account how the husband ought to regard her and treat her . . . As the holy soul, and as the purchased church is fair and lovely in the eyes of God, and dignified by him; so let the deserving wife be esteemed by her happy spouse." Human marriage would, in turn, inspire believers to strive for union with their other, greater spouse. Winthrop hoped that his and Margaret's "consideration" of their love for one another "could make us raise up our spirits to a like conformity of sincerity and fervency in the love of Christ our lord and heavenly husband; that we could delight in him as we do in each other." Heavenly and terrestrial marriages thus became symbiotic, their similarities as striking and instructive as their differences.[52]

When clerics advised their flocks to think of human marriage as "a lively emblem of what passes between the Lord Jesus Christ and his church," they offered a means to ease the tension between their exaltation of marriage and continued distrust of carnal relations. Just as Christ's sacrifice eclipsed Adam and Eve's lapse, so the savior's promised espousal with the elect enabled human marriage to rise above its association with the primal couple's sinfulness. Such was the thinking that underlay John Winthrop's hope that his and Margaret's love would form "into the similitude of the love of Christ and his church." Rather than seeking to transcend his corrupted flesh, Winthrop wanted to resanctify it through a form of typological regimen. Instead of seeing marriage primarily as a corrupt legacy of human history's origins, he could treat it as a presage of the joys accompanying that history's culmination. Cotton Mather hoped that couples who modeled their marriages on that of Christ, the second Adam, would "abate and prevent much of the curse, which every marriage in this world, is likely to be more or less encumbered and embittered withall." As Edward Taylor put it, Christ's "love was ne'er adulterate, e're pure." Marriage and marital sex thus became a foretaste of what the redeemed would experience when they joined their divine husband in heaven.[53]

Spousal imagery peppered New England sermons, devotional texts, diaries, and personal correspondence throughout the seventeenth and early eighteenth centuries. But there was a dramatic shift in the ways ministers used marital images as they engaged with their own and their flocks' spiritual journey. The first and second generations of New England pastors often deployed negative metaphors of adultery and estrangement to dramatize human sin; that recurrent theme reflected the spiritual disillusionment many Puritans felt after arriving in New England and also the ministers' growing fears of declension.[54] Thomas Shepard, the minister at Cambridge, Massachusetts, was far more inclined to bemoan his "widow-like separation and disunion" from his savior than to celebrate their union, just as Michael Wigglesworth constantly berated himself in his diary for "going awhoring . . . after vanities," thus wounding his "head and husband," Jesus Christ, "by not loving and delighting in his presence; by my liking other loves more than him." Wigglesworth, a young tutor at Harvard College, thought of the Sabbath as "blessed seasons wherein poor wandering harlots may return to their husband again." Occasionally he would fantasize about scenes of ardent reconciliation: "will the Lord now again return and embrace me in the arms of his dearest love? will he fall upon my neck and kiss me?" But in most of his diary entries, Wigglesworth lacerated himself for his "whorish desertions" and "brutish, swinish heart."[55]

The emphasis in both public and private writings during the first forty years of settlement lay on the failure of the bride to remain faithful and either Christ's forbearance or God's righteous anger.[56] But by the last quarter of the century, New England ministers changed their tune in a bid to reverse an apparent decline in spiritual fervor. Their message became much more affirmative: instead of threatening their flocks with punishment for their infidelities, pastors now sought to seduce them with promises of a loving and fruitful relationship with Christ. As clerics began to reconceptualize the believer's relationship to divinity so as to stress nurturing love over inspirational terrorism, they recast spousal imagery to support their new message. Images of Christ as a wronged husband and of God as a vengeful father were eclipsed by those of Christ the supportive lover and God the welcoming parent. The prospect of imminent doom in the hands of a father outraged by the harlotry of his prospective daughter-in-law was exchanged for that of ravishment in the bosom of a smiling husband.[57] Not coincidentally, that recasting of the evangelical message could be expected to appeal especially to young people who were contemplating both the choice of a husband or wife and also whether or not to apply for church membership. If the ministers' strategy worked, these two decisions would converge as New England's youth embraced a double marriage.

Clerical references to divine espousal became more frequent and more extensive, as well as more positive in tone. Sewall even criticized a guest speaker at his church in 1689 for not using "the metaphor of bridegroom and bride" to render more "profitable" a sermon on the "interest and duty of Christians to rejoice in Christ." During the last quarter of the seventeenth century and the first quarter of the eighteenth, pastors such as Samuel Willard and Cotton Mather described the soul's marriage to Christ in ever more elaborate detail, occasionally devoting entire sermons to the subject.[58] In doing so, they acted not only as teachers whose duty it was to explicate a recurring scriptural metaphor but also as self-styled "friends of the bridegroom" who courted on Christ's behalf. The days on which ministers preached became Christ's "wooing days," when the savior would "deck and array himself with all his glory and beauty," like a suitor hoping to bedazzle the object of his love. Since pastors were also prospective brides in their own right, they served simultaneously as interpreters, advocates, and potential recipients of the redeemer's advances.[59]

The ministers' use of marital imagery in these turn-of-the-century sermons was literal-minded and appealed blatantly to self-interest. According to clerical descriptions of "marriage" with Christ, the souls of the redeemed and their savior were united through "a regular procedure" that bore a close resemblance to earthly marital arrangements. First, God consented to the match: he "firmly engaged" to adopt his son's brides and "to carry to us in all things as a father."[60] Next, Christ would approach the soul and make his offer of marriage. His clerical advocates encouraged acceptance by detailing both the personal felicity and the "unsearchable riches" to be derived from the "transcendent match." So beautiful was Christ that "the believing soul" could not help but become "enamoured with him." In addition to securing a partner who was "altogether lovely," the bride would "wear the name of her husband," would share "in the glory of the person of Christ, as the wife is honoured by the dignity which her husband enjoys," and would become joint heir "with him who is the heir of all things."[61] Union with Christ began to sound like a social climber's dream marriage, as the groom's advocate exclaimed, almost salivating as he did so, "What a vast jointure hast thou!" But ministers recognized that the prospect of so unequal a match, between "a miserable sinner" and "the only begotten son of God," might be more intimidating than enticing. They urged the prospective bride not to back away because of her "want of a dowry." After all, Christ had laid down "an honourable preferment" in its place, covenanting "his estate to redeem her, to pay her debt, to purchase her freedom, her furniture, and her felicity." Like any husband, Christ assumed responsibility for his wife's debts: "He has suffered to make satisfaction to God for all our sins, which are our debts."[62]

Presented with this humbling yet aggrandizing proposal, the soul had only to utter one word of compliance and the betrothal would become "unquestionable." As in earthly marriage, betrothal was followed by a period of waiting. The "contraction" between soul and savior occurred "in this world," but "consummation" would take place in "the world to come." Meanwhile, believers "could but now and then steal a sight of him, or obtain a kiss from him" in brief "interviews" between which they "pined away with love-sickness." Their consolation was that once married, their "caresses" would be "both full and uninterrupted."[63] In the interim, God had ordained the Lord's Supper as a prenuptial celebration through which the betrothed could regularly and "solemnly renew" their marital covenant. Private prayer gave opportunity for more intimate communion: as one pastor remarked, "can a lover refrain from secret meetings with his beloved[?]"[64] When the nuptial day itself arrived, an occasion coincident with the Day of Judgment, the righteousness imparted by Christ would appear as the bride's wedding garment, "an embroidery with grace inlaid, of sanctuary white most fair." Thus "drest in heavens fashion rare," the souls of the saved would ascend to "the holy court," where their bridegroom would greet them "with widened arms" and "the most tender embraces," present them to his father, and then take them away to "his own home," where they would live together in "eternal cohabitation" and "joy unspeakable."[65]

In addition to shedding its earlier monitory tone, marital imagery became more intimate and familial toward the century's close. The individual believer would become not only a bride in his or her own right but also part of a loving family, the sum of the elect. Once in heaven, the redeemed would unite with each other, their mutual husband, the angelic host, and the heavenly Father to constitute the "family of God." Earlier descriptions of the saved as a group had tended to be quite impersonal, but ministers such as Cotton Mather and John Davenport now claimed that in heaven the saints would be "each of them as dear to another, as if all relations of husbands and wives, of parents, and children, and friends, were in every one of them." According to Edward Taylor, this close-knit family had "all one father" and were "all children of one mother Jerusalem that is above." They had "all one nature, the New Man" and were "all of one spirit and temper." They were "all of one family, the household of God"; they were "all brethren and sisters." They lived "all the same life," were "maintained all by the same food," were "employed in the same service, walking in the same path, making to the same mark." They were "all arrayed in the same apparel, viz., the wedden garment, and all guests at the same wedden, and discumbitants at the same table." Thus, Taylor concluded, "they are all alike excellent, as to the sort of excellency, and knit together in the same bond of love." Their "distinct love" for each other arose from the fact that they were "brethren" and "love[d] as brethren."[66]

Images such as those arrayed by Taylor comport well with the tribal spirit that became an increasingly prominent feature of New England Puritanism during the second half of the seventeenth century. As pastors became disheartened by the spiritual intransigence they discovered among many New Englanders, they directed their efforts more pointedly toward church members and their children rather than the entire community. Meanwhile, half-way membership was granted to the unconverted children of full members, and with more of these families intermarrying, the covenanted community began to resemble a tribal network. Ministers sought to justify these developments by arguing that most of the elect were descended from godly parents. Just as the covenanted community resembled more and more an extended family, so late-seventeenth- and early-eighteenth-century descriptions of spiritual marriage described the "affinity" between redeemed souls in terms of the bonds that tied "kindred" together. When Samuel Willard declared of the redeemed, "we are the children of one father, the spouse of the same Christ, the temple of the same spirit," he invoked an extended family of fellow saints, a consummation of the tribal community from which brides of Christ were destined to emerge.[67]

Descriptions of espousal late in the century focused much more than previously not only on an intimate sense of familial community but also on the sensual and even sexual connotations of Christ's union with the souls of the elect. Ministers encouraged their flocks to feel Christ's love as a romantic, voluptuous experience. "Here he comes," rhapsodized Willard, "to give us the caresses of his love, and lay us in his bosom and embraces. And now, oh my soul! Hast thou ever experienced the love of a saviour?" The redeemed would "ly in Christ's bosom, and be ravished with his dearest love, and most intimate embraces." Recall from the opening vignette of this chapter Edward Taylor's portrayal of his heavenly lover as "a spotless male in prime." The Christ of Taylor's imagination was a tender and compassionate lover, offering affectionate solace and protection to his soul-mate:

> Peace, peace, my honey, do not cry,
> My little darling, wipe thine eye,
> Oh cheer, cheer up, come see.
> Is anything too dear, my dove
> Is anything too good, my love
> To get or give for thee?

He fantasized that redeemed and redeemer would consummate their love in a "feather-bed . . . with gospel pillows, sheets, and sweet perfumes" where they would conceive together "the babe of grace." Taylor's poetry was exceptionally vivid, but his choice of imagery was neither idiosyncratic nor heterodox.[68]

It would be misleading to suggest that earlier discussions of union with Christ had never used erotic imagery. John Cotton, who differed from most of his first-generation colleagues in using marital imagery primarily to seduce rather than to chastise, invited his audience in 1651 to contemplate redemption in sexual terms: "Have you a strong and hearty desire to meet him in the bed of loves, whenever you come to the congregation, and desire you to have the seeds of his grace shed abroad in your hearts, and bring forth the fruits of grace to him[?]" Cotton was confident that Christ's allure could rescue unmarried young men from illicit desires. He urged those who were "troubled with lust after women" to "turn the strength of [their] affection to another, that is white and ruddy, the fairest of ten thousand." Once they understood Christ's love for them, they would "find little content in any other thing besides."[69] But whereas the majority of spousal references in earlier sermons had been monitory rather than anticipatory, the emphasis now shifted in favor of positive reinforcement and often explicit eroticism.

Samuel Willard, Cotton Mather, and their contemporaries often used sexual and reproductive metaphors to convey Christ's bestowal of grace. The soul would "receive him," declared Mather, and "bring forth fruit unto him." References to grace as "a seed that is sown within us" invoked rich symbols of human as well as agricultural fecundity.[70] Thomas Foxcroft's 1722 vision of redemption was particularly graphic: "As Christ that pure prolific corn of wheat fell into the ground and died, and arose again; so (the grave being made fertile by his dead body lying in it) the saints shall be impregnated, and spring up; sprout upon his stalk, and (being ripe to the harvest of glory) be gathered into the garner of paradise." Just as Foxcroft's saints became "impregnated," so Christ's "enliven[ing]" of grace after its "infusion . . . into the soul" was often referred to as "quickening," a word also used to describe the first stirrings of new life in the womb. The process of "excitation," explained Samuel Willard, was both "moral" and "physical": "the Spirit of God . . . invites, and useth arguments with the man, and so it is moral; but he withall puts in his finger, and makes a powerful impression."[71]

Equally suggestive was the language used by ministers to describe the "soul-ravishing communion" of individual prayer, from which the believer would emerge "refreshed with those close embraces which he receives from him whom his soul loves." Cotton Mather, admittedly idiosyncratic in many regards, confided to his diary the extravagantly sensual experiences that he underwent during spiritual exercise. He dwelt on "the rapturous praelibations of the heavenly world" in which he was "swallowed up with the ecstasies of [Christ's] love." So "inexpressably irradiated from on high" was Mather on some occasions that he was "not able to bear the ecstasies of the divine love, into which [he] was raptured": "they exhausted my spirits; they made me faint and sick; they were insupportable; I was forced even to withdraw from them, lest I should have swooned away under the raptures."[72]

SPOUSAL METAPHORS ENVISAGED ALL BELIEVERS, male and female, as prospective brides of Christ. Men as well as women were to yearn for "the caresses of his love" and prepare their wedding gowns for the nuptial celebration after which their "glorious espousal" would be consummated. Puritan men often described themselves as being "ravished" by the savior, a word choice that emphasized their sexual passivity in Christ's overpowering embrace.[73] Such images provoke intriguing questions about the gendering of roles in early New England culture and the willingness of men to adopt seemingly feminine qualities. That willingness depended upon conceptions of gender that were in some respects remarkably fluid and capacious. Puritans characterized certain roles as masculine and others as feminine, but these were not attached inflexibly to male and female bodies. Women could assume masculine roles in particular circumstances and be treated as if male figures by men and women around them, just as men could assume feminine roles without discomfort. That flexible relationship between biological and cultural gender informed social, civic, and spiritual interactions. It had clear limits, especially where women were concerned, but it did allow male believers to assume a bridal role without any sense of personal or social calamity.[74]

Puritan men who understood their theology had no reason to believe that their masculinity would be threatened by their union as brides to Christ: the son of God was to marry not men and women but the souls of men and women. That distinction was important since souls did not adopt the sex of the bodies they inhabited. Ministers generally characterized the soul as either female or sexually indeterminate. Whereas they used the generic masculine to describe human beings nonspecifically or collectively, they preferred neutral and feminine pronouns when referring to the soul. "It is now entertained by Christ as his spouse, the marriage completed," declared Willard expectantly, "it is with him at his own home . . . God the Father receives it, with the most inlarged expressions of his divine love to it." "The soul hence gives itself," Shepard explained, "like one espoused to her husband, to the Lord Jesus." The use of neutral and feminine pronouns to characterize the soul reflected the two gendered perspectives from which ministers viewed the spiritual realm. On the one hand, biological differences between men and women, though crucial in this world, were irrelevant in discussions of the soul, which was immortal and transcended carnal identity. In that sense, the soul need not be referred to in gendered terms; to avoid doing so would underline its transcendence of earthly bounds. On the other hand, "carnal similitudes" such as marriage were best able to convey the union of redeemed and redeemer. Thus, the soul could appropriately become feminine when discussing its union to Christ.[75]

But even men who were not punctilious about such distinctions would have had little cause for discomfort in assuming a bridelike posture before Christ, because they were trained to adopt that role in other contexts as well. Winthrop equated a citizen's "subjection to authority" with a wife's "subjection to her husband" and that of "the church under the authority of Christ, her king and husband." That last phrase was telling in its equation of spiritual, political, and bridal comportment.[76] Power was clearly gendered in early New England, but the role of wife was not always attached to women. New Englanders made sense of themselves and their society in terms of responsibilities and dependencies that involved everyone, men and women, in the assumption of male and female roles. Social and political order rested just as firmly on male as on female submission to those placed above them. That men could become gendered as female reveals a culture of intricate possibilities. Formal authority did rest in most circumstances with men and was conceived in male terms, placing concomitant restrictions upon women. Engendering authority as male and subordination as female had clear patriarchal implications, and the use of graphic spousal imagery to describe relations between savior and saved surely reinforced gender hierarchy within the family. But Christ was much more than a masculine role model for men: they developed a range of social capacities by relating to him as brides as well as emulating him in the role of bridegroom.[77]

Just as men were expected to become bridelike as citizens and Christians, yet Christlike as husbands, so women's roles were also multifaceted in ways that complicated both gender identity and social prerogative. A "worthy matron" related to others in manifold capacities, as a wife, a mother, a household mistress, a neighbor, and a member of the Christian community. Some of these roles involved her exercising a "wisely aweful" authority, others requiring that she defer "obedient[ly]." Though clearly subordinate to male household heads, women wielded considerable moral and practical authority both in the household and the larger community. They also exerted significant influence as church members, despite their lack of formal power within congregations. And if a husband was unable for some reason to fulfill his duties as a household head, his wife took his place as a "deputy husband." Neighbors and business associates were expected to treat these female surrogates as though they had become their husbands, suggesting, in the words of historian Laurel Thatcher Ulrich, "a certain elasticity in premodern notions of gender." [78] That gender flexibility applied only within particular contexts. Women who spoke or behaved like men in unauthorized settings could find themselves excommunicated, diagnosed as insane, or accused of witchcraft.[79] But male and female roles were quite compatible within the same person, man or woman, so long as the articulation of those roles obeyed prescribed protocol.

In the spiritual realm especially, New Englanders were encouraged to eschew a distinct feminine or masculine identity. Ministers did sometimes depict women as more vulnerable than men to diabolical temptation.[80] But their portrayal of redemption made no such distinction. As Benjamin Wadsworth put it, there was "no difference between men and women" as potential members of the elect: they "equally need[ed] Christ."[81] Believers of either gender could become potent only through recognizing their own spiritual impotence and reliance upon their savior: ministers assured their flocks that those who submitted to God's will would become "members of Christ," dedicated to his service and empowered by their regeneration.[82] Significantly enough, contemporaries used the word "member" to denote a penis. Puritans often wrote about their "spiritual ejaculations," ostensibly referring to spontaneous prayer but surely aware of the word's double meaning. Cotton Mather pledged himself "to lead a life of heavenly ejaculations."[83] Thus, though the awakened souls of both men and women surrendered themselves to be penetrated and fertilized by their savior, they also became phallic and ejaculatory extensions of Christ. The repeated use of a male phallic image to denote spiritual power reminds us that gender fluidity within Puritan culture had its limits. But it is significant that within the spiritual realm women could assume a masculine, even phallic, persona and become correspondingly potent. A virtuous woman, as much as any man, had "the image of Christ and God upon her" and, on the Day of Judgment, her soul would "be marvellously changed into the likeness of the Lord Jesus Christ himself." We should bear in mind that spiritual and physical realms were equally real to Puritans.[84]

Just as the redeemed exhibited both masculine and feminine sexual qualities, so images of the divine in clerical writings were sometimes maternal and reproductive. Willard referred to "the womb of providence" and spoke of the world as "a sucking infant depending on the breasts of divine providence." Nehemiah Walter urged his readers to "lay" their "lips unto the breasts of the gospel" so as to take "spiritual food" from it. Clergymen and the congregations over which they presided could also assume a maternal, reproductive persona. William Adams drew on Galatians 4:19 in describing ministers as "travailling in birth with souls till Christ be formed in them." And Samuel Danforth, reminiscing about the early years of settlement, recalled the "pious care" taken of "sister churches, that those that wanted breasts might be supplied." [85] Just as pastors and churches could resemble fecund mothers, so too could the institution at which clergymen were trained. John Wise described Harvard College as "our dear mother," producing "fair, and numerous offspring" in the 1720s after a difficult period during which she had brought forth only a few children each year, "with abundance of groans" and sometimes "nothing but dead embryoes, or abortions." [86]

The Puritans' clear commitment to order in gender relations as in all other matters should not blind us to the permeability and reciprocity that characterized many of the roles and metaphors through which they made sense of their lives. The use of marital and romantic imagery in a spiritual context did not pose a problem for male New Englanders since notions of gender were in some respects remarkably fluid. Women and men thought of themselves in terms of discrete roles rather than as embodying a packaged gender identity: the bridal image evoked not femininity as such but instead a role that both men and women were expected to assume in various contexts. Puritans inhabited a world in which earthly bridegrooms could anticipate eagerly becoming heavenly brides, in which both men and women embraced a polymorphous sexuality through which they would bear "the babe of grace" even as they rejoiced in their phallic credentials as "members of Christ."

JOHN WILLIAMS, the pastor at Deerfield, Massachusetts, gave a sermon in 1698 to mark the execution of Sarah Smith for the murder of her illegitimate child. Williams warned that unrepentant sinners would be delivered "not to a bed decked with coverings of tapestry, with carved works, with the linen of Egypt, perfumed with myrrh, aloes and cinnamon; but to a lake burning with fire and brimstone; a righteous allotment from God, to all them that burn in their filthy lusts here." The Deerfield pastor might appear to be contrasting carnal pleasure with the horrors to which the carnal would be consigned. But when Williams spoke of a bed decorated with perfumed linen and gorgeous tapestries, he evoked not the sensual pleasures of this world but the voluptuous afterlife of Christ's soul-brides. Just as mortal sex within the "due bounds" of matrimony was an ordained expression of love and fellowship, so union with Christ in heaven would provide sensual and sexual as well as emotional and spiritual fulfillment.[87]

Sexual passion was crucial to the Puritans' double marriage: it expressed with appropriate exuberance one's love for a human husband or wife and also the heavenly bridegroom, bridging this world and the next. Illicit sex, on the other hand, had ghastly implications for those involved, and so the guardians of Puritan orthodoxy fought hard to protect their charges from the snares of the flesh. As we are about to see, pastors and their lay allies sought to redeem brethren who succumbed to "uncleanness" through exhortation, informal counseling, and more public chastisement. But New England's spiritual leaders became increasingly convinced that seduction as much as direful warnings and discipline should play a central role in winning hearts and souls. Those not yet "changed by the regenerating grace of the spirit of God," lamented Increase Mather, "usually live in some unclean lust or other. Either fornication, or self-pollution, or in secret wanton pranks of darkness."[88] Ministers hoped to entice the unconverted, including and especially the young, not by persuading them to become ascetics but by evoking for them an alternative realm of sensuality. How many of the young men and women who became church members were drawn by the prospect of "love raptures" in the afterlife we will never know, since they rarely left behind them a detailed record of their interior life. But for New Englanders like Edward Taylor who did embrace that prospect, Puritan sensibility offered a way to spiritualize sex and sexualize the spirit in a glorious and torrid symbiosis.

3

"Pregnant with the Seeds of All Sin"

Regulating Illicit Sex in Puritan
New England

LIKE ANY CONSCIENTIOUS PURITAN PASTOR, Thomas Shepard was anxious that his congregation in Cambridge, Massachusetts, should resist spiritual complacency. "What though thy life be smooth, what though thy outside, thy sepulcher, be painted," he intoned, "O, thou art full of rottenness, of sin, within." All men and women, Shepard reminded his flock, inherited a depraved nature. Because sexual sin was founded in universal corruption, the temptation to engage in "uncleanness" afflicted everyone. Even those who avoided actual sin entertained sinful thoughts. Such individuals might appear virtuous, but the Almighty knew otherwise: "God looks to the heart; guilty thou art therefore of heart whoredom, heart sodomy, heart blasphemy, heart drunkenness, heart buggery, heart oppression, heart idolatry; and these are the sins that terribly provoke the wrath of Almighty God against thee." Given this lamentable state of affairs, there could be no justification for treating those guilty of actual sins as utterly distinct in their culpability. Samuel Danforth impressed upon his congregation at Roxbury that the exposure and punishment of sinners should make "aweful impressions upon the hearts of the spectators," who, if truth be told, "deserve[d] the like judgements." Samuel Willard declared in a Boston sermon that our awareness of "unchaste thoughts" within ourselves "should keep us humble, [even] tho[ugh] we should have the grace to resist them."[1]

All those who aspired to godliness must keep constant vigil against "unchaste thoughts, words, and actions," their own and those of all other men and women with whom they had contact. As young Joseph Green, a recent Harvard graduate and future minister, noted in his commonplace book, that enterprise required relentless self-surveillance: "Have you done what in you lay to preserve your own and your neighbor's chastity in heart, speech, and behavior? Did you never willingly entertain unclean thoughts of sinful objects? If so, remember that every sinful thought shall be brought into judgment." Green saw within himself "the seed of Apostate Adam" and believed that only God's restraining hand had kept him from acting out "that rebellion of Adam, in which we are all partakers." If left to his own depraved instincts, Green feared that he would have "run into all manner of sin." Those men and women who surrendered to "unclean" impulses posed a threat both to themselves and to those around them, since they might contaminate their neighbors, especially those less vigilant of their own depravity. Puritans sought to chasten sexual malefactors in part from altruistic motives but also for self-serving reasons. If an erring individual resisted exhortations to repent and reform, Danforth declared, the "rotten and putrid member" must be "cut off" to "prevent the spreading of the infection." In 1652 New Haven magistrates prosecuted three young men who confessed to having often "put down their breeches and whipped one another and handled one another's members." The court was particularly anxious to act against the young men because gossip about their sexual antics had "spread abroad among many youths" who "would be in danger of being further corrupted if they were not publicly witnessed against."[2]

Some New Englanders were remarkably assiduous and largely effective in seeking to quell their unauthorized sexual urges, but others were either less successful in their efforts or saw no compelling reason to try. This chapter examines the various arenas in which the Puritan community engaged with sexual malefactors and also the spirit of that engagement. Judicial prosecutions and ecclesiastical hearings provided the most dramatic assertion of a strong and officially backed commitment to moral surveillance and discipline, but these formal procedures were by no means the only expression of that commitment. Although much of the surviving information about illicit sex comes from court records, townspeople and villagers did not see such behavior primarily as a legal problem. The godly dedicated themselves to a regimen of informal stewardship within their local communities, hoping thereby to prevent offenses that would make formal action necessary. That enterprise was often compromised by ambiguities in social etiquette and expectations of hospitality that made it extremely difficult to guard against illicit intimacies. Nonetheless, individuals who were identified as behaving suspiciously or who seemed to be on the verge of an unauthorized liaison would be warned of their danger by neighbors or elders and then watched carefully so as to protect them from temptation. Sometimes an individual who had already lapsed would be reprimanded informally in the hope that gentle ministrations would suffice to reclaim the sinner. In other cases, formal institutions would be called upon to admonish or punish the malefactor.

The Puritans' dedication to "search, inquisition, and due punishment" can all too easily be misread as a single-minded and brutal determination to inflict the greatest possible penalty upon those who violated moral norms.[3] Yet the underlying motivation for discipline within congregations was not punitive but redemptive. Ideally, the repentant transgressor would embark upon a course of reformation, inspired by the prospect of Christ's mercy and of the community's forgiveness. The godly were expected to welcome back into their hearts and lives those who did repent. Discipline was framed, then, in terms of mutual care and forgiveness; only obdurate sinners would suffer the full force of righteous judgment. That spirit of compassion was at least partly self-referential. Given the universality of sin, those standing in judgment today might very well become the judged tomorrow. The impulse to redeem and rehabilitate brothers and sisters in Christ was driven by an awareness that everyone, without exception, needed to be forgiven. As much an expression of concern about oneself as of solicitude for others, it was heartfelt in its very narcissism.

Like ministers and church members, New England's magistrates sought to caution those teetering on the precipice of sexual transgression and to redeem actual sinners. They saw themselves as fulfilling a religious as well as a legal function. Offenders who manifested appropriate repentance were much more likely to be treated with compassion and even leniency than those who remained recalcitrant under judicial investigation. Sentences often involved some form of public shaming, intended to stimulate remorse and so aid in the process of spiritual resurrection. But magistrates did have a formal responsibility to punish those who broke laws prohibiting a range of sexual acts. Even those colonists who did not take Puritan values seriously and who could not be disciplined by fellow church members because they had never joined a congregation were, nonetheless, subject to legal prosecution if they violated sexual norms. Once offenders found themselves in court on criminal charges, they faced the possibility of a fine, public flogging, or even execution.

Yet the judicial system was much more lenient in practice than New England's laws would suggest. This was due in part to the self-conscious restraint of magistrates and jurymen, who generally refused to convict even those who seemed obviously guilty unless the evidence before them satisfied strict legal standards. Judicial process was by no means always weighted against the accused; in particular, prosecutions involving sex offenses that carried the death penalty were often hamstrung by fastidiousness about legal proof. Even clergymen, notwithstanding their denunciations of the unclean, shared their judicial colleagues' dedication to scrupulousness and so paved the way for many an acquittal. The courts' narrow definition of sex crimes further limited their ability to impose the maximum permissible sanctions on defendants. Because they focused on whether or not specific acts of intercourse had taken place, the magistrates could not treat desire or intent, however obvious, as compelling evidence of guilt. In sodomy and bestiality cases, deponents sometimes suggested that some men had an underlying disposition toward specific kinds of sexual partners, a ongoing propensity that ordinary folk saw as significant and relevant. Just as popular attitudes toward premarital sex were by no means always consistent with official teachings, so there were New England settlers who came close to identifying in themselves or others what we might call a sexual orientation, even though such a notion had no place within Puritan ideology. But positing a distinct sexual proclivity, however helpful to villagers and townsfolk as they sought to understand patterns of behavior in their own communities, proved irrelevant in court. That disjunction between official and popular attitudes benefited the accused: ironically, the paradigm on which magistrates relied in adjudicating such cases actually reduced the likelihood of conviction.

ONE OF THE MOST formidable weapons available to clergymen in their crusade against "uncleanness" was sermonic exhortation. Because all New Englanders were legally obligated to attend regular church services, ministers had a captive audience. In their sermons, Puritan teachers invoked the manifold threat posed by "unclean" thoughts and deeds, not only through carefully constructed arguments but also in the colorful language that they used to describe illicit sex. That vocabulary divided into four overlapping categories. The first signified a dearth of spiritual gravity: *light, dallying, uncomely, folly.* The second indicated lack of self-control and a tendency toward self-indulgence: *loose, incontinent, wanton, debauched, vain, lewd, lascivious.* A third related to desecration of the body: *polluting, defiling, unclean, vile, base.* And finally, a number of recurring words indicated disobedience to or deviation from the ordinances of God: *unlawful, uncivil, disorderly, irregular, rebellion, misdirection, idola-*

try, adultery. These words conjured up images that conveyed effectively the substance and consequences of sexual sin within the Puritans' mental world. In failing to exercise control over "wanton" impulses and in devoting themselves to "loose" pleasures, men and women rebelled against God's laws and became the agents of chaos; they defiled their bodies and jeopardized their souls.[4]

Ideally, listeners would take that message to heart and maintain tireless guard over themselves, watching for signs of encroaching sin and acting swiftly to quell the demon within. Michael Wigglesworth's diary from the 1650s provides a vivid example of Puritan self-surveillance and anxiety about "filthy" urges. Then a young man in his twenties, Wigglesworth felt overwhelmed by "unresistable torments of carnal lusts." He masturbated frequently and suffered from wet dreams, all of which he recorded and bemoaned in a catalog of self-flagellation. The following entry is typical: "The last night a filthy dream and so pollution escaped me in my sleep for which I desire to hang down my head with shame and beseech the Lord not to make me possess the sin of my youth and give me into the hands of my abomination." Wigglesworth's preoccupation with sexual continence was certainly not unique. Eighteen-year-old Cotton Mather committed himself "in a special manner to watch and pray against lascivious thoughts." He hoped "to be always exemplary for [his] chastity" and lamented moments of spiritual lassitude that made way for temptation "unto some degrees of wantonness." Joseph Moody, another young Harvard graduate, referred frequently in diary entries to his "defiling" himself and worried about the cumulative impact of his giving way so frequently to "lust":

After I had got up, I knowingly and intentionally defiled myself. I do not know whether I shall be able to bear the burden of my sin.

I defiled myself before I went to sleep. Little by little I indulge my lust until at the end it will come to have dominion.

Each of these young men had already been trained to enter the ministry. That clergymen internalized the moral imperatives of their faith is perhaps not surprising, and it is unfortunate that most of the confessional diaries extant from seventeenth-century New England were written by ministers. We will never know how many other godly youths experienced similar disquietude without recording their feelings or did so in diaries and journals that have not survived. It is clear, though, from church and court records, that conscientious Puritans were eager to identify and confront signs of "uncleanness" among their neighbors and brethren.[5]

The principal arena in which New Englanders sought to reinforce each other in their efforts to discipline the flesh was not institutional but rather the neighborhoods in which they dwelled. The godly resorted to churches and courts for regulation of sexual behavior only after informal stewardship by the local community had failed. Their main weapon in the war against carnal lusts was the very fabric of their everyday lives: the physical layout and communitarian ethos of the settlements themselves. Puritan leaders were determined that colonists should provide mutual support in the constant struggle against sinful impulses by keeping watch over each other and counseling those who seemed on the verge of sin. Resident officials had a particular responsibility to act as moral guardians: magistrates, grand jurors, and selectmen; sheriffs, constables, and watchmen; ministers, elders, and deacons. But all townsfolk were enjoined by their pastors to maintain "watchfulness" and "to admonish one another" when necessary. Failure to protect brethren from their own moral frailty was itself a sin of omission. "If the neighbor of an elected saint sins," declared Cotton Mather, "then the saint sins also."[6]

The spatial organization of New England communities quite self-consciously facilitated the regimen of "watchfulness" to which Puritans committed themselves. Most families received two lots of land, one for a dwelling in the town center and another for farming outside the residential area. Houses were generally clustered around the meetinghouse in close proximity to each other. Farming lots tended to be long, narrow strips of land, so that townsfolk worked as well as resided alongside their brethren. Under these circumstances, those who engaged surreptitiously in illicit activities faced the constant threat of discovery by a neighbor. William Bradford, Plymouth Colony's governor for many years, pointed out that because New Englanders lived in tiny, nucleated communities they were "made conspicuous to the view of all." When Hanah Gray was summoned to the Essex County Court in 1674, charged with "lascivious and wanton carriages," Mary Sollas deposed that, passing by Thomas Woodbery's house, she had heard Gray laughing and "going in quick without knocking, the door being open, she being a neighbor, saw said Hanah and Andrew Davis together." Sollas, "being a neighbor," had the opportunity, right, and responsibility to investigate.[7]

New England townsfolk took seriously their duty to watch over each other. John Leigh and Sarah Row of Essex County had been close friends for many years, and their neighbors had expected them to marry. When Row became another man's wife and yet continued her close friendship with Leigh, suspicions about the nature of their friendship began to spread. Judith Browne later told the court that she and her husband, Nathaniel, had become worried when Leigh and Row began to spend time "together at her house three or four hours at a time, until her husband, noticing their intimacy, warned them from the house." The Brownes noted with disapproval that Leigh and Row "would have the outer door shut and the latch pulled in and sometimes would withdraw into an inner room." The two friends were watched closely: according to Grace Hogskins, "Leigh had left his team at Sarah's house from morning till noon until she told him folks wondered why he did it." Neighbor Mary Wilson "had occasion to call at Sarah Row's house, and seeing somebody in bed, asked if her husband were at home, and she said that he was at sea." Wilson did not claim to know for certain that the "somebody in bed" was Leigh, but the implication was clear. And John Sinnett, another neighbor, "bade [Row] leave her tricks or she would come to the gallows." When Leigh and Row found themselves in court, neither would admit to sexual impropriety, but they both acknowledged that their imprudent intimacy had given ample cause for suspicion.[8]

Clandestine lovers faced considerable challenges as they sought to avoid detection in tightly clustered communities where neighbors were constantly bearing witness, sometimes accidentally and sometimes quite deliberately, to one another's lives. When James Creeke was tried in 1682 "for heinous, lascivious, and adulterous carriages with Elizabeth, wife of Luke Perkins," one of his neighbors testified as follows: "John Browne, aged forty-five years, deposed that he went down to his pasture to turn hogs out of it and when he came back through some Indian corn in his orchard, he saw James Creeke and Elizabeth, Luke Perkins' wife, tickling one another about the ribs. He was so ashamed that he went into his own house. One moonlight night near Haly's shop window at about nine o'clock when the moon shone very bright, he saw him kiss her." Browne may not have intended to intrude upon Creeke's illicit trysts with Perkins, but his wife deliberately positioned herself to spy on them. One Sunday she and her husband had seen Creeke and Perkins walking toward the orchard next to their house. Goody Browne told the court that "she had heard about the[ir] actions and now she might catch them if it were possible, so standing at the end window next to their orchard she could see them handling linen with their heads close together." In another instance of premeditated surveillance, fifty-year-old Clemant Coldam, "hearing that John Pearce was accustomed to take the widow Stanard to his house at night and she was seen to go away in the morning," went to Pearce's house "and looked in at the window." He then called Anthony Dey and Deacon Stevens, "and they saw enough to warrant a complaint against said Pearce."[9]

The imperatives of mutual stewardship led to a constant flow of information about people's behavior that could provide the basis for informal intervention by concerned neighbors or formal proceedings against an alleged offender. Whether particular tongues were wagging in the service of moral surveillance or prurient gossip is and would have been at the time difficult to determine, especially since the former could serve as an alibi for the latter. Even meetings for ostensibly unimpeachable purposes were open to suspicion. In 1638 John Underhill was called to account by his church in Boston after being found on several occasions alone with the wife of cooper Joseph Faber in her house with the door locked from the inside, which "had an appearance of evil in it." Underhill claimed that Faber's wife had been "in great trouble of mind," that he "resorted to her to comfort her," and that when the door was found locked they were "in private prayer" together. The church elders warned him that it would not have "been of good report for any of them to have done the like" and that he should have called in "some brother or sister" so as to avoid giving cause for "suspicion of incontinency." In Underhill's case, such suspicions turned out to be justified. Two months later, "a godly young woman" accused him of having "solicited her chastity under pretence of Christian love." She also claimed that he "confessed to her that he had his will oftentimes of the cooper's wife."[10]

It was all very well to insist that settlers pay close attention to moral decorum in their everyday interactions, but determining in practice where the boundary between appropriate and inappropriate behavior lay was no easy matter. Ensuring sexual propriety within New England communities was frequently complicated by ambiguities in social and moral etiquette. Consider the multipotential significance of a kiss. English moralist John Downame condemned embracing and kissing "in wanton dalliance between those who are light and lascivious," but conceded that either could be harmless if used "after a civil and honest manner to express our love one to another." The distinction sounded clear enough in theory, but it was sometimes less so in practice. When James Creeke was summoned by the Essex County Court to answer for his "adulterous carriages" with Elizabeth Perkins, much of the evidence against him related to their having been seen kissing one another. One witness testified that she saw them "kiss on the street, which made deponent much ashamed to be seen in their company." Creeke "accounted his kissing her to be good manners, and as other men did." The court was not convinced, but not everyone who heard about the case agreed that kissing another man's wife was necessarily improper. John Edwards Sr. apparently told John Hadly "that he had kissed the wife of Hugh Marsh of Newbury in the face of the court, and there was no harm in it." In 1704 the wife of a Boston ship-master, Sarah Knight, criticized the authorities in Connecticut for having been "very rigid in their administrations towards such as their laws made offenders, even to a harmless kiss or innocent merriment among young people."[11]

But one person's "harmless kiss" was another's "wanton dalliance." Some of the kisses reported to the authorities were clearly lascivious. William Knap, a man in his seventies, paid five shillings for a kiss with Phoebe Page and apparently declared that "young men would only give a touch but he would give her a cleaving kiss." Samuel Weed was dared by six friends to enter Thomas Wells's bedchamber while he was away on business and kiss Goodwife Wells, "which he accordingly performed, John Colby holding the light as a witness that the wager was carried out." But other incidents were more ambiguous, as when Benjamin Graves and recently married Ruth Briggs were seen "kissing one another and so near together as if they were hugging one another." Briggs claimed "that he did salute her and wished her joy after her marriage." This was a plausible explanation, but the fact that he and Briggs had been sexually involved before her remarriage gave those who saw the "salute" reason to doubt its propriety.[12]

Townsfolk who were eager to uphold moral standards did not always have the upper hand. Those who were reluctant to participate in or to condone prurient gossip-mongering found themselves in a delicate posi-tion when socializing with neighbors who were less sensitive about the tone and content of conversation: extreme zeal about such matters might prove unpopular and self-isolating, yet lack of concern would make the individual an accessory to "unclean" words. When Sarah Tuttle visited the house of Cornelis and Mariah Melyen, she not only cuddled with her beau Jacob but also gossiped about John Potter and his wife, married that day. She commented "that they were both lame" and "wondered what they would do at night." Mariah Melyen later claimed that it was a "matter of sorrow and shame to her" that such a conversation had taken place under her roof, "but there was company with her in the room, and she was in a strait," implying that the other visitors saw nothing wrong with such bawdy gossip and that she was afraid to appear overly particular about such matters. The court told Mariah that she "should not have suffered" such conversations to take place in her house. Whether Mariah was truly offended by the gossip or manufactured disapproval in retrospect in order to mitigate her offense in the eyes of the court, it is not difficult to imagine the social pressure that she could have felt as her friends and neighbors chatted about the newly married couple. There was a fine line between taking seriously one's responsibility as a moral steward and becoming a killjoy.[13]

The lack of private space in most homes created, furthermore, temptations and opportunities for illicit sexual contact against which it was difficult to guard. However determined the proponents of Puritan morality may have been to prevent illicit sex, they often ended up reacting to instead of preempting unauthorized intimacies. New Englanders did not expect to sleep alone: they shared bedchambers and beds with family members, servants, and strangers in need of accommodation. Maintaining "due modesty" under these circumstances cannot have been easy. Inevitably, there were those who exploited such physical proximity, although the circumstances that created the opportunity also facilitated exposure. The wife of John Lyford, a minister who was later expelled from Plymouth Colony, complained that "she could keep no maids but he would be meddling with them." She sometimes caught him fondling them "as they lay at their bed's feet."[14]

The emphasis placed on hospitality in early modern English culture created another potentially dangerous ambiguity. Robert Hill, who visited his lover Mary Wharton while her husband Phillip attended Sabbath services, boasted of his trysts in a way that showed his wry awareness of the fine line between hospitality and undue familiarity. When Dorcas Morris found him "trimming himself" one Sunday morning and asked why, he rather foolishly told her that he was off to "a church with a chimney on it" and that Mary Wharton "entertain[ed] a stranger lovingly." She had told him, Hill confided, that he could help himself to tobacco from the Whartons' cellar. The expectation that households would open their doors to neighbors in need made women vulnerable to predatory guests, especially if the house was isolated. This became increasingly likely as land shortages within town centers forced families to settle on outlying lots. Elizabeth

Goodell felt that she had particular reason to fear attack, living as she did "remote from neighbors." Brother-in-law John Smith made sexual advances toward Goodell when he was working in a swamp near her house and "called to her for fire," and when he "fetched her from her house to help his wife when she lay in, so that she jumped from the horse on which they rode." On both occasions he took advantage of their being alone to abuse her goodwill as neighbor and kin.[15]

Regardless of where a family's house was located, it was, of course, impossible to maintain constant surveillance so as to prevent abuses of hospitality. James Waters left a visitor, Patrick Morril, alone with his wife Mary for just a few minutes in order to fetch some cider from their cellar. While he was gone, Morril "assaulted said Mary, who told her husband of it, and asked him not to leave her alone with him." A few days later, Waters went off to cut wood at the ironworks. Morril saw him there and headed over to the Waters's house. Mary was there, "alone with my child," as she later recalled, "and no neighbors within call." At first she refused to let him in, but "he then said, may not a man light his pipe?" Her fears temporarily overshadowed by considerations of hospitality, Waters responded that she was "not against lighting his pipe in a civil way" and opened the door, whereupon he entered the house and tried to rape her. Mary managed somehow to get out of the house with her child and hurried off to seek protection. Henry Greenland gained access to the Newbury home of Mary Rolfe one night in 1663 while her husband, John, a fisherman, was away on a trip to Nantucket. Greenland claimed, like Morril, that "he desired but to light a pipe of tobacco." Betty Webster, a single woman who was staying with Mary, had refused to let him in at first, but Greenland complained of the cold outside and "vowed he would not touch them." After entering the house, he removed his clothes and got into bed with Goody Rolfe, who fainted from shock and fright.[16]

People who witnessed or became the objects of illicit passion sometimes decided against reporting what they had seen or experienced because they preferred to deal with the matter informally. The offender's social status could act as a powerful deterrent against public accusation. Henry Greenland was a physician who had recently arrived in town. Mary Rolfe feared that other townsfolk might not take a complaint against him seriously because of his standing and reputation: "he is in credit in the town, some take him to be godly and say he hath grace in his face, he has an honest look, he has such a carriage that he deceives many: it is said he is in credit with those that are in authority in the country: it is said the governor sent him a letter counting it a mercy such an instrument was in the country, and what [can] such a poor young woman as I do in such a case, my husband being not at home." Others shared Mary's reluctance to risk a public confrontation with Greenland. On the night that he gained access to her house on the pretext of lighting his pipe, eighteen-year-old Henry Lesenby heard a shriek as he was passing by. He "went straight into the house" and saw that Greenland had got into Goody Rolfe's bed. Lesenby and Rolfe "went out adoor to consider what was best to be done." They decided that "because he was a stranger and a great man it was not best to make an uproar but to let him go away in a private manner" and "to speak of it to some friends."[17]

But intimidation was not the only reason to hold back from lodging a formal complaint. Neighbors, friends, and family members might want to give malefactors a chance to reform before initiating legal prosecution, which carried serious and, in some cases, potentially fatal consequences. They might also want to avoid open conflict. When John Smith made sexual overtures toward his sister-in-law, Elizabeth Goodell, in the early 1670s, Goodwife Goodell decided not to report his "abuse" of her for several reasons. She feared friction with her husband's relatives and "was afraid [that] Smith would do her harm, as she was often alone with her children and remote from neighbors." Goodell hoped that he would agree to mend his ways and, "being a relation," she "thought a private healing might make it up." Neighbors also advised against a public complaint "because it would as they thought ruin his family." Goodell had, however, told several confidantes about her experiences with Smith, "foolish words" that she lived to regret once they took on a life of their own. Local "scandal" led to a public investigation and thus thwarted her desire for a "private" resolution of the matter.[18]

Those who preferred "private healing," for whatever reason, took a considerable risk. If the malefactor failed to mend his ways or if the offense came to light, they themselves could be censured for neglecting their responsibility as moral stewards. When Thomas Robinson of New Haven repeatedly tried to force himself upon Goodwife Fancy in the early 1640s, she "acquainted her husband with Robinson's lewd lustful attempts upon her" and "pressed him to complain to the governor." William Fancy refused to do so, afraid that his wife, who had previously been convicted of theft, "should not be believed." Goodwife Fancy, however, was unable to maintain complete silence: when she heard from neighbor Goody Thomas that Robinson had accused her of theft, she lost her temper and told Thomas about his "filthiness" toward her, declaring bitterly, "save one from the gallows and he will hang you or cut your throat if he can." She then told Robinson himself that she had informed Goody Thomas of his behavior and he, distraught that the matter had "come forth," told his wife, apparently calculating that she had better hear about it from him than Goodwife Thomas or another neighbor. Robinson's wife wanted the matter to be "taken up in a private way if it might be," and they "pressed Goodwife Thomas to that purpose." Goody Thomas agreed to keep quiet "if she might see a general reformation in his course" but told them that Robert Usher already knew "and must by a due acknowledgement be satisfied."

Thomas Robinson went to visit Usher that night, ostensibly to "acknowledge" his transgression and promise reformation. But he made the mistake of trying to trivialize the accusations, claiming that "it was but a word in jest" and that Goody Fancy had "wronged him." The Thomases later testified that they also had not been impressed by Robinson's private "acknowledgement" of his "miscarriages": some he confessed "weakly" and others he denied altogether. Robinson attempted, moreover, to bribe Goodman and Goodwife Fancy, "that there might be no further prosecution." In response to this insufficiently penitent behavior, Robinson's neighbors "resolved" to bring a formal complaint against him. He was subsequently whipped for his attempts to rape Goody Fancy, but magistrates also sentenced the victim and her husband to a whipping for "concealment" of the crime. The court deplored that Goodman Fancy, who "should have been her protector," failed to act and so became "as a pandar to his wife."[19]

Household heads had a particular duty to protect their dependents and restrain those under their charge from sexual lapses. Masters who failed to discipline licentious servants were deemed accessories to any offenses committed in their households. When John Knight, a servant in the home of William Judson, was tried for his "filthy" advances toward fellow servant Mary Clarke, the judges were "much unsatisfied" that the Judsons and Mary's parents had known of Knight's sexual aggression toward her and yet failed to take action. Mary had complained to her parents, yet they "let her stay there and [did] not complain of him to public authority." The Clarkes claimed that the Judsons had promised to send Knight away. Goodwife Judson had apparently urged Mary to keep quiet about the young man's behavior and later told the court that "she thought he had enough upon him already": she knew that Knight had been punished for "filthiness" before and had narrowly escaped the death penalty after being accused of "loathsome" behavior toward minors. She may also have sought to keep his behavior under wraps for fear of being censured for having enabled such things to occur under her roof. Even after the Judsons "counselled Mary Clarke to conceal it," the magistrates noted, they had often left her and Knight alone together. The court judged that the Judsons had "neglected their trust and duty towards Mary Clarke and her parents."[20]

Whereas some of those who became aware of misbehavior in their midst determined to avoid public revelation, others urged that "these things are not to be kept private, [or] we may justly provoke God, that further mischief may follow and then we will come under great blame."[21] Once an individual had actually committed a sexual offense, household members or neighbors who knew what had transpired were expected to report it so that appropriate action could be taken. If the offender belonged to the local church, he or she would be called to account at a disciplinary meeting. But when a congregation discovered that one of its brethren had committed a sexual offense, its primary response was redemptive, not punitive. Pastors and church members sought to help errant brothers and sisters understand the gravity and implications of their sins; this was the first step toward spiritual renewal and reaffirmation as a member of the covenanted community. The congregation might resort to informal counseling, formal admonition, or outright expulsion. But even the latter was not intended as a permanent rejection of the individual: excommunicates were cut off from the spiritual fellowship and protection of the church so that they would experience in isolation the power of Satan; having recognized their own frailty and endangerment, repentant sinners could return in sorrowful confession, pledge themselves to reformation, and be welcomed back into the congregation. Those sinners deemed truly repentant, then, were to be reintegrated and forgiven by their brethren. In 1700 Abigail Bixby of Topsfield, who "had played the whore," appeared before her congregation "to acknowledge her sin and folly in that respect and accordingly, on her sober and modest behavior of herself for the future, was to be looked on as in that capacity as if the matter had never been." That final phrase, "as if the matter had never been," bears striking testimony to the spirit of forgiveness and faith in the possibility of renewal that lay at the heart of disciplinary hearings.[22]

Individual congregations developed different strategies for guiding sinners toward an appropriate state of contrition. Some churches were much readier than others to excommunicate sexual malefactors, then restoring them to membership once they had demonstrated satisfactorily their sense of contrition. John Cotton, son and namesake of the renowned minister, was excommunicated by Boston's First Church in 1664 "for lascivious unclean practices with three women and his horrid lying to hide his sin." He was then readmitted a month later "upon his penitential acknowledgement, openly confessing his sins." In 1712 the same church summoned Rachel Preson to answer for the sin of fornication: she had a confession read for her, along with "a desire of pardon," but she was nonetheless excommunicated until such time as she gave "full proof of the sincerity of her repentance."[23] In sharp contrast, the Dorchester congregation and the Second Church at Boston generally forgave those who acknowledged sexual lapses without proceeding to formal censure. In 1704, when Richard and Sarah Withington "acknowledged their sin of fornication before marriage," Dorchester brethren immediately accepted the confession "as a token and sign of repentance."[24]

Under Cotton Mather's leadership, the Second Church at Boston proved remarkably forbearing even when dealing with egregious malefactors. Mather argued that "public acknowledgement before the whole church" should suffice in most cases; only those who failed to manifest an appropriate repentance for their transgression should be formally admonished or worse. Consider a particularly colorful disciplinary case from 1699. Edward Mills was a raffish fellow who tried the patience of many a saint in the congregation. Mills's first offense had been to seduce his married landlady, formerly "a young woman of a very laudable character." Once his "lewd, vile, and lascivious carriages towards her" became common knowledge, Mills left town. The congregation took no action against him, although they could have censured him in absentia. When he returned, the church merely "suspended him [for] certain months from the communion, with private admonition," trusting that "his future conversation would by its exemplary penitence and piety recover his reputation." Instead, Mills proceeded to spend his evenings at a local tavern, gaming and "in lewd company." On his way home at night, he would awaken and "vex" his neighbors. It also came to the church's attention that he had written "wicked and profane letters" to friends in London, "boasting" of his behavior. He had apparently "defamed several young gentlewomen in the neighborhood of an unspotted character; and reported them to be infamous whores." Despite this catalog of degeneracy, the congregation still held back from expelling Mills, on condition that he "expressed the least symptom or shadow of repentance." It was only when he "manifested such an obduration as was to [their] astonishment" that they proceeded to excommunication, "for which those miscarriages and impenitences had ripened him." Mills's "miscarriages" alone would not have earned him expulsion from Mather's church.[25]

The one sure way for sinners to alienate brethren was to remain obdurate. Church records noted carefully which errant members acknowledged their sins and which of them "persist[ed] impenitently therein," further damning themselves through "untruths," "self-justifyings," or "proud expressions and railing accusations." In 1668 Joshua Fletcher was excommunicated by the Wenham congregation because of his recalcitrant attitude when elders questioned him about secret and nocturnal visits with a young woman (which suggested "some intended act of lewdness and dishonesty"). The church had "several meetings" with Fletcher, characterized by "much agitation" as the members found him "still to grow more stiff and obstinate." Fletcher "answered all along boldly and as without shame." As a result, he was cast out from the church. The Roxbury congregation excommunicated Hannah Goffe in 1684 for "wicked fornication" and her "contumacy" in refusing to meet with the church. Considering the forgiveness usually extended to Roxbury members who confessed, Goffe's "contumacy" seems to have been the crucial factor leading to her expulsion.[26]

New England's civil magistrates, though formally charged with the punishment of sexual and other crimes, were also committed to the redemption of offenders. They urged malefactors to ponder the spiritual implications of their crimes and to mend their ways. Weybro Lovell, presented to a Boston court for "light and whorish behavior" in 1637, was "seriously admonished to repent, and [to] walk humbly, chastely, and holily." Judges often took evidence of contrition into account when punishing criminals. In 1665 the General Court of Massachusetts convicted John Evered of "wanton and shameful dalliance" with his wife's niece: he was fined twenty pounds, disfranchised, and stripped of his civic and military appointments. But the court noted a year later that Evered, having paid his fine, "carried it humbly and submissively, and under a due sense of his sin." Consequently, the other penalties were rescinded. In 1666 the same court found Anna Page, charged with adultery, to be "guilty of much wickedness" but declined to punish her (beyond paying the costs incurred by witnesses in the case) because it had "seen the fruits of her repentance" in a voluntary and public acknowledgment of her "great offences."[27] But John Knight was executed in 1655 for repeatedly assaulting fellow servants and minors (male and female) once the New Haven court became convinced that its earlier attempts to induce reformation had failed: "there seems to be no end of his filthiness nor no means will reclaim him, whether punishment or private warnings." Knight had been sentenced to wear a halter after a previous trial, but not even sustained public humiliation had worked. He was executed in large part because he seemed incorrigible.[28]

Public shaming, Puritans believed, could play an important role in prompting or reinforcing contrition. The judicial process itself, which involved appearance in court as an indicted criminal, presentation of evidence, and admonition by the magistrates, must have been mortifying for most offenders. Judges often required as part of the sentence that those convicted of sex crimes confess their transgressions not only in court but also in some other public setting. When William and Elizabeth Middleton appeared before the Suffolk County Court for having premarital sex, they were sentenced to "make a satisfactory acknowledgement in the public congregation where they usually hear." If they failed to do so within a month, they would be whipped. Corporal punishment was both physically painful and a humiliating form of exposure, literally so if the whipping was administered on the bare back. As with Hawthorne's fictional Hester Prynne, some sex offenders were made to wear either a letter that represented their crime or a label on which was written a fuller description of the offense, exposing them to censure and humiliation before the community. In 1639 John Davies was whipped in both Boston and Ipswich for "gross offences and attempting lewdness with diverse women." He was also made to wear the letter U (for *unclean*) "upon his uppermost garment" for six months. Thomas Jay, presented to the Suffolk County Court in 1676, was made to stand "upon a block or stool in the Boston marketplace with a paper upon his breast written in large characters, FOR LASCIVIOUS CARRIAGES TOWARDS YOUNG WOMEN."[29]

In addition to prodding sinners toward repentance and reformation, magistrates sought to protect potential criminals from their own moral frailty. Public shaming would hopefully deter onlookers from following in the malefactor's footsteps. And all "single persons" were ordered to live with relatives or a respectable family in their community so as to enable close surveillance of their behavior. John Littleale, a resident of Haverhill, was summoned in 1672 for living alone, "whereby he is subject to much sin and iniquity, which ordinarily are the companions and consequences of a solitary life." He was ordered to "settle himself in some orderly family in the town, and be subject to the orderly rules of family government," or leave Haverhill altogether.[30] The Massachusetts General Court worried that women such as Mary Rolfe might succumb to "sin and iniquity" while their husbands were away on business and therefore ordered in 1674 that no "single woman or wife in the absence of her husband" should "entertain or lodge any inmate or sojourner" without permission from the town selectmen.[31]

Magistrates regularly cautioned men and women whose "familiarity" with neighbors had given rise to suspicion. Abigail Gill was admonished for "drinking and dancing" in the company of "several men" (none of them her husband) at Arthur Keyne's house. And Thomas Waite was reported for "frequenting the company of Sara Gowen at unseasonable times." Joseph Rogers of Namassakeasett was summoned before a Plymouth court in 1665 after having been seen with Mercy Tubbs, a married woman, "in a way and after such manner as hath given cause at least to suspect that there hath been lascivious acts committed by them." Rogers was told to leave Namassakeasett and warned that he would be whipped if found at her home or in her company elsewhere. Mercy's husband, William Tubbs, was "strictly charged not to tolerate [Rogers] to come to his house or where he hath to do at any time."[32]

NEW ENGLAND COURTS allied with church congregations and watchful neighbors to prevent and expose sin. They enjoined those apparently on the verge of misdeed to take better care of themselves and encouraged in actual malefactors an appropriately penitent frame of mind. But however sincerely committed the judicial system may have been to spiritual and social rehabilitation, its most obvious responsibility was to enforce New England's laws, including those against illicit sex, by punishing individuals who flouted them. Couples who became sexually intimate before marrying and other single persons who had sex risked prosecution for "fornication" and, if convicted, faced a substantial fine or public whipping. Each of the northern colonies included several sex offenses in their list of capital crimes, citing Scripture to justify the death penalty. New Englanders who committed adultery, rape, incest, sodomy, or bestiality could be sentenced to death.[33] The language used to frame these laws made manifest their theological inspiration, alluding to "unclean carriages," "carnal copulation," "filthiness," and "abomination." Their tone as much as the penalties they prescribed bespoke harsh and unequivocal denunciation.

The sheer number of sex cases in surviving court records from seventeenth-century New England testifies to the zeal with which officials carried out their responsibility to discipline those who committed sexual misdemeanors. But the adjudication of such cases was often much more restrained than rhetorical formulations in the legal codes, let alone clerical diatribes on the subject, might lead us to expect. This was due in part to recognition by some magistrates that contrition should constitute a mitigating factor. But perhaps the most striking characteristic of sex prosecutions in early New England was that defendants were often punished for lesser versions of the crime in question. New England courts refused to convict individuals, especially if the penalty was death, unless the evidence satisfied fully the standards of proof laid down by the judicial system; in a capital case, this meant either confession or at least two independent witnesses. Furthermore, the courts defined sex very specifically as the act of intercourse. Thus, they could convict only if there was clear proof that copulation had taken place; neither intention nor an unsuccessful attempt would suffice. Given that there was often only one witness to an illicit tryst and that such witnesses could rarely testify with confidence that they had seen actual intercourse occur, those accused of capital offenses rarely suffered execution: they were much more likely to be whipped or fined for either suspicious behavior or an attempted crime. New England courts were committed to the punishment of sex offenders, but they were equally determined to proceed in a scrupulous and cautious spirit.

In adultery cases, for example, juries often handed down verdicts that asserted the likelihood of guilt but recognized the absence of proof that illicit intercourse had actually taken place. When Bethiah Bullen and Elizabeth Hudson, both married, were accused of adultery with Peter Turpin in 1667, a Massachusetts jury found them guilty "of being in bed" with Turpin but declared itself uncertain whether that made them guilty of adultery "by law." Bullen and Hudson were both sentenced to stand on a ladder under the gallows as a warning of the fate they might have suffered, had the evidence been more compelling. When David Ensigne was tried for committing adultery with Sarah Long in 1681, his jury in Connecticut found him "suspiciously guilty." The court, acknowledging that it was "difficult to find out such notorious wickedness, notwithstanding all care used," noted the "great appearance of guilt" and told Ensigne to keep away from Goodwife Long. For this and other misdemeanors ("spreading of false reports concerning the death of the King" and "contempt of authority"), Ensigne was disfranchised and bound to good behavior.[34]

Because of insufficient evidence, New England courts often found individuals accused of adultery "not guilty according to indictment" but nonetheless "guilty of lascivious, gross, and foul actions tending to adultery."[35] Consider the experience of Henry Dawson and Ann Hudson. In 1645 Bostonian William Hudson departed on a trip to England and "committed the care of his family and business" to his servant Henry Dawson, whose own wife was in England. Dawson was "a young man of good esteem for piety and sincerity," but during Hudson's absence he and his master's wife, Ann Hudson, became "over familiar." She was "with him oft in his chamber," and one night two servants saw him "go up into their dames' chamber." Dawson and Hudson confessed before the Court of Assistants "not only that he was in the chamber with her in such a suspicious manner, but also that he was in bed with her." Yet "both denied any carnal knowledge." According to Winthrop's account, many of the magistrates and town elders "judged them worthy of death," but the jury found them guilty only of "adulterous behavior." Its reasoning was as follows:

1: That seeing the main evidence against them was their own confession of being in bed together, their whole confession must be taken, and not a part of it.

2: The law requires two witnesses, but here was no witness at all, for although circumstances may amount to a testimony against the person where the fact is evident, yet it is otherwise where no fact is apparent.

3: All that the evidence could evince was but suspicion of adultery: but neither God's law nor ours doth make suspicion of adultery (though never so strong) to be death.

The court sentenced Dawson and Hudson "to stand upon the ladder at the place of execution with halters about their necks one hour." They were each to pay a fine of twenty pounds or be whipped.[36]

Rape cases reveal a similar pattern. Seventeenth-century New England courts took charges of sexual assault very seriously, but men were much more likely to be accused and convicted of attempted rape than of the actual crime. In some cases the offense was described as an attempt for the straightforward reason that the attacker had been interrupted. In November 1674 Richard Nevers assaulted seventeen-year-old servant Elizabeth Knight in her master's cowshed. She "clapt one hand on the ground and held fast the cow's teat with the other hand and cried out and John Abbot came."[37] But courts also characterized sexual assault as attempted instead of actual "ravishment" if the attack did not include penetration, since the courts understood rape, like other sexual crimes, strictly in terms of intercourse. Consider a case that magistrates John Pynchon and Elizor Holyoke referred to the Middlesex County Court in Massachusetts after having been asked by the General Court to determine whether it should be treated as a capital crime or as a lesser misdemeanor.

In early October 1655, Robert Bartlett of Northampton had offered to assist Sarah Smith, a married woman, in searching for two calves. According to Goody Smith, Bartlett had drawn her away from frequented areas into a deserted swamp and then had assaulted her. He had, she claimed, thrown her down and kissed her, mounted her, and, as she put it, "shamefully handle[d] [her] nakedness." She had been "very earnest with him to let [her] go," and eventually succeeded in getting him to desist. She later told the magistrates that "he did no more offer ill to me, only he told me that he could have done it [i.e., penetrated her] whether I would or no." Bartlett confessed to having "laid hold of her through the violence of the temptation, and that he threw her down and kissed her and that he did handle her nakedness." He said "that he did urge her twice or thrice to yield to him, but that she refused, and desired him to let her go, and at last he sayeth God smote him with a trembling that he let her go." There was no other testimony, "excepting something related by an Irish youth who could not be well understood, besides what he said was contradictory to himself and he accorded not with the man and woman about the place where this wickedness was attempted, they agreeing therein." Pynchon and Holyoke were dismayed by the incident: "O that rivers of water might run down our eyes because men keep not God's law." Bartlett had clearly assaulted Smith, but neither party claimed that penetration had occurred, and there were no reliable witnesses to the incident other than the victim and the perpetrator. Accordingly, Pynchon and Holyoke recommended that the matter be dealt with in court as a misdemeanor, not as a capital offense.[38]

The records that survive from sodomy and bestiality cases testify to the extreme caution used by New England courts even when dealing with categories of illicit sex that ministers condemned with particular vehemence as "abominable" and deserving of "death, without mercy." Judicial reluctance to convict on charges of sodomy or bestiality unless intercourse had clearly taken place reflected the rigorous standards of proof that magistrates sought to enforce in all capital cases and also the courts' conception of sex as a specific physical act, namely, intercourse. This goes a long way toward explaining the virtual absence of sodomy cases involving women, even though ministers quite explicitly included women in denunciations of same-sex intimacy. Because lawmakers and judges thought about sex in terms of phallic penetration, they found it difficult to conceive of a sexual situation that did not involve a man. As a result, there was little room for the recognition or prosecution of sex between women.

New England laws against sodomy generally followed clerical example in defining the crime as an act that involved two human beings "of the same sex." But the legal codes focused much more specifically on male sex than did clerical pronouncements. Whereas ministers referred to the "unnatural lusts of men with men, or woman with woman," the Plymouth, Massachusetts, Connecticut, and New Hampshire laws all quoted Leviticus 20:13: "If any man lyeth with mankind, as he lyeth with a woman, both of them have committed abomination; they both shall surely be put to death."[39] Rhode Island adopted the language of Romans 1:26–27, defining sodomy as "a vile affection, whereby men given up thereto leave the natural use of woman and burn in their lusts one toward another, and so men with men work that which is unseemly."[40] There were two exceptions to this male-oriented view of sodomy on the part of New England's lawmakers. A code drawn up by John Cotton in 1636 at the request of the Massachusetts General Court described sodomy as "a carnal fellowship of man with man, or woman with woman." Cotton's formulation was consistent with those produced by his fellow ministers, but the court declined to follow his lead and omitted women from the Massachusetts law against sodomy. New Haven's law, passed in 1655, did include sex between women as a capital offense. Neither Cotton's proposal nor the New Haven law gave any clue as to how sex between women was to be defined or proven.[41]

On only two known occasions did women appear before New England courts on charges of "unclean" behavior with each other. In 1642 Elizabeth Johnson was whipped and fined by an Essex County quarterly court for "unseemly practices betwixt her and another maid." Sara Norman and Mary Hammon, both of Yarmouth, Plymouth Colony, were presented in 1649 for "leude behaviour each with other upon a bed." In neither case does the brief court record suggest that the magistrates categorized the offense as sodomitical or that they categorized it at all save as "lewd" and "unseemly." The use of these vague adjectives may reflect judicial uncertainty as to how sexual intimacy between women should be classified, as well, perhaps, as a reluctance to describe the acts in question.[42]

New Haven's sodomy law differed in other respects from the codes adopted elsewhere in New England. It was much more detailed and included a broad range of sexual acts. Its definition of sodomy incorporated sex between women as well as between men; anal penetration by men of women and children, male or female ("carnal knowledge of another vessel than God in nature hath appointed to become one flesh, whether it be by abusing the contrary part of a grown woman, or child of either sex"); and vaginal penetration of a girl prior to puberty ("carnal knowledge of . . . [the] unripe vessel of a girl"). Each of these acts was to be treated as a capital crime. The law added that masturbation "in the sight of others . . . corrupting or tempting others to do the like, which tends to the sin of sodomy, if it be not one kind of it," could also justify death, "as the court of magistrates shall determine." The sexual acts encompassed by the New Haven law had two common characteristics, as the law itself explained. Each was nonprocreative, "tending to the destruction of the race of mankind," and each was "unnatural . . . called in scripture the going after strange flesh, or other flesh than God alloweth." Unlike clerical formulations and the laws enacted elsewhere in New England, the New Haven code viewed sodomy as a range of acts that frustrated reproduction, not simply as uncleanness between members of the same sex. The assistants focused on the misuse of genital organs, not the gender of the persons to whom they were attached. Seen from this perspective, sodomy became a catchall term for any nonreproductive and therefore unnatural act committed by human beings. The act need not even involve a penis, since the law encompassed sex between women.[43]

Why New Haven rejected a simple restatement of biblical injunction in favor of a lengthy, unusually explicit, and broadly conceived formulation is a mystery. If this sodomy law had been the first to appear in New England, it might be tempting to argue for a narrowing definition of the crime as years passed. Yet other northern colonies had already adopted laws that specified sex between men as their purview. New Haven's code was thus anomalous, not part of a trend. The General Court may have hoped that a far-reaching definition of the crime would facilitate legal process in dealing with sexual malefactors, reacting against the restrictive format used elsewhere. If so, no other colony followed New Haven's example. The New Haven law remained in effect for only ten years: the colony united with Connecticut in 1665 and thereafter came under Connecticut's legal code.

Excepting New Haven, New England's sodomy laws referred only to sex between men. Yet magistrates were sometimes willing to consider broadening their conception of sodomy, especially during the first few decades of settlement, which were avowedly experimental. In 1642 the Massachusetts General Court thought about treating vaginal sex between a man and a prepubescent girl as sodomy. Dorcas Humfry, the daughter of a Bay Colony magistrate who lived in Salem, had charged three men with having "used her" over a period when she was between six and ten years old.[44] The court faced a serious problem in that the crimes had been committed before the enactment of a law against rape. The assistants were reluctant to apply the law retroactively, and in any case, it did not apply to children under the age of ten. In the absence of an appropriate law, the magistrates contemplated defining the abuse of Dorcas Humfry as sodomy. They did so on the grounds that Scripture prescribed death for that crime, whereas the rape of a child "was not capital by any express law of God." Thus, the three men could be executed for sodomy with scriptural mandate as a justification, regardless of whether the General Court had passed a law against the crimes in question.[45] John Winthrop, writing in 1641, had argued that sex between a man and "a girl so young, as there can be no possibility of generation" should carry the death penalty since it was "against nature as well as sodomy and buggery." From this perspective, similar to that adopted in the New Haven law, any nonreproductive act might be equivalent to sodomy. And yet the assistants eventually decided that Humfry's ordeal did constitute rape, which left them with no choice but to hand down sentences far short of execution. On that same day, the General Court amended the law against rape so as to enable use of the death penalty in future cases of child molestation. It is abundantly clear that the magistrates were eager to execute the three men for what they had done, but judicial caution triumphed over moral outrage.[46]

Sex between men was incontrovertibly sodomitical. But there was room for doubt as to the point at which same-sex physical intimacy became a capital offense, given a lack of consensus among English legal experts as to whether penetration was necessary for conviction. Edward Coke held that there must be "*penetratio,* that is, *res in re* [one thing inside another]," though he added that "the least penetration maketh it carnal knowledge."[47] Yet this restrictive view of the crime was rejected in the

1631 Westminster trial of Mervyn Touchet, second earl of Castlehaven, who was accused of "abetting a rape upon his countess" and "committing sodomy with his servants." The attorney general argued that the law of 1563 did not actually require that penetration had taken place: it described the crime "in general terms, and *ubi lex non distinguit, ibi non distinguendum* [where the law does not distinguish, no distinction should be made]." The lord chief justice followed the same line of reasoning, insisting that the law made "no distinction" between ejaculation without penetration and penetration itself. Their eagerness to convict Castlehaven led the lords impaneled for the trial to embrace an expansive interpretation of the law that had disturbing implications for future defendants.[48]

Within the New England magistracy, a measure of initial uncertainty over legitimate grounds for conviction soon gave way to a carefully constricted policy. In 1642 the Massachusetts General Court sought advice from ministers and magistrates throughout the northern colonies, asking them "*an contactus et fricatio usque ad effusionem seminis sit sodomia morte plectenda* [whether physical contact and friction leading to ejaculation should be punishable by death as sodomy]." Not only was English jurisprudence ambiguous on this issue, but scriptural references to sodomy were also extremely vague, a crucial concern since New England law looked to Scripture for inspiration. It was not unusual for magistrates to consult the clergy on points of law since the latter were often better read than the former in legal as well as theological scholarship. But transposing biblical injunction into legal code and then determining what that meant in practice was a daunting task, especially when official horror of the crime clashed with commitment to judicial rigor. As Thomas Shepard wrote to Winthrop that year, "in discussing these questions we generally walk in untrodden paths."[49]

The stakes were high. A series of recent cases in Plymouth Colony had involved sexual dalliance between men that apparently did not culminate in actual penetration. In 1637 the Plymouth court found John Allexander and Thomas Roberts "guilty of lewd behaviour and unclean carriage one with another, by often spending their seed one upon another." The occurrence of ejaculation established beyond doubt their "unclean" conduct, but there was no evidence to support a charge of outright sodomy. In 1641 William Kersley was presented for "unclean carriages towards men that he hath lain withall." This indictment also made no mention of sodomy itself, presumably because the court did not anticipate finding any concrete proof. Kersley's case does not appear to have proceeded further, suggesting that the testimony available against him was too flimsy to substantiate even a crime of lesser degree. Edward Michell was whipped the following year for "his lewd and sodomitical practices tending to sodomy with Edward Preston." Depending on the advice given by the clerics and judges consulted by the General Court in Massachusetts, misdemeanors such as these might become offenses punishable by death.[50]

Surviving answers from three Plymouth ministers illustrate the broad range of interpretations that the laws against sodomy could accommodate. John Rayner defined sodomy as "carnal knowledge of man or lying with man as with woman, *cum penetratione corporis* [with penetration of the body]." However, he continued, "full intention and bold attempting" might be as damnable as actually performing the act. Moreover, "*contactus* and *fricatio usque ad effusionem seminis*" might be "equivalent to penetration" if performed frequently and over an extended period of time. Like Rayner, Charles Chauncy argued that not only penetration but "all the evident attempts thereof" might be capital offenses. He suggested that "lying with" could signify both copulation and "other obscure acts preceding the same." But Ralph Partridge wrote that there were several reasons to doubt this broad reading of the law. Partridge held that "the intended act of the Sodomites (who were the first noted masters of this unnatural art of more than brutish filthiness)" was expressed in Genesis 19 "by carnal copulation." Moreover, penetration was crucial to the act of sodomy "among the nations where this unnatural uncleanness is committed." (Partridge did not specify the nations.) Finally, he claimed that indictments in English sodomy cases spoke explicitly of penetration.[51]

Others in Plymouth Colony must have agreed with Partridge's narrower view, since Bradford, writing to Massachusetts governor Richard Bellingham on behalf of his colleagues, argued that though "high attempts and near approaches" in capital crimes may be "as ill as the accomplishment" in God's eyes, yet it was doubtful whether they were punishable by death according to law "if there be not penetration." According to Winthrop's account, "most of them answered negatively, and that there must be such an act as must make the parties one flesh." This straightforward interpretation fit well with judicial standards of proof for other capital sex crimes and became the standard used by New England courts in handling sodomy cases, even though it militated against conviction.[52]

Subsequent trials for sodomy hinged on the crucial issue of whether penetration had occurred. Courts rarely accepted either intent or physical intimacy short of intercourse as grounds for execution. They took care to distinguish between sodomy, attempted sodomy, and other acts tending toward sodomy. Securing evidence that would justify a conviction was no easy matter. Most courts had only circumstantial evidence on which to base their deliberations: deponents may have seen the accused in compromising circumstances, but they rarely claimed to have witnessed penetration itself. The two-witness rule made conviction even less likely, and so in most cases the court could find only that relations to some degree sodomitical had taken place. When Nicholas Sension was charged with sodomy in 1677, the frank and detailed testimony presented to the court by neighbors and acquaintances left no room for doubt that Sension had made sexual advances to many men in his community over a period of three decades. Sension was notorious for his "sodomitical actings" in and around Windsor.[53] But although several men came forward at the trial to describe his overtures, only one claimed that Sension had actually "committed the sin of sodomy." Daniel Saxton told the court that he saw Sension get into bed with Nathaniel Pond "and make the bed shake," which led Saxton to believe that intercourse had indeed occurred. But Sension denied having sodomized anyone, and Pond could not speak for himself since he had recently perished in Metacomet's War. Because the court lacked the two witnesses required by law for a capital conviction, Sension could be found guilty only of attempted sodomy.[54]

Given this restrictive reading of the law, it is not surprising that only two individuals, William Plaine and John Knight, are known to have been executed for sodomy in seventeenth-century New England. And in neither case was the route to conviction straightforward. Plaine appeared before the assistants at New Haven in 1646, accused of having "committed sodomy with two persons in England" and of having "corrupted a great part of the youth of Guilford [in New Haven Colony] by masturbations, which he had committed, and provoked others to the like above a hundred times." Despite this impressive record, the governor refused to condemn Plaine until he had sought the advice of magistrates and ministers in Massachusetts. Only when his consultants declared that Plaine "ought to die" did the court sentence him accordingly. It is unclear whether his conviction was based on his having committed sodomy "with two persons in England" or his encouraging young people in Guilford to masturbate, or both. In 1655 the same court found John Knight guilty only of "a sodomitical attempt" upon a teenage boy, but the assistants eventually decided that Knight's clear intention to commit sodomy, in conjunction with other "defiling ways" and his having been found guilty of similar offenses by a previous court, justified the death sentence. Knight's failure to show any sign of contrition for his many offenses was doubtless also a crucial factor in the decision to execute him. It is probably no coincidence that both of these executions took place in New Haven, where the law defined sodomy much more broadly than did those in other New England colonies.[55]

Even when dealing with bestiality cases, which inspired clergymen and magistrates to their most vehemently condemnatory rhetoric, the courts were careful to ensure that legal requirements were enforced conscientiously. If the accused was willing to confess or if there were at least two witnesses, the court would proceed with conviction and execution. But anything short of that was problematic. In 1641 a Salem woman who had been prevented "by some infirmity" from attending Sunday worship looked out of her window and "espied" William Hackett, who was apparently having sex with a cow. At his trial, Hackett "confessed the attempt and some entrance, but denied the completing of the fact." With only one witness and an incomplete confession, the local court was unwilling to convict and so referred the matter to the General Court, where there was also "much scruple." The court finally decided to convict, but Governor Bellingham, "being doubtful of the evidence, refused to pronounce the sentence," and Deputy-Governor Endecott had to act in his place.[56]

In most cases, the absence of clear evidence from either witnesses or the accused that intercourse had taken place led to conviction for a lesser offense such as suspicious behavior or attempted bestiality. In 1657 John Ferris confessed that he had "attempted" the crime "and drew out his member to that purpose," but "his own conscience condemned the sin as odious and caused him to withdraw." The court was reluctant to believe him, suspecting that Ferris would have proceeded had he not been interrupted by the arrival of Henry Accerly, who gave testimony against him in court. Nevertheless, "taking it in the most sparing way according to his own confession," the court decided against execution and sentenced him instead to two separate whippings, a heavy fine, and wearing a halter around his neck. In 1681 Thomas Saddeler of Plymouth, who was also found guilty of attempting but not of actually committing bestiality, was whipped, made to sit on the gallows with a rope around his neck, branded with a P ("to signify his abominable pollution"), and ordered to leave the colony. The harshness of these punishments dispels any doubt as to the court's disapproval of the crime, but magistrates were not willing to re-lax their standards of proof even in cases that struck them as particularly heinous.[57]

Some of those accused of bestiality came under suspicion after the birth of deformed animals with features similar to those of the defen-dant. The unfortunately named Thomas Hogg was suspected of having coupled with a sow after the birth of a piglet with features resembling his own. Hogg had frequently offended his neighbors by appearing in pub-lic with torn breeches and his genitals clearly visible, "seeming thereby to endeavor the corrupting [of] others." Goodwife Camp had given him needle and thread to mend the breach in cloth and etiquette, "but soon it was out again." Hogg was also reputed to be a liar and a thief, all relevant given the interconnectedness of sin in the Puritan mind. However, Hogg denied having fathered the deformed pig, and there were no witnesses to his having been sexually intimate with animals, so he was acquitted of bestiality, whipped for "his filthiness, lying, and pilfering," and ordered to "be kept with a mean diet and hard labour, that his lusts may not be fed."[58]

The legal system's commitment to rigor led in some cases to acquittal even when the evidence seemed clearly damning. In 1676 Thomas Michel-son of Cambridge told the court that he had seen John Lawrence of Sud-bury "standing on a tree that lay along on the ground having his face to-wards his mare's tail and his hand clasped about her buttock and after a while he saw him withdraw himself a little from the body of the mare and as he thought he turned the mare's tail on the one side and then he again clasped his hands about her buttocks as before and wrought with his body against her." Michelson saw his neighbor Isaac Amsden coming along the highway and told him what he had seen. The two men confronted Law-rence, who denied having "wrought" with the mare. Amsden "was too far away to witness the act," and so Lawrence was acquitted in the absence of a second witness. Michelson's evidence, however compelling, was in-sufficient.[59]

JUDICIAL CAUTION WAS clearly a crucial factor in the acquittal or rela-tively lenient punishment of most New Englanders indicted for sodomy or bestiality. But there was another obstacle to conviction in such cases: an underlying disjunction between official ideology and popular responses to these two categories of sexual behavior. Puritan theologians and jurists ascribed meaning and value to sex in terms of its impact upon the spiritual drama in which each individual played a part: marital sex embodied the sanctified love between husband and wife, cementing a union that would nurture their mutual quest for redemption; any other form of sex testified to the pernicious influence of inherited depravity, polluting the body and endangering the soul. In other words, they conceived of sex as a component of spiritual endeavor, not as a manifestation of sexuality. The modern notion of sexuality as a distinct and pivotal aspect of human identity that gives rise to sexual urges and acts had no place in their ideological framework. Nor did they make any fundamental distinction based on the gender of those involved in a sexual act (as in the modern paradigm of homo- or heterosexuality). Any individual had the potential to commit any sexual sin, be it masturbation, fornication, adultery, incest, or sodomy; each of these offenses enacted universal depravity. Yet ordinary folk did not necessarily see things in quite the same way, which further hampered court proceedings.

Some New Englanders apparently recognized in particular individuals an ongoing preference for certain kinds of sexual partners. Legal depositions reveal occasions on which colonists, sensing that official ideology was of limited use in making intelligible their actual experiences and observations, created what seemed to them more appropriate categories and frameworks of meaning. They did not go so far as to posit sexual identity as such, but they did perceive in particular neighbors and acquaintances a persistent inclination that transcended the sexual acts themselves. In court depositions, they testified to both actual behavior and an ongoing sexual proclivity that reinforced claims of sexual criminality. But that inchoate notion of sexual predisposition was of no interest to magistrates: their insistence upon proof of intercourse in cases of sodomy and bestiality, as in other capital sex crimes, illustrates both their rigor and their understanding of sex as an act with nonsexual roots rather than as an expression of sexuality.[60]

As witnesses against Nicholas Sension recounted his "sodomitical actings" over a period of several decades, they clearly recognized in him an ongoing predilection for members of the same sex. As Daniel Saxton put it, "You'll never leave this Devilish sin till you are hanged." New Englanders occasionally revealed in court that they were well informed about sodomitical behavior in their midst and the attempts of those who were so inclined to establish local networks. John Allexander of Plymouth Colony was tried in 1637 for "lewd behaviour and unclean carriage" with Thomas Roberts. Allexander was found by the court "to have been formerly notoriously guilty that way." He had apparently sought "to allure others thereunto." Some men clearly did have an ongoing sexual interest in members of the same sex that was recognized as such by their neighbors, even though the proclivity that they identified was not acknowledged in official pronouncements.[61]

Sension himself characterized his persistent sexual overtures toward other males as a distinct realm of activity. When neighbor William Phelps berated Sension for attempting to seduce various men in the vicinity, Sension apparently admitted that he had "long" practiced "this trade," which he "took up at the school where he was educated." It is not clear from Phelps's deposition whether he or Sension introduced the word *trade* into their conversation; Phelps may have used it retroactively. But the application of the term to Sension's "sodomitical actings" by whomever is significant in that *trade* implied a specific calling or way of life. Use of that word to describe Sension's behavior indicates a sense of its significance, distinctiveness, and permanence in his life. The designation "trade" went well beyond the act-oriented view of sodomy propounded in official statements. Indeed, it fitted Sension's own experience much better than did authorized categories. Phelps's deposition, then, provides a rare glimpse of ordinary people creating their own sexual taxonomy.[62]

Some of those New Englanders who practiced bestiality also viewed their behavior as an ongoing propensity. An unnamed man who fled Massachusetts in 1640 to escape "the hand of justice" confessed "to some" before his flight that he was "given up to bestiality" and "never saw any beast go before him but he lusted after it." William Potter of New Haven, condemned to death for bestiality at the age of about sixty in 1662, confessed that he had first committed the crime when he was an apprentice in England, about eleven years old, "and after when he came to New England these temptations followed him." Though "sometimes they left him some years together," they always "returned again." Potter claimed that he "had some dislikes of it, but was overcome still." His wife had found him "in flagrante" with a bitch ten years previously: "he then excused his filthiness, as well as he could, unto her" and "conjured her to keep it secret." After his daughter had a dream about his execution for an unspecified crime, apparently before she knew of his proclivities, "these warnings did so awaken his conscience as to make him for a time leave off his infernal debauches." Eventually, however, Potter's son chanced upon him "conversing with a sow" and made public what he had seen. On the one hand, Potter characterized the recurrence of these lusts in terms of external "temptations" that "followed him" throughout his life rather than as intrinsic to his own identity. Yet on the other, he understood his behavior not as a lark, as an isolated lapse, or as youthful experimentation, but as a lifelong condition that had haunted him and his family.[63]

The gap between official and popular attitudes on this issue should not be overdrawn. Saxton's remark about Sension's "Devilish sin" was, after all, framed in religious terms. John Enno "heard Sension pray God to turn him from this sin he had so long lived in."[64] And Potter referred to his "infernal debauches." To argue that New England townspeople and villagers identified distinct sexualities would be to stretch the evidence far beyond the bounds of credibility. But exposure to the recurrent impulses of men like Nicholas Sension does seem to have led neighbors and acquaintances to treat sodomy as a specific and consistent impulse; it became in their minds a habitual course of action that characterized some men throughout their lives. When inhabitants of Windsor told court officials about Nicholas Sension's long history of attraction toward young men, their remarks were of little use in proving a legal charge of sodomy unless they had seen penetration occur; nor did their perspective fit with the theological paradigm that emphasized a sinner's inclination toward all manner of depravity. Yet relating Sension's male-oriented sexual appetite made sense to them.[65]

JUDICIAL PUNISHMENT OF sexual malefactors was, then, moderated by the magistrates' narrowly circumscribed and fastidious conception of what constituted compelling proof. Moreover, in New England's courtrooms as in church disciplinary meetings, a commitment to encourage repentance and rehabilitation could and often did soften the blow of moral condemnation. That spirit of compassion combined with punctilious restraint to create a sexual regime that was much less ruthless and more understanding of human frailty than official rhetoric might lead us to expect. Meanwhile, ministers' exaltation of marital union in this world and the next provided their flocks with a positive context in which to embrace and channel their sexual urges.

The sexual agenda contained within Puritan ideology remained nonetheless quixotic: it demanded of colonists not only an extraordinary degree of self-control but also strict observance of a sexual and marital protocol that ran counter to longstanding popular traditions, including and especially the widespread condoning of premarital sex. Such traditions proved resilient among covenanted as well as less godly settlers.

Though some colonists espoused a moral worldview that was exclusively and rigorously orthodox, others who saw themselves as devout and respectable members of the community combined principles handed down to them from the pulpit with beliefs that diverged from official teaching. (Puritan leaders readily acknowledged the elusiveness of their goals, though they framed the problem rather differently: sexual sins, Bradford wrote, were inevitable because of "the corrupt impulses present in all men and women.")

The tenacity of unauthorized beliefs within the cultural hybrid that was seventeenth-century New England complicated and limited the sexual revolution that ministers and magistrates had hoped to bring about. Their attempts to create a society in which practice matched their ideals was further compromised by the challenges of a colonial environment in which large-scale mobility made enforcement of sexual and marital codes extremely difficult. Though New England's leaders conceived of law enforcement primarily as a moral enterprise, they also recognized its implications for civic order and cultural identity, both of which became precarious in a colonial setting. As officials up and down the Atlantic seaboard bemoaned, preserving even the fundamentals of English "civility" could not be taken for granted in a "wilderness" where "savage" inhabitants threatened to "corrupt" and "debase" English settlers. Defining those fundamentals was itself controversial, given the disparities between official and popular assumptions; as we will see, the latter were in some respects closer to those of nonwhite Americans than to the norms laid down by church and state. Issues of sex, race, and civility thus became closely entwined in the moral politics of British America, including New England but especially in the southern colonies. Those debates and struggles over cultural and racial integrity take center stage in the three chapters that follow.

II

Sex and Civility

4

"Living in a State of Nature"

Sex, Marriage, and Southern Degenerates

ON 21 JULY 1721 John Urmstone wrote to the secretary of the Anglican Society for the Propagation of the Gospel, announcing with palpable relief that he had just arrived in London after "a tedious and expensive voyage" from North Carolina, where he had served as a missionary "among an ungrateful people" for almost twelve years. Urmstone had "struggled with [the] great inconveniences of living in such an obscure corner of the world inhabited by the dregs and gleanings of all other English colonies." Like most other missionaries who spent time in the Carolinas, he had been plagued by illness. The humid, swampy environment had "driven many clergymen out of it, not being able to stay so many months as I have years, and brought others to their graves." But Urmstone was equally demoralized by the "loose, dissolute, and scandalous lives" of the settlers among whom he was expected to minister. He had been shocked to discover that migrants often abandoned legal spouses elsewhere and then entered adulterous relationships or bigamous marriages once settled in the Carolinas. Urmstone understood this "loose" behavior in terms of a widespread criminal mentality among settlers in the colony. In 1711, soon after his arrival, he had described North Carolina as "a nest of the most notorious profligates on earth . . . chiefly peopled by such as have been educated at some of the famous colleges of Bridewell, Newgate, or the Mint" (prisons in London). In 1719 he complained that his maidservant was "a notorious whore and thief" who had been "bred a trader in Spitalfields [a district of London], but followed the music houses most and other vile courses which brought her to Bridewell and from thence transported hither." She knew "nothing of household affairs" and yet was "preferable to any that can be hired here, notwithstanding all her faults."[1]

Similar denunciations of Carolina colonists and their behavior pervade the writings of Charles Woodmason, an Anglican minister who set out from Charleston in 1766 to minister in the South Carolina backcountry for six years. Woodmason characterized the region as "a stage of debauchery" on which polygamy was "very common," "concubinage general," and "bastardy no disrepute." The population was "composed of the outcasts of all the other colonies . . . the off-scouring of America." Settlers passed from one relationship to another with flagrant disregard for legal or ecclesiastical requirements, "swopping their wives as cattle, and living in a state of nature." The lack of sartorial decorum in backcountry communities seemed to him indicative of the settlers' "abandoned morals." Women and men wandered about "barelegged and barefoot," males wearing "only a thin shirt and [a] pair of breeches or trousers," females "only a thin shift and under petticoat." The young women arranged what little they wore to accentuate their physical allure, or so it seemed to the clearly titillated Woodmason: "They draw their shift as tight as possible to the body, and pin it close, to show the roundness of their breasts and slender waists (for they are generally finely shaped), and draw their petticoat close to their hips to show the fineness of their limbs." Woodmason "hope[d] to bring about a reformation" in dress and behavior, but found many of the colonists unreceptive to his exhortations. What scandalized him most of all was the shamelessness with which settlers engaged in what Woodmason saw as "gross licentiousness, wantonness, lasciviousness, rudeness, lewdness, and profligacy": "they will," he wrote, "commit the grossest enormities before my face and laugh at all admonition."[2]

Urmstone and Woodmason were utterly unexceptional in their condemnation of "licentiousness" and "debauchery" among inhabitants of the eighteenth-century Carolina backcountry. Perhaps the most striking aspect of these diatribes was that once the writers passed from vague denunciation to more specific comments, they tended to focus on a common pattern of behavior. Ministers and government officials worried that colonists often formed and dissolved cohabitational relationships without observing marital formalities: dissolute though some settlers undoubtedly were, it was not so much rampant promiscuity as the informality of ongoing sexual relationships that preoccupied observers of the Carolina interior. Given contemporary thinkers' emphasis upon marriage as a bulwark of social order, it is not surprising that James Glen, writing as governor of North Carolina to the Lords of Trade in 1753, made a connection between marital irregularities in the backcountry and the generally degraded nature of life there. Glen lamented that couples came together "without any previous ceremony," their "loose embraces" producing children whom they then raised with as little regard to education and decency as one would "a litter of pigs" ("their children," he wrote, "are equally naked and full as nasty").[3]

Unmarried, serial, and bigamous relationships occurred in all the North American colonies, even in New England, but they were much more prevalent in those regions of British America where the guiding hands of minister and magistrate were ineffective or nonexistent among white settlers. Southern governments had a much harder time establishing a marriage-centered sexual culture than did their northern counterparts: an imbalanced sex ratio and the inability of most servants to marry, scattered settlement, a much less godly population, the lack of governmental institutions in recently settled areas, and a chronic shortage of clerics combined to create a situation that was highly unconventional. Even free adults who wanted to get married often could not do so because no one in their vicinity was qualified to officiate at a wedding. But others saw no need to do so: southerners who lived together though not formally wed or who did marry and then passed on to another relationship without formally dissolving the previous union did not necessarily consider their behavior to be illicit.

Enforcing the laws governing sex and marriage under these circumstances was no easy matter. In Virginia and Maryland, the rapid proliferation of judicial and administrative agencies facilitated regulation; an influx of ministers toward the end of the century gave a much larger proportion of colonists ready access to ecclesiastical marriage. Further south in the Carolinas, however, bringing popular mores into line with official guidelines proved a daunting enterprise. Conditions that in most other colonies existed only on the western borderlands predominated throughout much of North and South Carolina. Many settlers either did not care about sexual and marital protocol or acted on assumptions far removed from those espoused by religious and legal authorities. The lack of effective institutions at a local level made it extremely difficult for clerical or lay reformers to have any lasting impact. Even in those areas where courts and parishes had been established, officials representing church and state often failed to regulate inhabitants effectively: by no means all officials believed in or sought to enforce the codes with which they were entrusted; those who did advocate moral reform were themselves divided and often lacked credibility.

This state of affairs appalled those who sought to establish in the south a conventionally law-abiding and Christian society. Though few southerners advocated the degree of spiritual fervor and moral exactitude that New England's leaders sought to impose, members of the southern elite nonetheless cared deeply about issues of civility and order. Even though they were situated, as one of them put it, "here at the end of the world," that did not mean that inhabitants should be allowed to live like "a litter of pigs."[4] Contemptuous descriptions of colonial America that appeared in eighteenth-century England tended to stereotype all European settlers across the Atlantic as boorish bumpkins. It is hardly surprising, then, that throughout the colonial period members of the elite sought to refine, as far as possible, the behavior and values of their social inferiors, including and especially those who occupied the interior. It was certainly in their own interest to civilize the "gross" settlers with whom they were so often conflated.[5] As political and religious leaders worried about the apparent degeneration of poorer southerners into barbarism, they articulated their concerns largely in sexual terms. This chapter examines their efforts to modify the sexual mores of ordinary folk in the Chesapeake and the Carolinas. By no means all officials and members of the elite agreed that establishing a civilized colonial society necessitated marital or sexual reform. In the lower south especially, those who did share that conviction faced an uphill struggle against formidable odds. Indeed, the quest for thoroughgoing reform in the Carolinas remained downright quixotic throughout the colonial period.

THE FIRST CONTINGENT of migrants traveling to Virginia in 1607 consisted of 104 men and boys. Jamestown was initially an all-male settlement. It was not until the fall of 1608 that "the first gentlewoman and woman-servant" arrived. The former was already married to colonist Thomas Forrest; the latter would soon join in wedlock with John Laydon, "the first marriage" to be solemnized in the southern colony.[6] More women crossed the Atlantic to Virginia and Maryland in subsequent years, but they remained relatively few in number: male colonists outnumbered women by roughly six to one in the 1620s and by four to one in later decades. The Chesapeake's skewed gender ratio made it extremely difficult for men to find wives and establish conventional family households. It also meant that most colonists did not have access to sexual relations with English women during the initial period of settlement; there seems, furthermore, to have been little sexual contact with Indians during these

years.[7] It is difficult to believe that a group of young and notoriously unbridled men remained celibate for an extended period of time. It seems
likely that some male settlers deprived of female companionship would
have turned to each other instead.

Settlers in the seventeenth-century Chesapeake often paired off to form
all-male households, living and working together. As one recent scholar
has remarked, "it would be truly remarkable if all the male-only partner-
ships lacked a sexual ingredient." Some men may have turned to each
other out of desperation, whereas others may have taken advantage of an
unusual situation to form relationships that would have been more controversial under normal circumstances. But whatever their motives, men
who coupled sexually with other men are unlikely to have been anomalous in such an environment. It seems reasonable to assume that much of
the sex that took place in the first few years of settlement in the south was
sodomitical.[8]

Just as New Englander Nicholas Sension preyed upon young males in
his employ, so southern men may well have sought to exploit their authority over male servants for purposes of sexual gratification. Twenty-
nine-year-old William Couse complained in late 1624 that Captain Richard Cornish had raped him that August aboard the ship *Ambrose* ("then
riding at anchor in James River"). Cornish, who was apparently drunk,
had called Couse to put some clean sheets on his bed, then got into the
bed and invited the indentured servant to join him. When Couse declined
the invitation, Cornish got out of bed, cut Couse's codpiece, made him
get into the bed, "and there lay upon him, and kissed him, and hugged
him," declaring "that he would love [Couse] if he would now and then
come and lay with him." Cornish then "by force" turned Couse "upon
his belly, and so did put [him] to pain in the fundament and did wet him."
On a number of subsequent occasions, according to Couse, the captain
"put his hands in [Couse's] codpiece and played and kissed him."[9]

As a result of the servant's testimony, Captain Cornish was convicted
of sodomy and hanged. His execution aroused heated controversy among
the colonists. The death sentence was certainly open to question, since
no one had witnessed the captain's assault of his servant. Edward Nevell
pointed out to his shipmates aboard the *Swan* that there was no clear corroborative testimony against Cornish and declared that the captain had
been "hanged for a rascally boy wrongfully." On his return to Virginia
from Canada, where he made these remarks, Nevell was arrested for his
criticism of the court and sentenced "to stand on the pillory with a paper

on his head showing the cause of his offense in the market place, and to lose both his ears, and to serve the colony for a year." Thomas Hatch also claimed that Cornish had died "wrongfully." When one of his companions warned that such talk was dangerous and could cost him his ears, Hatch replied, "I care not for my ears, let them hang me if they will." Hatch was whipped, made to stand on the pillory, lost one of his ears, and had his period of service extended by seven years.[10]

This is the only sodomy case for which records survive in the early-seventeenth-century Chesapeake. Cornish's execution and the merits of the case evidently became a common topic of conversation at social gatherings during the months that followed his death. The government was clearly determined to silence those who criticized its handling of the case. As women arrived in greater numbers, enabling the formation of more conventional households and marriages, the authorities may have wanted to make an example of Cornish, both as a rapist and as a sodomite. Those who gathered to discuss the case and attack the court may have been anxious about the vulnerability of other men, perhaps including themselves, especially if incidents of sexual aggression were to become capital offenses on the basis of an accusation without corroborative evidence. It is striking that none of the reported conversations suggested any revulsion toward sodomy itself. Some Virginians may have felt that a veil of silence regarding sexual activity between men in the fledgling colony was being ripped away, much to their consternation.

The development of a family-based society that centered on the institution of marriage between a man and a woman was delayed in the Chesapeake not only by the skewed gender ratio and horrifying mortality rates (due to malnutrition and disease) that ended the lives of many colonists within a few years of their arrival but also by the predominance of indentured servitude. An overwhelming majority of immigrants to the seventeenth-century South, male and female, spent several years paying for their transportation across the Atlantic by working as indentured servants. This had critical consequences for sexual relations since servants were not allowed to marry without the consent of their master or mistress. Female servants sometimes married their own masters; others escaped their indentures early because planters who wished to marry them had the means to buy them out of servitude.[11] But servants who married without their employer's consent could be taken to court for breach of contract; either they or their lovers would have to make reparation to the aggrieved master. Because women were in short supply and sex outside marriage was illegal, most young people in the early South were in effect denied access to a licit sexual relationship.[12]

Unmarried servants who engaged in sexual relations could find themselves in court charged as economic and moral liabilities. Such cases were generally initiated by the master of a female servant whom he knew or suspected to be sexually active: even employers unperturbed by the moral implications of extramarital sex were likely to worry about a female servant becoming pregnant, a development that would incapacitate her and so deprive the master of labor. Planters occasionally reported young men who had been caught misbehaving themselves with female servants. In 1627 William Garret was summoned to appear before the General Court of Virginia to answer for "his lewd behaviour with Katherine Lemon, his fellow servant."[13] But most cases involving fornication were prompted by the birth of "bastard" children to female servants; illicit affairs were, after all, most likely to be exposed if pregnancy ensued. Maryland and Virginia law mandated that the fathers of illegitimate children borne by female servants should pay damages to "the masters or owners of such servants." If the mother was either unable or unwilling to identify her child's father, or if he could not be tracked down, she bore the burden of compensation, usually serving extra time at the end of her indenture. Servants who were prevented from marrying by their circumstances thus found themselves in a double bind: they had to choose between celibacy and criminality.[14]

YOUNG PEOPLE WHO spent several years as indentured servants and so were denied access to marriage could wed once their period of service came to an end—assuming that they lived that long, which in the early South was far from certain. Yet many of those couples who were free to wed did not do so; instead, men and women often lived together as husband and wife without observing the marital formalities prescribed by church and state. Nor was it exceptional to have several committed relationships in the course of a lifetime; these serial monogamists might marry all, some, or none of their partners. Because divorce was rarely an option, those who had been married before but then lived informally with a new partner were, at least officially, adulterers; those who married again were, strictly speaking, bigamists.

As legislators and local magistrates labored to impose law and order in the southern colonies, one of their principal targets was unauthorized cohabitation. After all, couples who lived together without formal sanction committed a criminal act every time they had sex together. Colonial assemblies in Virginia and Maryland passed laws requiring that couples wed in public and condemning all other forms of domestic union. They did so on principle and also because informal unions deprived church and state of the opportunity to regulate domestic relationships. This was, then, a question of power as well as of propriety. In those parts of the seventeenth-century Chesapeake that were served by regular court sessions, a steady stream of settlers were charged with "living together in the sin of fornication" or "cohabiting in adultery."[15]

But relationships that court officials denounced as illegal and immoral were often perceived quite differently by the couples concerned and their neighbors. Consider an informal but committed marriage that came to the attention of Maryland magistrates when they heard a case in 1719 concerning the will of Kenelm Cheseldyne, who had recently died. The will named as administratrix of Cheseldyne's estate a woman whom he had never formally wed but whom nonetheless he had considered his legitimate wife. Cheseldyne and Mary Phippard had "married in private" in or around 1712; no official or any other witness had been present. When they subsequently had a baby together, the local constable, John Greaves, went to arrest Mary on the grounds that she had borne an illegitimate child. But Greaves withdrew once Kenelm informed him that "there was not any such person as Mary Phippard" because "she was his lawful wife." Until 1753 a private declaration of marriage was valid according to English law; a couple could demonstrate to a court that they were wed merely by showing that they lived together in harmony. Maryland law insisted upon public marriage, yet once Greaves realized that the Cheseldynes and their neighbors considered this to be a reputable union, the constable decided that he had no business arresting Mary for bastardy. After Kenelm's death in 1718, members of the local community came forward to confirm that he and Mary were effectively a married couple, citing as supportive evidence their peaceful cohabitation, monogamous sexual relationship, and public comportment. "Cheseldyne called her his wife," deposed a local midwife, "took care of her as such, and owned the children." "Cheseldyne came with her publicly to church," declared a neighbor, "and helped her off and on her horse, and showed her the respect due to a wife." In the eyes of those who lived around them, Kenelm and Mary behaved like a married couple and so were in effect married.[16]

But court officials were rarely willing to acknowledge marriages that had been contracted in private, as William Mitchell discovered in 1652 when he was summoned to appear before Maryland's Provincial Court, charged with having lived "in fornication" with a "pretended wife," Joan Toast. In April 1651 Mitchell had invited a neighbor "to go home with him" in order to witness an informal ceremony between himself and Toast whereby "he took that woman to [be] his wife." Mitchell declared "that if there should be any antipathy in nature betwixt them they would part or live asunder, but he would allow her means," adding that he "hope[d] in God it would never be so." He apparently delivered a little homily in which he "brought a comparison from Adam, that was, that God created man and he being alone, God thought fit to give him a meet helper, or to that effect." Toast declared in court that since "her joining together" with Mitchell that day "in way of marriage," they had been "as man and wife in reference to the marriage bed." The couple lived together as though married and believed that they had quite legitimately wed themselves. But the court ordered that they separate "till they be joined together in matrimony in the usual allowed manner."[17]

The depositions that survive from cases such as that involving Mitchell and Toast enable us to glimpse popular attitudes toward cohabitation, sex, and marriage that were far removed from official requirements. When Edward Coppedge and Elizabeth Risby were prosecuted by a Maryland court in 1652 for unlawful cohabitation, neighbor Jane Hood declared that Risby was innocent because the couple was indeed married "but only for the ceremony." Some couples expressed their commitment to each other by performing a simple ritual such as coin-breaking that neither church nor court would recognize and yet was laden with significance for the parties concerned and their local communities. Quintin Counyer and Bridget Nelson apparently married themselves "by breaking of a piece of silver," which they "divided between them for the purpose aforesaid." When Elizabeth Lockett was tried in 1661 for bearing an illegitimate child and named Thomas Bright as the father, she swore in court that "there was a piece of money broken betwixt them and that he promised her marriage before the child was got." Francis Nash had heard Bright say "that there was a piece of money broke betwixt him and Elizabeth Lockett." Robert Martin Jr., however, declared that "to the best of his knowledge" there had been no "money broken." The plaintiff evidently believed that a pledge of commitment mitigated the offense. Neighbors disagreed about the veracity of Lockett's story, but they evidently shared her belief that a couple's degree of commitment to each other (not their official status) determined whether sexual relations between them constituted a misdemeanor. The very reason so many couples saw premarital sex as unprob-

lematic was that they considered private declarations to be more significant than public confirmation of the relationship.[18]

Couples sometimes lived together without having formalized their relationship because they had no other option. As Virginia's population increased almost tenfold between 1630 and 1670, settlers spread rapidly inland; yet the number of clergymen living in the colony remained roughly
the same until the 1670s. As a result, many parishes had no ministers to
conduct services or officiate at marriages. In Maryland, which Lord Baltimore founded as a refuge for Catholics, Protestant colonists who wanted
to be married by a minister of their own faith rarely had the opportunity until a modest influx of clergymen toward the end of the seventeenth
century improved the situation. In 1665 an unnamed woman living in the
house of Gils Tomkinson in Charles County, Maryland, was accused of
being "illegitimately got with child." But Tomkinson declared that the
woman was actually "his lawful wife" and that they had wed prior to
the child's conception, albeit informally. He argued that their "marriage
was as good as possibly it could be made by the Protestants, he being
one," but he went on to explain that circumstances had dictated an informal approach to wedlock. Tomkinson acknowledged that the legiti-
mation of a marriage normally required "the parties' consent and publication thereof before a lawful churchman." The former was "apparent,"
but the latter had been impossible "because that before that time and ever
since there hath not been a Protestant minister in the province." If that
was a problem from the court's perspective, he declared, "for the world's
satisfaction they here publish themselves man and wife till death them
do part." [19]

Further south, in the Carolinas, ministers remained in short supply
throughout the colonial period, which deprived many settlers of access to
a church marriage. The region's lack of clergy had led the colonial assembly to pass a law in 1669 that enabled couples to marry by declaring before
the governor or a member of the council "that they do join together in the
holy state of wedlock and do accept one the other for man and wife." In
1741 the assembly empowered justices of the peace to conduct weddings
in districts without a minister; if there was a local clergyman, they had
to obtain his permission before doing so. But given the scattered nature
of settlement in the Carolinas and the scarcity of officials in remote areas,
it would have been extremely difficult for many couples to reach a member of the council or even a justice of the peace. Some colonists did not
see the need for such formalities, but others who would have preferred

to be married by a minister or licensed official had to settle for informal cohabitation.[20]

Missionaries found that at least some of those who were living together as man and wife without having been formally married welcomed an opportunity to have their unions solemnized. One eighteenth-century South Carolina couple who had "lived together as man and wife, without benefit of matrimony, and had had two children," approached a visiting minister, informed him of "their misery and unchristian life," and asked to be married. The husband had never been baptized, but this omission was now corrected. The couple was then married formally and their children also baptized. These settlers may have become interested in formalizing their union once they became parents so as to have their children baptized. It is possible that they exaggerated their distress and sense of contrition in order to secure the minister's cooperation. But the couple might quite sincerely have wanted—but not previously been able—to marry in an officially sanctioned and public ritual.[21]

Anglican itinerant Charles Woodmason actively sought out couples who had not yet presented themselves to be formally wed. He adopted a strategy that combined pastoral outreach with naked threats. In each place that he visited, he offered to marry without charge "all who had lived in a state of concubinage," but he also warned that he would prosecute in the local courts "whoever did not attend to be legally married." According to Woodmason, a significant number of couples accepted this offer, were duly married, and had their children baptized. "Several" of those who identified as Anglicans had been married previously by "dissenting" clergymen, presumably because they considered that preferable to no ceremony at all, but now "desired to be remarried by the [Anglican] liturgy." There were also couples who had been "joined" by magistrates and who now "applied likewise to be remarried, as judging such their former marriage temporary only." Settlers who were uncomfortable about having cohabited informally sometimes pressed the clergyman who eventually married them to do so as discreetly as possible, "through shame after many years [of] cohabitation."[22]

Many women who did formally wed were already visibly pregnant. Charles Boschi, who served as the parson of St. Bartholomew's Parish in South Carolina from 1745 to 1747, reported that all "except two or three" of the brides whom he had married were pregnant. He was even "obliged sometimes to call for a chair to make the woman to sit down in the time of marriage because they were fainting away." Not all pregnant couples were complacent about their having become sexually intimate prior to marriage. Woodmason noted that some of the settlers preferred to get married by dissenting ministers "to prevent their being registered, as therefrom the birth of their children could be traced." These embarrassed couples may have regretted giving in to sexual urges prior to wedlock; or they may have entered relationships without the imprimatur of formal marriage because there was no immediate prospect of finding an official to marry them. But other couples who were pregnant or even parents by the time they married did not consider premarital conception to be problematic. Popular attitudes toward premarital sex were, after all, much more permissive on both sides of the Atlantic than church or legal officials would have liked.[23]

The children of couples who lived together without having formally married were, in the eyes of church and state, illegitimate. In order to prevent unwed mothers and their infants from becoming a charge on the public purse, local courts required that men who sired out-of-wedlock children acknowledge financial responsibility for their offspring in bastardy bonds. This is one of those instances in which official records can be very deceptive: a brief perusal of the bastardy papers would suggest a staggering number of sexual liaisons that resulted in pregnancy but not marriage; yet many of these children had been borne to parents who, although not formally wed, were living in a committed domestic relationship. Edward Bonney was presented in 1717 "for leaving his wife in Virginia and keeping a whore" in Bertie County, North Carolina. Bonney and his so-called whore had "several bastards." Robert Butler and Jean Mitchell were presented in 1755 for "cohabiting together and begetting bastard children." Offspring such as these were legally "bastards" because their parents were unmarried in the eyes of the law. But in both cases the parents may well have been effectively, though not legally, married. Traveling along the border between Virginia and North Carolina in the late 1720s, planter William Byrd met a young woman whom he described as living "in comfortable fornication" with a man by whom she had "several children." This was another illegal but apparently stable and "comfortable" household.[24]

In both the upper and the lower South, the ways in which relationships often ended were as problematical from a legal and ecclesiastical perspective as the ways they frequently began. Official recognition that a marriage had collapsed was rarely forthcoming. Maryland legalized divorce in the early eighteenth century, but the other southern colonies made no such provision in their legal codes. Although English subjects could apply to the House of Lords in London for a divorce by private Act of Parliament, that was prohibitively expensive for most people. Alienated couples did very occasionally persuade magistrates to ratify a separation if the marriage seemed broken beyond repair. In 1656 Maryland magistrates granted Cornelius and Susan Cannady permission "to live asunder" after a hearing to ascertain if the couple could be "reconciled." Three years later, officials in Charles County, Maryland, allowed Robert and Elizabeth Robins to disavow each other as husband and wife. Robert had accused his wife of adultery two years earlier and petitioned then for a separation. The court had refused his request on the grounds that there was insufficient proof of Elizabeth's infidelity but promised to reconsider if evidence emerged to show that "the child now in her arms was not begotten by her said husband." Perhaps he had since then produced more compelling evidence; or perhaps the court now realized that their breach was irremediable. But officially sanctioned separations such as these were exceptional.[25]

Just as settlers sometimes used unauthorized rituals such as coin-breaking to mark the beginning of a committed union, so married couples whose relationships had collapsed and who either had no access to a court or doubted that officials would grant them a legal dissolution of their union might turn to an alternative form of ritual severance. In eighteenth-century England, people sometimes gave notice of separation and remarriage by a procedure known as "wife sale." This generally took place in a public venue such as the local market or a tavern and was believed to release a husband from future liability for his now former wife's actions and debts. In most cases the wife seems to have approved of the exchange: the purchaser was usually her new lover, so the procedure marked a transition, signifying both the end of one relationship and the beginning of another. The public setting served to legitimate the transaction; sometimes the parties also drew up a written agreement and arranged for formal witnesses. But although wife sales were widely assumed to be legally binding, a court would not have endorsed the transaction. If the previous relationship had taken the form of a legal marriage, the new couple could be charged with adulterous cohabitation (if they decided to live together informally) or bigamy (if they married).[26] Nevertheless, in 1781 William Collings of Charleston, South Carolina, sold his wife, "for ever and a day, with her bed, clothing, etc.," to Thomas Schooler for "two dollars and half dozen bowls of grogg." Whether Collings's wife and Schooler were lovers is unknown. Collings had the deal recorded in writing and corroborated by a subscribing witness. This is the only record of a wife sale known to have survived from the region, but it may not have been the only time the procedure was used.[27]

In most cases of separation, a husband and wife would part company without any formal ceremony. They might dissolve their relationship by mutual consent, or one partner might simply run away to live with someone else. North Carolinian Dorothy Steele absconded with her lover, William Lee, and an impressive collection of "goods and chattels" from Steele's house. They seem to have been planning to set up a home together elsewhere; if so, they had chosen an economical, though rather callous, way of doing so.[28] A deserted spouse might resist unilateral separation and seek legal assistance in forcibly reconstituting the marriage. In 1687 the Albemarle County Court received a petition from Joseph Alford "to have his wife home" and accordingly "ordered that she forthwith go along with her husband."[29] But even if an informal separation was consensual, the couple risked legal prosecution, especially if they subsequently entered into new relationships while still formally married. Grace Morgan was presented to North Carolina's General Court in 1721 "for having two husbands and living in adultery." Six years later, the same court summoned Solomon Hews "for leaving his lawful wife and cohabiting with another woman, in which time the woman has had two children." Yet unions such as these were not necessarily illicit from the perspective of those involved. Presentments for unmarried, adulterous, or bigamous cohabitation often transformed personal histories of informal marriage and serial monogamy into criminal records. They embodied a persistent struggle between two versions of marital and sexual protocol as many colonists sidestepped formal procedures, sometimes willfully and sometimes because there seemed to be no other choice.[30]

POPULAR ATTITUDES TOWARD the formation and dissolution of cohabitational relationships horrified those who believed that sexual unions were licit only if the parties concerned had become husband and wife in accordance with the protocol laid down by church and state. From that punctilious perspective, unauthorized marriages were objectionable in large part because they provided a specious justification for illicit sex. The linkage between marital procedure and sexual respectability was made explicit in a 1662 Virginia law, which ordered that children born into an illicit marriage "be esteemed illegitimate, and the parents suffer such punishment as by the laws prohibiting fornication ought to be inflicted."[31]

Southern legislators and magistrates sought with varying degrees of determination and success to impose their version of marital and sexual respectability upon the population. The assemblies in both Maryland and Virginia passed laws to suppress informal unions and to ensure that settlers who wished to marry were free to do so. But the geographical mobility of many colonists complicated such efforts. Officials were instructed to determine "to their utmost skill and power" that applicants for marriage licenses were single and neither servants nor minors, "as they will answer the contrary at their peril." Yet legislators acknowledged that it was extremely difficult to confirm that "strangers" who applied for a license were qualified. And Maryland's governor pointed out in 1699 that the laws did not specify "what certificate shall be sufficient for any persons pretending to have been married together in Pennsylvania, Virginia, or any other adjacent government, so as to tolerate their cohabiting together as such." [32]

The degree to which official restrictions could be enforced depended in large part upon the strength and determination of regional and local governing bodies. During the course of the seventeenth century, Virginia and Maryland developed court systems that proved to be active and, on the whole, quite efficient in bringing to account those who disregarded the laws governing sex and marriage. But in the Carolinas, advocates of strict marital and sexual regulation were often thwarted by the notorious weakness of law enforcement agencies. "The government there is so loose and the laws are so feebly executed," wrote Byrd in the late 1720s, that "everyone does just what seems good in his own eyes." Even magistrates who "had virtue enough to endeavour to punish offenders" (a rare species, according to Byrd) were "quite impotent for want of ability to put it in execution." Woodmason was barely exaggerating when he wrote in the 1760s, "The civil force is hardly yet established." [33]

The North Carolina assembly did take legislative steps to enable and regulate formal marriage, but such measures had little impact, since the infrastructure needed to enforce them was generally nonexistent in remote areas of settlement and elsewhere often weak or corrupt. Laws that permitted civil marriage in the absence of ministers were intended to bring relief to settlers who wanted to marry and had not been able to do so; but, as already noted, many inhabitants had as much trouble finding a justice of the peace as they had in gaining access to a minister. And implementing laws against informal cohabitation required an efficient network of officials and institutions that was notably lacking throughout much of the region. In 1715 the assembly passed a law that was designed to rid the colony of immigrant couples who could not prove that they were legally wed. All those "accused by credible report or common fame" of not being "lawfully married" would have to produce a certificate of marriage or, "at least," a written confirmation that they were "taken and reputed to be man and wife in the government where they last resided." If they failed to do so, they would be "treated as vagabonds and expelled [from] the government." Almost two decades later, Governor George Burrington noted that the measure, "like most laws of this kind," was "little regarded." The assembly's repeated attempts to ensure careful registration of marriages, an important step toward suppressing adulterous and bigamous relationships, also foundered. According to Governor Tryon, writing in 1767, this was "chiefly owing to the extensive residence of most of the parishioners from the parish clerks or readers in their respective parishes or counties, many of which are from forty to fifty square miles and upwards."[34]

Even in those regions where local institutions had been established and officials appointed, policing the inhabitants was extraordinarily challenging. Settlements were scattered across vast territories and often isolated from each other by forests and swamps that were dangerous to traverse and also provided refuge for those who wished to make themselves scarce. Getting those accused of breaking the law into court so that a trial could take place was no easy task, since suspects would often disappear without trace into the black hole that was the Carolina interior. The accused would be presented repeatedly, year after year, until they were finally tracked down or the magistrates gave up. Most colonial courts experienced occasional difficulty in bringing suspects to trial and sometimes failed to do so, but the lengthy delays and rate of failure within the Carolina judicial system were exceptional. Consider the Bertie County Court's lackluster record in bringing sex offenders to account. Of seven presentments for fornication in 1741, four were continued until 1751, after which they were dropped without any definite resolution. A fifth was quashed after two years in 1743. Only two individuals were fined, one in 1743 and the other in 1744. Of twelve presentments for sexual misdemeanors in 1748 (nine for fornication, three for adultery), none went to trial: four were dismissed for lack of evidence and a fifth case was abandoned because the accused was now dead; the others were eventually dropped without being resolved.[35]

This problem was not restricted to local institutions. In April 1720 the General Court issued a presentment against John Hassell "for cohabiting with Sarah Wilkinson." He had been summoned the year before "for living in adultery many years," and the court now noted that it had issued "several orders" demanding that he cease living with Wilkinson. In November 1720 Hassell was again presented for "in a lewd and dishonest manner liv[ing], cohabit[ing], and keep[ing] company with one Sarah Wilkinson . . . in contempt, disobedience, and contrary to an order or command or orders or commands of the General Court." Hassell finally appeared the following March and was fined. By the standards of the North Carolina judicial system, this was a not inconsiderable achievement. But whether Hassell would actually end his relationship with Wilkinson was quite another matter.[36]

When magistrates issued an order to prevent or end an illegal liaison, their directive might well be ignored, if it even reached its target. The president of North Carolina's General Court heard at the beginning of the eighteenth century that James Blount of Bath County was planning to marry Mary Tylor, having previously been married to Mary's sister Katherine. He sent letters "to all persons who he thought might be instrumental in the matter" so as to prevent the union, which he condemned "as abominable in the sight of God and prohibited by the laws of the church." But the man charged with "speedy delivery" of the letters "delayed and neglected to deliver the said letters, in contempt of the aforesaid charge," so that the marriage went ahead anyway. Whether the courier was sympathetic to the couple in question and deliberately procrastinated or was merely inefficient is unclear, but he was whipped all the same.[37]

Not all government officials could be relied upon to enforce the laws and regulations with which they had been entrusted. We should always take care not to confuse official norms with the officials who supposedly imposed them. Some of those appointed to administer civil marriages were negligent, incompetent, or simply corrupt. The governor of North Carolina claimed in 1755 that there were "many irregularities throughout the province with regard to the obtaining and granting of licenses." One of his predecessors had been accused of selling marriage licenses for fees far in excess of those established by law and of failing to ensure that applicants were qualified: "he makes merchandizes of them," council members had complained, "exposing them to sale to any purchaser at ordinaries, ale houses, or public taverns, employing people keeping such houses as his brokers to dispose of them through the province; by which means any young persons may and many actually are married without and even contrary to the consent of their parents or guardians."[38]

And then there were local officials who themselves committed the very offenses that they were supposed to report and prosecute. Gideon Johnston, an Anglican missionary in South Carolina, was aghast that "polygamy and incestuous marriages" were "often countenanced" in his parish, but then he discovered that the clerk responsible for registering marriages was himself a polygamist. Johnston had the clerk dismissed and campaigned "both in and out of the pulpit to promote a general prosecution of those that are guilty of immorality and profaneness in this province." He managed to cajole leading colonial officials into organizing a crackdown on offenders but fell ill just as the authorities were beginning their investigation and was confined to his bed "whilst the prosecution lasted." Once recovered, he "expostulate[d] with the Judge and Attorney General concerning the remissness of this prosecution in several instances." Had he not been incapacitated, Johnston assured his masters back in London, he would have done all that he could "to have it carried on with greater severity."[39]

Another South Carolina missionary, Francis Le Jau, lamented that he could neither prevent "notorious adulterers" from "being chosen to be in authority" nor secure their removal. Consequently, he declared, "all vice reigns here scandalously and without any notice taken of vicious men." Le Jau wrote repeatedly to the Society for the Propagation of the Gospel about his campaign to form a local association that would spearhead moral reform. In February 1710 he predicted that any such proposal would be "warmly opposed" and that only once the "chief men" were willing to "stand for us" was there any point in proceeding. Six months later, he reported that he had "the promise of several honest men and of the best sort to encourage us." Even so, the odds were not encouraging: "the libertinism and wicked morals of some men, even considerable here, are too open and scandalous." Le Jau requested that "some books and directions relating to the beginning and carrying on of the excellent work of Reformation of Manners may be sent to be distributed." He also wanted "some large sheets containing the penalties for offences fit to be fixed on boards and put up in churches and the houses of our magistrates," which he "believe[d] would have a good effect." A year later, in July 1711, he was much less sanguine about gaining sufficient support from leading inhabitants of his parish: "I am afraid our design to promote a Reformation of Manners will not succeed so soon, and we must content ourselves to pray and edify and exhort one another as we have opportunities: the evil cannot be stopped for want of authority to repress it; we of the clergy have hardly the liberty to speak and our chief men are little inclined to compell men to be less scandalous."[40]

PASTORS SUCH AS Gideon Johnston and Francis Le Jau rarely had access to nearby clerics for support and encouragement as they battled to save Carolinian souls. Ministers remained scarce in the Carolinas throughout the colonial period, so that many inhabitants had no local pastor. Some settlers were doubtless quite comfortable with that state of affairs, but others were not. Those Carolinians who considered themselves a belea-guered moral minority and who wanted things to change pressed the gov-ernment to establish parishes and to provide funding for ministers who could then lead campaigns for a reformation of attitudes toward sex and marriage. In 1746 residents of Purrysburg, South Carolina, petitioned to be recognized as a parish in order to bring their vicinity "the benefit of the parochial government and discipline": "for want of church wardens or other proper parish officials," they explained, "many lewd women had and did come there to be delivered of their bastard children, and other ir-regularities had been committed." A 1749 petition from settlers in Craven County, South Carolina, asked for land to be granted on which a minis-ter could settle, so as "to suppress the vice and immorality now greatly prevailing in those parts of this province."[41]

These petitioners clearly expected the government to take responsi-bility for moral reform by establishing and sustaining religious as well as judicial institutions. Such expectations did not fall on entirely deaf ears. Several of North Carolina's eighteenth-century governors called repeat-edly for assemblymen and local officials to promote "the knowledge of true religion and the practice of morality and virtue," according to Arthur Dobbs "the first and greatest principal and foundation of all social hap-piness." Dobbs urged the assembly in 1752 "to take the most effectual measures for promoting religion and virtue and suppressing vice and im-morality, which are come to such a dreadful height in this province." In 1771 Josiah Martin issued a proclamation "for the encouragement of reli-gion and virtue," stressing the "indispensible duty" to "discourage and suppress all vice, profanity, debauchery and immorality" and charging all officials to be "vigilant and strict" in acting against "immoral or dis-orderly practices." Such declarations should not be dismissed as empty rhetoric, accompanied as they were by persistent advocacy of public fund-ing for clergymen and schoolmasters throughout the colony. Dobbs em-phasized in letters to London and in speeches to his assembly that the chronic shortage of ministers and teachers in North Carolina was a major obstacle to moral reformation: "gross immoralities," he declared, "prevail for want of properly instructing and educating the rising generation." Several bills providing funds to that end were introduced and debated. The assemblymen claimed, in some cases no doubt sincerely, that they supported the governor in his objectives. But competing demands on the public purse, the reluctance of some assemblymen to make clergymen financially independent of their parishioners by paying them from the colonial government's coffers instead of via local collection, seemingly endless objections by the government in London to the wording of various clauses in proposed bills, and the apathy of at least some representatives combined to blight legislative provision for ministers and schools.[42]

Clergymen and ecclesiastical institutions were not, of course, the only possible agents of moral reclamation. In seventeenth-century Virginia, magistrates had responded to the absence of church courts by assuming themselves a sacerdotal mantle. Throughout the first half-century of settlement, they required that individuals convicted of fornication perform rituals of penance. In 1639 the Northampton County Court sentenced four married couples who had committed "the sin of fornication before marriage" to "stand in the church three several Sundays doing penance according to the canons of the church." Two years later, Christopher Burrough and his wife, Mary Soames, were convicted of the same offense in Lower Norfolk County and made to "do penance in their parish church the next sabbath the minister preacheth at the said church, standing in the middle alley of the said church upon a stool in a white sheet, and a white wand in their hands, all the time of divine service." Such penitential rituals did not always work out as the authorities planned: when Thomas Tooker and Elizabeth Hauntine were given a similar sentence that same year, Elizabeth, "like a most obstinate and graceless person, [did] cut and mangle the sheet wherein she did penance." She evidently rejected the notion that premarital sex was a sin.[43]

Some Carolina magistrates also saw themselves as fulfilling an almost priestly function. Nicholas Trott, who served as chief justice of South Carolina at the beginning of the eighteenth century, condemned Sarah Dickenson, Edward Beale, and Joshua Brenan to death in 1703 for conspiring to murder Dickenson's husband. Sarah and Edward were lovers and had "defile[d]" the dead man's bed. Trott devoted the bulk of his judgment to an appraisal of their crimes as sin with the explicit intention of bringing the three miscreants to a sense of their spiritual peril. He refrained from giving "particular directions . . . that being more properly the office of a divine," but he did subject the condemned trio to a lengthy exhortation that was designed to make them "sensible" of their "deplorable condition" and thus more inclined to become "truly repentant." Trott offered them "any of the ministers of this province" as "ambassadors of Christ," though there were very few to choose from. At least partly by default, he himself was performing that role.[44]

Much later in the eighteenth century, court officials in Pasquotank County, North Carolina, sometimes lent their proceedings a spiritual character by deploying religious language in presentments. Samuel Lowman was summoned in 1758 for committing adultery, "the sacerdotal order not regarding, but the rites and ceremonies of the church altogether despising." In 1770 Amos Upton was presented for having "entice[d] and seduce[d] a certain Martha Sikes from her virtue and religion to commit with him the horrid, abominable, and unchristian sin of adultery." He had "carnally and adulterously know[n]" her on several occasions, "in open violation of the laws of God and his country to the evil example of all others." In 1788 David Davis was also accused of having committed adultery, "in no manner regarding the religion of the said state and divine revelation, and in open contempt and violation of the Christian faith, wickedly intending and devising to destroy all order and decency in the marriage state." Such language, which might seem more plausible in seventeenth-century New England, suggests the tone that at least some magistrates and clerks hoped to establish in their courtrooms and, by extension, in the communities over which they had jurisdiction.[45]

But the primary responsibility for spiritual reclamation rested with religious leaders and institutions. These were frequently ineffective when dealing with the scattered and often intransigent Carolinians. The most successful of those who championed a particular version of sexual and marital propriety may well have been the Quakers, who evangelized successfully in North Carolina during the last three decades of the seventeenth century and remained a force to be reckoned with well into the eighteenth. Although the Friends had neither a formal ministry nor a conventional ecclesiastical structure, their cooperative ethos and energetic pursuit of informal alliances within and between settlements enabled them to develop communities of moral enterprise that for the most part eluded Anglicans. The Quakers' concern that couples presenting themselves for marriage be "free" or "clear" of impediments, including preexisting "marriage entanglements," was particularly apropos in the Carolinas. An applicant who had arrived only recently in a particular vicinity had to produce a certificate of "clearness" from the monthly meeting in his or her previous place of residence. Careful inquiries into the personal histories of fellow believers rapidly became an important part of corporate Quaker activity in North Carolina. In 1680, when Christopher Nicholson and Ann Atwood announced their intention to marry, fellow Quakers in Perquimans Precinct sought to verify that "the man was clear from all other women and the maid clear from all other men." In 1711 the Friends' Monthly Meeting in Pasquotank Precinct appointed Henry Keaton and John Symons to investigate William Everigin's "life and conversation and clearness in respect of marriage" when he and Elizabeth Henley "declared their intention of marriage."[46] Given the extensive network of contacts developed by Friends in the region, Quakers may well have been better equipped than many court officials to mount credible investigations. In some cases, the investigators found impediments. Robert White was forbidden to marry Rebecca Overman in 1719 because he had "a former wife living," even though she had abandoned him to live with another man. And in 1756 the Symons Creek Friends rejected Benjamin Morris's application to marry the "widow Hendly" because he had previously promised to wed Elizabeth Nixon, with whom he had been sexually intimate. The monthly meeting declared that Morris remained bound in conscience to marry Nixon "as long as she the said Elizabeth lives single and declares a willingness to marry."[47]

In sharp contrast to Quakers, who operated without official endorsement, Anglican ministers might have been expected to score considerable success in enforcing their moral agenda. The Church of England was, after all, the established faith in the Carolinas; at least in theory, ministers worked in tandem with local courts as the joint guardians of "morality and virtue." In practice, however, the situation was rather different. Anglican ministers were few in number and cut off from fellow pastors by vast forests and swampland; they were, moreover, frequently disabled by their inability to work effectively with potential lay allies and by the high-handed attitude that they brought to bear upon their mission. Those ministers who envisaged that they would join with local government officials in fighting for moral reformation were often sorely disappointed: they found themselves in competition rather than alliance with magistrates and local clerks.

Rivalry and tension between clergymen and secular officials focused on their joint responsibility to formalize marriages. Justices were supposed to marry couples only in the absence of a minister or, if there was a resident pastor, with his express permission. But they were sometimes eager to discharge this function even if a clergyman was readily available and willing to perform the ceremony himself; there was, after all, a fee involved. Ministers were outraged to discover that some officials valued the prospect of financial remuneration over their duty to respect ecclesiastical perquisites and the law. John Garzia, the pastor in St. Thomas's Parish, Beaufort Precinct, complained to the North Carolina General Court in 1735 that Henry Crofton, a justice of the peace, had married a couple in April of the previous year despite the fact that Garzia was "resident and incumbent in the said parish, contrary to the act of assembly." Garzia had repeatedly asked Crofton to hand over the five pounds prescribed by the act as a penalty for so doing, "one half thereof to the use of him the said John as a minister, and the other half to the use of the said parish." Crofton had refused to pay up, and so Garzia requested assistance from the court, "in behalf of himself as of the poor of the parish." This was not an isolated incident. According to Garzia, Crofton had married another three couples later that same year, also in violation of the act. In 1772 Governor Martin condemned "collusive malpractices" involving magistrates and court clerks that prevented ministers from marrying couples in their parishes and so augmenting their often meager incomes. He had heard from the rector of St. Luke's in Rowan County that the clerk responsible for issuing marriage licenses "encourage[d] people . . . to go to magistrates to solemnize their marriages in preference to the rector" and "conceal[ed]" from the rector "the number of licenses granted, by which means he [was] deprived of his dues."[48]

Sectarian politics also divided ministers who could have worked together as advocates for sexual reform. As well as causing tension between Anglican ministers and government officials, marriage fees proved a crucial issue in denominational rivalry. Not until 1776 were "all regular ministers of the Gospel of every denomination" in North Carolina authorized "to celebrate matrimony according to the rites and ceremonies of their respective churches."[49] But non-Anglican ministers had nonetheless performed marriages throughout the century: adherents to a particular denomination understandably wanted to be wed by a preacher of their own faith, and as we have already seen, couples who conceived children before marrying sometimes turned to a dissenting minister so as to elude registration and thus avoid later questions from local officials about the length of time between marriage and the birth of their first offspring. Anglican clergymen were, not surprisingly, irritated when they found out that their rivals were marrying people "in defiance of all laws and regulations." Not least of their objections was that this was another source of competition for fees: "if there is a shilling to be got by a wedding or funeral," Woodmason declared, "these impudent fellows will endeavour to pocket it."[50]

The insults that flowed from venom-tipped tongues and pens engaged in denominational warfare were often sexual in nature. Dissenters were scathing in their denunciations of Anglican clergymen for their failure to suppress immorality among their parishioners. Gideon Johnston conceded in his 1713 report to the Society for the Propagation of the Gospel that "one of their grand objections and principal causes of separation from us" was "that open profaneness and immorality which is too visible among us." Anglicans in turn equated evangelical religion with sexual license and were eager to believe any accusation of impropriety against its practitioners. Woodmason claimed that the very nature of revivalist gatherings encouraged libidinous tendencies. Their "love feasts," devotional gatherings that featured the "kiss of charity" (an opening, in Woodmason's opinion, to all manner of "filthy" behavior), took place in the evening. That necessitated that young people return home afterward "in the dark" or spend the night "at some cabin . . . sleeping together either doubly or promiscuously." The "lewdness and immorality" that surely resulted "scandalized" religion and caused "all devotion to be ridiculed." Not only did the physical manifestations of conversion at evangelical meetings involve "indecent postures and actions" (some women "falling on their backs, kicking up their heels, exposing their nakedness to all bystanders"), but those undergoing baptism wore "thin linen drawers" that once wet "expose[d] the nudities" as much as if the wearers were "strip[ped] wholly into buff." Such occasions drew "lascivious" spectators "as to a public bath." The arrival of evangelical preachers had thus advanced the cause of debauchery in the Carolinas. "There are rather more bastards," he declared, "than before."[51]

Anglican clerics could, then, become distracted from the task of redeeming their flocks by conflicts with secular officials and dissenting ministers, as well as by vicious attempts on all sides to expose denominational rivals as sexually permissive. But clergymen who lived or traveled well beyond the reach of competing authority figures found that battling to redeem sinners as isolated warriors was equally problematic. Local inhabitants did not always take kindly to pastoral denunciations of their behavior, so that ministers who went on the offensive could find themselves the targets of considerable lay hostility. Some Carolinians paid little regard to moral conventions of any kind and either ignored or mocked clerics like Charles Boschi, who denounced conception by unmarried couples as a "most abominable crime." But those who considered themselves reputable citizens, even though their understanding of what constituted acceptable behavior differed from that of the church, became upset if clergymen attacked them. When Boschi asked his parishioners sarcastically if it was "the fashion of this country to lie with the woman before they are married," some "made a jest" in response, but others "made no answer, and w[ere] displeased at my interrogation." According to Boschi, the local inhabitants were "so delicate that they do not like it that a clergymen should say anything against their faults." Indeed, he was "blamed" for "exclaim[ing] too much against the profaneness and iniquities that reign in the parish." Boschi claimed that such concerns lay behind his parishioners' reluctance to give him a permanent appointment: they preferred to "keep him under subjection," since a minister in that position would "be very cautious not to guide them in so rigorous a manner as he is bound in duty to exclaim against iniquity."[52]

Boschi was not the only Anglican missionary working in the Carolinas to claim that he paid a heavy price for criticizing the sexual mores of his parishioners. According to John de la Pierre, the "gradual depression and degradation" of his standing among parishioners began when he spoke out against a "great man" who had entered an openly incestuous marriage. Other residents had committed "incest or polygamy" and were evidently displeased by his public denunciation of such practices (perhaps also his lack of respect toward a "great man"). John Garzia had a similar experience: "upon my preaching [against] any prevalent and predominant sin, I must be prepared to stand the persecution of those who are guilty of it, especially in my resident parish, in which adultery, incest, blasphemy, and all kinds of profaneness has got such deep root." When Woodmason gave a sermon "against immorality," a local tavern keeper was "affronted . . . as if [it were] aimed at him" and "vow[ed] vengeance."[53]

One way of responding to unwelcome lectures on sexual morality was to accuse the minister himself of improper behavior. A striking number of missionaries suffered exactly that fate. According to Woodmason, dissenters sought to malign his name by framing him as a hypocrite. Two men, he reported in his journal, entered his house one night while he was asleep and stole his gown. One of them put on the gown, "then visiting a woman in bed, and getting to bed to her, and making her give out next day that the parson came to bed to her." The scheme, apparently "laid by the Baptists," was exposed and the two men seized by friends of Woodmason. But the constable released the culprits without charging them, much to Woodmason's chagrin.[54]

Some of those accused were doubtless guilty as charged. In 1744, when Stephen Roe appeared before the Anglican Commissary in South Carolina to answer allegations that he had committed adultery in Boston, the missionary confessed that he had impregnated "a daughter of the house where he lodged" and then fled the city after she "brought forth a child, the fruit of their wickedness." Michael Smith was dismissed in 1756 from Prince Frederick Church in Georgetown County, South Carolina, largely as a result of "immoral conduct" during "travels into the interior parts of the parish." So "indiscreet" was his behavior, claimed the vestry, that he alienated people "instead of bringing them over and joining of them to the communion of our church." Smith had returned from "one of his late rambles" with a woman named Margaret Jordan, whom he called his wife and with whom he lived, "though on our strictest examination of him on this head he could produce no witness or voucher of the celebration of marriage with her." The vestry suspected that either the couple had never formally wed or that Smith had married himself. The latter would be consistent with "assertions" he had made "in public company" that "it was in his power as a priest to marry himself to any woman whatever without the intervention of a third person." He was also alleged to have put up "a scandalous and libertine paper" at the Black River Church "in justification of fornication from scripture." (Exactly what kind of behavior he sought to condone and on what scriptural grounds the vestry did not specify.)[55]

Other allegations were more problematic and may well have been concocted in order to tar particular clergymen with the same brush that they had been brandishing against their parishioners. As two Maryland ministers wrote in 1727, accusations of sexual impropriety against members of the clergy were "very common in these parts of the world where people give too much liberty to their tongues to blacken the character even of the most innocent." Soon after missionary John Urmstone's departure from North Carolina in 1721, an anonymous letter was sent from the colony to Urmstone's masters in London. The writer claimed that Urmstone had led a "wicked and scandalous" life and that he was a "notorious drunkard," known for "swearing and lewdness." According to the letter, "for these and other of his vices he was so much disliked of the people he was among that scarce any of them came to hear him." The author sought to impress upon the society that Urmstone was "unfit" to serve as a missionary, yet he offered no specific or corroborative evidence against the cleric. Urmstone had himself admitted some years earlier that he was unpopular, but he gave a different explanation for the inhabitants' hostility toward him. "My sacred character," he wrote, "is sufficient to draw hatred and contempt upon me from a pack of profligate and loose people and zealous sectarists whose whole endeavour it is to load me with reproaches." By "sacred character" Urmstone meant not only his office but also, with typical self-righteousness, his own piety and virtue. Urmstone's sense of moral propriety was unbending and unforgiving: he disowned his own son when he discovered that the young man had "got a servant wench with child." It seems quite possible that the author of the letter was one of those who disliked Urmstone's "sacred character" and sought in a spirit of vicious irony to blacken the minister's name by accusing him of the very "profligacy" for which he had denounced his parishioners.[56]

Even if a minister accused of sexual impropriety had behaved inappropriately, it was not necessarily the offense itself that prompted his parishioners to accuse him. In 1756 St. Helena's Parish in South Carolina informed Alexander Garden that it was dismissing William Peasely for sexual misconduct. The vestry described his behavior as "so open and shameless as to disgust all ranks and degrees of people." Peasely had given "great umbrage" by paying frequent visits to "a woman who lived in this town" with whom he was assumed to be having a sexual relationship. Peasely had promised at a vestry meeting "never to make her any more visits, but they were notwithstanding repeated that very afternoon and continued so publicly that we [members of the vestry] were obliged to remind him of his promise which only served to whet his passion or purpose with assiduity in them to such a degree that scandalous advertisements were put up in public places by persons unknown, so obviously levelled at those nocturnal and other meetings that they seemed to give every person (but he who was most concerned) the greatest disgust." There was, however, a good deal more than moral outrage dividing the inhabitants of St. Helena's Parish from their minister. In a letter to Peasely, the vestry alluded to "animosities and feuds which ha[ve] so long subsisted in the parish, and which are now swelled to such a degree as to keep the people from the church and communion." One of the issues that had caused dissension between Peasely and his parishioners was financial remuneration, a thorny topic that poisoned relations between many missionaries and their parishes. But in a letter to clergymen in Charleston, the vestry "omit[ted] a detail [i.e., detailed description] of many feuds and the occasion of them between him and the great part of the parish," claiming that the vestry had no part in these "feuds" and that in any case describing the whole history would be "too prolix for a letter." Peasely may or may not have had an illicit relationship, but there was a prior history of contention between minister and parishioners that the vestrymen sought to de-emphasize because they wanted to focus attention on the issue of sexual impropriety; the latter was most likely, they realized, to bring about Peasely's "disgrace and ruin."[57]

Missionaries elsewhere in British America were also dogged by accusations of sexual impropriety. As in the South, some were clearly framed by their enemies.[58] Colonists were well aware that sexual allegations could serve as deadly weapons against missionaries of whom they wished to rid themselves. And many emissaries from the Society for the Propagation of the Gospel were extremely unpopular. Most of these missionaries came to North America after trying and failing to secure positions in England. They were bitter men who did not appreciate having to spend time in what Urmstone called "this hell of a hole." Hungry for a professional status that had been denied them across the Atlantic, they expected grateful obedience from the inhabitants and were not slow in reminding parishioners of what they conceived to be their prerogatives. They insisted upon theological and liturgical as well as sexual and marital orthodoxy. Yet colonists often had a quite different set of priorities, expected their ministers to answer their needs, and were outraged by the missionaries' punctilious demands. Laypersons in general on both sides of the Atlantic cared a good deal less about doctrinal niceties than ministers would have liked, but the weakness of clerical authority in the seventeenth-century colonies other than New England and the emergence by the early eighteenth century of a religious marketplace in which denominations increasingly had to compete for popular allegiance made for a degree of lay confidence and even pugnacity for which the missionaries were utterly unprepared.[59]

Given this scenario, it is not surprising that missionaries frequently came into conflict with the local inhabitants and that these controversies were often accompanied by accusations of personal misconduct against the ministers: if missionaries were going to demand obedience to spiritual orthodoxy, how better to undermine their position than to portray them as having violated moral conventions. This strategy was particularly appropriate in the Carolinas, since missionaries there launched determined, vehement, and often unwelcome campaigns against what they saw as widespread debauchery. One of North Carolina's governors urged in a 1767 letter to Anglican leaders in London that "the strictest caution and care" was "absolutely necessary in the recommendations of gentlemen who come to settle as ministers in this province." The settlers were "strict inquisitors and if the clergyman is not of a moral character, and his life regular and exemplary, he will attract but little esteem to himself and less benefit to his parishioners for whom he must undergo patience and fatigue in the service of his calling." This insistence that only men of "exemplary" character should be sent to the colony as missionaries was doubtless driven in part by a straightforward desire for clergymen who would inspire by their own example. But the personal conduct of missionaries became especially significant because sex was so frequently a topic of contention between representatives of the society and their parishioners. William Byrd commented that missionaries often left North Carolina without effecting much improvement in their parishioners, either because the minister was "too lewd for the people" or ("which oftener happens") because the people were "too lewd for the priest." What Byrd did not note was that allegations against a cleric sometimes arose as a result of the pastor's own complaints regarding parishioners. Such men were effectively tarred with their own brush.[60]

Eighteenth-century evangelical preachers who offended southerners by impugning their moral values also became the targets of sexual accusation. As Baptist and Methodist itinerants traveled far and wide to spread their message, critics alleged that they took advantage of their intense communion with female converts and seduced women whose souls they had already ravished. Some evangelical preachers did worry about temptations of the flesh. In one extreme case, twenty-four-year-old Jeremiah Minter became so anxious about the potentially sinful nature of his connection with a married convert named Sarah Jones that he had himself castrated. By becoming "an eunuch for the kingdom of heaven's sake," he could "devote [himself] entirely to the Lord in a single life." Others used less drastic measures to resist temptation; a few may well have succumbed. But as with Anglican missionaries, the underlying motive for allegations of sexual impropriety, whether or not founded in fact, seems to have been resentment of the ministers' intrusive and reformist creed.[61]

NOT ALL CAROLINIANS were opposed to the careful supervision of sexual behavior and marriage protocol. In 1752 a group of "inhabitants on Peddee River above the mouth of Lynche's Creek" requested the setting up of a county court to punish local criminals, among whom they included people "cohabiting with their neighbors' wives" and those "living in a most lascivious manner while the petitioners have no way or means to suppress them." Other communities recognized that at least some couples would marry if they had the opportunity to do so and therefore requested the appointment of local officials who could issue marriage licenses and officiate at weddings. Settlers who disapproved of the informal relationships so prevalent in many districts were not averse to informing on their neighbors, even urging the prosecution of kinfolk whom they presumably hoped to rescue from a life that they considered to be lawless and depraved. In 1695 Edward Jones complained to the Albemarle County Court that his son and namesake was "cohabit[ing]" with Sarey Minkings "in unlawful lust." He had "often admonished" his son and urged him "to leave of those wicked and ungodly practices."[62]

Carolinians may have impressed outside observers as a crew of devil-may-care degenerates, but at least some settlers cared deeply about sexual respectability. As shown in slander suits prompted by ribald remarks about sexual behavior, the victims of such jests clearly believed that "the good will and esteem" of "neighbours and others" depended in part upon moral reputation. Sexual defamation, the plaintiffs claimed, was socially damaging.[63] A 1760 case involving slander and retaliatory assault illustrates the bitter, even violent, divisions that could grip local communities over issues of sexual propriety. Richard Spaight, a justice of the peace in New Bern, North Carolina, found himself in court as a defendant after he whipped Richard Core for making "scurrilous" claims about his wife. Spaight was accused of acting arbitrarily and abusing his position as a magistrate, but he claimed to have whipped Core in a "private" capacity, not "by any judicial authority." He had acted "in the heat of passion for the affront and indignity with which his wife was treated." Spaight argued that he had struck a blow on behalf of those who cared about sexual reputation against those who did not: "in this new settled country, as the most of the people are from mean originals, they don't much stand upon character, which makes it incumbent upon those that do, to exert themselves in their own defense." James Parkinson, a merchant, had already "severely beat" Core for "writing or copying a libel against him." Indeed, "several of the inhabitants" had been "vilified by scurrilous libels full of ribaldry almost daily published." Those New Bern denizens who "st[oo]d upon character" saw themselves as waging a defensive war against those who reveled in "ribaldry." Like the districts from which settlers wrote to request official assistance in suppressing "vice and immorality," New Bern was riven by different expectations regarding sexual behavior and conversation. In common with settlers who sought to discredit reforming ministers by accusing them of sexual impropriety, those in New Bern who saw no need for moral reform may have intended to undermine the credibility of righteous neighbors by besmirching them or their families as sexually loose.[64]

Carolinians who favored sexual and marital reform lobbied for more effective regulation throughout the eighteenth century. During the revolutionary period, some citizens voiced their concern that legal disruptions might prevent the punishment of couples who failed to marry or whose marriages were illicit. The Instructions from Mechlenburg to North Carolina's Provincial Congress in 1776 included an injunction "to obtain a law to prevent clandestine marriages," whereas Orange demanded "a law for making the marriage contract notorious [i.e., public and proven]." In 1778 the state assembly passed a law regulating "rites of matrimony," and in 1788 it resolved that North Carolina needed legislation "to punish bigamy and polygamy." There was clearly a need for clarification: in September of that year, magistrate Spruce Macay recorded in his notebook the conviction of one Garnel Smithers for bigamy, but he added, "query whether punishable in this state."[65] A bill was introduced soon thereafter "to punish persons guilty of the sin of adultery, incest, and polygamy." The law that finally passed in 1790 focused on the latter offense, its purpose "to restrain all married persons from marrying again whilst their former wives or former husbands are living." It denounced in particular the "many evil-disposed persons" who, "going from one part of our country to another, and into places where they are not known," exploited their anonymity to enter bigamous marriages in full knowledge that their previous spouses were alive.[66]

But those who favored such laws and their rigorous enforcement continued to be thwarted by much more pragmatic and permissive attitudes toward sex and marriage. In 1796 the General Conference of Methodists, meeting in Baltimore, advised ministers "not to receive any person into society who had put away a wife or husband and married again, no matter what the crime was that caused them to part." William Ormond, an itinerant on the Tar River circuit in North Carolina, noted in his journal, "This I do not approve of." Ormond may have objected to the inflexible prohibition on compassionate grounds, but he must also have realized that taking the recommended position would make the task of attracting and retaining followers in North Carolina much more difficult.[67]

That many citizens of North Carolina did not share the concerns of moral reformers became abundantly clear during a political scandal that erupted a decade later in 1809. John Clary of Perquimans County had recently married a widow of apparently "respectable connections, irreproachable character, and affluent fortune." Not content with these manifold blessings, he had entered into a sexual liaison with his stepdaughter, Leah Toms, who became pregnant and bore his child.[68] Clary was indicted for his criminal behavior and heavily fined. A group of six men, including one of his stepsons, dragged him out of his house one night and tarred and feathered him. (Clary brought them up on charges and all six were fined, though the governor later remitted the penalties.) But many of Clary's neighbors were willing to forgive and forget. A few months later, in August 1809, he was elected to the state assembly by a large majority. The *Edenton Gazette* condemned vehemently the election of a man whose crime "might appal the grim court of Pandemonium." An editorial declared that every man who voted for him had effectively "given his sanction to the crime and, though silently, yet emphatically ha[d] declared that, placed in similar situation, he could be guilty of the same unparalleled wickedness." The lower house moved to eject Clary on the grounds that his crime "manifested an utter depravity of heart, and destitution of moral principle." Clary resigned to preempt ejection and promptly put himself up as a candidate for the vacated seat; he was reelected with an even larger majority. The assembly now formally ejected him (by 68 to 28). We will never know whether or not Clary's enemies were justified in portraying him as a "fiend-like" predator who had despoiled an innocent beauty just entering "the dawn of womanhood." But it is clear that Clary's opponents were scandalized by his electoral success: "Among the many causes which tend to corrupt the human heart and to nourish the seeds of vice and profligacy, none is more powerful than that countenance and support we sometimes see given to the perpetrators of crimes, at which humanity should revolt." Clary's election suggested that a majority of North Carolinians were still far from fastidious about the observance of sexual boundaries and taboos held dear by those who characterized themselves as "the virtuous few."[69]

MANY OF THOSE who advocated a reformation of sexual mores in the colonial South bemoaned a lack not only of virtue but also of fundamental civility among white settlers. Members of the southern elite remarked scornfully upon the barbarism of their social inferiors, including and especially their lack of sexual decorum. Recall Governor Glen's comment about the "loose embraces" of folk who lived like "pigs" and Woodmason's description of colonists "swopping their wives as cattle." Virginia planter William Byrd declared of a backcountry couple that "these wretches live[d] in a dirty state of nature and were mere Adamites, innocence only excepted."[70] It is no coincidence that political and religious leaders used similar criteria and language in assessing the behavior of African slaves and Indians, who also seemed sexually fickle and promiscuous. Anxiety about the apparent savagery of poorer white settlers was informed in part by racial perceptions and sometimes framed quite explicitly in terms of comparison with nonwhite behavior.

When observers portrayed those living in the southern backcountry as primitive and depraved, they often compared them to Native Americans. The baron of Graffenfried, who traveled to North Carolina with a group of Palatine colonists in 1710, averred that the settlers already living in the colony's interior were "such a criminal and ungodly set of people that it is no wonder if the Almighty has punished them by means of the heathen, for they were worse than these." William Byrd characterized the inhabitants of North Carolina's "lubberland" ("lubber" meaning loutish and clumsy) as "just like the Indians." Woodmason described South Carolina settlers as "rubbing themselves and their hair with bear oil and tying it up behind in a bunch like the Indians . . . Indeed, nakedness is not censurable or indecent here, and they expose themselves often quite naked, without ceremony." As far as Woodmason was concerned, the settlers conducted themselves "more irregularly and unchastely than the Indians." And missionary James MacSparren wrote in 1753 that North Carolina "may still pass for a pretty wild and uncultivated country, and excepting few of the better sort, its white inhabitants have degenerated into a state of ignorance and barbarism not much superior to the native Indians."[71]

As planters and missionaries turned their attention toward the interior, their anxiety about the behavior of white settlers and their similarity to Indians living nearby was doubtless compounded by analogous impressions of the African slave population. African sexual mores also struck white commentators as shockingly permissive and depraved. The very same clergymen who condemned white southerners for their marital inconstancy also berated slaves for "changing of wives and husbands." Francis Le Jau, for example, observed of slaves in South Carolina that

SEX AND CIVILITY

"when a man or woman's fancy does alter about his party, they throw up one another and take others, which they also change when they please." When Le Jau and others observed slaves engaging in serial or polygamous relationships that would have been deemed licit in African societies, they generally assumed that such patterns of behavior were rooted in a savage and depraved nature. The depiction of blacks as incapable of sexual loyalty was reinforced by the instability of family life among slaves, itself caused by the conditions under which they lived. Slave unions had no legal standing: masters were under no obligation to respect such relationships, and slave couples faced the constant threat of separation, should their owner decide to sell one but not the other. Meanwhile, the widespread rape of black women by masters and overseers violated not only the victims themselves but also their sexual and emotional ties with other slaves. The treatment of female slaves as sexual objects and the difficulties that blacks experienced in sustaining marital relationships combined with the persistence of distinct cultural practices that seemed licentious to confirm a reputation for sexual depravity. The equation of Africans as well as Indians with promiscuity must have influenced profoundly the ways in which planters and missionaries responded to the similar sexual behavior of white settlers: their own countrymen were apparently turning into savages.[72]

The key issue here was fear of cultural atrophy. In a sermon advocating greater public investment in schools for the backcountry, Woodmason pointed out that just as "detestable practices" persisted among the Indians "for want of due instruction," so similar deprivation was reducing the settlers to a comparable depravity: "Would we wish to see any of our own complexion, descendants of freeborn Britons, in such a state of barbarism and degeneracy? And yet we begin to be almost on the borders of it." If the Indians were "but one degree removed from the brute creation," much the same could be said of the backcountry settlers, "as rude in their manners as the common savages, and hardly a degree removed from them." From that perspective, it was deeply unfortunate that such people had regular contact with Indians. Implicit in Woodmason's diatribe about "descendants of freeborn Britons" verging upon "barbarism and degeneracy" was the danger of cultural decay via contamination. Contemporaries emphasized the inferiority of Indians and Africans not only to justify their mistreatment but also to reaffirm the differences between "civilized" Englishmen and "savage" nonwhites, despite the debilitating influence of a "wilderness" environment. Yet the behavior of

152

poorer whites threatened to erode that distinction. That European people "of our own complexion" could be "as rude in their manners as the common savages" horrified members of the southern elite who were anxious to replicate English civility in the New World. The interweaving of sex with issues of cultural allegiance played, then, a crucial role in shaping perceptions of sexual and marital diversity within white communities. As the next two chapters illustrate, it also bedeviled interracial relations in British America.[73]

5

The Dangerous Allure
of "Copper-Coloured Beauties"
Anglo-Indian Sexual Relations

WHEN ROGER WOLCOTT sat down to compose a celebratory poem about the early history of Connecticut, he devoted two particularly effusive stanzas to the English colonists' first encounter with the land on which they planned to settle:

> As when the wounded amorous doth spy
> His smiling fortune in his lady's eye,
> O how his veins and breast swell with a flood
> Of pleasing raptures that revive his blood!
> And grown impatient now of all delays,
> No longer he deliberating stays;
> But through the force of her resistless charms,
> He throws him, soul and body, in her arms.

> So we, amazed at these seen delights,
> Which to fruition every sense invites,
> Our eager minds, already captive made,
> Grow most impatient now to be delayed,
> This most delightful country to possess;
> And forward, with industrious speed, we press,
> Upon the virgin stream, who had, as yet,
> Never been violated with a ship.

When Wolcott characterized the land in North America as a virginal beauty, drawing the infatuated English to take possession of her charms, he drew on a well-established tradition of eroticizing the New World. Captain Seagull, a character in the 1605 play *Eastward Ho*, had characterized Virginia as a "maidenhead" waiting to be deflowered by rollicking

Englishmen. The decision to name England's first successful colony across the Atlantic Virginia bespoke not only a desire to flatter and memorialize Elizabeth I but also a perception of the New World as an unspoiled and enticing land that beckoned to those who were able and willing to plumb its riches. John Hammond, who lived first in Virginia and then in Maryland, waxed lyrical about these "two fruitful sisters" and wrote that he shifted to Maryland after becoming "amoured on her beauty." Thomas Morton, similarly charmed by "the beauty of the country" and "her natural endowments," likened New England to "a fair virgin, longing to be sped and meet her lover in a nuptial bed, decked in rich ornaments to advance her state and excellence, being most fortunate when most enjoyed." English "art and industry," he wrote, would fertilize "her fruitful womb."[1]

Early explorers used equally provocative language to portray the New World's native inhabitants. The Indians were apparently "very well favoured" with "exceeding smooth and well proportioned" bodies. The women went about "naked, saving that their privy parts were covered," and looked like "beautiful dryads or the native nymphs or fairies of the fountains whereof the antiquities speak so much."[2] John White's drawings of southeastern Algonquians, first printed in 1590 as illustrations for Thomas Harriot's best-selling *Briefe and True Report of the New Found Land of Virginia,* presented native women as bare-breasted and otherwise scantily clad; since the English invested nudity with sexual connotations, these images must have been highly suggestive to many readers (see fig. 2). Seventeenth-century Englishmen traveling to North America corroborated earlier claims that Indian women had "comely forms," their physical beauty "enriched with graceful presence."[3] John Josselyn described New England's native women as both attractive and alluring: "many of them have very good features, seldom without a 'come-to-me' or 'cos amoris' [whetstone of desire] in their countenance." English commentators tended to depict Indian women as libidinous and sexually available. They were, as one author put it, "very hot and disposed to lecheredness."[4]

Descriptions of Indian life almost always mentioned sexual customs, and many such accounts portrayed native behavior as licentious. "Incredible it is," wrote William Strachey of the Indians whom he observed in Virginia, "with what heat both sexes of them are given over to those intemperances." The oft repeated claim that Indians were lustful and promiscuous can be traced in large part to three facets of native culture that drew the attention of explorers and colonists. Many Indian nations con-

FIG. 2. *"A younge gentill woeman doughter of Secota,"* drawing by John White. *Engraved by Theodor de Bry and printed in the 1590 edition of Thomas Harriot's* Briefe and True Report of the New Found Land of Virginia. *Courtesy Library of Congress.*

doned sexual experimentation among young people prior to marriage; they also sanctioned polygamy within their elites, usually in the service of political and diplomatic goals; and those Indians who were not allowed to take more than one spouse at a time could nonetheless enjoy several relationships during the course of their adult lives, since marriage was not perceived as necessarily permanent. Richard Eden reported that an Indian man had "as many women as he listeth," discarding them "at his plea- sure." He described native sexual practices as "filthy and without shame . . . rather a horrible licentiousness than a liberty." A visitor to New En- gland claimed that the Indians turned to polygamy in order to satisfy a voracious sexual appetite: "wives they have two or three, according to the ability of their bodies and strength of their concupiscence." And Strachey suggested that "immoderate use and multiplicity of women" might have weakened the Indians' reproductive capacity, which would help to ex- plain the relatively small native population in the Chesapeake. "Many women dividing the body," he wrote, "and the strength thereof, make it generally unfit to the office of increase."[5]

It is hardly surprising that the Indians' sexual and marital customs fascinated early modern Englishmen. The campaign for moral reformation that was currently being waged back in England saw sexual attitudes as symptomatic of the broader values that prevailed in a given society. The claim that North American natives were debauched as well as heathen seemed to confirm by negative example the notion that sexual restraint was an essential ingredient of godliness and civility. That logic also coincided with the interests of colonial adventurers, since portraying Indians as depraved in sexual as in other respects would help to justify their denigration and mistreatment. There were, furthermore, sound commercial reasons for including sexual comments in published accounts of the New World: the portrayal of Indian life as erotically charged had a voyeuristic appeal; it would doubtless help to sell copies.

A significant number of seventeenth-century commentaries challenged conventional wisdom regarding native "licentiousness." Edward Winslow refused to generalize, writing that some Indian women were "very chaste," whereas others were "light, lascivious, and wanton." Roger Williams stressed that although Indians considered "single fornication" to be "no sin," they had "a high and honourable esteem of the marriage bed" and considered "the violation of that bed abominable." Although Williams acknowledged that a man or woman could "put away" at will a marriage partner, he assured his readers that he knew "many couples that ha[d] lived twenty, thirty, forty years together."[6] Several writers recognized that polygamy was used only within native elites. William Wood, the author of *New England's Prospect,* insisted that "men of ordinary rank" had "but one" spouse, "which disproves the report that they had eight or ten wives apiece." Even members of the elite, he wrote, "seldom use[d]" the option of polygamy.[7] Some observers also noted the "modesty" of native women. Even though they exposed their breasts to the general view, Indian females were fastidious about covering their genitals, which these writers seem to have considered a somewhat redeeming sign of propriety.[8] And Gabriel Archer, who visited New England in 1602, wrote that Indian women "would not admit of any immodest touch."[9] But other commentators paid little attention to evidence of sexual decorum or self-control among native peoples. Those who commented on Indian customs and demeanor often misconstrued them as being much more permissive than they actually were. As Robert Beverley wrote at the end of the seventeenth century, Englishmen often assumed that because Indian women were "frolicksome" and "full of spirit," their sexual behavior must also be unbridled: "this is ground enough for the English, who are not very nice [i.e., particular] in distinguishing betwixt guilt and harmless freedom, to think them incontinent."[10]

English settlers were for the most part loath to join in sexual communion with Native Americans. Seventeenth-century colonists certainly found native women attractive, but a combination of factors—the general perception of Indians as loose and immoral, fear of the unfamiliar, and the dark specter of cultural contamination—inhibited intimate relations between English settlers and Native Americans. For all their condescension toward native inhabitants, colonists were far from confident that they would emerge culturally ascendant from "a nuptial bed" in which they united with Indian lovers. On the one hand, interracial unions might well provide an opportunity to convert and otherwise assimilate native partners; but on the other, settlers worried that intimate contact with Indians might compound the challenge of retaining a civilized identity while living in a far-flung wilderness. They feared that they themselves would degenerate and become "Indianized."

Many seventeenth-century English settlers had neither need nor opportunity to intermarry with Indians. In the northern colonies, a relatively balanced gender ratio enabled colonists to find marriage partners within their own community, so that there was little reason to look elsewhere for companionship. A combination of disease, warfare, and land appropriation soon pushed native inhabitants inland, away from English settlements on the seaboard. But even during the first phase of settlement in the Chesapeake, when English women were in short supply and Native Americans lived close at hand, relatively little sexual contact seems to have taken place between the colonists and Indians. This was probably due in no small part to lack of native interest, but many of the settlers were also extremely reluctant to form liaisons, fleeting or otherwise, with Indian women.[11]

It was not until the eighteenth century that a significant pattern of intermarriage emerged in British America. Most of these unions took place along and beyond the frontier, far removed from established and heavily populated regions of colonial society. That distance may have given white traders and other men who ventured into the interior a sense of freedom from otherwise overpowering cultural inhibitions. It also left them isolated and vulnerable: intermarriage provided a measure of security as well as access to services and goods that were otherwise unavailable to white men living on the margins of empire. The initial motives of both partners tended to be far from romantic, but although some of these relationships lasted only as long as they served their practical purpose, others evolved into loving and lasting unions. Meanwhile, visitors from the eastern seaboard and across the Atlantic continued to admire Indian women and invoked their charms for readers back home in suggestive, sometimes downright pornographic, descriptions. Yet even in the context of literary voyeurism, fascination by native beauty was still offset by fears of cultural pollution that lurked in Anglo-American minds as the deadly price of interracial desire.

CAPTAIN JOHN SMITH, who crossed the Atlantic to Jamestown with the first contingent of settlers in 1607, was a self-made man, a shameless braggart, and an unapologetic martinet. In addition to being one of Virginia's most colorful and controversial leaders, he was also a prolific (and unsparing) chronicler of the colony's early years. In 1612 he published two books, *A Map of Virginia* and *The Proceedings of the English Colony in Virginia*, in which he included extensive descriptions of the Chesapeake's native inhabitants and their way of life. Reinforcing the general view that Indians were sexually permissive, Smith noted that Powhatan, a powerful sachem with whom he had many dealings, enjoyed "as many women as he will" and that once he became "weary of his women, he bestowe[d] them on those that best deserve[d] them at his hands." According to Smith, Englishmen visiting native settlements could themselves benefit from this largesse: when a guest stayed overnight at an Indian village, they would "set a woman fresh painted red with pocones and oil to be his bedfellow." Smith claimed that he himself had been offered such hospitality. He described an "antic" (a fantastic or grotesque entertainment) provided by his Indian hosts: "thirty young women came naked out of the woods (only covered behind and before with a few green leaves), their bodies all painted." After almost an hour of singing and dancing, "they solemnly invited Smith to their lodging, but no sooner was he within the house, but all these nymphs tormented him more than ever, with crowding, and pressing, and hanging upon him, most tediously crying, love you not me?"[12]

Like much else that Smith wrote, these descriptions of native hospitality cannot have pleased the Virginia Company. The prospect of sexual contact between Englishmen and Indians aroused considerable perturbation among colonial leaders. The recent colonizing venture in Ireland had taught English adventurers that settlers were all too prone to adopt the customs and manners of native inhabitants with whom they intermixed. Reports lamented that "some of our English in small time have grown wild in Ireland, and become in language and qualities Irish, few of whom do in exchange become civilized and English." The threat of cultural degeneration in a colonial setting became particularly acute if settlers engaged in sexual relations or intermarried with native inhabitants. In a 1609 sermon to planters leaving for Virginia, minister William Symonds urged his audience to "keep them to themselves." The colonists must not marry "the heathen," he declared. "The breaking of this rule may break the neck of all good success of this voyage."[13]

As it turned out, Chesapeake colonists showed little interest in Indians as lovers or wives, despite a chronic shortage of women in the early years. According to Smith, the Indians were amazed that the English "had no women, nor cared for any of theirs." Smith's generalization should not blind us to the fact that there were, of course, exceptions: minister Patrick Copland later acknowledged that some of the colonists had "carried themselves dissolutely amongst the heathens." The "Laws Divine, Moral, and Martial" of 1610, introduced to address disciplinary problems in the colony, prescribed the death penalty for any man who raped an Indian woman or ran away to live with the Indians. A number of men had apparently assaulted native women or fled Jamestown to seek female companionship and also a more reliable food supply in native settlements. The colony's president, Sir Thomas Dale, refused to countenance either loss of labor through desertion or the less tangible but equally disturbing prospect of cultural apostasy that went along with such flights. Dale meted out brutal punishment to those who abandoned the English in favor of Indian company. "Some he appointed to be hanged," wrote a contemporary, "some burned, some to be broken upon wheels, others to be staked, and some to be shot to death; all these extreme and cruel tortures he used and inflicted upon them to terrify the rest [from] attempting the like."[14]

Whether refugees were driven primarily by hunger or lust is open to conjecture, but the early colonists who stayed in Jamestown showed little inclination to partner with Indian women. Though fear of official retribution may well have been a powerful inhibiting factor, at least some colonists were doubtless constrained by beliefs and anxieties that they held in common with their leaders. Most fundamental of these were biblical injunctions against marriage to non-Christians and English disdain for the Indians' "barbaric" way of life. As the colonists struggled to survive in a new environment and were forced initially to rely upon Indian assistance, they sought to shore up their battered sense of superiority by maintaining a self-conscious boundary between the "savage" natives and their "civilized" selves; Anglo-Indian marriage threatened that strategy both literally and figuratively. On a more practical level, colonists harbored suspicions that the Indians might use intermarriage as a way to infiltrate colonial settlements; Indian wives might, as one account put it, "conspire with those of their own nation to destroy their husbands." Religious and cultural inhibitions, insecurity, and naked fear doubtless held back many Anglo-Virginians from marrying native women. Even individuals who did not share these feelings must have worried about being stigmatized by fellow colonists and becoming vulnerable to suspicions of disloyalty (a realistic prospect for those who married Indians, as we will see).[15]

Perhaps the most eloquent expression of colonial discomfort with the idea of Anglo-Indian union was contained, ironically, within a marriage proposal. When John Rolfe petitioned Governor Dale in 1614 for permission to marry Pocahontas, the daughter of Powhatan, he dwelt at length on possible objections to their marriage and his own ambivalence toward the union. Rolfe was well aware that his "settled and long continued affection" for Pocahontas might be mistaken for sexual desperation and that "the vulgar sort, who square all men's actions by the base rule of their own filthiness," might "tax or taunt" him for his choice of partner. Rolfe claimed that he was driven by unadulterated love, "not any hungry appetite, to gorge myself with incontinency." He insisted that this was not a union of last resort: he had marital prospects back in England and meanwhile could, if he were "so sensually inclined," find English women who would readily satisfy his "carnal" needs. (This was remarkably optimistic, given the scarcity of women in Jamestown at the time.) Not only would such partners be "more pleasing to the eye," but the sin of fornication would be less egregious, he claimed, if committed with an English instead of an Indian woman. Rolfe assured Sir Thomas that he was in "no way led" to marry Pocahontas by "the unbridled desire of carnal affection." Theirs was an affair of the heart.

Yet Rolfe acknowledged that he himself had only recently come to believe that marrying Pocahontas was defensible. His petition expressed profound anxiety about cultural and spiritual contamination through union with a "strange" and "barbarous" woman. That anxiety had provoked a "mighty war in [his] meditations," as Rolfe sought to justify his "affection" to himself as well as to others. He had recalled "the heavie displeasure which almightie God conceived against the sonnes of Levie and Israel for marrying strange wives" and had weighed the "inconveniences" of uniting "in love with one whose education hath bin rude, her manners barbarous, her generation accursed," and "discrepant in all nurtriture" from himself. Scriptural injunctions and a fear of the "barbarous" combined with his suspicion that Satan himself had "hatched" his love for Pocahontas to form a lurid nightmare of self-destruction.

Seeking an escape from the "laborinth" in which he found himself "entangled and inthralled," Rolfe had "thoroughly tried and pared [his] thoughts even to the quick." He finally convinced himself that marrying Pocahontas would save her instead of destroying him. Their union would justify itself not only as a political alliance, "for the good of this plantation, for the honour of our country," but also and primarily as an evangelical enterprise, "for the converting to the true knowledge of God and Jesus Christ an unbelieving creature, namely Pocahontas." Dedicating his marriage to the spiritual redemption of Pocahontas would free him from the charge of seeking "transitory pleasures and worldly vanities." His responsibility "to labour in the Lord's vineyard, there to sow a plant, to nourish and increase the fruits thereof," overrode his "base fear of displeasing the world" and calmed his "troubled soul." Because the English understanding of conversion included the adoption of English clothing and modes of behavior, Pocahontas's spiritual redemption would also conveniently help to rescue Rolfe from the threat of cultural degeneration.[16]

Rolfe's "private controversy" may have been partly, or even wholly, concocted as a way to assure critics that he understood and even shared their objections to his marriage proposal; but even if a tactical ploy, it remains helpful in conveying the kinds of concern that Rolfe believed his union with Pocahontas would provoke in fellow colonists. Their marriage was clearly perceived by both Indian and English leaders as a political alliance. As such, it won their support. But it did not lead to a spate of Anglo-Indian unions. That few of the colonists followed Rolfe's example may have been due in part to their lack of interest in making the Chesapeake their permanent home: "the intentions of the people in Virginia," according to a 1625 account, "were no ways to settle there a colony, but to get a little wealth by tobacco, then in price, and to return for England." But when Sir Edwin Sandys sought a solution to this "defect" in the enterprise, he did not encourage the male colonists to partner with

Indian women. In 1619 he asked the Virginia Company back in London to send one hundred English women, to make the men living in Virginia "more settled and less moveable." [17] Rolfe's view of intermarriage as a high-minded conjunction of spiritual duty and romantic fulfillment did not prove influential among his contemporaries. Englishmen clearly found Indians beguiling; native women also had a reputation for being hard-working and faithful as wives. But as Rolfe had expressed in his petition, there were powerful cultural and religious factors discouraging such unions.[18]

Indian women, moreover, had little reason to choose as husbands men who were generally much less adept at hunting, fishing, and other pertinent skills than prospective mates in their own communities. When native women did make overtures to Englishmen, their motives were not always as friendly as the colonists assumed: according to both Smith and Strachey, Indians used their sexual charms to "entice" Englishmen into traps. Powhatan did approve the marriage of his daughter Pocahontas to John Rolfe. "Intermarriage," Beverley wrote, "had been indeed the method [to secure peace] proposed very often by the Indians in the beginning." But the sachem subsequently rejected Dale's proposal for another political marriage involving the chief's youngest daughter.[19] As tension between native and English residents escalated into brutal warfare that lasted from 1622 until 1646, intermarriage became increasingly unlikely. Anglo-Indian sexual unions remained unusual in the decades that followed: the growing availability of English women lessened and eventually eliminated any need for intermarriage, while an explicit policy of segregation and the removal of most natives into the interior reduced opportunities for such relationships to occur.[20]

Scattered references in seventeenth-century Chesapeake court records suggest that colonists perceived Anglo-Indian unions to be degrading and potentially dangerous. A slander case in Northampton County, Virginia, was prompted by rumors that an English woman had "defiled herself" by having sex with an Indian. A doctor who lived in the neighborhood had penned a scurrilous verse that he left one night at the woman's house, offering his professional services to mend the "wound" that "a wild savage boar" had inflicted with his "tusk."[21] Mary Edwin complained to a Maryland court that a neighbor had slandered her by "saying she hath lain with an Indian for peake or roanoke." Edwin was married and may have been outraged by the allegation that she had committed adultery in exchange for goods, but the fact that Edwin explicitly mentioned the race of her purported lover suggests strongly that she considered this additional assertion to be a significant part of the defamation. And when Jacob Young's enemies impeached him for treasonous activities against Maryland's government, they included as crucial substantiating evidence the claim that Young "did contract marriage and take to wife an Indian woman of the Susquehannah Nation, by whom the same Jacob had several children, one or more of which is now amongst the Indians, and thereby he the said Jacob is more nearly concerned for these Indians even against his majesty's subjects." Young vehemently denied that he was married to an Indian and must have realized how damaging such a marriage would be to his defense. In many English minds, sexual union was the agent of cultural apostasy.[22]

FURTHER NORTH IN NEW ENGLAND, the Puritan leaders' reformative agenda provided them with an additional incentive to insulate their settlements from contamination by "savage" peoples and their "licentious" customs. Situated as they were in "a hideous and desolate wilderness," cut off "from all the civil parts of the world" and surrounded by "brutish men," it was essential that godly colonists guard closely their moral and cultural integrity. It seemed to Puritans that the Indians represented all that a pious and law-abiding New Englander ought not to be. Indeed, Native Americans proved an effective rhetorical foil for proponents of moral order. At the end of the century, when Cotton Mather railed against the prevalence of "evil manners," including laziness and parental indulgence, he characterized these "abominable things" as "Indian vices," declaring that the colonists had "degenerated" and become "shamefully Indianized."[23]

The first generation of New England settlers recognized that some degree of cooperation with the native inhabitants was essential to their survival, but they became extremely suspicious whenever individuals sought contact with Indians beyond what was clearly necessary for practical purposes, especially if they seemed to enjoy "brutish" company. Thomas Morton and his followers embodied most flagrantly the moral corruption that leading Puritans associated with Anglo-Indian intimacy. When Morton assumed control of Captain Wollaston's private plantation in 1626, Wollaston having left for Virginia, he renamed the settlement Merry Mount, with obvious sexual connotations. The godly settlers in nearby Plymouth Colony looked on in horror as Morton and his "dissolute" companions "pour[ed] themselves into all profaneness." They "set up a maypole, drinking and dancing about it many days together, inviting the Indian women for their consorts, dancing and frisking together." Morton also composed verses "tending to lasciviousness" that he attached to the maypole, including the following invitation: "Lasses in beaver coats, come away,/Ye shall be welcome to us night and day." The "licentiousness" that held sway at Merry Mount under its "Lord of Misrule" combined pagan festivities that the godly thought to have left behind them in England with erotically charged capers that involved Indian women. Morton himself characterized these high jinks as "harmless mirth made by young men" who "lived in hope to have [English] wives brought over to them." But his neighbors denounced what they saw as a reassertion of Old World "vices" in the company of New World "savages" who would further pollute the atmosphere at Merry Mount with their own brand of degeneracy. Given this peculiarly disturbing conjunction, it is hardly surprising that the Puritan worthies of Plymouth hated Morton with such ferocity.[24]

New England settlers, like those to the south, tended to associate Anglo-Indian unions with a broader cultural apostasy. In their view, such relationships either led to other forms of debasement or were symptomatic of the English partner's depravity and unreliability. Fur trader Edward Ashley became suspect in large part because he "lived among the Indians as a savage and went naked among them and used their manners." Significantly, "it was also manifest against him that he had committed uncleanness with Indian women." William Baker, wanted by the authorities in Connecticut for "uncleanness with an Indian squaw," confirmed the worst suspicions of those who feared such intimacies when he ran away to live with a group of Pequot refugees, "turned Indian in nakedness and cutting of hair, and after many whoredoms, [was] there married." Baker was eventually tracked down, taken back to Hartford, and "suffered for his much uncleanness two several whippings."[25] New Englanders clearly understood that allegations of sexual intimacy with Indians could serve well in blackening a person's name. In 1686 the northern and middle colonies were amalgamated under the governorship of Edmund Andros, an Anglican career soldier with autocratic tendencies. Enemies of the Andros regime sought to engender "a universal hatred against him" by spreading a rumor that "he admitted the squaws daily to him; or else he went out and lodged with them." And witnesses claimed at Salem in 1692 that accused witch John Alden had not only sold "powder and shot to the Indians and French," but also "l[ay] with the Indian squaws, and ha[d] Indian papooses."[26]

Because Puritans, like other Englishmen, saw the Indians' sexual and marital customs as an intrinsic component of their savagery, it is hardly surprising that New England missionaries singled out those particular aspects of native culture as they sought to save and civilize Indians. Predictably, they categorized any sexual activity prior to marriage as fornication; polygamy and serial monogamy, they insisted, should be understood as forms of desertion and adultery. The laws established for Indian praying towns prohibited specifically these three categories of behavior and also forbade women "to go with naked breasts." Confessions by converting Indians often laid great stress upon the renunciation of native sexual mores.[27] But the possibilities for misunderstanding must have been endless. Getting colonists who saw nothing wrong with premarital sex to change their ways proved challenging enough, but surmounting the linguistic and cultural barriers between colonial and native New Englanders so as to explain and promote an alien moral code was a task of altogether different proportions. When Indian chiefs met with English officials in 1644 to negotiate what the latter understood as terms of submission to English governance, colonial representatives were anxious to ensure that the Indians undertake henceforth "to commit no unclean lust." The chiefs responded rather vaguely that "though sometime some of them do it, yet they count that naught, and do not allow it." They were clearly asserting a commitment to sexual propriety, but whether they understood or accepted the official English version of proper conduct is a good deal less certain.[28]

Most New Englanders considered even Indian converts to be unsuitable as marriage partners, so that Anglo-Indian relationships appear to have been no more common in the northern colonies than in the Chesapeake. A fairly balanced sex ratio within New England's colonial population removed any practical justification for intermarriage; Indian demographic decline and removal into the interior also militated against interracial unions.[29] But relationships between seventeenth-century colonists and Indians were doubtless also inhibited in the northern as in the southern colonies by the stigma attached to such unions. In 1668 Elizabeth Stevens petitioned the General Court in Massachusetts for a divorce because of her husband's multiple adulteries, "and that not with those of our own nation only but [also with] the very heathen that live among us." The authorities were certainly eager to encourage such distaste. In 1639, when Mary Mendame of Plymouth Colony was convicted of "dalliance divers times" with Tinsin, an Indian man, the court ordered not only that she be whipped in public but also that she "wear a badge upon her left sleeve" announcing her criminality. New England minister Samuel Nowell drew a grim parallel between Anglo-Indian relations and Old Testament history: because "God intended the Canaanites to be destroyed, he did forbid Israel to marry with them: they were to be thorns to them, and Israel was to root them out in the conclusion."[30]

There were, of course, colonists who dissented from the prevailing attitude and who became sexually involved with Native Americans. In Essex County, Massachusetts, two servants working in the same household, Andrew Creek and Mary, an Indian, were whipped for fornication in 1654. The same county court fined William Rane in 1680 "for committing fornication with Ann, Mr. Samuel Gardner's Indian servant, and being in her company with other suspicious carriages at unseasonable times." Christopher Blake was sentenced to sit in the stocks at Yarmouth for "his unseemly carriages in his drunkenness with an Indian woman." And in Suffolk County, Samuel Judkin was punished for "being naught with Sarah, an Indian squaw."[31] Several Englishmen were prosecuted for trying to force themselves upon Indian women.[32] And native men were occasionally presented to New England courts on charges of attempted or actual rape, some of their alleged victims English and others Indian.[33] But prosecutions involving illicit sex between colonists and Indians were few and far between. The surviving documentation for such cases is, for the most part, extremely laconic, revealing little of the ways in which the defendants perceived their behavior.

Gauging Indian attitudes toward sexual contact or intermarriage with the English is as difficult in the context of New England as in that of the Chesapeake, because of the paucity of sources expressing native views. An encounter reported by Thomas Morton suggests that at least some native inhabitants had positive feelings about offspring resulting from interracial unions. Morton wrote that he had met an Indian man who proudly showed him his baby son's gray eyes. Indian eyes were "generally black," and so these were unusual and distinctive, "English men's eyes," as the Indian put it. Morton remarked with his characteristic lack of diplomacy that the infant must be a "bastard," to which the Indian responded that he "could not tell." But in any case he "desired" that the baby "might have an English name, because of the lightness of his eyes, which his father had in admiration, because of [its] novelty amongst their nation."[34] Native Americans living in the region were not automatically averse to interracial unions, at least if they occurred on their own terms: Englishmen who abandoned colonial settlements to live in Indian communities were allowed to marry Indian women, and colonists who had been captured during raids and subsequently assimilated into native communities generally partnered with Indian spouses. Since New England's native inhabitants had been decimated by disease even before the English established permanent settlements, they might have been willing to consider intermarriage for pragmatic reasons. New England colonists learned how to grow crops and provide for themselves much more quickly than their southern counterparts, which may have made them seem more viable as husbands in Indian eyes. Relations between English and native inhabitants were also less immediately tense than in the Chesapeake, though the bitterness engendered by land appropriation, the imposition of English law, and the peremptory treatment of Indian converts in praying towns must have alienated many native inhabitants over the years.

The English portrayal of Indians and their sexual behavior became much more negative during the 1670s, when tension between colonial and native New Englanders reached its height. Claims of sexual rapacity and barbaric sadism figured prominently in accounts of the devastating war that erupted in 1675.[35] The English had long feared that lustful Indians might force themselves upon white colonists. In 1625 an English woman had worried about leaving the settlement at Plymouth because she "feared to fall into the Indians' hands and to be defiled by them." Yet allegations of sexual assault by Indians were extremely unusual. Mary Rowlandson wrote of her captivity that "not one of them ever offered me the least abuse of unchastity to me in word or action."[36] It was in fact extremely unlikely that native warriors would rape captives. Since a principal objective in taking prisoners was to replace lost family and clan members, captive women might well become a warrior's relatives through adoption or marriage; sexual assault might turn out to be incest, which Native Americans abhorred. The Indians would also have avoided sexual contact with prisoners or other colonists during raids because of their belief in the need for sexual abstinence at time of war.[37]

Nonetheless, Nathaniel Saltonstall claimed in his narrative of the 1675–76 war that native warriors frequently raped their prisoners: "any woman they take alive they defile," he wrote, "afterwards put[ting] her to death." In a later account, he repeated his claim that Indians "forced [women captives] to satisfy their filthy lusts and then murdered them." In addition, he alleged that a group of native women had attacked and emasculated two English men: they "beat out their brains, and cut off their privy members, which they carried away with them in triumph." Cotton Mather also wrote that Indians had stripped a male captive, "scalped him alive," and then castrated him. Benjamin Tompson stretched to the limit both his modest abilities as a poet and his equally dubious claim to historical veracity when he invoked the sexual rampage that, he claimed, accompanied Indian raids:

> Will she or nill the chastest turtle must
> Taste of the pangs of their unbridled lust,
> From farms to farms, from towns to towns they post,
> They strip, they bind, they ravish, flea and roast.

Tompson went so far as to claim that lust for English women had been a significant driving force behind the Indian attacks. His account had Metacomet propose to his council, "We'll have their silken wives, take they our squaws." This one line expressed a potent blend of chauvinism and paranoia, assuming that the Indians would prefer English wives to their own and would actively pursue racial mixing through forcible appropriation.[38]

Not all contemporary accounts of the war included allegations of sexual violation. Neither Increase Mather nor William Hubbard claimed in their narratives that Indians had assaulted captive women in this way. But when Hubbard noted in one particular passage that Indian warriors had "offered" no "uncivil carriage to any of the females, nor ever attempted the chastity of any of them," he proceeded to reaffirm belief in the rapacity of Indian men by averring that they must have been "restrained" by God or "some other accidental cause."[39] Sexual barbarism had always figured prominently in unsympathetic portrayals of the Indians, and it was entirely consistent with that tradition that the deterioration of Anglo-Indian relations into bloody conflict should be accompanied by vicious sexual allegations. New England colonists had rarely considered Indians to be viable marriage material, but now they vilified Indian men as savage rapists, voracious beasts that must be driven away from the vineyard of the Lord.

THERE WERE ANGLO-AMERICANS who disagreed with that perspective. Two Virginia authors of the early 1700s characterized the colonists' repudiation of intermarriage as a lost opportunity. Robert Beverley, who inherited not only a handsome patrimony but also his father's propensity to question conventional wisdom, addressed the issue of Anglo-Indian unions in *The History and Present State of Virginia,* a far-from-rose-tinted account of the colony that was written in 1703 and published two years later. Had the colonists been willing to intermarry with the Indians, Beverley argued, "the abundance of blood that was shed on both sides would have been saved," and "the colony, instead of all these losses of men on both sides, would have been increasing in children to its advantage." Instead of "the frights and terrors" caused by Indian attacks, there would have been "success and prosperity," which would have drawn "others to have gone over and settled there." Intermarriage would also have worked, Beverley insisted, to the spiritual and demographic advantage of the Native Americans: "many if not most, of the Indians would have been converted to Christianity by this kind method," and "there would have been a continuation of all those nations of Indians that are now dwindled away to nothing by their frequent removals, or are fled to other parts."[40]

Writing just over two decades later, Beverley's brother-in-law William Byrd argued along similar lines. He also claimed that intermarriage would have benefited the English and enabled the spiritual assimilation of Native Americans (from his perspective, a blessing for the Indians as well as the colonists). The settlers' refusal to intermarry had caused the Indians to believe "that the English were ill-affected toward them," which in turn damaged Anglo-Indian relations and led to "various distresses." Byrd pointed out that the predominantly male colonial population in the seventeenth-century Chesapeake would have grown much more rapidly had the men been willing to marry Indians. Native women, he wrote, would have proven "altogether as honest wives for the first planters" as the English "damsels" who crossed the Atlantic, many of whom were rumored to have had shady pasts. Byrd argued, as had John Rolfe, that intermarriage could serve as a tool of conversion: "a sprightly lover," he wrote, "is the most prevailing missionary that can be sent amongst these or any other infidels." Anglo-Indian marriage would, furthermore, have prevented bloodshed by allowing the colonists to expand onto land deeded to them through dowry agreements: "the poor Indians would have had less reason to complain that the English took away their land if they had received it by way of a portion with their daughters."[41]

In criticizing seventeenth-century colonists for failing to see the benefits of intermarriage, Beverley and Byrd overlooked the fears and insecurities of their forebears in the Chesapeake. Now that the Indians had become a more distant and less menacing presence, it was easy to forget that native inhabitants of the Chesapeake had initially interacted with English settlers from a position of strength: as John Smith would have attested, Indian leaders had proved neither gullible nor tractable in their dealings with the starving and disease-ridden colonists. Eighteenth-century accounts of native culture tended in general to be somewhat more positive than most seventeenth-century representations, in large part because Native Americans seemed less immediately threatening. Beverley and Byrd could contemplate the benefits of intermarriage in ways that would have been unthinkable during most of the preceding century. Yet their blithe confidence that colonial interests and values would predominate in Anglo-Indian relationships was by no means pervasive even among their eighteenth-century contemporaries, some of whom still worried about the capacity of Indians to seduce white lovers into cultural degeneration and apostasy.[42]

In advocating intermarriage, both Beverley and Byrd challenged the predominant attitude among their contemporaries within colonial society. Most white men and women living in the settled regions of British America continued to shun relationships with Indians throughout the eighteenth century. There was, in any case, little opportunity for colonists living in eastern communities to form interracial unions since the Indians living there were few in number.[43] But the positive spin put on marriage with Native Americans by Beverley and Byrd would have seemed much less outlandish to Anglo-Americans who lived on the margins of empire. Traders who spent extended periods of time along and beyond the frontier often came together with Indians in casual and more lasting unions. They did so not only because they found themselves without English female companions but also because they realized how much else was to be gained by forming relationships with women in native communities. As we will see, the motives of all concerned were pragmatic and self-interested. But many such unions became loving relationships and proved enormously constructive as channels for cultural accommodation.

Eighteenth-century travelers who ventured into the frontier regions of British America often noted that fleeting sexual congress and more established relationships between Native Americans and Englishmen were commonplace. It is no coincidence that Byrd recommended intermarriage soon after traveling into the southern interior as a boundary commissioner. John Lawson, an English explorer and naturalist who traveled extensively through the Carolina backcountry in 1700-1701, observed stable relationships, more temporary liaisons, and casual encounters between Englishmen and Indians. It was Lawson's observation of such unions that led him also to advocate intermarriage in an account of his travels that he wrote several years later. Lawson recommended that "ordinary people" be given incentives ("land and some gratuity of money") to marry Indians and bring them into English settlements. Anglo-Indian marriage would give the English "a better understanding of the Indian tongue" and readier access to "all the Indians' skill in medicine and surgery," along with their knowledge of the regional topography. Like Beverley and Byrd, Lawson valued intermarriage in terms of its potential for assimilating Native Americans: "the whole body of these people would arrive to the knowledge of our religion and customs, and become as one people with us." Yet Lawson also recognized that the dynamics of life in the interior as well as the personal inclinations of the traders themselves sometimes led in quite different directions: a significant number of Englishmen living among the Indians became "as one people" with them.[44]

Sexual relationships had an important role to play in Anglo-Indian relations along and beyond the margins of British America. The colonists had every incentive to cultivate amicable relations with strong and populous Indian nations in the interior: at least for the time being, the English wanted their trade more than their land; they also feared the possibility that native warriors might ally with the French or the Spanish against them. Considerations such as these doubtless played a part in the reflections of Beverley and Byrd as well as in the conciliatory attitudes of many traders and officials. Anglo-Indian relations were often shaped by personal and physical interactions. As travelers, traders, soldiers, and diplomats dealt with Native Americans on territory and under circumstances that nobody fully controlled, their interactions, accommodations, cultural misunderstandings, and conflicts were as much sexual as they were economic, diplomatic, and military.[45] By no means all such interactions were constructive: sexual contact sometimes took the form of assault, and even unions that began under apparently promising circumstances could have disastrous consequences for one or both parties. But Anglo-Indian sexual relations bore witness to the many possibilities of intercultural contact:

they embodied not only the violence of colonial appropriation but also the mutual and successful accommodation of different peoples.

BYRD CLAIMED THAT the settlers' "squeamish" opposition to Anglo-Indian marriage was rooted in their "aversion to the copper complexion of the natives." But that assertion belies a more complex attitude toward native inhabitants as sexual objects that emerges from eighteenth-century writings. English culture did invest light-colored skin with connotations of virtue, cleanliness, and civilized beauty; visitors, migrants, and Anglo-Americans proved themselves true Englishmen by expressing disdain for nonwhite complexions. Yet just as explorers and early colonists had found the native inhabitants of North America aesthetically pleasing and sexually attractive, so prejudicial attitudes toward skin color did not prevent their eighteenth-century counterparts from finding Indians physically striking and desirable.[46]

Eighteenth-century visitors from across the Atlantic and white Americans who traveled westward to the edges of colonial settlement often commented on the beauty of Indian women, even though they usually framed their remarks with defensive reservations about the natives' skin color or lack of hygiene. We should bear in mind that such remarks came overwhelmingly from genteel travelers and reflected a preoccupation with cleanliness and fashionable, leisured pallor (a tan indicating the need to labor outside) that colonists outside the elite would most likely not have shared. Lawson declared at the beginning of the century that Indian women were "as fine-shaped creatures (take them generally) as any in the universe . . . not so uncouth or unlikely as we suppose them." Beverley described native women as "generally beautiful, possessing an uncommon delicacy of shape and features, and wanting no charm but that of a fair complexion." They were, he wrote, "remarkable for having small round breasts, and so firm that they are hardly ever observed to hang down, even in old women." Byrd himself commented that native women had "an air of innocence and bashfulness that with a little less dirt would not fail to make them desireable." He referred admiringly to "copper-coloured beauties." Robert Hunter, a young merchant who traveled in North America during 1785–86, collecting debts owed to his father's firm in London, described Native American women as "handsome . . . notwithstanding their color." Luigi Castiglioni, a Milanese botanist traveling through the United States in 1785–87, declared that they were "very dirty and ill-smelling" but often "combine[d] a pretty figure with a vivacious face."[47]

Officials who traveled westward on government business, soldiers on campaign, and scientists in search of indigenous flora and fauna found Indian women both charming and beguiling. In published narratives of their journeys, they sought to pass on that impression, portraying Native Americans in language that was clearly intended to titillate prurient readers. Indeed, the voyeuristic fascination with Indian bodies that had characterized early descriptions of the New World reemerged as a feature of eighteenth-century travel narratives. Consider a description of "American aborigines" by William Bartram, a Philadelphian naturalist who traveled through the Carolinas, Georgia, and Florida in 1773–77: "The Muscogulge women, though remarkably short of stature, are well formed; their visage round, features regular and beautiful; the brow high and arched; the eye large, black, and languishing, expressive of modesty, diffidence, and bashfulness; these charms are their defensive and offensive weapons, and they know very well how to play them off." In shifting from a purely physical description to discussion of actual behavior, Bartram encouraged his readers to envisage Indian women as sexual partners. "Under cover of these alluring graces," he warned in the more overtly piquant sentence that followed, native women "concealed the most subtle artifice." He added for good measure that they were, "however, loving and affectionate."[48]

Along with admiration came fantasies of possession and conquest. In another passage that began with an extravagantly lyrical evocation of native beauty, Bartram used idyllic motifs to frame, and partly camouflage, an account of thwarted sexual assault. He conjured for his readers an enticing image of "primitive innocence," set in "a vast expanse of green meadows and strawberry fields" that Bartram and his companions chanced upon as they traveled through the South Carolina backcountry:

> Companies of young, innocent Cherokee virgins, some busily gathering the rich fragrant fruit, others having already filled their baskets, lay reclined under the shade of floriferous and fragrant native bowers of Magnolia, Azalea, Philadelphus, perfumed Calycanthus, sweet Yellow Jessamine and cerulian Glycine frutescens, disclosing their beauties to the fluttering breeze, and bathing their limbs in the cool fleeting streams; while other parties, more gay and libertine, were yet collecting strawberries or wantonly chasing their companions, tantalising them, staining their lips and cheeks with the rich fruit.

The strangers' arrival threatened to transform this charming and sensual scene into one of sexual violence. The prospect of "sylvan nymphs," Bartram wrote, was "perhaps too enticing for hearty young men to continue idle spectators" and so they crept down toward the young women, determined "to have a more active part in their delicious sports." Bartram admitted that their interest in the "Cherokee virgins" was at least potentially sexual and predatory:

> Although we meant no other than an innocent frolic with this gay assembly of hamadryades, we shall leave it to the person of feeling and sensibility to form an idea to what lengths our passions might have hurried us, thus warmed and excited, had it not been for the vigilance and care of some envious matrons who lay in ambush, and espying us gave the alarm, time enough for the nymphs to rally and assemble together.

The defensive maneuvers executed by the "matrons" and perhaps also a sudden realization that Indian men might be close at hand jolted the travelers into a more circumspect and gentlemanly comportment. Once Bartram and his companions convinced the "matrons" that they were willing to restrain themselves, tension dissipated and the strangers were invited to join them in eating some fruit, "encircled by the whole assembly of the innocently jocose sylvan nymphs." Bartram's account allowed readers to delight in visions of Edenic innocence while participating vicariously in the travelers' voyeurism and their barely contained lust for the native women. In this way, he invited them to appropriate his own experiences and fantasies into a pornographic gaze upon the New World.[49]

Other eighteenth-century authors admitted that white travelers who came into contact with native inhabitants were often eager to sample "their favors." In October 1711, when Byrd took part in military exercises not far from an Indian settlement, he noted in his diary that he and other militiamen entertained themselves by cavorting with native women. One morning, they "rose about 6 o'clock and then took a walk about the town to see some Indian girls, with which we played the wag." In the evening of the following day, he wrote, "some of my troop went with me into the town to see the girls and kissed them without proceeding any further." That night, "an Indian girl" named Jenny "got drunk and made us good sport." (It is not clear from Byrd's laconic entry how far the "sport" went and to what extent Jenny was a willing participant.) Two decades later, after leading an expedition to investigate the boundary between Virginia and North Carolina, Byrd recalled his colleagues' sexual escapades with Native Americans whom they met along the way. When the commissioners stayed overnight as the guests of an Indian tribe, William Dandridge and several other "gentlemen" went "hunting" through the night. Their ruffles, "discoloured with puccoon [red dye]," gave them away the next morning. Byrd sought to explain away Dandridge's behavior by suggesting that "curiosity made him try the difference between them and other women." He was less concerned that their subordinates had been frolicking with the native women, since these men were, after all, "not quite so nice [i.e., particular]." The next day, Byrd and Dandridge visited "most of the princesses at their own apartments," intending to admire their beauty at close quarters, "but the smoke was so great there, the fire being made in the middle of the cabins, that we were not able to see their charms." As with Bartram's description of his encounter with the "sylvan nymphs," Byrd's account of his sojourn in the Indian village combined voyeurism with the tantalizing possibility of sexual possession, salacious material for the reader's and his own imagination.[50]

Sexual interest in native women did sometimes result in violent assault, but it would be wrong to assume that English advances were always unwelcome or that the advances always came from the English. The authors of eighteenth-century travel narratives pointed out that many Indian tribes condoned sexual experimentation prior to marriage and that single native women were often eager to have sexual relations with white men. Some accounts made sweeping generalizations on this as on many other aspects of Indian mores. "The 'Flos Virginis,'" wrote Lawson, "so much coveted by the Europeans, is never valued by these savages." But other writers recognized that not all Indian nations had the same attitude and noted carefully for the benefit of prospective travelers which ones seemed to be sexually permissive. Diron D'Artaguiette, a French official in Louisiana, reported that young Illinois women were "the mistresses of their own bodies (to use their own expression)" and welcomed the attentions of European visitors, whereas Arkansas women were not available (their menfolk had convinced them, "if one cares to believe the interpreters," that they would die if they had sex with Europeans). Thomas Nairne, a soldier and diplomat in South Carolina during the early eighteenth century, wrote that Chickasaw mores forbade the sexual license allowed young women elsewhere: "you shall not see them ogle and splite glances as the other savages' ladies usually do." Under the guise of praising such nations for preventing "scandalous liberties," such passages warned which Indian women could not be approached without risking native anger and retribution.[51]

Travelers found that native women generally expected some kind of gift in exchange for a sexual encounter. Byrd wrote that Indian women were "a little mercenary in their amours and seldom bestow[ed] their favors out of stark love and kindness." When four Saponi women offered themselves to Byrd and his companions, "the price they set upon their charms" was "a pair of red stockings." Europeans and white Americans tended to assume that such women were prostituting themselves, an interpretation that conveniently debased Native American women and reduced them to vendible goods. But the Indians themselves would have perceived such encounters very differently. The notion of reciprocal exchange was universal in Native American cultures, providing a fundamental structure with accompanying rituals of civility for any interaction, including courtship. Young women who asked for goods in exchange for sexual intimacy were insisting upon a social etiquette that Europeans frequently misinterpreted, blind as they were to the underlying cultural logic.[52]

Consider Lawson's account of sexual commerce in the Native American societies that he encountered. Certain young women, he wrote, were "set apart" to be "trading girls," their "particular tonsure" distinguishing them from other women, who were available for marriage. Most of their income went to "the king," whom Lawson characterized as "the chief bawd, exercising his prerogative over all the stews of his nation, and his own cabin (very often) being the chiefest brothel-house." The "trading girls" apparently "led that course of life for several years," using abortive medicine to end any incidental conceptions; their marital prospects were not, so far as he could discern, damaged by their "having been common to so many."[53] Lawson's perspective was, to put it mildly, skewed. From the Indians' point of view, "trading girls" may well have operated not only as a commercial proposition but also as a component of diplomatic ritual. Beverley reported that visitors "of great distinction" were provided with "a brace of young beautiful virgins," and Byrd also referred to "the compliment of bedfellows" as an "Indian fashion." Since diplomacy and commerce were bound together in Indian exchange culture, it would not be surprising if sex as diplomatic courtesy and sex as trade were sometimes conflated. Lawson noted that when another of his companions refused a trading girl offered to him by a sachem, "his majesty flew into a violent passion to be thus slighted, telling the Englishmen they were good for nothing." The sachem may have been frustrated by his failure to extract goods from the traveler in return for the woman's services, but he may also have been enraged by the white man's lack of manners in rejecting a gesture of welcome.[54]

In some cases, native women used their bodies to procure goods of value for their kin network, cannily exploiting hunger for female companionship. English forts offered ample opportunities for Indians to deploy female bodies as a medium of exchange. Some women functioned as temporary companions to officers who could afford to support them. Visiting Fort Niagara in 1785, Robert Hunter observed an "abundance of squaws" who were "mostly kept by the gentlemen who reside there." Hunter noted disapprovingly that these women would "immediately leave their keeper" if "any little quarrel" occurred and take up with someone else. Even while being "kept," they would, "before their keeper's face, go with anybody else who will offer them some rum, which they are extravagantly fond of." The women were willing to partner irrespective of English racial distinctions: "everybody is alike indifferent to them, black, white, or Indian." The picture that emerges from Hunter's account is of a fluid and multiracial sexual marketplace in which native women provided services, apparently on their own terms, to the troops in residence, either in the form of brief encounters or as part of a temporary domestic relationship. Whether the initial decision to engage sexually with the fort's inhabitants had been made by the women themselves or by relatives is unclear (this presumably varied from nation to nation), but Hunter's description of the women's behavior at the fort suggests that they considered themselves free of English control and indeed empowered by demand for their services. The goods that they procured as a result of these sojourns would presumably make their way back to kinfolk. Hunter commented that "one squaw" was "much more expensive than three or four white women, for you are sure to have the whole family to maintain."[55]

Sexual exchange could sometimes take a more inadvertent form. Travel narratives warned that venereal disease, that "hateful distemper," was "frequent in some of these nations." As D'Artaguiette put it, "the malign influences of Venus are so common that those who are wisest restrain themselves and go bridle in hand." Lawson was "assured that the pox had its first rise (known to us) in this new world, it being caught of the Indian women by the Spanish soldiers that followed Columbus in one of his expeditions to America," and who then passed on their "pocky spoils" to other Europeans.[56] Images of alluring nymphs frolicking in Edenic landscapes were juxtaposed in European minds with fears of physical (as well as cultural) contamination. The problem became so serious in French Louisiana by the early 1720s that a hospital was being planned specifically to treat "venereal" infections. Fortunately, D'Artaguiette wrote, the Indians knew "how to cure all sorts of venereal diseases" and "healed numerous Europeans."[57] Observers often commented upon the Indians' "exquisite knowledge" of medicine and their "admirable cures" for various maladies, including sexually transmitted ailments.[58]

Lawson did recognize that venereal infections were transmitted in more than one direction. Eighteenth-century Indians, he wrote, often caught the disease from "English traders that use amongst them."[59] Traders who spent most of their time traveling beyond the frontier and who often lived in native communities for prolonged periods had by far the most sustained and intimate contact with Indians. Those among them who succeeded in establishing a cordial, trusting rapport with their hosts became valuable diplomatic as well as economic intermediaries between native and colonial societies. It was not unusual for traders to enter relationships with Indian women, which not only satisfied personal needs but also eased their acceptance into the local community. However, whereas some traders settled into at least temporarily stable and monogamous relationships, others were notoriously promiscuous: hence their responsibility in Lawson's account for the spread of venereal disease in many Indian communities. The traders who attracted the most attention from colonial officials were those who treated the Indians with the least respect. Their abusive and violent behavior, which often manifested itself in sexual form, could poison Indian attitudes toward both the individual concerned and Englishmen in general, undermining decades of patient diplomacy. Although it is clear that many traders dealt peaceably and respectfully with the native peoples among whom they lived, the outrages perpetrated by their colleagues often overshadowed the more constructive results of trading activity in both Indian and colonial minds.

Maverick and abusive sexual behavior toward Indians disturbed colonial officials and English ministers for ethical and practical reasons. Anglican missionaries touring the backcountry complained that trading licenses had been granted to "profligate and debauched" individuals, "utter strangers to the virtues of temperance and chastity." Clergymen such as Robert Maule feared that the Indians would be discouraged from converting by the "vile and unjust behavior of these and some others who call themselves Christians." Such concerns were not without foundation: in 1725 a Cherokee "priest" in conversation with trader and interpreter

Alexander Long expressed (presumably ironic) amazement that "those white men who live amongst us," despite "such good priests and such knowledge as they ha[d]," were "more debauched and more wicked than the beastliest of our young men."[60]

Government officials also lamented "the evil impressions which those savages are liable to receive from the rudest of mortals" and worried about the disruption of peaceful relations by the abusive and insulting behavior of the traders, some of whom were "more savage than them." In 1710 the commissioners for Indian trade in South Carolina received a report that trader Philip Gilliard "took a young Indian against her will for his wife." Gilliard had apparently "cruelly whipped" this woman and her brother when she gave him some beads, "to the great grief of the Indians there present."[61] Fearing the negative impact of such behavior upon diplomatic relations, the commissioners repeatedly enjoined agents "to regulate the lives of the traders, so that they give not the Indians offence."[62] Other members of the colonial elite shared this concern. William Byrd, though far from immune to the charms of Indian women, worried that sexual contact along the frontier could turn violent. He was convinced that the misconduct of Carolina traders toward the Indians, "abusing their women and evil entreating their men," was "the true reason of the fatal war which the nations round about made upon Carolina in the year 1713."[63]

The Indians themselves were not reticent in expressing outrage when traders preyed on their women. In 1752 leaders of the Lower Creek nation met with an agent of the South Carolina government and "complained very heavily of the white people in general for debauching their wives and mentioned several in particular that were found guilty, and said if his Excellency would not punish them for it, the injured persons would certainly put their own laws in execution." At a 1765 meeting with representatives of the new English government in Louisiana, Choctaw chiefs protested "the behaviour of the traders towards our women," claiming "that often when the traders sent for a basket of bread and the generous Indian sent his own wife to supply their wants, instead of taking the bread out of the basket they put their hands upon the breast of their wives." The chiefs warned that such "indecent freedom" threatened to produce "very great disturbances."[64]

The colonial authorities also worried about sexual abuse of Indian women by English soldiers. In the late 1750s, officials in South Carolina learned that the French were trying to undermine English relations with the Indians by telling them that English officers took native women into forts "before their husbands' faces" to be "used by the soldiers." Although English agents assured the Indians that such claims were "all French lies," they were evidently none too sure of that: "I hope this is not true," one of them wrote. It is clear that British soldiers did rape Indian captives. In 1761 the lieutenant governor of South Carolina informed the colony's governing council that soldiers were assaulting native women held captive in Charleston during the Cherokee War: "Colonel Grant had been with him, and informed him that great abuses were daily committed by the soldiers on duty at the main guard upon the Cherokee women, prisoners in part of the said guardhouse." The colonel said that it "was not in his power effectually to remedy" the soldiers' behavior and so "desired [that] the Cherokee prisoners confined in the guardhouse might be removed to some other proper place."[65]

Yet, although government officials focused their attention on the political damage wrought by "debauched" traders and soldiers, eighteenth-century travelers often encountered white men whose dealings with native peoples were peaceful and constructive. Traders who lived in Indian communities for an extended period of time often established stable domestic relationships with native women for the duration of their stay. One trader pointed out to Lawson a "cabin" that belonged to his "father-in-law": "he called him so by reason the old man had given him a young Indian girl, that was his daughter, to lie with him, make bread, and to be necessary in what she was capable to assist him in, during his abode among them." As Lawson observed, marriage among the Indians was "no further binding than the man and woman agree[d] together." Either was at liberty to dissolve the union as he or she saw fit. The temporary arrangements that traders made were, then, broadly compatible with Indian custom. They were also consistent with the widespread practice of informal and serial marriage among white colonists in the backcountry.[66]

In addition to functioning as "she-bed-fellow[s]" to traders, "dressing their victuals," and performing other forms of labor, native wives could help their English "husbands" to learn the local language more quickly and become acquainted with "the affairs and customs of the country." Traders who became involved with Indian women were given privileges otherwise unavailable to outsiders. Bartram, for example, mentioned a man who, "being married to a Cherokee woman of family, was indulged to keep a stock of cattle." Most traders were "fully sensible" how much they stood to benefit "in matters of trade and commerce" by securing the "affections and friendship" of women in the communities where they were staying. Such women, Bartram wrote, were usually energetic in promoting "the interests and views of their temporary husbands": "they labour and watch constantly to promote their private interests, and detect and prevent any plots or evil designs which may threaten their persons, or operate against their trade or business." By "taking a mistress," explained another eighteenth-century observer, Englishmen "procure[d] kindred among the Indians." Should conflict arise between a trader and members of the community in which he was living, the kin associations he had acquired through his marriage could offer some measure of protection. At the very least, his wife could warn him that all was not well. In 1751 the Indian Trade Commissioners in South Carolina received a report that "the white people" living among the Cherokee had heard from their "Indian wenches" that they were in danger; the women "bid them be gone." Familial ties with Indians could also protect traders from the English authorities. When Captain Paul Demere arrived at an Indian settlement in 1758 with a warrant for the arrest of Englishman Samuel Jarron, the Indians refused to produce him. "He has lived among us several years," they informed the captain, "he has had some of our women, and has got children by them. He is our relation, and shan't be taken up."[67]

From the perspective of Indian wives and their kinfolk, marriage to an English trader, whether temporary or lasting, had much to offer as they drew the Englishman, along with his goods, into their kinship orbit.[68] Eighteenth-century observers paid little attention to the practical advantages that native women derived from such relationships. Lawson claimed that Indian women were "prone to European attachments" because their own menfolk were "not so vigorous or impatient in their love as we are." Yet such unions could confer considerable status, given the important economic and diplomatic roles played by trader-husbands, and enabled women to gain access to valuable goods that they then passed on to their kin. This did not always sit well with other Indians interested in acquiring such items. In 1753 representatives of the Lower Creek Nation complained that traders had inflated their prices in order to compensate for the expense of "giv[ing] away such quantities to their wives."[69]

As contemporary accounts occasionally recognized, "temporary husbands" could serve to further the interests of shrewd, sometimes ruthlessly ambitious, women. Bartram related the trials of a susceptible trader from North Carolina living among the Seminoles who had apparently become the dupe of a "beautiful savage":

Her features are beautiful, and manners engaging. Innocence, modesty, and love appear to a stranger in every action and movement; and these powerful graces she has so artfully played upon her beguiled and vanquished lover, and unhappy slave, as to have already drained him of all his possessions, which she dishonestly distributes amongst her savage relations.

The trader was "now poor, emaciated, and half-distracted, often threatening to shoot her, and afterwards put an end to his own life." Yet he had "not resolution even to leave her" but instead "endeavour[ed] to drown and forget his sorrows, in deep draughts of brandy." The Seminole woman had used her "powerful graces" to invert the European male vision of domination that pervades Bartram's narrative. Bartram himself was careful to emphasize, in deference to "the virtue and moral conduct of the Seminoles, and American Aborigines in general," that her conduct was "condemned and detested by her own people, of both sexes."[70]

Just as traders who entered relationships with Indian women might find sexual dominion more elusive than they had anticipated, so individuals who violated Indian mores by, for example, bedding an Indian's wife discovered that their lusts were subject to the conditions and boundaries laid down by the community in which they lived. The frontier and beyond did not, after all, constitute a sexual playing field without rules or restrictions; traders with maverick libidos found themselves in a highly vulnerable and dangerous position. Bartram was acquainted with a trader, referred to as Mr. T——y, who had married a chief's daughter in the Creek town of Muklasa, where he was living. He was subsequently "detected in an amorous intrigue" with the wife of another chief, who "with his friends and kindred resolved to exact legal satisfaction." The punishment for adultery in this nation was "cropping," the removal of both ears. The trader was seized, stripped, and beaten but managed to escape before the cropping could take place. After hiding in a swamp, he "finally made a safe retreat to the house of his father-in-law," who "gave his word that he would do him all the favour that lay in his power." A "council of the chiefs of the town" decided "that he must lose his ears, or forfeit all his goods, which amounted to upwards of one thousand pounds sterling." The cuckolded chief still wanted his life. Bartram promised the trader that he would ask George Galphin, an influential and wealthy trader based at Silver Bluff, South Carolina, to intercede on his behalf. When he did so, Galphin remarked that the trader was "in a disagreeable predicament, and that he feared the worst, but said he would do all in his power to save him." (Unfortunately, Bartram's account ends here, presumably because he did not know how the situation resolved itself.)[71]

The case of Mr. T——y served as a reminder to Europeans that those who passed through or lived in native communities did not enjoy sexual impunity. He who assumed otherwise did so at his peril. But most traders were committed to establishing and maintaining a peaceful coexistence with the native peoples among whom they lived, and they behaved accordingly. They understood that obtaining sexual access to Indian women, whether through a relationship or as a casual encounter, was usually quite straightforward if they were willing to abide by native prohibitions and codes of reciprocity and courtesy.

Some Englishmen doubtless became "temporary husbands" with little hesitation or scruple, but others were initially uncomfortable with the custom. Nicholas Cresswell, a young unmarried man who migrated from Derbyshire to North America in 1774 and traveled through "Indian country" the following year, wrote in his diary at the end of his journey that it was "absolutely necessary to take a temporary wife" if one had "to travel amongst the Indians." Yet at first he had found the prospect of a native "bedfellow" distasteful. Cresswell acknowledged early in his travels through the interior that some of the Indian women were "very handsome," but he "pretended to be sick" on the first occasion that one of them "invited [him] to sleep with her." Two weeks before, Cresswell had spent the night with "a fine blooming Irish girl," so his reluctance was hardly due to shyness or a chaste character. He was less evasive a few days later when another Indian woman offered herself to him. She had taken care of his horse at the end of the day, "then spread my blankets at the fire and made signs for me to sit down." After supper, she lay down "very near" and he "began to think she had some amorous design": "In about half an hour she began to creep nearer me and pulled my blanket. I found what she wanted and lifted it up. She was young, handsome, and healthy." The following day, Cresswell's "bedfellow" guided him through the woods to his next destination and he gave her a "coat, with which she seemed very well pleased."[72]

Cresswell was now beginning to understand the dynamic at work, sex figuring as one of several components in the exchange of goods and services. A few days after this, a Mohawk host "offered" Cresswell his sister "to sleep with" and he felt "obliged to accept." The following morning, she offered to accompany him on his journey. "I must often meet with such encounters as these," Cresswell wrote, "if I do not take a squaw to myself." This particular woman was "young and sprightly, tolerably handsome," and could "speak a little English," so he "agreed to take her." It was "an odd way of travelling," he confided to his diary, but "squaws" were "very necessary" for practical purposes ("fetching our horses to the camp and saddling them, making our fire at night and cooking"). One must therefore "submit to it," he wrote. Cresswell feared that "conscientious people" might consider such a union "base" (he did not specify whether because it was temporary and informal, or because it might resemble prostitution in English eyes, or because the companion was an Indian—perhaps all of these). But he clearly warmed to the custom, became fond of his companion, and found parting with her just over a month later an "affecting experience."[73]

The attitude of traders and Indian women toward such relationships was pragmatic but not necessarily cynical. As Bartram put it, though "fully sensible" of the practical advantages that such "marriages" offered "upon principles of reciprocity," the couple's "love and esteem" for each other became in many cases quite "sincere." Relationships between traders and Indian women were often intended to last only for the duration of the Englishman's residence, but some developed into lasting marriages. The frequent use by contemporaries of derogatory words such as "wench" to describe the traders' female companions indicates a fundamental lack of respect for "temporary wives" on the part of many observers and even some of those who engaged in such liaisons. But not all traders viewed their native lovers with contempt or merely as a temporary convenience. Lawson acknowledged that it was not unusual for traders to settle permanently in native communities, drawn by their personal attachments to native women as well as by the Indians' way of life:

> We often find that Englishmen, and other Europeans that have been accustomed to the conversation of these savage women, and their way of living, have been so allured with that careless sort of life, as to be constant to their Indian wife, and her relations, as long as they lived, without ever desiring to return again amongst the English, although they had very fair opportunities of advantages amongst their countrymen; of which sort I have known several.

Other colonists whose business took them westward sometimes found personal happiness and material opportunities among native peoples.

At Pittsburgh, actor-manager John Bernard met a land surveyor named Wools, whose surveying "had led him among the Indians near the Mississippi, where he had married a king's daughter" and received "a tract of land which he soon contrived to convert into a handsome independence." Wools had married his wife in an Indian ceremony.[74]

Englishmen who settled with Indian partners in Indian territory on Indian terms struck most observers as bizarre and disturbing. Like white captives who refused to return to colonial society and settlers in the backcountry who dressed and behaved "as Indians," they brought into question both the resilience and the superiority of English culture.[75] "Temporary marriage" functioned as a cultural compromise from which both parties stood to benefit. But when such unions became permanent, they raised potentially vexing issues of cultural allegiance. These became most pressing when Englishmen had children with Indian women. Regardless of whether the context was a casual sexual liaison, a temporary relationship, or a lasting marriage, decisions had to be made about the children's upbringing. According to Lawson, it was "a certain rule and custom amongst all the savages of America" that children stayed with their mothers if the parents parted company. He considered this a "great misfortune" since it meant that the offspring of Anglo-Indian couples were "seldom educated any otherwise than in a state of infidelity." But this was clearly an unwarranted generalization. Nathaniel Osborne, an Anglican missionary, mentioned in a 1715 report that he had recently baptized five "mulatto children," the offspring of "our Indian traders, by Indian women during their abode amongst them." Alexander Cameron, British agent among the Cherokee from 1764 to 1781, married an Indian woman who resided with him at his plantation, Lochaber, and bore him three children, all of whom were later sent to England. And Bernard Elliott, a military recruiting agent who was traveling through South Carolina in 1775, stayed as a houseguest with trader George Galphin, whose daughters by an Indian woman were "politely enough educated with music, etc."[76] Most traders, however, lacked the resources of Cameron or Galphin and were themselves no longer fully committed to an English way of life. Their children often built lives that straddled the physical and cultural frontier: by the middle of the eighteenth century, many of the traders were themselves offspring of Anglo-Indian relationships.[77]

The ritual through which a mixed couple formalized their marriage had far-reaching implications for cultural power within the relationship and could be fraught with anxieties for those involved. Trader James

Adair mentioned an Englishman who married an Indian, Dark-Lanthorn, "according to the manner of the Cherokee," but then took her to an English settlement in order to remarry in an English ceremony, which involved having Dark-Lanthorn baptized. According to a Frenchman who traveled through North America in the 1790s, marrying according to Indian custom appealed to some European men because native marriage was "but a transitory union" and divorce "very frequent": a man who declared himself wed "in the Indian manner" could legitimate his relationship and yet treat the ceremony as binding him "no longer than he himself chooses." But in this case the Englishman worried about the apparent transience of native marriages and the implications of the matriarchal system within which they were contracted: "observing that marriages were commonly of a short duration in that wanton female government," he decided that he had a better chance of "ingrossing her affections, could he be so happy as to get her sanctified by one of our own beloved men with a large quantity of holy water in baptism." She could then "be taught the conjugal duty, by virtue of her new Christian name, when they were married anew." The personal negotiations and educative process involved in preparing for a marriage of this sort must have been challenging, regardless of which culture predominated. Dark-Lanthorn became increasingly impatient as a minister subjected her to detailed examination prior to the marriage ceremony. Her husband, acting as interpreter, "recommended to her a very strict chastity in the married state," the importance of which he clearly feared she did not appreciate. When the clergyman continued to question her about religious doctrine and lectured her on the need for "a proper care in domestic life," she called him an "Evil Spirit" and instructed her husband to "tell him his speech [was] troublesome and light."[78]

Adair finished his account by noting sardonically that the minister later had to erase Dark-Lanthorn's name from his book of converts "on account of her adulteries," but he gave no clue as to the circumstances under which these alleged "adulteries" took place. If, for example, Dark-Lanthorn left her husband without a formal divorce and then initiated a sexual relationship with another man, this would have counted as adultery from an English legal or ecclesiastical perspective but not necessarily from an Indian point of view. Whatever the actual train of events, Adair saw the collapse of their marriage as a warning to those contemplating unions with women from cultures not only "savage" but also subject to "wanton female government." Such marriages involved the risk that one's spouse might not prove susceptible to patriarchal expectations, a particularly horrifying testimony to the backcountry's abandonment of "civilized" norms and to the dangers of intimacy with "brutish" peoples. It was all very well for authors such as Byrd and Beverley to enthuse about the benefits of intermarriage, assuming that the Indian spouse would assimilate and abide by her husband's will, but the realities of Anglo-Indian union were complex and by no means automatically weighted in favor of an English partner.

COMPROMISE, ACCOMMODATION, CONFUSION, tension, and fracture: all of these figured in the relationship between Dark-Lanthorn and her unnamed English husband. They also encapsulate more generally the range of dynamics produced by Anglo-Indian erotic and romantic relations along and beyond the eighteenth-century frontier. The surviving evidence suggests that sexual contact between Indians and Englishmen created a broad spectrum of intercultural scenarios, with violent coercion at one extreme and respectful, loving unions at the other. As Indians and Englishmen eroticized the middle ground between their cultures, they bore testimony together to the possibilities of their meeting as well as to its dangers. Rape was doubtless more common and relations in general more contested than the extant sources, with all their biases, suggest; but we should not ignore evidence for more positive interactions. Indians and Englishmen could and sometimes did enjoy each other, love each other, and live together in peace.

Eighteenth-century commentators responded to Anglo-Indian sexual relations with prurient ambivalence. Most of these observers sought to distance themselves, at least rhetorically, from such intimacies: they adopted a tone that combined to varying degrees condescending humor, disapproval, and incomprehension, even as they reveled in the voyeuristic possibilities afforded by such interactions. Their determination to sustain a sense of cultural difference and superiority demanded no less. Sexual contact with Indians was a tempting yet perilous prospect, since those attracted to "savages" might be "beguiled and vanquished" in more ways than one. Given that the Indians' apparently licentious behavior figured in contemporary accounts as a crucial expression of their barbarism, it followed that Englishmen who had sexual encounters or relationships with Indian partners ran the risk of becoming debased themselves. Native American customs served handily as a measure of moral laxity when criticizing behavior within the white colonial population. As we saw in chapter 4, officials, clergymen, and other travelers frequently compared backcountry settlers to Indians so as to underline their "ignorance and barbarism." The seemingly unbridled sexual and marital lives of those living in the interior combined with their lack of clothing, personal dirtiness, and other "barbaric" traits to render them Indian-like. That threat of cultural debasement in a primitive setting was compounded by the possibility of direct contamination through sexual intimacy with Indian neighbors. Whereas traders who abused native women might arouse official ire because they endangered Anglo-Indian relations, those who settled in native communities as the husbands of Indian women were threatening in more insidious ways: they demonstrated the precarious ascendancy of English identity and the potential for cultural apostasy. In going native, they made evident the dangerous allure of "copper-coloured beauties."

6

"The Cameleon Lover"
Sex, Race, and Cultural Identity
in the Colonial South

VIRGINIA PLANTER WILLIAM BYRD was a passionate and lustful man. We have already encountered his salacious interest in Indian women whom he met during his travels along the frontier. In diary entries and private correspondence, Byrd recorded his many other sexual cravings and escapades, marital and extramarital. These occurred at home on his plantation at Westover; in Williamsburg, the seat of Virginia's colonial government; and across the Atlantic in London. Through his writings, Byrd crafted for himself a distinct sexual persona. The patriarch of Westover was determined that all his relationships, public and private, should serve to fulfill his image of himself as a gracious yet masterful gentleman. The significance he ascribed to sex as an extension of his social and cultural identity was never clearer than in the language he used to describe sexual relations with his first wife, Lucy Parke. In diary entries that cataloged their moments of intimacy, Byrd usually wrote either that he "gave [his] wife a flourish," or that he "rogered" her. On 4 November 1710 Byrd bestowed "a flourish in which she had a great deal of pleasure." Several weeks later, on 22 December, William and Lucy "played at billiards" in the afternoon. He "laid her down and rogered her on the trestle."[1]

As Byrd recorded these incidents in his diary, he chose to bring into play a vocabulary with specific and significant connotations. The word *flourish* was used in early modern English to describe an elaborate physical gesture or rhetorical expression, a mark of one's social grace and sophistication. Byrd thus described sex with Lucy as a stylish parade of his ability to perform as an accomplished gentleman. The word also had a military connotation, and Byrd was not unusual in using soldierly terms such as "salute" and "mount the guard" to describe kissing and sexual intercourse.[2] Sex as an expression of cultured panache was closely allied in Byrd's mind to sex as an act of potent masculinity. In writing that he "rogered" Lucy, Byrd used a colloquialism current back in England that turned the noun *roger* (a slang term for the penis) into a verb. Byrd in effect portrayed sex as an extension of his own penis and so endorsed a phallic view of intercourse in which his member became the active force that defined sex. This colloquialism originated with the common practice of giving the name Roger to bulls. In "roger[ing]" his wife, Byrd presented himself as a virile, domineering figure. He enhanced this impression of phallocratic mastery by noting from time to time that he bestowed "a powerful flourish" or "rogered" his wife "with vigor."[3]

By the time of William Byrd's early-eighteenth-century flourishes, the demonstration of gentility had established itself as a conspicuous feature of southern elite culture. The initial contingent of migrants to Virginia had included the offspring of wealthy, landed families back in England, but a much larger proportion of the southern elite that established itself during the seventeenth century came from commercial backgrounds. As these self-made men and their sons acquired social and political power, they sought also to present themselves as convincing gentlemen; their lack of hereditary pedigree and their awareness of the stigma attached to trade in polite society across the Atlantic made them especially eager to acquire the trappings of gentility. Affluent planters were determined to distinguish themselves from common southerners and to prove themselves worthy members of a transatlantic ruling class, despite their often modest origins and colonial status. Their quest to demonstrate social grace and cultural legitimacy both to themselves and to others inspired the design of ostentatious plantation homes filled with imported goods from England and an elaborate social etiquette that reinforced hierarchical distinctions. Even religious services became artfully choreographed pageants of display as elite families paraded in and out of the church, their dress and bearing a testament to their sense of themselves.[4]

Sex had an important role to play in the southern elite's articulation of power and gentility. When planter Robert Bolling sketched the floor plan for a splendid new house in his notebook, he drew above it two winged objects, an escutcheon and an erect penis. The display of wealth, assertion of aristocratic pedigree, and a glorified sexual potency came together in a triad of self-spectacularizing images (see fig. 3).[5] Like libertines in contemporary England, southern planters sought to portray sexual relations as an expression of the freedom and panache intrinsic to a genteel

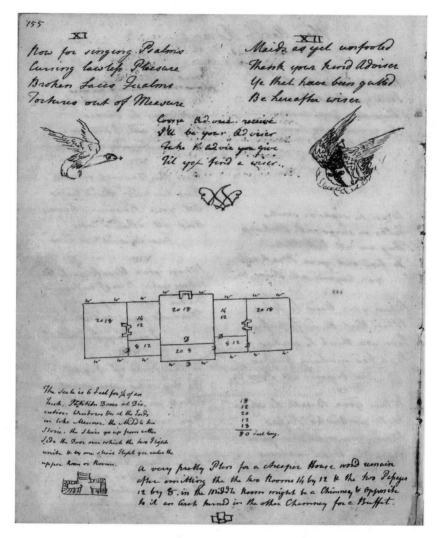

FIG. 3. *Robert Bolling's plan for a new house, with winged genitalia and escutcheon overhead, from Bolling's notebook, "La Gazetta di Parnasso . . ." Reproduced by permission of the Huntington Library, San Marino, California.*

way of life. Byrd sometimes used the word "gallantry" to denote sex in his correspondence, describing prostitutes sardonically as "ladies of universal gallantry" and writing on another occasion of "the inconveniences that attend accidental and promiscuous gallantry." From this perspective, even venereal infections could be gentrified as a "fashionable" or "polite disorder." Robert Carter characterized three slaves who were apparently suffering from venereal disease as "men of gallantry," a cruelly ironic extension of genteel euphemism to those systematically excluded from social grace.[6]

The tone of polite exuberance that affluent planters cultivated in sexual as in other matters furthered their cultural aspirations by asserting a common identity with the ruling classes in England. But it also sought to obscure a grim sexual regime over which they presided, a regime that was predicated upon exploitation and brute force. Planters sometimes treated even elite women with a good deal less consideration than Byrd's "flourish" would suggest. The wives and female relatives of supposedly "gallant" gentlemen sometimes viewed male behavior from an altogether different and much less flattering perspective. The sexual contact that white masters had with their servants and slaves was often much more overtly abusive: planters used sex to articulate crude power as they appropriated and violated laborers' bodies. The institution of slavery fostered a general sense of sexual entitlement among white planters: the transformation of southern colonies into slave societies affected profoundly the ways in which people living in the region related to each other across lines of status and gender as well as of race. If the courtly "flourish" exemplified one aspect of a planter's sexual repertoire, the rape of social subordinates epitomized another.

Stung by English ridiculing of all colonists as crude and boorish, wealthier planters asserted their own genteel credentials and sought to distance themselves from their social inferiors. Even in the aftermath of Independence, they continued to cultivate a republicanized version of gentility that emphasized social grace and cosmopolitan sophistication.[7] Yet widespread sexual contact between masters and their slaves undercut that enterprise. Members of the southern elite might vilify blacks as savage and depraved, but in the eyes of outside observers they proved themselves degenerate by lusting after their slaves. These "licentious and even unnatural amours" testified to the "vitiated taste" of southern whites.[8] Few members of the planter elite would have admitted to any contradiction between their mistreatment of bound laborers and their own claims to civility. But some southerners did express quite openly their concern that miscegenation might compromise white identity. Anglo-Americans believed that interracial sex could transform those involved: not only would white men and women who had sex with slaves produce a "mulatto" race, but they themselves might undergo metamorphosis, becoming culturally tainted and, at least metaphorically, "blackened" by their lusts. Although by no means all white residents feared interracial sex, legislation against miscegenation did express clear anxiety within the southern gentry about the contamination of white women through intimate contact with black men; as we will see, some people worried also about the impact of sexual intermixing upon white men. From that perspective, miscegenation struck a potentially fatal blow to the much vaunted distinction between "civilized" Englishmen and "savage" Africans as well as that between genteel planters and boorish commoners. The dynamics of sexual interaction between planters and the laboring underclass exposed the masquerade of genteel performance as little more than a tragic farce.

The prevailing atmosphere in which eighteenth-century elite southern families raised their sons was indulgent and permissive. Visitors and residents commented upon the "unbounded licentiousness" that "taint[ed] the morals" of "young gentlemen" growing up in the region. As one traveler put it, "all their whims are indulged." According to Jonathan Boucher, tutor to George Washington's stepson John Custis, there were "many complaints of children spoiled by parental indulgence." Boucher bemoaned in 1770 that it was well nigh impossible to insulate his young charge from the corrupting influence of dissolute friends. Custis "seldom or never [went] abroad without learning something [Boucher] could have wished him not to have learned" and often spent his nights "in company with those who do not care how debauched and vicious his conduct may be." A series of penmanship exercises written by another tutor for his pupils at Bluff Plantation, a South Carolina estate not far from Charleston, contained moral strictures intended to offset the combined impact of "indulgent parents," "unreasonable liberty," and "profligate companions." The exercises urged youths to "curb" their "vicious inclinations, fierce unruly passions, and inordinate appetites."[9]

The libertine sensibility that prevailed in London's beau monde exercised a significant influence over the values and behavior of young southern gentlemen who were sent across the Atlantic to acquire education and social polish. These visitors to the metropolis found themselves in an environment that not only condoned but even celebrated sexual promiscuity. They responded enthusiastically. Young Peter Manigault, for example, was described by his companion in London as a "gay Lothario," given up to "the pleasures of . . . frisking and capering."[10] William Byrd was much older than Peter Manigault when he resided for several years in London as a widower, but his diary and correspondence attest to the possibilities for sexual adventure that awaited southern gentlemen of any age in the metropolis. Byrd engaged in "amours" with women of his own social rank and had dozens of sexual encounters with prostitutes whom he met on the streets, at the theater, and in brothels that he frequented.[11] Venereal disease ran rampant in eighteenth-century London. As a colonial almanac for 1734 remarked sardonically, young "sparks" who visited London to become acquainted with "fashions" and "the world" often returned with "nought but these to show, new wig above, and new disease below." Given Byrd's promiscuity while in London, it is hardly surprising that during the voyage back to Virginia he dreamed that he "was clapped."[12]

Some contemporaries worried that "scarce any" of the young men sent to Europe for their education returned "without having his morals corrupted." Thomas Jefferson, writing in 1785 from Paris to an acquaintance back in North America, urged "the disadvantages of sending a youth to Europe," most of which involved moral corruption: "he is led by the strongest of all the human passions into a spirit for female intrigue destructive of his own and others' happiness, or a passion for whores destructive of his health, and in both cases learns to consider fidelity to the marriage bed as an ungentlemanly practice and inconsistent with happiness." That sexual libertinism across the Atlantic could inspire and serve to justify licentious behavior back in the colonies became very clear to North Carolinian Thomas Burke in 1773 when his brother tried first to seduce and then to assault Burke's wife. The brother "endeavored to debauch her principles and recommended to her the example of persons of rank in England and flatly proposed what he called an amour."[13]

Establishing the tone of sexual encounters within the southern elite is no easy matter, given the dearth of surviving journals and correspondence in which individuals recorded their personal experiences and impressions. William Byrd may well have been unique in the extent to which he wrote about sex and the place that it occupied in his mental world. But other eighteenth-century southerners did occasionally leave behind accounts that reveal the aggressive physicality of male attentions. In 1760 Robert Bolling, son of a wealthy Virginia planter, fell in love with and wooed Anne Miller, daughter of a Scottish merchant. Bolling made no great effort to control his "pleasing passion" for Anne, which he characterized as an "involuntary inclination." On one occasion, "coming by accident into a chamber where she was sitting, extremely pensive, on a bed," Bolling was "overcome by an excess of passion": "I threw myself thereon, and pressed her to my bosom, with a rapture which can scarce be conceived . . . While we were together on the bed, I overlaid and broke a fan of hers; a necklace too had already fallen a sacrifice to my caresses."[14]

We have no way of knowing what Anne Miller thought about her suitor's "excess of passion," the broken fan, or her scattered necklace beads. But several entries in fellow Virginian Lucinda Lee's diary from the 1780s suggest that she resented bitterly the aggressive sense of entitlement displayed by young men in their flirtatious attentions toward women in their social circle. On one occasion, "two horrid mortals," related to Lucinda by marriage, "seized" her as she and a cousin were leaving the house for an evening walk: "[they] kissed me a dozen times in spite of all the resistance I could make." One of them also "plagued" Lucinda and her companions when he found them outside, "chased" them "all over the garden, and was quite impertinent." "They really think," Lucinda wrote indignantly, that "now they are married, they are privileged to do anything." Men marrying into Lucinda Lee's family seem to have treated their female in-laws as fair game for sexual horseplay, apparently seeing this as their automatic right.[15]

Women within the southern elite were by no means "privileged to do anything." They were expected to embody the very ideals of decorum and self-restraint so flagrantly disregarded by their menfolk. The *South Carolina Gazette* for 22 June 1734 included a prayer for young ladies that called on "Virgin Powers" to defend them against "amorous looks" and "saucy love." When tempted to commit an indiscretion, respectable women should arm themselves with "honour" and "a guard of pride." Young gentlemen, in contrast, were expected to be "abandoned" and "debauched." Outsiders observing the eighteenth-century southern elite commented on the sharp contrast between male and female standards of behavior. Timothy Ford, a New Jersey lawyer who moved to Charleston in 1785, wrote that "the ladies" there were "circumscribed within such narrow bounds" of acceptable behavior that they "carr[ied] formality and scrupulosity to an extreme," whereas the gentlemen were "more sociable" and "generally very dissipated."[16]

We should, of course, beware of reducing southern gentlemen as sexual beings to a performative role or stereotype. William Byrd's physical relationship with his first wife consisted of much more than a display of his gentlemanly bravado. Byrd's affectionate love for Lucy is evident throughout his diary, notwithstanding their frequent arguments. "About ten o'clock we went to bed," he wrote in April 1709, "where I lay in my wife's arms." "I rose at eight o'clock," he noted later that year, "because I couldn't leave my wife sooner."[17] Byrd was not an entirely selfish lover and certainly expected that Lucy would derive pleasure from their intercourse; he made sure to record on 30 April 1711 that his "powerful flourish" gave her "great ecstasy and refreshment." He also recognized that his spouse had an appetite of her own: "my wife made me lie in bed and I rogered her." Nonetheless, he expected his wife to acknowledge his mastery over her and the primacy of his will. When Lucy was "much indisposed" from one of her pregnancies, he still went ahead with a sexual encounter from which, he admitted, "she took but little pleasure." There is, unfortunately, no surviving account of the physical relationship between William and his wife from Lucy's perspective. She may have perceived her husband's "flourishes" and "rogering" in quite different terms.[18]

Byrd's sense of sexual entitlement, physical aggressiveness, and insensitivity was also evident in his dealings with elite women other than his wife. In November 1709, when Lucy joined her husband in Williamsburg, they invited some friends back to their room. He played cards with Mrs. Chiswell "and kissed her on the bed till she was angry and [his] wife also was uneasy about it, and cried as soon as the company was gone." Byrd's response provides a telling counterpoint to Lucinda Lee's diary entry about being manhandled by her cousins' husbands. He finished his own entry by expressing remorse for his behavior, but his comment related to the illicit nature of his desire and the proprietary rights of Mrs. Chiswell's husband, not the two ladies' discomfort: "I neglected to say my prayers," he wrote, "which I should not have done, because I ought to beg pardon for the lust I had for another man's wife."[19]

Although Byrd was eager to cultivate in his diary an image of himself as sexually exuberant and masterful, he did not condone utter licentiousness in himself or anyone else. Libertinism was by no means the only version of gentility to which planters such as Byrd were exposed. Rival models of genteel behavior in eighteenth-century English society promoted self-control and virtuous moderation.[20] Byrd claimed in a self-portrait that he had always aspired to be rational and morally upstanding, despite "the lively movement of his passions." He does seems to have tried, albeit often unsuccessfully, to restrain his sexual appetite when it strayed outside the bounds of marriage. Byrd was clearly torn between rival versions of "polite" behavior. As he put it, a "civil war" raged within him: "sometimes grace would be uppermost and sometimes love, [but] neither would yield and neither could conquer." The "principles" of self-control that battled with Byrd's "inclinations" toward dissipation figured in his diary entries as religious in nature. Byrd cared deeply about spiritual as well as social grace, and it was usually in a religious context that he expressed qualms about his sexual behavior. One evening in London, he "picked up two women" and had sex with one of them (the other refused). He later "repented of what [he] had done and begged pardon of God almighty." On another occasion, he thanked God when he "endeavoured to pick up a woman, but could not." Given the almost daily references in Byrd's diary to prayer, his constant examination of his spiritual condition, and his frequent reading of religious literature, there seems to be no good reason for distrusting these expressions of guilt. Though pangs of conscience did not prevent Byrd from entertaining impulses that he considered illicit, he did aspire to self-restraint.[21]

Byrd was well aware that some planters were much less punctilious about such matters and did not hesitate to indulge their sexual appetites, especially when directed toward social subordinates. As the leading member of a commission to investigate the boundary between Virginia and North Carolina in 1728, Byrd witnessed a chain of sexual assaults that he condemned and apparently sought to prevent. Indeed, one of the recurring themes in Byrd's narrative of the expedition was sexual aggression by his colleagues toward women whom they encountered. On 9 March some of the commissioners "broke the rules of hospitality by several gross freedoms they offered to take with our landlord's sister," prompting Byrd "to send her out of harm's way." A week later, William Little, the attorney general of North Carolina, took their host's daughter to see the tent in which most of the men would be sleeping "and might have made her free of it, had not we come seasonably to save the damsel's chastity." This predatory behavior characterized auxiliary members as well as the leaders of the expedition. Richard FitzWilliams's servant made "boisterous" overtures toward a young woman "and employed force, when he could not succeed by fair means." Fortunately, "one of the men rescued the poor girl from this violent lover," although he was "so much his friend as to keep the shameful secret from those whose duty it would have been to punish such violations of hospitality."[22]

These incidents were symptomatic of a generally aggressive and maverick sexual ethos within the southern male culture to which Byrd belonged; according to his diaries, it was an ethos that he himself exhibited on occasion. Though Byrd portrayed himself as having restrained sexual aggressors during the expedition, each of his surviving diaries records his own predatory advances toward servants and slaves. During his first marriage, Byrd appears to have gone no further than a little kissing and groping. These extramarital encounters usually took place during visits to Williamsburg. "I sent for the wench," he wrote in 1709, "to clean my room and when she came I kissed her and felt her, for which God forgive me." A decade later, Byrd was widowed and living in London. There he frequently "kissed the maid till [his] seed ran from [him]." On a November morning in 1719, he "made the maid feel [his] roger." Back in Williamsburg a year later, Byrd took a white maid "by the cunt." She managed to stop him from going any further by telling him that "she was out of order, else she would not mind it" (probably a reference to menstruation). A week afterward, "the maid of the house" came into his room after he had retired for the night: "I felt her and committed uncleanness but did not roger her."[23]

Servants could find themselves under intense pressure to gratify their masters and risked retaliation if they resisted such advances.[24] Sexually abused servants did have the option of complaining to the authorities, and neighbors who suspected that a household head was making inappropriate advances toward those working for him might pressure the servants concerned to speak out against their master.[25] But intimidation, fear of reprisal, and the challenge of proving an allegation must have inhibited many victims from coming forward. Not all sex between masters and servants was coercive. Seventeenth-century planters often ended up marrying the young women whom they purchased as servants. Because women were in short supply and must have known that other men would gladly take them as wives, most of those who wed their masters presumably did so of their own volition. Some of the sex that occurred between masters and female servants in the early Chesapeake may have been regarded by both parties as premarital and entirely consensual.[26]

The extent and tone of sexual contact between masters and their servants must have varied from one household to another. But when a household head did proposition his servant, the advance must often have come across as at least implicitly coercive, overshadowed by issues of status and authority. Consider William Byrd's behavior toward Annie. After his return from London to Virginia at the beginning of 1720, still a widower, Byrd focused his sexual energies on this particular maidservant, whom he had engaged while still in London. Sometimes he "only kissed her" or toyed with a part of her body ("I felt Annie's belly this morning"), but on other occasions he "spent" (i.e., ejaculated). Byrd seems to have convinced himself that he did not actually force himself upon her. His comment in a May 1720 entry that he "made Annie feel about [his] person" implies an element of coercion, yet on 9 August 1720 Byrd urged her "to come to bed but she would not consent." On 4 September 1720 he wrote that she would not let him "feel her," and on 9 March 1721 that "she would not be prevailed with." It is not clear from the diary whether Annie was sexually attracted to Byrd, whether she was testing the limits of permissible resistance to unwanted advances, or whether she sought to ensure that encounters she enjoyed took place on her terms. The fact that Annie and her master were engaged in an ongoing liaison may have caused Byrd to accord her a degree of respect that was not necessarily granted to all of the women whom he propositioned. But even nominally consensual sex between master and a servant was doubtless colored in many instances by a servant's awareness of the authority that her master wielded over her and the possibility of reprisals if she dared to resist him.[27]

VULNERABLE THOUGH SERVANTS WERE to sexual aggression from their masters, they could at least seek protection and redress if they experienced abuse. The legal system saw indentured laborers as prospective members of free white society, accorded them basic rights, and sought to defend them against obvious mistreatment. Slaves had no such recourse: they were defined legally as chattels rather than as persons, which encouraged a much more absolute sense of possession and entitlement on the part of masters. The sexual exploitation of slaves was facilitated by their exclusion from legal marriage, which in turn denied them sexual respectability. Only free persons had the legal right to marry. English law authorized sexual acts only if they took place within a formal marriage, which meant that all sex between slaves could be treated as illicit unless a master saw fit to confer informal legitimacy upon particular relationships. When a white man appropriated for his own gratification a slave who was in a committed relationship with another slave, he violated that union as well as the victim herself. But depriving slaves of the right to marry enabled those in authority over them to ignore such considerations.

White men who raped slaves and disregarded relationships that bound African men and women together could and doubtless did draw on wide-

spread preconceptions about African savagery and licentiousness to ratio-
nalize their treatment. Contemporaries claimed that Africans were "prone
to debauch and venereal excess," as "libidinous and shameless as mon-
keys, or baboons."[28] According to one account, Africans "laugh[ed] at
the idea of marriage, which ties two persons together indissolubly," con-
ceiving of love as "free and transitory." Though some masters and overseers did become involved in regulating sexual activity among their slaves,
there was no concerted attempt to impose English sexual norms upon
the black labor force: after all, their alleged depravity served to justify
their exploitation and abuse.[29] Sexual encounters between slaves and their
owners or overseers sometimes took place in the context of ongoing
and affectionate relationships from which slaves could derive substantial benefits. But the underlying reality of a master or overseer's power
and the likelihood of brutal recrimination against those who challenged
that power must have compromised the meaning of consent in any sexual
union between a white man and a slave over whom he had authority.
Many black women were subjected to straightforward and brutal assault.
Their experiences embodied in the most intimate of contexts the violence
and degradation that lay at the heart of the slave system.

In neither the upper nor the lower South was there any room for
doubt that miscegenation was taking place on a large scale. As a minister in Charles City County, Virginia, put it, "the country swarms with
mulatto bastards." Henry Muhlenberg, a Lutheran minister, saw "many
slaves" in Charleston who were "only half black, the offspring of those
white Sodomities who commit fornication with their black slave women."
Another pastor, Johann Bolzius, observed disapprovingly that "white
men live in sin with negresses and father half-black children who walk
around in large numbers to the shame of the Christian name." And Ebenezer Hazard, who traveled through the southern states in 1778 as surveyor of the post roads, wrote that "the number of mulattoes" testified to
"a vitiated taste in their inhabitants." Throughout the South, miscegenation remained widespread despite an increasing preoccupation with racial
purity and the enactment of laws prohibiting interracial sex. The prevalence of miscegenation gave rise to profound anxiety within the southern
elite, especially in the Chesapeake but also further south. That anxiety focused on the threat of contagion: at least some whites feared that colonial
society would become polluted and degenerate through sexual contact
with blacks. This in turn would undermine the efforts of wealthy planters

to achieve respectability within a transatlantic elite. Interracial sex thus imperiled their quest for cultural legitimacy.[30]

RELATIONS BETWEEN ENGLISH colonists and Africans in the Chesapeake had been somewhat fluid during the early decades of settlement. White and black laborers worked together, socialized together, and became lovers. In punishing colonists who committed sexual misdemeanors, magistrates do not appear to have discriminated between interracial and intraracial couplings. It was only later in the century that legislators began to codify racial distinctions in sexual as in other matters. A 1662 Virginia law began that process by requiring that courts differentiate between extramarital sex involving two persons of the same race and that involving an interracial couple. It stated that "if any Christian shall commit fornication with a negro man or woman, he or she so offending shall pay double the fines imposed by the former act." This clearly established race as a distinct and significant element in computing the seriousness of a sex crime.[31]

The 1662 law made no distinction between interracial liaisons involving white men and those in which white women coupled with black men; thus, English planters who had sex with their female slaves did, at least in theory, fall within its purview.[32] But a new statute prohibiting miscegenation and intermarriage, enacted in 1691, focused more specifically on white women who produced illegitimate children with a nonwhite lover. Although the law forbade intermarriage regardless of whether the white partner was male or female, it raged quite specifically in its preamble against "that abominable mixture and spurious issue" that resulted from "English or other white women" marrying "negroes, mulattoes, and Indians." Its primary aim was to prevent the sexual pollution of white women, passing over in silence the sexual degradation of female slaves by white masters and overseers, as well as any lasting relationships between white men and black women. Maryland laws passed at the end of the seventeenth century used similar language: they described interracial unions as "unnatural and inordinate copulations," condemning English women for marrying "negroes or other slaves . . . to the satisfaction of their lascivious lustful desires, and to the disgrace not only of the English but also of many other Christian nations." These telling formulations framed moral, spiritual, and cultural integrity in specifically gendered terms. They required that white women become a bulwark of racial purity even as white men continued to breach racial boundaries.[33]

Prior to the passage of the 1691 law in Virginia, interracial marriages were far from unknown in the colony. Hester Tate, an English servant in Westmoreland County, married a slave named James. Their masters had evidently given permission for the marriage to take place. One of their four children was apprenticed to the mother's master, James Westcomb; the other three were placed with their father's owner, Patrick Spence. In Northampton County, a white woman named Aymey wed Francis Payne, a free black. And in Northumberland County, attorney William Greensted married Elizabeth Key, a mulatto woman, after suing successfully for her freedom.[34] Although some mixed-race couples actually married, others chose to live together without legal sanction (as did many white couples in the early South). Recent research has uncovered a tangled skein of unmarried interracial relationships among poorer inhabitants of seventeenth-century Virginia. The 1691 law banning intermarriage was evidently controversial: later that decade, a group of Norfolk County residents submitted a petition "for the repeal of the act of assembly against English people's marrying with negroes, Indians, or mulattoes."[35]

After 1691 the number of interracial sex crimes adjudicated by Virginia courts rose rapidly. These prosecutions targeted almost exclusively unions that involved white women. The agenda was all too clear: hardly any white men were brought to trial for "inordinate mixture" with black women.[36] This wave of prosecutions seems to have had its effect: the number of white women presented in court for producing children of mixed race fell significantly by the middle of the eighteenth century. This decline in prosecutions was certainly not due to any relaxation in attitudes toward miscegenation between white women and black men. Other evidence suggests that racist attitudes were hardening and that for white women to seek out black men as sexual partners was becoming increasingly unacceptable. In 1729 one woman berated another for being "a negro whore and negro[']s strumpet" who "would have jumped over nine hedges to have had a negro." And in 1769 a Calvery County planter renounced his wife, Mary Skinner, in the *Maryland Gazette* because she had, "after all the love and tenderness which could possibly be shown by man to a woman, polluted my bed by taking to her in my stead her own negro slave, by whom she hath a child, which hath occasioned so much disgrace to me and my family, that I have thought proper to forbid her my sight any more."[37]

White men continued to have sex with female slaves and to sire mixed-race offspring throughout the eighteenth century, but they did so for the most part in secret. A Frenchman who traveled through Maryland and Virginia in the late eighteenth century reported that a white man fathering a mulatto child "would be scorned, [and] dishonored; every house would be closed to him, he would be detested." According to another Frenchman who visited the region in the 1790s, "public opinion" was "so much against this intercourse between the white people and the black" that it took place "by stealth and transiently." Plantation "stewards or bailiffs" were generally "accused of producing this mongrel breed" on the grounds that they were "liable to temptation," being "young and constantly amidst their slaves," as well as "enjoy[ing] the power of gratifying their passions because they [were] despots." This handily diverted attention away from the clandestine activities of planters themselves.[38]

Young men doubtless experimented sexually with slaves belonging to their parents and learned at an early age that white male privilege could include the physical appropriation of enslaved women. In March 1774 Robert Carter's son Bob teased his eighteen-year-old brother, Ben, about a rumor that was circulating in the neighborhood: Ben had allegedly taken Sukey ("a plump, sleek, likely negro girl, about sixteen") into the stable and stayed there with her "for a considerable time." Later that same year, when someone broke into the nursery at night, "either to rob the house, or commit fornication with Sukey," it was "whispered" that Ben might be the culprit. But Philip Fithian, the tutor who recorded these incidents in his journal, preferred to believe that the suspicions regarding Ben were a "calumny" and that "more probably it was one of the warm-blooded, well fed young negroes, trying for the company of buxom Sukey." It is fitting that these interactions between Ben and Sukey (if they took place) remained the stuff of rumor, gossip, and "whispers" in the Carter household. Regardless of what Ben's father thought about miscegenation in private, he would not have been likely to condone openly his son's alleged behavior.[39]

By the late eighteenth century, candidly acknowledged relationships between white men and slave women had become extremely unusual in the Chesapeake. One can, of course, find exceptions. Thomas Wright, a planter in Bedford County, Virginia, lived in an open and obviously affectionate relationship with Sylvia, one of his slaves, during the 1780s and 1790s. Sylvia bore Thomas four children, the oldest of whom became free in 1791 and inherited his father's estate in 1805. But most unions were more secretive. John Custis never openly acknowledged his relationship with his slave Alice, though he did provide for their son in his will.[40] The contrast between public repudiation and private accommodation of inter-racial unions in eighteenth-century Virginia is striking. Consider Thomas Jefferson, whose declared "aversion to the mixture of colour" stood in stark contrast to both his own behavior and that of relatives and associates whom he liked and respected. Jefferson's father-in-law, John Wayles, had a long-term relationship with his slave Elizabeth Hemings, who bore him six offspring. On Wayles's death, Hemings and her children came to live with the Jeffersons as favored house servants at Monticello. One of Eliza-beth's daughters, Sally Hemings, became Jefferson's lover and gave him several children. None of their offspring remained in slavery as adults; significantly enough, the only slaves whom Jefferson freed were members of the Hemings family. Mary Hemings, another of Elizabeth's daugh-ters, was leased to Thomas Bell in the 1780s, became his lover, and bore him two children. Jefferson later sold Mary and her offspring to Bell; that he did so at her request suggests a mutual affection between Bell and Hemings. They lived together as a couple for the remainder of Bell's life. George Wythe of Williamsburg, who taught Jefferson law, apparently lived with a black mistress by whom he had a son. (Jefferson's youngest grandson was named after this teacher.) The Monticello patriarch was, then, surrounded by and willing at some level to accept racial mixing, de-spite his public position on the subject.[41]

The covert nature of interracial intimacies in the eighteenth-century Chesapeake was due largely to the conflation of sex, race, and civility in the minds of planters such as William Byrd. Recall Byrd's quest to em-body the refined panache of an English gentleman. His transformation of a romp with his wife Lucy into a courtly "flourish" provides a per-haps extreme but nonetheless revealing example of the role that sex could play in the performance of gentility. Byrd was well aware that libertinism figured as one of the ways in which members of the beau monde across the Atlantic displayed their "gallantry." But in a 1735 letter to England, he confessed that he had no "stories" of sexual "scandal" or "intrigue" to share with his correspondent, at least none that would pass muster in "the fine world." It was, he wrote, "a mighty misfortune for an epistolizer not to live near some great city like London or Paris, where people play the fool in a well-bred way, and furnish their neighbors with discourse." It is surely no coincidence that Byrd's diary referred to having sex with slaves as "play[ing] the fool." Miscegenation was not "well-bred" from Byrd's perspective and certainly not the ideal way for eighteenth-century Virginian planters like Byrd to "furnish their neighbors with discourse."

In a particularly revealing passage, he wrote as follows: "Our vices and disorders want all that wit and refinement which make them palatable to the fine world. We are unskilled in the arts of making our follies agreeable, nor can we dress up the D[evil] so much to advantage, as to make him pass for an angel of light." Byrd equated Virginian "follies" with the Devil, the epitome of darkness and depravity. Given the images of blackness, savagery, and evil that recur in contemporary descriptions of African people, it is difficult not to read Byrd's remark as a coded reference to miscegenation. Virginians had their sexual "vices and disorders," but these could not be dressed up so as to make them "palatable to the fine world."[42]

Byrd's equation of social refinement with angels of light and of colonial foolery with black devils was rooted in a commonplace racial construct that had insidious implications for all concerned, including white residents of the South. Anglo-Americans were convinced that skin color expressed cultural worth (or the lack thereof), but they also believed that both were mutable. Early modern Englishmen had often used the phrase "to wash an Ethiop white" as a synonym for impossibility.[43] Yet commentators in North America claimed that miscegenation could achieve just that. When Byrd criticized seventeenth-century settlers for not having intermarried with Indians, he insisted that the issue of color would have faded as the progeny of interracial marriages became paler with each passing generation: "if a Moor may be washed white in three generations," he wrote, "surely an Indian might have been blanched in two." By the early eighteenth century, there would have been no "reproach" attached to such a union because the physical signs of intermarriage would have disappeared. The early colonists, Byrd argued, should have focused on the Indians' potential for "improvement," physical and otherwise. Their "complexion" and "talents" could have been "improve[d]" through becoming anglicized.[44]

Many Anglo-Americans believed that Africans were more fundamentally different from them than were Indians. Yet even Africans could be "blanched" through miscegenation. Byrd recounted in his commonplace book a story about a West Indies planter who "had an intrigue with an Ethiopian princess, by whom he had a daughter that was a mulatto." The planter sired another child with that daughter and then another with his granddaughter. That great-grand-daughter was "perfectly white and very honorably descended." The planter boasted that "he had washed the

blackamoore white." As with the Indians, amelioration through miscegenation would be evident in much more than physical changes. "The improvement of the blacks in body and mind," wrote Jefferson, "in the first
instance of their mixture with the whites, has been observed by everyone."
Their "inferiority," he concluded, was "not the effect merely of their condition of life," yet they were apparently susceptible to "improvement."[45]

Unfortunately for those invested in English "complexion" and "talents," it seemed that they just as much as the Indians and Africans were
mutable. Across the Atlantic, that capacity for change had enabled progress from barbarism to civilization. In their *Briefe and True Report of the
New Found Land of Virginia,* Thomas Harriot and John White had provided drawings not only of the Indians but also of ancient Picts, "for to
show how that the inhabitants of the late Bretannie have been in times past
as savage as those of Virginia."[46] But that process of physical and cultural
metamorphosis could work in the other direction. It was all very well for
an eastern planter such as Byrd to wax lachrymose about the squandered
possibilities of Indian assimilation via intermarriage, but contemporaries
were well aware that traders who became involved with Indian women
often settled permanently in native communities and became assimilated
to an Indian way of life, not quite the "opportunities of improvement"
that Byrd had in mind.

The threat posed by Africans was much more immediate and alarming.
By the early eighteenth century, slave importation had transformed the
Chesapeake. Though slaves did not constitute a majority of the population, as was the case in South Carolina and the West Indies, some contemporaries nonetheless found the African presence overwhelming. "They
import so many negroes hither," wrote Byrd in 1736, "that I fear this
colony will some time or other be confirmed by the name of New Guinea."
Widespread miscegenation exposed the world that southern planters inhabited as fundamentally different from that across the Atlantic. Neither
a black lover, nor the offspring from such a union, nor indeed a master
who had sex with slaves could "pass as an angel of light."[47] Byrd may not
have been a typical Virginia planter (he did, after all, spend almost half
his life in England), but his anxiety about becoming blackened in his own
and other minds was not anomalous. Consider Robert Bolling's telling description of a colonist returning from Virginia to England: "men were surprised to behold him so white. All thought that Virginians were blacker
than night." Anxiety about the possibility of physical and cultural debase-

ment through miscegenation combined with the colonial elite's insecurities to ensure that interracial unions were for the most part clandestine.[48]

WHEREAS CHESAPEAKE PLANTERS became increasingly committed to a conspiracy of silence about the widespread occurrence of interracial sex, South Carolinians were much more inclined to acknowledge miscegenation and debate its implications for white identity. In eighteenth-century South Carolina, as in the West Indies, black slaves constituted a majority of the population (by 1730 there were two Africans for every European). A visitor to Charleston in the 1770s saw so many "black faces" that he began to suspect he had come not to an American city, but "to Africa, or Lucifer's court." Another remarked that there were "swarms of negroes about the town and many mulattoes." Some white residents were disturbed by widespread miscegenation and voiced their objections; others admitted to such unions quite openly. Charlestonians discussed this aspect of their sexual lives with a frankness that would have been inconceivable in the Chesapeake.[49]

The lack of surviving documentation from South Carolina in the late 1600s makes it impossible to gauge the extent to which Englishmen and Africans formed interracial unions during the first few decades of settlement. The spirit of interdependence that characterized the pioneer colony, as blacks and whites worked and lived together in crude and challenging conditions, would suggest more rather than less. But in any case, as Africans became a majority in the colony, legislators enacted repressive slave codes that imposed rigid racial distinctions and outlawed miscegenation. A 1717 act decreed that any white servant who bore a black man's child should serve an additional seven years; any free white woman who did so would become a servant for seven years, as would any free black man who sired a child by a white woman. The law ordered that "any white man that shall beget any negro woman with child, whether free or servant, shall undergo the same penalties as white women."[50]

But the prohibition of sex between white men and black women was largely ignored. Bolzius noted that "such mixings" were "not allowed by the laws" but went ahead anyway. Samuel Dyssli, a Swiss immigrant, was also struck by the impunity with which settlers engaged in such liaisons: "if a white man has a child by a black woman, nothing is done to him on account of it. Such swinishness is not punished in this country." Visitors from Europe and the northern colonies were astounded by the frankness with which white Charlestonians acknowledged and discussed such matters. Bolzius wrote that it was "considered little or no shame" for "leading gentlemen" to "disgrace" themselves "with such heathen folk." And New Englander Josiah Quincy was shocked to discover in 1773 that "the enjoyment of a negro or mulatto woman" was "spoken of as quite a common thing" with "no reluctance, delicacy, or shame." Such matters could even become the topic of humorous conversation between members of "polite" society: "It is far from being uncommon to see a gentleman at dinner, and his reputed offspring a slave to the master of the table. I myself saw two instances of this, and the company would very facetiously trace the lines, lineaments, and features of the father and mother in the child, and very accurately point out the more characteristic resemblance. The fathers neither of them blushed or seem[ed] disconcerted." Such men, Quincy added, "were called men of worth, politeness, and humanity." He found this a "strange perversion of terms and language."[51]

Carolina planters often developed lasting relationships with slave women. In many cases, they freed their lovers and the children that resulted from these interracial unions, either during their own lifetimes or in their wills. One-third of recorded manumissions in colonial South Carolina involved mulatto children; three-quarters of the adults manumitted were women. Although masters rarely stated their reasons for freeing particular slaves, it seems likely that they were often emancipating their mistresses and offspring. Charleston merchant Hopkin Price freed his mulatto slave Sylvia on his death in 1781 and left her an annual income of 143 pounds.[52] South Carolina law limited the value of bequests that a married man with legitimate children could leave to a mistress or illegitimate offspring; assemblymen were evidently worried that a master's affection for his slave lover and their children might endanger the material prospects of white heirs, which speaks volumes about the emotional commitment that was assumed to underpin many such relationships. A contributor to the *South Carolina Gazette* in 1772 complained that some planters avoided matrimony with a white woman altogether: "to such a pitch of licentiousness have some men arrived, that they cohabit as husbands with negro women, treating them as wives even in public, and do not blush to own the mongrel breed which is thus begotten, maintaining the spurious progeny as well as the mother in splendor."[53]

Interracial unions in South Carolina were clearly not limited to sexual contact between masters and their slaves. White men of any social status had diverse opportunities to meet, flirt with, and become sexually intimate with black women. Ebenezer Hazard wrote that "many of the first gentlemen (so called)" attended events known as "black dances" ("a peculiarity which I did not hear of in any other state"); these were "balls given by negro and mulatto women, to which they invite the white gentlemen."[54] Meanwhile, the notoriously wild nightlife that Charlestonians at the other end of the social scale enjoyed along the waterfront and in nearby streets had an interracial component that clearly disturbed at least some citizens and prompted the following threat in a 1736 issue of the *South Carolina Gazette:* "Certain young men of this town are desired to frequent less with their black lovers the open lots and the Chandler's house on the Green between old Church Street and King's Street, there being something intended to cool their courage and to expose them."[55]

That announcement was not unique as an expression of local concern about interracial sex involving white men. In 1743 the Grand Jury in Charleston also took a stand: "We present the too common practice of criminal conversation with negro and other slave wenches in this province, as an enormity and evil of general ill-consequence." Some Carolinians repudiated the double standard that allowed white men to cross racial boundaries in pursuit of pleasure while stigmatizing white women who had relationships with black men. Anxiety about interracial sex was not gender-exclusive, and some people worried that any form of miscegenation threatened to subvert the racial and cultural order. There does seem to have been a consensus in the lower as well as the upper South that respectable white women should stay away from black men. According to Bolzius, interracial unions involving Carolina women were in actuality much less common than those between white men and black women. And it is no surprise that most defamation cases involving allegations of interracial sex stemmed from the slandering of white women. But men did occasionally sue because of reports that they had been sexually intimate with black women. These male plaintiffs claimed that their reputations had been "blackened" as a result of such claims, suggesting that at least some folk disapproved of interracial sex regardless of whether the white partner was male or female.[56]

A lively exchange that took place in the *South Carolina Gazette* during the 1730s provides us with a revealing glimpse of the anxieties that underlay opposition to interracial sex involving white men. In 1732 the newspaper published a poem entitled "The Cameleon Lover":

> If what the curious have observed be true,
> That the Cameleon will assume the hue

Of all the objects that approach its touch;
No wonder then, that the amours of such
Whose taste betrays them to a close embrace
With the dark beauties of the sable race
(Stained with the tincture of the sooty sin)
Imbibe the blackness of their charmer's skin.

According to the poem, white men who engaged in sexual relations with "dark beauties" might well transform and degenerate: "stained" by that "close embrace," they would take on "the blackness" of their lovers. The tone of the poem was ambiguous, perhaps deliberately so: it could be interpreted either as a serious attack on miscegenation and the threat of racial pollution or as a humorous lampoon upon such fears. But the anxieties to which it referred, whether sympathetically or satirically, were clear enough. They focused on the threat of contagion.[57]

Such concerns resonated throughout the debate that ensued in the *Gazette*. One reader read the poem as an inappropriate "smattering of wit" and wrote a letter in response that the *Gazette* published in its next issue. The author, who rather redundantly assumed the pseudonym "Albus [white]," denounced interracial sex as "subvert[ing] and defac[ing] the order and beauty which this our all-wise Creator has discovered to us through all his works." That "scandalous offence" showed "base ingratitude" for the "form and complexion" that God had "thought fit to bestow upon us" and should be seen for what it was, "the grossest affront upon his wisdom." It was "too shocking to see an evil of this kind spreading itself among us, too gross to be suffered to pass in silence." The author hoped that "the man whose taste is thus unhappily vitiated" would "fall into the utmost confusion to see in the product of such an amour the exact features of his own face, sculking beneath the base thin disguise of a tawny complexion." If not, he was indeed "an incorrigible son of darkness." This final metaphor invoked both the entrenched association between blackness and depravity in early modern Anglo-American culture and the danger of contagion on which "The Cameleon Lover" had focused. Whether through physical contact or through the moral degradation that such contact necessarily involved, the white lover would become blackened, or Africanized.[58]

Another reader was offended by "The Cameleon Lover" for an entirely different reason. He had read the poem as a serious attack on interracial sex and submitted a piece entitled "Cameleon's Defense," urging the pub-

lisher to print his contribution so as to "avoid the imputation of par-
tiality." The "Defense," though acknowledging that miscegenation was
one of those "follies" to which men were led "through the dark turnings of
a dubious maze," urged compassion for its perpetrators, since they were
under the thrall of "love" and therefore helpless:

> Love is the monarch passion of the mind,
> Knows no superior, by no laws confined;
> But triumphs still, impatient of control,
> O'er all the proud endowments of the soul.

The poem also pointed out that even "wise" men had been engaging in
such "follies" since time immemorial:

> The eldest sons of wisdom were not free,
> From the same failure you condemn in me.
> If as the wisest of the wise have erred,
> I go astray and am condemned unheard,
> My faults you too severely reprehend,
> More like a rigid censor than a friend.

The publisher printed this poem in the same edition that featured the diatribe by "Albus." But whereas the latter was included without comment,
"Cameleon's Defense" was followed by an editorial that doubted the merits of a defense on the grounds "that my great-grandsire had as vitiated a
taste as myself." It also "beg[ged]" the author "not to mention a word of
the 'proud endowments of his soul' after having stooped to so very low
an amour."[59]

Four years later, the *Gazette*'s publisher felt that it was safe to revisit
the subject of interracial sex in a humorous context. But it provoked a
spirited, if rather crass, defense of white women's sexual prowess by implying that the appeal of black women lay in their superior stamina. The
offending paragraph reported the alleged advice of women from Bermuda
who had "lately arrived in this province," addressed to "distressed bachelors and widowers" in Charleston who were "in a strait" for female companionship. Such men should wait for the next shipment "from the coast
of Guinny," the piece declared: "African ladies are of a strong, robust constitution; not easily jaded out, able to serve them by night as well as by
day." The following week, a letter in response insisted that "our country-
women are full as capable for service either night or day as any African
ladies whatsoever, unless their native constitution is much altered." The

irritated reader continued: "In all companies wheresoever I have been, my country-women have always the praise for their activity of hips and humoring a jest to the life in what posture soever their partners may fancy, which makes me still hope that they'll have the preference before the black ladies in the esteem of the widowers and bachelors at Charleston." Another contributor to that week's issue also condemned white men who sought out "black lovers," pointing out that there were "buxom" and "tender-hearted" women "of their own colour" who "no doubt [would] comply easily with their request on small rewards to cure their itch and courage." The *Gazette* had clearly touched a sensitive nerve.[60]

The debate in Charleston's newspaper during the 1730s indicates that at least some Carolinians were troubled by the implications of miscegenation, but others apparently treated the issue as a joking matter. A very different ethos prevailed within the lower South's white elite from that which characterized affluent planters in the Chesapeake. Charlestonians were eager to imitate the opulence and freewheeling libertinism of London's beau monde, but in general they seem to have been much less anxious than their counterparts in the upper South to camouflage the differences between their world and English society across the Atlantic. That difference was exemplified by frank acknowledgment of and open debate about miscegenation, both strikingly absent in the upper South. It is doubtless no coincidence that emigrants from the West Indies were prominent among those who settled in South Carolina. West Indies planters were much further removed from illusions of cultural commonality and accompanying imperatives. They made little or no attempt to disguise the kind of society they had constructed, the prevalence of interracial sex, or their attachment to slave mistresses. The scandal that erupted on the mainland in 1802 over Jefferson's alleged relationship with his slave Sally would have made little sense to West Indies masters. Their much more blatant "enjoyment" of slaves, in circumstances that ranged from violent assault to openly acknowledged informal marriage, provides a telling contrast with the dynamics of interracial sex on the mainland, especially in the Chesapeake.[61]

THE SUGAR ISLANDS in the West Indies were justifiably notorious for the extreme brutality of their slave regimes. It is no surprise, then, that the most shocking descriptions by far of eighteenth-century slave rape come from journals kept by white men living in the West Indies. Thomas Thistlewood arrived in Jamaica in 1750 at the age of twenty-nine. From

1751 until 1767, he worked almost continuously as overseer at Egypt Plantation, working for William Dorrill and then his son-in-law John Cope. He later bought an estate of his own, where he lived until his death in 1786. Thistlewood's laconic but nonetheless revealing journal lays bare the sexual violence to which slaves were subjected. According to his entry for 12 March 1755, a gang rape occurred that evening when Cope arrived at Egypt Plantation with six male companions. Four of the guests, Thistlewood wrote, "heartily drunk, hawled Eve separately into the water room and were concerned with her." One of them raped her "twice, first and last." On 9 October 1756, Cope was "in his tantrums" and "like a madman most part of the night." He "forced Egypt Susanah in the cookroom." And in February 1758, the bookkeeper got Coobah "into the boiling-room by strategem" and then "attempted to ravish her, stopped a handkerchief into her mouth, etc.," but Thistlewood was nearby and prevented the rape from taking place.[62]

Thistlewood's journal is not the only brutally frank account of sexual coercion on West Indies plantations to have survived. John Gabriel Stedman, a young lieutenant in the Scots Brigade, spent just over four years in Surinam, from 1773 to 1778, as part of a volunteer military corps sent to reinforce local troops as they countered attacks by bands of escaped slaves. Stedman kept a journal, which he later expanded into an account of his years in Surinam that was first published in 1796. Stedman appears to have been genuinely appalled by the widespread rape of slave women on Surinam and was evidently moved by the plight of black couples who found themselves unable to resist sexually predatory owners or overseers: "if a negro and his wife have never so great an attachment to each other, the woman if handsome must yield to the loathsome embraces of a rascally manager, or see her husband cut to pieces by the whip for daring to think of preventing it, which truly drives them to distraction." On one occasion, Stedman came across a young slave "tied up with both arms to a tree ... lacerated in such a shocking condition ... that she was from her neck to her ankles literally dyed over with blood." She had received two hundred lashes for "firmly refusing to submit to the loathsome embraces of her despicable executioner," the overseer, who "construed" her refusal as "disobedience" and so had her "skinned alive."[63]

Hardly any eighteenth-century slaves left behind descriptions of their experiences, but Olaudah Equiano was an exception. Kidnapped by slave traders from the Ibo tribe in present-day Nigeria at the age of eleven, Equiano spent ten years as a slave, became free in 1766, and two decades later wrote an account of his life as a contribution to the antislavery movement. Working as a slave at Montserrat in the mid–eighteenth century, Equiano frequently witnessed the sexual abuse of African women: "it was almost a constant practice with our clerks, and other whites," he wrote, "to commit violent depradations on the chastity of the female slaves." That Equiano was "unable to help them" clearly tormented him. The women were equally vulnerable in transit from one island to another:

> When we have had some of these slaves on board my master's vessels, to carry them to other islands, or to America, I have known our mates to commit these acts most shamefully, to the disgrace not of Christians only but of men. I have even known them to gratify their brutal passion with females not ten years old; and these abominations, some of them practised to such scandalous excess, that one of our captains discharged the mate and others on that account.

According to Stedman, sexual assault was one of the major grievances cited by rebel slaves, who demanded that planters keep "a more watchful eye" on "drunken managers and overseers" prone to "debauching their wives and children." When one plantation manager who was taken prisoner by rebels begged a slave whom he recognized to intercede on his behalf, the slave apparently reminded the prisoner that he had "ravished" his mother and "flogged" his father "for coming to her assistance." This had taken place in the "infant presence" of the slave who was now expected to show mercy but instead decapitated the manager.[64]

The sexual abuse described by Equiano, Stedman, and Thistlewood was not limited to the West Indies. Yet that region was distinctive in ways that had a profound impact upon sexual relations between Africans and Europeans living on the sugar islands. Slaves outnumbered white residents by an overwhelming majority. At the time of Stedman's arrival, about three thousand Europeans were living in Surinam, along with some fifty thousand slaves. By the early eighteenth century, Africans constituted around 90 percent of Jamaica's population, which was skewed along gender as well as racial lines: within the white population, men outnumbered women by roughly four to one; they often never married. Immigrants were especially likely to remain bachelors, many of them assuming that their residence in the West Indies would be temporary and that they would return home after making their fortune. Thomas Atwood, writing about Dominica in the late eighteenth century, acknowledged the white male settlers' "great aversion to forming matrimonial connections." But as Atwood and other commentators emphasized, widespread bachelor-hood did not mean widespread celibacy. Assuming that they would stay "only for a few years," white immigrants "content[ed] themselves with the company of a mulatto or negro mistress."[65]

White men living in the West Indies were infamous for their promiscuous relations with slaves, and Thistlewood's journal certainly gives credence to claims that white residents were sexually hyperactive. Between 1751 and 1764, Thistlewood recorded having intercourse 1,774 times with 109 black women; of these partners, 18 had sex with him more than ten times, 69 only once.[66] Thistlewood generally named his sexual partners, though occasionally he would mate with a "negress unknown." He often noted the place where the encounter took place: with Susannah "in the curinghouse gangway" and "in the cornloft in the curinghouse," with Mirtilla "in the entrance into [the] standing lime kiln," with Maria "sup. terra [on the ground] among the shrubs, in the Rockey island, on the left-hand side, going to the wild olive tree," and with Abba "sup. [on the] bench, under [the] shed in [the] new garden."[67] Sometimes he made note of the sexual position (including "stans [standing]" or "backwards") and the quality of the experience (occasionally "non bene").

Given the scale of sexual activity on plantations such as Egypt, it is hardly surprising that Thistlewood and his slaves suffered frequent and severe bouts of venereal disease, which he recorded in gruesome detail. On 30 September 1751, for example, he "perceived a small redness" in his groin, but did not regard it [take it seriously]." He spent that night with Dido. On 1 October, he noticed "a greater redness, with soreness, and scalding water [urine]." A "running" of "a yellow greenish matter" now began, and over the next few days things got much worse. Thistlewood realized that he had "a rank infection" ("flying pains . . . breaking out on the thighs . . . loathsome linens") and so he sought medical assistance from Dr. Joseph Horlock. He "was 44 days curing, from 11th of October to 23rd November, in which time was blooded, and took 24 mercurial pills, 4 at a dose; 3 single mercurial pills, and one dose of 5 ditto." He had "some doubts" as to whether his recovery was "perfect." However unpleasant and painful such infections may have been, Thistlewood did not allow caution to get in the way of sexual gratification. He noted on 19 May 1759 that his employer, John Cope, spent the night at Egypt Plantation and had sex with Little Mimber. Thistlewood wrote that he "suspect[ed]" Cope had "the clap," yet he himself enjoyed Little Mimber five days later.[68]

Other contemporary accounts suggest that Thistlewood's experience and attitude were far from atypical. Planter Edward Long lamented that "a promiscuous commerce on their first arrival with the black and mulatto women, and this with so little prudence and caution," made white men extremely vulnerable to "being very speedily infected." Stedman noted in his journal that on the day of his arrival in Surinam he went to the house of a planter who had offered him hospitality while Stedman was still on board ship. His host was away from home, but Stedman settled in and "f[uc]k[ed] one of his negro maids." White men were "encouraged" to "persevere in this unheeding course" by "the facility with which the milder symptoms of the virus [were] removed." Long criticized physicians for being "too fond" of prescribing mercury cures, the "pernicious effects" of which weakened their patients so that they then fell prey to other diseases and often died of ailments that under normal circumstances could have been "easily removed."[69] Hans Sloane, who spent twenty months in late-seventeenth-century Jamaica as physician to the island's governor, also reported that venereal disease was "very common" and that he treated many slaves for the disease during his stay on the island. According to Sloane, planters took "great care" of slaves when "in danger of being disabled or of death," because they were worth "a great deal of money."[70]

But infected slaves were often reluctant to trust overseers or masters. In 1779 the overseer at Hope Plantation, Jamaica, complained that slaves "quack[ed] themselves" instead of "making application to the [white] doctor." Long wrote that slave women who served or wanted to serve as wet nurses were particularly reluctant to reveal that they had been infected. Because this position was "anxiously coveted," they were "sure to keep secret any ailment they labour[ed] under, however detrimental to the child." Slaves who distrusted white medicine might turn to medical experts within their own community. According to Sloane, a black overseer named Hercules was "not only famous amongst the blacks on his master Colonel Fuller's plantation but [also] amongst the whites in the neighborhood for curing several diseases, and particularly gonorrheas." Even though European treatments were often either ineffective or had deadly side effects, that did not prevent Sloane from criticizing "Indian and black doctors" who were "suppose[d] to understand and cure several distempers," yet could not "perform what they pretend[ed], unless in the virtues of some few simples." According to Sloane, the "ignorance" of such "doctors" made their treatments not only "useless" but even "hurtful to those who employ[ed] them." Hercules had himself suffered from the disease and thought that he had cured it but came to Sloane "complaining of a very great heat in making water with intolerable pain and scalding." Sloane told Hercules to take "some mercurial medicines" but was unable to track his progress because he left the island soon afterward.[71]

Venereal infection was not the only unwanted consequence of sexual intercourse on sugar island plantations. According to eighteenth-century observers, slave women often used abortifacients to terminate pregnancies that resulted from sex with white men, sometimes killing themselves in the process. As a Scottish woman visiting the West Indies wrote, "they have certain herbs and medicines, that free them from such an incumbrance, but which seldom fails to cut short their own lives, as well as that of their offspring. By this many of them perish every year." Some women may have aborted because they had been raped and could not bear to go ahead with a pregnancy that resulted from violation. Others may have wanted to avoid producing children who would become slaves and suffer as they had. Sloane reported that African women sometimes came to see him "pretending themselves ill" in the hope that the medicine he gave them would "cause abortion" of unwanted children. In one case, a woman who discovered that she was pregnant "endeavoured to hide it, and took violent medicines designing abortion." Despite her drinking down "mercury sublimate in broth," she "went out her time, and after violent vomitings, and great spitting for some time, she was privately delivered, and the child buried in a field." The mother was exposed when carrion crows uncovered the infant corpse.[72]

Not all slave women who had sex with white men were raped. Given the power dynamic at work, most slaves doubtless felt that they had little choice but to accommodate their master or overseer's wishes.[73] Yet sexual relationships that began under circumstances that were at least implicitly coercive did sometimes develop into committed and loving unions. Thistlewood, for example, developed an enduring relationship with a slave named Phibbah that both parties seem to have found emotionally fulfilling as well as beneficial in more practical ways. The couple lived together from 1754 until Thistlewood's death in 1786; he arranged in his will for Phibbah to be manumitted, and she became legally free in 1792. They had a son together named John, whose freedom Thistlewood purchased in 1762; he sent him to school and had him apprenticed as a carpenter. (John died as a young man, his life cut short in 1780 by fever.)

John's parents seem to have been fond of each other: they tended to and worried about each other when sick, exchanged gifts, and even went on walks together. When Thistlewood left Cope's employment in 1757 (temporarily, as it turned out) and departed the Egypt estate, Phibbah "grieve[d] very much" during the days preceding their separation, and Thistlewood "could not sleep." He was "vastly uneasy" about leaving Phibbah "in miserable slavery." He "begged hard of Mrs. Cope to sell or hire Phibbah" to him, but "she would not," even though her husband "was willing."[74] Like any couple, Thistlewood and Phibbah argued from time to time, but their relationship appears to have become increasingly harmonious as the years went by. Thistlewood referred occasionally to Phibbah's "keep[ing] away" after they had quarreled, which suggests that she could refuse him when she wished. Neither seems to have expected the other to be monogamous. Thistlewood did become anxious in 1754 about the nature of Phibbah's relationship to Cope, and on 3 October they "had great words . . . in bed" on the subject. Phibbah in turn was worried in 1757 about Thistlewood's intimacy with Aurelia at Kendal estate.[75] But the issue on both of these occasions seems to have been fear of abandonment in favor of another principal partner, not sexual infidelity.

Phibbah belonged to a cadre of slave women who chose to have sex mostly or exclusively with white men. Contemporary claims that "young black wenches la[id] themselves out for white lovers" were doubtless unwarranted in their generalizations, but they were grounded in reality. Thistlewood's nephew John recorded in his own diary that "a negro wench" came to see him on 3 February 1765, "to persuade me if possible to lay with her." She "wanted to have a child for a master" but thought "she would never have one" by her own.[76] If a woman like Phibbah succeeded in balancing her loyalties to a white lover on the one hand and her fellow slaves on the other, she could become a key mediating figure in the plantation community, benefiting herself, her lover, and her fellow slaves. Phibbah secured her freedom and amassed considerable property, at one point lending Thistlewood money.[77] We should, of course, beware a rose-tinted view of such liaisons. During their lengthy relationship, Thistlewood recorded only one occasion on which he gave Phibbah "some correction." But the brutality of the labor system could and did extend into ongoing and nominally consensual relationships. Thistlewood wrote that a fellow overseer on the island "ill treated and greatly abused a white girl wh[om] he had kept some time by beating, trampling upon her, tearing her private part with his finger." Another man "cut off the lips, upper lip almost close to her nose, of his mulatto sweetheart in jealousy, because he said a negro should never kiss those lips he had."[78]

Visitors to the West Indies were astonished to behold the "spurious race of children" produced by interracial unions. Lady Nugent, who lived in Jamaica from 1801 to 1805 as wife of the governor, claimed that "white men of all descriptions, married or single, live[d] in a state of licentiousness with their female slaves." She found herself surrounded by mulatto "daughters of members of assembly, officers, etc, etc." At Golden Grove Plantation, Nugent learned from the housekeeper that Simon Taylor, the bachelor owner, "had a numerous family, some almost on every one of his estates." Earlier that same day, a "little mulatto girl" had been "sent into the drawing room to amuse" Lady Nugent, who now learned that she was one of Taylor's daughters. Edward Long wrote that it was not unusual for white and mulatto children, "all claimed by the same married father," to be "bred up together under the same roof." However shocking this may have been to newly arrived Europeans, "habit" and "the prevailing fashion" soon reduced the "abhorrence" caused by "such scenes."[79] Masters often arranged for their mulatto children to receive baptism, apprenticeships, land for farming, equipment for the practice of assorted trades, and testamentary bequests. So concerned did the Jamaica assembly become about the size of bequests being left to slave mistresses and their children that in 1761 it passed a law limiting inheritance by "negroes" and the "issue of negroes" to two thousand pounds. According to Long, many settlers opposed this measure "with great warmth." Whereas the mainland colonies treated all children of mixed race borne by slave women as legally indistinguishable from the offspring of African couples, the Jamaica assembly had assigned a distinct status to the offspring of interracial relationships, along with many rights and privileges elsewhere reserved for white residents.[80]

Fathers who did not actually own their mulatto children were often quite open about their paternity as well as their desire to save their offspring from a life in bondage. The overseer at Hope Plantation, a fellow named Concanon, requested "title to a mulatto child about four years of age" in a 1779 letter to his employer back in England, the duchess of Chandos, offering to pay "whatever your attorneys value him at." He made no secret of his reasons for wanting to purchase the infant: "My motive for making this request is that I have reason to think the child to be nearly related to me." As he wrote in a subsequent letter, "his being my son makes me impatient to have him manumitted." The duchess's agent, Edward East, recommended that she grant Concanon's request, exchanging the boy for an adult male slave: "such children are seldom serviceable to an estate," he pointed out, "from the indulgence they get when young." He informed the duchess that there were "several of these children on the estate" and averred that it would be in her interests "to exchange all you can on the same terms." The duchess did give her permission for the exchange to go ahead, and East promised in a letter dated 12 September 1780 to ensure that Concanon provided "an able negro in place of him." He had evidently received orders "to do the like with all the other mulattoes that are upon the estate."[81]

The affection and concern shown by many white masters toward their slave families confounded those observers who assumed that love could not cross racial boundaries. Janet Schaw, who traveled to the West Indies in the 1770s, "sincerely believe[d]" that planters were "excited to that crime by no other desire or motive but that of adding to the number of their slaves." Yet even she conceded that "they often honour[ed] their black wenches with their attention" and claimed to "love" them. Schaw's assertion that sex with slaves served principally to augment a planter's assets conveniently obscured the attraction of white men toward slave women and the emotional ties that sustained some interracial unions. But though Schaw may have been willfully blind to such ties, planters' wives were less so.[82]

Although a significant proportion of white males living in the sugar islands arrived as single men and remained unmarried, by no means all of those who had slave mistresses were bachelors. In the West Indies, as in mainland southern colonies, white women were expected to embody ideals of sexual restraint and racial purity that did not apply to men. They were to practice "sobriety and chastity" while their menfolk indulged themselves in what one observer called "goatish embraces."[83] Stedman commented sardonically on the double standard that governed interracial sex in Surinam: on the one hand, sexual relationships between white men and slaves were widespread, "to the no small mortification" of white women; yet "should it ever be known that a European female had kept a carnal intercourse with a slave of whatever denomination, the first is detested, and the last loses his life without mercy."[84] According to Stedman, white women who married planters and then found themselves neglected in favor of black lovers vented their resentment upon "the negro and mulatto girls," whom they blamed as "the causes of their disgrace." Thus, even a slave whose sexual contact with a master was largely positive could find herself "persecute[d] with the greatest bitterness and most barbarous tyranny" by his wife. Stedman gave several ghastly examples of "revenge" that "ill-treated ladies" inflicted upon black rivals. One wife "put an end to the life of a young and beautiful Quodroon girl by the infernal means of plunging a red hot poker in her body, by those parts which decency forbids to mention." This fatal parody of the sexual act was motivated by "jealousy," though the husband claimed it was unfounded.[85]

Outsiders were struck not only by the scale of interracial sex that occurred in the West Indies but also by the openness with which white men pursued slave women. Long wrote that they made no secret of their "infatuated attachments to black women" and that any man "who should presume to show any displeasure against such a thing as simple fornication would for his pains be accounted a simple blockhead, since not one in twenty can be persuaded that there is either sin or shame in cohabiting with his slave." Instead of embracing "the pure and lawful bliss derived from matrimonial, mutual love" and so producing "a race of unadulterated beings," white men "of every rank, quality, and degree" preferred to "riot in these goatish embraces," spawning "a vast addition of spurious offsprings of different complexions." Their "licentious and even unnatural amours," declared Schaw, "seems to have gained sanction from custom."[86] One of the principal distinctions between sexual attitudes in the West Indies and those prevailing in the mainland southern colonies was that most white men in the former region do not seem to have been troubled by interracial sex, unless it involved a white woman. White residents of South Carolina were much more divided on the subject, and Chesapeake planters mostly refused to acknowledge their sexual relationships with slave women. A merchant from Jamaica, visiting Charleston in 1773, remarked in a letter written during his stay there that unions crossing racial boundaries in the South Carolina city were "carried on with more privacy than in our West India islands."[87] But the contrast between attitudes in Jamaica and those prevailing in the Chesapeake was much more dramatic. Interracial sex was clearly widespread in the upper South, but it was characterized by "stealth" and "whispers" instead of frank acknowledgment and open debate.

INTERRACIAL SEX BETWEEN free white men and enslaved black women had profound and ambiguous implications for eighteenth-century southern society. Widespread sexual coercion confirmed the dominion of masters and overseers over bound laborers and their bodies; it exemplified power of appropriation. Yet it also compromised the racial segregation that southern legislators had taken pains to codify in detail as slavery became embedded in the region. Southerners who feared physical and cultural pollution as a result of "mixing" with blacks were, not surprisingly, disturbed by the evidently widespread occurrence of miscegenation: such couplings betokened the debasement of their society. As we have seen, the degree to which southern whites feared interracial unions varied from region to region: Chesapeake planters were least inclined to acknowledge or discuss miscegenation, whereas many of their counterparts further south were, as one observer put it, "less scrupulous" about such matters.[88] White men living in the West Indies were strikingly casual about the prevalence of interracial sex on the sugar islands and engaged quite openly in long-term relationships as well as brief encounters with black women. Given contemporary expressions of anxiety about the growing number of "black faces" visible among southerners, it might be tempting to explain these regional differences in demographic terms. Yet whites were outnumbered not in the Chesapeake but in South Carolina and especially the West Indies, those areas where miscegenation aroused less, not more, anxiety.

Cultural imperatives and, in particular, the degree to which planters were invested in emulating an English way of life provide a much more compelling basis for understanding the variance in concern about interracial sex among southern whites. For those Carolina and West Indies planters who identified with members of the English elite primarily in terms of material ostentation and genteel libertinism, otherwise recognizing that they inhabited an utterly different world, such unions represented much less of a problem. But for those who sought a more thoroughgoing replication of English society, miscegenation threatened to undermine their sense of themselves. Ironically, the labor system on which such planters pinned their hopes for self-aggrandizement transformed the southern region of British America into a "blackened" realm that resembled "Africa, or Lucifer's court," more closely than England itself. Interracial sex embodied that transformation and compounded the fears of planters such as Byrd that they and their apparently debased society were far from "palatable to the fine world."

As some white southerners struggled with the implications of the sexual culture that they had brought into being, British colonies further north were also struggling to come to terms with a growing tension between cultural norms and practice. Enforcing the reformative sexual agenda espoused by Puritan leaders had proven a daunting challenge even in early New England, but demographic and cultural shifts in the late seventeenth and early eighteenth centuries led to nothing less than a sexual revolution as young people declared their independence and embraced a more permissive sexual ethos. Once Americans cut their ties with Britain, their efforts to nurture and sustain republican virtue became closely entwined with attempts to contain the implications of that concurrent sexual revolution. The interplay between sexual morality and notions of civility that had driven earlier campaigns to suppress unorthodox patterns of sexual behavior among ordinary settlers and had poisoned interracial relations now became crucial in a new context as citizens of the United States pondered the significance of sexual mores for their republican enterprise. Once again, sex would function for early Americans as an emblem of their larger moral and civic identity.

III

The Sexual Revolution

7

"Under the Watch"

The Metamorphosis of Sexual Regulation in Eighteenth-Century New England

As THE EIGHTEENTH CENTURY got under way in Boston, Puritan worthies such as Samuel Sewall felt that they and their values were increasingly held up to ridicule. In February 1712 a mortified Sewall noted in his diary that a "mock-sermon," "full of monstrous profaneness and obscenity," had been delivered at one of the Boston taverns on Shrove Tuesday. Sewall was particularly shocked to discover that a number of prominent citizens had attended and failed to prevent or condemn the performance. Veterans of the Puritan enterprise beheld a changing world and were not encouraged by what they saw. Their moral vision still enjoyed considerable influence, but increasingly it had to compete with other priorities and points of view. In 1685 Sewall and his friends had prevented Francis Stepney from setting up a dancing school by using their influence with the General Court. But when organist Edward Enstone, brought over from England in 1714 to play at King's Chapel, augmented his salary by giving dancing lessons, they could only look on disapprovingly. Sewall did persuade the governor not to attend a ball given by Enstone in 1716, but such affairs, which Cotton Mather had denounced in 1700 as "provocations to uncleanness," would go ahead anyway.[1]

It was all too easy for men such as Sewall and Mather to forget that enforcing their moral agenda had always been an uphill struggle. They now invested the past with a purity of spirit that was rhetorically potent but historically problematic. Yet a momentous shift had taken place as New England developed into an economically and socially sophisticated province of the British empire. That shift had been symbolized powerfully by the new charter granted to Massachusetts in 1691, which made property ownership instead of church membership the prerequisite for voting rights. The changes under way had important consequences for sexual mores and the regulation of sexual behavior. Not only was New England's increasingly diverse population less predominantly Puritan in its outlook, but in addition the legal mechanisms that had previously enforced a godly agenda increasingly served other interests. Eighteenth-century courts took less and less interest in the enforcement of moral values as their caseloads became dominated by financial and commercial issues.[2]

That redirection in legal energies represented a significant change in the tone of public life; nevertheless, the pace of change was slow, and many New Englanders remained committed to a culture of sexual surveillance and regulation. Local institutions still sought, for example, to discourage and punish sexual intimacy during courtship. It was only toward the middle of the eighteenth century that county courts ceased to prosecute married couples for having engaged in premarital sex. New England congregations continued to demand public confessions for that offense until the final decades of the century. Meanwhile, informal moral stewardship continued to play an important role within local neighborhoods. In 1773 two Boston women glanced through an open window and caught sight of Adam Air committing adultery with Pamela Brichford. They marched into the house and "asked him if he was not ashamed to act so when he had a wife at home."[3] Recourse to legal presentment had always been the last resort of a regulatory ethos that was predominantly informal in its orientation. But as the courts disengaged gradually from the enterprise of moral discipline, eighteenth-century New Englanders developed new and often highly effective strategies for policing sexual behavior from within their own homes and communities. And there were still ways in which New Englanders could mobilize the courts to reinforce unofficial pressure upon errant individuals. The judicial system's shift in priorities led not to the deregulation of sex but to the metamorphosis of sexual regulation.

This chapter examines the persistence of a regulatory ethos in eighteenth-century New England and also the sexual culture that it sought to govern. Perhaps the most striking facet of sexual behavior during the 1700s was a steady rise in premarital pregnancy, which began at the close of the previous century. In New Haven County, Connecticut, 19 percent of women who married during the 1690s were pregnant, up from a mere 2 percent in the 1670s. By the revolutionary era, between 30 and 40 percent of brides in some New England towns were already expecting.[4]

Seventeenth-century couples who had become sexually intimate during betrothal had acted in accordance with English popular tradition, ignoring legal and ecclesiastical prescriptions. The increase in bridal pregnancy rates throughout New England during the eighteenth century was due in part to the resurgence of traditional sexual mores as Puritan values loosened their grip on the population. But the rise was also caused by a transformation in familial politics. During the first half of the century, a slackening of parental control paved the way for a less restrictive sexual climate, which then seems to have been further encouraged by the spirit and disruptive impact of the American Revolution. Young people took full advantage of that increasingly permissive atmosphere, experimenting sexually not only within the context of courtship but also as they dallied in more casual and transitory liaisons.

Yet they did so, for the most part, in their parents' homes and with their parents' permission. As it became increasingly difficult to prevent unmarried sons and daughters from becoming sexually active, parents responded pragmatically. By the second half of the eighteenth century, it was not unusual for young women to spend the night with their sweethearts under the familial roof with the knowledge and consent of their parents. This enabled older adults to supervise and protect their offspring, especially unwed women: if relatives knew the identity of a male lover, they could ensure that he took responsibility for any children that resulted. By the late eighteenth century, there had emerged a clear double standard in criminal cases dealing with unwed pregnancy as magistrates focused increasingly upon the punishment of unmarried mothers instead of targeting both male and female partners. Eighteenth-century Americans were well aware, however, that greater sexual freedom brought with it greater risk for women; families were determined to hold unwed fathers accountable and often succeeded in doing so by threatening or, if necessary, actually bringing paternity suits against them. Knowing who was involved with whom enabled parents to protect young women from the hazards inherent in sexual experimentation. By condoning physical intimacy between unmarried young people within the home, they both maintained watch over and effectively domesticated a potentially perilous realm of sexual activity.

NEW ENGLAND'S COUNTY courts remained actively involved in the regulation of unmarried and premarital sex through the first half of the eighteenth century. The prosecution of single men and women for "fornication" and of married couples whose firstborn were conceived prior to their formal entry into wedlock accounted for just over half (53%) of all criminal prosecutions in Essex County, Massachusetts, between 1700 and 1785. Just over two-thirds (69%) of the criminal cases that came before New Haven County's court in Connecticut between 1710 and 1750 involved sex between unmarried persons.[5] Prosecutions for premarital sex continued until midcentury. Between 1731 and 1737, twenty-four married couples were presented to the Worcester County Court in Massachusetts for having conceived children prior to wedlock. But the punishments meted out in such cases became lighter over time, suggesting that the courts now saw the misdemeanor as less serious. In Essex County, the average fine fell from more than two pounds at the beginning of the century to five shillings by 1785; no couples were whipped for that offense after 1725.[6]

Prosecutions for premarital sex declined throughout New England during the 1730s and 1740s, becoming rare thereafter. That trend may have been due in part to religious revivals that swept through New England during those decades. This is not to suggest that young people were less likely than before to engage in sex prior to marriage, but they were becoming church members in larger numbers and often confessed to that offense as part of the application process. Judicial prosecutions would have decreased in number as church confessions became more numerous, since eighteenth-century courts often protected couples against double jeopardy by not targeting those who had already confessed in church. A broader change was also under way as the legal system reoriented itself away from overseeing New England's moral economy and toward the regulation of commercial transactions. By the second half of the century, the quarterly courts dealt only with fornication that resulted in out-of-wedlock births and so gave rise to economic as well as moral concerns.[7]

Like the county courts, church congregations dealt with sexual infractions on a regular basis during the first half of the century. In 1746, when Remember Backhouse confessed to her congregation in Barnstable that she had "fallen into the great and heinous and repeated sin of fornication, to the dishonoring of God, to the just grief of his people, to the scandal and reproach of my profession [of faith], and to the wounding of my own soul," she submitted to a still vital process of ecclesiastical surveillance and public shaming.[8] Long after the courts ceased to pay attention, churches continued to demand that their members and those applying for membership confess to premarital sex. Of 200 people owning the baptismal covenant in the church at Groton, Massachusetts, between 1761 and 1775, 66 confessed to having had sex before marriage, as did 9 of the 16 couples admitted to full communion in 1789–91. In Chebacco Parish, Ipswich, applicants for church membership regularly made "sincere apology" for having committed the same offense. The Dedham congregation heard 25 confessions to premarital sex between 1756 and 1781, 14 of them within the latter ten years.[9]

Actual and potential members of New England congregations still underwent painstaking inquisition if suspected of engaging in illicit sex. When Abigail Noyes named Isaac Abbot Jr. as the father of her "bastard" twins in 1754, and again in the following year when John Danforth was accused of having sired Elizabeth Chamberlain's illegitimate child, officials from the South Andover Church subjected the parties involved to detailed questioning: "in private," "before witnesses," and in "church meetings." Abbot was applying for admission; Danforth was already a member. The thorough investigation by church officials of both these allegations must have served as a reminder to the community that sexual relations were still very much a matter of public concern, "under the watch" of the local church. The confessional process was no more perfunctory in the eighteenth century than it had been in the seventeenth. The key criteria for forgiveness were still open acknowledgment of sin and apparently heartfelt repentance. In 1754 John Smith and his wife were excommunicated from the Dorchester church "for committing fornication together before marriage" and because "they being questioned for it before the church did conceal their sin." That same year, William Robinson was excommunicated for "lasciviousness" and, significantly, "his obstinancy in not hearing, the church having before admonished him." But those who atoned for their sins would benefit, like their forebears, from the faith of brethren in the possibility of rehabilitation. Ebenezer Knight, a member of the First Church at Marblehead, Massachusetts, had been suspended from communion in 1732 for his "long series of uncleanness" with other men but was restored to full membership after spending six years in Boston and convincing the membership that he had seen the error of his ways. Why the church finally took action against Knight is unclear, but his expressions of repentance (and perhaps the assuaging effect of an extended absence) brought about his reacceptance into the church community.[10]

Throughout the century, confessions to fornication more often than not took place in the context of an application for church membership by parents who were anxious to have their children baptized. Jeremiah

Ballard Jr. and his wife appeared before New Salem's church in 1754, "made satisfaction for the sin of fornication, owned the covenant, and gave up their child to God in baptism." Congregations were well aware that some parents might deliver insincere avowals of contrition for their children's sake. Mercy Cary, wife of Stephen, had to give "Christian satisfaction for the sin of fornication" and "also for her saying that she had rather confess that she had been guilty of the sin though she was innocent than not have her children baptized." The church members at Groton worried that "less conscientious" applicants for membership who had engaged in premarital sex might be tempted "to belie their consciences" by giving false assurances of repentance, thus "adding sin to sin." They also worried about the difficulty of proving that a baby was conceived prematurely rather than born early. The congregation decided in 1740 that it would no longer require "persons suspected of fornication" to confess in public. The minister would instead encourage them to repent "of all known sins" and to "watch against sins of uncleanness in particular." But the church subsequently reversed its decision, and other congregations remained confident that they could and should ascertain whether couples were telling the truth when they denied that they had sinned or professed contrition.[11]

Couples who refused to confess that they had engaged in premarital sex, claiming that their babies had been born prematurely, could face a thorough investigation. Clerics and congregants generally sought to balance respect for apparently sincere declarations of innocence with a commitment to quasi-judicial rigor. In 1728 Samuel Hardy and his wife approached Ebenezer Parkman, the minister at Westborough, Massachusetts: they "desired baptism for their child, born three days within seven months after the parents' marriage." Parkman asked the church members to "give [him] their minds and make what opposition they would ever offer." One townsman declared that they should withhold judgment until the local court had determined whether or not the birth was premature, but other brethren felt that they had sufficient information before them to reach an independent decision. The mother had been in a "fright," the congregation heard, "occasioning it was believed the hasty birth." The couple submitted, moreover, a "serious declaration that they were innocent," and so the congregation decided that it had no objection to its pastor's baptizing the infant. Parkman, however, met a few days later with the couple to question them further; he also called on the midwife who had delivered the baby and then consulted with colleagues before proceeding with the ceremony.[12]

Forty years later, the congregation at Westborough was still demanding corroborative testimony when couples claimed premature birth and exercising considerable rigor in its investigation of apparent sexual lapses. In 1770 Levi and Deborah Warrin wrote to Parkman about their application to become church members. Some of the brethren were "uneasy" because the couple had "a child born so soon after marriage." The Warrins acknowledged that it was "the duty of every person overtaken in a fault to give glory to God by confessing it," but they refused to admit to an offense that they had not committed ("which we think no Christian can desire"). They rejected the "judgment" of women present at the birth that the child was fully grown, "and that the truth of it may not be scrupled we have taken the pains to get a certification from the doctor that delivered the mother of the child." But they were clearly not optimistic about their chances of winning over the congregation and finished by expressing the "hope" that "being debarred of church privileges will not debar us of an interest in our Lord and sav[ior] Jesus Christ."[13]

Parkman clearly included sexual surveillance in his array of pastoral duties and left townsfolk in no doubt that their sexual lives were his business. In 1747, for example, he visited the home of Eleazer Bellows "to admonish his daughter Charity for her repeated fornications." Although Parkman sometimes informed church members of illicit behavior so that they could proceed with disciplinary hearings, he often dealt with errant brethren in private and informally. Unless a minister kept notes recording his meetings with parishioners and their subject matter, private interventions such as these went unrecorded. Yet they were a crucial part of the regulatory skein that still wove through community life. Parkman was called upon to intervene informally as a moral steward in December 1746 when a sexual crisis intruded unexpectedly into the household of a local family. Joanna Fay of Southborough, "an unmarried young woman," had come to nurse Solomon Woods's wife, who was about to give birth. But on the fourth day of her visit, Fay herself went into labor. Following the birth and almost immediate death of the illegitimate child, Parkman was asked to visit Fay and "accordingly talked with the girl." Fay "seemed penitent but would not tell who was the father of her child." Since the baby was already dead, financial support was not an issue, so Parkman's interest in identifying the man responsible was clearly driven by a desire to provide moral counseling. But Parkman was concerned about the practical as well as spiritual consequences of extramarital birth. In 1754 he secured from Francis Wheeler a written commitment "that the child which might be born of his daughter in Westborough should not be a town charge."[14]

Westborough's pastor worked hard as a private intermediary to reconcile aggrieved parties when disputes arose involving sexual and other offenses, though informal resolution was not always possible. When Abijah Gale, a member of his congregation, was accused of sexually assaulting Isaac Amsden's wife in June 1754, the pastor visited both families to attempt "a reconcilement," but he was unsuccessful. That September, Parkman was summoned to court as a witness. He was evidently uncomfortable in that role, pointing out to the court that he knew "no otherwise than by report and conversation as any other neighbors might do." He had expected to attend only "to hear the cause (being Mr. Gale's pastor)" and to testify to his "unblemished reputation till this affair." Parkman declined to repeat his conversation with Mistress Amsden ("I could not think it fit or just for me to utter what was so brokenly and imperfectly remembered"), though under pressure he did testify that what she said then "did not carry the matter so far as the complaint she has made upon oath." After the court found Gale guilty of assault, Parkman secured "reconcilement" between Gale and the Westborough congregation. Gale had been told "to stay away from communion till the cause can be heard." That November his "acknowledgement of acting foolishly and imprudently with the wife of Isaac Amsden" was read and "the church voted satisfaction with what he offered," enabling his restoration to full communion.[15]

New England communities had always looked first to town leaders such as Parkman to solve problems by unofficial intervention; only when such mediations failed did they turn to formal procedures. But during the first half of the eighteenth century, it became increasingly common to handle sexual crises in private, eschewing any external or formal intervention. This shift away from institutional mediation did not result solely from the legal system's reorientation toward commercial and administrative matters. Equally significant was a growing preoccupation with privacy as a desideratum in its own right. Whereas seventeenth-century New England Puritans had resorted frequently and enthusiastically to public shaming as an instrument of moral renewal, their eighteenth-century descendants became increasingly uncomfortable with such exposure and humiliation. As early as 1727, the First Church at Boston agreed that members who were now living "in a distant town" should confess to fornication only "in the place where they at present reside, and so be healed without spreading the report of their fall any further than necessity requires." In midcentury Billerica, a number of members objected to the inclusion of their confessions to premarital sex in the permanent church records. However common premarital pregnancy may have become, at least some couples were concerned about its impact on their reputations and wanted to move on with their lives as discreetly as possible. The pastor responded by erasing the entries.[16]

As the avoidance of exposure became a priority, so the impulse to preserve individual and institutional reputations began to counterbalance other considerations. When John Seccomb, the pastor at Harvard, Massachusetts, was accused of sexual impropriety in 1739, neighboring minister Parkman recommended against having a "council of churches" deal with the matter, "further publishing and spreading the evil, already too great," if "by any good methods they could heal their grievance at home." Two decades later, another clerical sex scandal exemplified similar concerns. In 1756 Stephen Gorton, minister at the Baptist church in New London, Connecticut, was suspended from his position for "unchaste behaviour with his fellow men when in bed with them." Gorton had apparently exhibited his attraction to men "in many instances through a number of years." He had appeared before the New London County Court in 1726 for "hav[ing] lasciviously behaved himself towards sundry men, endeavouring to commit sodomy with them." But the charge had been dismissed for lack of evidence, and it was not until 1756 that the General Meeting of Baptist Churches judged that his "offensive and unchaste behaviour, frequently repeated for a long space of time," necessitated action.[17]

Gorton's congregation initiated proceedings against him only after his activities became a public embarrassment. According to his opponents in 1756, the pastor's interest in men had caused such discomfort that "many" members left "on that account," and the church had "been broken thereby." Yet most of the correspondence relating to this dispute between pastor and congregation addressed not Gorton's exploits but the fact that "rumour, offense, and reproach" arising from them had now reached "distant parts and different churches." The primary concern seems to have been that rumors had "spread abroad in the world." Church elders may well have berated Gorton informally prior to 1756, hoping that he would mend his ways without their having to take formal action, which would cause a public scandal and damage the church. But "rumor, offense, and reproach" spread anyway, rendering obsolete their reasons for avoiding formal censure and making action imperative.[18]

The very notion that men and women should acknowledge their sexual lapses in public settings came increasingly under attack. In 1767 the author of an anonymous letter to the *Connecticut Courant* complained that two young women who had already made "humble" confession to "fornication" in church were now "exposed" in court, their names put on "lasting record" for the "malicious to make use of at pleasure." The correspondent insisted that such cases should be dealt with in private before individual judges. In 1786 a new clause was added to the Massachusetts law "for the punishment of fornication, and for the maintenance of bastard children." Women could now avoid an appearance in court by confessing privately before a justice of the peace and paying a fine. In the latter part of the century, criminal cases in general were delegated more and more to individual justices as the general sessions became preoccupied with administrative and economic issues. Thus, even those incidents of illicit sex still subject to judicial regulation tended to be dealt with in more private settings. New England churches also introduced procedural reforms that enabled sexual transgressors to avoid public humiliation. During the last quarter of the eighteenth century, a series of congregations voted to end public confessions for premarital sex. The First Church at Salem did so in 1779, Dedham in 1781, Cambridge in 1788, Milton in 1789, Sheffield in 1794, Leominster in 1795, Groton in 1803, and Palmer in 1812. In doing so, these churches were not condoning such offenses: they were merely shifting the venue for confession, so that sinners would acknowledge their infractions either before church members in a closed session or in a private meeting with the minister. Even within an ecclesiastical setting, the public exposure of sexual lapses had gone out of fashion.[19]

NEITHER THE LEGAL SYSTEM'S shift in priorities nor increasing sensitivity about issues of privacy should be mistaken for lack of concern about sexual matters on the part of eighteenth-century New Englanders. Nothing could be further from the truth. Families and local communities evinced particular anxiety about the behavior of young people within their purview. Just as Puritans had to grapple in the late 1600s with a maturing generation that had not chosen to settle in New England and did not necessarily identify with godly values, New Englanders in the 1700s faced problems with young people that were also rooted in demographic and cultural change. A shift in practical circumstances and prevailing values brought about a more permissive sexual environment, which in turn became a matter of public and private controversy.

Parental control of young adults and their sexual behavior relied upon effective moral instruction, the bonds of familial affection, deference to parental authority, and also the practical dependence of children upon parents for land as they planned to marry and settle in homes of their own. By the second quarter of the century, it was becoming increasingly difficult for parents to provide children with adequate plots because the land in densely settled communities had been divided and subdivided from generation to generation. Some parents abandoned the principle of partible inheritance that had governed the transmission of property throughout the seventeenth century in New England and gave most or all of their land to the oldest son so as to ensure a viable family property. Sons with no prospect of inheriting land either went into trade or, more often, moved away to settle on cheap and plentiful land further west. These men tended to marry at a younger age, since they had no reason to wait for their fathers to divide and hand over land on which to settle. Household heads also began to settle their oldest sons on land earlier than before, perhaps to match the greater autonomy of younger siblings. Parental authority based on control of inheritable land was thus undermined by population pressure.[20]

Ideological trends reinforced these practical developments. In the educational realm, eighteenth-century advice literature embraced a less authoritarian approach to child-rearing. And in politics, the prerogatives of patriarchal absolutism became less fashionable on both sides of the Atlantic as political theorists laid increasing emphasis upon the rights of the subject. That shift away from unconditional obedience would be dramatized and intensified in New England as elsewhere in British America by the rhetoric of the revolutionary period. The pursuit of individual happiness, a recurring priority in Enlightenment writings, combined with the invocation of liberty by revolutionary leaders to justify youthful insistence upon personal freedom. In the aftermath of Independence, a pastor in Philadelphia complained that young people in his parish were now "insisting on their capacity and right of choosing for themselves," "having no idea of parental authority," and declaring themselves "free and independent."[21]

During the course of the eighteenth century, young people choosing marital partners became less and less inclined to follow their parents' wishes. They now made decisions based primarily upon their own personal and romantic inclinations.[22] One of the ways young adults declared their new sense of independence was by having sex during courtship. They not only married earlier and with less regard to parental opinion, but they also became sexually active prior to marriage in far greater numbers than before. It is surely no coincidence that premarital pregnancy rates rose sharply during this period: as both the reality of filial dependence and its ideological justification weakened, adult children felt at liberty to ignore pressure from parents who wanted them to refrain from sex until after marriage. The rising bridal pregnancy rate is doubtless a conservative indicator of how many betrothed couples were having sex and also of how many sexually active couples conceived prior to marriage. New Englanders were evidently familiar with abortifacients, and some young people undoubtedly chose to use them, especially if an engagement was broken off after conception occurred.[23] The validity of moral conventions that demanded premarital abstinence was now open to question even within the very institution that trained New England's ministers. A student club at Harvard College debated in 1722 "whether it be fornication to lie with one's sweetheart (after contract) before marriage." A 1728 broadside published in Springfield, Massachusetts, blamed a recent earthquake in part on "the notion advanced by some that it is no breach of the seventh commandment for persons that have made private promises to one another to have carnal knowledge of one another, although not joined in marriage."[24]

It is hardly surprising, then, that Ebenezer Parkman worried in his joint capacity as parent and pastor about the flirtatious high jinks of Westborough's rising generation. He noted in September 1739 that a group of young people had "met at a frolick and continued late," to his "great trouble and disquietment." At the raising of the frame for a new meetinghouse in 1749, he observed "the impudence of young men with the young women." Their behavior, he wrote, was "shameless." Parkman fretted about "young people's disorderly night walking," including that of his own children and other young adults living with his family, who ventured out late at night "contrary to the advice and counsel which I am frequently giving them." He inveighed in his sermons "against company keeping and unchastity," warning young people "with respect to unclean practices" and the kinds of "behavior among youth which lead thereto."[25]

Jonathan Edwards, the pastor in Northampton, Massachusetts, perceived a direct link between the decay of "family government" and what he characterized as licentious behavior on the part of young adults. Edwards lamented that the youth of his parish were "many of them very much addicted to night-walking, and frequenting the tavern, and lewd practices, wherein some by their example exceedingly corrupted others." "It was their manner," he wrote, "very frequently to get together in conventions of both sexes, for mirth and jollity, which they called frolics; and they would often spend the greater part of the night in them, without any regard to order in the families they belonged to, and indeed family government did too much fail in the town." In a 1738 sermon, Edwards claimed that "commonly in those towns where most frolicking is carried on, there are the most frequent breakings out of gross sins; fornication in particular." A few years back, he recalled, frolicking had been abandoned as the result of a religious revival, but now that the upsurge in spirituality had passed, "young people of both sexes" were once again "getting together in companies for mirth, and spending the time together till late in the night in their jollity." Edwards urged young people to "avoid not only gross acts of uncleanness, but all degrees of lasciviousness, both in talking and acting." Frolics were particularly dangerous as a likely catalyst for sexual impropriety: "we ought not," he declared, "to go on in a practice that leads and exposes to sin."[26]

A few years later, in 1744, Edwards's fear that "getting together in companies" would lead young people in his parish to commit "all degrees of lasciviousness, both in talking and acting," was vindicated when he discovered that they had been meeting to pore over "immoral books."[27] The volumes in question were gynecological manuals ("books written on the business of midwives"). Rebecca Strong reported that the book she saw contained "pictures" showing "parts of a woman's body." Midwifery books did indeed contain illustrations, along with explicit textual descriptions of the female (and, to a lesser degree, male) genitalia. Many of them also discussed sexual relations, often in graphic detail. Midwifery manuals could serve pornographic as well as gynecological purposes, and the authors of such volumes sometimes expressed concern that their books not "fall into the hands of any obscene or wanton person."[28] These particular volumes were probably purchased for medical purposes and then appropriated by young adults in Northampton who were eager to acquire and then parade the sexual information that such books provided. Young men apparently "made sport of what they read" and "boasted" that "they knew about girls," much to the horror of those who considered such material "exceeding unclean to the top of baseness." John Lancton held forth "uncleanly and lasciviously" on the subject to a group of young women, and when one of them "checked" him, "he laughed." The women agreed with each other "after he was gone" that they had "never heard any such talk come out of any man's mouth whatsoever." It seemed "almost as bad as tongue could express." But enthusiasts spoke of a manual that they had perused as the "young folks' bible," a striking testimonial to its authority in their minds and also its subversive potential.[29]

When Edwards heard about this alternative "bible" and its devotees among the young people of Northampton, he responded rather tactlessly. He launched an investigation, gathered detailed testimony, and denounced from the pulpit not only those who had read aloud from the books but also all those present at such readings. His public condemnation of the young people concerned cost him the support of several influential families in the town and was a contributing, if not crucial, factor in his dismissal from the Northampton pastorate in 1749. But however angered parents may have been by the open humiliation of their children, at least some of them doubtless shared their minister's dismayed response to this latest example of youthful license. Parents who fretted about their increasing inability to contain the sexual curiosity of teenage and adult offspring might well encourage pastors such as Edwards to counsel and discipline errant young people, albeit discreetly. Local ministers were, after all, their natural allies in such an enterprise.

Yet the credibility and trustworthiness of ministers as guardians of sexual morality came into question during that same period as a result of the scandals and vicious insinuations that accompanied a wave of religious revivals sweeping through New England, referred to by historians as the Great Awakening. Evangelical ministers such as Jonathan Edwards forsook their regular parishes and toured from community to community, seeking to reawaken New England spirituality from what they characterized as "great decay and deadness." They brought about a chain of mass conversions during which "the operation of the divine spirit" provoked frenzied grief followed by paroxysms of joy as converts experienced first the full horror of their depravity and then "sweet tastes of redeeming love." Critics condemned the "ungoverned passions" and "disorderly tumults" that erupted during these meetings. "Indecent behaviors" that struck hostile observers as at least implicitly erotic in nature combined with a number of sex scandals on the fringe of the movement to besmirch not only the revivals themselves but also the reputation of preachers associated with them.[30]

Evangelical ministers clearly did not intend to be sexually permissive. They attacked not only the alleged "deadness" of early-eighteenth-century spirituality but also what they saw as an increasingly licentious and immoral society. Yet according to their opponents, revivalists fostered, whether wittingly or not, the very culture of immorality that they claimed to abhor. The outpouring of emotion at revival meetings (accompanied by screaming and moaning, writhing, swooning, and "strange unusual bodily motions") was seen by some observers as both indecent in its own right and conducive to other forms of unbridled behavior. Antirevivalist Charles Chauncy hinted darkly of the "gross disorders" to which this "commotion in the passions" gave rise; William Douglas, a Boston deist, accused George Whitefield of promoting "wantonness between the sexes" by encouraging converts to embrace each other at revival meetings. Anglican Timothy Cutler passed on to the Bishop of London a damning account of sexual frenzy intertwined with evangelical ardor that he claimed to have received from Samuel Johnson, the pastor at Stratford, Connecticut. According to Johnson, Cutler wrote, the revivalist "humor" in that town began "with an old whimsical maid, crazed with love for a young man." Her unrequited passion caused her to "turn towards this imaginary religion, and set her to crying for she knew not what." Two of the "four or five young women" taken with "the humor" in Johnson's parish "married soon after these religious raptures, and had each of them a child in six or seven months."[31] Whether or not the basic facts in this account were true, Cutler's implication that revivalism and fornication were intrinsically linked seems dubious as well as tendentious: there was, after all, nothing unusual about bridal pregnancy by the second quarter of the eighteenth century. Nonetheless, Edwards himself warned against "a counterfeit of love" among some of the "wildest enthusiasts" whereby the expression of "Christian love" through "mutual embraces" and "holy kisses" degenerated into "unclean and brutish lust."[32]

Opponents of revivalism claimed that such degeneration did take place and that evangelical ministers themselves engaged in "unclean" practices. Theodorus Jacobus Frelinghuysen, a leading evangelical within the Dutch Reformed Church, was accused of having a sexual relationship with his close associate Jacobus Schuurman, who "often embraced him and kissed him." Their enemies charged that Schuurman had "attempt[ed] scandalous undertakings by night upon the person of more than one man with whom he happened to sleep."[33] Other evangelical ministers were dogged by allegations that they had seduced female devotees and "had bastards in this or that place." The ardent veneration that charismatic itinerants inspired in some of those who came to hear them provided ample grist for vicious rumor mills. Consider the following extravagant tribute to the preaching of Andrew Croswell, penned by Sarah Parsons Moorhead:

> My soul by you its glorious power has felt,
> My bosom warms all my affections melt:
> I should not think a thousand winters long,
> While Jesus' love sounds sweetly from your tongue.
> Many such times has sovereign love returned:
> By many instruments my heart has burned;
> Then blame me not if I should take the part
> Of all whom God has made to reach my heart.

Moorhead claimed to love and laud Croswell as the emissary and mouthpiece of her savior's love, but there was a fine line between "burn[ing]" for Christ, whose "love sound[ed] sweetly from [Croswell's] tongue," and "burn[ing]" for Croswell himself. Worshipers such as Moorhead may have maintained that distinction, but less generous observers feared the worst. A woman who followed Whitefield's retinue from town to town declared that "she wanted nothing but Christ, and Christ she would have," yet it was Whitefield to whom she had attached herself. It is perhaps not surprising that critics, green with envy as itinerants performed before thousands of adoring fans, should have accused them of exploiting their almost cultic status.[34]

Evangelists revived and deployed with dramatic effect the rhetoric of sensualized spirituality so popular among the previous generation of Puritan ministers (a rhetoric increasingly eschewed by other New England pastors as they shifted their focus from passionate to more rational aspects of faith).[35] Edwards compared "the union between a faithful minister and a Christian people" to "that between a young man and virgin in their marriage." That pastoral union prefigured the ultimate marriage between Christ and his church, which Edwards characterized in passionately romantic and erotic language. The feminized faithful would be "offered up to him in the flame of love," their union "most tender and ardent." The savior would "give her his loves; and she shall drink her fill, yea, she shall swim in the ocean of his love." Edwards quoted lavishly from Canticles 4: "Thou hast ravished my heart, my sister, my spouse; thou hast ravished my heart with one of thine eyes, with one chain of thy neck . . . How fair is thy love, my sister, my spouse! how much better is thy love than wine! . . . Thy lips, O my spouse, drop as the honeycomb: honey and milk are under thy tongue." Edwards stressed that the union between a minister and his congregants was a mere "shadow" of that between Christ and the saints, and that it was a pastor's duty "not only to espouse the church to her husband, but to present her a chaste virgin to Christ." Yet his use of sensual, even torrid, imagery to describe spiritual marriage in a sermon ostensibly discussing the union between a minister and his flock must have had a powerful impact on his audience, particularly given his own widely recognized charisma. Such rhetoric was, of course, open to misconstruction.[36]

The relationship between spiritual and human marriage became a crucial and highly controversial issue for a group on the fringe of the revivals, known as the Perfectionists or Immortalists. Perfectionists believed that conversion freed them from the external dictates of law and social convention, in place of which they could rely upon inner direction provided by the Holy Spirit. Members of this group argued that they could set aside unawakened husbands or wives in favor of partners whom they identified, through the power of the Holy Spirit, as their spiritual soul mates. They used 2 Corinthians 6:14 ("Be ye not unequally yoked together with unbelievers") to justify doing so. Those who entered into soul marriages with fellow believers claimed that their relationships were purely spiritual, but others had their doubts.

In at least some cases, that skepticism proved well founded. At the end of the 1740s in Cumberland, Rhode Island, Ebenezer Ward permitted his daughter Molly to live with Solomon Finney while her husband, Joseph Bennet, was away at sea. Ward apparently told Molly that "it was sinful for her to cohabit" with Bennet because he was "unconverted." Her new relationship was supposedly a spiritual marriage: neighbor Samuel Bartlett heard Molly say "that Solomon Finney and she was man and wife internally but not externally . . . they was man and wife in the sight of the Lord and it was made known to them that it was so." The soul mates promised Ebenezer Ward that they would sleep with a Bible between them, but neither the physical impediment nor its contents seem to have been effective in restraining them. Molly became pregnant by Finney, and Joseph Bennet, who returned from sea to find his wife living with another man, obtained a divorce in 1749 on grounds of adulterous cohabitation.[37] A few weeks later, the General Assembly of Rhode Island passed a law "against adultery, polygamy, and unlawfully marrying persons; and for the relief of such persons as are injured by the breach of marriage covenants." This appears to have been a direct response to the practice of spiritual marriage, which had just been exposed as a good deal less exclusively spiritual than its advocates claimed.[38]

The scandal surrounding Ward and Finney was not an isolated incident. According to Isaac Backus, kindred spirits in the neighboring communities of Easton, Norton, Attleborough, and Taunton also acted on their belief that they could reject "legal bonds" in order "to take their true mate, if they saw who it was." Once they had been baptized, wrote Backus, "parting from their lawful husbands and wives, and taking of others, immediately followed; until some bastard children were born among them, with many other abominations." In 1747 Ebenezer Parkman visited the minister at Grafton, Solomon Prentice, whose wife had declared herself a "Separate" after falling under the influence of an Immortalist named Shadrach Ireland. Rumor had it that she "used to lie with Ireland as her spiritual husband." Parkman warned Prentice's wife against "giving occasion to others to suspect criminal freedoms with the other sex under the splendid guise of spiritual love and friendship." She denied any impropriety, and Prentice stood by his wife when rumors began to circulate about her beliefs and behavior. His congregation dismissed him, however, and the family had to leave town.[39]

Revivalists were well aware that allegations of promiscuity against those on the extreme fringe of their movement endangered the reputation of evangelicals in general. Enemies such as Charles Chauncy claimed that "many" had "fancied themselves acting by immediate warrant from heaven" while "committing the most undoubted wickedness" and that there was "scarce anything so wild, either in speculation or practice, but they ha[d] given in to it." Evangelical churches tried to restrain members from behavior that might fuel such attacks. In 1751 a council of Separate churches investigated Ebenezer Titus for "promiscuous dancing of men and women and kissing his wife—not in token of her being his wife but in token of his fellowship with another man in his wanton dancing with her."[40] The Baptist congregation in New London, Connecticut, may have been particularly sensitive to "rumor" and "reproach" caused by Stephen Gorton's "unchaste behavior" because of the damaging insinuations as well as actual scandals by which evangelical churches were already burdened. The gossip that "spread abroad in the world" may well have sought to reinforce the association between evangelicals and sexual license. Its primary purpose may have been broadly political rather than to attack Gorton personally.

However damaging sexual scandals may have been to individual congregations and their ministers, they do not seem to have had an immediate impact on the credibility of sexual regulation by New England churches. The surge in confessions to premarital sex by applicants for membership during the middle decades of the eighteenth century bespoke widespread conviction that such matters still came under the legitimate purview of church congregations. Evangelical churches may have encouraged these rituals of sexual cleansing in order to compensate for allegations of sexual license directed against them by their enemies. But many families were already loath to air embarrassing lapses in a public setting; the vicious use of alleged improprieties to besmirch the reputation of evangelical preachers may have reinforced the growing tendency on the part of New Englanders to deal with sexual crises as discreetly as possible within their own homes and neighborhoods to avoid public scandal and opprobrium. The tawdry ruckus that surrounded the Great Awakening quite possibly encouraged a long-term shift toward informal and privatized sexual regulation as families and communities developed new ways of policing and protecting their members.

THAT NEW ENGLANDERS were increasingly eager to avoid exposure in a public venue does not mean that an earlier commitment to sexual surveillance and regulation had dissipated. It is surely no coincidence that townsfolk began using extralegal shaming rituals to disgrace adulterers and wife-beaters in the middle decades of the eighteenth century, just as the courts retreated from moral regulation. By riding malefactors around town on a rail in a raucous procession or otherwise humiliating them in public, local residents punished individual offenders and reasserted the standards of behavior that they had violated. Some transgressors were whipped, a clear assumption of punitive rights previously exercised by the courts. That most of the individuals subjected to these processions of ridicule were men indicates that New Englanders were not willing to let a decline in judicial watchfulness translate into male impunity for moral infractions. A similar spirit of informal surveillance and intervention characterized attitudes toward unwed fathers.[41]

As a growing proportion of young couples became sexually intimate and conceived children prior to marriage, relatives and neighbors sought to ensure that the men concerned either married their pregnant girlfriends or at least provided for the children that resulted from out-of-wedlock intercourse. Some of these couples had every intention of marrying, so that there was no need to exert pressure. But engagements could turn sour and suitors could prove fickle. Greater sexual freedom brought with it significant risk, especially for young women who might agree to have sex in expectation of marriage and then find themselves abandoned by their lovers. In order to ensure that unwed fathers were held accountable, it was essential that people other than the lovers themselves know that they had been involved with each other. If couples were forced to find secret venues in which to have sex, families and neighbors would have to rely on rumor and guesswork in figuring out who had impregnated their daughters. But if parents accommodated the personal freedom that young adults now clearly asserted by condoning physical intimacy and allowing it to occur within their homes, they would be much better able to protect pregnant daughters, should the need arise.

By the middle of the eighteenth century, it was increasingly common for courting couples to spend the night together under the auspices of parents, other relatives, or neighbors. Some did so on condition that they would remain at least partly clothed, a practice known as bundling; older adults apparently hoped that remaining at least partially dressed would inhibit the couple from engaging in actual intercourse.[42] Given the challenges of traveling home late at night, especially in bad weather along primitive roads, allowing suitors to stay overnight may have represented innocent hospitality in some instances. But the high incidence of premarital pregnancy suggests that many such sojourns were far from innocent and that sartorial restraints were often ineffective. However, if the couple did conceive, the parents would know who was responsible and could pressure the father to marry or at least support the mother. Permissive courtship functioned for the families concerned as a pragmatic accommodation between the greater sexual freedom that young people now enjoyed and the desire of parents to maintain protective surveillance over their children.

Allowing people who were unmarried to sleep together would not have seemed anomalous to colonists. Because of the lack of space and beds in most homes, eighteenth-century Americans were quite accustomed to sleeping with relatives, friends, and even strangers. It was not unusual for travelers to share beds even with single young women who lived in the household that was providing them with lodging; the women remained at least partially clothed, and some accounts by European travelers suggest that locals referred to this also as bundling.[43] But contemporaries understood that bundling as courtship was a distinct phenomenon. Europeans who traveled through North America during the second half of the century often noted its widespread use in the northern and middle colonies. Andrew Burnaby, a young Englishman who toured Massachusetts in 1759–60, wrote about the custom: "At their usual time the old couple retire to bed, leaving the young ones to settle matters as they can, who, after having sat up as long as they think proper, get into bed together also, but without pulling off their undergarments, in order to prevent scandal." Visitors were amazed by the openness with which young men and women spent the night together. "I have entered several bedchambers," wrote Alexandre Berthier, "where I have found bundling couples, who are not disturbed and continue to give each other all the honest tokens of their love." Johann Schoepf, who toured the region in 1783–84, assured his readers that "the young woman's good name [was] no ways impaired" by such nocturnal intimacies. Visits took place neither "by stealth" nor only after the young couple was "actually betrothed": "on the contrary, the parents are advised, and these meetings happen when the pair is enamored and merely wish to know each other better." Schoepf was not the only traveler to report that young people spent the night together after brief acquaintance. Luigi Castiglioni, who traveled through the United States in 1785–87, found himself in company with a fellow who had just spent the night with a young woman "after having courted her not more than six hours." He also claimed that overnight visits cast "no shadow upon the character of the girl."[44]

Most eighteenth-century commentators who mentioned bundling portrayed the custom as predominantly rural and used primarily by "the lower people."[45] In matters of courtship, argued John Adams, "persons of rank and figure" had something to learn from their social inferiors. Condemning the "prevailing practice" within New England's elite of "concealing" young women "from all males till a formal courtship is opened," he pointed out that bundling enabled suitors to test their compatibility with potential wives without risking either their own or their sweethearts' reputation. In a 1761 essay, written during his own courtship of Abigail Smith, Adams recommended that young ladies "associate . . . in some good degree, and under certain guards and restraints, even privately with young fellows." In Adams's opinion, the custom benefited both parties. "Though discretion must be used, and caution, yet on [considering] the whole of the arguments on each side, I cannot wholly disapprove of bundling."[46]

The journal kept by Abner Sanger, a young farmer in late-eighteenth-century Keene, New Hampshire, confirms that all-night courting was common. Sanger made frequent references to nocturnal visits by himself and other young men. He called the practice "staying with" or "girling of it." Some of these meetings took place in the context of an ongoing courtship that led to marriage, but others seem to have been casual or perhaps a preliminary exploration of intimacy that might or might not lead to more serious involvement. One July afternoon in 1780 Joseph Reed and Zadock Dodge were "plowing among corn" when Susanna Wyman, Grate Willard, and Hephzibah Crossfield arrived to pick currants. Reed and Dodge abandoned their task in order to flirt with the three women and ended up spending the night at Major Willard's house with Grate Willard and Crossfield. The next day, Joseph gave Sanger "an account of his and Dodge's girling of it at Major Willard's and of Dodge's being over-come by the fatigue of the last night with Hephzibah." They now finished the plowing, but Reed was apparently "dumpish" and Dodge "asleep." Sanger made no mention of these pairings being repeated; neither resulted in serious courtship or marriage.[47]

"Girling of it" seems to have provided Keene townsfolk with regu-lar and titillating material for gossip. On 24 August 1782 Sanger noted: "Captain Benjamin Ellis passes twice to Ash Swamp and back again. He coddles Rachel Morse as he goes backward and forward as is storied at Bailey's." But there is no suggestion in Sanger's journal that those who "stayed with" each other were secretive about the practice or that it caused much controversy in the town. Esther Scovill and Sanger did have a confrontation in August 1782 because he was "staying with" two women that summer, Poll Bailey and Rachel Morse. But whether Scovill was "mad" because Sanger was visiting two women at once, or because she disapproved of the practice altogether, or because she wanted him to "stay with" her is not clear.[48] Sanger sounded a disapproving note only when recording the nocturnal visits of his rivals for the attention of par-ticular Keene women. The young man launched a series of unsuccessful courtships in the late 1770s and early 1780s before finally marrying in 1784. He watched with resentful fascination as more successful suitors paraded quite openly in and out of nearby bedchambers, in some cases "staying with" the women he had been pursuing.

Sanger was particularly obsessed by the antics of Ebenezer Bragg with Abigail Washburn and of Prentice Willard with Hephzibah Crossfield, each "girling of it" with gusto. The thwarted Sanger nicknamed Willard "Lord Bugger" and "Lord Debauche," making snide comments in his journal about "fucksters" and "Lord Bugger's manoeuvers." But this was clearly the voice of envy, not of opposition on principle to such "manoeuvers." Sanger referred to Bragg as "Unction" and maintained a jealous surveillance over the comings and goings of the dandified suitor, "fire red in an old red, threadbare coat, a shining ribbon and loop on his hat." Sanger was a dedicated voyeur:

> I spy Unction before sunrise coming from old Mr. Washburn's very gaily dressed.

> By and by I spy Unction to full satisfaction that he has been with Nabby Washburn all night.

> I spy Unction dressing himself in Thomas Field's bedroom [Field, a blacksmith, was married to Mary Bragg] to go and see Abigail Washburn. After he went off I soon discover a light [in] Washburn's chamber.

Bragg's all-night visits began in February 1779 and continued until his marriage to Washburn in October 1780; he had been "staying with" her for over a year when they announced their intention to marry in May 1780. The degree of intimacy enjoyed during these nocturnal meetings must have varied from one couple to the next. Abigail Washburn was not pregnant when she married, but given the premarital pregnancy rate of between 30 and 40 percent for late-eighteenth-century New England, at least some "girling of it" must have involved sexual intercourse. Sanger himself imagined Bragg and Washburn "in great delight," and Joseph Reed had reported that Zadock Dodge was "overcome by the fatigue" due to his night with the same woman.[49]

Contemporaries may have perceived overnight visits as an extension of the easygoing sociability that enabled young people to spend time together, sometimes with and sometimes without older relatives or neighbors in attendance. Thomas Anburey, a lieutenant in the British army, noted that "young folks" were "accustomed to go afrolicking" in late-eighteenth-century New England, setting off in the evening to "dance and carouse" in groups of "thirty or forty" without adult supervision (a practice that, he averred, "would be esteemed extremely imprudent" back in England). Venues for "frolicking" included work-related gatherings such as quiltings and huskings, parties to celebrate elections or other significant occasions, and excursions for snowballing and sleighing. Martha Ballard of Hallowell, Maine, worried when her "young folk," who had gone off to a husking and quilting, "came home late." On another occasion, she noted, they went sleigh riding and did not return home until after midnight. And then there were spontaneous get-togethers: it was not unusual for Sanger to visit one of his neighbors on an errand and then stay for several hours chatting and sometimes doubtless flirting with daughters, servants, and other young women who happened to be working indoors.[50]

In considering the ease with which young adults in towns such as Keene slipped in and out of sexual liaisons, we need to bear in mind the relaxed physicality that characterized day-to-day interactions between unmarried men and women in New England at that time. David Shepard's diary reveals a young man who could mix comfortably and playfully with the women around him. Born in 1777, Shepard was living with his parents on their farm in Chester, Massachusetts, as the century drew to a close. Shepard spent many unsupervised hours with female friends and relatives, lounging in the bedchambers of various houses in town, merrily gossiping and flirting. One diary entry mentioned his sitting upstairs in a chamber with his sisters, his cousin Polly, and neighbor Melinda, "talking of girls and fellows keeping company, etc." Another recorded his "tumbling cousin Lucy's bed and chatting with her." Cousin Polly was his "confidential friend," and they talked tête-à-tête for hours on end, sometimes sitting together on a bed and sometimes with Polly perched on his lap. They were clearly fond of each other, and neither seems to have felt any need to maintain physical distance. It is striking that David and Polly were allowed to spend so much time alone together. Such familiarities were rife with possibilities for offense and dispute. Shepard's delight in "playing with cousin P" sometimes went too far, becoming at least implicitly sexual and making Polly uncomfortable (even he described his behavior around her as "hairbrained" and "giddy"). On one occasion, he "pull[ed] her on the bed till she was almost affronted," and on another, after getting into bed with Polly and his sister, he "spent a few minutes in hugging and kissing the former, while the latter was scolding at me." On the whole, however, their physical intimacy failed to raise hackles, because it was apparently quite normal.[51]

However much Shepard may have enjoyed his coltish friendship with cousin Polly, the young man focused his romantic energies on neighbor Ellen Savage. With Ellen he also developed a close and physically affectionate relationship. David relished "hugging, talking to, and sometimes kissing my sweet girl." When he walked her home at night, they would often find "the little bedroom empty and a good fire," beside which they "spent the evening sweetly." Ellen's family was evidently making an effort to provide the young couple with some measure of privacy (he called the bedroom "our little room"). As their courtship became more serious, David wanted to advance from "kissing" and "hugging" to more explicitly sexual forms of congress. In June 1798, a few days after his twenty-first birthday, he "began to use some endeavors to get her in the bed" with him, but his efforts were "fruitless." Two months later, he "made a further trial," but "found her inflexible." On both occasions, he wrote that he respected her refusal and "prized her the more," but he was clearly disappointed.[52]

Negotiating the degree of physical intimacy that would occur within a premarital relationship could give rise to tension and manipulation. Elihu Ashley, a medical student living with Dr. William Williams in Deerfield, Massachusetts, kept a diary for 1774 in which he recorded his courtship of another Polly, who lived next door. The two young people were able to spend a good deal of time alone together, apparently with Williams's blessing, not only in the kitchen but also in Elihu's garret.

> About eleven I came home, spent my time in writing till dinner, after which I came into the garret. About three Polly came up. She tarried till five with me, was very sociable.

> The company broke up about eleven. After they were gone, supper being over, I took Polly and went into the kitchen and sat up till two — a very fine evening we had.

That fall, Elihu and Polly discussed the possibility of "our being married." Elihu evidently saw that prospect as justification for sexual intimacy. But Polly, although very "sociable" when alone with him, wanted to wait until after they were wed. On one occasion, when Polly complained that "something always happened" when they spent time alone together, Elihu threatened to "throw the courtship up," to which Polly replied that "we had better put an end to it by marrying." It is not clear whether Elihu and Polly did ever spend the night together (on one occasion Ashley wrote that they "retired to bed," but did not specify whether it was together). Ashley left Deerfield without marrying Polly.[53]

While couples such as these quarreled over whether they should have sex during courtship, New Englanders in general debated whether physical intimacy prior to marriage was defensible on moral or practical grounds. That ministers denounced permissive courtship is hardly surprising, since it raised issues not only of sexual morality but also of parental stewardship, which New England pastors had long portrayed as a bulwark of piety and order. In 1738 Jonathan Edwards drew his congregation's attention to "certain customs, too common among young people," in particular the custom of "young people of different sexes reclining together." The "custom" was apparently unexceptionable in many people's eyes, but, declared Edwards, "however little is made of it, and however ready persons may be to laugh at its being condemned," it was nevertheless "one of those things that lead and expose to sin" and "one main thing that has led to the growth of uncleanness in the land." Edwards condemned the practice, furthermore, as "violating all family order," implying that parents who condoned or failed to prevent such behavior were failing in their responsibility to maintain discipline and moral standards within their households. Samuel Hopkins, speaking in 1753, "cautioned" parents and their children on the same subject in a sermon attacking "youthful lusts" and "all those things which have any tendency and lead to the gratification of lust," which included "unseasonable company-keeping" and "lying on the bed of any man with young women." Hopkins averred that "if women had suitable regard to their virtue and honor, they would not do it." There was, he declared, a clear "need of this caution and warning at this day, when the acts of uncleanness are in so many instances visible." [54]

Pastors sought to combat the "wicked practice" not only in general pronouncements but also in private confrontations with individual offenders. Ebenezer Parkman awoke one morning in lodgings at Upton to "the silent sight of a young fellow in the room getting up from his girl in the other bed in the same room with us." Parkman was taken aback as much by their "astonishing boldness and impudence" as by their "unchastity." He and his traveling companions gave the woman "a brief lecture" before she left but "kept the matter from the parents for the time," perhaps hoping that their words of admonition would effect a change of behavior. [55] The parents of this particular couple may not have approved of their spending the night together. Pastors could sometimes rely on townsfolk to join them in condemning the custom and its practitioners. In 1742 Joseph Tucker had to defend himself in a church meeting at Canton against the allegation that he and Susannah Pelton had been seen "early in the morning in bed together, covered with bedding," if true "a thing of no good report." During the 1750s, several New England towns tried to prohibit the practice, doubtless with the encouragement and support of local ministers. But overnight courtship and bundling were becoming firmly embedded in popular culture and enjoyed considerable support.[56]

Rival positions in the controversy over bundling were voiced in popular verses and songs that blended bitter invective with wry humor and revealing social commentary. Not surprisingly, some opponents of the practice claimed that it was irreligious and that those who bundled would pay with their souls:

> Down deep in hell there let them dwell,
> And bundle on that bed;
> There burn and roll without control,
> Till all their lusts are fed.

But another ditty, in defense of bundling, questioned where these critics found biblical justification for their fulminations:

> In Genesis no knowledge is
> Of this thing to be got,
> Whether young men did bundle then,
> Or whether they did not.

> The sacred book says wives they took,
> It don't say how they courted,
> Whether they in bed did lay,
> Or by the fire courted.

As yet another song recognized, those pastors who took a stand on the issue risked alienating their congregants, many of whom saw nothing wrong with young people spending the night together:

> Dissatisfaction great appeared,
> In several places where they've heard
> Their preacher's bold, aloud disclaim
> That bundling is a burning shame.

Clerical tirades against "courting in a bed of love" could prove counterproductive, since those who disagreed were likely to respond with equally "bold" voice and indeed "justified the custom more than e'er was known or heard before."[57]

Most of the poems and songs that condemned or defended bundling focused on practical rather than spiritual issues, debating whether or not it really prevented young lovers from having sex during nocturnal visits.

Opponents of the custom argued that physical proximity would draw couples into behavior from which they might otherwise refrain. "Seized in some lover's arms," many a young woman had "grown weak with Cupid's heat and lost her virgin charms." Clothing alone, they insisted, would not deter "unruly horses" determined to "push the fence."[58] Apologists countered that bundlers were no more likely to have sex than lovers who met under other circumstances. The determining factor would always be whether the men and women concerned were able or willing to restrain themselves:

> Let coat and shift be turned adrift,
> And breeches take their flight,
> An honest man and virgin can
> Lie quiet all the night.

> But if there be dishonesty
> Implanted in the mind,
> Breeches nor smocks, nor scarce padlocks
> The rage of lust can bind.

This song pointed out that "bastards" were "not at all times got in feather beds." The rhymester continued, "Perhaps there's more got on the floor than any other way."[59]

The fundamental issue underlying the controversy over bundling was not whether sex should be regulated but whether that regulatory impulse should seek to prevent or merely to monitor premarital intimacy between young people. Lovers who had sex "on the floor" were probably doing so in secret, whereas those who conceived "in feather beds" were more likely to be meeting with parental knowledge. The latter could be held accountable and so were more likely to marry. An opponent of bundling averred that it was a "great source of matches undesigned" and that such matches were more likely to be shadowed by "quarrels and strife." But without this sanctioned and supervised "course," women who became "undesigned[ly]" pregnant were more likely to be abandoned by irresponsible male lovers.[60]

Some parents doubtless tolerated nocturnal courtship only grudgingly. But others did so wholeheartedly. According to a song that appeared in a 1785 almanac, mothers were notably supportive of the custom:

> Some mothers too will plead their cause,
> And give their daughters great applause,

And tell them, 'tis no sin or shame,
For we, your mothers, did the same;
We hope the custom ne'er will alter,
But wish its enemies a halter.

Mothers may have been especially aware that a more permissive sexual environment left young women vulnerable to unwed pregnancy and abandonment. Some may have hoped that bundling would prevent nocturnal courtship from becoming overtly sexual; others who were less anxious to prevent premarital sex may nonetheless have realized that they could much more effectively demand satisfaction from a daughter's lover if pregnancy arose from relations about which they knew because they occurred within their homes.[61]

PARENTAL SANCTIONING OF nocturnal courtship epitomized both the relaxation of restraints upon young people in eighteenth-century New England and the continued surveillance of their behavior. Those who conceded the likelihood that couples would become sexually active prior to marriage and who allowed such relations to take place under their supervision were much better placed to keep an eye on their children, know with whom they were intimate, and protect daughters from the possibility of abandonment by exerting pressure upon their lovers to behave honorably in the event of a pregnancy. As we are about to see, most families that found themselves in this situation were able to maneuver unmarried fathers into wedlock or child support settlements without formal intervention by the courts. But the judicial system was not irrelevant to their successful insistence upon paternal accountability. Unwed mothers and their families in the late 1700s could and did threaten paternity suits in order to rein in men who were reluctant to take responsibility for their offspring. Legal action proved highly effective as a prospective means of retaliation that could be used to intimidate and corral wayward fathers.

Official court records might give the impression that responses to unwed pregnancy in the late eighteenth century enacted a double standard in favor of men. County courts continued to hear fornication cases involving out-of-wedlock births, but almost all of those prosecuted were women. Of the eighty-three individuals prosecuted for fornication in Lincoln County, Maine, between 1761 and 1785, only ten were male. Seventeenth-century courts had generally held men and women equally accountable for "bastard" offspring, but toward the end of that century, unwed fathers had sought in increasing numbers to evade liability by fleeing justice or contesting allegations of paternity. As a growing proportion of accused men refused to confess, unwed mothers faced the considerable challenge of proving their allegations. That challenge became greater as the courts sought to adhere more closely to English legal procedures and evidentiary standards. Whereas most seventeenth-century courts had been willing to accept a woman's word against the man whom she named as the father, by the early eighteenth century the courts required corroborative testimony. Only half of the women prosecuted for fornication in eighteenth-century Essex County formally accused a man of fathering the child in order to secure paternity support. It would seem that fornication was now seen as a woman's crime and that men who sired out-of-wedlock children were rarely held accountable for their actions.[62]

Such an impression would be misleading. The preponderance of women among those prosecuted for fornication in the late 1700s by no means represented a consistent pattern of male impunity. Young women who found themselves pregnant out of wedlock sometimes voluntarily confessed to fornication as the first step toward accusing their lovers of paternity and securing either marriage or financial support for the child. This strategy involved acknowledging culpability and undergoing a humiliating confession, whether before an individual judge or in the Court of General Sessions, but unwed mothers evidently thought the price worth paying.[63] There was, of course, no guarantee that accused men would be found guilty, but corroborative evidence was now much more likely to be available, because parents were allowing young unmarried couples to sleep together at home. That it was seldom necessary for such testimony to be produced and recorded by the final decades of the eighteenth century speaks to the effectiveness of preliminary legal pressure. Men who chose to settle out of court and so avoid public embarrassment would never appear in the court records, thus creating a false impression of impunity. In 1794 Mary Crawford of Bath, Maine, confirmed in writing "that Samuel Todd of said Bath hath agreed to make me satisfaction for getting me with child by promising to marry me, therefore, I wish that the prosecution I commenced against him for so doing may be squashed." As a result of this agreement, Samuel Todd did not have to appear in court or the sessions record, but he had "made satisfaction" to the mother of his child; he did not elude accountability.[64]

By and large, New England communities seem to have engineered an orderly progression from sexual intimacy between young adults to male acceptance of responsibility for its consequences, whether in the form of marriage or financial support. More than a third of the first births that Maine midwife Martha Ballard attended between 1785 and 1797 were conceived out of wedlock. But more than three-quarters of these mothers had married by the time they gave birth, either because the couple had committed to marry before they became sexually intimate or because pressure had been exerted on the father to do so, as in the case of Samuel Todd. Out-of-wedlock pregnancies could mire young women and their families in temporary crisis, but most New England women who became pregnant before marriage either wed their lovers or received child support and went on to marry other men.[65]

Communities evidently perceived this process in terms of reining in young males, whence the wry custom in late-eighteenth-century New England of electing all men married in the previous year as hogreeves. These were the local officials responsible for ensuring that hogs were ringed or yoked and prevented from straying onto neighbors' property. The office had become largely redundant as fences had become more ubiquitous and reliable, but it was kept on to serve as a humorous recognition that another batch of young men had been duly bridled. In June 1792 Martha Ballard's son Jonathan was elected as a hogreeve along with six other newly married men in Hallowell, Maine. His bride was Sally Pierce, who had given birth to an illegitimate child the previous October, named Ballard as the father, and then initiated a paternity suit against him. Their marriage took place a month before Ballard was due to appear in court. The suit was canceled, but Ballard's neighbors must have appreciated the irony of his election as a yoker of stray animals.[66]

Matrimony was not the only form that acknowledgment of paternal responsibility could take, but arranging a financial settlement instead involved decoupling sexual relations and reproduction from marriage. Not surprisingly, some New Englanders refused to condone that disconnection. Others were more pragmatic, giving priority to the wishes of the couple and weighing the likelihood of a successful marriage. A controversy that arose over precisely this issue at midcentury illustrates the potential for acrimonious disagreement as individuals, families, and communities chose between different kinds of accountability.[67] In early 1748 Martha Root, an unwed Northampton woman, gave birth to twins and named Elisha Hawley as the father. That May, the county court awarded her 155 pounds "in full satisfaction for and toward the support and maintenance of a bastard child, now living." (The other baby had presumably died.) Elisha was away on military service, so his brother Joseph negotiated with the county court as to the size of the financial settlement. Shortly thereafter, the Northampton church excommunicated Elisha in absentia for refusing to marry Martha. Her father was one of the wealthier householders in Northampton, ranking in the top fourth of the town's taxpayers. But Elisha's family was considerably richer, and he subsequently married Elizabeth Pomeroy, whose father was within the top tenth of taxpayers.[68] The difference in economic standing between the two families may have been an issue in preventing their union. But neither of the lovers wanted to marry. It was the church, not Martha or her family, that was pressing for the couple to do so ("the woman declares against taking you," wrote Joseph, "as also her father and mother"). Martha's family apparently recognized that she and Elisha were personally (perhaps also socially) incompatible and that a financial settlement constituted a satisfactory solution for all concerned. Elisha's family may have been hoping for a more advantageous marital alliance, and they got one, but the Hawleys did recognize the possibility of a private commitment between the lovers that would, on grounds of honor, necessitate a union. Joseph had cautioned his brother in a letter that he should search his conscience and memory as to whether there had been any prior and "binding" agreement "that nobody else knew of." Either there was no such agreement, or neither of the lovers wished to invoke it.

Elisha's excommunication was, of course, an extreme sanction with serious consequences. His family decided to challenge the church's decision, and a council of ministers met in June 1749 to consider the matter. Jonathan Edwards, speaking on behalf of his congregation, conceded that "in some cases" the man might be permitted to "make reparation . . . without marrying the woman." But "moral obligation," "the well being of the society and the nature of things" required that marriage occur "at least in all ordinary cases." The ministers sitting in judgment on this case rejected Edwards's reasoning: although "far from determining that Lieutenant Hawley [was] not bound in conscience to marry Martha Root," they nonetheless decided that "it must be left to the determination of his own conscience." They recommended that he be readmitted as a church member, "upon his making a penitent confession of the sin of fornication." The Northampton congregation had voted to uphold the principle that sexual relations necessarily involved marital obligation. According to their pastor, "the order, decency, and health of society" required that Martha and Elisha become man and wife. The gathered ministers and

Elisha's family took a somewhat different tack, arguing that whether or not a marriage took place should be left to the "conscience" of those involved. However, neither they nor local magistrates absolved Elisha of responsibility for his offspring.

But what of relationships between men and women of markedly different social status that resulted in pregnancy? One might assume that young men who belonged to the upper echelons of colonial society could sow their wild oats with impunity. In 1740 the *Boston Evening Post* reprinted a piece from the *London Magazine* mocking the notion that men of whatever rank who "seduce[d] young girls" should "be obliged to marry them."[69] Whether the newspaper intended to endorse the writer's point of view is unclear, but in practice young men from New England's elite families could be held accountable by female lovers and their families, even if of a much lower social rank. In 1763 Massachusetts lawyer Robert Treat Paine wrote to Justice of the Peace Ephraim Keith on behalf of Keith's son and namesake, who had recently graduated from Harvard and was studying law in Taunton. The young man had become sexually involved with an unnamed woman who became pregnant by him. She had submitted a formal complaint to a local justice as the first step toward a paternity suit. Ephraim junior had apparently "endeavored to settle the matter" (on what terms Paine did not specify), "but in vain, and this afternoon the officer appeared in Taunton Green with his warrant." Paine understood that the complaint was intended to "scare" Ephraim into settling the matter out of court "by some disadvantageous accommodation of the matter." The woman's social status was evidently such that neither the prospective father nor Paine considered her suitable as a wife for an aspiring young lawyer. Ephraim had "conceal[ed] himself" until he could flee the town so as "to avoid the severity of the law" and the "anger of an offended father." Paine had encouraged the young man to stay hidden until he could consult with Ephraim senior about a financial settlement. "Money," he wrote, "answers all ends."

Both Paine and Ephraim junior attempted to make light of the matter by introducing a satiric tone into their prose. "And all," penned the young man, "merely for the peccadillo of begetting my own likeness." Paine wrote to the father: "In short, honest Ephraim, your shamefaced, dutiful son Ephraim, is too handsome. A Dighton girl (heavens screen us from the girls) laid amorous hands on him, as Joseph's mistress did on him, but being more good-natured than Joseph, she saith he did not resist." Ephraim was, nonetheless, clearly terrified by the position in which he found himself, and Paine also understood the gravity of the situation. The pregnant young woman was determined that her lover should take responsibility for "the fruits of love" and so followed what had become standard practice in New England. Ephraim may well have thought that the affair was casual and fancied himself a freewheeling libertine, but he now found himself subject to moral and practical expectations that did not exempt men of status. Ephraim Keith had been pressured successfully by the mother of his child and the local authorities to accept liability for his actions.[70]

Yet extracting an acknowledgment of responsibility often involved a struggle, even when the parties were of roughly equivalent social status. Pregnant women and their families could find themselves pitted against slippery and duplicitous young men. Consider the behavior of Benjamin Gilbert, a junior infantry officer in the Continental Army, who returned to his hometown of Brookfield, Massachusetts, during a three-month leave in early 1782. While on furlough, Gilbert made frequent visits to the home of Colonel James Converse, with whose daughter Patience the young ensign was on intimate terms. That September Gilbert learned that Patience Converse was pregnant and that she had named him as the father. Colonel Converse demanded that Gilbert marry his daughter. The young man replied in a penitential and ingratiating tone, averring that the "misfortunes" afflicting Patience and himself were "just punishments for our unwarrantable practices" and that to "bring a scandal" upon the Converse family was "a crime so capital" that he was "totally at a loss how to atone" for it. His duties with the army prevented him from traveling immediately to Brookfield, but he promised to do so that fall or during the winter so as "to compromise the matter and do justice to [the] person and character of your daughter." In subsequent letters, however, Gilbert tried to foist the blame upon other men in the vicinity. Despite his initial admission, he now claimed "that if no man is more guilty than myself, she has conceived without the seed of man." In March 1783 he informed Colonel Converse that "quitting the field" was still impossible "without relinquishing every idea of honour" as well as "interest" and "expectation of reward for past services."[71]

Contemporaries feared that the code of conduct absorbed by patriot soldiers such as Gilbert was in fact far from honorable. Quite apart from all the talk of liberty that young people could and did apply to aspects of their lives certainly not intended by those who crafted revolutionary ideology, young men who served in the Continental Army were exposed

to opportunities for sexual license that most of them would not have encountered in their own communities. These included access to prostitutes.
In 1782–83, Gilbert and his fellow officers made frequent visits to "the
girls" in a "seraglio" near their encampment at New Windsor.[72] Military
leaders were anxious to insulate their soldiers from "lewd women" and
repeatedly gave orders that no "woman of ill fame" should be allowed
in camp.[73] But this was easier said than done. Gilbert mentioned in his
diary the presence in his tent at night of women who were subsequently
thrown out of the camp. As early as 1777, parents had become reluctant
to let their sons enlist, in part because of the revolutionary army's reputation as a moral cesspool. "The prevalence of dissipation, debauchery,
gambling, profaneness, and blasphemy," wrote John Adams, "terrifies the
best people upon the continent from trusting their sons and other relations among so many dangerous snares and temptations." Gilbert may
have become a rake while away in the service. At the very least, his experiences in and around military encampments would have encouraged
his rakish tendencies. The ideological currents of the revolutionary era,
wartime disruption, and the less savory components of a soldier's education thus contributed to an already transformed sexual climate and may
well have fostered the irresponsibility of unwed fathers such as Gilbert.[74]

But the Converse family had no intention of allowing Gilbert's evasive tactics to succeed. That November, when Gilbert finally arrived back
in Brookfield, he was served with a warrant "on Patience Converse's
account." Gilbert now surrendered. He "rode to Colonel Converse's,"
where he "settled with him and his daughter": "Gave them thirty pounds,
fifteen of which I paid down, the other fifteen to be paid twelve months
from the settlement. I then took a full acquittal from the father and daughter and rode to Colonel Reed's and acknowledged it." Patience subsequently married Nathan Prouty from neighboring Spencer; at the time
of their wedding in late 1784, she was again pregnant. Benjamin Gilbert
married Mary Cornwall of Danbury, Connecticut, in early 1786. The effi-
cacy of informal pressure and legal threats in cases such as this must have
been enhanced by the fact that the pregnant woman's family knew about
the relationship and had observed its progress at close quarters. Transparent relationships were ultimately much safer for the women concerned,
enabling surveillance and protective intervention. What Patience and her
family had feared was that she would be left a single mother without any
man acknowledging responsibility. Marriage to the father or a financial
settlement constituted an acceptable, if not ideal, outcome; both regis-

tered obligation to the mother and thus her comparative respectability. Abandonment would have signified shame.[75]

The Marquis of Chastellux, traveling through Connecticut in November 1780, encountered an example of the latter scenario when he stayed overnight at Dorrance's Tavern in Voluntown (now Sterling Hill). The Dorrances, a "kind and obliging" couple, had five children. The elder of their two daughters, who was around twenty years old, "kept her chamber and did not show herself." Chastellux "learned that she was with child and near her confinement." She had been "deceived by a young man, who after promising to marry her, absented himself and ha[d] not returned." The Frenchman observed that "great care was taken of her," but the "chagrin" of being abandoned, along with "the consequences of her situation," had left the young woman depressed and listless. When Chastellux passed through Voluntown again a few months later in January 1781, he stayed at the same tavern and discovered that the daughter had given birth in the interim. Although the family was "consoling and taking care of her," the young mother was utterly despondent. Her circumstances moved and enraged Chastellux. "May that man," he wrote, "be banished from the bosom of society who is so barbarous as to leave this unlucky girl a prey to a misfortune he is capable of repairing."[76]

This woman's ordeal did have a happy ending. Almost two years later, Chastellux visited Voluntown yet again to find that "her lover had returned, and had married her." He had apparently "expiated all his wrongs," and she appeared to be "perfectly happy." Prior to this turn of events, she at least had relatives who were able and willing to support her, but such was not always the case. Janette Day, another New Englander who bore a child outside wedlock, found herself "helpless, friendless, [and] almost reduced to want." Her sense of self-worth had also been battered: she was "sunk in [her] own opinion" and indeed bereft of "internal satisfaction." Some potential suitors might very well be alienated by a previous sexual history if it resulted in unmarried motherhood and had not been mitigated by some acknowledgment of responsibility on the father's part; the latter provided, after all, not only financial support but also a degree of respectability that abandonment denied. Even those, like Miss Dorrance, who ended up happily married might spend months or years fearing otherwise.[77]

IN EARLY 1783, while trying to evade responsibility for Patience Converse's pregnancy, Benjamin Gilbert had the nerve to lament the perfidy of young men in a letter to his sisters, twenty-two-year-old Esther and seventeenth-year-old Mary: "gallantry and amorous intrigues ha[ve] become so prevalent, [that] (with sorrow I aver it) a great many of your sex are deceived and debauched thereby." Gilbert advised Esther and Mary that "chastity" was "a virtue worthy the pursuit of every noble mind" and indeed "pursued by the female world in general." He made no such claim for the male sex but hoped that his sisters would bear this principle in mind whenever "in danger of being overpowered."[78] Setting aside for a moment the gendered implications of Gilbert's remarks about chastity and virtue, the crucial issue underlying this solicitous letter, as in his negotiations with the Converse household, was abandonment. At the close of the eighteenth century, New Englanders remained committed to an ethos of familial and community stewardship. Yet that ethos, however effective in many cases, could not guarantee the safety of young women who became sexually active prior to marriage. Greater personal freedom gave rise to widespread anxiety about the vulnerability of women who became trusting lovers. Having examined the practical and remarkably pragmatic strategies developed by New Englanders of the 1700s who sought to contain the dangers attendant upon that freedom, we now turn our attention to parallel responses in the literary sphere, most significantly a shift in the gendering of moral virtue. That shift, evident in late-eighteenth-century didactic writings, was designed on the one hand to restrain young women from exercising sexual freedom and on the other to protect them from the personal tragedy of seduction and abandonment.

8

"A Hint to Young Ladies"
Courtship, Sexual Danger, and Moral Agency in Revolutionary America

ON 8 MARCH 1784 THE *Boston Gazette* included a poem entitled "The Forsaken Fair One." This short but vivid piece featured a distraught young woman named Smiletta who confided to her friend Patty that she had been seduced and then cast aside by "a smart young fellow" with "charming face" and "persuasive tongue." He had "promised fair" and she had "believed" him. However, once "the deceiver had [her] virtue stained," he announced "flatly" that "all his ends were gained" and henceforth "shun[ned]" her. Smiletta warned Patty to "trust not mankind: your ruin they pursue, smile to entrap, flatter to undo." Patty agreed that caution was clearly in order:

> Let us, from what is past, this lesson reap,
> That girls should always look before they leap.

Yet that was often easier said than done, given just how charming young men could be. In October 1785 the same newspaper featured another poem, entitled "The Inconstant Swain," in which Silvia lamented her attraction to Damon, "the brightest of all the gay swains." This "bewitchingly sweet" fellow was notorious for his "falseness," and she found herself torn between desire and distrust:

> His speeches, like poison, thrill through all my veins,
> And much I'm inclined to believe.
> Ah, Silvia, beware, for thy lover but feigns,
> His pleasure is still to deceive.

Silvia felt that her situation was "wretched" whether or not she gave way: "refusing or granting I die."[1]

A HINT TO YOUNG LADIES

During the second half of the eighteenth century, scores of "moral tales" and didactic essays that appeared in magazines, newspapers, and almanacs dwelt upon the dangers facing young white women who became sexually active before marriage. According to these pieces, even seemingly devoted suitors could turn out to be cads of the deepest dye who took their pleasure and then deserted their lovers, leaving them to bear the consequences. Moralists warned that an unwed mother whose lover abandoned her faced social ruin, her reputation and marital prospects shattered. Short stories, melodramatic poems, and more expansive narratives in contemporary novels depicted pregnant women fleeing their homes and communities in shame, sometimes forced to leave by parents who condemned and disowned them; outcast and destitute, they ended their broken lives as penniless vagrants, sometimes completing their degradation by turning to prostitution. "Every town and village," declared an essay in the *Massachusetts Magazine* for November 1791, "affords some instance of a ruined female, who has fallen from the heights of purity to the lowest grade of humanity."[2]

In chapter 7 we observed New England communities seeking to ensure that pregnant women were not deserted by irresponsible or unscrupulous lovers. As young people availed themselves of greater sexual freedom, eighteenth-century parents developed strategies for preventing the abuse of that liberty. Indeed, the relatives and neighbors of unwed mothers often succeeded in pressuring young men to take responsibility for children that they sired during courtship, whether by marriage or financial provision. But there were no guarantees that surveillance and stewardship of physical intimacy between young people would always protect women from abandonment; some men simply disappeared once they had had their way with women who believed that their suitors were committed to them. It is extremely difficult to tell how many young women were in fact "ruined" because they surrendered their chastity to men who then deserted them. But it is clear that the possibility of abandonment had given rise to profound and widespread anxiety that was not limited to New England.[3] Seduction literature reflected and responded to that anxiety. As rising literacy rates among both women and men in eighteenth-century North America created a much broader reading public, and as the proliferation of lending libraries enabled less affluent readers to obtain publications that they could not have afforded to purchase, the wide-ranging discussion of courtship, sexual danger, and moral responsibility that now took place in printed matter could reach out and

265

engage a new social class of readers, including a much enlarged constituency of women.[4]

Most contributors to seduction literature were avowedly sympathetic toward deserted women, launching vitriolic tirades against the villainous men who took advantage of trusting young innocents. However, they also sent out a clear message that women should take responsibility for their own safety. Didactic essays on the subject were mostly addressed to women, offering warnings and advice on how to conduct oneself during courtship. Since society could not always protect them, women should gauge carefully the characters of men with whom they consorted and beware sexual temptation. Women were apparently much better equipped than men to withstand such temptations. It was their allotted task, these writers opined, not only to defend their own sexual honor but also to inspire in their suitors a moral rectitude of which men were often incapable if left to their own instincts. By the late 1700s, moralists regularly portrayed women as the guardians of sexual virtue.

That apparently affirmative role had insidious implications. However skillful and dastardly the seducers who tricked and ruined young women, their victims were portrayed as having failed themselves in giving way. Writers rarely went so far as to exculpate men for their seduction and abandonment of women, but the assumption that women had a greater capacity for moral resilience did, at least implicitly, deflect moral responsibility away from men. Furthermore, the obligations that accompanied moral guardianship restricted the freedom of women to act as they pleased, if they intended to remain socially respectable. The danger posed by rakish irresponsibility was not the only consequence of a less restrictive sexual environment: young women as well as men now enjoyed greater personal freedom. The etiquette espoused by didactic literature sought to replace external restraints that were no longer effective with new internal inhibitors that did not apply to men; it contained women's agency even as it placed moral authority in female hands.[5]

Yet the notion of moral guardianship did represent a dramatic shift away from earlier representations of women as lewd and morally untrustworthy. The tone of publications discussing sexual relations changed dramatically over the course of the century: characteristics previously associated with women, especially lust and deceit, were transposed onto men. Seduction literature sought to regulate courtship by operating from within rather than upon women and men who were tempted to have sex outside marriage. It sought nothing less than the moral reconstruction of the individual, especially of women, in order to meet the challenges of an increasingly permissive society. This chapter investigates the transformation in sexual images of women during the course of the eighteenth century. It examines the huge body of ephemeral literature on seduction and abandonment in which writers offered strategies for self-stewardship in an environment that they viewed as fraught with sexual danger. And it considers the political implications of concern about seduction. Just as revolutionary ideology and the disruptive impact of the War for Independence encouraged an increasingly permissive sexual climate, so the widespread occurrence of sexual assault during the war and the use of rape as a rhetorical motif in patriot propaganda intensified public concern about the sexual safety of young women. Given widespread emphasis upon virtue as the cement that would hold the new republic together and the clear association of women with the guardianship of virtue, both personal and political, the threat of sexual degradation had significance above and beyond the personal welfare of victims and their families: seduction and abandonment debased those who represented and guaranteed the fledgling nation's moral integrity.

PRUDERY IS NOT THE WORD that first comes to mind when contemplating the tone of English society in the early eighteenth century. The predominant mood both within and outside the social elite was crude and scurrilous. Much of Restoration society had embraced an exuberantly bawdy spirit, in part a reaction to the rather dour atmosphere fostered by the Cromwellian regime of the 1650s. The ribald tone that now prevailed had a distinctly misogynist ring to it. Satire of the late 1600s and early 1700s often targeted women, especially in terms of their sexual power over men. According to this literature, women were lustful, insatiable, and deceitful: they would stop at nothing in their relentless quest for sexual pleasure, deploying with irresistible cunning an array of seductive stratagems that lured men into debauchery. Men were often depicted as helpless against feminine wiles: their moral and rational instincts overpowered, they found themselves plunged into an exhausting and degrading servitude, emasculated by an unquenchable female lust. Medical and marital handbooks portrayed women's sexual appetites as debilitating both for men and for themselves. One such guide, *The Mysteries of Conjugal Love Revealed,* claimed that "neither hellfire nor the earth" were "so devouring as the privy parts of a lascivious woman." It averred that women had a shorter life span than men because they were "much more amorous": their "heat . . . consume[d] them by degrees."[6]

Bawdy and misogynist humor was also commonplace in eighteenth-century colonial society. Consider the experience of Alexander Hamilton, a rather straitlaced Scottish physician who emigrated to Maryland in 1739. Hamilton traveled northward five years later, hoping to escape the summer heat and so alleviate his tuberculosis symptoms. The good doctor was dismayed by the lewd conversation to which he was subjected on his journey. In New York City, his host one rainy September day claimed to know "an infallible cure" for "hysterics and vapours in women." The appropriately named Mr. Hog went on to explain "that a good mowing was a cure for such complaints," which piece of "bawdy" he spoke "before his wife, who did not seem to be much surprised at it." Hamilton was appalled. That evening, he went out for a quiet meal with a friend, hoping no doubt to put the "inexcusable piece of rudeness" that he had witnessed at the Hog residence out of his mind. The two men were "expecting to sup and have some chat snugly by [them]selves" but "were interrupted by three young rakes who bounced in upon us, and then the conversation turned from a grave to a wanton strain." The young men wanted to talk of nothing "but ladies and lovers," including along the way "a good deal of polite smut." The threesome eventually departed to go "awhoring." A week or so later in Philadelphia, even an "agreeable" gathering that included the governor "and several other gentlemen of note" was somewhat marred in Hamilton's view by the "particular fondness" of some people present "for introducing gross, smutty expressions."[7]

The private writings of eighteenth-century elite men often included "expressions" relating to sex and womanhood that were explicitly hostile and derogatory. Given the determination of southern planters to emulate English fashions, it is hardly surprising that at least some of them adopted the misogynistic tone that was in vogue across the Atlantic. "I don't think," wrote Landon Carter, "there can be a more treacherous, enterprising, perverse, and hellish genius than is to be met with in a woman." Eve, he lamented, had "suffered the devil to tempt her," though "at the very hazard of paradise," and "of such a tendency ha[d] her sex been" ever since. There was nothing idiosyncratic about Carter's mordant perspective. Robert Bolling portrayed Adam as the first henpecked husband, seduced into thralldom by a guileful Eve and thereafter "truckling to a haughty scold." He referred to womankind as "that inconstant, faithless sex, ordained to rule, betray, [and] perplex." They might appear "guiltless," but so did "adders" that lay "repos[ing], 'till something comes in reach." Beauty made women "powerful," wrote Charles Carroll Jr. in a letter to his father: "I would defy an ugly woman endowed with the sagacity of a sphinx ever to entrap me." Bearing this information in mind, no doubt, Charles Carroll Sr. urged his son to avoid "intimacy or familiarity with the fair sex" (other than to "soften and polish" his manners). The "power of that sex," wrote a Yorktown merchant, could prove fatal to men drawn by its allure. Though "a virtuous woman" was "ever a blessing," others were "nothing better than moth in a garment, for they not only ruin[ed] fortune but [also] constitutions, that great blessing."[8]

Striking though these remarks may be, William Byrd's voluminous writings exhibit most clearly the influence of contemporary English attitudes upon southern planters. Byrd, who spent almost half of his life in England, was well versed in the tone of London's polite (or rather, impolite) society, including its bawdy humor and far-from-graceful sentiments regarding womankind. His letters and his commonplace book reveal a deep-seated distrust of women and their sexual power. Byrd's attitude toward marriage was profoundly cynical: he described it as a "galling yoke," a "contagion," a "distemper," and "a troublesome sea," "making everybody sick that comes near it." That matrimony so often became miserable and embittered owed a great deal, in his view, to sexual disillusionment. Byrd remained convinced throughout his life that a marriage could not work without personal compatibility based on physical attraction. The promise of sexual gratification was for him a crucial factor in the choice of a spouse: he referred in a 1740 letter to the marrying off of young women as "put[ting] them to bed to agreeable husbands." Yet Byrd also believed that the physical allure used by women to attract men was more often than not a carefully prepared artifice, the exposure of which after marriage generally led to disappointment and alienation.[9]

Byrd defined love as "a longing desire to enjoy any person, whom we imagine to have more perfections than she really has." Once men fell in love, they became "idolaters" and "fondly fanc[ied] a kind of divinity in their mistresses." According to an entry in Byrd's commonplace book, women understood and exploited this tendency: "When a mistress wishes her gallant every thing that is good, she excepts always good sense, which might open his eyes and make him despise charms which owe their being to imagination only." Byrd portrayed courtship as a game of deception, even fraud, in which women held the trump cards. Women, he wrote, were more skilled than men in "the arts of dress and disguise." They knew "how to place their perfections in the fairest light, and cast all their blemishes in shade, so that the poor men who know no better take them to be cherubins and gems without flaw." But once the male victim of a woman's skillful deception gained "better acquaintance" as a husband and began "to judge a little by sense and not altogether by fancy," the woman's physical "irregularities" and "failings" became clear. The man's "vast expectations" were dashed, and disappointment led him to seek satisfaction elsewhere: "the appetite will naturally pall, and after we have missed of paradise in one place, we are apt to look for it in another."[10]

The ultimate responsibility for this pattern of behavior, Byrd wrote, lay with wives, not their errant husbands: "the inconstancy of our sex is owing to the disappointments it meets from yours, who are too solicitous to hide their blemishes before they throw themselves into a man's arms and too little afterwards." In a 1729 letter, Byrd suggested in jest that when a couple was contemplating marriage, "the parties should view each other stark naked through an iron gate for the space of half an hour." This would prevent them from "concealing their personal defects" and so would "hinder their being surprised after marriage with any deformities and disproportions which they did by no means expect." Beneath the superficial playfulness of this passage lurked a distrust of women's apparent beauty that pervades Byrd's writings. In his mind, male naïveté and yearning for an idealized female body combined with feminine deceit to make a heady but dangerous potion with which men were drugged and duped into unsatisfactory marriages.[11]

Byrd's distrust of women was usually camouflaged in his correspondence by a coating of humor and counterbalanced in his letters to women by a tone of solicitous gentility. In the privacy of his commonplace book, however, he allowed himself to express more overtly and maliciously his fear of female beauty and sexual power; the humor deployed in these passages was more spiteful and so deepened instead of lightening the overall vituperative tone. Byrd entered into this volume a series of anecdotes and aphorisms that together constitute a bitter and paranoid commentary on sex and marriage. One extract drew a parallel between "the bite of a deadly serpent" that would "putrify your body" and "the kisses of a beautiful woman" that would "imprison your soul." Entries described in lurid detail the insatiable nature of female lust, so potent that one woman in love with a social inferior could overcome her incommodious "concupiscence" only by "drinking the blood of her beloved," and so unrelenting in its demands that male victims faced utter prostration and sometimes actual annihilation. One extract related how a man, "finding his vigour begin to abate," had one of his legs cut off "so that the blood and spirits which used to nourish that limb might add strength to those which remained, and increase his abilities with the alluring sex." Some women dispensed with men altogether, either by becoming pregnant "without losing their maidenhead" or by rejecting sex with men in favor of "Lesbian" pleasures. In entry after entry and page after page, Byrd built up a nightmarish collage of women, their voracious appetites, and the predatory wiles that trapped men in a destructive and debilitating cycle of helpless desire and humiliation.[12]

Byrd's expressions of anxiety and distrust regarding women were exceptional only in their volume. The tone of his comments was consistent with that of other early-eighteenth-century American writers, especially those in the South and elsewhere who evinced a modish cosmopolitan sensibility. Consider this passage from a satiric history of New York politics, written in the late 1720s by Lewis Morris. A local resident is showing a visitor to the colony a picture on the wall of the assembly's chamber that shows "a creature of the imagination whose upper part is a woman and whose lower part is a rapacious beast." Our guide rejects an interpretation claiming "the upper part to be reason which is to guide and govern the passions and brutal appetites," arguing that "the female figure doth not signify reason for if that had been intended the representation had been by a male figure." Instead, "being by a woman joined to a rapacious beast it shows that inveterate rancour, implacable hatred, and irreconcileable resentment is to be concealed under the appearance of a smooth front and smiling countenance and that our enemies are to be lured by the female arts of flattery and dissimulation till brought within reach of the lion's paw and then no mercy to be shown."[13]

Misogynist satire and bawdy humor circulated not only within the elite but also among less privileged early Americans through the medium of ephemeral print. Almanacs and newspapers featured a wealth of salacious material that was often hostile toward women. These two kinds of publications had somewhat different audiences: newspapers targeted primarily an urban, educated, and commercially minded constituency, whereas almanacs catered to a less sophisticated sensibility and rural households as well as town-dwellers. But together they reached a remarkably broad-based readership. That eighteenth-century printers, deferential as they were to the tastes of their audience, included bawdy and misogynist items in these publications suggests that an extensive audience existed for this kind of material. We have already seen that the testimony submitted to colonial courts was often extremely earthy, reflecting the ribald tone of everyday gossip in towns and villages throughout British America. During the early decades of the eighteenth century, there emerged a culture of ephemeral print that gratified and encouraged an appetite for lewd and often hateful fare that transcended social rank and occupation.[14]

Yet the colonists' initial experiments with ephemeral print had been decidedly prim. British America had no regular newspaper until 1704, but the printing press in Cambridge, Massachusetts, had been producing almanacs throughout the seventeenth century. These publications evinced neither the salacious tone nor the vitriolic attitude toward women that would characterize their eighteenth-century descendants. This is not surprising, given that the press was owned by Harvard College, a bastion of Puritan sensibility. Ministerial exaltation of family life as the basis for godly society and of women as "helpmeets" within the household precluded attacks upon either in the almanacs coming out of Cambridge. Harvard's monopoly came to an end in 1675, when John Foster set up the first Boston printing press, but official censorship prevented the publication of bawdy and otherwise questionable material.[15] In the more permissive atmosphere of the early eighteenth century, the tone of New England almanacs depended to a significant degree upon the attitude of individual printers. James Franklin, for example, was by nature an irreverent fellow; his *Rhode Island Almanac* series of the late twenties and early thirties regularly included bawdy material. Nathaniel Ames, in sharp contrast, produced unimpeachably respectable almanacs that doubtless appealed to a quite different segment of the population; in a 1758 almanac, Franklin's son and namesake lampooned the Ames style as "starched."[16]

Meanwhile, Philadelphia readers who were so inclined could purchase almanacs containing material that was both lewd and frankly hostile toward women. Benjamin Franklin included in his *Poor Richard* series a steady stream of verses and aphorisms casting doubt upon the sexual probity of women both before and after marriage. The following are typical of his barbed style:

Neither a fortress nor a maidenhead will hold out long after they begin to parley.

Three things are men most liable to be cheated in,
A horse, a wig, and a wife.

Men did not emerge unscathed from these barbs, destined as they often were in Franklin's satiric mind's eye to be cuckolded, but women figured in his almanacs as by far the less meritorious of the sexes. Franklin was more daring than most of his competitors. Titan Leeds's Philadelphia almanacs were generally much less ribald, though he also cast aspersions upon women:

> In marriage are two happy days allowed,
> A wife in wedding-sheets and in a shroud,
> How can the marriage state then be accurs'd,
> Since the last day's as happy as the first?

> Regard not woman's passions, nor her smiles;
> With passion she ensnares, with tears beguiles.

Leeds did occasionally include moral homilies aimed primarily at men. "If thou desire to be chaste in wedlock," he advised in the 1721 issue, "keep thyself chaste before thou weddest; he that hath known pleasure unlawfully will hardly be restrained from unlawful pleasure." But more typical was an item in the 1728 issue that focused attention upon female infidelity, averring that venereal disease was "fit sauce for the drab, that from her good husband does stray."[17]

By the mid–eighteenth century, almanacs published in the northern, middle, and southern colonies regularly included bawdy material that characterized women as lustful and manipulative. A 1754 almanac warned that "young females" were "sly and mischievous," forever "contriving tricks to tempt" potential mates. Just as William Byrd had claimed that men were duped by "the arts of dress and disguise," a 1761 almanac claimed that "gay appareled women" used their physical appearance as "bait to catch" their prey. Far from embracing sexual restraint once married, the wives depicted in almanac doggerel were habitually adulterous and, moreover, taunted their husbands with the possibility that they had cuckolded them. According to one such item that appeared in 1767, "a certain gentleman" declared, "The Devil take all the cuckolds, I wish they were all in the river," to which his wife replied, "O, dear husband, how can you make such a wish, when you know you cannot swim." Women apparently remained sexually voracious throughout their lives. A 1762 almanac included a mock petition from "the Maids of Philadelphia" complaining that widows, "more subtle than a fox," purloined the choicest "young fellows," leaving "no lovers to adore us."[18]

Items relating to women and sex ran the gamut from light-hearted wordplay to snide insinuation to blatant misogyny. Consider these literary gems from the *Virginia Almanack* for 1764:

> Mary, a chambermaid, a brown-eyed lass,
> Complained that she all day in labour was;
> I laughed at her simplicity, and said,
> Surely at night then you'll be brought to bed.

> If you a sweetheart go about,
> Valentine's Day may help you out;
> But mind your hand, and still take care,
> You be not drawn into a snare.

> This world's a prison in every respect,
> Whose walls are the heavens in common;
> The gaoler is sin, and the prisoners men,
> And the fetters are nothing but women.

Many items vilified marriage, recommending bachelorhood as far preferable to a scolding and all too often cuckolding wife. "To wed, or not to wed," a parody of Hamlet's famous soliloquy, replaced the uncertainties and horrors of death invoked by the Danish prince with "the dark perplexed ways of wedlock." Given "the dread of something after honeymoon (that gaily-fleeting period, whose sweet joys few loves, alas! survive)," bachelors might well conclude that the tribulations of a single life ("the harlot's impudence, the prude's disdain, the pangs of love despised") were by comparison quite trivial (see fig. 4).[19]

Whereas most of the bawdy items included in almanacs were brief and generic, colonial newspapers featured a much broader range of sexually related material that was designed to inform, entertain, and titillate readers. Some items were only a few lines long, but others were lengthy and detailed. Like almanacs, newspapers were increasingly prone to include material that portrayed women in a negative light. But men were much more likely to be condemned for illicit behavior in newspapers than in almanacs, largely because they often figured as criminals in news reports. Though women did not always receive sympathetic coverage in such articles, journalists readily cast men as malefactors. This relatively equitable approach spilled over into bawdy stories that appeared in newspapers: though sometimes demeaning to women, these regularly poked fun at men and most often were evenhandedly satirical.

The BATCHELOR's SOLILOQUY.

TO wed, or not to wed—that is the queſtion :
Whether 'tis better ſtill to rove at large
From fair to fair, amidſt the wilds of paſſion ;
Or plunge at once into a ſea of marriage,
And quench our fires ?—To marry,—take a wife,
No more—and by a wife to ſay we quell
Thoſe reſtleſs ardours, all thoſe nat'ral tumults
That fleſh is heir to ;—'tis a conſolation
Devoutly to be wiſh'd.—Marry,—a wife,
A wife,—perchance a devil :—ay, there's the rub ;
For 'mongſt that angel-ſex what dev'ls are found,
When they have ſhuffled off the virgin-maſk,
Muſt give us pauſe.—There's the reſpect
That keeps a prudent man ſo long a Batchelor.
For who would bear the taunts of longing maids,
The harlot's impudence, the prude's diſdain,
The pangs of love deſpis'd, coquette's delay,
The inſolence of beauty, and the ſpurns
Which merit bears, when fools become their fav'rites,
When he himſelf might his *quittus* make   [bear
With one kind woman ?—Say, what youth could
To wiſh and ſigh alone the weary night,
Or dangle after belles, coquettes, and wenches,
But that the dread of ſomething after honey-moon,
(That gaily-fleeting period, whoſe ſweet joys
Few loves, alas ! ſurvive) puzzles the will,
And bids us rather linger in the path,
The well-known, ſimple path of ſingle life,
Than tempt the dark perplexed ways of wedlock ?
Thus forethought does make Batch'lors of us all ;
And hence the face of many a willing maid
Is ſickly'd o'er with the pale caſt of languiſhment ;
And many a youth of no ſmall pith and moment,
With this regard, ſpends all his days in whoring,
And damns the name of huſband.

FIG. 4. *"The Batchelor's Soliloquy," from* The American Calendar, or, An Almanack for the Year of Our Lord 1768 *(Philadelphia, 1767).* Courtesy Library of Congress.

From the early decades of the eighteenth century, newspapers printed in New England, mid-Atlantic, and southern colonies reported the occurrence and punishment of sexual crimes on both sides of the Atlantic. The *Boston Gazette* for 9 January 1727 reported the trial of John and Mary Harwood for "keeping a disorderly house" in London and for "entertaining sodomites," which included "willingly permitting them to commit . . . divers sodomitical obscenities." The *South Carolina Gazette* for 11 November 1732 informed readers that "a negro man" had just been convicted in Springfield, Massachusetts, of rape "committed on the body of a white woman about eighteen years old, belonging to Suffield, of a good reputation." And the *Pennsylvania Gazette* for 11 November 1762 told of an unintentionally incestuous marriage between a tradesman in London and a woman who turned out to be the daughter of his estranged wife by a subsequent relationship; this "so afflicted him, that he took to his bed, and is since dead." Most of this news coverage was highly sensationalist. It invited voyeuristic readers to envisage pirates running amok and ravishing maidens to "gratify their brutish passion" (though according to the *Boston Gazette* for 25 March 1734, one "damsel" committed suicide "to preserve her chastity"). It recounted the scandalous lecheries of wanton priests and lascivious nuns, mostly in France. And the *Boston Gazette* for 20 September 1725 described the flight from a burning London brothel of the establishment's "lady governess, together with her doxies and their companions," making sure to let readers know that they had "just time enough to escape in their shifts." Laconically but effectively, the report invoked an image of nubile wenches silhouetted in flimsy undergarments against the flames that licked the brothel walls. This doubtless titillated more than a few readers.

Some of the sexual items included in colonial newspapers were designed exclusively to entertain. There were bedroom farces, one involving a lecherous constable who had agreed to a nocturnal tryst with "a neighboring female" but "unluckily mistook the window" and joined another woman whose husband was "lying on a couch not far distant." This "good woman, perceiving presently by the extraordinary fondness of her bedfellow that it could not possibly be her husband, made so much disturbance as to wake the good man," who then "lay about him unmercifully." In another tale of mistaken identity, two young gentlemen, "strongly united in friendship" and "married about the same time," had each been trying without success to produce an heir. They underwent medical examinations to assess the relevant "faculties" and embarked with their wives on a series of trips to health spas, "but without effect." One night the two couples arrived late at their destination and could find only one vacant room with two beds; the men went out for an evening walk. On returning to the room, they climbed into the wrong beds; each gamely made another attempt to solve their problem, and the next morning the four awoke to find themselves in considerable embarrassment. Nine months later, "each lady presented her husband with a son." Since the two men wanted their own sons to inherit from them and neither mother wanted to be parted from her child, "an exchange was made" whereby the inadvertent wife swap became a permanent arrangement. And then there were shorter anecdotes, one featuring a young lady who omitted the first syllable of *obey* when reciting her wedding vows, hoping that "she was bound to perform no more than she said." The parson objected, but her groom recommended that he "let it pass," assuring the reverend, "Ere the business is done, I'll make her cry, O!"[20]

These crimes and comedic misadventures took place in North America, England, Ireland, various European countries, and more exotic locations. But by far the most frequent source for sexual items was London, a characteristic entirely consistent with the overall composition of these publications. Decade by decade, colonial newspapers devoted more and more space to English news and the advertisement of manufactured goods imported from England as early Americans increasingly saw themselves as part of a larger English culture.[21] More specifically, imported snippets detailing adulterous affairs, elopements, and other scandals within the metropolitan beau monde gave colonists access to a libertine sensibility with which some clearly identified and to which others aspired.[22] It is no coincidence that newspapers, which served a more affluent and self-consciously cosmopolitan constituency than did almanacs, were much more inclined to feature sexual license in a transatlantic context. When members of the colonial elite waxed libertine, they liked to think that they did so in good company. Almanac readers, it would seem, were less affected in their bawdiness.

But during the second half of the century, as Americans became increasingly troubled by the implications of a more permissive sexual culture, especially as it affected young women, the tone and content of ephemeral print underwent a transformation. Humorous bawdry was counterbalanced and increasingly overshadowed by earnest discussion of predatory libertinism and its consequences; hostile portraits of women as lustful seducers were displaced to a considerable degree by sympathetic images of innocents who fell victim to male seduction. Instead of presenting womankind in general as sexually voracious and deceitful, magazines, newspapers, and almanacs increasingly distinguished between respectable women who embodied moral rectitude and those who either embraced depravity or were ruined by seductive rakes.[23] A similar shift had taken place in English publications by the mid–eighteenth century, which doubtless influenced colonial printers and their audiences. But the changing tone of ephemeral print in the British colonies of North America was not merely mimetic: the seduction genre appealed to Americans because it spoke to troubling issues with which they were all too familiar.[24]

STORIES, POEMS, AND ESSAYS that addressed the potentially tragic consequences of male infidelity became increasingly commonplace in ephemeral literature of the late 1700s. Two extracts from Philadelphia almanacs printed in the early 1760s exemplify the sympathetic attitude and monitory tone of this emerging genre:

> Hard is the fortune that your sex attends;
> Women, like princes, find few real friends;
> All who approach them their own ends pursue;
> Lovers and ministers are seldom true.
>
> Therefore guide each step with caution,
> For just like glass is reputation;
> Both broke to pieces in once falling.
> For ever lost, and past recalling.[25]

Earnest items such as these did not immediately gain ascendance over bawdy and sometimes callous humor. In 1774 an almanac from the same series that featured these two poems included a joke at the expense of abandoned women:

> Says Dolly, "Me, Thomas, you promised to wed,
> And I, silly girl, believed all that you said."
> "That I promised to wed you, and love you, 'tis true,
> But I've tried you, my Doll, and I find you won't do."

Yet those Philadelphians who used a competing almanac for that year would have read a much more melancholic ditty on the subject:

> My daughter, once the comfort of my age,
> Lured by a villain left her native home,

278

Is now abandoned on the world's wide stage;
And doomed in scanty poverty to roam.[26]

During the 1780s, material dealing with courtship, marriage, and sex became predominantly serious and sympathetic toward women. Smutty humor did not disappear from the pages of ephemeral print even then, but it was overshadowed in the late eighties and nineties by the sheer mass of didactic stories and essays devoted to the perils of premarital sex.[27] Widespread rape during the Revolutionary War had exacerbated public anxiety about the sexual dangers facing young women, while the emphasis within republican ideology upon women's role as moral exemplars reaffirmed the need to protect female virtue. As we will see, the sustenance of public and private virtue became tightly interwoven during the closing decades of the century, which in turn gave new significance to discussion of courtship and sexual politics.

Score upon score of cautionary tales and essays appeared in newspapers, almanacs, and especially the magazines that proliferated during the second half of the eighteenth century, discussing the difficulties that faced women as they decided whether or not to trust suitors who wanted to have sex with them. Although short stories and poems addressing this issue were obviously intended to entertain, their primary purpose was didactic. As one author put it, "morality shall be my guide, and utility my object."[28] Not all of the suitors who figured in didactic tales turned out to be incorrigible villains. But most of the stories that appeared in ephemeral publications featured "ruined" maidens who had to endure unmarried pregnancy alone, having been seduced by bewitching young rakes who then absconded to ply their charms elsewhere. Through these monitory tales, women could experience vicariously the possibilities and perils of sexual freedom; they could learn without risk and then conduct themselves in real life with due regard to their own safety. Doomed heroines learned "by sad experience" what "happier females" would "only know by report, that an ingenuous soul is ever in danger from the machinations of a designing world."[29] Seduction literature cast doubt upon the probity of mankind in general and advocated premarital chastity over trust as a young woman's best bet. "A Hint to Young Ladies" warned "imprudent young maids who grant favours to deceitful lovers, upon their swearing they will marry you," that such men "despised" those whom they seduced and cared nothing for their "honour" or "future happiness." Women could not afford to be trusting, given "how inconceivably base" some men turned out to be. They should "learn a lesson of prudence" from the tragic fate of duped heroines.[30]

Many seduction tales were set in exotic locations and involved melodramatic twists of fate that were far removed from ordinary experience. Yet the fundamental issues that they addressed would have been familiar to most readers in the late eighteenth century. The authors of didactic essays and short stories often used words associated with "the fashionable world" such as "libertine" and "rake" to describe men who seduced and then betrayed the trust of young innocents. As one author pointed out, however, even "the little retired village" had been "contaminated" by "the volatile salt of perfidious refinement." All too often, "the young, infatuated, and thoughtless" confused "an incessant round of pleasure" with true "happiness." Young women who grew up in the countryside were now notorious for "levity bordering on licentiousness." Even worse, their male contemporaries were driven by "an unbounded thirst in the pursuit of interest and pleasure." Floretta, the heroine of this particular morality tale, "saw through the misleading glare of lawless pleasures and shuddered at the danger she was daily exposed to." The "village swains" found her "impenetrable":

> They sung, they danced, and they piped in vain. She saw that they assailed her virtue, not her heart. They did not seek for connubial delights in her society, but for momentary gratifications in her seduction. Aware of their ends, she had strength and virtue enough to defeat them.

Floretta's reward came in the form of Florio, a virtuous fellow whose "ardour" was matched by "the sincerity of his heart." But Florio, alas, was not your average "swain": even a village lass was likely to find herself surrounded by "volatile" and "perfidious" lovers; she had best take care.[31]

Authors warned repeatedly against the specious pleasures of immediate gratification. In a lush and gothic piece that appeared in the *Massachusetts Magazine* for September 1791, "the young and beauteous Cleanthe," who was taking a walk at sunset, "strayed into a thick forest that reared its aweful shade behind the stately castle of the baron her father." She fell into a reverie, from which she was roused by the sound of a lute, which then faded away into "deep silence." Cleanthe realized that she had wandered "out of her knowledge" and had no idea how to find her way back to "the peaceful parental asylum she had unwarily quitted." She now heard "mournful and piercing shrieks," along with "the howlings of savage beasts" that "resounded on every side." She fled in terror and soon found herself in "the ruins of an ancient abbey." There, "at the foot of an alter half destroyed by time," a woman lay "as if expiring, with eyes fixed, and features pale and ghastly." Blood was trickling from her bosom, where "her hand convulsively grasped a rusty and leaden hilted poignard." The "miserable wretch" opened her eyes, fixed her gaze upon the petrified Cleanthe, and in a "hollow tone of voice" declared, "Whoever thou art, behold in me the fatal effects of heedlessness, vice, and criminal despair!" She then expired. The earth trembled; the sound of thunderbolts and rushing water filled the air; and Cleanthe "sunk lifeless on the ground."

On "returning to life and recollection," Cleanthe found herself in "the most delicious garden, surrounded with all that could charm and delight the sense." As she arose, a "beauteous" young man "for whom her gentle bosom had long sighed in secret" approached, knelt at her feet, and "poured out vows of tenderness and ardour." He then "conducted her to a temple sacred to the loves," where "a train of young beauties crowded around, and with siren voices hailed her fairest of the throng." One of these nymphs presented Cleanthe with "a bowl of an intoxicating mixture" and bade her drink. Her admirer took the bowl, "drank deep of its contents," and passed it back to Cleanthe, who was about to imbibe herself when "a low and mournful voice sounded in her ear": "Forbear! Call to remembrance the ghastly figure, the pavement dyed with blood, the convulsive pangs, the dying groans! Heedlessness has already betrayed thee into danger—temptation is now plunging thee into vice! Despair, death, destruction follow!" Cleanthe flung the bowl and its "fatal beverage" away from her. She heard "a loud shriek," followed by "a hideous crash," and then "the whole vision faded away." Cleanthe was once again on the edge of the forest at the rear of her father's castle. She rushed indoors "and in the soothings of parental affection sought consolation and repose for her agitated spirits."[32]

It was no coincidence that Cleanthe had strayed "unwarily" from "the peaceful parental asylum" before undergoing this unnerving experience. Cautionary tales often drew attention to the dangers of personal autonomy and also the ambiguities inherent in a parent's relationship with adult but as yet unmarried children, especially daughters. On the one hand, illicit affairs and elopements were sometimes prompted by disagreement between parents and children over the choice of a marriage partner. Fathers who privileged considerations of wealth or status over the romantic attachments of their offspring were roundly condemned in these tales and essays. Authors warned parents that "thwarting the affections" of children might drive lovelorn sons and daughters to ruinous expedients.[33] On the other hand, many of the seductions that took place in these stories were made possible by unsupervised courtship. An unscrupulous suitor named Orlando, for example, was "with little ceremony permitted to visit" Narcissa "as a candidate for her affections." He enjoyed frequent and private access to the young woman, during which meetings he deployed his "wiles" to seduce her.[34]

Seduced and abandoned heroines were mostly consigned to a life of shame, grief, and sickliness. She who "gave too soon her virgin-heart" and submitted to the "flame" of a "cruel despoiler" became "the sport of every babbling tongue." As "all her joy and all her hopes" disappeared, "the roses that adorned her face" faded away, "the fire that sparkled in her eyes" grew dim, and "her form no more retain[ed] its wonted grace."[35] Some of these deserted and pregnant young heroines fled their homes rather than face their parents, but others were forced to leave by families who condemned and disowned them.[36] Now doubly abandoned, the heroine found herself homeless and destitute. In the standard scenario, she turned to prostitution, a measure of her desperation and also of her moral degradation. An elegy entitled "The Dying Prostitute" invoked "the miseries of a wretched maid" whose "health and fame" had been "sacrificed" to the "brutal passion" of an "unfeeling man." She now wandered the streets "wan and sallow, changed with sin and care," forced "by pining want" to proposition "each hideous form" that passed her by. Even those disowned women whose lovers did not abandon them nonetheless faced a grim future: the "amiable and virtuous female" who had "sacrificed the sublime delights of parental approbation to gratify the volatile passion of youth" now "trim[med] the almost expiring taper, and wait[ed] in torturing suspense for her beloved partner, while he, callous to every tender feeling of humanity, [was] squandering away the future prospects of an infant family at the destructive and ever detested gambling table."[37]

Seduction literature inveighed bitterly against rakes for exploiting the innocence and credulity of their victims. Denunciations of male artifice and treachery were as colorful as they were commonplace: "The man who lays a snare to entrap innocence, however shielded by the specious names of gallantry or gaiety of disposition, is a fiend and a monster that should be shunned and detested by society." Those outraged by such depredations could take comfort in the knowledge that a rake's life of pleasure was built upon a "tottering base," its "joys" a "delusive show." Debt, disease, and disgrace would soon enough supplant the seeming glories of the moment. The seducer's "unfeeling triumph" would eventually give way to repentance as he lay "writhing on death's gloomy bed." "Rest assured," wrote one commentator, "that the burden of misery which awaits yourself is heavier far than any you have heaped on another." Another hoped that "no sweet forgiveness" would then "descend from heaven" and that the "wretch" would instead be consigned "to the rigor of relentless fate."[38]

Yet some authors gave the impression that libertines could be inspired to repent and reform long before they lay on their deathbeds. The catalyst was almost always feminine virtue. One rakish fellow apparently promised to mend his ways after receiving a letter from a female friend in which she chastised him gently and outlined an appropriate course of conduct for the future. Another was redeemed by his introduction to "the lovely Olivia" during a visit to his father's country estate. Dorcas now "looked back with horror at his former debaucheries, and was convinced that there was no real felicity but when a mutual passion prevailed." They married and lived happily ever after. According to a poem purportedly written "by a lady in New England," "the rake" was a man of "open heart" and "generous mind" who had temporarily lost his way, "a thousand virtues misapplied" as "reason floats on passion's tide." His ability to "judge of right" may have been "banished from its practice quite," but neither "his nobler wit" nor his conscience had deserted him entirely:

> He knows his fault, he feels, he views,
> Detesting what he most pursues.
> His judgment tells him, all his gains
> For fleeting joys, are lasting pains.

This type of young man, "a wretched, self-condemning creature," would welcome the redemptive ministrations of a virtuous woman.[39]

Mistreated women could apparently inspire their lovers to reform by means of their very suffering. One tale featured "a fashionable voluptuary" who seduced and eloped with a trusting young maiden. As Sir Edward observed "anguish" and "guilt" cast their shadow over his lover's spirits and demeanor, he came to feel "the deepest remorse" and "curse those false ideas of pleasure which had led him to consider the ruin of an artless girl." He accordingly married her and settled into virtuous domesticity.[40] Magazine articles and stories trumpeted the ability of virtuous wives "to reform the disposition" of unfaithful husbands. One adulterous libertine was moved to repentance and reformation by his long-suffering wife's tender ministrations after he received a wound in a duel with "another gentleman of fashion" who had insulted his mistress. "To suffer with patience," the author declared, "to rise superior to misfortune, and to repay unmerited ill-treatment with benevolence, are virtues which not only promote the happiness of those who can exercise them, but frequently recall the licentious to the paths of their duty."[41]

Implicit in these accounts of redemption was the notion that women could seduce men into virtue, a reversal of earlier writings that portrayed womankind as luring male victims into vice. Consider the case of Louisa, a young widow who was abducted from the coast of England by Algerian privateers and consigned as a slave to the harem of a Turk named Osmen. Louisa proved more than equal to the challenge of her new surroundings. She "wrought such a change in Osmen's bosom" by means of her "virtues" and enlightened "conversation" (much of it concerning the sterling qualities of George Washington) that he decided to free his slaves, including Louisa.[42] By the early nineteenth century, the idealized virtuous woman was also a desexualized, passionless woman. But images of virtuous femininity in the late 1700s still allowed that women's sex appeal could prove an effective tool in controlling men. An essay about Amazonian women claimed that on one occasion these formidable warriors averted imminent defeat at the hands of a neighboring tribe by "laying aside all measures of resistence" and "rush[ing] out with naked breasts to meet the enemy." When the advancing army responded "with enthusiasm" to this provocative gesture and ended hostilities, the Amazon women "relinquished their bows and their spears, and resolved in future to trust more to their weakness than their strength."[43]

Wives who wished to ensure or recover their husband's loyalty must seduce them literally as well as metaphorically. One piece advised that a wife must not only "be strictly virtuous" but also adorn herself beguilingly if she was to retain her husband's love. Though "indispensably necessary" before marriage, a pleasing appearance was "still more so" afterward: "nothing can be more fatal to conjugal happiness than that carelessness of dress, that loose and disorderly attire, to which too many married ladies give themselves up," since "indifference, if not disgust," would "undoubtedly ensue," prompting the husband to "rove abroad, like the bee, in search of new sweets." In "The School for Husbands and Wives," a man sought "affection which he imagined himself unable to obtain from his wife" in "a celebrated courtesan" named Nina. The distraught wife determined "to rekindle the flame of her husband's conjugal affection" and so visited Nina in disguise to ask her advice. The courtesan suggested that she watch from a closet while she entertained a client, who turned out to be the husband in question. Having to watch their tryst was, of course, a mortifying experience, but the new skills with which she plied her husband on his return "astonished and delighted him." He stopped visiting the courtesan, and the couple "continued to live in love and harmony to the end of their days."[44]

But just how strong were the twin weapons of inspiring virtue and beguiling beauty when pitted against male depravity? Although some writers enthused about women's redemptive power, others averred that most libertines were incapable of reform. Skeptics questioned the "common" adage that "a reformed rake" made "the best husband," pointing out that such individuals had "little left to boast but a shattered constitution, empty pocket, tradesmen's bills, bad habits, and a taste for dress and vices of every denomination." Men of this stripe needed wives to replenish their coffers and had most likely feigned reformation for that purpose. Once "the poor wife's fortune" had been squandered, she would find herself "despised by her friends" and most likely neglected by her husband. Even the rake who had sought with some degree of sincerity to reform would be "tempted by the power of long habit to return to his old ways." His "insatiable love of variety" would "lead him astray from the finest woman in the world."[45]

Authors who doubted the possibility of a "reformed rake" justified their pessimism in terms of male infirmity. When it came to pleasures of the flesh, they argued, men were constitutionally incapable of either self-restraint or fidelity: "so frail" was their sense of loyalty, "so addicted" were they to change, "so transitory" were their affections, "that the greatest of blessings, when once enjoyed, bec[a]me matters of mere neutral concern"; thus "sated," the lover was easily distracted by new "objects of pursuit."[46] In theory, man's rational capacity should enable him to quell his passionate urges. But these writers suggested that neither reason nor morality could be relied upon to triumph in practice. When given "an occasion of gratifying his wishes," the typical man might "fancy he will go to such and such lengths, and no further," but "passion" would "hurry him imperceptibly from liberty to liberty." Young men in particular were "slaves to the irregular motions of passion": rational and virtuous instincts had little chance against the "extravagant desires, tumultuous thoughts, and amorous fires" that "rage[d]" within the youthful male bosom.[47]

Many of these writers claimed that the typical young libertine was "vicious contrary to his inclination" and despite his "natural love for virtue." According to an essay in the *American Magazine,* "a hundred good qualities" were "rendered useless" by his "impotence of mind." He was compelled not only by the inner workings of passion but also by social pressure and fear of "ridicule" by friends who themselves "seduce[d]" and "ensnare[d]" him into "the stream of vice." The *South Carolina Gazette* lamented that many a young "buck" was "dazzled" by "men of pleasure" and so became a "servile imitator." In other words, he was "dissolute rather from fashion than inclination." The *Massachusetts Magazine* lamented that it had become "in some measure necessary for a young fellow to give in to the fashionable follies, and practise vices to which he ha[d] a real abhorrence, if he would establish the character of a man of taste, or show himself tolerably well acquainted with the world." Some authors complained that virtuous men had to pose as rakes if they were to attract young ladies with redemptive impulses. A piece entitled "Thoughts on Gallantry, Love, and Marriage" lamented that "the lady of merit" actually encouraged libertines to court her because she thought herself "possessed of charms sufficient" to "reclaim the wanderer, and fix him unalterably hers." This contributor claimed to "have known a fellow whose behavior was really virtuous" and yet who was "very solicitous to be thought a libertine by the girl to whom he paid his addresses." The lesson was clear: "a man can take no more effectual method to secure himself the esteem of our modern ladies, in general, than by appearing a rake, at least in practice, if not in principle."[48]

Whether driven by "fashion" or "impotence of mind," men evidently could not be relied upon to exercise self-restraint. Even those authors who had faith in women's ability to reform rakish suitors warned that they must take care when dealing with potential recruits to the cause of virtue. If it was true that most men were enslaved to their lusts, then it followed that "young ladies" must fill the moral vacuum: the "only remedy," opined a piece in the *American Museum,* was for women "to act in their own defense" by exercising "their unquestionable capacity to judge what is amiable and virtuous, and their indefeasible right in all matters of moral conduct to follow their own judgment." Essays discussing seduction and abandonment routinely denounced those men who "imposed on the honest and obliging credulity of the virtuous fair." But they focused most of their attention on the implications for female comportment.[49]

A steady stream of articles addressed to "young unmarried ladies" offered "friendly hints" about appropriate conduct in the presence of men. "Caution and circumspection," warned one such piece, "ought ever to be on the watch, and externally pleasing appearances examined with an eagle's eye." Those who gave way to "wild passion" and "suffer[ed] unbridled desire to warp the true bent of the soul," ignoring "the voice of calm reason," would soon repent of their folly. However tempting it might be to consort with rakes in the hope of reforming them, young women should shun indiscreet and corrupting persons of either sex, limiting themselves as far as possible to intercourse with those from whom they were "least liable to receive any taint or infection." To do otherwise was "the height of folly and stupidity." After all, men were unlikely to "regard the honour and happiness of a woman" who "shew[ed] but little regard to her own." [50]

Eschewing company and behavior that might compromise one's moral integrity, reputation, or personal safety did not necessitate prudery or self-isolation. Conduct manuals appearing in the late eighteenth century advised young women to steer a middle course between undue familiarity, which was dangerous, and cold reserve, which made them undesirable. Magazine and newspaper articles gave similar advice. As one author put it, a young woman's conduct should be "free and unconstrained so far as is consistent with modesty." She who wished to maintain a lover's interest without surrendering her virtue should avoid "too easy compliance" without "run[ning] into the opposite extreme." She should avoid either "reprehensible" or "outrageously virtuous" manners.[51]

Emphasis upon a young lady's "unquestionable capacity to judge what is amiable and virtuous," a capacity that was not to be expected of male suitors, placed a heavy burden of responsibility upon her shoulders. It also imposed strict limits upon her freedom of action, without placing any such restrictions upon the men with whom she interacted. Conduct books warned women not to do anything that might encourage men to take liberties with them, but they rarely lectured young men about the need for self-control. Likewise, essayists in magazines and newspapers seldom addressed advice concerning courtship etiquette specifically to men.[52] Whereas seduction literature often portrayed libertine behavior as compulsive and even involuntary, women were presented as much more fully in control of themselves. Most contributions to that genre insisted that women must assume responsibility for appropriate behavior during courtship, protecting themselves and inspiring men to virtuous behavior. A letter from "Adolescens" to the *Philadelphia Minerva* in 1795 urged women not to associate with libertine men on the grounds that they could best reform rakes by discountenancing them. "Ladies," he wrote, "much depends on you, towards a reformation in the morals of our sex." A response the following week from "Dorothy Glibtongue" declared that women must admit rakes into their company so as to exert their influence over them. Both perspectives vested power in women.[53]

Ephemeral publications had become increasingly committed to the notion that women were by temperament more virtuous than men and better able to withstand temptation. Whereas earlier satiric writings had portrayed men as the helpless victims of female manipulation and lust, late-eighteenth-century literature tended more and more to present men as enslaved to their passions and thus dangerous to women. These depictions seem quite different, and in some respects they were, but the assertion of male helplessness remained constant. Consider Joseph Shippen's effusively admiring poem about the "striking charm," "pleasing excellence," and "various graces" of Philadelphia ladies gathered in an assembly room. Shippen described the women whom he encountered there as "commanding all" through their charms, "enchanting," "conquering," and inspiring "awe" as they "please[d]," so that men such as himself "must soon submit to love." An almanac essay entitled "Love and Acquaintance with the Fair Sex" averred that men were incapable of "resistance" against "the attractive charms of an enchanting outside in the sprightly bloom of happy nature; against the graces of wit and politeness; against the lure of modesty and sweetness." Thus, even as the heroines of seduction tales fell victim to overpowering male predators, they held the key to their own salvation. "Let the fair ever remember," warned one author, "that their peace, dignity, and character chiefly depend on themselves." "It will then," declared another, "be your own fault if you are not happy."[54]

THE NUMEROUS DIDACTIC STORIES and essays that appeared in magazines, newspapers, and almanacs were, for the most part, limited by considerations of space to a laconic treatment of their subject matter. Two of the first novels published in the United States, William Hill Brown's *The Power of Sympathy* (1789) and Hannah Webster Foster's *The Coquette* (1797), examined the etiquette of courtship and the threat posed by seductive, rapacious suitors in much greater detail. In common with the "moral tales" that appeared in ephemeral print, their message was complex and ultimately ambiguous: both novels sympathized with the plight of young women, condemned men who mistreated them, and yet suggested that women who fell victim to rakes should have taken better care of themselves. Their heroines bore a significant and insidious moral burden.

Eighteenth-century novels from across the Atlantic had found an enthusiastic audience throughout the British colonies. A striking proportion of these volumes placed women center stage, focusing on their experience of love and the tribulations of sexual temptation. It is surely no coincidence that two of the most popular novels among early Americans were Samuel Richardson's *Pamela* (1740) and *Clarissa* (1747–48): each presented an epic struggle between a virtuous young woman and an unscrupulous admirer who had determined to breach her chastity. *Pamela, or, Virtue Rewarded* concerns an attractive and self-possessed fifteen-year-old maidservant who is preyed upon by Mr. B., her master. Pamela's stubborn refusal to surrender her chastity eventually vanquishes and redeems Mr. B., who repents of his past behavior and commits himself to reformation. Once Pamela becomes convinced of his sincerity, she agrees to marry him, and the couple settle into virtuous domesticity. *Clarissa, or, The History of a Young Lady* has a much less cheerful ending. The heroine is being wooed by a captivating young rake named Lovelace. Clarissa is charmed, but her family insists that she marry a wealthy gentleman named Solmes, whom she loathes. When Clarissa proves intransigent, they lock her up. Lovelace persuades Clarissa to escape with him, promising to broker a reconciliation with her relatives. But instead he deposits the fugitive in a brothel and attempts to debauch her. Clarissa repudiates his advances repeatedly, and Lovelace becomes increasingly obsessed by the challenge of overcoming her scruples. He eventually drugs and rapes her. Clarissa is devastated by the loss of her chastity. She escapes from the clutches of Lovelace and is cared for by the virtuous Belford, but her constitution has been hopelessly compromised by her ordeal, and her condition slowly deteriorates. Following Clarissa's death, one of her cousins challenges Lovelace to a duel and kills him.

Both of these novels were explicitly didactic in tone. Their championing of virtuous young women who resisted sexual temptation even under extreme pressure was hugely popular with early American readers.[55] But the way Richardson resolved the two plots and the general tone of his novels proved controversial. New Englander Esther Edwards Burr complained in her journal that Richardson had "degraded our sex most horridly, to go and represent such virtue as Pamela falling in love with Mr. B. in the midst of such foul and abominable actions." That Pamela could "forgive Mr. B. all his devilish conduct so as to consent to marry him" did "not well agree with so much virtue and piety." She considered this "a very great defect in the performance."[56] A 1784 magazine essay bemoaned that Richardson portrayed "some of his wicked characters as more agreeable than was necessary to his plan, which may make the example dangerous." Lovelace was so "adorned with youth, beauty, eloquence, wit, and every other intellectual and bodily accomplishment" that "thoughtless young men may be tempted to imitate, even while they disapprove him." The reviewer also objected to Lovelace's honorable death by the sword. He would have preferred "a series of mortifications, leading him down gradually to infamy, ruin, and despair, or producing by probable means an exemplary repentance." That "would have been more useful in a moral view, and perhaps more interesting." Another assessment, published in 1790, warned that Clarissa should be "read with caution, and under the direction of a guide," since it "laid open scenes which it would have been safer to have kept concealed" and "excited sentiments which it would have been more advantageous to early virtue not to have admitted." Though "written with the purest intentions of promoting virtue," it inadvertently encouraged readers to lose sight of "the moral view" by presenting "love scenes which interest the passions more than the understanding."[57]

Novels in general became increasingly controversial among Americans during the postrevolutionary period. Critics warned that although some volumes had "moral merit" and included "lessons of prudence and virtue," many more were dangerous because of their "immoral tendency" or "romantic turn." A steady stream of essays published during the 1790s lamented "the sorrowful effects of reading novels and romances" upon young women. Because vices were often "painted in captivating colors" and "intrigues as genteel gallantries," readers might be corrupted by "such a course of reading" and then fall "an easy prey to the first boy who assume[d] the languishing lover." Any seducer with a flair for histrionics could achieve his object simply by imitating the heroic type familiar to those "much conversant with sentimental novels."[58] One writer went so far as to argue that novels had democratized libertinism: "fashionable depravity" was no longer "confined to the higher circles of life" but had now become common "in the middling orders of society." The underlying message of these attacks was that women would be less instead of more capable of defending themselves against seduction as a result of reading novels. When a woman was seduced and abandoned, declared a contributor to the *Massachusetts Magazine,* blame did not rest solely with "the arts of the seducer." Many "a ruined female" had herself "open[ed] the broad gate that leads to destruction," her moral scruples having been dulled by reading novels, "the literary opium that lulls every sense in delicious rapture." Novels, then, impelled female readers to "act improperly, owing to the romantic turn of thinking [that] they imbibe[d] from their favourite studies."[59]

Both Brown and Foster were well aware of such concerns. They sought to preempt criticism of their own novels by giving especial prominence to didactic passages that discussed appropriate behavior during courtship and the need for women to protect themselves against unscrupulous suitors. Brown conceded in his preface to *The Power of Sympathy* that novels had "not been received with universal approbation." He even had one of his characters declare that "many fine girls" had been "ruined by reading novels" that were "not regulated on the chaste principles of true friendship, rational love, and connubial duty." Only those volumes dedicated to "strict morality" were "fit to form the minds of women." Brown and Foster clearly intended that their volumes should combine the thrill of a novel with the instructive tone of a conduct book. Their work was as much indebted to the etiquette manual genre as to authors such as Richardson.[60]

Both *The Power of Sympathy* and *The Coquette* condemned predatory men who seduced and ruined young women, but they also insisted that women be held accountable as accomplices in their own downfall. Like many of the short stories published in the late eighteenth century, Brown described his male despoilers in language reminiscent of the serpent's victory over Eve in the Garden of Eden. In one of the novel's subplots, Ophelia kills herself after being seduced and abandoned by her brother-in-law, Mr. Martin. "By a series of the most artful suggestions, suggested by a diabolical appetite," Martin "insinuated himself into her affection," "prevailed upon the heart of the unsuspicious Ophelia, and triumphed over her innocence and virtue." In another passage, Brown wrote of "the fell seducer's wiles." But just as theologians had often insisted that Eve was partly to blame for her own misfortunes (and those of her husband), one of the characters entrusted with the delivery of moral lessons throughout the novel points out that "a woman may be accessory to her own ruin": "when a woman, by her imprudence, exposes herself, she is accessory; for though her heart may be pure, her conduct is a tacit invitation to the seducer." "It is hardly worth while," the moralist insists, "to contend about the difference between the meaning of the terms 'accessory' and 'principal.' The difference, in fact, is very small."[61]

The theme of female responsibility is much more prominent in *The Coquette*. The flawed heroine, Eliza Wharton, writes that she is "the victim of her own indiscretion" as well as of "a designing libertine." The novel begins soon after the death of two men, Eliza's father and the man whom he has selected as her "future guardian and companion." Eliza has deferred to "the will and desire of [her] parents" in the choice of a husband but now finds herself altogether freed from the "shackles" of male authority. As she sets out from Hartford to stay in New Haven with a married friend, Mrs. Richman, Eliza revels in leaving behind, figuratively as well as literally, the "paternal roof" and in the "egotism" that she can now indulge: "Let me then enjoy that freedom which I so highly prize. Let me have opportunity, unbiased by opinion, to gratify my natural disposition in a participation of those pleasures which youth and innocence afford." But reconciling "pleasure" with "innocence" proves to be more difficult than Eliza has anticipated. Granted "independence" as a result of these two deaths, she fails to exercise that "freedom" responsibly and considers herself at least partly to blame for what ensues. "I am sensible that the power is in my hands," she acknowledges, "but the disposition (shall I confess it) is wanting!"[62]

Eliza experienced "freedom" and "independence" to an unusual degree, but her situation was emblematic of social change in the eighteenth century: parental authority may not have died, but it had weakened; young people were freer to court as they wished and must accordingly assume a greater share of responsibility for their own safety.[63] Negotiating freedom was no easy matter, especially if male suitors were often too weak to resist corrupt inclinations. In *The Coquette* as in other moral tales of the period, this meant that women must take the moral initiative. The novel's concluding message was addressed explicitly to women: "From the melancholy story of Eliza Wharton, let the American fair learn to reject with disdain every insinuation derogatory to their true dignity and honor. Let them despise, and for ever banish the man, who can glory in the seduction of innocence and the ruin of reputation. To associate is to approve; to approve is to be betrayed." In other words, she who was betrayed must first betray herself. Eliza's misuse of her freedom, pursuit of pleasure, and lack of self-control resulted in her loss of virtue, which in turn destroyed her happiness and ended her life.[64]

WORRIED DISCUSSION OF women's sexual and moral endangerment reached its height in the years following the War of Independence. This was not a coincidence. Two facets of the revolutionary experience gave additional resonance to images of female defilement and moral degradation. The first was rape, both literal and metaphoric. Official reports, newspapers, and diaries from the period contain numerous accounts of women "ravished" and "shamefully abused" by the British.[65] Whether or not all such accounts were true, they became common currency. Like seduction literature, these reports stressed the youth and innocence of the victims, along with the cruel and callous depravity of those who attacked them. Both sets of women lost their chastity to men who had no intention of marrying them or acknowledging paternal responsibility in the event of pregnancy. Most tales of seduction and abandonment differed from rape accounts in that they featured women who consented, at least nominally, to have sex. Yet late-eighteenth-century literature characterized seduction as a form of predatory violation; its victims were usually described as having been overwhelmed in some way, albeit by false words rather than physical force. And just as libertines deceived the objects of their lust, reports of wartime rape sometimes claimed that British soldiers lured women into situations where they could be assaulted more easily, using "vile artifices for the delusion and ruin of the virtuous and innocent."[66]

As magazine stories and newspaper articles often associated rakish seducers with metropolitan degeneracy, so rape served as a potent metaphor for British decadence, brutality, and tyranny during the revolutionary period. Patriots claimed that their way of life was being violated by the imperial government's repressive policies. They conflated attacks on political freedom with sexual degradation in visual and rhetorical images that served to dramatize their cause. Consider "The Able Doctor, or, America Swallowing the Bitter Draught," a 1774 print that portrayed the British response to the Boston Tea Party in terms of assault: Lord North forced the spout of a teapot into the mouth of a scantily clad woman representing America, grasping her throat in a demonstration of force while another man lifted her skirt and peered lasciviously up toward her thighs and genitalia (see fig. 5). As it indicted the abusive depravity that

FIG. 5. *"The Able Doctor, or, America Swallowing the Bitter Draught,"* 1774. *Reproduced by permission of the Beinecke Rare Book and Manuscript Library, Yale University. This pro-colonial print first appeared in the* London Magazine, *April 1774, and then was reproduced for Americans by Paul Revere in the June issue of the* Royal American Magazine *(Boston).*

allegedly characterized British government, this cartoon insisted upon a tight link between sexual, moral, and political integrity. Thomas Paine's *Common Sense* claimed that "the domestic tranquility of a nation depend[ed] greatly on the *chastity* of what may properly be called national matters." Paine urged the impossibility of reconciliation between Britain and its American colonies in terms of sexual degradation and its irreversibility: "Can ye give to prostitution its former innocence? Neither can ye reconcile Britain and America. The last cord now is broken, the people of England are presenting addresses against us. There are injuries which nature cannot forgive; she would cease to be nature if she did. As well can the lover forgive the ravisher of his mistress, as the continent forgive the murders of Britain." The British government was not the only political force accused of preying upon innocents during this period. John Adams drew a direct parallel between the "artful villain" in seduction novels who "pursue[d] the innocent lovely girl to her ruin and her death" and the corrupting, manipulative influence of populists. "Democracy is Lovelace," he wrote, "and the people are Clarissa."[67]

But women figured in revolutionary and postrevolutionary rhetoric as much more than victims. They also assumed a crucial role in the forging of a new republican sensibility. That role depended upon exactly the same qualities that enabled women to protect themselves against seduction and inspire men to set aside their baser sexual instincts. In the absence of a monarchy and the loyalty that it inspired, political writers insisted that Americans must find a new sentiment that would bind them together and propel them to place the interests of the whole before their own selfish concerns. Eighteenth-century political philosophers generally held that a republic could not survive without civic virtue, a benevolent and disinterested concern for the common good.[68] Two fundamental aspects of civic virtue and its place in late-eighteenth-century American politics concern us here. First, postrevolutionary writers argued that private and public virtue were closely intertwined: the former sustained the latter. A society in which people fixated upon their own gratification, regardless of ethical or altruistic considerations, could not sustain political freedom, which required a high-minded citizenry.[69] Second, since women were now generally perceived as better equipped than men to withstand moral corruption and promote virtue, they became a crucial component in the republican vision: as women had to nurture men's more honorable instincts in private life, so now they must encourage their husbands and sons to embrace and exercise public virtue.[70]

During the early decades of the republic, political writings emphasized women's role as guardians of public as well as private virtue. Tangible forms of power would remain in male hands, but moral authority was now vested in the sweethearts, wives, and mothers who would inspire men to public-spirited behavior. A young woman could apparently "mould the taste, the manners, and the conduct of her admirers, according to her pleasure." She could "even to a great degree change their tempers and dispositions, and superinduce habits entirely new." Once married, the republican wife must ensure that her husband's conduct as a public and private citizen met the highest ethical standards. "It rests with her," the *New York Magazine* pointed out, "not only to confirm those virtuous habits which he has already acquired, but also to excite his perseverance in the paths of rectitude." Women thus bore a mighty and onerous burden: they should always bear in mind "their high importance in society" and "reflect how much the virtue and happiness of mankind depend[ed] upon them." One essay quoted Milton's famous line, "The world lies all before them," and applied it specifically to women, declaring that the world was "theirs to mould into what shape they please."[71]

But if republican wives were to appeal successfully to men's higher instincts, they must be properly equipped to do so. A host of postrevolutionary writers argued that greater attention to female education would make women more effective not only as household mistresses but also as informed and astute companions to politically engaged and responsible male citizens. The need to expand and improve formal schooling for girls and young women became an important component in discussions of women's role in the sustenance of republican virtue.[72] Contemporaries recognized, though, that informal education through reading was also crucial if women were to realize their full potential as the moral lodestars of the nation. And that brings us back to the seduction literature that flooded American households in the 1790s. The education of a good republican woman involved the acquisition of skills related not only to literacy and numeracy but also to social interaction and moral self-preservation. As we have seen, seduction literature was avowedly didactic: it sought to prepare young women for the challenges of personal freedom and sexual temptation. That enterprise had clear political implications in the climate of the 1780s and 1790s, given the central roles allotted to virtue and to women in sustaining a healthy republic.[73]

The trials and temptations undergone by ingenue heroines in late-eighteenth-century moral tales paralleled closely those of the new nation. As young women should recognize the dangers that accompanied greater personal independence and eschew licentious behavior, so the citizens of the United States must grapple with the challenges of exercising political freedom and protect civic virtue from corruption. Male villains who stalked the pages of novels and short stories embodied the forces of corruption and depravity that might overwhelm the republic if civic virtue faltered; the fate of young women such as Eliza Wharton dramatized the grim consequences of giving in to dishonorable impulses. A carefully designed governmental structure could minimize the dangers, just as familial and community surveillance could protect young women to some degree from male abuse of sexual freedom. But safety in both contexts depended in large part upon individual virtue and perspicacity. Given the frequency with which Americans of this period insisted upon the interdependence of personal and public virtue, these parallels would have been obvious to readers. John Adams's equation of politicians whom he considered corrupt with Lovelace and of novice citizens with the much abused Clarissa was neither obscure nor far-fetched in the cultural context of the new republic.[74]

But men could not be expected to learn these lessons without the assistance of their womenfolk. In both personal and political realms, responsibility for awakening and sustaining virtue lay primarily with women. The redemption of initially ill-fated relationships such as that between Pamela and Mr. B. came to serve as a model for the virtuous republican marriage in which wives saved their husbands from corruption and inspired them to disinterested feats of which they might otherwise have been incapable. Stories that placed moral authority in the hands of women became so popular in the 1790s because they played out in the most intimate of contexts the grandiose redemptive and inspirational role that women were expected to perform in the republican experiment now unfolding. Women could and must ensure moral order by using their hold over men to shape their conduct as suitors, husbands, fathers, and citizens. Heightened concern for the physical safety and moral welfare of women in the new republic was bound up with widespread discussion of their mission to guide men away from corrupt political impulses; women had to be kept inviolate because so much rested upon their integrity.

GIVEN THE EMPHASIS in postrevolutionary political discourse upon the inspirational role that republican wives and mothers were to play in the creation of a virtuous new republic, it is hardly surprising that celebrations of matrimonial and familial bliss became a staple of ephemeral print in the 1790s. Whereas a poem printed in 1763 and sardonically entitled "The Happy Pair" had regaled readers of *Father Abraham's Almanack* with the mutual and multiple adulteries of a married couple, a piece carrying the same but now more literally appropriate title in an almanac at the end of the century described the joyful reunion of a family at the end of each day with cloying sentimentality: "Their imaginations could picture nothing softer, nothing happier than themselves."[75] But we should not exaggerate the degree to which the tone of available printed matter had changed by the late eighteenth century. Abner Sanger, the young New England farmer whom we met in chapter 7, had reading habits that exemplify the heterogeneity of items in circulation. On the one hand, he read and transcribed from a borrowed copy of *The Ladies Library*, a didactic three-volume set that adopted an affirmative and respectful attitude toward women. On the other, he owned and lent out *Female Policy Detected*, a crudely misogynistic tract that promised to educate young men in the "allurements, inconstancy, love, revenge, pride, and ingratitude" of women, so as to provide "armour" against "the attracting sorcery of these bewitching load-stones." This latter volume, originally published in 1695 by a London printer, appeared in several American editions during the second half of the eighteenth century.[76]

The overall shift in emphasis is unmistakable, yet the varied tone of publications available in the new republic reflected the ambiguity of its sexual culture. Celebrations of chaste courtship and of marital fidelity emphasized the safety that these afforded to all concerned, responding to the dangers and anxieties that accompanied a less restrictive sexual climate:

> No husband wronged, no virgin's honour spoiled,
> No tender parent weeps his ruined child.
> No bad disease, nor false embrace is here,
> The joys are safe, the raptures are sincere.[77]

Didactic literature sought to reform sexual mores, yet many contributors to that genre proceeded on the assumption that it was extremely difficult, if not impossible, to refashion the attitudes of young men toward white women with whom they had unmarried sex. Indeed, the continued availability and popularity of bawdy and misogynist material doubtless fed the widespread concern that underlay more high-minded discussion of sex and gender relations. It is also surely no accident that most of the publications discussed in this chapter were printed in major cities, where the sexual climate left much to be desired from the perspective of moralists. Cities were notorious as dens of debauchery and exemplified in particularly grim fashion the perils of sexual freedom, especially for women. Monitory literature was prompted not only by a generally more permissive atmosphere but also by the specific sexual climate that prevailed in cities, to which we now turn our attention.

9

"Martyrdom to Venus"

Sexual Freedom in Post-Independence Philadelphia

SALLY DAWSON WAS "determined and did go to a play this evening."
Thus wrote Elizabeth Drinker, the chagrined wife of an affluent Philadelphia merchant, on 12 March 1803. Dawson, a servant in the Drinker
household, "did not come home till midnight" and, moreover, "ha[d] a
beaux after her." From the viewpoint of a respectable Quaker mistress
such as Drinker, the combination of staying out late, attending a theatri-
cal entertainment, and having a "beaux" was ample cause for distress.
Drinker was not alone in worrying about her servants' nighttime activities and the possibility of untoward intimacies while away on such jaunts.
Lewis Farmer complained to the vagrancy court in June 1792 that his servant Philipina Deitrick had "frequently gone out of the house after the
family had retired to rest, remaining out during the night in company
with disorderly men." The nocturnal seaport culture into which Dawson and Deitrick disappeared was boisterous and bawdy: sailors, servants of both sexes, laborers, apprentices, and journeymen drank, sang,
and brawled; single, married, widowed, deserted, and runaway denizens
flirted, groped, and fornicated. The merrymaking often got out of hand:
in March 1799 a young man was arrested after being "stripped naked"
in the street. Highly visible among these carousing pleasure-seekers were
women working as prostitutes. Readily available in taverns and brothels
or outside in thoroughfares and byways, these "ladies of pleasure" were
"so numerous," observed a visitor to the city, "that they flood[ed] the
streets at night." This was hardly the kind of company in which employers
such as Drinker wanted servants to spend their free time.[1]

Dawson's and Deitrick's worrisome absences testified not only to the
opportunities for recreation afforded by an urban environment but also

to the changing circumstances of servants and the generally libertarian atmosphere of postrevolutionary Philadelphia. As wage labor gradually superseded indentured servitude in the city's increasingly cash-oriented economy, servants such as Dawson evinced an independent spirit as free laborers that defied expectations of deference and obedience. Employers complained of increasing "impertinence and irregular conduct." "Times are much changed," Elizabeth Drinker lamented, "and maids are become mistresses."[2] In the closing decades of the eighteenth century, Philadelphia embodied a brave new world. During the revolutionary period, it had provided the setting for a radical popular upsurge that resulted in one of the most democratic state constitutions to be ratified in the new republic.[3] Considering the strength of that populist movement and the implications of a transformed labor system, it is hardly surprising that young people living in Philadelphia were aggressive in asserting their rights and liberty. Happy to escape the restrictive surveillance of their employers, servants tended to leave the homes in which they lived and worked "as soon as night ha[d] arrived" and often could not "be persuaded to return until eleven-thirty or midnight." They reveled meanwhile in the freedom of the city's streets and taverns, where they could gossip and drink with friends, flirt with strangers, and perhaps nestle in the arms of a lover.[4]

By the mid–eighteenth century, Philadelphia was the largest city in North America. Capital of the United States until the end of the century, it exemplified the greater personal freedom made possible by urban life and also its troublesome consequences. The sexual climate in Philadelphia was remarkable for its lack of restraint. Casual sex, unmarried relationships, and adulterous affairs were commonplace, much to the dismay of more straitlaced residents who held that sex should not occur outside marriage. The city swarmed with young women and men who had migrated there in search of work, some from the surrounding countryside and others from across the Atlantic. Most of these young people had come to Philadelphia on their own and found themselves free to act pretty much as they pleased. The constant flow of people in and out of the city combined with the greater anonymity of urban life to facilitate casual encounters and informal liaisons. Sexual surveillance and effective stewardship by relatives and neighbors was much less viable in a bustling seaport than in smaller communities: there was comparatively little pressure upon the city's unmarried inhabitants to think of sexual involvement as a component of courtship; if lovers conceived a child, they were much less likely to marry than if they had been residents of a small agricultural town. Meanwhile, husbands and wives inclined to cheat on their spouses found ample opportunity to do so: married Philadelphians had sex with strangers whom they met on the streets and in taverns, with workers in their own homes, and with prostitutes.[5]

The city's most notorious symbols of disorder and sexual license were taverns and whorehouses. Taverns were infamous for "drunkenness," "gaming," and other "vicious pleasures," as well as "the receipt of stolen goods, and concealment of offenders." In such establishments, "all the loose and idle characters of the city, whether white, black, or mulatto," could "indulge in riotous mirth and dancing til dawn." Brothels were in plentiful supply and seem to have done a roaring trade. Particularly renowned were the establishments in Southwark, a ramshackle and rapidly growing district of the city that served as home to poorer artisans, unskilled laborers, and mariners. But bawdy houses were scattered across the city and frequented by men from every walk of life, ranging from sailors to skilled artisans to more affluent residents. A French visitor in the 1790s declared it a matter of common report that "a great many husbands" visited whorehouses as a "means of libertinism." Although some of these men sought to conceal their patronage of brothels, maintaining an air of specious respectability, others made no secret of doing so.[6]

Philadelphians of the late 1700s could, if they wished, enjoy remarkably uninhibited sex lives. But the price of that freedom was often very high: venereal infection ran rampant among the city's residents, and out-of-wedlock pregnancies also became increasingly common. City-dwellers could purchase contraceptives: Moreau de St. Mery, a refugee from Robespierre's Reign of Terror, ran a bookstore in the city from 1794 to 1798 that "carried a complete assortment" of prophylactics, apparently "in great demand." But many Philadelphians were either unaware of these options, or could not afford them, or did not care. The Guardians of the Poor, who worked with unwed mothers to extract financial support from the fathers of their children, recorded more than five hundred cases of bastardy during the 1790s; the actual incidence of out-of-wedlock births was doubtless higher, since not all unwed mothers would have wanted to involve the authorities.[7]

Young women who had neither financial means nor a local support network could be plunged into crisis by unexpected pregnancy. Unlike indentured laborers, hired servants could be fired at will; thus, expectant mothers working in that capacity faced the very real possibility of being thrown onto the streets once they were no longer able to carry out their duties. Such women could gain admission to the almshouse for the period of their lying-in, but that provided only a temporary solution to their predicament. We have already seen that premarital pregnancy became much more common in agricultural communities by the latter part of the eighteenth century. What distinguished urban from rural environments was the number of women who became pregnant and never married. The majority of nonmarital conceptions seem to have occurred as the result of a casual encounter or a short-term affair, but some unwed mothers may have agreed to have sex because their lovers promised to marry them. Ensuring that men lived up to such promises was much more difficult for single women living alone in a city than for their counterparts in a small, tight-knit community. Despite the efforts of city officials to extract financial support from the fathers of illegitimate children, women were much more likely to suffer economically and otherwise as a result of bearing a child outside marriage than were the men concerned.[8]

As Philadelphia's inhabitants grappled with the practical consequences of a sexually permissive environment, their responses were shaped in part by the judgments that they made about the character of those concerned. Some contemporaries reveled in the freedom afforded by a large city, but others condemned such behavior as immoral, disorderly, and criminal. The ways Philadelphians conceived of licentious behavior differed according to rank and sex. Those gentlemen who embraced a libertine sensibility would have pointed to their sexual exploits and infidelities as an expression of their modish dissipation. Yet they, along with more fastidious members of the urban elite, used highly derogatory terms to characterize women of whatever status and poorer men who engaged in promiscuity. The treatment of prostitutes illustrates most clearly the ways in which social condescension, a gendered ideology of virtue, and continued commitment in some quarters to a particular version of moral order shaped responses to the medical problems and personal tragedies associated with Philadelphia's unbridled atmosphere. Prostitution exemplified a conception of sex as a recreational activity disassociated from marriage, but discussion of sexual commerce also dramatized the dangers of a polyamorous culture, both for the individuals concerned and for society as a whole.

PROMISCUITY IN LATE-EIGHTEENTH-CENTURY Philadelphia was not limited to any one district of the city or any segment of the population. Some city-dwellers were, however, a good deal franker than others about their sexual activities. St. Mery commented sardonically on those inhabitants who "pretend[ed] to be virtuous" but whose "morals" were actually far from impeccable. On first arriving in the city, he had been taken in by such pretensions. His store's supply of contraceptives had been "primarily intended for the use of French colonials," but he soon found that the items were "in great demand among Americans, in spite of the false shame prevalent among the latter." And *The Philadelphiad,* a collection of satiric poems and anecdotes about life in the city, poured scorn upon the religious hypocrite who was "always preaching morals" and yet had fathered "a score" of "bastard" offspring and was "known to every old procuress in the town." But whereas some philandering Philadelphians maintained a facade of moral rectitude, others saw no reason to conceal their recreational activities and visited brothels "at all hours" of the day. According to St. Mery, "a certain well-known gentleman" left "his horse tied to the post outside one of these houses, so that everyone knows when he is there and exactly how long he stays." Those conversant with genteel libertinism could, of course, draw on that sensibility to justify their engagement in casual sex and extramarital affairs. Benjamin Rush lamented that one of the criteria for being considered a fashionable "gentleman" in Philadelphia at the end of the century was "getting bastards" (along with swearing, regular inebriation, and indebtedness).[9]

Rush gave several examples of prominent Philadelphians who met this criterion with brazen enthusiasm. Governor Mifflin "lived in a state of adultery with many women during the life of his wife" and "educated in his own family" the illegitimate offspring whom he sired during these affairs. According to Rush, Mifflin's wife died of "a broken heart in consequence of his conduct towards her," but neither that nor his notorious infidelities prevented him from being elected as governor soon thereafter. William Wister, an affluent Quaker merchant, was apparently a "kind, charitable, generous, friendly, and even just" bachelor, but he "had one vice, viz. an unlimited commerce with women." He had "four mistresses in keeping" at the time of his death in 1801. Wister was denied burial in the Friends' graveyard because he had expired "in the house of one of his mistresses," but the Baptists took him in. John Hay, a much-respected minister, abandoned his wife and children to cohabit, quite openly, with one of his congregants. Hay "rode with her and his child by her through the streets of Philadelphia, regardless alike of public opinion and of the public eye."[10]

Reconstructing the attitudes of Philadelphians who engaged in casual sex and adulterous affairs is extremely challenging, especially once we venture outside the social elite. But there does survive one remarkably vivid account of sexual promiscuity penned by an anonymous diarist, probably a sawyer, who inserted a year-long series of entries in an account book belonging to lawyer and businessman James Wilson at some point during the 1790s. The diarist, who was married, noted in his first entry that he had "topped" thirty-six "wenches" during the previous year. Subsequent entries suggest no abatement in his extramarital activities. The sawyer had sex with women whom he met in taverns, brothels, the thoroughfares in and around the city, and even in his own house. On 14 March he lay with "a great vigorous wench" whom he met "in the inn" and who had apparently "ogle[d]" him "with lecherous eye." In May he visited "a house of joy on Dock Street" that was "chiefly for sailors." He had sex with a "wench" who "enveloped" him "dearly and sweet." On his way to the Schuylkill Falls later that same month, he "got one Mistress Anne King near the road and in some bushes." She was apparently "a brave wench, thin in flesh but great in motion." (It was "all over in ten minutes.") And when Ludowick Richard's wife, endowed with "a nice person [i.e., body]," started washing for the sawyer and his wife that December, he "rolled her over and fuddled her."[11]

Not all of these encounters were consensual. In January he danced with Mistress Young at a "soiree," which "aroused all of my passion." According to the sawyer, "she resisted much, holding her limbs together, but my flame being up I thrust her vigorously and she opened with a scream." He described the encounter as "a real joyful fuddle," but Mistress Young may not have felt the same way. Some of the women whom our diarist "enjoyed" were working in his house, and he seems to have assumed that they were therefore sexually available; these employees may or may not have been willing partners, but in either case they may have felt that they must accede if they wanted to keep their jobs. The sawyer's lecherous intentions were sometimes thwarted by other men who understood only too well what he was up to, as this March entry suggests: "Passing along the quad a wench eyed me from a house—I entered—a man with a gun requested me to depart—I tarried not."[12]

Dangers of that sort were the least of his worries. Far from resting complacent about his behavior, the sawyer voiced concern repeatedly in his diary about the moral and medical implications of his promiscuity. On 1 January he "promise[d]" himself "in the coming year to avoid lewd women," who were "the bane of [his] life." But a week later he had sex with Mistress Young, and a week after that he "lay" with a cook. "Why oh why," he wrote plaintively on that occasion, "can I not resist?" The diarist portrayed himself as "a poor weak man with great passion and no self-restraint." He seems to have internalized the notion promulgated in ephemeral print during this period that men had no control over their lusts. In one entry, noting that he had just had sex with Maria, a "chamber woman," he claimed that he "could not resist her charms." In another, he again wrote that he "could not resist" temptation, whereas his sexual partner, Amanda, could and should have done so, but "would not." As far as he was concerned, women had no excuse to fall back on: he was helpless, whereas they were irresponsible.[13]

Our diarist's motivation for trying "to avoid lewd women" seems to have been partly religious, though spiritual compunction stood little chance against his attraction to the pleasures of the flesh. "God forgive me," he declared in one entry, "but it was good." When he recorded having had sex with Maria, a "chamber woman," he "cried 'God help me' as [he] thrust her." But the sawyer's antics posed a threat to his physical as well as spiritual welfare. In June, when he experienced "a great itching in his parts and breech," his physician diagnosed the "clap" (gonorrhea). "What an evil a bad woman is," he wrote, and "how dangerous too." This was not the first time that the sawyer had become infected ("oh my again," he declared), and that December he had another bout, along with "much itching in my flopper." Yet such episodes, however painful and recurrent, did not deter him from his sport.[14]

This energetic fellow was evidently far from anomalous in his maverick adulteries. Philadelphian women petitioning for divorce in the late eighteenth century often cited their husbands' promiscuous infidelity. According to Margaret Erben, her husband Adam had committed adultery with "lewd and wicked women" whom he visited "in several different houses of bad fame in the City of Philadelphia." Erben had boasted to his brother-in-law about his "frequenting bawdy houses . . . naming the lewd women with whom he had been engaged in a criminal and adulterous intercourse." Another married man, David Pemble, regularly visited brothels in the city with his friend Thomas Lyons during the late 1790s. The two men, both tailors, would exchange details after emerging from the rooms in which they were entertained by prostitutes (on one occasion, Pemble "complained of her not being clean"). Sexual bragging seems to have been quite common in male company. In 1778, at a tavern just outside Wilmington, Delaware, an officer "entertained" Charles Peale "with his many feats in the wars of Venus, which necessar[il]y led to the discovery of some of those houses of nightly revel in the city of Philadelphia." He also shared "the secret history of the debauchery of some married men amongst [Peale's] acquaintance." Just as some of these stories may have been exaggerated, not all allegations made by divorce petitioners and their supporters are necessarily reliable, but late-eighteenth-century Philadelphians must have realized that claims of rampant promiscuity would appear only too credible.[15]

Wives figured in divorce proceedings and other contemporary accounts of sexual license as much more than the neglected victims of male wanderlust. Men were not the only ones running amok. Rachel Lakine, a servant in the household of John and Catharine Mulloway, saw her mistress "kiss and toy" with one man; another had to "run into the street with his breeches down" after a tryst with Mistress Mulloway was interrupted. Charlotte Bennett had apparently "given herself up to lewd practices and to the having adulterous conversations and intercourses with lewd men"; Catharine Britton had cuckolded her husband William "with a certain Garret Burns and others," kept company with "debauched persons," and "live[d] frequently in lewd houses."[16] But whereas some Philadelphia gentlemen were quite blatantly promiscuous, their female counterparts within the elite were much more discreet. This is hardly surprising, given the emphasis placed upon women's mission as guardians of virtue in the new republic and the double standard that this entailed: men were held to be morally frail and unable to restrain themselves; women were depicted as having a much greater capacity for self-control and so were obliged to assume responsibility for sexual propriety. Literature of the period taught that young ladies who forsook their calling as exemplars of moral integrity would suffer an ignominious fall from social grace. Thus, overt debauchery was not an option for women of rank who valued their reputation.

Depictions of women outside the elite were quite different. A 1790 magazine essay claimed that "not every one" had "a mind capable of loving" and that "vulgar minds" in particular lacked the "organs" requisite for that exalted emotion; they experienced only lust. Poorer women still tended to be characterized as naturally lustful and licentious: whereas ladies were blessed with virtue and should take care not to lose it, their lowlier sisters were apparently depraved by nature. In 1793, when a wealthy New Yorker named Henry Bedlow was tried for the rape of Lanah Sawyer, a seventeen-year-old seamstress whom he met on a stroll, befriended, and then allegedly assaulted, the defense argued that Sawyer could not be considered a victim: she must have known that Bedlow's "aim" in making her acquaintance was "lust and nothing else"; she herself must have been motivated to spend time with him by a "desire of gratifying her passions." A number of women testified that Sawyer was "of good character, modest, and virtuous," but Bedlow's attorneys responded that these witnesses were "of the same condition of life," "an obscure set of people, perhaps of no character themselves." Such women were doubtless "accustomed to levity" and "to allowing male friends liberties," so the court had "a right to doubt what they mean[t] by these terms."[17]

Whereas members of the elite often characterized women of modest social background as "husseys" and "wenches" of dubious morality, popular ditties from the period depicted them in more neutral or even celebratory terms as acknowledging their sexual urges and welcoming opportunities to indulge them. "The Longing Maid" featured a young woman who thirsted for sexual experience "with some jolly brisk man," admitting quite candidly that she "wearied" of "lying alone." And a poem entitled "The Orange Woman" gave voice to "a hearty, buxom girl" from Ireland who knew what she wanted and did not hesitate to say so:

> I always fancy pretty men,
> Whenever I can find 'em.
> I'll never marry, no indeed,
> For marriage causes trouble:
> And after all the priest has said,
> 'Tis merely hubble bubble.
> The rakes will still be counted rakes,
> Not Hymen's chains can bind 'em,
> And so preventing all mistakes,
> I'll kiss whene'er I find 'em.

This down-to-earth and lusty lass made no secret of her delight in the company of "pretty men," but her distrust of marriage as a guarantee of male fidelity led her to stay single and seek sexual pleasure in casual encounters, for which she made no apology.[18]

That spirit of insouciance was not merely a literary artifact. Some Philadelphia women evidently responded with enthusiasm to opportunities for nonmarital sex that came their way or actively sought pleasure in casual encounters and transient affairs. Louisa Lovinger, caught in the act of adultery and castigated by a neighbor in 1797, declared that she had no reason to feel ashamed, because "her husband was away the whole week at the store and she had not good of him." Louisa did not plan to "stay with him much longer" and meanwhile had taken a lover to meet needs that he was not fulfilling. Eleanor Lightwood left her husband Jacob in 1788 because he was "a little ugly fellow" and "she saw a number of faces that she liked abundances better." She settled in the Northern Liberties, a suburb of Philadelphia, and supported herself by working as a hired servant. Lightwood became known as a woman prone to "go after men" and bore a "bastard" child fathered by Simon Hetcher, who was employed in the same household. When her master fired Hetcher, she declared that she would "have connection" instead with a black servant who also worked for Fulmer: "if she could not get a white man, she would have him."[19]

ALL NONMARITAL ENCOUNTERS and relationships were, of course, illegal and, from an ecclesiastical perspective, immoral. But as we have seen in other contexts, some relationships deemed illicit by officials and moralists were in fact committed unions that ordinary folk considered quite unexceptionable. Serial monogamy and informal marriage were common in late-eighteenth-century Philadelphia: in passing from one cohabitational relationship to another, city-dwellers often paid scant regard to marital formalities that religious and judicial authorities took very seriously. Some Philadelphians remained ostensibly committed to their husbands or wives while actually betraying their marriage vows; but others who seemed to be committing adultery or bigamy had already severed their ties with previous partners, albeit informally. Personal histories were further complicated by the demographic transience characteristic of large seaports such as Philadelphia. Behavior that some contemporaries condemned as "licentious" is sometimes better understood in terms of alternative sexual and marital codes. As a visitor to Pennsylvania noted, local inhabitants who separated generally did so "with no great formality, either quietly or, after the event, by giving notice in the public prints." (Philadelphia husbands sometimes announced in the local newspaper that they would no longer take responsibility for their wives' debts because they had separated.) Official action was necessary in order for a separation to become "completely valid and legal," but, he remarked, "it is not always that the trouble is thought worth the taking."[20]

After the Revolution, divorce reform gave Pennsylvanians easier access to formal termination of failed marriages, and a substantial number of Philadelphians did petition for divorce in the closing decades of the century. But some couples preferred to manage such matters themselves, drawing up "a mutual agreement of separation" that marked the dissolution of marriage without involving the courts.[21] Others did not see any need to formalize the end of their relationships. Divorce petitions often described scenarios in which individuals had left their legal spouses, in some cases after many years of marriage, and entered other relationships without formally dissolving their previous marital commitments; they either cohabited informally with new partners, which was officially adulterous, or entered what were legally bigamous marriages. Mary Dicks left her first husband, John, after one year of marriage to live with William Ford; they lived together for several years and had six children together. She then entered into a formally bigamous marriage with William Pierce and subsequently, after he was lost at sea, cohabited with William Humphreys. John Jones, a mariner, returned from sea to find that his wife had left him to live nearby with John Collins, a carpenter. And Susanna Evans sought a divorce after her husband departed from Philadelphia and entered a bigamous marriage in New Jersey. In each of these cases, a former spouse had decided that he or she wanted a formal divorce, perhaps paving the way for remarriage and so expressing deference to legal requirements. But Mary Dicks, Catharine Jones, and William Evans may not have considered their subsequent relationships to be illicit, since they were de facto separated; or they may not have cared. Their personal histories comprised a succession of formal and informal unions that either ignored or defied official protocol.[22]

Evans was not unique in departing the state as well as his wife.[23] But such men were not necessarily driven away by fear of legal retribution. Philadelphians often stayed put, establishing new relationships quite openly and with impunity. Matthias Conrad left his wife Catherine and entered into a second, bigamous marriage within the same city. William Brown deserted his wife Joanna after ten years of marriage to live nearby with Hannah Pope.[24] Few women would have had the resources to move away, but remaining in Philadelphia does not seem to have been particularly risky: even those neighbors who knew about the personal histories of people living in what was legally adultery or bigamy rarely cared enough to report them. Very occasionally individuals were prosecuted for these offenses. In June 1791 Christopher Armstrong confessed before the Mayor's Court in Philadelphia to having married Mary Holmes, "at the same time being previous[ly] married to, and then and still being the husband of Elizabeth Lodge." Four years later, John Lloyd was found guilty by the Philadelphia Quarter Sessions of having married one woman in April 1794 and then another the following February; Mary Lloyd, the first of these two wives, noted that recent conviction in her petition for divorce, submitted in the summer of 1795. But keeping track of marital histories in a large and chaotic metropolis was extremely challenging, so that bigamy and adulterous cohabitation seldom came to the courts' attention save in the context of divorce petitions.[25]

Because it was not unusual for eighteenth-century Americans to uproot themselves and resettle, often at a great distance from their previous place of residence, it could prove well nigh impossible for individuals contemplating remarriage to ascertain whether a previous spouse was even alive, let alone cohabiting with someone or remarried. When Benjamin Franklin and Deborah Read wanted to marry in the late 1720s, they had to decide how best to deal with Deborah's previous and complex marital history. Several years earlier, she had married a potter named Rogers, but she "soon parted from him, refusing to cohabit with him or bear his name, it being now said that he had another wife." Rogers had since then moved to the West Indies in order to escape his creditors and was rumored to have died in a fight. But there was no "certain" information regarding his death (merely "a report"). Moreover, although "a preceding wife was said to be living in England," this "could not easily be proved because of the distance." If Benjamin and Deborah married without first securing proof either that Rogers was dead or that an earlier marriage invalidated his later one, they themselves could be liable to punishment as adulterers and bigamists. They "ventured, however, over all these difficulties" and Franklin "took her to wife." But Deborah simply came to live with Benjamin and assumed his name; they never formalized their relationship in a public ceremony. Fortunately for them, the previous husband never resurfaced. Franklin and his wife doubtless felt that they were making the best of a difficult situation. Though Pennsylvania law required public marriage, the Franklins do not appear to have been stigmatized for their failure to comply with that requirement.[26]

Those Philadelphians who wanted to marry in a formal ceremony often had their own ideas as to the circumstances under which they should be allowed to do so. Nicholas Collin, the rector of Gloria Dei, a Swedish Lutheran church located in Southwark, condemned "licentious manners which in this part of America, and especially in Philadelphia, are evidently striking, and which in matrimonial affairs are so pernicious." This reads at first glance like an attack upon loose morals, but the primary issue exercising Collin was not so much immorality as disregard for official marriage requirements. The institution of matrimony was far from moribund in Southwark: during his forty-five-year tenure at Gloria Dei, Collin married more than three thousand couples. But many more he refused to accommodate. Although these unsuccessful candidates clearly saw formal marriage as desirable, their notion of what qualified them to wed was quite different from his own.[27]

Many of those who approached Collin assumed that they should be free to marry as and when they saw fit, regardless of their legal status or previous spousal commitments. What mattered from their perspective was that they wanted to live together as man and wife; nothing else should interfere. Over half of those turned away by Collin could not prove that they were free to wed. The pastor refused to marry couples if he suspected that one or both of the parties had been previously married and neither divorced nor widowed. In January 1795 he would not wed a seaman to an alleged widow because he "found reason to believe that she had a second husband living." The couple was subsequently "married by some other clergyman," perhaps because this colleague was oblivious of the possibly bigamous nature of their union. Couples often realized that Collin would have his own ideas about marital requirements and so tried to adapt their stories to his expectations, usually by lying. Marriage applications sometimes turned into a battle of wits between the minister and those who sought to trick him into wedding them. Collin's principal motive in keeping a record of unsuccessful applications was to "prove the prudence of [his] conduct against blame for cases against which no caution can secure." One such incident came to light in January 1794 when a man came "to ask whether a certain Mary White had been married." Collin told him that she had indeed been wed "on the 10th of December last, as per record." The man "declared her to have been his wife, though she pretended widowhood."[28]

Collin required that young people who were unaccompanied by their parents or guardians provide written proof of their consent; he also wanted to see freedom papers, since those who were bound by apprenticeship or indenture could not marry without a master's permission.[29] It was not unusual for young adults without the necessary documentation to try to deceive Collin. In January 1800 an applicant named Thomas Snowden "asserted that he had come from England to the West Indies when a boy, and from there to Philadelphia; that he was a comedian, belonging to the theatre here; [and] that he was not in the least related to

any of that name in the city." But he turned out to be the son of a Philadelphian. His bride, who "had assumed a false name," also came from a
local family. Other applicants were quite honest about their not having
parental consent and tried to persuade Collin that he should marry them
anyway. A young man who arrived at Collin's door in September 1794
"sincerely confessed that his father was not willing" and yet hoped that
they could proceed. The following January, another candidate "strongly
entreated" the pastor "to dispense with certificate of the father's consent."
Some "begged very hard" and were furious when their entreaties proved
ineffectual. One thwarted couple "went off in a vicious manner, throwing
a large stone against the entry door."[30]

Young couples whom Collin turned away were often perplexed or enraged by what they saw as an infringement upon personal liberty, "insisting on their capacity and right of choosing for themselves," regardless of
whether they met the legal criteria. One pair, turned away by Collins because there was no proof of permission from the bride's father, "thought
it very odd, as many others, having no idea of parental authority." A shoemaker whom Collins refused to marry because he could not produce freedom papers departed in a "miff, saying he was free and independent." He
"behaved otherwise civilly, but ha[d] no idea of civil order."[31] Couples
evidently believed that they should be "free" to marry on impulse and that
their own desires should be the only qualifications that mattered. One
"bridegroom gave as a strong reason for his importunity, that his love
was so violent that he might suffer if he refrained from bedding with her
that night." Another "young couple" arrived at his door, "without previous notice, at ten in the evening." Collin "refused until they brought
evidence" and became even less sympathetic when "the girl" responded
"with levity." She declared, "if I do not now marry him, I never shall, for I
may marry his rival." This young woman claimed to have "earnest desire
of the rite," but neither her understanding of matrimonial requirements
nor her manner met with Collin's approval. "Liberty! Liberty," lamented
the pastor, "in a shape often seen by me! Wretched manners!"[32]

Premarital pregnancy also created tension between Collin and those
who believed that marriage procedures were there to serve them as they
saw fit. Some couples sought to conceal their having been sexually intimate prior to marriage by having ministers antedate their marriage certificates. These Philadelphians took seriously the notion that sex should not
precede marriage: they had not complied with it, but they did expect the
clergy to cooperate in making it appear that they had done so. There were

pastors in and around Philadelphia who were willing to falsify marriage dates. But the punctilious Collin refused to cooperate. In April 1800 he recorded that "a young man in trade, of good connections, applied three times with earnest sollicitations and offers of reward for being married with antedating the certificate, in order to conceal his premature connection with the bride, for whose reputation he expressed great anxiety." Collin "refused with ample demonstration of the necessity for official veracity, and the pernicious consequence of falsifying records." Later that same year, another couple made a similar request: they "could not be made to comprehend," wrote Collin, "my reasoning on the impropriety and many bad consequences of such fraud."[33]

Other couples lived together for substantial periods of time without marrying and then decided, for whatever reason, to formalize their relationship. In March 1794 Collin joined in matrimony a man and a woman who had "cohabited for six years." He was doubtless happy to oblige on this occasion since their union would now become licit in the eyes of church and state. Collin recognized that the very strictness of marriage protocol could drive some committed couples to settle for informal cohabitation. He predicted that one man whom he refused to marry would probably try his luck with "one or two other clergymen" and then, if they also turned him away, "either quit the woman or live with her without wedlock." Along with those who cohabited without formalizing their union, bigamists also contributed to what Collin saw as an "extreme want of order" in personal relationships. Collin focused his outrage upon those who had "two or more wives by getting married in diverse places," a ploy that seafaring men were occasionally discovered to have used. Most bigamists in eighteenth-century Philadelphia were, however, not polygamists but serial monogamists. Insistence by city-dwellers that they should be "free and independent" to establish and dissolve marital relationships in whatever manner suited them was doubtless encouraged by the spirit of the revolutionary period, but there was nothing new about the attitudes that Collin and others condemned as immoral and licentious. Such attitudes had proved themselves remarkably resilient throughout and beyond the colonial period, despite vociferous opposition from those invested in legal and ecclesiastical norms.[34]

YET WE CANNOT DISMISS all contemporary reports of "licentious" behavior as the product of differing perspectives upon sexual and marital propriety. Eighteenth-century Philadelphia's sexual culture had become increasingly unbridled, as the widespread circulation of sexually transmitted disease and large numbers of "bastard" children made abundantly clear. As early as the 1720s, when Benjamin Franklin first came to Philadelphia, the atmosphere was already both permissive and hazardous. Franklin later admitted to having sowed many a wild oat in his youth: "that hard-to-be-governed passion of youth had hurried me frequently into intrigues." He managed to avoid venereal infection, "a distemper which of all things I dreaded, though by great good luck I escaped it." However, at about the same time that Franklin married Deborah Read, he did acquire an illegitimate son. There survives no reliable information about the mother's identity or her ultimate fate; the infant, named William, was brought into the Franklins' home and raised there. But not all children born outside marriage were so lucky, and unwed pregnancy often had dire consequences for the mothers concerned.[35]

Social rank was a significant factor in shaping a woman's experience of unmarried pregnancy. Single women from affluent families could be sent away to bear in secret out-of-wedlock children for whom no man had acknowledged responsibility; the offspring would then be disposed of discreetly. If young ladies were to pass as exemplars of sexual morality and so attract a respectable husband, they could do no less. The establishment of academies for women in the decades following the American Revolution seems to have provided relatives with a convenient alibi for such absences. According to a foreign traveler staying in the city, it was not unusual for families to claim that a daughter had gone to attend the academy in nearby Wilmington when she had in fact departed from the city "to hide her state."[36] Gendered conceptions of virtue and moral guardianship were less relevant to poorer unwed mothers living in Philadelphia, but many of these women faced problems of a different nature. Although there were official mechanisms in place to assist them in extracting support from the fathers of their children, such men could prove elusive. Unmarried mothers often found, moreover, that their employment opportunities were severely curtailed, leaving them destitute and desperate with no relatives at hand to care for them.

Pregnant women who were working as hired servants could find themselves thrown onto the streets by unsympathetic employers. The greater independence that came with a shift from indentured servitude to hired labor was, as these young women discovered, a double-edged sword. Consider the very different experiences of two servants working in the Drinker household, one indentured and the other hired. In August 1794 the Drinkers discovered that Sally Brant was pregnant by Joe Gibbs, a black servant working for the household who was dismissed soon afterward.[37] Because Brant was an indentured servant and so could not be fired, her master and mistress had little choice but to shoulder the cost of her pregnancy, including loss of labor, the child's delivery that December, and the infant girl's burial when she died the following July.[38] Elizabeth Drinker clearly resented the disruption and expense that resulted from Sally Brant's pregnancy. Drinker's response to the baby's death is telling: "'tis gone, and no doubt but all's for the best."[39] There had been no such inconveniences or distasteful responsibilities when Polly Moore, a hired servant working in the Drinker household, turned out to be pregnant. Moore arrived on 24 November 1781 and left three months later. As Drinker explained in her diary, "she has been near a quarter here, and is now near lying in, I was glad to get rid of her." Moore was allowed to stay as long as she was still able to work but no longer.[40]

Brant's dependent status had its price. She wanted to name the infant Hannah and give her Joe's surname, but Drinker insisted that the child be named Catherine Clearfield, after the Drinkers' summer home where the baby was born. Drinker was determined to prevent Sally from having any further contact with Joe and had the infant nursed elsewhere, so as to avoid "bringing the parents together, or reviving the former liking to the sire." On 14 February 1795 Drinker "intercepted a letter today from J.G. to our S.B.," and a week later Henry Drinker, her husband, "overtook Joe a few doors from our house." Elizabeth Drinker recorded approvingly that Henry "laid his cane over [Joe's] back, and told him, if he found him sculking about our neighbourhood he would lay him by the heels." Joe "looked sheepish, and walked off without reply." But Brant was at least taken care of. The Drinkers had no contractual obligation toward Moore and so got rid of her once pregnancy began to interfere with her work for them.[41]

Employers such as Elizabeth and Henry Drinker expected their servants to abide by strict moral standards, yet such expectations clashed with the increasingly permissive atmosphere of the city in which they lived as well as the greater freedom asserted by servants in the aftermath of Independence. Drinker expected that the pregnant Sally Brant would exhibit some sense of shame, especially after having been brought up from her "tenth year" in such a respectable household. However, the young woman "appear[ed] to be as full of glee as if nothing ailed her but what was right." Drinker had "more trouble" with Sally Brant in April

1795, when she was seen "ogling" with "a fellow opposite our kitchen." The same man had apparently "been talking with and kissing her" in the Drinkers' yard. This gave the mistress of the house "much uneasiness," since Brant was not the only servant living in and Drinker was "afraid of her bad example." Brant's "vile propensity" struck Drinker as particularly unfortunate in that she was otherwise "one of the most handy and best servants we have ever had, and a girl of very pretty manners." Moralist Benjamin Rush urged employers to keep a close eye on servants at all hours, including "the evening, when they cease[d] to be subject to government" and were "in the most danger of corruption." But this was easier said than done, especially when dealing with hired servants, whose time when not actually working was very much their own. Nonindentured laborers who proved to be unsatisfactory could, however, be discharged. That was Polly Moore's experience.[42]

Relationships that began on "evening promenades" could, then, leave single women more permanently out on the streets or in the almshouse. In theory, there were mechanisms in place to protect single mothers and their children from indigence. Out-of-wedlock births had become, as one contemporary put it, "extremely common in Philadelphia," and the city's officials were eager to prevent women who bore "bastards" from becoming a drain upon the public purse. The Guardians of the Poor administered a procedure for registering unwed fathers and extracting from them bonds ensuring paternity support.[43] Some unwed mothers, however, either did not know who had fathered their children or had no idea where they were. A "black wench" with whom our anonymous sawyer spent the night gave him "much fright" by asking where he lived so that "in case of increase from contact she would make known to me the fact." He replied that he lived "in the Carolinas" and "fled." She may have believed him and so assumed that, in case she became pregnant, he could not be reached or held accountable. Mary Johnson, admitted pregnant to the almshouse in May 1796, said "that the father of her child [was] one James Steel, a sailor with whom she ha[d] been long intimate and familiar at her place of service and frequently elsewhere, that she had informed him of her condition to which he made little reply [and that] the last time she saw him was about a month ago, since when she ha[d] heard that he [was] gone to sea."[44]

Unmarried mothers who were unable to call upon the fathers of their children for assistance could find themselves in desperate straits. Many of the single women living in Philadelphia had come to the city alone and had no relatives or friends nearby to provide support if needed. Mary

McAllen, "a pregnant woman lately arrived from Ireland," was admitted to the almshouse in September 1796. A man named Hugh Black had brought her into the city "as a redemptioner" (that is, she would be bound out as a servant in exchange for the cost of her transport across the Atlantic). But on "finding he could not dispose of her time under existing circumstances," Black "abandoned her to her fate." For those women who reached the end of their pregnancies unemployed and homeless, the almshouse was usually the only alternative to giving birth in the streets. The refuge that it provided, however, was only temporary. Sophia Fitzpatrick secured admission on 6 May 1800, gave birth to a daughter on 3 June, and was discharged three weeks later. Fitzpatrick now faced the considerable challenge of finding and keeping employment as the mother of an infant child.

Some mothers, driven to desperation by indigence or shame, either abandoned their babies or put them to death. In August 1780 Drinker noted in her diary that "a new born infant was taken out of the river this afternoon with a wound in its neck—supposed to have been murdered." In January 1799 a Portuguese visitor to the city reported in his journal that "a newborn child" had been found in front of the house in which he was staying, "lying dead in the snow." This child was not necessarily the victim of infanticide: it may have been abandoned after dying of natural causes; or it may had been left outside the house alive in hope that the residents would take it in and then died before its discovery. Indictments for infanticide were few and far between. This is hardly surprising, since the size and constant movement of the city's population would have made it extremely difficult to identify and trace the parents of such children. But the houseguest was horrified that "no investigation was made" about the infant or the circumstances under which it perished.[45]

If abandoned infants survived the ordeal of exposure, they were taken to the almshouse and eventually bound out to local families. But many of them were in poor condition when they arrived and had little chance of living that long. The almshouse clerk noted in July 1794 that "an unknown foundling child, which was found at a door in the Northern Liberties and then sent here where it was put in care," had now died. Some of the infants brought to or born within the almshouse were suffering from venereal infections that were passed on by their parents. In February 1790 the almshouse admitted Elizabeth Nicholson, "a poor feeble infant of between two and three years old, deserted by her parents" and apparently infected "with the venereal disease from her birth." Edward Griffin, born on the premises in March 1790, was, like his mother, "very bad with the venereal disease." A month later, the infant died "in a miserable way."

Venereal disease constituted a major medical problem in Philadelphia at this time. Contemporaries used the term to describe both syphilis ("the pox") and gonorrhea ("the clap"). Most medical experts held that both conditions were caused by the same "poison" and that gonorrhea was a manifestation of syphilis. Some city-dwellers overcame or at least contained infection by drawing on the expertise of neighborhood doctors. On 4 May 1772 Dr. Thomas Anderton announced in the *Pennsylvania Packet* that he had set up facilities in his "large commodious house, next door to his flint-glass store" in the city "for a private reception and cure of venereal patients," promising "secrecy" and "every suitable accommodation to render their short stay agreeable." In February 1791 another physician located in Black Horse Alley placed an advertisement in *Dunlap's American Daily Advertiser,* announcing that he specialized in curing "venereal complaints." For individuals such as the sexually voracious sawyer, venereal infection seems to have been a manageable, albeit unpleasant, problem. But over time the disease could take a terrible toll as it worked its way through the body. The Pennsylvania Hospital admitted scores of men and women in advanced stages of infection. Venereal patients were placed in separate wards, located "in a little building on the other side of the court" from the main structure. In addition to the hospital's patients, a significant number of those admitted to the almshouse were described in the register as "venereal," "highly venereal," or "eaten up with the venereal disease." Around 10 percent of those who entered the institution between June 1800 and June 1801 were listed as infected (9% of the men and 16% of the women). As in the hospital, these inmates were treated in separate "venereal" wards.[46]

Infected men and women arrived at the almshouse gate because they were too sick to support themselves. Mariners figured prominently among the "venereal" men who sought refuge there. Daniel Smith, an Irish sailor who had lived in the city for ten years and "sailed out of it in the employ of several merchants," applied for admission in October 1800, "now very lame and venereal and not capable of contributing towards his living by any kind of labour." But others had worked as carpenters, bricklayers, ironworkers, shoemakers, printers, tailors, blacksmiths, and shipbuilders. John Harkins, "a young man and shoemaker" admitted in September 1790, was "so emaciated with the effects of venereal diseases as not to be able to do anything at his trade." William Cronkleton had been employed "slating stone" in various Pennsylvania quarries, but by the fall of 1794 could no longer work because he was "so far gone in the venereal disease." That October he was found in a "distressed condition in the streets and sent here in a wheelbarrow."

Married men who contracted venereal disease while visiting whorehouses or having casual sex with women whom they met in the city might then pass on infections to their wives. When our anonymous diarist came down with the "clap" and complained of "much itching in [his] flopper," he also noted his intention to "keep away from [his] wife" while infected.[47] We have no way of knowing whether he kept to this resolution, but a woman named Elizabeth Smith informed almshouse officials that she had caught the disease from her husband, a laborer at Clark's Ferry. She was admitted in December 1789 and died the following July "in a mortified state." The clerk noted in June 1792 that Submit Hickman's husband, "a tailor by trade," had "communicated that fatal disease to this poor woman." She died a month after admittance. And Andrew Duncan, a sailor, apparently infected his wife Sarah before going to sea; she sought admission in December 1796.

The majority of "venereal" women admitted to the almshouse were prostitutes, too ill to continue plying their trade and without means of support. Ann Brown was brought to the almshouse in January 1793 "from a bawdy house in Southwark." She was "in a deplorable situation" and died that March. Like other almshouse inmates, prostitutes often resented the strict regulations to which they were subjected and so "jumped the fence" before they had fully recovered. Hannah Levy eloped, "though not yet half cured," in July 1795. When she returned the following February, the clerk complained that "there [was] no such thing as keeping [her] in or out." A month later, after receiving medical attention and putting up with the restrictions upon her freedom as long as she could bear it, she made her escape. The clerk wrote caustically that she had eloped again and "gone forth to propagate, not the gospel (for she is a Jewess) but the disease." Whether or not Levy did infect others, the reluctance of venereal patients to stay in the confining atmosphere of the almshouse until fully recovered made recurrence of the disease and its further circulation highly likely. In August 1792 the almshouse clerk described two prostitutes as "town boiling ladies," a reference to their contagious effect upon sexual partners. John Roberts, who was "known as a tender or waiter among the fish sellers" (in other words, a pimp), had been "cooked" by "the dirty husseys" and was admitted, "highly venereal," in July 1797.[48]

The treatment that "venereal" patients received was itself grueling and ghastly, which further helps to explain why so many of them eloped from the almshouse though only "partly" or "nearly" cured. Venereal disease had become the subject of intense study by the late eighteenth century. Though medical experts disagreed as to how such infections spread through the body, they were virtually unanimous in arguing that mercury-based therapies were by far the most effective in combating both "local" and "constitutional" manifestations of the disease. John Hunter, one of England's foremost pioneers in experimental pathology, was no exception. Hunter published his influential *Treatise on the Venereal Disease* in 1787; an abridged version was printed in Philadelphia that same year. Hunter did recognize that other substances such as gaiac "possess[ed] some power over the disease" and reported that recent experiments with electricity had yielded promising results in the treatment of venereal warts, but mercury was "the only medicine to be depended upon." Like other doctors, Hunter recommended a range of mercury treatments, internal and external. He favored, for example, an external ointment made of "crude mercury and fresh hogslard" as well as mercury gargles for ulcers of the mouth and throat. For venereal warts, he counseled that "stimuli applied to their surface" would "make them wither and die" and that they could also be "cut off with a pair of scissors." "An inflammation excited around them" would "often make them drop off." A "caustic" such as "the rust of copper and powder of savine leaves" should then be applied to the base.[49]

The prominence of abrasive therapy in the treatment meted out by almshouse physicians is underlined by the official record's repeated description of the ward set aside for that purpose as "the polishing room." The clerks frequently used nautical metaphors to characterize prostitutes and their medical treatment. Drawing a sardonic parallel between the treatment given in the "polishing room" and the overhaul of barnacled and leaky boats, they described the condition of prostitutes on leaving the almshouse as "new bottomed but not thoroughly repaired," "somewhat patched or mended up," "rebottomed and fit to proceed," or "well enough to go out of dock and proceed on a cruise."[50] Eleanor Murren was discharged in July 1797 after having been "careened, boot-topped, hovedown, and polished over; and though all her leaks may not be stopped, yet many worm holes may, and though not coppered she hath sailed again." Just as prostitutes in early modern London were sometimes referred to as "punks" (small sailing ships), so the almshouse records conjure up an image of the institution as a harbor to which damaged vessels came for repair before setting off on another cruise.

Mercury treatments could, of course, prove fatal to much more than the venereal infection. Hunter recommended the use of opium in conjunction with both internal and external treatments. Mercury was, he warned, especially dangerous if applied to "weakly persons" or those "labouring under any chronic disease." He claimed that external applications were less risky in that the skin was "capable in itself of bearing much more than the stomach," so that the treatment would "affect the constitution much less."[51] But any form of mercury treatment was, as Hunter acknowledged, harmful in its own right. The Philadelphia almshouse was well acquainted with the perils of such therapies. In August 1792 Hannah Giles arrived in a cart, "having lost the use of her limbs by too much familiarity with mercury." Andrew Courtney, who was admitted in May 1798, was scarred by "venereal relics" and suffering in his throat "from mercurial applications."

THE ALMSHOUSE CLERKS rarely devoted space in their entries to expressions of sympathy for the unfortunates passing in and out of their institution. But they were especially inclined to callous remarks when dealing with prostitutes: they used a range of derogatory epithets to describe these women, including "vile strumpet," "dirty venereal trollop," "common hussey," and "infamous trull." Officers of the law were no less hostile toward "women of ill fame," referring to them in presentments as "idle, lewd, and disorderly." Philadelphia prostitutes had customers aplenty, but they also provoked much controversy and outrage among city-dwellers. Sexual commerce attracted attention as the most visible symptom of the city's uninhibited sexual culture, combining the treatment of sex as a form of recreation with a marketplace mentality. Prostitution struck moralists as having a disruptive impact upon marriage and family life, as well as occasioning chronic "disorder" outside the household, not least of all in the form of violence that erupted in and around brothels. And images of "fallen," "immoral," and "disorderly" women provided an ominous foil to the holy trinity of femininity, moral virtue, and national welfare so prominent in republican rhetoric at the close of the eighteenth century. While republican wives and mothers strove to sustain the new nation's moral fiber, prostitutes threatened to undermine it.

By the middle of the century, sexual commerce had become an entrenched and highly visible part of seaport culture. Alexander Hamilton, who visited New York City in 1744, was told by a customs officer that prostitutes frequented the battery, "a great half moon or semicircular rampart bluff upon the water." This helpful fellow informed Hamilton "that to walk out after dusk upon this platform was a good way for a stranger to fit himself with a courtesan." There was apparently "a good choice of pretty lasses among them, both Dutch and English." The expansion of maritime trade and of the ports that functioned as commercial hubs ensured a growing demand for prostitutes, as did the presence of troops in these cities during the Seven Years' War and then the War of Independence.[52] The ranks of those offering sexual services were swollen by the presence in seaports of women who found themselves dislocated, widowed, and often desperate as a result of the wars that raged in the middle and later decades of the eighteenth century. By the revolutionary period, most of the New York prostitutes lived in a neighborhood several blocks north of the battery. This district, adjacent to St. Paul's Chapel and owned by the Episcopal Church, was referred to by waggish locals as "the Holy Ground." St. Mery noted that there were "many houses of debauchery" in the Holy Ground and that "whole sections of streets" were "given over to streetwalkers for the plying of their profession." Women "of every colour" could be found there, "particularly after ten o'clock at night, soliciting men and proudly flaunting their licentiousness in the most shameless manner."[53]

Bored and sexually frustrated soldiers stationed in New York provided steady work for the city's prostitutes. In 1776 Lieutenant Isaac Bangs, who had joined the Continental Army that January, heard that "many of our officers and soldiers" were spending time at the Holy Ground and visited the district "out of curiosity" to see the women who allured them. Bangs was horrified not only by the "impudence," "immodesty," and "brutality" of the "horrid wretches" who worked there but also by the danger of venereal infection to which his fellow officers and subordinates exposed themselves repeatedly, "notwithstanding the salutary advice of their friends, till the fatal disorder seized them and convinced them of their error." Bangs learned to his consternation that venereal disease was affecting a significant proportion of the troops: "I am informed that not less than forty men of one regiment which last Sunday set off for Quebec were infected with that disorder." These men, he ruminated, were in no condition "to undergo a fatiguing march."[54]

Concern about prostitution was not limited to those such as Lieutenant Bangs who feared its impact upon the moral and physical well-being

of soldiers. While many city-dwellers, sailors, and other visitors partici-
pated eagerly as consumers in this market (some more conspicuously than
others), critics of prostitution pointed to the immorality, disorder, and
violence that it fostered. Some of these attacks were laced with humor,
but even satiric disquisitions on the subject often gave voice, however
obliquely, to disquietude about prostitution as the most obvious manifestation of a more permissive and less family-oriented sexual culture. The
fictional biography of a prostitute and brothel owner named Moll Placket-
Hole (her surname referring none too subtly to the opening in a woman's
skirt), published for the entertainment and edification of Philadelphians
in 1765, illustrates well the kinds of anxiety aroused by sexual commerce.

Moll was born in a bawdy house run by her mother "in a lane in the
City of Brotherly Love." Her father's identity was unknown. Moll grew
up in the brothel and spent much of her childhood "prying into the mystical employment of her mother's customers," peeping through "every
crevice" she could find to observe "scenes" that the author deemed "too
indecent to be described here." Her mother's business was "failing" by
the time Moll reached the age of twelve, and so she "sold" her daughter's
"virginity" to a gentleman who "was soon cloyed and abandoned her."
Moll now "commenced open prostitute and dealt out her favours to the
highest bidder." There followed seven years of "nothing very remarkable"
save "common occurrences to women of her profession," such as "poxes,
claps," and several visits to "houses of correction." Moll was now about
twenty and found that "she could not get a livelihood any longer in this
way," since her body was already "broken by disease." Having watched
her mother at work since infancy, "she understood the trade and set up
a bawdy house" of her own. Moll "furnished" her establishment with
"handsome husseys," and her business did extremely well: "she herself
became rich, and bought a house and sundry lots of ground."

But her "trade became at last so public that it gave offense to her sober
neighbors." Mothers "mourned for their children, unguarded youths who
had been drawn in there"; ministers "declaimed against the vice, both
in public assemblies and private companies." The city magistrates "resolved to punish all such offenders as could be found out," and so Moll
"disappeared till the storm blew over." On returning "in triumph," she
rather foolishly "exulted" in her impunity and "insulted everyone who,
she believed, had complained against her." Citizens enraged by her "in-
solence" and "escape from justice" proceeded to retaliate by "set[ting] a
mob (many of whom had been her beneficiaries) upon her." The rioters

"pulled down her house and destroyed her furniture," but the resourceful and ruthless Moll threatened to publicize the names of her customers unless they built her "a better house." Terrified by the prospect of exposure, her clients "opened a subscription, and a hundred pounds were subscribed in one day." There the brief account ended. "What the latter part of her life may be," the author wrote, "God knows."[55]

Although Moll's story was intended to titillate, its themes of youthful corruption, illegal commerce, violence, and blackmail were hardly frivolous. The author ended his tale on an unequivocally serious note. Most predictably, he railed against brothel houses as "seats of idleness and debauchery." In addition to violating "the divine law which declares that whoremongers and adulterers God will judge," prostitution "destroy[ed] the bodies and estates of the people," as well as "discourag[ing] matrimony, the best seminary for raising good members of a commonweal." Since the family remained a potent symbol of both order and morality in American society, it is hardly surprising that denunciations of sexual commerce often noted its impact upon family life. The *New York Gazette* complained in 1766 that the authorities were not doing more to shut down houses of ill-repute, thus depriving "virtuous wives" of the "pleasure of their husbands' company at home." And Philadelphian Charles Peale was aghast that "married men amongst [his] acquaintance" frequented such establishments. "How horrid," he wrote in 1778, "that a man who has a family where he might find all the enjoyments of a domestic life should go abroad to herd with a set of prostitutes."[56]

Critics of sexual commerce objected to the violence that often broke out in and around brothels as well as the moral license that they fostered.[57] By no means all such critics were members of the urban elite. In 1790 worried residents of Southwark, a poor and rowdy district of Philadelphia, formed an association devoted to "suppressing vice and immorality." The members wanted to close down all houses "of bad character," including brothels and the more notorious taverns. An article in the *Federal Gazette* enthused about their campaign, especially given its potential to save young people from "destruction" in such establishments. This group had apparently ceased to operate by the middle of the decade. But in August 1795 *Aurora* announced that "several citizens of the district of Southwark," inspired by a recent speech in which the mayor of Philadelphia had asked for public "countenance and support in the preservation of the order of the city and in the suppression of vice and immorality," had formed a new organization. Their objective was "to aid the civil officers in bringing disorderly persons to punishment and to prevent the growth and spreading of immoral or vicious practices."[58]

By the end of the decade, frustrated Southwark residents were ready to take the law into their own hands. In August 1800 a brawl between a boatswain and a blockmaker broke out at "a house of ill fame" known as the China Factory (so called because china had been manufactured in a building on the same site in the 1770s). The reason for the quarrel is now obscure, but as it escalated into a fight, "their mistresses" apparently "encouraged neither to yield." The brawl resulted in the death of the blockmaker. Both women and the boatswain were arrested, but that was not enough to satisfy locals. The coroner's verdict of manslaughter provoked a mob to attack and demolish the China Factory as well as several other brothels in the neighborhood. A newspaper report noted that "police officers" had "made few and feeble (if any) efforts" to check the mob. It conceded that any such effort "would have been useless": these establishments had been "for a long time the subject of regret by all the well-disposed citizens of Southwark; and the eagerness with which this opportunity was seized for their destruction is sufficient proof of the detestation in which their infamous occupants was held by the public." Elizabeth Drinker copied the newspaper report into her diary, commenting that she was "pleased to hear that such creatures were routed" but "could wish that a more justifiable power had taken them in hand long ago." That "any such houses" should be "suffered" was "a shame to our police."[59]

Philadelphia's constables had not completely ignored the presence of prostitutes and brothels in the city. Along with drunken brawlers and other unruly types, they regularly detained women such as Margaret Britton, who was found "skulking about country wagons in High Street at a late hour" in the hope of finding sexual partners "to get money." Prostitutes who walked the streets in search of clients were often presented for vagrancy as well as immoral behavior. From the perspective of city officials, it was not just their "lewd purpose" but also their "perambulating the streets of this city at late hours of the night," along with their "insolent" and often "riotous" behavior that made such women a menace to law and order.[60] Brothel-keepers were also occasionally charged with criminal activity. Such was the fate of Frederick and Mary Foy, found guilty in June 1798 of "keeping a bawdy house." The court fined them both and sentenced them to imprisonment with hard labor. The following March, Maria Cashman was convicted on an identical charge. Yet offenders such as these were soon back out on the streets. City officials mounted no systematic campaign against "strumpets" or the "houses of ill fame" in which many of them worked. As a foreign visitor pointed out in the 1790s, it was only when "neighbours complain[ed] of any exterior scandal" that whorehouses were "shut, and the inhabitants carried to the house of correction." Otherwise, "the municipal police connive[d] at this sort of house."[61]

The ad hoc nature of official responses to prostitution was exemplified by the Philadelphia almshouse and its treatment of ailing "strumpets" who, having been "worn out in the service," sought refuge within its walls. Until the 1760s, Philadelphia's Overseers of the Poor had provided relief to the city's destitute in the form of money, food, and firewood. But as the cost of providing relief increased along with the number of those seeking assistance, officials decided that it would be more economical to provide institutional care for the poverty-stricken in an almshouse where able-bodied inmates could be made to work for their keep. A building was constructed for that purpose in 1767, but the almshouse sought to provide only temporary shelter for the indigent and sick; it offered no lasting solution to the plight of those admitted. Some adults were bound out as indentured servants, but the primary purpose of doing so was to reimburse the institution for the expense of caring for them. City officials would occasionally note the desirability of binding out a young woman "in the country" as "a means of reclaiming her from the lewd and vicious courses which she ha[d] followed."[62] But they developed no coherent strategy for addressing the long-term fate of prostitutes who came within their purview: just as "strumpets" who were arrested and sentenced by the vagrancy courts to imprisonment and hard labor were usually released a month later, those who gained admittance to the almshouse were expected, sooner or later, to leave and fend for themselves in the precarious world outside. Officials treated these women as disorderly, degenerate, and mostly incorrigible. They witnessed and recorded the downward spiral of disease, debility, and destitution into which prostitutes often fell. But they saw that suffering as the price of immorality and lawlessness. Absent from their responses to the plight of individual women was an appreciation of the practical circumstances that drove women into sexual commerce.

Those circumstances were clear enough to a French nobleman, the duke of Rochefoucault-Liancourt, who visited Philadelphia at the close of the century. Rochefoucault noted that it was women "without sure means of subsistence" who turned to "this illicit practice," especially "the wives of seafaring men" and other married women whose husbands had died, abandoned them, or were working elsewhere. We might add that single young women also turned to prostitution because they lacked "sure means of subsistence." What united all these women was their economic vulnerability as free laborers in an urban seaport economy. A growing proportion of Philadelphia's women—single, married, separated, abandoned, and widowed—worked as hired servants. Unless they had capital behind them, there were few alternative forms of employment. Whereas servitude had constituted one stage in the life cycle of many colonial women, it now became a permanent condition for a growing proportion of female laborers, especially those living in large cities such as Philadelphia. Immigrants generally worked first as indentured and then as hired laborers. Though pregnant women no longer able to work at normal capacity and those ailing from various diseases were particularly likely to find themselves unemployed and on the streets, hired servants were in general extremely vulnerable, even if healthy and fully productive. Only eight of fifty women working for the Drinker family between 1760 and 1800 stayed for more than one year. Some servants doubtless left positions voluntarily or because they proved unsatisfactory, but employers took full advantage of their freedom to hire and fire servants at their own convenience. A downturn in the general economic situation or a particular family's fortunes could result in the dismissal of domestics whose services were no longer affordable. Some jobs were by their very nature temporary or seasonal. Given the meager wages paid to servants, few would have been able to save for hard times.[63]

Faced with the challenge of supporting themselves in an unpredictable and often hostile job market, scores of women living in Philadelphia turned to prostitution. When female servants joined other Philadelphians at night in the city streets and taverns, they would have observed "ladies of pleasure" plying their trade. Some servants apparently augmented their salaries by "traffic[king] in their charms" while out on their "evening promenade." For those who supplemented their wages in this way, prostitution may have seemed a promising option if they found themselves out of work, offering a way to capitalize on the city's permissive culture and their own personal freedom. It could prove lucrative, at least in theory, and furthermore, a prostitute did not have to put up with the restraints imposed by employment in a genteel household. There were other possible attractions. Destitute and friendless women may have found a much-needed haven in bawdy houses. Glove Hunt suspected that his run-away servant, Mary McCormick, was "harboured in some lewd house." Charlotte Bennett's husband claimed in a divorce petition that she had been seen "frequenting houses of ill fame" and that she lived with "an avowed prostitute" after leaving him. Bennett presented this information to illustrate his wife's alleged depravity, but she and other women such as McCormick may have sought "harbour" among those who worked in "houses of ill fame" at least in part because that seemed the best way to survive. Sexual commerce created a female subcommunity that must have been tenuous and yet provided some measure of support for other-wise solitary and desperate women. Diseased prostitutes who had to seek refuge and treatment in the almshouse were often taken there by other women in the same business. Maria Carr was "brought in a carriage by two of her equals" in December 1797. These women could not afford to support each other through illness, but neither did they simply abandon sick friends.[64]

Not all women who turned to prostitution remained permanently in that occupation. Rochefoucault claimed to have heard "many examples of this description of women, who leave those situations, place them-selves as servants, or are married, and make faithful domestics and hon-est wives."[65] But although some women may have used prostitution as a temporary means of survival, for others it became a deadly trap. Making enough money to survive, let alone save for the future, was often thwarted by the occupational hazard of venereal disease. Consider the experience of Mary McCullock, who had migrated from Ireland, "served her time" as an indentured servant in Philadelphia, and was working the streets as a prostitute by the early 1790s, when she began to seek refuge in the almshouse during bouts of infection. Amelia Wheeler "served her time" in Baltimore and then came to Philadelphia in search of work. She also ended up supporting herself through prostitution; like McCul-lock, she stayed in the almshouse while incapacitated by venereal and other ailments. Given the prevalence of sexually transmitted infection in late-eighteenth-century Philadelphia, women who turned to prostitution faced the distinct possibility of a gradual and gruesome descent into in-firmity. Some of the "worn out unhappy strollers," wrote the almshouse clerk in February 1790, spent their time in "almost a perpetual round between the jail, workhouse, hospital, and this place." Margaret Hurst, who would often arrive "dirty and diseased," departing once she had been "somewhat patched up" only to return again in as bad or worse condition, was readmitted "very helpless" and for the last time in June 1797; she died that October. Ann Gallagher was another frequent and "highly diseased" visitor whose gradual degeneration during the 1790s was detailed in the almshouse records. In December 1795 she was found "in a suffering or almost perishing condition in a saw pit." She eloped the following March but was readmitted in November 1796, having been "found laying in a yard by Thomas Earnest near his house in a situation supposed near dying." She was "brought in a cart" and expired the following night.[66]

City officials responded to the vicissitudes of women such as these on an occasional basis, showing little regard for their long-term fate. It would be misleading, however, to claim that no Philadelphians pondered why women became prostitutes or cared about their welfare. The most coherent and sustained attempt to engage with the individual lives and struggles that underlay sexual commerce was informed by a moral paradigm. When a group of concerned citizens met in February 1800 at the Quaker schoolhouse on Pine Street to plan a concerted response to what they saw as the scourge of prostitution, they took their cue from the deluge of literature on seduction and sexual degradation that had appeared over the preceding decades in magazines, newspapers, and novels. Members of the Magdalen Society, as this group named itself, committed themselves to work for the redemption of "unhappy females" who had been "seduced from the path of innocence and virtue" by "wicked and abandoned men." The members did acknowledge that women turned to prostitution through economic desperation and lack of familial or community support, but they saw moral corruption as the root cause of both predicaments. The society planned to establish an asylum in which a combination of religious instruction and hard work would promote the virtues of chastity and industry, "recovering to honest rank of life" those "affected with remorse" and "desirous of returning to a life of rectitude."[67]

Rather than providing a temporary refuge of last resort, the Magdalen Society's asylum was intended to incarcerate, segregate, and redeem the inmates through relentless discipline and spiritual instruction. Unfortunately for all concerned, this ambitious scheme was based on priorities and goals quite different from those of the women whom it sought to save. As a result, once the program got under way, its executioners encountered a good deal of resistance from Philadelphia's Magdalens. Few women sought refuge within the asylum walls ("a matter of surprise and of deep regret to the managers"), whereas some of those who did soon became convinced that they would be better off elsewhere: a high fence had to be built around the asylum in 1811, partly to protect the inmates from "prying eyes" but also "to prevent the escape of discontented Magdalens."[68]

SINCE MOST DISCUSSIONS of prostitution at the close of the eighteenth century were framed as morality tales, it is hardly surprising that the Magdalen Society followed suit. Seduction and abandonment narratives depicted prostitutes as having been reduced to that way of life by a fatal lapse of judgment, usually brought on by the deceitful blandishments of a rakish admirer. That genre was generally sympathetic toward deserted women who became outcasts and, in many cases, prostitutes. But other contemporary depictions of prostitution were less compassionate. Literary representations of the trade and its participants varied considerably in terms of who figured as villains and victims.

Brothel-keepers almost always appeared in accounts of prostitution as less than sympathetic figures. The author of Moll's "life and adventures" minced no words with regard to the abusive nature of sexual commerce. He excoriated "mercenary harpies" who ensnared young women and "deluded" them into "such practices." Moll herself had "inveigle[d] unwary girls" whom she found in the market: one target "discovered the design" before it was too late, and another was rescued by a client who recognized her as "the daughter of his friend," but a less fortunate woman was "now languishing in a hospital," presumably afflicted by venereal disease. According to The Philadelphiad, brothel-keepers would assume an air of pious respectability ("a nun-procuress" with "well-dissembled looks" and "pious prejudice for heav'nly books") in order to win the trust of young women whom they hoped to recruit. "Prone to deceive and watchful to beguile," they "trap[ped] the unwary female" by "seeming fair and kind." These images of ensnared and exploited young innocents were much indebted to current literary motifs. The whorehouse matron became the female equivalent of the villainous male seducer.[69]

But young women lured into prostitution by manipulative whorehouse matrons were not the only victims to appear in eighteenth-century depictions of sexual commerce. Once "estranged" from "modesty and virtue," the "poor, unfortunate, and miserable prostitute" became a seducer in her own right, "allur[ing] unwary youth by her fatal powers of delusion." Young men were apparently "enticed" by "ladies of pleasure" ("so pretty . . . so glittering") into a life of depravity, oblivious for now to the "fire below" that would later infect and wrack their bodies. A particularly lurid poem entitled "Bagnio" (common parlance for brothel in the eighteenth century) described how one "youth" was drawn to "court the low raptures of the harlot's bed":

> Delusive joys betray his tender heart,
> Ensnar'd, bewilder'd by the wanton's art;
> The leg half-naked and the breast quite bare,
> With all the studied ornament of hair,
> The garments loose to raise the warm desire,
> And touch the passions with a keener fire,
> Her syren voice that captivates the ear,
> With tempting gestures and inviting leer:
> These move his heart and youthful mind employ,
> Till fated pleasure proves 'tis baneful joy.

This rather slanted perspective on a young man's descent into disease-ridden debauchery fits well with prevalent assumptions about male susceptibility to female charms and the frailty of a man's higher faculties once lust had been inflamed. Images of womankind had now bifurcated: virtuous and responsible young ladies embodied chastity and restraint, whereas women deficient in either social or moral grace were still portrayed in terms of their lechery and untrustworthiness.[70]

Late-eighteenth-century accounts did occasionally recognize that some of those gentlemen who went with prostitutes were hardly victims. These "bucks" or "men of pleasure" lacked any moral scruple and even boasted of their "dirty low amours." They "swore that marriage was a wanton fit," and preferred "a bagnio" or "lift[ing] some trull" to domestic comforts. Callous and crude in word and deed, they made "rude" advances even "to harmless females as they harmless walk[ed]," assuming that any woman whom they met in the street at night must be sexually available. According to one depiction, their coarse and presumptuous behavior aroused violent hostility among less privileged Philadelphians. One "woman-hunting" gentleman apparently "account[ed] it a most manly precaution to carry a brace of pistols or a sword about him, when on his nocturnal revels." The "buck" related "that he and some of his companions [had] pick'd up a girl (his own phrase) and took her to the common (very gentleman-like indeed), that they were followed by some harmless tradesmen, whom after some words of altercation they shot and cut in a cruel manner, but somehow or other Johnny escaped punishment."[71]

That the recreational activities of "rakes" and "bucks" did in fact provoke popular outrage is confirmed by a 1793 riot that broke out in New York City after the acquittal of accused rapist Henry Bedlow. Lanah Sawyer, a young seamstress and daughter of a sailor, claimed that Bedlow had treated her to ice cream, taken her on a late evening stroll around the battery, and then dragged her forcibly to a bawdy house ran by a Mrs. Cary, where he deflowered her. Bedlow admitted that they had sex, but maintained that it was consensual. When the jury voted to acquit Bedlow, a large and "enraged" crowd of New Yorkers sacked Mrs. Cary's establishment. The rioters went on to attack several other brothels and also the homes of Bedlow's defense attorneys. Media coverage of these events was far from sympathetic to the "popular indignation" unleashed on Sawyer's behalf. Several newspaper accounts condemned the "shameful riots" and "indecent outrages" upon private property by "boys, apprentices, and negroes, as well as sailors." A second wave of commentaries appeared when a female correspondent signing as "Justitia" denounced Bedlow as "a wretch," referred caustically to the destruction of brothels as "a matter of great grief for many of our male citizens," and suggested that such establishments were much of the time left undisturbed because the magistrates who should have suppressed them were among their clients. One of several abusive responses accused "Justitia" of promoting "anarchy and misrule." A writer who called himself "Justitius" insisted that all citizens, "whatever may be their professional demerit," deserved "the protection of the law" and pointed out rather defensively "that in order to exterminate vice we must exterminate mankind." Justitia had clearly touched a nerve.[72]

Popular outrage regarding the sexual abuse and exploitation of poorer women by well-heeled urban males rarely surfaces in discussion of prostitution during this period. But in a striking parallel with Justitia's letter, Moll Placket-Hole's biographer acknowledged in his opening remarks that patrons frequenting brothels had a vested interest in the trade's continuation and that these customers included influential citizens who could prove formidable enemies to those who attacked the brothel business. Exposing "vice" that involved not only "the lower class of people" but also "the rich and great" was, he wrote, a perilous enterprise. The author referred tellingly to "lewdness or oppression joined with power," a phrase that encapsulated effectively the collusion of Philadelphia's male elite in an illegal and exploitative trade that benefited them as well as the assumptions made by privileged men regarding the sexual availability of poorer women. Seduction tales regularly denounced individual rakes, but this remark posited a more general, even systemic, abuse of status and authority. Such comments were, however, exceptional, and the main narrative of Moll's life focused attention upon her own depravity and blameworthiness.[73]

Given the widespread belief among postrevolutionary Americans that a stable republic required a virtuous citizenry and the central place accorded to women in nurturing that virtue, it is hardly surprising that officials, leading citizens, and writers at the end of the eighteenth century would have responded to prostitution in terms of the threat that its practitioners posed to order and morality in the new nation's metropolis. That these images of prostitutes and their employers appeared alongside celebrations of chaste young ladies who inspired their menfolk to forsake lives of debauchery was no coincidence. In chapter 8 we saw how anxious republican writers were that women should protect their own virtue, so that they could become and remain effective guardians of the new nation's moral integrity. Prostitutes symbolized the failure, or rather dereliction, of a woman's mission to embody and inspire virtue: the degenerate and chaotic atmosphere that surrounded them provided a grim metaphor for what would happen to the republic if its citizens slid into lives of self-serving pleasure and moral corruption. Narratives of seduction and abandonment often showed the descent of women from chaste respectability into ruinous depravity: such could be the fate of the United States. Meanwhile, prostitutes who satisfied the appetites of sexual consumers in Philadelphia and elsewhere often sought to avert more personal catastrophe. Those preoccupied by the specter of moral anarchy and national degeneration paid scant attention to the mundane deprivation that faced many of those women who turned to prostitution. Their primary concern was basic survival.

IN SEPTEMBER 1794 the Philadelphia almshouse clerk noted that Con McCue, a young Irishman admitted two months previously "in the last stages of the venereal disease," had now died and so "finished his martyrdom to Venus." There were many such martyrdoms during this period in Philadelphia, undergone by men and women whose intimate encounters bore deadly fruit. But the city's permissive sexual climate proved especially hazardous for women. Single female servants who became expectant mothers could lose their jobs once pregnancy impaired their performance at work and so find themselves on the streets without family or friends to assist them. Some of those women who, for whatever reason, could not find work in the city's harsh labor market turned to the sexual marketplace and sought to support themselves as prostitutes; in so doing, they often unwittingly signed their own death warrants.

The young people who came to live and work in Philadelphia during the latter part of the eighteenth century exemplify a gradual but fundamental shift that was taking place in American society. Less constrained than their parents and grandparents by ties of family, neighborhood, dependency, and deference, they operated as free individuals and asserted their right to do so; these young adults enacted the principles of independence and freedom that patriot leaders enshrined in their revolutionary declarations. We should not exaggerate the degree to which change had occurred in deeply rooted agricultural communities; nevertheless, for those who migrated westward or into coastal cities, such changes were very real. That new sensibility would become one of America's richest blessings, but its ramifications were ambiguous: as urban society became less organic and more individualistic, that left its members less protected as well as less restricted by the corporate and hierarchic ties of the past.

With personal independence came new forms of vulnerability. Institutions such as the almshouse proffered temporary assistance to the needy but then turned recipients back onto the streets, their underlying problems unresolved. Men and women who suffered misfortune in this brave new world had far fewer resources within the community to fall back on; for them, individual freedom must have been a lonely and frightening experience. Moralists insisted, meanwhile, that freedom should not be conflated with license and were seldom inclined to sympathy for those who became sick or needy as a result of apparently "vicious pleasures." Even amid social and economic atomization, reformers still sought to impose their own values upon other residents of the city. In Philadelphia and elsewhere, reconciling the new nation's rhetoric of righteousness with its commitment to individual freedom would prove a thorny and lasting challenge. Not surprisingly, eighteenth-century Americans were sometimes overwhelmed by the dilemmas and contradictions inherent in the society taking shape before their very eyes. Philadelphia embodied in extreme form the ironies of that new society. As pastor Nicholas Collin acknowledged sardonically, the cry of "Liberty!" had brought unexpected consequences.

Afterword

Late-eighteenth-century assertions of sexual independence found both an ideological pretext and further impetus in revolutionary ideology. That appropriation of political rhetoric galled people like Southwark minister Nicholas Collin, who sought to de-legitimate what they saw as "false ideas of liberty." The greater personal freedom now enjoyed by those who lived in urban centers such as Philadelphia as well as by young adults in northern rural communities reflected a momentous transformation that had taken place over the preceding century as organic conceptions of society gave way to more individualistic notions. That public debate relating to sexual propriety in New England had shifted from attacks on mixed dancing to disputation over the circumstances under which young people were to spend the night together suggests how much things had changed. Yet neither the reality of that sexual revolution, nor the adoption of emancipatory rhetoric by those who deemed themselves "free" to form and dissolve personal relationships as they saw fit, nor the horrified reaction of those wedded to a more restrictive version of sexual order should blind us to an underlying continuity. Issues of sexual and marital protocol had divided inhabitants of the British colonies in North America throughout the colonial period; even the very meaning of sexual respectability had been deeply contested from the early decades of settlement and remained unresolved at the close of the eighteenth century.

That ongoing struggle over sexual morality did not simply pit two opposing camps, one espousing and the other rejecting moral order, against each other. Instead, it took the form of a tripartite engagement between those who championed official values, those who adhered to alternative sexual codes, and those who disregarded issues of morality altogether or gloried in sexual license as an expression of genteel libertinism. In seventeenth-century New England, the authorities had done their best to quell rambunctious folk who sang dirty songs, ran naked around the local pond, and otherwise delighted in offending more straitlaced neighbors. But they also had to deal with settlers who saw themselves as decent, respectable members of the community and yet defined sexual propriety in terms quite different from those mandated by church and state. The New Haven court "laboured hard" to convince Benjamin Graves that he had sinned in having sexual relations with a woman to whom he was not married, "but little prevailed" because Graves had considered himself betrothed at the time and believed that premarital sex was quite inoffensive.[1] Further south, a generally less fastidious population and the frequent unavailability of officials who could conduct marriages resulted in widespread recourse to informal cohabitation, often without any sense of wrongdoing on the part of those involved. When officials accused such couples of living together illicitly, they and their neighbors would sometimes respond by pointing out that they were in effect married; such unions were, from their perspective, neither morally or socially problematic.[2]

The contentious sexual culture of early America was shaped in part by heterogeneous values and practices that the colonists brought with them across the Atlantic. The varying priorities and demographic characteristics of settlers in each region of British America influenced sexual mores just as they did all other aspects of colonial life. But these attitudes and behavioral patterns took on new forms and clashed with each other in new ways as they found expression in novel settings. Interaction with Indian and African peoples in North America complicated that interplay of values as colonists pondered new possibilities for sexual expression and the cultural dangers that came with them. Sexual intimacy that crossed racial boundaries had profound implications for colonial self-perception, especially in terms of the settlers' need to sustain a sense of their own civility: interracial unions exemplified the distinctive and seemingly de-based nature of the new world in which they found themselves. The prevalence of miscegenation in southern slave societies, despite the passage of legal codes forbidding interracial unions, dramatized the lack of consensus over where sexual boundaries should lie. Interracial sex troubled not only those who eschewed such intimacies but also some of those who did engage in sexual relations with their slaves. This issue divided southerners within themselves as well as from each other as patterns of sexual behavior collided with the imperative to preserve civility through racial segregation.

Whether debating interracial unions or sexual and marital protocol within the white population, moral critics emphasized that the dynamics of sexual behavior had broad social significance. According to these critics, sexual mores both expressed and shaped the moral values of society as a whole. Puritans held that sex played a crucial role in nurturing or undermining the spiritual health of individuals and the society in which they lived; reformers in the South feared that apparent moral laxity among white settlers betokened a general dereliction of civility; and opponents of miscegenation worried that such "mixings" would taint white partners and result in their overall decomposition as civilized persons. For those who feared that a colonial setting might facilitate degeneration into savagery as well as those who later emphasized the need for virtue in a republican society, the articulation and regulation of sexual ethics were especially significant.

Anxieties about miscegenation and the gradual erosion of restraints upon sexual behavior within the white northern and urban population during the course of the eighteenth century each provoked explicitly gendered responses that had lasting and ambiguous implications for women. Southern fear of interracial sex led to particular emphasis upon the need for white women to avoid intimate relations with black men; women became the repositories of sexual virtue and racial purity, an arrangement that conveniently enabled male planters to consort with black women while continuing to exalt ideals that their wives and daughters embodied. As young white couples further north became freer to experiment sexually prior to marriage and as urban centers facilitated uninhibited behavior, women were enjoined to avoid the dangers of seduction and abandonment by exercising careful judgment and self-control during courtship. In each of these contexts, women were expected to exert a restraint of which men were often deemed incapable. This representation of women as guardians of sexual morality exalted them as an invaluable cultural commodity and simultaneously limited their personal freedom. Meanwhile, denigration of men as morally frail and involuntarily lustful could operate as an alibi for male sexual license. Thus, the apparent veneration of women as ethical exemplars created an insidious double standard. This combined with an emerging belief that men and women had distinct personalities to create a gendered conception of moral order that rapidly gained ascendancy in republican society. By the early nineteenth century, idealized images of womanhood exhibited morally impeccable, increasingly desexualized figures who could and should inspire men to transcend their own more depraved instincts. But wives and mothers, now conse-

SEXUAL REVOLUTION IN EARLY AMERICA

crated by a cult of domesticity as the priestesses of moral order, were effectively prisoners in their own temples; those who forsook normative roles or whose lack of means prevented them from embracing domesticity and its ideals would be branded as having failed in their mission as women.[3]

Republican ideology reinvigorated a conception of society in which the sexual morality of individuals sustained both public order and cultural legitimacy. Yet sexual mores remained diverse and contested. City-dwellers were deeply divided in their responses to the permissive sexual environment of seaports such as Philadelphia; likewise, the widespread occurrence of bundling in northern rural communities gave rise to spirited debate. Southerners were equally heterogeneous in their codes of conduct. Recall itinerant minister William Ormond's objection in the 1790s to a ruling by the General Conference of Methodists that applicants for church membership should not be admitted if they had "put away a wife or husband and married again." Serial monogamy, including informal separation and subsequent marriages that the law condemned as bigamous, had by no means died out in the area of North Carolina through which Ormond traveled; the pastor realized that this ruling might exclude significant numbers of well-meaning men and women who wished to become members of his church. The furor that broke out in the first decade of the nineteenth century over John Clary's election to the North Carolina assembly after having been convicted of "fornication" with his stepdaughter centered on disagreement as to whether moral virtue and civic aptitude did indeed go together.[4]

Moral commentators today who argue that only certain kinds of sexual relationships should be accorded cultural legitimacy often point to colonial society as an ideal from which modern Americans have degenerated. Yet those in search of a usable past would do well to bear in mind that our own struggles over the delineation of sexual and marital respectability (including recent debates over the legal status of domestic partnership and gay marriage) offer striking parallels with those fought by settlers in the British colonies of North America and citizens of the new republic. Modern conceptions of sexuality and of sexual orientation are far removed from the categories through which early Americans made sense of their sexual urges and behavior. The fundamental issues driving sexual debate remain the same, however: competing sexual codes that stress either exclusive or more inclusive standards for judging intimate relationships still struggle to coexist; Americans continue to frame that debate in terms of the correlation between sexual mores and the character of society as a whole; and as the great republican experiment continues into the twenty-first century, the quest for personal freedom still collides with a hankering after moral community. Defining and sustaining sexual ethics as a crucial part of who we are, individually and collectively, remains a daunting enterprise.

Notes

Dates are represented throughout the notes in an abbreviated, numerical style and should be read as day/month/year.

Introduction

1. *Measure for Measure* was performed before James I on 26/12/1604. It was probably written earlier that year for performance at the Globe after its reopening in April; London's playhouses, inns, and brothels had been shut down through 1603 and into early 1604 because of the plague.

2. Quotations from *Measure for Measure*, act 1, sc. 1, 2, 3.

3. Ibid., act 1, sc. 2; act 2, sc. 1, 4; act 3, sc. 1.

4. For discussion of the reformist agenda and its impact, see Patrick Collinson, *The Religion of Protestants: The Church in English Society, 1559-1625* (Oxford, 1982); Christopher Haigh, *Reformation and Resistance in Tudor Lancashire* (Cambridge, 1975); and Christopher Haigh, *English Reformations: Religion, Politics, and Society under the Tudors* (Oxford, 1993); William Hunt, *The Puritan Moment: The Coming of Revolution in an English County* (Cambridge, Mass., 1983); and Barry Reay, "Popular Religion," in Barry Reay, ed., *Popular Culture in Seventeenth-Century England* (London, 1985).

5. Quotation from *Measure for Measure*, act 1, sc. 2.

6. For the contents of this paragraph and the preceding one I am much indebted to Martin Ingram, *Church Courts, Sex, and Marriage in England, 1570-1640* (Cambridge, 1987), esp. chaps. 4 and 7. See also David Cressy, *Birth, Marriage, and Death: Ritual, Religion, and the Life-Cycle in Tudor and Stuart England* (Oxford, 1997); and J. A. Sharpe, *Defamation and Sexual Slander in Early Modern England* (York, Eng., 1980). The campaign against premarital sex was also driven by worsening economic conditions and local concern about the implications of bastardy for poor relief: churchwardens were well aware that if an engaged couple had sex, conceived, and then failed to marry, the illegitimate child that resulted might well become a public charge. See Keith Wrightson and David Levine, *Poverty and Piety in an English Village* (New York, 1979), esp. 132-33.

7. William Bradford, *Of Plymouth Plantation, 1620-1647*, ed. Francis Murphy (New York, 1981), 70; William Byrd I to Daniel Horsmanden, 8/8/1690, in Marion Tinling, ed., *The Correspondence of the Three William Byrds of Westover, Virginia, 1684-1776*, 2 vols. (Charlottesville, Va., 1977), 1:136.

8. Thomas Morton, *The New English Canaan* (1637; Boston, 1883), 114, 179; George Chapman, Ben Jonson, and John Marston, *Eastward Ho*, ed. R. W. Van Fossen (Baltimore, 1979), 137–38; Henry Neville, *The Isle of Pines, or, A Late Discovery of a Fourth Island Near Terra Australis, Incognita* (London, 1668).

9. See Winthrop D. Jordan, *White over Black: American Attitudes toward the Negro, 1550–1812* (Chapel Hill, N.C., 1968), 4–9.

10. These references to "improvement," "blanching," and "blackening" are discussed and cited in chap. 6. Jordan also links the Protestant Reformation and its promotion of self-scrutiny with the ways Englishmen envisaged nonwhite peoples, though the psychological dynamic that he posits is somewhat different from the one suggested here. According to Jordan, Englishmen were "inclined to discover attributes in savages which they found first but could not speak of in themselves" (ibid., 40). I would argue that Englishmen on both sides of the Atlantic were eager to "discover" savagery in other peoples precisely because contemporaries were so vocal about the depravity that they saw in themselves and their fellow countrymen.

11. Quotations from *The Tempest*, act 1, sc. 2.

12. James Glen, governor of North Carolina, to Lords of Trade, 25/10/1753, *Public Records Office Transcriptions*, 25:350–51; [James MacSparran,] *America Dissected* (Dublin, 1753), 9–10.

13. The legality of private marriage ended with Lord Hardwicke's Marriage Act of 1753, which required a public ceremony. Church marriage not only reinforced ecclesiastical prerogative but also benefited couples by bestowing upon their unions a public recognition and certainty that unchurched marriage could not offer. See Cressy, *Birth, Marriage, and Death*, 316–17; Ingram, *Church Courts, Sex, and Marriage*, esp. 132; and Lawrence Stone, *Road to Divorce: England, 1530–1987* (New York, 1990), 64–66. Although most couples did marry in a public ceremony, private espousal had by no means died out, and church courts often cited couples for informal cohabitation (Cressy, *Birth, Marriage, and Death*, 329).

14. John Miller, *A Description of the Province and City of New York . . . in the Year 1695* (London, 1843), 14–16. For the law enabling justices to formalize marriages, see John D. Cushing, ed., *The Earliest Laws of New York* (Wilmington, Del., 1978), 149–50.

15. John Winthrop, "A Model of Christian Charity," in Alan Heimert and Andrew Delbanco, eds. *The Puritans in America: A Narrative Anthology* (Cambridge, Mass., 1985), 90.

16. William Hand Browne et al., eds., *Archives of Maryland*, 72 vols. (Baltimore, 1883–1972), 54:9, 10.

17. For an analogous distinction in the realm of supernatural belief, see Richard Godbeer, *The Devil's Dominion: Magic and Religion in Early New England* (New York, 1992), esp. 16. E. P. Thompson identifies in eighteenth-century England "a rebellious traditional culture . . . rebellious in defence of custom" (*Customs in Common* [New York, 1991], 9).

18. David M. Halperin, *One Hundred Years of Homosexuality, and Other*

Essays on Greek Love (New York, 1990), 18; see also Bruce R. Smith, *Homosexual Desire in Shakespeare's England: A Cultural Poetics* (Chicago, 1991), 10-11; and Robert A. Padgug, "Sexual Matters: On Conceptualizing Sexuality in History," *Radical History Review* 20 (1979): 16. John H. Gagnon and William Simon develop the concept of sexual "scripts" (ranging from those shared by all members of a given society to "intrapsychic scripts" that express an individual's most private and idiosyncratic desires) in *Sexual Conduct: The Social Sources of Human Sexuality* (Chicago, 1973), esp. 1-26; and John H. Gagnon and William Simon, "Sexual Scripts," *Society* 22 (1984): 53-60. There has been lively debate among scholars as to the cultural contingency of sexual categories; see Edward Stein, ed., *Forms of Desire: Sexual Orientation and the Social Constructionist Controversy* (New York, 1990). Readers unfamiliar with recent theories of sexuality will find a lucid introduction to the field in Joseph Bristow, *Sexuality* (New York, 1997).

19. Byrd's conceptualization of sex is discussed in chap. 6.

20. Though same-sex desire surfaces repeatedly as a significant issue in this book, there is no separate chapter on the subject: I have deliberately chosen to place issues that we might consider distinct in conjunctions that made sense to early Americans; that approach will, I hope, bring us closer to understanding the place that sex occupied in their lives.

21. Literacy was more widespread in New England than elsewhere in the seventeenth-century colonies because of the importance that Puritans attached to reading Scripture. Reading and writing skills improved dramatically throughout British America over the course of the eighteenth century, but literacy still varied significantly according to social status, sex, and race. For discussion of early American literacy and the scholarly debates centering on this issue, see Hugh Amory and David D. Hall, eds., *A History of the Book*, vol. 1, *The Colonial Book in the Atlantic World* (Cambridge, 2000); David D. Hall, *Worlds of Wonder, Days of Judgment: Popular Religious Belief in Early New England* (New York, 1989), chap. 1; and Cathy N. Davidson, *Revolution and the Word: The Rise of the Novel in America* (New York, 1986), chap. 4.

22. Roy Porter, "Forbidden Pleasures: Enlightenment Literature of Sexual Advice," in Paula Bennett and Vernon A. Rosario, eds., *Solitary Pleasures: The Historical, Literary, and Artistic Discourses of Autoeroticism* (New York, 1995), 91.

1. "Chambering and Wantonising"

1. Religious dissenters in general were often smeared with charges of sexual license; see David S. Lovejoy, *Religious Enthusiasm in the New World: Heresy to Revolution* (Cambridge, Mass., 1985), chap. 2.

2. C. H. Firth, ed., *An American Garland, Being a Collection of Ballads Relating to America, 1563-1759* (Oxford, 1915), 29-30.

3. J.W., "A Letter from New-England," in George Parker Winship, ed., *Boston in 1682 and 1699* (Providence, R.I., 1905), 3-4, 5, 9.

4. *Records and Files of the Quarterly Courts of Essex County* (henceforth

ECR), 9 vols. (Salem, Mass., 1911–78); Richard S. Dunn, James Savage, and Laetitia Yeandle, eds., *The Journal of John Winthrop, 1630–1649* (Cambridge, Mass., 1996), 51, 56, 93, 97, 141, 264, 269, 319, 330, 342–43, 350, 368–69, 370–74, 374–76, 500–502; William Bradford, *Of Plymouth Plantation, 1620–1647*, ed. Francis Murphy (New York, 1981), 351; Samuel Eliot Morison and Zechariah Chafee, eds., "Records of the Suffolk County Court, 1671–1680," *Colonial Society of Massachusetts Publications* 29–30 (1933); and Robert Roetger, "Order and Disorder in Early Connecticut: New Haven, 1639–1701" (Ph.D. diss., University of New Hampshire, 1982), chap. 3.

5. Bradford, *Of Plymouth Plantation*, 351–52.

6. Ibid., 356–57.

7. See Daniel Vickers, *Farmers and Fishermen: Two Centuries of Work in Essex County, Massachusetts, 1630–1850* (Chapel Hill, N.C., 1994), esp. 188–89; and Christine Leigh Heyrman, *Commerce and Culture: The Maritime Communities of Colonial Massachusetts, 1690–1750* (New York, 1984), esp. 218–21.

8. Middlesex County Court Records (henceforth MCCR), Massachusetts State Archives, Columbia Point, Boston: Order Book for 1681–1686 (transcribed by David Pulsifer), 22; file 97.

9. MCCR: Order Book for 1681–1686, 130, 140; file 109.

10. MCCR: Sessions Records for 1692–99, 46–49, 57–58, 62; files 162, 201.

11. M. Halsey Thomas, ed., *The Diary of Samuel Sewall*, 2 vols. (New York, 1973), 1:140.

12. Promoters of the ironworks to John Winthrop Jr., 13/3/1648, Samuel Eliot Morison et al., eds., *Winthrop Papers*, 5 vols. (Boston, 1929–47), 5:209. Stephen Innes discusses the ironworks venture, the arrival of laborers such as the Leonards, and the implications for Puritan society, in *Creating the Commonwealth: The Economic Culture of Puritan New England* (New York, 1995), chap. 6.

13. *ECR*, 5:351–55.

14. *ECR*, 6:1. Subsequently, the Leonards made at least some effort to identify with community values: in 1679 four members of the family contributed to the church fund supporting a new minister for Topsfield (7:237–38).

15. Bradford, *Of Plymouth Plantation*, 357; "[Francis] Higginson's Journal of His Voyage to New England," in Stewart Mitchell, ed., *The Founding of Massachusetts* (Boston, 1930), 71; Nathaniel B. Shurtleff, ed., *Records of the Governor and Company of Massachusetts Bay, in New England*, 5 vols. (Boston, 1853–54), 1:52, 54; Morison and Chafee, "Records of the Suffolk County Court," 149–50.

16. Morison and Chafee, "Records of the Suffolk County Court," 1061; Joseph H. Smith, ed., *Colonial Justice in Western Massachusetts, 1639–1702: The Pynchon Court Record* (Cambridge, Mass., 1961), 224, 276–77.

17. Both quotations from Worthington C. Ford, ed., *The Diary of Cotton Mather*, 2 vols. (1911; New York, 1957), 1:55. See also William Hubbard, *The Benefit of a Well-Ordered Conversation* (Boston, 1684). Jane Kamensky discusses Puritan attitudes toward the spoken word in *Governing the Tongue: The Politics of Speech in Early New England* (New York, 1997).

18. John Noble and John F. Cronin, eds., *Records of the Court of Assistants of the Colony of Massachusetts Bay, 1630-1692*, 3 vols. (Boston, 1901-28), 2:104; Franklin Dexter, ed., *New Haven Town Records*, 2 vols. (New Haven, 1917-19), 1:245-46, 2:149-50.

19. *ECR*, 3:90.

20. Mary Beth Norton discusses the social functions of gossip in *Founding Mothers and Fathers: Gendered Power and the Forming of American Society* (New York, 1996), 253-69.

21. MCCR: Order Book for 1649-1663, 295; file 34. For more detailed discussion of such manuals, including those attributed to Aristotle, see chap. 7.

22. Nathaniel B. Shurtleff and David Pulsifer, eds., *Records of the Colony of New Plymouth in New England*, 12 vols. (Boston, 1855-61), 4:47, 177; *ECR*, 1:166; Dexter, *New Haven Town Records*, 1:55-56. The combination of drinking and "filthy" singing at Langden's house would not have surprised ministers or magistrates. "When drink is got into the brain," averred Increase Mather, "then out come filthy songs . . . where there is rioting and drunkenness, there is wont to be chambering and wantonness" (Increase Mather, *Two Sermons Testifying Against the Sin of Drunkenness* [Cambridge, 1673], 13-14; see also Cotton Mather, *A Serious Address to Those who Unnecessarily Frequent the Tavern* [Boston, 1726], 6, 23; and Shurtleff, *Records of the Governor and Company*, 1:107, 2:100-101).

23. John Williams, *Warnings to the Unclean* (Boston, 1699), 22.

24. Shurtleff, *Records of the Governor and Company*, 4B:143, 513; Morison and Chafee, "Records of the Suffolk County Court," 82-83. The General Court waged a concerted campaign against illicit sex in the late 1660s and early 1670s. In addition to its order regarding fornication in 1665, the court set up (in 1668) a standard procedure for establishing paternity and child support in cases of bastardy (393-94), clarified (in 1669) the law concerning sex with underage children (437-38), confirmed (in 1670) the illegality of marriage to a deceased wife's sister (454), and passed (in 1672) a law against brothels (513, 532). There was, however, no sudden improvement in law enforcement that would explain the surge in prosecutions. See also J. Hammond Trumbull and Charles J. Hoadly, eds., *The Public Records of the Colony of Connecticut*, 15 vols. (Hartford, 1850-90), 2:282.

25. Roger Thompson shows that young people were highly successful in evading adult supervision and that it was not unusual for offspring from godly families to experiment sexually before embracing respectability; see his *Sex in Middlesex: Popular Mores in a Massachusetts County, 1649-1699* (Amherst, Mass., 1986), pt. 1, esp. 103, 104-5; see also Roger Thompson, *Women in Stuart England and America* (London, 1974), 148-53.

26. Dexter, *New Haven Town Records*, 2:228-29.

27. MCCR: file 38.

28. See Thompson, *Sex in Middlesex*, 20.

29. MCCR: file 52; Dexter, *New Haven Town Records*, 2:65-71.

30. Dexter, *New Haven Town Records*, 1:497-99, 505-7.

31. Charles J. Hoadly, ed., *Records of the Colony and Plantation of New Haven* (Hartford, Conn., 1857), 81, 84; Charles J. Hoadly, ed., *Records of the Colony or Jurisdiction of New Haven* (Hartford, Conn., 1858), 366.

32. Dexter, *New Haven Town Records*, 2:186; Shurtleff, *Records of the Governor and Company*, 5:63.

33. MCCR: Order Book for 1649-1663, 217-18; file 25. Neither Stearns nor Fleming was enrolled at the college.

34. "A Letter from the Rev. Mr. Thomas Shepard to His Son at His Admission into the College," *Colonial Society of Massachusetts Publications* 14 (1913): 193, 197.

35. Quoted in Thompson, *Sex in Middlesex*, 87-88.

36. Ibid., 148; Dexter, *New Haven Town Records*, 1:125-26, 450-52; 2:26-31, 42-44.

37. Cotton Mather, *An Holy Rebuke to the Unclean Spirit* (Boston, 1693), 60.

38. Increase Mather, *An Arrow Against Profane and Promiscuous Dancing* (Boston, 1686), 2, 3, 14, 16, 27. Cotton Mather, who also attacked "the dancing humour," did acknowledge that "persons of quality" might justifiably "employ a dancing master, with due circumstances of modesty, to instruct their children how to carry themselves handsomely in company" (Cotton Mather, *A Cloud of Witnesses* [Boston, 1700], 1).

39. Thomas, *Diary of Samuel Sewall*, 1:83, 88; M. G. Hall, ed., "The Autobiography of Increase Mather," *Proceedings of the American Antiquarian Society* 71 (1961): 319; "Diary of Increase Mather," vol. 11, 12/2/1704, Massachusetts Historical Society, Boston. Richard P. Gildrie discusses attempts to sustain a reformist impulse during these years; see *The Profane, the Civil, and the Godly: The Reformation of Manners in Orthodox New England, 1679-1749* (University Park, Pa., 1994).

40. See Godbeer, *Devil's Dominion*, chaps. 1 and 2.

41. Bradford, *Of Plymouth Plantation*, 95.

42. Members of the clergy in Massachusetts were authorized in 1692 to perform marriages; Connecticut followed suit two years later. See Chilton Powell, "Marriage in Early New England," *New England Quarterly* 1 (1928): 323-34.

43. Mary Beth Norton discusses "disagreement between lawmakers and ordinary English settlers" on this issue in *Founding Mothers and Fathers*, esp. 66-69. According to Norton's data for the first half-century of settlement in New England, 43.5% of fornication defendants were married couples (466 n. 48).

44. "Boston Second Church Records," Massachusetts Historical Society, vol. 4, 1689-1717, cases of Elizabeth Denham (3/2/1692) and Stephen Johnson (25/11/1701). See also William Upham, ed., *Records of the First Church in Beverly, 1667-1772* (Salem, Mass., 1905), 12, 18, 47, 48, 49, 55; "Records of the Congregational Church in Topsfield," *Historical Collections of the Topsfield Historical Society* 14 (1909): 11-12, 14, 18, 19, 21, 22; and Richard D. Pierce, ed., *Records of the First Church in Salem, Massachusetts, 1629-1736* (Salem, Mass., 1974), 140,

173, 175, 177, 194, 209, 224, 239, 247, 249, 261, 274, 296, 297, 300, 313, 318, 319, 321, 322.

45. Two-thirds of the couples prosecuted for this offense in Middlesex County during the second half of the seventeenth century included at least one person from a covenanted family (Thompson, *Sex in Middlesex*, 65).

46. Hoadly, *Records of the Colony and Plantation of New Haven*, 75, 77–78; William Brigham, ed., *The Compact with the Charter and Laws of the Colony of New Plymouth* (Boston, 1836), 79–80, 246.

47. Hoadly, *Records of the Colony and Plantation of New Haven*, 435; Dexter, *New Haven Town Records*, 2:160–61.

48. Dexter, *New Haven Town Records*, 2:11.

49. "Early General Records of the Colony of New Haven," 1B:328–31, Connecticut State Library, Hartford; for their marriage, see Norton, *Founding Mothers and Fathers*, 467 n. 59.

50. MCCR: file 52. Sarah's sister, Mary, told the court that Christopher had made advances toward her as well. According to Mary, Christopher had said that "he would marry me if I would yield to him, but because I would not he gave me a box on the ear and said, 'Get ye gone, you dirty slut, now I will go to your sister.'"

51. Shurtleff, *Records of the Governor and Company*, 1:132–33; MCCR: file 163. See also *ECR*, 9:96. For an exceptional case in which a woman was accused of having "ensnared and deluded sundry young men upon pretense and promise of marriage to countenance and cover unlawful familiarity with them," see Dexter, *New Haven Town Records*, 2:160–61.

52. *ECR*, 7:316–18.

53. William Whitmore, ed., *The Andros Tracts*, 3 vols. (Boston, 1868–74), 3:15.

54. *ECR*, 8:101.

55. John Russell Bartlett, ed., *Records of the Colony of Rhode Island and Providence Plantation in New England, 1636–1677*, 10 vols. (Providence, R.I., 1856–65), 2:99–103; see also G. Andrews Moriarty, "Herodias (Long) Hicks-Gardiner-Porter: A Tale of Old Newport," in *Genealogies of Rhode Island Families from Rhode Island Periodicals* (Baltimore, 1983), 599–606.

56. Bartlett, *Records of the Colony of Rhode Island*, 2:99–103. Soon thereafter, Horod Long married John Porter, a prominent Rhode Islander who was himself recently divorced. Their petitions were submitted to the same court session and may well have been coordinated.

57. Ibid., 1:187; 2:103–5.

58. *Records of the Court of Trials of the Colony of Providence Plantations, 1647–1670*, 2 vols. (Providence, R.I., 1920–22), 2:48.

59. Norbert B. Lacy, ed., "Records of the Court of Assistants of Connecticut, 1665–1701" (M.A. thesis, Yale University, 1937), 55–56. Elizabeth Jarrad sought a legal termination of the marriage several years later.

60. Morison and Chafee, "Records of the Suffolk County Court," 517; *ECR*, 1:199. For other examples of extralegal renunciation, written and oral, see Cornelia Hughes Dayton, *Women before the Bar: Gender, Law, and Society in Connecticut, 1639–1789* (Chapel Hill, N.C., 1995), 116-18.

61. Morison and Chafee, "Records of the Suffolk County Court," 1158. See also Lacy, "Records of the Court of Assistants of Connecticut," 37-38, 53-54, 105, 118, 615, 673.

62. Lacy, "Records of the Court of Assistants of Connecticut," 96; *ECR*, 9:535-38.

63. Noble and Cronin, *Records of the Court of Assistants*, 2:89; Shurtleff, *Records of the Governor and Company*, 2:86. In some instances the authorities received incriminating information that enabled them to preempt bigamous unions. See, e.g., Trumbull and Hoadly, *Public Records of the Colony of Connecticut*, 1:351-52; Morison and Chafee, "Records of the Suffolk County Court," 232, 943.

64. Short-term visitors and those "come over to make way for their families" were automatically exempted. Shurtleff, *Records of the Governor and Company*, 2:211-12; Trumbull and Hoadly, *Public Records of the Colony of Connecticut*, 1:350.

65. *ECR*, 1:123-24. For other cases in which settlers were sent to rejoin spouses, see Noble and Cronin, *Records of the Court of Assistants*, 2:67, 89; Morison and Chafee, "Records of the Suffolk County Court," 23, 108, 119, 232, 425, 518-19, 720, 779-80, 811, 942, 943; *ECR*, 1:274, 275, 306.

66. Shurtleff and Pulsifer, *Records of the Colony of New Plymouth*, 5:33, 6:44-45; Bartlett, *Records of the Colony of Rhode Island*, 3:164.

67. "Boston Second Church Records," vol. 4, 1689-1717: case of Hannah Bishop (23/1/1696).

68. See, e.g., Trumbull and Hoadly, *Public Records of the Colony of Connecticut*, 2:328. For cases relating to this law, see 1:362; 2:129, 293, 322; and Shurtleff, *Records of the Governor and Company*, 3:277, 5:188. In England, the Bigamy Act of 1604 had forbidden remarriage within the lifetime of an earlier spouse unless he or she had been missing for seven years, or the couple had been divorced, or the first marriage had been annulled because one or both parties were underage (Ingram, *Church Courts, Sex, and marriage*, 150).

69. Lacy, "Records of the Court of Assistants of Connecticut," 55-56.

70. For the transcripts from Sension's trial, see "Crimes and Misdemeanours," 1st ser. (1662-63 to 1789), vol. 1, nos. 85-102, Connecticut Archives, Connecticut State Library; and Lacy, "Records of the Court of Assistants of Connecticut," 67-68. Jonathan Ned Katz discusses this case in *Gay/Lesbian Almanac: A New Documentary* (New York, 1983), 111-18. See also Linda Auwers Bissell, "Family, Friends, and Neighbors: Social Interaction in Seventeenth-Century Windsor, Connecticut" (Ph.D. diss., Brandeis University, 1973), 123-28; and Richard Godbeer, " 'The Cry of Sodom': Discourse, Intercourse, and Desire in Colonial New England," *William and Mary Quarterly* 52 (1995): 259-86. Lim-

ited biographical information is contained in Henry Reed Stiles, *The History and Genealogies of Ancient Windsor, Connecticut . . . 1635-1891*, 2 vols., rev. ed. (Hartford, Conn., 1891-92). Sension's date and place of birth are unknown. His wife was admitted to church communion in January 1649, but Sension himself does not appear to have been a church member.

71. "Crimes and Misdemeanours," 1st ser., 1:87a, 88a, 101.

72. Ibid., 1:89.

73. Ibid., 1:99.

74. Ibid., 1:88a, 91, 95b.

75. Ibid., 1:96a, 96b. Not all of those who engaged in sodomy took religious doctrine seriously: when questioned in 1646 about "the lawfulness of such a filthy practice," William Plaine "did insinuate seeds of atheism, questioning whether there were a God" (John Winthrop, *The History of New England from 1630 to 1649*, ed. James Savage, 2 vols. [Boston, 1825-26], 2:265). See also Alan Bray, *Homosexuality in Renaissance England* (London, 1982), 63-66.

76. "Crimes and Misdemeanours," 1st ser., 1:89.

77. Ibid., 1:87a, 88b, 93, 98.

78. Ibid., 1:99. E. P. Thompson argues that whether sex offenders in English communities became the targets of active local hostility could also depend in large part upon "personal histories" and whether the culprits were unpopular for other reasons; see Thompson's *Customs in Common*, 515-16.

79. "Crimes and Misdemeanours," 1st ser., 1:89, 95b. Katz has suggested that since Sension's marriage was childless, the servant may also have been motivated by hopes of an inheritance (Katz, *Gay/Lesbian Almanac*, 114).

80. This fits well with Alan Bray's argument that sex between men in Renaissance England expressed the "prevailing distribution" of economic and social power (Bray, *Homosexuality in Renaissance England*, 49-51, 56). Bruce Smith identifies the myth of "Master and Minion" as an important component in the "cultural poetics" of same-sex desire in the English Renaissance. That particular configuration "reinforced the hierarchical relationships in which Renaissance readers defined themselves as individuals, as members of society, and as partners in love" (Smith, *Homosexual Desire in Shakespeare's England*, 193).

81. Bray suggests that "a sluggishness in accepting that what was being seen was indeed the fearful sin of sodomy" may have protected perpetrators from social or official retribution as well as from condemnation by their own consciences (Bray, *Homosexuality in Renaissance England*, 76).

82. Roger Thompson's claim that official condemnation of sodomy translated into an equally intense "public hostility" seems unwarranted by the evidence (Thompson, "Attitudes towards Homosexuality in the Seventeenth-Century New England Colonies," *Journal of American Studies* 23 [1989]: esp. 31, 34). Nor do popular attitudes toward sodomitical behavior in early modern England seem to have been particularly disapproving. As B. R. Burg argues, although sodomy was not "an accepted form of conduct," it had "little inherent capacity to evoke passionate detestation." There were few prosecutions for

sodomy in part because the law could not be enforced without local cooperation; see Burg, *Sodomy and the Pirate Tradition: English Sea Rovers in the Seventeenth-Century Caribbean* (New York, 1984), 40; and Bray, *Homosexuality in Renaissance England*, 70–71.

83. "On The Wearing of The Hair" [extracts from sermons by Michael Wigglesworth], *New England Historical and Genealogical Register* 1 (1847): 371.

2. "A Complete Body of Divinity"

1. Thomas M. Davis and Virginia L. Davis, eds., *The Unpublished Writings of Edward Taylor*, 3 vols. (Boston, 1981), 3:37–41.

2. Ibid., 3:37–38.

3. Donald E. Stanford, ed., *The Poems of Edward Taylor* (New Haven, Conn., 1960), 142, 164, 212, 230, 248, 259, 295, 362–63, 448.

4. H. L. Mencken, quoted in Randall Stewart, *American Literature and Christian Doctrine* (Baton Rouge, 1958), 4. For examples of Hawthorne's fictional Puritans and their sexual world, see esp. *The Scarlet Letter* and "The Minister's Black Veil."

5. Over half a century ago, Edmund Morgan argued that Puritans had a positive and healthy attitude toward sex within marriage and that they showed a compassionate, sympathetic understanding of human nature when dealing with sex offenders (Edmund S. Morgan, "The Puritans and Sex," *New England Quarterly* 15 [1942]: 591–607). More recent scholars have countered with a darker version of Puritan sexuality, arguing that Puritan attitudes toward sex even within marriage were shadowed by "wariness, distaste, even horror" and that the godly "could not countenance carnal pleasure for its own sake" (Kathleen Verduin, "'Our Cursed Natures': Sexuality and the Puritan Conscience," *New England Quarterly* 56 [1983]: 223; Michael Zuckerman, "Pilgrims in the Wilderness: Community, Modernity, and the Maypole at Merry Mount," *New England Quarterly* 50 [1977]: 265).

6. Thomas Hooker, *The Soul's Implantation* (London, 1637), 158.

7. In the High Middle Ages, for example, it was not unusual for the devout to address Jesus as a mother and to use feminine imagery in their descriptions of Christ and God; see Caroline Walker Bynum, *Jesus as Mother: Studies in the Spirituality of the High Middle Ages* (Berkeley, Calif., 1982), 110–69.

8. William Whateley, *The Bride Bush* (London, 1617), 268; Davis and Davis, *Unpublished Writings of Edward Taylor*, 3:38; Samuel Willard, *A Complete Body of Divinity* (Boston, 1726), 609; Edmund S. Morgan, "Light on the Puritans from John Hull's Notebooks," *New England Quarterly* 15 (1942): 100. Historians such as Lawrence Stone have argued that the rise of "companionate marriage" was an eighteenth-century phenomenon (Lawrence Stone, *The Family, Sex, and Marriage in England, 1500–1800* [New York, 1977], chaps. 7, 8). We should not, however, underestimate the importance of affection and passion in many earlier marriages. See Alan Macfarlane's review of Stone in *History and Theory* 18 (1979): 103–26; David Cressy, *Birth, Marriage, and Death: Ritual, Religion, and the Life-Cycle in*

Tudor and Stuart England (Oxford, 1997), 260-63, 297; Lisa Wilson, "A Marriage 'Well-Ordered': Love, Power, and Partnership in Colonial New England," in Laura McCall and Donald Yacovone, eds., *A Shared Experience: Men, Women, and the History of Gender* (New York, 1998), 78-97; and Edmund Leites, "The Duty to Desire: Love, Friendship, and Sexuality in Some Puritan Theories of Marriage," *Journal of Social History* 15 (1981-82): 383-408.

9. Robert C. Winthrop, ed., *The Life and Letters of John Winthrop*, 2 vols. (Boston, 1864-67), 1:135, 139, 195, 226-27, 301, 389, 391; 2:39.

10. Seaborn Cotton, "Commonplace Book," New England Historical and Genealogical Society, Boston.

11. Jeannine Hensley, ed., *The Works of Anne Bradstreet* (Cambridge, Mass., 1967), 225, 226-27.

12. William Gouge, *Of Domesticall Duties* (1622; Norwood, N.J., 1976), 182, 234. This was not, however, to condone deliberately nonprocreative sex. In his account of the sex scandal surrounding Plymouth Colony pastor John Lyford, William Bradford noted with horror that the reverend not only "satisfied his lust" by "defil[ing]" a young woman but also "endeavoured to hinder conception," which exacerbated his offense (William Bradford, *Of Plymouth Plantation, 1620-1647*, ed. Francis Murphy [New York, 1981], 187).

13. John Cotton, *A Meet Help* (Boston, 1699), 15, 16; *The Crown and Glory of a Christian* (Boston, 1684), 46; Edward Taylor, "Commonplace Book," Massachusetts Historical Society, Boston; Willard, *Complete Body of Divinity*, 675.

14. Willard, *Complete Body of Divinity*, 669, 674, 682; Richard D. Pierce, ed., *The Records of the First Church in Salem, Massachusetts, 1629-1736* (Salem, Mass., 1974), 175-76; Nicholas Noyes, "An Elegy upon the Death of Mrs. Mary Brown," in Cotton Mather, *Eureka the Virtuous Woman Found* (Boston, 1704), 5.

15. Richard D. Pierce, ed., "The Records of the First Church in Boston, 1630-1868," *Colonial Society of Massachusetts Publications* 39 (1961): 26-27; Nathaniel B. Shurtleff and David Pulsifer, eds., *Records of the Colony of New Plymouth in New England*, 12 vols. (Boston, 1855-61), 4:93, 106, 107-8, 121, 125-26; Middlesex County Court Records, Massachusetts State Archives, Columbia Point, Boston, file 42. A woman's reputation could also be damaged by rumors that she withheld sex from her husband; see, e.g., Franklin Dexter, ed., *New Haven Town Records*, 2 vols. (New Haven, Conn., 1917-19), 1:389.

16. Nicholas Culpeper, *The Compleat Practice of Physick* (London, 1655), 503. See Mary Fissell, "Gender and Generation: Representing Reproduction in Early Modern England," *Gender and History* 7 (1995): 433-56, and Thomas Laqueur, *Making Sex: Body and Gender from the Greeks to Freud* (Cambridge, Mass., 1990).

17. Charles J. Hoadly, ed., *Records of the Colony or Jurisdiction of New Haven* (Hartford, Conn., 1858), 123. Ruhamah Doane of Plymouth, Massachusetts, reported in 1708 that her master, David Melville, had forced himself upon her while his wife was away in Boston. He was apparently hopeful that Doane "would not prove with child," because she had been "so unwilling in the time

of action." He doubted that she could conceive without experiencing pleasure (Record Book for 1700-1714, 235, and file 7640, Supreme Court of Judicature, Massachusetts State Archives, Columbia Point, Boston).

18. *Aristotle's Masterpiece* (London, 1684), 189; Samuel Eliot Morison and Zechariah Chafee, eds., "Records of the Suffolk County Court, 1671-1680," *Colonial Society of Massachusetts Publications* 29-30 (1933): 838; John Noble and John F. Cronin, eds., *Records of the Court of Assistants of the Colony of Massachusetts Bay*, 3 vols. (Boston, 1901-28), 3:67.

19. Hoadly, *Records of the Colony or Jurisdiction of New Haven*, 586; Norbert B. Lacy, ed., "Records of the Court of Assistants of Connecticut, 1665-1701" (M.A. thesis, Yale University, 1937), 10; Noble and Cronin, *Records of the Court of Assistants*, 3:67; Morison and Chafee, "Records of the Suffolk County Court," 837, 838. Thomas A. Foster discusses attitudes toward impotence in "Deficient Husbands: Manhood, Sexual Incapacity, and Male Marital Sexuality in Seventeenth-Century New England," *William and Mary Quarterly* 56 (1999): 723-44.

20. Willard, *Complete Body of Divinity*, 669, 675; Gouge, *Of Domesticall Duties*, 234; Lacy, "Records of the Court of Assistants of Connecticut," 55-56; Taylor, "Commonplace Book." See also *Onania; or, The Heinous Sin of Self-Pollution* (Boston, 1724), 44-45.

21. John Williams, *Warnings to the Unclean* (Boston, 1699), 56; Hensley, *Works of Anne Bradstreet*, 52; "The Commonplace Book of Joseph Green," *Publications of the Colonial Society of Massachusetts* 34 (1943): 236; Worthington C. Ford, ed., *The Diary of Cotton Mather*, 2 vols. (1911; New York, 1957), 2:118; Willard, *Complete Body of Divinity*, 296, 299, 357.

22. John Cotton, *A Practical Commentary* (London, 1656), 126, 200; *The Works of Thomas Shepard, First Pastor of the First Church, Cambridge, Massachusetts*, 3 vols. (1853; New York, 1967), 1:26; Winthrop, *Life and Letters of John Winthrop*, 1:193; Ford, *Diary of Cotton Mather*, 2:523, 727; see also 1:121. For further discussion of the link between sexual lust and idolatry in Puritan minds, see Verduin, "'Our Cursed Natures,'" 229-31.

23. Jonathan Mitchell, "Continuation of Sermons upon the Body of Divinity," 10, 24/1/1657, and 7/2/1657, Massachusetts Historical Society, Boston; Willard, *Complete Body of Divinity*, 502; Cotton Mather, *The Pure Nazarite: Advice to a Young Man* (Boston, 1723), 17-19.

24. John Rogers, *Death the Certain Wages of Sin to the Impenitent* (Boston, 1701), 98; Williams, *Warnings to the Unclean*, 6; Samuel Danforth, *The Cry of Sodom Enquired Into* (Cambridge, 1674), 7.

25. Cotton Mather, *An Holy Rebuke to the Unclean Spirit* (Boston, 1693), 48; Ford, *Diary of Cotton Mather*, 2:75.

26. Cotton Mather, *Ornaments for the Daughters of Zion* (Cambridge, 1692), 12; Jeremiah Dummer, "Diary, 1709-11," 18/3/1710, Massachusetts Historical Society, Boston.

27. Dummer, "Diary," 22/12/1709.

28. Bradford, *Of Plymouth Plantation*, 351.

29. Danforth, *Cry of Sodom*, 6, 8-9, 18-19; *Records and Files of the Quarterly Courts of Essex County, Massachusetts* (henceforth *ECR*), 9 vols. (Salem, Mass., 1911-78), 1:44; John Winthrop, *The History of New England from 1630 to 1649*, ed. James Savage, 2 vols. (Boston, 1825-26), 2:265.

30. Thomas Shepard, *Eye-Salve* (Cambridge, 1673), 42; Willard, *Complete Body of Divinity*, 671. See also Joshua Moodey, *Soldiery Spiritualized* (Cambridge, 1674), 20. David Hibler, in "Sexual Rhetoric in Seventeenth-Century American Literature" (Ph.D. diss., Notre Dame University, 1970), chap. 4, explores the Puritans' use of sexual imagery and innuendo to bolster religious polemic.

31. Willard, *Complete Body of Divinity*, 684; Cotton Mather, *A Christian At His Calling* (Boston, 1701), 43; Jonathan Mitchell, "Continuation of Sermons Concerning Man's Misery," 1/2/1653, Massachusetts Historical Society, Boston. See also Samuel Willard, *Useful Instructions for a Professing People in Times of Great Security and Degeneracy* (Cambridge, 1673), 12; and Williams, *Warnings to the Unclean*, 16. The importance of Sodom as an inspiration to collective discipline is discussed in Michael Warner, "New English Sodom," *American Literature* 64 (1992): 19-47.

32. Danforth, *Cry of Sodom*, 3-5; Willard, *Complete Body of Divinity*, 681-82.

33. Bradford, *Of Plymouth Plantation*, 351; Mitchell, "Sermons Concerning Man's Misery," 21/6/1654.

34. Charles Chauncy, in "Opinions of Three Ministers on Unnatural Vice" (1642), in William Bradford, *Of Plymouth Plantation, 1620-1647*, ed. Samuel Eliot Morison (New York, 1952), 410; Cotton Mather, *The Sailor's Companion and Counsellor* (Boston, 1709), viii. See also the denunciations by Ralph Partridge in "Opinions of Three Ministers," 407; by Mitchell in "Sermons Concerning Man's Misery," 15/8/1655; and by Increase Mather in *Solemn Advice to Young Men* (Boston, 1695), 37. John Rayner did concede that in one respect sodomy's nonprocreative nature made it less threatening than adultery or rape, either of which could intrude illegitimate offspring into a family's line of inheritance: "there was not," he wrote, "the like reason and degree of sinning against family and posterity in this sin as in some other capital sins of uncleanness" ("Opinions of Three Ministers," 405).

35. The drunkard, for example, "ma[d]e himself a beast" (Cotton Mather, *A Monitory and Hortatory Letter* [Boston, 1700], 6).

36. Danforth, *Cry of Sodom*, 16; Cotton Mather, *Magnalia Christi Americana*, ed. Thomas Robbins, 2 vols. (1852; New York, 1967), 2:405-7. John Canup discusses the link between images of the wilderness and attitudes toward bestiality in *Out of the Wilderness: The Emergence of an American Identity in Colonial New England* (Middletown, Conn., 1990), esp. 33-46. For a comprehensive survey of bestiality cases in early America, see John M. Murrin, "'Things Fearful to Name': Bestiality in Colonial America," supplemental issue of *Pennsylvania History* 65 (1998): 8-43.

NOTES TO PAGES 68-72

37. Rogers, *Death the Certain Wages of Sin*, 95; Thomas Shepard, *The Sincere Convert: Discovering the Small Number of True Believers* (Cambridge, 1664), 42.

38. Mather, *Holy Rebuke*, 42-44; Danforth, *Cry of Sodom*, 9.

39. Mather, *Solemn Advice*, 24; Thomas Foxcroft, *Cleansing Our Way in Youth* (Boston, 1719), 16; Increase Mather, *Some Important Truths* (Boston, 1684), 145; Cotton Mather, *Addresses to Old Men, Young Men, and Children* (Boston, 1690), 73. In addition to brief discussions in writings of the 1600s and the early 1700s that addressed a broad range of sins, two publications focused specifically on masturbation: Cotton Mather's *Pure Nazarite;* and *Onania; or, The Heinous Sin of Self-Pollution,* an anonymous tract published first in London and then on three occasions in Boston (1724, 1726, and 1746).

40. Winthrop, *History of New England*, 2:265. See also *Onania*, 1.

41. Mather, *Pure Nazarite*, 2; Danforth, *Cry of Sodom*, 16.

42. Mather, *Pure Nazarite*, 6; Mather, *Holy Rebuke*, 46, 47; *Onania*, 15-16, 17-18.

43. Mather, *Pure Nazarite*, 6-7, 8; see also *Onania*, 17.

44. Mather, *Holy Rebuke*, 42; Charles Morton, "Compendium Physicae," *Collections of the Colonial Society of Massachusetts* 33 (1940): 143. See also Cotton Mather, *Early Religion* (Boston, 1694), 9.

45. Danforth, *Cry of Sodom*, 16; Cotton Mather, *Pillars of Salt* (Boston, 1699), 42; and Mather, *Pure Nazarite*, 7. See also *Onania*, 20.

46. Danforth, *Cry of Sodom*, 7-8; Mather, *Early Religion*, 71.

47. Cotton, *Practical Commentary*, 131; Mather, *Holy Rebuke*, 65.

48. M. Halsey Thomas, ed., *The Diary of Samuel Sewall*, 2 vols. (New York, 1973), 2:864, 882, 891; Increase Mather, *Practical Truths Plainly Delivered* (Boston, 1718), 59-60; Ford, *Diary of Cotton Mather*, 2:540; Cotton Mather, *A Glorious Espousal* (Boston, 1719).

49. Amanda Porterfield, *Female Piety in Puritan New England: The Emergence of Religious Humanism* (New York, 1992), chap. 1. See also Peter Brown, *The Body and Society: Men, Women, and Sexual Renunciation in Early Christianity* (New York, 1988); E. Ann Matter, *The Voice of My Beloved: The Song of Songs in Western Medieval Christianity* (Philadelphia, 1990); and Dyan Elliott, *Spiritual Marriage: Sexual Abstinence in Medieval Wedlock* (Princeton, N.J., 1993).

50. That more benign view of the marital relationship was bound up with their particular focus upon family life as a primary agent of grace and social order, which required a close and mutually supportive alliance between husband and wife. See Carol Karlsen, *The Devil in the Shape of a Woman: Witchcraft in Colonial New England* (New York, 1987), 160-66; Larzer Ziff, *Puritanism in America: New Culture in a New World* (New York, 1973), 14; and John Demos, *A Little Commonwealth: Family Life in Plymouth Colony* (New York, 1970).

51. For discussions of marital imagery in early modern English literature, see Barbara Kiefer Lewalski, *Protestant Poetics and the Seventeenth-Century Religious Lyric* (Princeton, N.J., 1977); Stanley Stewart, *The Enclosed Garden: The Tra-*

dition and the Image in Seventeenth-Century Poetry (Madison, Wis., 1966); and Jonathan Jong-Chu Won, "Communion and Christ: An Exposition and Comparison of the Doctrine of Union and Communion with Christ in Calvin and the English Puritans" (Ph.D. diss., Westminster Theological Seminary, 1989).

52. Winthrop, *Life and Letters of John Winthrop*, 1:136, 193; Benjamin Colman, *The Honour and Happiness of the Virtuous Woman* (Boston, 1716), 26.

53. Cotton Mather, *The Mystical Marriage* (Boston, 1728), 15; Winthrop, *Life and Letters of John Winthrop*, 1:161; Mather, *Glorious Espousal*, 46; Stanford, *Poems of Edward Taylor*, 199 (see also 139).

54. See Emory Elliott, *Power and the Pulpit in Puritan New England* (Princeton, N.J., 1975), chap. 3; Patricia Caldwell, *The Puritan Conversion Narrative: The Beginnings of American Expression* (New York, 1983), chap. 3; and David Cressy, *Coming Over: Migration and Communication between England and New England in the Seventeenth Century* (New York, 1987), chap. 8.

55. *God's Plot: The Paradoxes of Puritan Piety, Being the Autobiography and Journal of Thomas Shepard*, ed. Michael McGiffert (Amherst, Mass., 1972), 98; Edmund S. Morgan, ed., *The Diary of Michael Wigglesworth, 1653–57* (New York, 1946), 13, 17, 54, 82.

56. Porterfield shows that Thomas Hooker and Thomas Shepard "most often used the analogy between Christian life and wifely devotion in negative terms, defining sin against God in terms of the failure of wifely affection." John Cotton's use of spousal imagery was much more positive and seductive, but he was atypical of his generation in that regard (Porterfield, *Female Piety in Puritan New England*, 55, 66–79).

57. See Elliott, *Power and the Pulpit*, 13–14, 175. Ministers continued, of course, to express concern about the soul-bride's fidelity, as in Increase Mather, *A Sermon* (Boston, 1682), 10; Joseph Rowlandson, *The Possibility of God's Forsaking A People* (Boston, 1682), 20; William Adams, *God's Eye on the Contrite* (Boston, 1685), 25; Samuel Wakeman, *Sound Repentance* (Boston, 1685), 28–29; Willard, *Complete Body of Divinity*, 627–28; and Francis G. Walett, ed., *The Diary of Ebenezer Parkman, 1703–1782* (Worcester, Mass., 1974), 36 (September 1729).

58. Thomas, *Diary of Samuel Sewall*, 1:202. The printing explosion toward the end of the century played a role in increasing the number of references to espousal in published works, but they became proportionally more prominent as well. By no means all New England ministers approved of such imagery, as Michael Winship points out in "'Behold the Bridegroom Cometh': Marital Imagery in Massachusetts Preaching, 1630–1730," *Early American Literature* 27 (1992): esp. 172–73. But Winship's claim that "marital imagery largely disappeared from discourse after the turn of the eighteenth century" exaggerates the speed with which such language vanished from New England sermons.

59. Mather, *Ornaments for the Daughters of Zion*, 64 (see also Mather, *Glorious Espousal*, 12; Mather, *Mystical Marriage*, 6; Cotton Mather, *A Union with the*

Son of God by Faith [Boston, 1692], 14-15); Joshua Moodey, *A Practical Discourse Concerning the Choice Benefit of Communion with God in his House* (Boston, 1685), 24-25.

60. Mather, *Glorious Espousal*, 14-20; Willard, *Complete Body of Divinity*, 489. See also Cotton Mather, *Bethiah* (Boston, 1722), 11.

61. Increase Mather, *The Greatest Sinners Exhorted* (Boston, 1686), 5; Mather, *Ornaments for the Daughters of Zion*, 64-65; Mather, *Union with the Son of God by Faith*, 15, 21; Willard, *Complete Body of Divinity*, 488, 557. See also Increase Mather, *Renewal of Covenant* (Boston, 1677), 7; and Mather, *Practical Truths*, 59-60.

62. Mather, *Mystical Marriage*, 1, 13; and Mather, *Ornaments for the Daughters of Zion*, 69; Edward Taylor, *Treatise concerning the Lord's Supper*, ed. Norman S. Grabo (East Lansing, Mich., 1966), 185; Mather, *Practical Truths*, 60.

63. Mather, *Glorious Espousal*, 9, 20; Willard, *Complete Body of Divinity*, 557.

64. Taylor, *Treatise concerning the Lord's Supper*, 17 (see also Moodey, *Practical Discourse*, 24-25); James Fitch, *Peace the End of the Perfect and Upright* (Cambridge, 1672), 4.

65. Stanford, *Poems of Edward Taylor*, 453; Willard, *Complete Body of Divinity*, 533, 556; Mather, *Bethiah*, 30.

66. Mather, *Ornaments for the Daughters of Zion*, 99; John Davenport, *The Saint's Anchor-Hold* (London, 1682), 28; Taylor, *Treatise concerning the Lord's Supper*, 170-71. The saints would not engage in "conjugal union" with each other. Such relations would "cease and be useless," because the redeemed now found themselves in a transcendent "union" with Christ (Willard, *Complete Body of Divinity*, 546).

67. Stanford, *Poems of Edward Taylor*, 47; Willard, *Complete Body of Divinity*, 879. Edmund S. Morgan first identified and examined this "tribal attitude" in *The Puritan Family: Religion and Domestic Relations in Seventeenth-Century New England* (1944; New York, 1966), chap. 7.

68. Samuel Willard, *The High Esteem Which God Hath of the Death of His Saints* (Boston, 1683), 15; and Samuel Willard, *Some Brief Sacramental Meditations* (Boston, 1711), 4; Stanford, *Poems of Edward Taylor*, 212, 362-63, 414, 448. Taylor drew extensively on the language of Canticles. See, for example, his adaptation of "Let him kiss me with the kiss of his mouth" (Cant. 1:2) in ibid., 254-55, and of "I am my beloved and my beloved is mine" (Cant. 6:2) in ibid., 323-25.

69. John Cotton, *Christ the Fountain of Life* (London, 1651), 36-37; and Cotton, *Practical Commentary*, 131. See also Thomas Shepard, *The Parable of the Ten Virgins* (London, 1660), 25-26; John Norton, *Three Choice and Profitable Sermons* (Cambridge, 1664), 20-21; and Samuel Whiting, *A Discourse of the Last Judgment* (Cambridge, 1664), 102. John Winthrop had invoked Christ in 1630 as "my love, my dove, my undefiled" and prayed that he might be "possesse[d]" by his savior in "the love of marriage," but his language lacked the overtly erotic tone of Taylor's poetry (Winthrop, *Life and Letters of John Winthrop*, 1:397). For references by Ann Hutchinson to "the voice of my beloved," see David D. Hall,

ed., *The Antinomian Controversy, 1636-1638: A Documentary History* (Durham, N.C., 1990), 272, 337.

70. Mather, *Ornaments for the Daughters of Zion*, 68; Willard, *Complete Body of Divinity*, 821 (see also 849-50).

71. Thomas Foxcroft, *A Funeral Sermon Occasioned by Several Mournful Deaths* (Boston, 1722), 27; Mather, *Bethiah*, 46 (see also Mather, *Glorious Espousal*, 23; Mather, *Union with the Son of God by Faith*, 17; Ford, *Diary of Cotton Mather*, 1:222; Taylor, *Treatise concerning the Lord's Supper*, 210); Willard, *Complete Body of Divinity*, 458-59. The reproductive emphasis in sexual imagery used by ministers may also have been prompted in part by Puritan tribalism. Once ministers began encouraging their congregations to hope that grace was hereditary, physical procreation and spiritual fecundity became closely related in Puritan minds.

72. Mather, *Practical Truths*, 175; Willard, *Complete Body of Divinity*, 892; Ford, *Diary of Cotton Mather*, 1:98, 426, 471, 483.

73. See Marilyn Westerkamp, "Engendering Puritan Religious Culture in Old and New England," *Pennsylvania History* 64 (1997): 115.

74. For further discussion of gender fluidity in early modern culture, see Richard Godbeer, "Performing Patriarchy," in Francis J. Bremer and Lynn A. Botelho, eds., *The Worlds of John Winthrop* (Boston, forthcoming 2002). Mary Maples Dunn, Gerald Moran, and Amanda Porterfield have argued that the increasing use of spousal imagery was linked to changes in the sexual composition of church membership as women came to outnumber men in most congregations by the late seventeenth century (Mary Maples Dunn, "Saints and Sisters: Congregational and Quaker Women in the Early Colonial Period," in Janet Wilson James, ed., *Women in American Religion* [Philadelphia, 1980], 593; Gerald Moran, "'Sisters' in Christ: Women and the Church in Seventeenth-Century New England," also in James, *Women in American Religion*, 61; Porterfield, *Female Piety in Puritan New England*, 8). Yet to argue for a causal link between membership sex ratios and the use of marital imagery is problematic. As Margaret Masson and Laurel Thatcher Ulrich have pointed out, the increasing use of spousal language during the 1670s and 1680s coincided not with a decline but with a rise in male church membership. Moran has shown convincingly that the long-term trend was toward female majorities, but his own numbers demonstrate that that movement was temporarily reversed during the very period in which clerics increased their use of marital and romantic imagery (Margaret W. Masson, "The Typology of the Female as a Model for the Regenerate: Puritan Preaching, 1690-1730," *Signs* 2 [1976]: 315; Laurel Thatcher Ulrich, "'Vertuous Women Found': New England Ministerial Literature, 1668-1735," in James, *Women in American Religion*, 84 n. 65; Moran, "'Sisters' in Christ," 51, fig. 1). The larger trend did resume during the last decade of the century, so one could argue for a gradual or delayed impact. But as Laurel Thatcher Ulrich points out, "church membership was one of the few public distinctions available to women." That seems to me a much more promising explanation of why women of the sec-

ond and third generations became church members in disproportionate numbers. One would not expect first-generation settlers to fit this pattern, since so many of the men as well as women migrated specifically to become part of a covenanted community (Laurel Thatcher Ulrich, *Good Wives: Image and Reality in the Lives of Women in Northern New England, 1650–1750* [New York, 1982], 216–26).

75. Willard, *Complete Body of Divinity*, 534; *Works of Thomas Shepard*, 2:31. Jonathan Mitchell referred to the soul as "it" repeatedly in his "Continuation of Sermons upon the Body of Divinity." For discussion of the soul as a female entity, see Elizabeth Reis, *Damned Women: Sinners and Witches in Puritan New England* (Ithaca, N.Y., 1997), chap. 3.

76. Winthrop, *History of New England*, 2:281. See also Richard Dunn, James Savage, and Laetitia Yeandle, eds., *The Journal of John Winthrop, 1630–1649* (Cambridge, Mass., 1996), 588. For English use of marital metaphor in political discourse, see Mary Lyndon Shanley, "Marriage Contract and Social Contract in Seventeenth-Century English Political Thought," *Western Political Quarterly* 32 (1979): 79–91.

77. Lisa Wilson emphasizes the dependency of men as well as of women in *Ye Heart of a Man: The Domestic Life of Men in Colonial New England* (New Haven, Conn., 1999).

78. Hensley, *Works of Anne Bradstreet*, 204; Ulrich, *Good Wives*, 50. For discussion of women as "deputy husbands" and church members, see ibid., chaps. 2, 12. Mary Beth Norton shows that "the symbolic relationship between family and state that characterized early seventeenth-century Anglo-American thought and practice" also created "ambiguities in women's status." Women as mothers "legitimately wielded some authority within the family; because of the intimate link between family and state, they consequently could not be wholly excluded from the category of those who wielded power in the society at large." Furthermore, women who became household heads as widows and elite female colonists who had precedence over low-status men could exercise a form of social authority that would be denied them once public and political power became separated from familial analogies. Norton points out that "women's voices" could have influence not only informally within their communities but also in formal contexts such as the courtroom (Mary Beth Norton, *Founding Mothers and Fathers: Gendered Power and the Forming of American Society* [New York, 1996], 8, 10, 21).

79. See "Proceedings of Excommunication against Mistress Ann Hibbens of Boston," in John Demos, ed., *Remarkable Providences: Readings in Early American History* (Boston, 1991), 262–82; Dunn, Savage, and Yeandle, *Journal of John Winthrop*, 570; and Karlsen, *The Devil in the Shape of a Woman*.

80. Reis points out that "colonists shared with their English brethren the belief that women's bodies were physically weaker than men's" and that therefore "the devil could more frequently and successfully gain access to and possess women's souls" (Reis, *Damned Women*, 108, 110). That four-fifths of accused

witches in New England were women was surely due, at least in part, to the currency of these assumptions about female vulnerability among both men and women. See also Karlsen's discussion of Adam and Eve's fall as related by Willard in *The Devil in the Shape of a Woman*, 173–77; and Mather, *Ornaments for the Daughters of Zion*, 19–20.

81. Benjamin Wadsworth, *Unchast[e] Practices Procure Divine Judgments* (Boston, 1716), 5–6. See also Masson, "Typology of the Female," 305, 315; Ulrich, "Vertuous Women Found," 75; and Charles Cohen, *God's Caress: The Psychology of Puritan Religious Experience* (New York, 1986), 222–23.

82. See, for example, Willard, *Complete Body of Divinity*, 543–47.

83. Ford, *Diary of Cotton Mather*, 1:4. Mather referred to his spiritual "ejaculations" in diary entries throughout his life; see also Peter Thacher, "Diary," 5, 6/9/1682, Massachusetts Historical Society, Boston.

84. Mather, *Ornaments for the Daughters of Zion*, 39, 42.

85. Willard, *Complete Body of Divinity*, 131, 145; Nehemiah Walter, *Unfruitful Hearers Detected and Warned* (Boston, 1696), 52; William Adams, *The Necessity of the Pouring Out of the Spirit* (Boston, 1679), A4; Samuel Danforth, *A Brief Recognition of New England's Errand into the Wilderness* (Cambridge, 1671), 12. John Oxenbridge likened the role of a magistrate to that of "a nursing father" who "bears the sucking child" (John Oxenbridge, *New England Freemen* [Cambridge, 1673], 36–37).

86. John Wise, *A Word of Comfort to a Melancholy Country* (Boston, 1721), 11. For an extended discussion of maternal imagery in Puritan literature, see David Leverenz, *The Language of Puritan Feeling: An Exploration in Literature, Psychology, and Social History* (New Brunswick, N.J., 1980).

87. Williams, *Warnings to the Unclean*, 9–10.

88. Increase Mather, *A Call From Heaven* (Boston, 1679), 109.

3. "Pregnant with the Seeds of All Sin"

1. Thomas Shepard, *The Sincere Convert: Discovering the Small Number of True Believers* (Cambridge, 1664), 42; Samuel Danforth, *The Cry of Sodom Enquired Into* (Cambridge, 1674), 11; Samuel Willard, *A Complete Body of Divinity* (Boston, 1726), 682.

2. "The Commonplace Book of Joseph Green," *Publications of the Colonial Society of Massachusetts* 34 (1943): 218, 235, 238, 242; Danforth, *Cry of Sodom*, 15; "New Haven Town Records," 142–44, typescript, Connecticut State Library, Hartford. New Englanders were also taught to believe that God punished entire communities for allowing sexual and other transgressions to occur. Ministers interpreted harvest failures, epidemics, and other collective misfortunes as judgments upon the colonists for sins committed among them, which testified to their laxity as moral stewards.

3. Quotation from William Bradford, *Of Plymouth Plantation, 1620–1647*, ed. Francis Murphy (New York, 1981), 352.

4. Harry S. Stout discusses preaching as a "medium of public communication" in *The New England Soul: Preaching and Religious Culture in Colonial New England* (New York, 1986); see esp. 3–4.

5. Edmund S. Morgan, ed., *The Diary of Michael Wigglesworth, 1653–57* (New York, 1946), 4, 5; Worthington C. Ford, ed., *The Diary of Cotton Mather,* 2 vols. (1911; New York, 1957), 1:3–4, 38, 90; Philip McIntire Woodwell, ed., *Handkerchief Moody: The Diary and the Man* (Portland, Maine, 1981), 144, 150.

6. Cotton Mather, *Bonifacius: An Essay upon the Good,* ed. D. Levin (Cambridge, 1966), 85.

7. Bradford, *Of Plymouth Plantation,* 351–52; *Records and Files of the Quarterly Courts of Essex County* (henceforth *ECR*), 9 vols. (Salem, Mass., 1911–78), 5:291.

8. *ECR,* 5:143–47.

9. Ibid., 5:231, 8:285–88. New Englanders did make a distinction between legitimate watchfulness and gratuitous intrusion or voyeurism; for examples, see ibid., 3:90, 8:23.

10. Richard Dunn, James Savage, and Laetitia Yeandle, eds., *The Journal of John Winthrop, 1630–1649* (Cambridge, Mass., 1996), 264, 269.

11. John Downame, *Four Treatises Tending to Dissuade All Christians From Swearing* (n.p., 1609), 195–201; *ECR,* 8:285–87; "Journal of Madam Knight," in Wendy Martin, ed., *Colonial American Travel Narratives* (New York, 1994), 63.

12. Middlesex County Court Records (henceforth MCCR), Massachusetts State Archives, Columbia Point, Boston: Order Book for 1649–1663, transcribed by David Pulsifer, 6; *ECR,* 7:283; Franklin Dexter, ed., *New Haven Town Records,* 2 vols. (New Haven, Conn., 1917–19), 2:160.

13. Dexter, *New Haven Town Records,* 1:450–52.

14. Bradford, *Of Plymouth Plantation,* 185. For further discussion of privacy issues, see David Flaherty, *Privacy in Colonial New England* (Charlottesville, Va., 1972), esp. 76–83.

15. Samuel Eliot Morison and Zechariah Chafee, eds., "Records of the Suffolk County Court, 1671–1680," *Colonial Society of Massachusetts Publications* 29–30 (1933), 914; *ECR,* 5:53, 54. Laurel Thatcher Ulrich points out that the distance between "affability" and a dangerous "accessibility" was "shorter than we might think" in *Good Wives: Image and Reality in the Lives of Women in Northern New England, 1650–1750* (New York, 1982), 95–96.

16. *ECR,* 3:53, 5:21–22.

17. Rolfe became prey to several sexual predators during the extended absence of her husband. Laurel Thatcher Ulrich provides a detailed and insightful analysis of these incidents in *Good Wives,* chap. 5. The depositions relating to Mary Rolfe's ordeal are found in *ECR,* 3:47–55, 65–66, 70, 75, 88–90, 97–98.

18. *ECR,* 5:52–55. Elizabeth Goodell was not the only target of John Smith's errant libido. When Lott Killum's wife claimed that Smith propositioned her, he also "dealt with said Smith privately."

19. Charles J. Hoadly, ed., *Records of the Colony and Plantation of New Haven* (Hartford, Conn., 1857), 233–39.

20. "Early General Records of the Colony of New Haven," 1B:89–92, Connecticut State Library, Hartford. See also Charles J. Hoadly, ed., *Records of the Colony or Jurisdiction of New Haven* (Hartford, Conn., 1858), 137–39.

21. *ECR*, 3:52.

22. "Records of the Congregational Church in Topsfield," in *Historical Collections of the Topsfield Historical Society* 14 (1909): 17. For a detailed discussion of confessional rituals, see David D. Hall, *Worlds of Wonder, Days of Judgment: Popular Religious Belief in Early New England* (New York, 1989), 172–86.

23. Richard D. Pierce, ed., "The Records of the First Church in Boston, 1630–1868," *Colonial Society of Massachusetts Publications* 39 (1961): 60, 61, 181; see also the case of James Mattock (26–27, 36). The congregations at Salem and Beverly were similarly cautious; for examples, see Richard D. Pierce, ed., *Records of the First Church in Salem, Massachusetts, 1629–1736* (Salem, Mass., 1974), 106, 121, 126, 134, 140, 166–67, 171, 173, 185, 193; and William Upham, ed., *Records of the First Church in Beverly, 1667–1772* (Salem, Mass., 1905), 12, 17, 18, 51, 62.

24. *Records of the First Church at Dorchester in New England, 1636–1734* (Boston, 1891), 130. See also 102, 118, 123, 125, 127, 128, 130; and "Boston Second Church Records," vol. 4, 1689–1717, cases of Abigail Lordson (17/2/1698), Stephen Johnson (25/11/1701), and Susanna Fling (25/10/1709), Massachusetts Historical Society, Boston.

25. Cotton Mather, *Ratio Disciplinae Fratrum Nov-Anglicorum* (Boston, 1726), 134–57 (quotation on 144); "Boston Second Church Records," vol 4, 1689–1717, case of Edward Mills (23/5/1699); see also case of Mary Cooly (19/1/1694).

26. Pierce, "Records of the First Church in Boston," 22, 28, 48, 55; "Notebook of the Reverend John Fiske," *Colonial Society of Massachusetts Publications* 47 (1974): 209–12; *Roxbury Land and Church Records: Sixth Report of the Record Commissioners* (Boston, 1881), 98. In 1673 Samuel Danforth had reminded the Roxbury congregation that to continue "inpenitently in the same sins" despite "solemn warning" of "God's judgments executed upon the wicked" was "a great aggravation of sin and provocation of wrath" (Danforth, *Cry of Sodom*, 13–14). See also Pierce, *Records of the First Church in Salem*, 140; and Abigail Merrifield's case in *Records of the First Church at Dorchester*, 81, 82–83, 106.

27. John Noble and John F. Cronin, eds., *Records of the Court of Assistants of the Colony of Massachusetts Bay, 1630–1692*, 3 vols. (Boston, 1901–28), 2:65; Nathaniel B. Shurtleff, ed., *Records of the Governor and Company of Massachusetts Bay, in New England*, 5 vols. (Boston, 1853–54), 4B:156–57, 307, 309. See also Morison and Chafee, "Records of the Suffolk County Court," 518, 558. Some of those who declared themselves contrite may have done so cynically, hoping to mollify the court and so secure a lighter sentence; others were doubtless sincere.

28. Hoadly, *Records of the Colony or Jurisdiction of New Haven*, 138. Walter

Knight was presented in 1642 for "glorying in his and his wife's illegal relations before marriage" (*ECR*, 1:52).

29. Morison and Chafee, "Records of the Suffolk County Court," 90–91, 697; Noble and Cronin, *Records of the Court of Assistants*, 2:81, 87. See also Nathaniel B. Shurtleff and David Pulsifer, eds., *Records of the Colony of New Plymouth in New England*, 12 vols. (Boston, 1855–61), 2:28; 3:111–12; and *ECR*, 5:239. For further discussion of reformative shaming, see Jane Kamensky, *Governing the Tongue: The Politics of Speech in Early New England* (New York, 1997), esp. 142, and citations in ibid., 261 n. 81.

30. *ECR*, 5:104. For more detailed discussion of the laws against living alone and their enforcement, see Edgar J. McManus, *Law and Liberty in Early New England: Criminal Justice and Due Process, 1620-1692* (Amherst, Mass., 1993), 39; and Flaherty, *Privacy in Colonial New England*, 175–79.

31. Shurtleff, *Records of the Governor and Company*, 5:4. The court had ordered previously that even "boyes and girls be not suffered to converse together, so as may occasion any wanton, dishonest, or immodest behavior" (2:7).

32. *ECR*, 9:29; Morison and Chafee, "Records of the Suffolk County Court," 941; Shurtleff and Pulsifer, *Records of the Colony of New Plymouth*, 4:42.

33. The penalty for adultery varied from colony to colony. In neither Plymouth Colony nor Rhode Island was the crime punishable by death. In Connecticut it became noncapital in 1672; henceforth, adulterers would be whipped, branded, and made to wear a halter. Adultery also ceased to be punishable by death in Massachusetts once the colony became a royal province at the end of the century. See *Book of the General Laws of the Inhabitants of the Jurisdiction of New Plymouth* (Cambridge, 1672), 5; John D. Cushing, ed., *The Earliest Acts and Laws of the Colony of Rhode Island and Providence Plantations, 1647-1719* (Wilmington, Del., 1977), 65; *Book of the General Laws for the People Within the Jurisdiction of Connecticut* (Cambridge, 1673), 3; and *Acts and Laws of His Majesty's Province of the Massachusetts Bay* (Boston, 1699), 65–66. Only in New Haven and Connecticut did the legal codes specify that incest was a capital offense; a 1702 law removed the death penalty for that crime in Connecticut, which by that time had incorporated New Haven (*New Haven's Settling In New England* [London, 1656], 35; *Book of the General Laws . . . of Connecticut*, 9; and *Acts and Laws of His Majesty's Colony of Connecticut* [New London, Conn., 1715], 74–75).

34. Noble and Cronin, *Records of the Court of Assistants*, 3:191–93; Norbert B. Lacy, ed., "Records of the Court of Assistants of Connecticut, 1665–1701" (M.A. thesis, Yale University, 1937), 96–98.

35. Noble and Cronin, *Records of the Court of Assistants*, 1:73–74, 234; see also 56–57, 252.

36. Dunn, Savage, and Yeandle, eds., *Journal of John Winthrop*, 609–10.

37. Quoted in Roger Thompson, *Sex in Middlesex: Popular Mores in a Massachusetts County, 1649-1699* (Amherst, Mass., 1986), 81.

38. Joseph H. Smith, ed., *Colonial Justice in Western Massachusetts, 1639-1702: The Pynchon Court Record* (Cambridge, Mass., 1961), 389–91. For the

record of the proceedings against Bartlett in the Middlesex County Court, see MCCR: Order Book for 1649-1663, 113.

39. Charles Chauncy, in "Opinions of Three Ministers on Unnatural Vice" (1642), in William Bradford, *Of Plymouth Plantation, 1620-1647*, ed. Samuel Eliot Morison (New York, 1952), 411; see also Samuel Whiting, *Abraham's Humble Intercession for Sodom* (Cambridge, 1666), 46, and Shepard, *Sincere Convert*, 67. The Plymouth code of 1636 merely listed capital crimes (Shurtleff and Pulsifer, *Records of the Colony of New Plymouth*, 11:12), whereas the much fuller General Laws of 1671 incorporated the Levitical injunction (*Book of the General Laws . . . of New Plymouth*, 4). See also "The Capital Laws of New England," *Colonial Society of Massachusetts Publications* 17 (1913-14): 117; *Book of the General Laws and Liberties Concerning the Inhabitants of the Massachusetts* (Cambridge, 1648), 5-6; J. Hammond Trumbull and Charles J. Hoadly, eds., *The Public Records of the Colony of Connecticut*, 15 vols. (Hartford, Conn., 1850-90), 1:77, 515; *Book of the General Laws . . . of Connecticut*, 9; and "Capital Lawes," in John D. Cushing, ed., *Acts and Laws of New Hampshire, 1680-1726* (Wilmington, Del., 1978), 205. Massachusetts adopted a new law in 1697 that combined biblical language with legal phraseology taken from the English statutes of 1533 and 1563 (*Acts and Laws of . . . the Massachusetts Bay*, 114). New Hampshire followed suit in 1718 (Cushing, *Acts and Laws of New Hampshire*, 141).

40. Cushing, *Earliest Acts and Laws of the Colony of Rhode Island*, 25-26, 64.

41. John Cotton, "An Abstract of the Laws of New England as They Are Now Established" (1641), *Collections of the Massachusetts Historical Society*, 1st ser., 5 (1798): 183; *New Haven's Settling in New England*, 19.

42. ECR, 1:44; Shurtleff and Pulsifer, *Records of the Colony of New Plymouth*, 2:137. That the courts thought about sex in terms of phallic acts is reinforced by their general portrayal of men as the instigators and primary actors in sexual situations, for which see Cornelia Hughes Dayton, *Women before the Bar: Gender, Law, and Society in Connecticut, 1639-1789* (Chapel Hill, N.C., 1995), 176-79. Surviving references to trials involving what we might term lesbianism are equally sparse in other parts of British America. For an exceptional case from early-eighteenth-century Georgia, see E. Merton Coulter, ed., *The Journal of Peter Gordon, 1732-1735* (Athens, Ga., 1963), 40-41. For discussion of theological and legal perspectives on sex between women in premodern Western society, see Louis Crompton, "The Myth of Lesbian Impunity: Capital Laws from 1270 to 1791," in Salvatore J. Licata and Robert P. Peterson, eds., *Historical Perspectives on Homosexuality* (New York, 1981), 11-25; Judith C. Brown, "Lesbian Sexuality in Medieval and Early Modern Europe," in Martin Bauml Duberman, Martha Vicinus, and George Chauncey Jr., eds., *Hidden from History: Reclaiming the Gay and Lesbian Past* (New York, 1989), 67-75; Randolph Trumbach, "London's Sapphists: From Three Sexes to Four Genders in the Making of Modern Culture," in Julia Epstein and Kristina Straub, eds., *Body Guards: The Cultural Politics of Gender Ambiguity* (New York, 1991), 112-41; and Emma Donoghue, *Passions between Women: British Lesbian Culture, 1668-1801* (New York, 1995).

43. *New Haven's Settling in New England*, 19.

44. John Winthrop describes this case in his *History of New England from 1630 to 1649*, ed. James Savage, 2 vols. (Boston, 1825–26), 2:45–48.

45. Deuteronomy 22:25 prescribed death for rape only if the victim was betrothed or married.

46. Dunn, Savage, and Yeandle, *Journal of John Winthrop*, 361; Winthrop, *History of New England*, 2:48; Shurtleff, *Records of the Governor and Company*, 2:12–13, 21–22.

47. Edward Coke, *The Third Part of the Institutes of the Laws of England* (London, 1644), 58–59.

48. For a detailed discussion of this case, see Caroline Bingham, "Seventeenth-Century Attitudes toward Deviant Sex," *Journal of Interdisciplinary History* 1 (1970–71): 447–72; quotations on 448, 456, 459. Cynthia B. Herrup reconstructs the Castlehaven scandal in *A House in Gross Disorder: Sex, Law, and the Second Earl of Castlehaven* (New York, 1999).

49. Thomas Shepard to John Winthrop, n.d. (ca. 1642), in Samuel Eliot Morison et al., eds., *Winthrop Papers*, 5 vols. (Boston, 1929–47), 4:345.

50. Shurtleff and Pulsifer, *Records of the Colony of New Plymouth*, 1:64; 2:28, 35.

51. "Opinions of Three Ministers," 404–13.

52. Bradford, *Of Plymouth Plantation*, 354; Winthrop, *History of New England*, 2:47.

53. "Crimes and Misdemeanours," 1st ser. (1662–63 to 1789), vol. 1, nos. 85–102, Connecticut Archives, Connecticut State Library, Hartford.

54. Ibid., 93, 95b; Lacy, "Records of the Court of Assistants of Connecticut," 67–68.

55. Winthrop, *History of New England*, 2:265; "Early General Records of the Colony of New Haven," IB:89–92.

56. Dunn, Savage, and Yeandle, *Journal of John Winthrop*, 374–76. At Benjamin Goad's trial in 1673, the jury declared him guilty only if confession "upon his first apprehension and examination," in conjunction with one witness, sufficed for a conviction. Otherwise, they declared, he was "not legally guilty of the fact but of a most horrid attempt." The magistrates decided that they were on firm ground and so sentenced him to death (Noble and Cronin, *Records of the Court of Assistants*, 1:10–11).

57. Hoadly, *Records of the Colony or Jurisdiction of New Haven*, 223–24; Shurtleff and Pulsifer, *Records of the Colony of New Plymouth*, 6:74–75. See also the cases of Simon Drake (1674) and Daniel Clark (1697) in Lacy, "Records of the Court of Assistants of Connecticut," 52–53, 262, 263–64.

58. Hoadly, *Records of the Colony and Plantation of New Haven*, 295–96. In a similar case, the accused did confess and so was executed (62–73).

59. Noble and Cronin, *Records of the Court of Assistants*, 1:87–88; depositions by Thomas Michelson and Isaac Amsden, 9/9/1676, Prince Collection, Boston Public Library.

60. Recent scholarship on attitudes toward sex and gender in eighteenth-century London and other major European cities has shown that modern notions of sexual identity began to develop long before the late nineteenth century, when a new scientific taxonomy of sexual behaviors based on sexual orientation emerged. See Alan Bray, *Homosexuality in Renaissance England* (London, 1982), 134–37; Stephen O. Murray, "Homosexual Acts and Selves in Early Modern Europe," in Kent Gerard and Gert Hekma, eds., *The Pursuit of Sodomy: Male Homosexuality in Renaissance and Enlightenment Europe* (New York, 1989), 457–77; Joseph Cady, "'Masculine Love,' Renaissance Writing, and the 'New Invention' of Homosexuality," in Claude J. Summers, ed., *Homosexuality in Renaissance and Enlightenment England: Literary Representations in Historical Context* (New York, 1992), 9–40; and chap. 9 of this volume, note 6. The New England evidence suggests that making a clear-cut distinction between premodern conceptions of sodomy as an *act* and the modern construction of a sexual *identity* is problematic not only for eighteenth-century urban culture but also for early modern popular attitudes in the provinces and colonies.

61. "Crimes and Misdemeanours," 1st ser., 1:87a (see also 93, 95); Shurtleff and Pulsifer, *Records of the Colony of New Plymouth*, 1:64. In 1642, when Edward Michell and Edward Preston appeared before the same colony's court for "lewd practises tending to sodomy," Preston was also accused of "pressing" a third man, John Keene, to join them. Keene had refused and reported the incident (2:35–36). It is not possible to tell whether any of those who engaged in sodomy (or acts "tending to sodomy") were gender-exclusive in their sexual tastes, but some were clearly not. Edward Michell, for example, had apparently engaged in "lewd carriages" with Lydia Hatch as well as "sodomitical practices" with Edward Preston.

62. "Crimes and Misdemeanours," 1st ser., 1:98b. The English case of George Dowdeney (an innkeeper from Hatch Beauchamp, Somerset) resembles that of Sension in that locals described many attempts by the accused during at least the previous fourteen years to seduce men and youths in the vicinity, presenting Dowdeney's interest in members of the same sex as an ongoing "course" analogous to Sension's "trade" (Somerset Record Office, Q/SR/40). This case is discussed in G. R. Quaife, *Wanton Wenches and Wayward Wives* (New Brunswick, N.J., 1979), 175–77; and Bray, *Homosexuality in Renaissance England*, 70, 74, 76, 128–29.

63. Dunn, Savage, and Yeandle, *Journal of John Winthrop*, 342–43; Hoadly, *Records of the Colony or Jurisdiction of New Haven*, 440–43; Daniel E. Williams, ed., *Pillars of Salt: An Anthology of Early American Criminal Narratives* (Madison, Wis., 1993), 67–69.

64. "Crimes and Misdemeanours," 1st ser., 1:96a, 96b.

65. Thomas Foster points out that New England courts "linked male sexual capacity and incapacity to larger character traits and standards of manhood." This officially validated notion that "sexual conditions" were indicative of "a larger sexual character or identity" could have made it easier for neighbors and

acquaintances of Sension, Potter, and others like them to interpret their behavior as a distinct propensity (Thomas A. Foster, "Deficient Husbands: Manhood, Sexual Incapacity, and Male Marital Sexuality in Seventeenth-Century New England," *William and Mary Quarterly* 56 [1999]: 743, 744).

4. "Living in a State of Nature"

1. *Colonial Records of North Carolina*, 1st ser., 10 vols. (Raleigh, N.C., 1886–90) (henceforth *CRNC*, 1st ser.), 1:767; 2:371–72, 431–32.

2. Richard J. Hooker, ed., *The Carolina Backcountry on the Eve of Revolution: The Journal and Other Writings of Charles Woodmason, Anglican Itinerant* (Chapel Hill, N.C., 1953), 6, 7, 15, 52, 61, 80–81.

3. James Glen to Lords of Trade, 25/10/1753, *Public Records Office Transcriptions*, 25:350–51.

4. William Byrd I to Daniel Horsmanden, 8/8/1690, in Marion Tinling, ed., *The Correspondence of the Three William Byrds of Westover, Virginia, 1684-1776*, 2 vols. (Charlottesville, Va., 1977), 1:136.

5. For discussion of these negative stereotypes in eighteenth-century English publications, see Michal Rozbicki, *The Complete Colonial Gentleman: Cultural Legitimacy in Plantation America* (Charlottesville, Va., 1998), chap. 3.

6. Philip L. Barbour, ed., *The Complete Works of Captain John Smith, 1580-1631*, 3 vols. (Chapel Hill, N.C., 1986), 2:184, 192.

7. For discussion of sexual relations between European settlers and Native Americans, see chap. 5.

8. Mary Beth Norton, *Founding Mothers and Fathers: Gendered Power and the Forming of American Society* (New York, 1996), 354. That Virginia's male colonists were willing to have sex with other men is suggested obliquely in a comment made by Captain John Smith, an invaluable chronicler of Jamestown's first few years. Smith wrote that sailors pilfered biscuit from supplies on board their ships "to sell, give or exchange with us, for money, saxefras, furs, or love" (Barbour, *Complete Works of Captain John Smith*, 1:210). When John Hammond bemoaned that Virginia "in its infamy and filth" had harbored "licentious men" and "vices," he was not necessarily referring only to illicit sex that involved a man and woman (John Hammond, "Leah and Rachel, or, The Two Fruitful Sisters, Virginia and Maryland," 1656, in Clayton Colman Hall, ed., *Narratives of Early Maryland, 1633-1684* [New York, 1910], 286, 287).

9. H. R. McIlwaine, ed., *Minutes of the Council and General Court of Colonial Virginia, 1622-1632, 1670-1676* (Richmond, Va., 1924), 34. John Murrin notes that a boy servant in Surry County was found dead with his thighs badly bruised; another young fellow named John Verone, who had been working for an all-male household, hanged himself for no apparent reason. We can only wonder if these deaths were prompted, at least in part, by sexual coercion (John M. Murrin, "'Things Fearful to Name': Bestiality in Colonial America," supplemental issue of *Pennsylvania History* 65 [1998]: 12).

10. McIlwaine, *Minutes of the Council and General Court of Colonial Virginia*,

78, 81, 83, 85, 93. The only other person on the ship when Cornish raped Couse was Walter Mathew, who had been working in an adjoining room. He overheard Couse saying that "he would not" and that "if he did so it would be an overthrow to him both in soul and body, and alleged the scripture to him." But Mathew could not tell what Couse was refusing to do. Later that day he asked him why he had been arguing with Cornish. Couse told him that their master "would have buggered him or [words] to that effect, but did not confess that the master did that fact" (42).

11. Robert Beverley, *The History and Present State of Virginia* (1705; Chapel Hill, N.C., 1947), 287; Lois Green Carr and Lorena S. Walsh, "The Planter's Wife: The Experience of White Women in Seventeenth-Century Maryland," *William and Mary Quarterly* 34 (1977): 549; James Horn, *Adapting to a New World: English Society in the Seventeenth-Century Chesapeake* (Chapel Hill, N.C., 1994), 212.

12. See, for example, McIlwaine, *Minutes of the Council and General Court of Colonial Virginia*, 469. In 1643 the Virginia assembly passed a law confirming the compensation due when servants entered into "secret marriages" (William W. Hening, ed., *The Statutes at Large: Being a Collection of all the Laws of Virginia, from the First Session of the Legislature in the Year 1619*, 5 vols. [Richmond, New York, and Philadelphia, 1809–23], 1:252–53). Masters did occasionally allow servants to marry each other; for an example see "Lower Norfolk County Records, 1636–1646," *Virginia Magazine of History and Biography* 39 (1931): 3–4.

13. McIlwaine, *Minutes of the Council and General Court of Colonial Virginia*, 154; see also William Hand Browne et al., eds., *Archives of Maryland*, 72 vols. (Baltimore, 1883–1972), 54:571.

14. Hening, *Statutes at Large*, 1:253; Browne et al., *Archives of Maryland*, 1:373–74. For examples of female servants who were sentenced to serve extra time for bearing "bastard" children, see McIlwaine, *Minutes of the Council and General Court of Colonial Virginia*, 238; and Browne et al., *Archives of Maryland*, 41:603–4; 54:540. For examples of suits for compensation brought against the fathers of illegitimate children borne to female servants, see ibid., 10:337, 365–66, 525–26; 41:14–18; 54:211–12, 291–92, 519.

15. See, for examples, Horn, *Adapting to a New World*, 213.

16. Testamentary Proceedings, Hall of Records, Annapolis, Md., 23:349–77.

17. Browne et al., *Archives of Maryland*, 10:173–74, 183, 185.

18. Ibid., 41:456; 54:9, 10, 205, 211–12. For an example of coin-breaking in early modern England, see David Cressy, *Birth, Marriage, and Death: Ritual, Religion, and the Life-Cycle in Tudor and Stuart England* (Oxford, 1997), 241.

19. Jon Butler, *Awash in a Sea of Faith: Christianizing the American People* (Cambridge, Mass., 1990), 45, 51–52, 102; Browne et al., *Archives of Maryland*, 53:599.

20. *CRNC*, 1st ser., 1:184, 201; *State Records of North Carolina*, 16 vols., numbered 11–26, to follow on from *CRNC*, 1st ser. (Winston and Goldsboro, N.C., 1895–1906), 23:1, 158–61. See also Hooker, *Carolina Backcountry*, 15.

21. Walter L. Robbins, ed., "John Tobler's Description of South Carolina," *South Carolina Historical Magazine* 71 (1970): 152.

22. Hooker, *Carolina Backcountry*, 15; Frank J. Klingberg, ed., *The Carolina Chronicle of Dr. Francis Le Jau, 1706-1717* (Berkeley, Calif., 1956), 175.

23. Florence Gambrill Geiger, ed., "St. Bartholomew's Parish as Seen by Its Rectors, 1713-1761," *South Carolina Historical and Genealogical Magazine* 50 (1949): 191; Hooker, *Carolina Backcountry*, 100. More than a third of the presentments brought before Virginia's Lower Norfolk County Court in 1654 targeted married couples who had engaged in premarital sex (Horn, *Adapting to a New World*, 214).

24. *Colonial Records of North Carolina*, 2d ser. (Raleigh, N.C., 1963-) (henceforth *CRNC*, 2d ser.), 5:127, 157; Bertie County, Bastard Bonds and Papers, North Carolina State Archives, Raleigh, N.C.; William Byrd, "The Secret History of the Line," in Wendy Martin, ed., *Colonial American Travel Narratives* (New York, 1994), 165.

25. Browne et al., *Archives of Maryland*, 10:471, 503, 504; 53:4, 33-34.

26. See E. P. Thompson, *Customs in Common* (New York, 1991), 404-66; Samuel Pyeatt Menefee, *Wives for Sale: An Ethnographic Study of British Popular Divorce* (New York, 1981); and Lawrence Stone, *The Family, Sex, and Marriage in England, 1500-1800* (London, 1977), 40-41. Sometimes a neighbor or friend would purchase and thus assume custodial responsibility for a woman in the event of marital breakdown. But "first and foremost," wife sales served "to replace discordant relationships with more harmonious liaisons" (Menefee, *Wives for Sale*, 67).

27. Records of Secretary of State, Miscellaneous Records, State Archives, Columbia, S.C., vol. SS:420.

28. *CRNC*, 2d ser., 3:88, 89, 90, 126, 128.

29. *CRNC*, 2d ser., 2:379. Abandoned spouses did not always want their partners back. In 1766 Solomon Ewell complained to the General Court about "the elopement of his wife Lydia and her living in adultery with one Samuel Colten of Northampton County." Ewell wanted his marriage dissolved (*CRNC*, 1st ser., 7:352). Husbands sometimes announced the elopement of their wives in printed advertisements and renounced any further financial responsibility for them, for examples of which see *South Carolina Gazette* (Charleston), 31/10/1768, 9/2/1769.

30. *CRNC*, 2d ser., 5:251, 6:420.

31. Hening, *Statutes at Large*, 2:49-51.

32. Browne et al., *Archives of Maryland*, 17:404-5; 22:342.

33. William Byrd, "History of the Dividing Line," in Louis B. Wright, ed., *The Prose Works of William Byrd of Westover* (Cambridge, Mass., 1966), 212; *CRNC*, 1st ser., 7:288.

34. *CRNC*, 1st ser., 3:180; 7:488; *State Records of North Carolina*, 23:5-6. In 1703 the South Carolina assembly resolved that the colony needed an act

"to punish men cohabiting with women with whom they are not married, and also against strumpets and bastardizing." But the legislation passed later that year addressed only the issue of bastardy (A. S. Salley, ed., *Journals of the Commons House of Assembly of South Carolina for 1703* [Columbia, S.C., 1934], 59, 95; John D. Cushing, ed., *The Earliest Printed Laws of South Carolina, 1692-1734*, 2 vols. [Wilmington, Del., 1978], 2:164-68).

35. Bertie County, Court of Pleas and Quarter Sessions, 1739-64, North Carolina State Archives. Donna J. Spindel gives another example of this recurrent problem in *Crime and Society in North Carolina, 1663-1776* (Baton Rouge, La., 1989), 96, though her overall impression of the court system's effectiveness is more positive than mine.

36. *CRNC*, 1st ser., 2:363, 401, 413, 437.

37. *CRNC*, 2d ser., 3:468-69.

38. *CRNC*, 1st ser., 3:367; 5:336. Maryland's lower house of assembly had declared in 1688 that sexual and marital irregularities were commonplace not because of any deficiency in the laws but because "the said laws are not put in execution against the offenders by those magistrates that are entrusted therewith" (Browne et al., *Archives of Maryland*, 13:181).

39. Frank J. Klingberg, ed., *Carolina Chronicle: The Papers of Commissary Gideon Johnston, 1707-1716* (Berkeley, Calif., 1946), 22, 77, 126.

40. Klingberg, *Carolina Chronicle of Dr. Francis Le Jau*, 27, 30, 69, 81, 94.

41. *Colonial Records of South Carolina*, 1st ser., 15 vols. (Columbia, S.C., 1951-96), 7:57; South Carolina Council Journal, vol. 17, pt. 2 (19/5/1749-16/12/1749), 522-24, South Carolina State Archives, Columbia, S.C.

42. *CRNC*, 1st ser., 4:1318; 5:213; 6:1091; 9:28-29. See also 6:223, 709-10, 1040.

43. Susie M. Ames, ed., *County Court Records of Accomack-Northampton, Virginia, 1632-40* (Washington, D.C., 1954), 151; Warren M. Billings, ed., *The Old Dominion in the Seventeenth Century: A Documentary History of Virginia, 1606-1689* (Chapel Hill, N.C., 1975), 102. See also McIlwaine, *Minutes of the Council and General Court of Colonial Virginia*, 31, 142, 477, 479, 483; and Susie M. Ames, ed., *County Court Records of Accomack-Northampton, Virginia, 1640-1645* (Charlottesville, Va., 1973), 236. Virginia's courts abandoned the use of penance rituals in the 1660s, "after Restoration church courts in England failed to regain jurisdiction over sexual offenses" (Kathleen M. Brown, *Good Wives, Nasty Wenches, and Anxious Patriarchs: Gender, Race, and Power in Colonial Virginia* [Chapel Hill, 1996], 190-91). That shift would have been reinforced by the dramatic increase in ministers and parish activity during the 1670s, which removed to a significant degree the need for secular courts to assume a spiritual role; see Butler, *Awash in a Sea of Faith*, 49-50.

44. L. Lynn Hogue, "An Edition of 'Eight Speeches Delivered At So Many Several General Sessions and Gaol Deliveries: Held at Charlestown . . . in the Years 1703, 1704, 1705, 1706, 1707,' by Nicholas Trott, Esq., Chief Justice of the

Province of South Carolina" (Ph.D. diss., University of Tennessee, 1972), 221, 223. See also L. Lynn Hogue, "Nicholas Trott: Man of Law and Letters," *South Carolina Historical Magazine* 76 (1975): 25-34.

45. Pasquotank County Criminal Action Papers, 1729-1800, North Carolina State Archives; see also the presentments of Robert Hosea (1758) and William Blackstock (1766).

46. Symons Creek Monthly Meeting Minutes, 1699-1785, 17, Friends Historical Collection, Guilford College Library, Greensboro, N.C.; Perquimans Monthly Meeting Minutes, 1680-1736, 1, Friends Historical Collection, Guilford College Library; *CRNC*, 1st ser., 1:813.

47. Symons Creek Monthly Meeting Minutes, 80, 354, 358, 367. For more detailed discussion of Quakers in early North Carolina, see James Le Shana, "'Heavenly Plantations': Quakers in Colonial North Carolina" (Ph.D. diss., University of California, Riverside, 1998); and Donald Vernon Dowless, "The Quakers of Colonial North Carolina, 1672-1789" (Ph.D. diss., Baylor University, 1989).

48. Memoranda from John Garzia to General Court of North Carolina, Papers Pertaining to Marriages, Colonial Court Records, North Carolina State Archives; *CRNC*, 1st ser., 9:267-68. See also Hooker, *Carolina Backcountry*, 40-41.

49. *State Records of North Carolina*, 23:997. A 1766 act giving Presbyterian ministers the right to marry people was soon repealed, and a 1771 act to the same end was vetoed by the crown (*CRNC*, 1st ser., 8:xliv-xlv; 9:284-85). For Presbyterian petitions requesting this right, see ibid., 8:80, 82-83; 10:1015-17.

50. Hooker, *Carolina Backcountry*, 43.

51. Amy Friedlander, ed., "Commissary Johnston's Report of 1713," *South Carolina Historical Magazine* 83 (1982): 261; Hooker, *Carolina Backcountry*, 99, 100, 102, 103. See also Christine Leigh Heyrman, *Southern Cross: The Beginnings of the Bible Belt* (New York, 1997), 181-84; and Cynthia Lynn Lyerly, *Methodism and the Southern Mind, 1770-1810* (New York, 1998), 158-60.

52. Geiger, "St. Bartholomew's Parish," 188-89, 191.

53. *CRNC*, 1st ser., 3:624; 4:604; Hooker, *Carolina Backcountry*, 12.

54. Hooker, *Carolina Backcountry*, 45.

55. Alexander Garden to Secretary of S.P.G., 10/10/1743 and 6/11/1744, S.P.G. Letterbooks (microfilm of originals at Rhode House Library, Oxford), Letterbook B, 12:78, 120; Register and Journal of Prince Frederick Episcopal Church, Georgetown County, 1713-78, transcript in 2 vols., vol. 2, Vestry to Bishop of London, 1/5/1756; Vestry to Secretary of the S.P.G., 1/5/1756, South Carolina Historical Society. See also George W. Williams, ed., "Letters to the Bishop of London from the Commissaries in South Carolina," *South Carolina Historical Magazine* 78 (1977): 133-34.

56. William Stevens Perry, ed., *Historical Collections Relating to the American Colonial Church* (1871; New York, 1969), 4:158; *CRNC*, 1st ser., 2:417, 431; 2d ser., 10:181.

NOTES TO PAGES 146-149

57. A. S. Salley, ed., *Minutes of the Vestry of St. Helena's Parish, South Carolina, 1726–1812* (Columbia, S.C., 1919), 74, 75, 182–83.

58. For examples, see Eugene R. Sheridan, ed., *The Papers of Lewis Morris,* 3 vols. (Newark, N.J., 1991), 1:47, 97; and Committee on Building a Church in New England to Bishop of London, 8/1/1721, S.P.G. Letterbook A, 16:269.

59. *CRNC,* 1st ser., 2:417. For the content of this paragraph, I am much indebted to Annette Laing, "'All Things to All Men': Popular Religious Culture and the Anglican Mission in Colonial America, 1701–1750" (Ph.D. diss., University of California, Riverside, 1995). See also Patricia U. Bonomi, *Under the Cope of Heaven: Religion, Society, and Politics in Colonial America* (New York, 1986), esp. 45; and Joan Gundersen, *The Anglican Ministry in Virginia, 1723–1766: A Study of a Social Class* (New York, 1989), chap. 6.

60. *CRNC,* 1st ser., 7:458; Byrd, "History of the Dividing Line," 207.

61. Jeremiah Minter, *A Brief Account of the Religious Experience, Travels, Preaching, Persecutions from Evil Men, and God's Special Helps in the Faith and Life etc. of Jeremiah Minter* (Washington, D.C., 1817), 13–15. See also Heyrman, *Southern Cross,* 131–32; and Lyerly, *Methodism and the Southern Mind,* 158–59.

62. Terry W. Lipscomb and R. Nicholas Olsberg, eds., *Journal of Commons House of Assembly, 1751–52* (Columbia, S.C., 1977), 163; J. H. Easterby, ed., *Journal of Commons House of Assembly, 1749–50* (Columbia, S.C., 1962), 428, 439; Civil and Criminal Papers, 1681–1710, North Carolina State Archives. Far from appreciating this solicitude for his moral welfare, the younger Jones had responded by slandering his father, "accusing him most falsely" of "felonious stealing of cattle."

63. Quotations from *John Clark vs. William Wynn, CRNC,* 2d ser., 5:164–67.

64. *CRNC,* 1st ser., 6:271, 275–76, 303. Factional divisions and issues of status clearly played into this affair. The accused magistrate declared that "had not party violence been carried with so high a hand, nothing would have been said upon that affair, as everybody was satisfied [Core] deserved much more for offering to meddle with persons of character." Indeed, Spaight claimed that Core had forgiven him for the whipping. Kirsten Fischer points out that in colonial North Carolina, sexual slander sometimes served as "a means of slighting the local elite." Insults directed against "the wives and daughters of prominent men also implied that since these patriarchs could not control the women in their families, neither were they fit to rule the public at large" (Kirsten Fischer, "'False, Feigned, and Scandalous Words': Sexual Slander and Racial Ideology among Whites in Colonial North Carolina," in Catherine Clinton and Michele Gillespie, eds., *The Devil's Lane: Sex and Race in the Early South* [New York, 1997], 143).

65. *CRNC,* 1st ser., 10:870e, 870g; *State Records of North Carolina,* 20:491–92; 24:164–65; Spruce Macay Notebook, Record of Trials in Morgan District, 1786–95, North Carolina State Archives.

66. *State Records of North Carolina,* 20:569; 25:74. Remarriage was permis-

sible if a spouse had been missing for seven years, if the union had been voided, or if a divorce had been granted.

67. Journals of William Ormond, 1791–1803, transcript in 2 vols., 2:39, Special Collections Library, Duke University.

68. *The Trial and Conviction of John Clary* (n.p., 1810), 25. The following account draws on the documents and editorial commentary printed in this pamphlet, which was sponsored by a group of those who opposed Clary's election to the state assembly.

69. Ibid., iii, 16, 21, 26, 29.

70. Byrd, "History of the Dividing Line," 180.

71. *CRNC*, 1st ser., 1:971; Louis B. Wright and Marion Tinling, eds., *William Byrd of Virginia: The London Diary (1717–1721) and Other Writings* (New York, 1958), 564, 573; Hooker, *Carolina Backcountry*, 15, 61; [James MacSparran,] *America Dissected* (Dublin, 1753), 9–10.

72. Klingberg, *Carolina Chronicle of Dr. Francis Le Jau*, 41–42, 60. For discussion of English and European perceptions of African sexuality, see Winthrop D. Jordan, *White over Black: American Attitudes toward the Negro, 1550–1812* (Chapel Hill, N.C., 1968), 32–40. Ira Berlin charts the persistence of African culture among North American slaves in *Many Thousands Gone: The First Two Centuries of Slavery in North America* (Cambridge, Mass., 1998).

73. Hooker, *Carolina Backcountry*, 56, 121–22.

5. The Dangerous Allure of "Copper-Coloured Beauties"

1. Roger Wolcott, "A Brief Account of the Agency of the Honorable John Winthrop, Esq. in the Court of King Charles the Second, Anno Dom. 1662," in *Massachusetts Historical Society Collections*, 1st ser., 4 (1795): 267; George Chapman, Ben Jonson, and John Marston, *Eastward Ho*, ed. R. W. Van Fossen (Baltimore, 1979), 137; John Hammond, "Leah and Rachel, or, The Two Fruitful Sisters, Virginia and Maryland," in Clayton Colman Hall, ed., *Narratives of Early Maryland, 1633–1684* (New York, 1910), 281, 300; Thomas Morton, *The New English Canaan* (1637; Boston, 1883), 114, 179. See also Philip L. Barbour, ed., *The Complete Works of Captain John Smith*, 3 vols. (Chapel Hill, N.C., 1986), 1:401. Annette Kolodny examines the feminization of the American landscape in *The Lay of the Land: Metaphor as Experience and History in American Life and Letters* (Chapel Hill, N.C., 1975).

2. Richard Eden, "The Decades of the New World" (1555), in Edward Arber, ed., *The First Three English Books on America* (Birmingham, Eng., 1885), 83; Arthur Barlowe, "The First Voyage Made," in Richard Hakluyt, *The Principal Navigations, Voyages, Traffiques, and Discoveries of the English Nation*, 12 vols. (1589; Glasgow, 1903–5), 8:302.

3. "[William] Morrell's Poem on New England," *Massachusetts Historical Society Collections*, 1st ser., 1 (1792): 135. See also William Strachey, *The History of Travel Into Virginia Britania* (1612), ed. Louis B. Wright and Virginia Freund (London, 1953), 71.

4. John Josselyn, *New England's Rarities Discovered*, ed. Edward Tuckerman (Boston, 1865), 157; "Of the New Lands and of the People Found by the Messengers of the King of Portugal Named Emanuel" (1511), in Arber, *First Three English Books*, xxvii.

5. Strachey, *History of Travel Into Virginia*, 113, 116; Eden, "A Treatise of the New India" (1553), in Arber, *First Three English Books*, 37; Eden's preface to "Decades of the New World," in ibid., 50; John Josselyn, "A Relation of Two Voyages to New England," *Massachusetts Historical Society Collections*, 3d ser., 3 (1833): 296.

6. "Governor [Edward] Winslow's Account of the Natives of New England" (1624), in Nathaniel Morton, *New England's Memorial* (Boston, 1855), 491; Roger Williams, *A Key into the Language of America*, ed. John J. Teunissen and Evelyn J. Hinz (Detroit, 1973), 205, 208. See also Robert Beverley, *The History and Present State of Virginia* (1705; Chapel Hill, N.C., 1947), 170.

7. William Wood, *New England's Prospect*, ed. Alden T. Vaughan (1634; Amherst, Mass., 1977), 99. See also Williams, *A Key*, 206; and Karen Ordahl Kupperman, *Indians and English: Facing Off in Early America* (Ithaca, N.Y., 2000), 147–48.

8. For examples, see Barbour, *Complete Works of Captain John Smith*, 1:161; "Morrell's Poem on New England," 131; and Williams, *A Key*, 185.

9. Gabriel Archer, "The Relation of Captain Gosnold's Voyage to the North Part of Virginia," in *Massachusetts Historical Society Collections*, 3d ser., 8 (1843): 77. See also Edward Porter Alexander, ed., *The Journal of John Fontaine, an Irish Huguenot Son in Spain and Virginia, 1710–1719* (Charlottesville, Va., 1972), 94.

10. Beverley, *History and Present State of Virginia*, 171.

11. Gary B. Nash, in *Red, White, and Black: The Peoples of Early America* (Englewood Cliffs, N.J., 1982), 282, argues that Anglo-Indian unions were "limited more by demographic considerations than by prior attitudes," whereas David D. Smits emphasizes English "aversion to race mixing" in "'Abominable Mixture': Toward the Repudiation of Anglo-Indian Intermarriage in Seventeenth-Century Virginia," *Virginia Magazine of History and Biography* 95 (1987): 157–92; and in his "'We Are Not To Grow Wild': Seventeenth-Century New England's Repudiation of Anglo-Indian Intermarriage," *American Indian Culture and Research Journal* 11 (1987): 1–31.

12. Barbour, *Complete Works of Captain John Smith*, 1:168, 174, 235–36.

13. Samuel Purchas, *Hakluytus Posthumus, or, Purchas His Pilgrims*, 20 vols. (Glasgow, 1905–7), 14:298; William Symonds, *A Sermon Preached at White-Chapel* (London, 1609), 35.

14. Barbour, *Complete Works of Captain John Smith*, 2:81; Patrick Copland, *Virginia's God Be Thanked* (London, 1622), 24; George Percy, "A True Relation," *Tyler's Quarterly Historical and Genealogical Magazine* 3 (1922): 280.

15. Beverley, *History and Present State of Virginia*, 287.

16. John Rolfe to Sir Thomas Dale, April 1614, in Warren M. Billings, ed.,

The Old Dominion in the Seventeenth Century: A Documentary History of Virginia, 1606-1689 (Chapel Hill, N.C., 1975), 216-19.

17. "The Discourse of the Old Company," in Lyon Gardiner Tyler, ed., *Narratives of Early Virginia, 1606-1625* (New York, 1907), 433-34; Susan Myra Kingsbury, ed., *Records of the Virginia Company of London,* 4 vols. (Washington, D.C., 1906-35), 1:256.

18. See Smits, "'Abominable Mixture,'" 166.

19. Ibid., 168-69; Barbour, *Complete Works of Captain John Smith,* 1:71, 2:249; Strachey, *History of Travel Into Virginia,* 60; Beverley, *History and Present State of Virginia,* 38.

20. See J. Douglas Deal, *Race and Class in Colonial Virginia: Indians, Englishmen, and Africans on the Eastern Shore during the Seventeenth Century* (New York, 1993), 41. For exceptions, see Smits, "'Abominable Mixture,'" 188-89.

21. "Northampton County Deeds, Wills, Etc., 1645-1651," quoted in Deal, *Race and Class,* 41-42.

22. William Hand Browne et al., eds., *Archives of Maryland,* 72 vols. (Baltimore, 1883-1972), 4:258, 7:370.

23. William Bradford, *Of Plymouth Plantation, 1620-1647,* ed. Francis Murphy (New York, 1981), 26, 70; Cotton Mather, *Magnalia Christi Americana,* ed. Thomas Robbins, 2 vols. (1852; New York, 1967), 2:663.

24. Bradford, *Of Plymouth Plantation,* 227; Morton, *New English Canaan,* 280. For an insightful discussion of the conflict over Morton's Merry Mount, see Michael Zuckerman, "Pilgrims in the Wilderness: Community, Modernity, and the Maypole at Merry Mount," *New England Quarterly* 50 (1977): 255-77.

25. Bradford, *Of Plymouth Plantation,* 242, 258; *Complete Writings of Roger Williams,* 7 vols. (New York, 1963), 6:67, 85, 95. See also William Hubbard, *A Narrative of the Troubles with the Indians in New England* (Boston, 1677), 59.

26. "A Particular Account of the Late Revolution," in Charles M. Andrews, ed., *Narratives of the Insurrections, 1675-1690* (New York, 1915), 197; Paul Boyer and Stephen Nissenbaum, eds., *The Salem Witchcraft Papers: Verbatim Transcripts of the Legal Documents of the Salem Witchcraft Outbreak of 1692,* 3 vols. (New York, 1977), 1:52.

27. Thomas Shepard, *The Day-Breaking If Not The Sun-Rising of the Gospel with the Indians in New-England* (London, 1647), 22; Thomas Shepard, *The Clear Sunshine of the Gospel Breaking Forth upon the Indians in New-England* (London, 1648), 4-5. Ann Marie Plane discusses Indian conversion narratives in *Colonial Intimacies: Indian Marriage in Early New England* (Ithaca, N.Y., 2000), chap. 2.

28. Nathaniel B. Shurtleff, ed., *Records of the Governor and Company of Massachusetts Bay, in New England,* 5 vols. (Boston, 1853-54), 2:56.

29. See Nash, *Red, White, and Black,* 279; James Axtell, *The Invasion Within: The Contest of Cultures in Colonial North America* (New York, 1985), 304; and Alden T. Vaughan, *The New England Frontier: Puritans and Indians, 1620-1675* (Boston, 1965), 209. No northern colony and only two southern colonies (Virginia and North Carolina) bothered to prohibit intermarriage with Indians; this

was doubtless due to the relatively insignificant number of Indians living on the eastern seaboard within a few decades of settlement. In March 1635 the General Court of Massachusetts did refer "the matter of marriage betwixt English and Indians" to "after consideration," but no record survives of further debate or resolution on this issue (Shurtleff, *Records of the Governor and Company,* 1:140).

30. Petition of Elizabeth Stevens to the governor and magistrates at Boston, 1668, quoted in Plane, *Colonial Intimacies,* 81; Nathaniel B. Shurtleff and David Pulsifer, eds., *Records of the Colony of New Plymouth in New England,* 12 vols. (Boston, 1855–61), 1:132; Samuel Nowell, *Abraham in Arms* (Boston, 1678), 14.

31. *Records and Files of the Quarterly Courts of Essex County,* 9 vols. (Salem, Mass., 1911–78), 1:337; 7:410; Shurtleff and Pulsifer, *Records of the Colony of New Plymouth,* 5:31 (see also 5:163); Samuel Eliot Morison and Zechariah Chafee, eds., "Records of the Suffolk County Court, 1671–1680," *Colonial Society of Massachusetts Publications* 29–30 (1933): 183–84. As Plane writes, "such unions certainly made up a part, however hidden, of New England's colonial past" (*Colonial Intimacies,* 36).

32. For examples, see Shurtleff and Pulsifer, *Records of the Colony of New Plymouth,* 3:180; 5:107, 255.

33. See John Noble and John F. Cronin, eds., *Records of the Court of Assistants of the Colony of Massachusetts Bay, 1630–1692,* 3 vols. (Boston, 1901–28), 1:21–22, 3:210, 216–17.

34. Morton, *New English Canaan,* 148.

35. It is perhaps significant that a disproportionate number of prosecutions involving sexual contact with Indians were clustered in the 1670s, though even during that decade, as Plane points out, there was "only a handful of such actions, making it impossible to draw conclusions of any statistical significance" (*Colonial Intimacies,* 82).

36. Bradford *Of Plymouth Plantation,* 185; Alden T. Vaughan and Edward W. Clark, eds., *Puritans among the Indians: Accounts of Captivity and Redemption, 1676–1724* (Cambridge, Mass., 1981), 70. For an exceptional allegation by a sixteen-year-old captive, see John Underhill, "News from America" (1638), in *Massachusetts Historical Society Collections,* 3d ser., 6 (1837): 18.

37. Daniel K. Richter, in *The Ordeal of the Longhouse: The Peoples of the Iroquois League in the Era of European Colonization* (Chapel Hill, N.C., 1992), esp. 32–38, 52–53, discusses the use of mourning wars to replace the dead. See also James Axtell, *The European and the Indian: Essays in the Ethnohistory of Colonial North America* (New York, 1981), 182; Sharon Block, "Coerced Sex in British America, 1700–1820" (Ph.D. diss., Princeton University, 1995), 236–38; an account of Indian behavior toward prisoners of war in the *Pennsylvania Gazette,* 25/7/1765; and Francois Alexandre Frederic, duc de La Rochefoucault-Liancourt, *Travels Through the United States of North America, the Country of the Iroquois, and Upper Canada* (London, 1799), 1:179.

38. Nathaniel Saltonstall, *The Present State of New England with Respect to the Indian War* (London, 1676), 6; Nathaniel Saltonstall, *A New and Further Nar-*

rative of the State of New England (London, 1676), 4, 14; Cotton Mather, "Decennium Luctuosum," in Charles H. Lincoln, ed., *Narratives of the Indian Wars, 1675-1699* (New York, 1913), 238; Benjamin Tompson, *New England's Tears for Her Present Miseries* (Boston, 1676), 11.

39. Hubbard, *Narrative of the Troubles,* 61; see also 78, 135.

40. Beverley, *History and Present State of Virginia,* 38-39.

41. Byrd, "History of the Dividing Line," in Louis B. Wright, ed., *The Prose Works of William Byrd of Westover* (Cambridge, Mass., 1966), 160-61.

42. For a helpful discussion of the shifting tone in colonial writings about Indians, see Gary B. Nash, "The Image of the Indian in the Southern Colonial Mind," *William and Mary Quarterly* 29 (1972): 197-230.

43. Alexander Spotswood wrote while serving as governor of Virginia in 1717 that the "inclinations" of the English precluded intermarriage and that there were no such marriages in Virginia at that time (A. Brock, ed., *The Official Letters of Alexander Spotswood* [Richmond, 1885], 227). The one context in which Anglo-Indian unions became common in eastern communities, albeit for a brief period of time, was slavery in South Carolina. Settlers there used Native Americans as slaves in the late 1600s and early 1700s: as we will see in chapter 6, the power that masters wielded over their slaves was often embodied in sexual coercion; that context of subjugation may have made white Carolinians feel less uncomfortable about miscegenation than their counterparts in the early Chesapeake (a situation in which Indians were not enslaved). A large number of children with Indian mothers and English fathers were born in and around Charleston during those years (See Nash, *Red, White, and Black,* 282).

44. John Lawson, *A New Voyage to Carolina,* ed. Hugh Talmage Lefler (Chapel Hill, N.C., 1967), 244-45. Most of the Anglo-Indian relationships mentioned in contemporary accounts were between English men and native women; for an exception, see Francis Harper, ed., *The Travels of William Bartram* (1791; New Haven, Conn., 1958), 11.

45. Richard White, in *The Middle Ground: Indians, Empires, and Republics in the Great Lakes Region, 1650-1815* (New York, 1991), esp. ix-x, characterizes this physical and cultural space as "the middle ground."

46. Byrd, "History of the Dividing Line," 161; Winthrop D. Jordan, *White over Black: American Attitudes toward the Negro, 1550-1812* (Chapel Hill, N.C., 1968), esp. 4-11. For a fuller discussion of colonial attitudes toward skin color and its relationship to sex, see chap. 6 of this book.

47. Lawson, *New Voyage to Carolina,* 189; Beverley, *History and Present State of Virginia,* 159, 166; Byrd, "History of the Dividing Line," 314; Louis B. Wright and Marion Tinling, eds., *Quebec to Carolina in 1785-1786, Being the Travel Diary and Observations of Robert Hunter, Jr., A Young Merchant of London* (San Marino, Calif., 1943), 55; and Antonio Pace, ed. and trans., *Luigi Castiglioni's 'Viaggio': Travels in the United States of North America, 1785-87* (1790; Syracuse, N.Y., 1983), 39. See also Henry W. Clune, ed., *A Journey through the Genesee Country, Finger Lakes Region, and Mohawk Valley* (Rochester, N.Y., 1978), 60-61.

48. Harper, *Travels of William Bartram*, 306–7.

49. Ibid., 225–26.

50. "Journal of Diron D'Artaguiette," in Newton D. Mereness, ed., *Travels in the American Colonies* (New York, 1961), 48; Louis B. Wright and Marion Tinling, eds., *The Secret Diary of William Byrd of Westover, 1709–1712* (Richmond, Va., 1941), 423–25; Byrd, "The Secret History of the Line," in Wendy Martin, ed., *Colonial American Travel Narratives* (New York, 1994), 113–14; Byrd, "History of the Dividing Line," 218, 222.

51. Lawson, *New Voyage to Carolina*, 41; "Journal of Diron D'Artaguiette," 58, 73; Alexander Moore, ed., *Nairne's Muskhogean Journals: The 1708 Expedition to the Mississippi River* (Jackson, Miss., 1988), 44. As White points out, the sexual behavior of young Indian women was often regulated by relatives in ways that Europeans would not have noticed or understood (*Middle Ground*, 64).

52. Byrd, "History of the Dividing Line," 218, 314.

53. Lawson, *New Voyage to Carolina*, 41, 194. Smith also wrote that the Indians had "harlots" or "common whores by profession" (Barbour, *Complete Works of Captain John Smith*, 2:128, 461).

54. Beverley, *History and Present State of Virginia*, 189; Byrd, "History of the Dividing Line," 218; Byrd, "Secret History of the Line," 113; Lawson, *New Voyage to Carolina*, 50.

55. Wright and Tinling, *Quebec to Carolina*, 110–11.

56. Moore, *Nairne's Muskhogean Journals*, 44; Lawson, *New Voyage to Carolina*, 226; "Journal of Diron D'Artaguiette," 48; Lawson, *New Voyage to Carolina*, 25–26.

57. "Journal of Diron D'Artaguiette," 48, 91. For more information on the hospital and its checkered history, see Carl A. Brasseaux, "The Moral Climate of French Colonial Louisiana, 1699–1763," *Louisiana History* 27 (1986): 38.

58. For examples, see Thomas Ashe, "Carolina, or, A Description of the Present State of that Country," 1682, in Alexander S. Salley, ed., *Narratives of Early Carolina, 1650–1708* (New York, 1911), 156; and Maurice Mathews, "A Contemporary View of Carolina in 1680," *South Carolina Historical Magazine* 55 (1954): 157. Alfred W. Crosby discusses the transmission of syphilis in *The Columbian Exchange: Biological and Cultural Consequences of 1492* (Westport, Conn., 1972), chap. 4.

59. Lawson, *New Voyage to Carolina*, 25.

60. William Tredwell Bull to Secretary of Society for Propagation of Gospel, 10/8/1715, *South Carolina Historical Magazine* 63 (1962): 25; Robert Maule to Secretary of Society for Propagation of Gospel, 2/8/1711, *South Carolina Historical Magazine* 61 (1960): 8–9; Alexander Long, "A Small Postscript of the Ways and Manners of the Indians Called Cherokees," *Southern Indian Studies* 21 (1969): 20. See also Frank J. Klingberg, ed., *Carolina Chronicle: The Papers of Commissary Gideon Johnston, 1707–1716* (Berkeley, Calif., 1946), 53.

61. Governor Johnstone to Don Antonio D'Ullua, 3/5/1766, in Dunbar Rowland, ed., *Mississippi Provincial Archives, 1763–1766: English Dominion* (Nash-

ville, Tenn., 1911), 312–13; W. L. McDowell, ed., *Colonial Records of South Carolina: Journals of the Commissioners of the Indian Trade, 1710–1718* (Columbia, S.C., 1955), 4.

62. McDowell, *Journals of the Commissioners of the Indian Trade, 1710–1718*, 30, 34. See also W. L. McDowell, ed., *Colonial Records of South Carolina: Documents Relating to Indian Affairs, 1750–1754* (Columbia, S.C., 1958), 81, 87–88, 135–36; and W. L. McDowell, ed., *Colonial Records of South Carolina: Documents Relating to Indian Affairs, 1754–1765* (Columbia, S.C., 1970), 560.

63. Byrd, "History of the Dividing Line," 311. See also David Crawley to William Byrd, 30/7/1715, in Marion Tinling, ed., *The Correspondence of the Three William Byrds of Westover, Virginia, 1684–1776* (Charlottesville, Va., 1977), 1:289.

64. McDowell, *Documents Relating to Indian Affairs, 1750–1754*, 306; Rowland, *Mississippi Provincial Archives*, 238–39, 241.

65. McDowell, ed., *Documents Relating to Indian Affairs, 1754–1765*, 371; South Carolina Council Minutes, 20/1/1761, CO5/477, fol. 35, Public Records Office, London.

66. Lawson, *New Voyage to Carolina*, 193.

67. Harper, *Travels of William Bartram*, 124, 221; Moore, *Nairne's Muskhogean Journals*, 60–61; McDowell, *Documents Relating to Indian Affairs, 1750–1754*, 70; McDowell, *Documents Relating to Indian Affairs, 1754–1765*, 456.

68. See Sylvia Van Kirk, *"Many Tender Ties": Women in Fur-Trade Society in Western Canada, 1670–1870* (Norman, Okla., 1983), 29. The emergence of substantial female majorities in many eighteenth-century Indian nations, resulting from an upsurge in warfare brought on by the colonists' presence, may have softened objections to marriage to whites and highlighted the advantages. Although a straightforward demographic explanation for Indian interest in intermarriage would be reductive, it may well have been part of the picture for at least some native peoples.

69. Lawson, *New Voyage to Carolina*, 193; McDowell, *Documents Relating to Indian Affairs, 1750–1754*, 407.

70. Harper, *Travels of William Bartram*, 71–72.

71. Ibid., 283–84, 292.

72. *The Journal of Nicholas Cresswell, 1774–1777* (1924; Port Washington, N.Y., 1968), 93, 100, 103–6, 122.

73. Ibid., 108, 113, 122.

74. Harper, *Travels of William Bartram*, 124; Lawson, *New Voyage to Carolina*, 192; John Bernard, *Retrospections of America, 1797–1811*, ed. Mrs. Bayle Bernard (New York, 1887), 182. See also Van Kirk, *"Many Tender Ties*," 33.

75. For discussion of Indian captives, see Axtell, *Invasion Within*, chap. 13; June Namias, *White Captives: Gender and Ethnicity on the American Frontier* (Chapel Hill, N.C., 1993); and John Demos, *The Unredeemed Captive: A Family Story from Early America* (New York, 1994).

76. Lawson, *New Voyage to Carolina*, 192; Nathaniel Osborne to Secretary of Society for Propagation of Gospel, 1/3/1715, *South Carolina Historical and Genealogical Magazine* 50 (1949): 175; John L. Nichols, "Alexander Cameron, British Agent among the Cherokee, 1764–1781," *South Carolina Historical Magazine* 97 (1996): esp. 100; "Bernard Elliott's Recruiting Journal, 1775," *South Carolina Historical and Genealogical Magazine* 17 (1916): 98–99.

77. Tom Hatley, *The Dividing Paths: Cherokees and South Carolinians through the Revolutionary Era* (New York, 1995), 60, 85. In 1731 the South Carolina assembly had passed legislation prohibiting Indians and the children of interracial couples from becoming traders or factors working for traders. Assemblymen evidently doubted the loyalty and trustworthiness of mixed-blood offspring (Thomas Cooper and David J. McCord, eds., *The Statutes at Large of South Carolina*, 10 vols. [Columbia, S.C., 1836–41], 3:330). But the law had little practical effect; for continued participation by those of mixed blood in the South Carolina trade, see Hatley, *Dividing Paths*, 37, 85, 220–21, 228.

78. James Adair, *The History of the American Indians* (1775; New York, 1973), 133–35; Rochefoucault, *Travels Through the United States*, 1:167, 180.

6. "The Cameleon Lover"

1. Louis B. Wright and Marion Tinling, eds., *The Secret Diary of William Byrd of Westover, 1709–1712* (Richmond, Va., 1941), 253, 275. Entries that describe Byrd as giving his wife "a flourish" or "roger[ing]" her pervade the diary.

2. See Kathleen M. Brown, *Good Wives, Nasty Wenches, and Anxious Patriarchs: Gender, Race, and Power in Colonial Virginia* (Chapel Hill, N.C., 1996), 328–29. The word *flourish* could also suggest spontaneous, even hasty, sexual intercourse (Francis Grose, *A Classical Dictionary of the Vulgar Tongue* [1785; New York, 1963], 149).

3. Wright and Tinling, *Secret Diary of William Byrd*, 337, 446, 583; see also Grose, *Classical Dictionary*, 289.

4. See Rhys Isaac, *The Transformation of Virginia, 1740–1790* (Chapel Hill, N.C., 1982), pt. 1. Michal Rozbicki discusses eighteenth-century genteel aspirations in *The Complete Colonial Gentleman: Cultural Legitimacy in Plantation America* (Charlottesville, Va., 1998). Kenneth A. Lockridge has argued that the planters' quest for gentility was psychologically destructive and, indeed, "almost pathological." See his *The Diary, and Life, of William Byrd II of Virginia, 1674–1744* (Chapel Hill, N.C., 1987); Kenneth A. Lockridge, *On the Sources of Patriarchal Rage: The Commonplace Books of William Byrd and Thomas Jefferson and the Gendering of Power in the Eighteenth Century* (New York, 1992); and Kenneth A. Lockridge, "Colonial Self-Fashioning: Paradoxes and Pathologies in the Construction of Genteel Identity in Eighteenth-Century America," in Ronald Hoffman, Mechal Sobel, and Fredrika J. Teute, eds., *Through a Glass Darkly: Reflections on Personal Identity in Early America* (Chapel Hill, N.C., 1997), quotation on 276.

5. Robert Bolling, "La Gazetta di Parnasso . . . ," Huntington Library, San Marino, Calif. Rozbicki discusses "the irresistable allure of heraldry" in *Complete Colonial Gentleman,* 43-49.

6. Marion Tinling, ed., *The Correspondence of the Three William Byrds of Westover, Virginia, 1684-1776,* 2 vols. (Charlottesville, Va., 1977), 1:227, 370; Maude H. Woodfin, ed., *Another Secret Diary of William Byrd of Westover, 1739-41, With Letters and Literary Exercises, 1696-1726,* trans. Marion Tinling (Richmond, Va., 1742), 278; *South Carolina Gazette* (Charleston), 26/1/1738; Robert Carter to Clement Brooke, 7/1/1783, Letterbook 5, Robert Carter Papers, Special Collections Library, Duke University, Durham, N.C.

7. See Gordon S. Wood, *The Radicalism of the American Revolution* (New York, 1992), esp. 194-97.

8. Evangeline Walker Andrews, ed., *Journal of a Lady of Quality; Being the Narrative of a Journey from Scotland to the West Indies, North Carolina, and Portugal in the Years 1774 to 1776* (New Haven, Conn., 1923), 112; H. Roy Merrens, ed., "A View of Coastal South Carolina in 1778: The Journal of Ebenezer Hazard," *South Carolina Historical Magazine* 73 (1972): 190. For the role played by slavery in "the confrontations between colonial and metropolitan elites," see Rozbicki, *Complete Colonial Gentleman,* 111-18.

9. "Observations in Several Voyages and Travels in America in the Year 1736," *William and Mary Quarterly,* 1st ser., 15 (1906-7): 222; Kenneth Roberts and Anna M. Roberts, eds. and trans., *Moreau de St. Mery's American Journey* (Garden City, N.Y., 1947), 54; Stanislaus Murray Hamilton, ed., *Letters to Washington and Accompanying Papers,* 5 vols. (Boston, 1898-1902), 4:41-43; Bluff Plantation Book, 1760-1773, South Carolina Historical Society, Charleston, S.C. See also Michael Zuckerman, "Penmanship Exercises for Saucy Sons: Some Thoughts on the Colonial Southern Family," *South Carolina Historical Magazine* 84 (1983): 152-66.

10. William Drayton to Peter Manigault, 18/4/1753, Manigault Family Papers, South Caroliniana Library, Columbia, S.C. See also Beverly McAnear, ed., "An American in London, 1735-36," *Pennsylvania Magazine of History and Biography* 64 (1940): 180. For a "mortified" response to such amenities, see Andrew Oliver, ed., *The Journal of Samuel Curwen* (Cambridge, Mass., 1972), 34, 48-49.

11. For examples, see Richard Godbeer, "William Byrd's 'Flourish': The Sexual Cosmos of a Southern Planter," in Merril D. Smith, ed., *Sex and Sexuality in Early America* (New York, 1998), 142-43.

12. *Poor Richard: An Almanack for the Year of Christ, 1734* (Philadelphia, 1733); Louis B. Wright and Marion Tinling, eds., *William Byrd of Virginia: The London Diary (1717-1721) and Other Writings* (New York, 1958), 356. For discussion of venereal infection in eighteenth-century London, see Randolph Trumbach, *Sex and the Gender Revolution,* vol. 1, *Heterosexuality and the Third Gender in Enlightenment London* (Chicago, 1998), chap. 7. Trumbach discusses metropolitan male libertinism in chap. 3. See also A. D. Harvey, *Sex in Georgian England: Attitudes and Prejudices from the 1720s to the 1820s* (New York, 1994);

G. S. Rousseau and Roy Porter, eds., *Sexual Underworlds of the Enlightenment* (Manchester, Eng., 1987); and Paul-Gabriel Boucé, ed., *Sexuality in Eighteenth-Century Britain* (Manchester, Eng., 1982).

13. Thomas Atwood, *The History of the Island of Dominica* (1791; London, 1971), 215; Julian P. Boyd, ed., *The Papers of Thomas Jefferson*, vol. 8 (Princeton, N.J., 1953), 636; Thomas Burke to Alexander McCullock, 3/3/1773, Thomas Burke Papers, 1769-83, North Carolina State Archives, Raleigh, N.C. See also Elise Pinckney, ed., *The Letterbook of Eliza Lucas Pinckney, 1739-1762* (Chapel Hill, N.C., 1972), 159; and Hamilton, *Letters to Washington*, 2:20.

14. J. A. Lemay, ed., *Robert Bolling Woos Anne Miller: Love and Courtship in Colonial Virginia* (Charlottesville, Va., 1990), 52, 55.

15. Emily V. Mason, ed., *Journal of a Young Lady of Virginia, 1782* [actually 1787] (Baltimore, 1871), 29, 41. A letter that appeared in the *South Carolina Gazette* for 20/7/1747 complained bitterly about male adultery. "Gallantry among the men," wrote an anonymous lady, "is at present so fashionable that a breach of the most sacred tie is accounted no crime."

16. *South Carolina Gazette*, 22/6/1734, 26/1/1738; Joseph W. Barnwell, ed., "Diary of Timothy Ford, 1785-86," *South Carolina Historical and Genealogical Magazine* 13 (1912): 190-91. Kathleen Brown discusses this double standard in *Good Wives, Nasty Wenches, and Anxious Patriarchs*, chap. 9.

17. Wright and Tinling, *Secret Diary of William Byrd*, 27, 101. Byrd clearly enjoyed his wife's companionship: they often read together, went on walks together, and applied themselves to chores around the plantation together. He also appreciated his wife's ability to play the role of a lady and commented on the "respect" that she inspired during her stay in London from "many persons of distinction, who all pronounced her an honour to Virginia" (Tinling, *Correspondence of the Three William Byrds*, 1:296).

18. Wright and Tinling, *Secret Diary of William Byrd*, 337 (see also 253), 344-45, 465 (see also 481).

19. Ibid., 101.

20. See Lockridge, *Diary, and Life, of William Byrd*, 22-25. Lockridge discusses Byrd's relentless self-control through reading, exercising, dietary, and spiritual regimens (6-9); see also Brown, *Good Wives, Nasty Wenches*, 324-28.

21. Woodfin and Tinling, *Another Secret Diary*, 276-77; Wright and Tinling, eds., *London Diary*, 133, 157. Byrd also lamented his frequent recourse to masturbation, which he described in biblical terms as "polluting" himself or "uncleanness." For examples, see ibid., 72, 77, 83, 85, 87.

22. William Byrd, "The Secret History of the Line," in Wendy Martin, ed., *Colonial American Travel Narratives* (New York, 1994), 95, 100, 106; see also 124.

23. Wright and Tinling, *Secret Diary of William Byrd*, 90 (see also 425); Wright and Tinling, *London Diary*, 68, 71, 72, 77, 83, 85, 87, 347 (the November 1719 incident), 479, 482.

24. For examples, see Peter Charles Hoffer and William B. Scott, eds., *Criminal Proceedings in Colonial Virginia* (Athens, Ga., 1984), 70; and H. R. McIl-

waine, ed., *Minutes of the Council and General Court of Colonial Virginia, 1622–1632, 1670–1676* (Richmond, Va., 1924), 34.

25. See, e.g., William Hand Browne et al., eds., *Archives of Maryland,* 72 vols. (Baltimore, 1883–1972), 54:211.

26. James Horn, *Adapting to a New World: English Society in the Seventeenth-Century Chesapeake* (Chapel Hill, N.C., 1994), esp. 212. Yet even a sexual relationship that ended in marriage might begin with coercion, as in the relationship between Jacob Lumbrozo, a physician in Charles County, Maryland, and his servant, Elizabeth Wild (Browne et al., *Archives of Maryland,* 53:387–91; Raphael Semmes, *Crime and Punishment in Early Maryland* [Montclair, N.J., 1970], 240–41).

27. Wright and Tinling, *London Diary,* 374, 382, 409, 437, 447, 505, 506; Lockridge, *Diary, and Life, of William Byrd,* 101. There are no suggestions in the diary of emotional intimacy between maid and master. Byrd's interest in Annie was certainly not exclusive; see, for example, Wright and Tinling, *London Diary,* 505. Sharon Block discusses the subtly coercive dynamics that could play a crucial role in nominally consensual encounters or relationships in "Lines of Color, Sex, and Service: Comparative Sexual Coercion in Early America," in Martha Hodes, ed., *Sex, Love, Race: Crossing Boundaries in North American History* (New York, 1999), esp. 147.

28. Edward Long, *The History of Jamaica,* 3 vols. (1774; New York, 1972), 2:383, 412. Winthrop D. Jordan discusses this stereotype in *White over Black: American Attitudes toward the Negro, 1550–1812* (Chapel Hill, N.C., 1968), esp. 32–40, 136–78.

29. Long, *History of Jamaica,* 2:415; see also Atwood, *History of the Island of Dominica,* 273; and Frank J. Klingberg, ed., *The Carolina Chronicle of Dr. Francis Le Jau, 1706–1717* (Berkeley, Calif., 1956), 41–42, 60. Philip D. Morgan discusses slave attitudes toward marriage in *Slave Counterpoint: Black Culture in the Eighteenth-Century Chesapeake and Lowcountry* (Chapel Hill, N.C., 1998), 530–40.

30. Peter Fontaine to Moses Fontaine, 30/3/1757, quoted in Robert E. Brown and B. Katherine Brown, *Virginia, 1705–1786: Democracy or Aristocracy* (East Lansing, Mich., 1964), 68; Theodore G. Tappert and John W. Doberstein, trans., *The Journals of Henry Melchior Muhlenberg,* 2 vols. (Philadelphia, 1942–45), 1:58; Johann Martin Bolzius, "Reliable Answers to Some Submitted Questions concerning the Land of Carolina," *William and Mary Quarterly* 14 (1957): 235; Merrens, "Journal of Ebenezer Hazard," 190. It is not possible to estimate reliably the number of mulattoes in the eighteenth-century South. Contemporary reports were impressionistic and inconsistent (see, for examples of the latter, Francois Alexandre Frederic, duc de La Rochefoucault-Liancourt, *Travels through the United States of North America,* 2 vols. [London, 1799], 2:82; and "Journal of an Officer," in Newton D. Mereness, ed., *Travels in the American Colonies* [New York, 1961], 406). Philip Morgan suggests that "the more evenly matched black

NOTES TO PAGE 202

and white populations of the Chesapeake provided more opportunities for racial intermixture than the heavily imbalanced black-white ratios of the Lowcountry" (*Slave Counterpoint*, 400). But this seems rather dubious, since in the West Indies white men were vastly outnumbered by the slaves around them and yet managed to engage in a prodigious amount of interracial sex, for which see discussion later in this chapter.

31. William W. Hening, ed., *The Statutes at Large: Being a Collection of all the Laws of Virginia, from the First Session of the Legislature in the Year 1619*, 5 vols. (Richmond, New York, and Philadelphia, 1809–23), 2:170. The evidence that survives from the early-seventeenth-century South is notoriously scanty, but in 1649 William Watts and a "negro woman" named Mary were found guilty of fornication and ordered "to do penance by standing in a white sheet with a white rod in their hands in the chapel of Elizabeth River in the face of the congregation," exactly the same punishment being meted out to intraracial sex offenders (Warren M. Billings, ed., *The Old Dominion in the Seventeenth Century: A Documentary History of Virginia, 1606–1689* [Chapel Hill, N.C., 1975], 161, 102). When Hugh Davis was sentenced in 1630 for having illicit sex with an African, both the punishment and the tone of the judgment was strikingly harsh: he was "to be soundly whipped before an assembly of negroes and others for abusing himself to the dishonor of God and shame of Christians by defiling his body in lying with a negro, which fault he is to acknowledge next sabbath day" (Hening, *Statutes at Large*, 1:146). Some historians have used this judgment to argue that even at this early stage interracial sex was viewed as more heinous than illicit sex between people of the same race (see, e.g., Brown, *Good Wives, Nasty Wenches, and Anxious Patriarchs*, 195). Yet the passage refers not to "a negro woman" or "a negro wench" or "a negress" but a "negro," suggesting that Davis may have had sexual contact with a male African. This specific punishment does not appear in any surviving sentence for an interracial sex crime that clearly involved a man and woman.

32. In practice, it was extremely unlikely that a master would be punished for having sex with his own slave. A slave owner had little reason, moreover, to bring charges against another white man who impregnated one of his slaves: the 1662 law ordered that the child of an interracial union follow the status of the mother, so that the master would gain a new slave, whose labor would compensate for the cost of upbringing. In practice, the doubling of the fine was likely to affect only white men who had sex with free black women or white women who became sexually involved with black men. See Paul Finkelman, "Crimes of Love, Misdemeanors of Passion: The Regulation of Race and Sex in the Colonial South," in Catherine Clinton and Michele Gillespie, eds., *The Devil's Lane: Sex and Race in the Early South* (New York, 1997), 128–29.

33. Hening, *Statutes at Large*, 3:86–88; Browne et al., *Archives of Maryland*, 7:204, 13:546–47, 22:552. Edmund Morgan points out that white women were "still scarce" in 1691, providing another reason for preventing unions with black

men (Edmund S. Morgan, *American Slavery, American Freedom: The Ordeal of Colonial Virginia* [New York, 1975], 336).

34. Morgan, *American Slavery, American Freedom*, 334; Warren M. Billings, "The Cases of Fernando and Elizabeth Key: A Note on the Status of Blacks in the Seventeenth Century," *William and Mary Quarterly* 30 (1973): 468-69. See also Martha Hodes, *White Women, Black Men: Illicit Sex in the Antebellum South* (New Haven, Conn., 1997), chap. 2.

35. J. Douglas Deal, *Race and Class in Colonial Virginia: Indians, Englishmen, and Africans on the Eastern Shore during the Seventeenth Century* (New York, 1993); Morgan, *Slave Counterpoint*, 400; H. R. McIlwaine, ed., *Legislative Journals of the Council of Colonial Virginia* (Richmond, Va., 1918), 1:262. Ira Berlin estimates, in "Time, Space, and the Evolution of Afro-American Society in British Mainland North America," *American Historical Review* 85 (1980): 69, that between a quarter and a third of the "bastards" born to white Virginian women prior to 1700 were of mixed race. The 1691 law ordered that illegitimate children of mixed race born to white women should serve as indentured servants until age thirty, six years longer than "bastards" born to a white servant and a white lover. But as Deal points out, some of the enslaved men with whom female servants produced out-of-wedlock children "may have looked upon relations with servant women as a way of having children who would some day be free" (*Race and Class*, 180).

36. Most of these cases involved servant women who became pregnant outside marriage. The courts may have been less eager to prosecute unbound white women for "bastardy" because there was no master to be compensated for loss of labor, but white women free from indentures may have felt less commonality with enslaved black men and so were more likely to abide by the double standard that deemed miscegenation incompatible with female respectability: the higher a woman's social status, the more she had to lose in terms of the stigma attached to an interracial union. See Brown, *Good Wives, Nasty Wenches, and Anxious Patriarchs*, 198-200.

37. Allan Kulikoff, *Tobacco and Slaves: The Development of Southern Cultures in the Chesapeake, 1680-1800* (Chapel Hill, N.C., 1986), 386-87, 395; Douglas Deal, "A Constricted World: Free Blacks on Virginia's Eastern Shore, 1680-1750," in Lois Green Carr, Philip D. Morgan, and Jean B. Russo, eds., *Colonial Chesapeake Society* (Chapel Hill, N.C., 1988), 279-80; *Maryland Gazette* (Annapolis), 12/10/1769.

38. Ferdinand-M. Bayard, *Travels of a Frenchman in Maryland and Virginia*, trans. and ed. Ben C. McCary (Williamsburg, Va., 1950), 20; Rochefoucault, *Travels Through the United States*, 2:82.

39. Hunter Dickinson Farish, ed., *Journal and Letters of Philip Vickers Fithian, 1773-1774: A Plantation Tutor of the Old Dominion* (1943; Charlottesville, Va., 1968), 86, 184-85.

40. Thomas E. Buckley, "Unfixing Race: Class, Power, and Identity in an

Interracial Family," *Virginia Magazine of History and Biography* 102 (1994): 349–80; Mechal Sobel, *The World They Made Together: Black and White Values in Eighteenth-Century Virginia* (Princeton, N.J., 1987), 150–52.

41. Annette Gordon-Reed, *Thomas Jefferson and Sally Hemings: An American Controversy* (Charlottesville, Va., 1997), esp. 128–30; and Jordan, *White over Black*, 465–68 (quotation on 467).

42. Tinling, *Correspondence of the Three William Byrds*, 2:461; Woodfin and Tinling, *Another Secret Diary*, 70, 93, 137, 155, 157, 166, 168, 174.

43. Jordan, *White over Black*, 15.

44. William Byrd, "History of the Dividing Line," in Louis B. Wright, ed., *The Prose Works of William Byrd of Westover* (Cambridge, Mass., 1966), 160, 221–22.

45. William Byrd, Commonplace Book, Virginia Historical Society, Richmond; Jordan, *White over Black*, 490.

46. Thomas Harriot, *A Briefe and True Report of The New Found Land of Virginia* (1590; New York, 1972), 75.

47. William Byrd to John Perceval, earl of Egmont, 12/7/1736, in Tinling, *Correspondence of the Three William Byrds*, 2:487. It is surely no coincidence that Byrd and Beverley sought to rehabilitate the notion of marriage with Indians just as the African-born slave population was rising sharply in the coastal South, along with miscegenation between whites and blacks.

48. Robert Bolling, "Hilarodiana," Special Collections, Alderman Library, University of Virginia, Charlottesville, quoted in Lockridge, "Colonial Self-Fashioning," 309.

49. *South Carolina Gazette*, 27/8/1772; Jordan, *White over Black*, 145. Philip Morgan draws attention to this regional contrast in *Slave Counterpoint*, 398–412.

50. Thomas Cooper and David J. McCord, eds., *The Statutes at Large of South Carolina*, 10 vols. (Columbia, S.C., 1836–41), 3:20.

51. Bolzius, "Reliable Answers to Some Submitted Questions," 235; Samuel Dyssli to his family in Switzerland, 3/12/1737, *South Carolina Historical and Genealogical Magazine* 23 (1922): 90; George Fenwick Jones, trans., "John Martin Bolzius' Trip to Charleston, October 1742," *South Carolina Historical Magazine* 82 (1981): 101; "Journal of Josiah Quincy, 1773," *Proceedings of Massachusetts Historical Society* 49 (1916): 463. For examples of interracial unions in North Carolina, despite legislation prohibiting intermarriage and miscegenation, see Kirsten Fischer, "'False, Feigned, and Scandalous Words': Sexual Slander and Racial Ideology among Whites in Colonial North Carolina," in Clinton and Gillespie, *Devil's Lane*, 144. For the laws against such unions, see *State Records of North Carolina* (Winston and Goldsboro, N.C., 1895–1906), 23:65, 160.

52. John D. Duncan, "Slave Emancipation in Colonial South Carolina," *American Chronicle, a Magazine of History* 1 (1972): 66; Walter J. Fraser, *Charleston! Charleston!* (Columbia, S.C., 1989), 130. See also Morgan, *Slave Counterpoint*, 408–9.

53. Benjamin James, ed., *Digest of the Laws of South Carolina* (Columbia, S.C., 1822), 66; *South Carolina Gazette*, 27/8/1772.

54. Merrens, "Journal of Ebenezer Hazard," 190. For other references to such events, see Morgan, *Slave Counterpoint*, 408.

55. *South Carolina Gazette*, 24/7/1736.

56. Ibid., 28/3/1743; Bolzius, "Reliable Answers to Some Submitted Questions," 235; Fischer, "'False, Feigned, and Scandalous Words,'" 145–47.

57. *South Carolina Gazette*, 11/3/1732.

58. Ibid., 18/3/1732.

59. Ibid.

60. Ibid., 17, 24/7/1736.

61. For discussion of the scandal and its implications, see "Forum: Thomas Jefferson and Sally Hemings Redux," *William and Mary Quarterly* 57 (2000): 121–210; Gordon-Reed, *Thomas Jefferson and Sally Hemings;* and Trevor Colbourn, ed., *Fame and the Founding Fathers: Essays by Douglas Adair* (New York, 1974), 160–91.

62. Thistlewood Journal, 12/3/1755, 9/10/1756, 19/2/1758. The original of Thistlewood's thirty-seven-volume journal is kept at the Lincoln County Record Office, England (Monson 31/1–37). I have used a microfilm copy in conjunction with a transcription that Trevor Burnard generously shared with me. For an introduction to Thistlewood's journal and life, see Douglas Hall, *In Miserable Slavery: Thomas Thistlewood in Jamaica, 1750–86* (London, 1989). More directly relevant to this study is Trevor Burnard's astute essay, "The Sexual Life of an Eighteenth-Century Jamaican Slave Overseer," in Smith, ed., *Sex and Sexuality in Early America,* 163–89.

63. John Gabriel Stedman, *Narrative of a Five Years Expedition against the Revolted Negroes of Surinam,* ed. Richard Price and Sally Price (Baltimore, 1988), 264–66, 529. The original of Stedman's journal is kept at the James Ford Bell Library at the University of Minnesota. A fairly reliable published version is available in Stanbury Thompson, ed., *The Journal of John Gabriel Stedman, 1744–1797* (London, 1962). For detailed discussion of Stedman's life, Surinam society at the time of his visit, and the history of Stedman's writings on his experience in the West Indies, see Stedman, *Narrative,* xiii–xcvii.

64. Robert J. Allison, ed., *The Interesting Narrative of the Life of Olaudah Equiano* (New York, 1995), 93–94 (see also 139); Stedman, *Narrative,* 71, 271 (see also 398). The inability of male slaves to protect their womenfolk from sexual abuse must have dramatized for them in a particularly wrenching context their own subjugation; black men were doubtless enraged and grief-stricken primarily on behalf of the victims, but they themselves must also have felt wounded and humiliated by such incidents.

65. Burnard, "Sexual Life of an Eighteenth-Century Jamaican Slave Overseer," 164; Atwood, *History of the Island of Dominica,* 209–10.

66. Burnard, "Sexual Life of an Eighteenth-Century Jamaican Slave Overseer," 171. Richard S. Dunn has calculated that on Mesopotamia Estate in Ja-

maica, at the end of the eighteenth century, a white man was twice as likely to father a slave baby as was a black man, "a find which provides some idea of the frequency of interracial sexual intercourse" ("A Tale of Two Plantations: Slave Life at Mesopotamia in Jamaica and Mount Airy in Virginia, 1799 to 1828," *William and Mary Quarterly* 34 [1977]: 48-49).

67. Thistlewood Journal, 1, 9/2/1765, 11/8/1774, 22/8/1774, 11/9/1774.

68. Ibid., 30/9/1751, 1, 3, 8, 9/10/1751, 26/11/1751; 19, 24/5/1759.

69. Long, *History of Jamaica*, 2:535-37; Stedman Journal, 9/2/1773.

70. Hans Sloane, *A Voyage to the Islands Madera, Barbados, Nieves, St. Christopher's, and Jamaica*, 2 vols. (London, 1707-25), 1:cxxii, cxxviii; see also ci, cxlv; and see Long, *History of Jamaica*, 2:433. On 18/8/1774, Thistlewood gave Cudjoe "a mercury pill" for "the clap." On 15 November Cudjoe was "ill of the clap again" and so he "gave him a dose of salts." Settlers doubtless shared information about various treatments. On 9/3/1774, Thistlewood noted that a newly arrived consignment of books included "a treatise on the venereal disease."

71. J. Concanon to Anna Eliza, duchess of Chandos, 6/5/1779, Stowe Collection, Huntington Library, San Marino, Calif., STB box 25, no. 31; Long, *History of Jamaica*, 2:276-77; Sloane, *Voyage to the Islands*, 1:cxli.

72. Andrews, ed., *Journal of a Lady of Quality*, 112-13; Sloane, *Voyage to the Islands*, 1:cxliii, cxlvii. See also Stedman, *Narrative*, 494.

73. See Burnard, "Sexual Life of an Eighteenth-Century Jamaican Slave Overseer," 176; and Brown, *Good Wives, Nasty Wenches, and Anxious Patriarchs*, 356.

74. Thistlewood Journal, 17, 19, 22/6/1757.

75. See, e.g., their row on 4/11/1757 (ibid.).

76. Andrews, *Journal of a Lady of Quality*, 112; John Thistlewood, Diary, 3/2/1765, Lincoln County Record Office, England (Monson 31/38).

77. Trevor Burnard has argued that Phibbah "was able to transcend slaves' powerlessness through her privileged position as the mistress of a white man" in "'Do Thou in Gentle Phibia Smile': Scenes from an Interracial 'Marriage' in Early Jamaica, 1754-86," unpublished paper given at the Huntington Library, San Marino, Calif., 24/1/1998, 5-6. See also Barbara Bush, "White 'Ladies,' Coloured 'Favourites' and Black 'Wenches'; Some Considerations on Sex, Race and Class Factors in Social Relations in White Creole Society in the British Caribbean," *Slavery and Abolition* 2 (1981): 253.

78. Thistlewood Journal, 6, 31/12/1765, 24/2/1779. See 20, 21/11/1775, 31/7/1778, and 8/10/1781, for Francis Ruecastle's physical abuse of Sappho (described revealingly as Ruecastle's "wife").

79. Atwood, *History of the Island of Dominica*, 210; Philip Wright, ed., *Lady Nugent's Journal of her Residence in Jamaica* (Kingston, Jamaica, 1966), 68, 87; Long, *History of Jamaica*, 2:330.

80. See Richard S. Dunn, *Sugar and Slaves: The Rise of the Planter Class in the English West Indies, 1624-1713* (Chapel Hill, N.C., 1972), 254; and Jordan, *White over Black*, 177.

81. J. Concanon to Anna Eliza, duchess of Chandos, 6/5/1779, 20/1/1780,

Stowe Collection, STB box 25, nos. 31, 32; Edward East to Anna Eliza, duchess of Chandos, 24/5/1779, 12/9/1780, Stowe Collection, STB box 25, no. 59; box 26, no. 8.

82. Andrews, *Journal of a Lady of Quality*, 154.

83. Atwood, *History of the Island of Dominica*, 212; Long, *History of Jamaica*, 2:328. See also Jordan, *White over Black*, 148; and Bush, "White 'Ladies,' Coloured 'Favourites' and Black 'Wenches,'" 249.

84. Stedman, *Narrative*, 242. This double standard was built into Surinam law, for which see R. A. J. Van Lier, *Frontier Society: A Social Analysis of the History of Surinam* (1949; The Hague, 1971), 76-77. For the legal situation in Antigua, Barbados, and Jamaica, see Dunn, *Sugar and Slaves*, 228, 253.

85. Stedman, *Narrative*, 49, 115; see also 340. For a gruesome case of spousal retaliation in Chowan County, North Carolina, in which a woman tarred the genitalia of a servant who had apparently slept with her husband, see Kirsten Fischer, "Dangerous Acts: The Politics of Illicit Sex in Colonial North Carolina" (Ph.D. diss., Duke University, 1994), 264-69.

86. Long, *History of Jamaica*, 2:327, 328; Andrews, *Journal of a Lady of Quality*, 112.

87. Jordan, *White over Black*, 145.

88. Bayard, *Travels of a Frenchman*, 20.

7. "Under the Watch"

1. M. Halsey Thomas, ed., *The Diary of Samuel Sewall*, 2 vols. (New York, 1973), 2:680, 838; Cotton Mather, *A Cloud of Witnesses* (Boston, 1700), 1. Shrovetide, traditionally an occasion for festive merrymaking, was one of many holidays that Puritans had sought to suppress. The performer was arrested, and Sewall, acting as a magistrate, had copies of the oration seized so as to "stop" his "lying mouth." But the damage had already been done.

2. See Sacvan Bercovitch, *The American Jeremiad* (Madison, Wis., 1978); Cornelia Hughes Dayton, "Turning Points and the Relevance of Colonial Legal History," *William and Mary Quarterly* 50 (1993): esp. 12-13; and Cornelia Hughes Dayton, *Women before the Bar: Gender, Law, and Society in Connecticut, 1639-1789* (Chapel Hill, N.C., 1995).

3. Quoted in Nancy F. Cott, "Eighteenth-Century Family and Social Life Revealed in the Massachusetts Divorce Records," *Journal of Social History* 10 (1976-77): 22.

4. R. W. Roetger, "The Transformation of Sexual Morality in 'Puritan' New England: Evidence from New Haven Court Records, 1639-1698," *Canadian Review of American Studies* 15 (1984): 254 (the percentage had been higher elsewhere in New England, but it was still in single digits); Robert V. Well, "Illegitimacy and Bridal Pregnancy in Colonial America," in Peter Laslett, Karla Oosterveen, and Richard M. Smith, eds., *Bastardy and Its Comparative History* (Cambridge, Mass., 1980), 353-54; and Daniel Scott Smith, "The Long Cycle in American Illegitimacy and Premarital Pregnancy," in ibid., 371-73.

5. Paul D. Marsella, *Crime and Community in Early Massachusetts: Essex County, 1700-1785* (Acton, Mass., 1990), 18; Dayton, *Women before the Bar*, 160 n. 5.

6. Franklin P. Rice, ed., *Records of the Court of General Sessions of the Peace for the County of Worcester, Massachusetts, 1731-37* (Worcester, Mass., 1883), 35-36, 52, 58, 61-62, 71, 73-74, 91, 103, 108, 118, 125, 129, 140, 151, 166, 181; Marsella, *Crime and Community*, 23. The penalty was also reduced in New Haven; see Dayton, *Women before the Bar*, 192.

7. Christine Leigh Heyrman, *Commerce and Culture: The Maritime Communities of Colonial Massachusetts, 1690-1750* (New York, 1984), 384; Marsella, *Crime and Community*, 20, table 5; Edgar McManus, *Law and Liberty in Early New England: Criminal Justice and Due Process, 1620-1692* (Amherst, Mass., 1993), 98; Dayton, *Women before the Bar*, 190-91. For the growing number of confessions at midcentury, see Emil Oberholzer, *Delinquent Saints: Disciplinary Action and the Early Congregational Churches of Massachusetts* (New York, 1956), 237-38; and Henry Bamford Parkes, "Morals and Law Enforcement in Colonial New England," *New England Quarterly* 5 (1932): 443-44. Dayton notes the continuation of legal prosecutions in New Haven County, Connecticut (*Women before the Bar*, 192).

8. Records of Barnstable West Parish, 1668-1853, 21/7/1746, photostat of original, Massachusetts Historical Society, Boston. Between 1710 and 1739, twenty-eight persons confessed to "fornication" before the First Church in Salem; at least twenty-two of these cases involved premarital sex (Richard D. Pierce, ed., *Records of the First Church in Salem, Massachusetts, 1629-1736* [Salem, Mass., 1974], 209, 224-25, 239-40, 247, 249-50, 261-62, 271, 274, 276, 296, 297, 300, 301, 313, 318-19, 321, 322, 328). See also William Upham, ed., *Records of the First Church in Beverly, 1667-1772* (Salem, Mass., 1905), 48, 49, 50-51, 51-52, 53-54, 55, 62, 64, 65; and Charles Francis Adams, "Some Phases of Sexual Morality and Church Discipline in Colonial New England," *Proceedings of Massachusetts Historical Society*, 2d ser., 6 (1891): 486-90.

9. Adams, "Some Phases of Sexual Morality," 493-95; Christopher Jedrey, *The World of John Cleaveland: Family and Community in Eighteenth-Century New England* (New York, 1979), 152. See also Francis G. Walett, ed., *The Diary of Ebenezer Parkman, 1703-1782* (Worcester, Mass., 1974), passim; New Salem Unitarian Church Records, 1742-70, Essex Institute, Essex, Mass.; Records of Second Church of Christ in Sutton, 1743-1910, American Antiquarian Society, Worcester, Mass.; and Henry Reed Stiles, *Bundling: Its Origin, Progress, and Decline in America* (Albany, N.Y., 1869), 76-77.

10. Records of South Andover Church, 1711-72, 24/11/1754, 8/12/1754, 10/12/1754, 19/12/1754, 26/1/1755, 4/2/1755, 9/2/1755, Andover Historical Society, Andover, Mass.; *Records of the First Church at Dorchester in New England, 1636-1734* (Boston, 1891), 163, 164, 166 (the Smiths were restored in 1755); Marblehead First Church Records, 1688-1800, Old North Church, Marblehead, Mass.

11. New Salem Unitarian Church Records, 1742-1770, confessions, 29/1/

1743, 18/8/1754; Samuel Abbott Green, ed., *Groton Historical Series,* 4 vols. (Groton, Mass., 1887–99), 1:41–42; 4:6, 16.

12. Walett, *Diary of Ebenezer Parkman,* 28 (3/1/1728), 31 (11, 13/3/1728). See also 10 (20/3/1726); and *Records of the First Church at Dorchester,* 137.

13. Levi and Deborah Warrin to Ebenezer Parkman, folder 2, 18/12/1770, Parkman Family Correspondence, American Antiquarian Society.

14. Walett, *Diary of Ebenezer Parkman,* 146 (8/12/1746), 163 (9/11/1747), 273 (29/3/1754). See also "Joseph Emerson's Diary, 1748–1749," *Massachusetts Historical Society Proceedings* 44 (1910–11): 278 (23/2/1749).

15. Walett, *Diary of Ebenezer Parkman,* 276 (5/6/1754), 279 (13, 14/8/1754), 281–82 (17, 18, 20, 28/9/1754, and 5, 7/10/1754), 283–84 (10/11/1754).

16. Pierce, ed., "Records of the First Church in Boston," 148; Oberholzer, *Delinquent Saints,* 136. See also Dayton, *Women before the Bar,* 223.

17. Walett, *Diary of Ebenezer Parkman,* 60 (7/2/1739); General Meeting of Baptist Churches to Stephen Gorton, 10/9/1757; New London congregation to General Meeting of Baptist Churches, 11/9/1756; General Meeting of Baptist Churches to Stephen Gorton, 13/9/1756, Backus Papers, Andover-Newton Theological School, Newton Center, Mass., box 7; June Term, 1726, New London County Court Records, Connecticut State Library, Hartford, loose files. See also Susan Juster, *Disorderly Women: Sexual Politics and Evangelicalism in Revolutionary New England* (Ithaca, N.Y., 1994), 90–92; and Richard Godbeer, "'The Cry of Sodom': Discourse, Intercourse, and Desire in Colonial New England," *William and Mary Quarterly* 52 (1995): 277–79.

18. New London congregation to General Meeting of Baptist Churches, 11/9/1756; General Meeting of Baptist Churches to Stephen Gorton, 13/9/1756, Backus Papers, box 7. Once Gorton acknowledged and confessed his sins, members voted by a two-thirds majority to restore him to the pastorate. This case, along with that of Ebenezer Knight in Marblehead, suggests a remarkable forbearance toward individuals who were recognized as having "sodomitical" proclivities, a forbearance that had also benefited Nicholas Sension in seventeenth-century Connecticut; see Godbeer, "'The Cry of Sodom,'" 277–78.

19. *Connecticut Courant* (Hartford), 19/10/1767; *The Perpetual Laws of the Commonwealth of Massachusetts* (Worcester, Mass., 1788), 245–47; Ronald Snell, "The County Magistracy in Eighteenth-Century Massachusetts, 1692–1750" (Ph.D. diss., Princeton University, 1971), 179–82; Oberholzer, *Delinquent Saints,* 136, 303 n. 55; Stephen Pascholl Sharples, ed., *Records of the Church of Christ at Cambridge in New England, 1632-1830* (Boston, 1906), 279–80; Green, *Groton Historical Series,* 4:32.

20. See Philip Greven, *Four Generations: Population, Land, and Family in Colonial Andover, Massachusetts* (Ithaca, N.Y., 1970), chap. 8; Kenneth A. Lockridge, *A New England Town: The First Hundred Years* (New York, 1970), chap. 8; Daniel Scott Smith, "Parental Power and Marriage Patterns: An Analysis of Historical Trends in Hingham, Massachusetts," *Journal of Marriage and the Family*

35 (1973): 419-28; Robert Gross, *The Minutemen and Their World* (New York, 1976), chap. 4; and Jedry, *World of John Cleaveland*, chap. 3.

21. "Remarkable Occurrences Concerning Marriage," 29/7/1797, 15/7/1805, 8/11/1806, in "The Records of Gloria Dei Church," Historical Society of Pennsylvania, Philadelphia. See Gordon S. Wood, *The Radicalism of the American Revolution* (New York, 1992); Edmund S. Morgan, *Inventing the People: The Rise of Popular Sovereignty in England and America* (New York, 1988); and Jay Fliegelman, *Prodigals and Pilgrims: The American Revolution against Patriarchal Authority* (New York, 1982).

22. This is not to suggest that seventeenth-century marriages were for the most part emotionally barren; see chap. 2, note 8. For discussion of earlier conventions that balanced parental wishes with personal choice, see Martin Ingram, *Church Courts, Sex, and Marriage in England, 1570-1640* (Cambridge, 1987), 134-40; and David Cressy, *Birth, Marriage, and Death: Ritual, Religion, and the Life-Cycle in Tudor and Stuart England* (Oxford, 1997), 255-60.

23. Most procedures of this kind would have taken place in secret and so did not make their way into the historical record, but one abortion scheme did become public because it went tragically awry. Cornelia Hughes Dayton reconstructs the scandal caused by Sarah Grosvenor's death in "Taking the Trade: Abortion and Gender Relations in an Eighteenth-Century New England Village," *William and Mary Quarterly* 48 (1991): 19-49. See also Susan E. Klepp, "Lost, Hidden, Obstructed, and Repressed: Contraceptive and Abortive Technology in the Early Delaware Valley," in Judith McGaw, ed., *Early American Technology: Making and Doing Things from the Colonial Era to 1850* (Chapel Hill, N.C., 1994), 68-113.

24. James D. Hart, *The Popular Book: A History of America's Literary Taste* (New York, 1950), 23; Mary Cable, *American Manners and Morals* (New York, 1969), 36.

25. Walett, *Diary of Ebenezer Parkman*, 68 (3/9/1739), 90 (12/1/1744), 108 (11/12/1744), 195 (3/5/1749), 196 (23/5/1749).

26. Jonathan Edwards, "A Faithful Narrative," in C. C. Goen, ed., *The Great Awakening* (New Haven, Conn., 1972), 146; Jonathan Edwards, "Joseph's Great Temptation and Gracious Deliverance," in Edward Hickman, ed., *The Works of Jonathan Edwards*, 2 vols. (London, 1835), 2:231-32.

27. Quotations relating to the Northampton book scandal are taken from Thomas H. Johnson, "Jonathan Edwards and the 'Young Folks' Bible,'" *New England Quarterly* 5 (1932): 37-54. The original documents are located at Yale University and at the Andover-Newton Theological School.

28. Quoted in Roger Thompson, *Unfit for Modest Ears: A Study of Pornographic, Obscene, and Bawdy Works Written or Published in England in the Second Half of the Seventeenth Century* (Totowa, N.J., 1979), 162. Printed material that could feed salacious appetites had been circulating in the North American colonies long before the 1740s, but interest in such reading material seems to have

grown during the early decades of the eighteenth century; see Roger Thompson, "The Puritans and Prurience: Aspects of the Restoration Book Trade," in H. C. Allen and Roger Thompson, eds., *Contrast and Connection: Bicentennial Essays in Anglo-American History* (London, 1976), esp. 50-52; and Peter Wagner, "Eros Goes West: European and 'Homespun' Erotica in Eighteenth-Century America," in Winfried Herget and Karl Ortseifen, eds., *The Transit of Civilization from Europe to America* (Tübingen, Germany, 1986). For discussion of the pornographic literature available in English-speaking societies during the seventeenth and eighteenth centuries, see David Foxon, *Libertine Literature in England, 1660-1745* (New York, 1965); Thompson, *Unfit for Modest Ears;* and Peter Wagner, *Eros Revived: Erotica of the Enlightenment in England and America* (London, 1988).

29. Others referred to it as "a Granny Book" (*Granny* being a colloquialism for nurse or midwife), "The Midwife Rightly Instructed," and "Aristotle." Many midwifery editions were falsely attributed to the Greek philosopher: numerous versions of *Aristotle's Masterpiece* were published in England during the seventeenth and eighteenth centuries; a number of editions were printed in North America during the second half of the eighteenth century, but copies from England were circulating in the colonies much earlier. See Otho T. Beall Jr., "*Aristotle's Masterpiece* in America: A Landmark in the Folklore of Medicine," *William and Mary Quarterly* 20 (1963): 207-22. I am much obliged to Mary Fissell, who is currently working on the evolution and significance of *Aristotle's Masterpiece,* for a helpful conversation on this subject.

30. "The Testimony and Advice of an Assembly of Pastors of Churches in New England," in Richard L. Bushman, ed., *The Great Awakening: Documents on the Revival of Religion, 1740-1745* (1970; Chapel Hill, N.C., 1989), 129-30; "The Testimony of the Pastors of the Churches in the Province of the Massachusetts Bay," in ibid., 128. For perceptions of sexual and gendered disorder during the revivals, see Erik R. Seeman, *Pious Persuasions: Laity and Clergy in Eighteenth-Century New England* (Baltimore, 1999), chap. 5.

31. Samuel Blair, "A Short and Faithful Narrative," in Bushman, *Great Awakening,* 73; Jonathan Parsons, "Account of the Revival at Lyme," in Alan Heimert and Perry Miller, eds., *The Great Awakening: Documents Illustrating the Crisis and Its Consequences* (Indianapolis, 1967), 200; Charles Chauncy, "A Letter from a Gentleman in Boston," in Bushman, ed., *Great Awakening,* 117, 120; J. M. Bumsted and John E. Van de Wetering, *What Must I Do to Be Saved? The Great Awakening in Colonial America* (Hinsdale, Ill., 1976), 144; Douglas C. Stenerson, "An Anglican Critique of the Early Phase of the Great Awakening in New England: A Letter by Timothy Cutler," *William and Mary Quarterly* 30 (1973): 484-85.

32. Jonathan Edwards, "The Distinguishing Marks of a Work of the Spirit of God," in Goen, *The Great Awakening,* 256-57; "Some Thoughts concerning the Present Revival," ibid., 468. Charles Adams suggested in 1891 that the "morbidly excited spiritual condition" induced by the Awakening, in his view "a species

of insanity," may indeed have led to "a period of sexual immorality" (Adams, "Some Phases of Sexual Morality," 502). But the increase in confessions to fornication during this period, cited by Adams as supporting his hypothesis, more likely points to the prevalence of sexual activity among unmarried young people in general, who now confessed to their previous behavior as they converted in large numbers. If young men and women were more likely to confess during this period, it was presumably because of a heightened religious sensibility rather than because the revivals had drawn them into a wave of sexual license. See also Cedric B. Cowing, "Sex and Preaching in the Great Awakening," *American Quarterly* 20 (1968): 641-42.

33. See Randall H. Balmer, *A Perfect Babble of Confusion: Dutch Religion and English Culture in the Middle Colonies* (New York, 1989), 110-22. For other rumors of "indecency" involving members of the same sex, see Philip Greven, *The Protestant Temperament: Patterns of Child-Rearing, Religious Experience, and the Self in Early America* (New York, 1977), 139.

34. William G. McLoughlin, ed., *The Diary of Isaac Backus*, 3 vols. (Providence, R.I., 1979), 1:35; Sarah Parsons Moorhead, "To the Reverend Mr. Andrew Croswell," in *To The Reverend Mr. James Davenport* (Boston, 1742), 7-8; *George Whitefield's Journals* (London, 1960), 471. Whitefield saw earthly affections as a distraction from spiritual effort; he lived almost exclusively for his ministry and would brook no rival passion. Yet he did, ironically, become an object of desire, at least spiritually if not otherwise. See Harry Stout, *The Divine Dramatist: George Whitefield and the Rise of Modern Evangelism* (Grand Rapids, Mich., 1991), chap. 7. Henry Abelove discusses the loving devotion that John Wesley inspired in *The Evangelist of Desire: John Wesley and the Methodists* (Stanford, Calif., 1990).

35. See Juster, *Disorderly Women*, 64-65; and Michael P. Winship, "Behold the Bridegroom Cometh: Marital Imagery in Massachusetts Preaching, 1630-1730," *Early American Literature* 27 (1992): esp. 178-80.

36. Jonathan Edwards, "The Church's Marriage to Her Sons, and to Her God," in Hickman, *Works of Jonathan Edwards*, 2:20-23. See also John Webb, *Christ's Suit to The Sinner* (Boston, 1741), 30-31. Seeman discusses lay use of sensual imagery in *Pious Persuasions*, 104.

37. The documents relating to this case are located at the Andover-Newton Theological Seminary and transcribed in William G. McLoughlin, *Soul Liberty: The Baptists' Struggle in New England, 1630-1833* (Hanover, N.H., 1991), 119-23. Molly and Solomon were married legally in 1750.

38. Ibid., 103.

39. Isaac Backus, *A History of New England*, 2 vols. (Newton, Mass., 1871), 2:185-86, 209; Walett, *Diary of Ebenezer Parkman*, 154 (18/5/1747), 292 (26/7/1755); Ezra Stiles reported the rumor that Prentice "used to lie with Ireland" in *Extracts from the Itineraries*, ed. F. B. Dexter (New Haven, Conn., 1916), 418.

40. Charles Chauncy, "Enthusiasm Described and Cautioned Against," in Heimert and Miller, *Great Awakening*, 232 (see also 243); "A Copy of what the

Council of the Lord did, Rehoboth, May 8th, 1751," Backus Papers, Andover-Newton Theological School.

41. For discussion of these shaming rituals (referred to by contemporaries as "rough music" or "skimmingtons"), see Alfred Young, "English Plebeian Culture and Eighteenth-Century American Radicalism," in Margaret Jacob and James Jacob, eds., *The Origins of Anglo-American Radicalism* (London, 1984), 184–212; Steven J. Stewart, "Skimmington in the Middle and New England Colonies," in Matthew Dennis, Simon Newman, and William Pencak, eds., *Riot and Revelry in Early America* (University Park, Pa., forthcoming 2002); and Brendan McConville, "The Rise of Rough Music: Reflections on an Ancient New Custom in Eighteenth-Century New Jersey," in ibid.

42. The most detailed study of bundling remains Stiles, *Bundling*. See also Dana Doten, *The Art of Bundling* (New York, 1938). Bundling was used in the British Isles and Europe during the early modern period; colonists did not invent the custom. There is no evidence for the use of bundling boards to separate courting couples in bed except among the Pennsylvania Dutch, who also used a pillow for the same purpose, giving rise to the proverb "He who cannot crawl over a pillow is no man" (Monroe A. Aurand, *Bundling Prohibited!* [Harrisburg, Pa., 1929], 27).

43. For references to this practice, see "Lettre écrite à M. Garat par un Officer Récemment Arrivé d'Amérique," *Mercure de France*, 29/3/1783; Thomas Anburey, *Travels through the Interior Parts of America*, 2 vols. (Boston, 1923), 2:25–27; John Bernard, *Retrospections of America, 1797-1811*, ed. Mrs. Bayle Bernard (New York, 1887), 246; Kenneth Roberts and Anna M. Roberts, eds. and trans., *Moreau de St. Mery's American Journey* (Garden City, N.Y., 1947), 316; "Autobiography of Peter Stephen Du Ponceau," *Pennsylvania Magazine of History and Biography* 63 (1939): 203; and Thomas Cajetan Wengierski's American diary, quoted in Miecislaus Haiman, *Poland and the American Revolutionary War* (Chicago, 1932), 145–46. For the lack of private sleeping space in eighteenth-century North America, see John S. Ezell, ed., *The New Democracy in America: Travels of Francisco de Miranda in the United States, 1783-1784*, trans. Judson Wood (Norman, Okla., 1963), 126; Rufus Rockwell Wilson, ed., *Burnaby's Travels through North America* (New York, 1904), 142; Abbe Robin, *New Travels Through North America* (Philadelphia, 1783), 26; "Diary of Elizabeth House Trist, 1783–84," 5, 7, 8, typescript, Elizabeth House Trist Papers, Southern Historical Collection, University of North Carolina at Chapel Hill; and David H. Flaherty, *Privacy in Colonial New England* (Charlottesville, Va., 1972), 76–79.

44. Wilson, *Burnaby's Travels Through North America*, 141–42; Alexandre Berthier, "Journal de la Campagne d'Amérique," ed. Gilbert Chinard, *Bulletin de l'Institut Francais de Washington* 1 (1951): 102–3; Johann David Schoepf, *Travels in the Confederation, 1783-1784*, trans. and ed. Alfred J. Morrison (New York, 1968), 101; Antonio Pace, ed. and trans., *Luigi Castiglioni's 'Viaggio': Travels in the United States of North America, 1785-87* (1790; Syracuse, N.Y., 1983), 254, 326 n. 43. For an overview of European commentaries on bundling, see Bernard

Chevignard, "Les voyageurs Européens et la pratique du 'bondelage' (bundling) en Nouvelle-Angleterre à la fin du XVIIIe siècle," *L'Amérique et L'Europe: Réalités et Représentations* 2 (1986): 75–87.

45. See, e.g., Wilson, *Burnaby's Travels Through North America,* 141. Samuel Peters claimed, exceptionally, that bundling was prevalent "among all classes," in his *General History of Connecticut* (London, 1781), 71. Castiglioni's reference to women who became pregnant as a result of bundling "withdraw[ing] to the country" suggests that it was not exclusively rural (Pace, *Luigi Castiglioni's 'Viaggio,'* 254).

46. L. H. Butterfield, ed., *The Diary and Autobiography of John Adams* (Cambridge, Mass., 1962), 1:195–96. Bernard wrote that bundling functioned as "a matrimonial ordeal" whereby lovers were "enabled to discover how their tempers would agree during darkness as well as daylight" (Bernard, *Retrospections of America,* 246).

47. Lois K. Stabler, ed., *'Very Poor and of a Lo Make': The Journal of Abner Sanger* (Portsmouth, N.H., 1986), 302–3 (21, 22/7/1780). For background information regarding Sanger, I am indebted to Laurel Thatcher Ulrich and Lois K. Stabler, "'Girling of it' in Eighteenth-Century New Hampshire," in Peter Benes, ed., *Families and Children* (Boston, 1987), 24–36.

48. Stabler, *Journal of Abner Sanger,* 431 (20/8/1782), 433 (24/8/1782).

49. Ibid., 229 (8/2/1779), 240 (2, 3/4/1779), 234 (2/3/1779), 267 (22/10/1779), 303 (22/7/1780), 419 (18/6/1782), 428 (5/8/1782).

50. Anburey, *Travels Through the Interior Parts of America,* 2:57; Robert R. McCausland and Cynthia MacAlman McCausland, eds., *The Diary of Martha Ballard, 1785–1812* (Camden, Maine, 1992), 86 [25/2/1788], 313 [7/10/1794]; Stabler, *Journal of Abner Sanger,* 232 (23/2/1779), 257 (31/7/1779). Ulrich and Stabler discuss opportunities for socializing, flirting, and courting in "'Girling of it' in Eighteenth-Century New Hampshire," 27. For other comments by Europeans on the freedom and informality of social interactions, see Louis B. Wright and Marion Tinling, eds., *Quebec to Carolina in 1785–1786, Being the Travel Diary and Observations of Robert Hunter, Jr., a Young Merchant of London* (San Marino, Calif., 1943), 145, 180; Marquis de Chastellux, *Travels in North America in the Years 1780, 1781 and 1782,* trans. and ed. Howard C. Rice, 2 vols. (Chapel Hill, N.C., 1963), 1:120; and Francois Alexandre Frederic, duc de la Rochefoucault-Liancourt, *Travels Through the United States of North America, the Country of the Iroquois, and Upper Canada,* 2 vols. (London, 1799), 2:675.

51. Alexander G. Rose, ed., *The Chester and Westfield, Massachusetts, Diaries (1795–1798) of David Shepard, Jr.* (Baltimore, 1975), 86, 145, 153, 158, 159, 162.

52. Ibid., 160, 170, 181, 204.

53. Elihu Ashley, "Diary," in George Sheldon, *A History of Deerfield, Massachusetts* (Deerfield, Mass., 1895–96), 686 (9, 13/9/1774), 687 (14/9/1774), 688 (18/9/1774), 691 (29/9/1774).

54. Jonathan Edwards, "Joseph's Great Temptation and Gracious Deliverance," 231, 232; Samuel Hopkins, "A Persuasive to flee Youthful Lusts," 11/3/

1753, Huntington Library, San Marino, Calif. Later in the century, Jason Haven, the pastor at Dedham, Massachusetts, also condemned from the pulpit the practice of "reclining together," perhaps in response to regular confessions of premarital sex by applicants for church membership (Erastus Worthington, *History of Dedham* [Boston, 1827], 108).

55. Walett, *Diary of Ebenezer Parkman,* 91 (15/2/1744). Parkman subsequently "requested young women to dismiss seasonably the young men that wait upon them" (237 [26/5/1751]).

56. Oberholzer, *Delinquent Saints,* 141; Peters, *General History of Connecticut,* 71.

57. Stiles, *Bundling,* 84, 108; Cable, *American Manners and Morals,* 36. See also Peters, *General History of Connecticut,* 71.

58. Stiles, *Bundling,* 88, 106; see also Edwards, "Joseph's Great Temptation and Gracious Deliverance," 231.

59. Stiles, *Bundling,* 97–98; see also Peters, *General History of Connecticut,* 71.

60. Stiles, *Bundling,* 105. The author also claimed that loose women (epitomized as "romp Moll") would "plead" for the custom as a way to ensnare men into wedlock (107).

61. Ibid., 83–84. See also Ellen K. Rothman, *Hands and Hearts: A History of Courtship in America* (New York, 1984), 47–48; and Laurel Thatcher Ulrich, *Good Wives: Image and Reality in the Lives of Women in Northern New England, 1650–1750* (New York, 1982), 122–23.

62. Laurel Thatcher Ulrich, *A Midwife's Tale: The Life of Martha Ballard, Based on Her Diary, 1785–1812* (New York, 1990), 148; Roger Thompson, *Sex in Middlesex: Popular Mores in a Massachusetts County, 1649–1699* (Amherst, Mass., 1986), 29–30; Dayton, *Women before the Bar,* 188, 194–97, 273; Marsella, *Crime and Community,* 20.

63. Ulrich, *Midwife's Tale,* 147–55. Dayton, in contrast, argues that "most single women at risk for prosecution experienced the criminal action as a coercive rather than a chosen process" (*Women before the Bar,* 201). She concedes, though, that unwed mothers in eighteenth-century New Haven could and sometimes did use civil suits as an alternative to criminal proceedings. An unmarried mother could thus initiate proceedings against the father and secure an out-of-court settlement without either of them ending up in the records (217–18).

64. Quoted in Ulrich, *Midwife's Tale,* 155. Ulrich uses a 1773–98 record book kept by Nathaniel Thwing, a justice in Woolwich, Maine, to show that only half of the women and a mere tenth of the men originally accused in the fornication or paternity cases that Thwing dealt with actually appeared in court. "It is important to emphasize," she writes, "that the charges were dropped, not that the men were acquitted" (154–55).

65. Ibid., 155–56.

66. Ibid., 147, 151, 155, 160. See also Ulrich and Stabler, "'Girling of it' in

Eighteenth-Century New Hampshire," 31; Betty Bandel, "Haywards and Bride-grooms," *New England Historic Genealogical Society Newsletter,* 2d preliminary issue, 1 (1984): 13-14; and Edward Cook, *The Fathers of the Towns: Leadership and Community Structure in Eighteenth-Century New England* (Baltimore, 1976), 218 n. 14.

67. The surviving documentation for the series of events examined here is to be found in the Letters and Papers of Major Joseph Hawley, 2 vols., 1:6-9, 12, New York Public Library; and in the Jonathan Edwards Papers, Andover-Newton Theological School, folder "no date," no. 1, item 11, and no. 2, item 15. Kathryn Kish Sklar discusses the Root-Hawley controversy in "Culture versus Economics: A Case of Fornication in Northampton in the 1740s," *Michigan Occasional Papers in Women's Studies* 2, special issue (May 1978): 35-56. See also Patricia Tracy, *Jonathan Edwards, Pastor: Religion and Society in Eighteenth-Century Northampton* (New York, 1980), 164-66.

68. Sklar, "Culture versus Economics," 39-41.

69. *Boston Evening Post,* 12/5/1740.

70. Stephen Riley and Edward Hanson, eds., "The Papers of Robert Treat Paine, 1757-1774," *Collections of Massachusetts Historical Society* 88 (1992): 251-54. For a reading of this incident that stresses the letters' satiric tone and down-plays the young man's actual plight, see Dayton, *Women before the Bar,* 227-28.

71. John Shy, ed., *Winding Down: The Revolutionary War Letters of Lieutenant Benjamin Gilbert of Massachusetts, 1780-1783* (Ann Arbor, Mich., 1989), 69, 77, 80-82, 88, 91.

72. Ibid., 98. See also Edward Bangs, ed., *Journal of Lieutenant Isaac Bangs* (Cambridge, 1890), 29.

73. For examples, see *Orderly Book of the Continental Forces* (Washington, D.C., 1877), 1:10; John C. Fitzpatrick, ed., *The Writings of George Washington,* 39 vols. (Washington, D.C., 1931-44), 9:129-30; and Colonel Alexander McDougall's orderly book, quoted in Holly A. Mayer, *Belonging to the Army: Camp Followers and Community during the American Revolution* (Columbia, S.C., 1996), 111.

74. Rebecca D. Symmes, ed., *A Citizen-Soldier in the American Revolution: The Diary of Benjamin Gilbert in Massachusetts and New York* (Cooperstown, N.Y., 1980), 30, 31, 32; John Adams to General Nathaniel Greene, 9/5/1777, quoted in Mayer, *Belonging to the Army,* 61.

75. Symmes, *Diary of Benjamin Gilbert,* 131, 133; Shy, *Winding Down,* 93 n. 194, 95.

76. Chastellux, *Travels in North America,* 1:67, 231-32. See also Rochefoucault, *Travels Through the United States,* 1:344.

77. Chastellux, *Travels in North America,* 1:254; Janette Day to Elizabeth Smith, 16/6/1769, quoted in Mary Beth Norton, *Liberty's Daughters: The Revolutionary Experience of American Women, 1750-1800* (Boston, 1980), 54.

78. Shy, *Winding Down,* 78.

8. "A Hint to Young Ladies"

1. "The Forsaken Fair One," *Boston Gazette,* 8/3/1784; "The Inconstant Swain," ibid., 10/10/1785.

2. "On Modern Novels and Their Effects," *The Massachusetts Magazine, or, Monthly Museum of Knowledge and Rational Entertainment* (Boston), November 1791, 663. Cathy N. Davidson, in *Revolution and the Word: The Rise of the Novel in America* (New York, 1986), examines novels of the late 1700s and the issues with which they engaged. The analysis of ephemeral literature that follows is based upon a reading of around 600 almanacs, 700 magazines, and 11,000 newspapers, mostly but not exclusively printed in Boston, Philadelphia, and Charleston.

3. Bundling was commonplace in the middle as well as the northern colonies (see chap. 7, notes 42–44). Courting couples in the eighteenth-century South were often allowed to spend time alone together, for discussion of which see "Journal of Jean-Francois-Louis, Comte de Clermont-Crevecoeur," in Howard C. Rice and Anne S. K. Brown, trans. and eds., *American Campaigns of Rochambeau's Army,* 2 vols. (Princeton, N.J., 1972), 1:66. John Harrower, a tutor living with the family of Virginian planter William Dangerfield in the 1770s, became increasingly aware of a young woman's plight if abandoned by a lover as he observed the progress and demise of a sexual relationship between overseer Anthony Frazier and Lucy Gaines, the housekeeper. See Edward Miles Riley, ed., *The Journal of John Harrower, an Indentured Servant in the Colony of Virginia, 1773–1776* (New York, 1963), 129–49 passim, 159. Daniel Scott Smith and Michael S. Hindus show, in "Premarital Pregnancy in America, 1640–1971: An Overview and Interpretation," *Journal of Interdisciplinary History* 4 (1974–75): esp. 556–59, that premarital pregnancy became more common among southerners during the eighteenth century.

4. Davidson discusses the implications of expanding literacy in *Revolution and the Word,* chap. 4.

5. Susan E. Klepp shows how American women applied "a revolutionary rhetoric of independence" to perceptions of fertility and "procreative physicality" in "Revolutionary Bodies: Women and the Fertility Transition in the Mid-Atlantic Region, 1760–1820," *Journal of American History* 85 (1998–99): 910–45. Kathryn Shevelow argues that "women's visible entrance into print culture" in early-eighteenth-century England had also been marked by "complementary processes" of "enfranchisement" and "restriction" (*Women and Print Culture: The Construction of Femininity in the Early Periodical* [New York, 1989], 1, 2, 6).

6. Nicholas de Venette, *The Mysteries of Conjugal Love Revealed* (London, 1707), 83, 123. For the contents of this paragraph, I am much indebted to Felicity A. Nussbaum, *The Brink of All We Hate: English Satires on Women, 1660–1750* (Lexington, Ky., 1984). See also Paul-Gabriel Boucé, "Some Sexual Beliefs and Myths in Eighteenth-Century Britain," in Paul-Gabriel Boucé, ed., *Sexuality in Eighteenth-Century Britain* (Manchester, Eng., 1982), esp. 41–43.

7. "The Itinerarium of Dr. Alexander Hamilton," in Wendy Martin, ed., *Colonial American Travel Narratives* (New York, 1994), 308–9, 319.

8. Jack P. Greene, ed., *The Diary of Colonel Landon Carter of Sabine Hall, 1752–1778*, 2 vols. (Charlottesville, Va., 1965), 2:1103; J. A. Lemay, ed., *Robert Bolling Woos Anne Miller: Love and Courtship in Colonial Virginia* (Charlottesville, Va., 1990), 98, 109, 110; Daniel Blake Smith, *Inside the Great House: Planter Family Life in Eighteenth-Century Chesapeake Society* (Ithaca, N.Y., 1980), 70; Frances Norton Mason, ed., *John Norton and Sons: Merchants of London and Virginia* (New York, 1968), 187.

9. Marion Tinling, ed., *The Correspondence of the Three William Byrds of Westover, Virginia, 1684–1776*, 2 vols. (Charlottesville, Va., 1977), 1:230 (5/8/1703), 392 (3/4/1729), 432 (28/7/1730); 2:564 (17/9/1740); and Maude H. Woodfin, ed., *Another Secret Diary of William Byrd of Westover, 1739–41, With Letters and Literary Exercises, 1696–1726*, trans. Marion Tinling (Richmond, Va., 1742), 250 (undated). Byrd's attitude may well have been intensified by the difficulties of his first marriage and a series of unsuccessful courtships in London following his first wife's death, for which see Kenneth A. Lockridge, *On the Sources of Patriarchal Rage: The Commonplace Books of William Byrd and Thomas Jefferson and the Gendering of Power in the Eighteenth Century* (New York, 1992), esp. 24, 75. But it would be misleading to portray these sentiments simply as a product of such experiences. Byrd expressed these views throughout his adult life and, in so doing, bespoke his membership in a transatlantic fraternity that celebrated male libertinism and yet feared male vulnerability to female predators.

10. Tinling, *Correspondence of the Three William Byrds*, 2:505 (20/3/1737); Commonplace Book, Virginia Historical Society, Richmond.

11. Tinling, *Correspondence of the Three William Byrds*, 1:401 (ca. June 1729), 2:505 (20/3/1737). Even if a woman's charms were real, he contended, sexual boredom often dulled them and sent husbands in search of new pleasures; see 1:393; and Woodfin, *Another Secret Diary*, 191.

12. For a more detailed discussion of the commonplace book, see Lockridge, *On the Sources of Patriarchal Rage*, chap. 1.

13. Eugene R. Sheridan, ed., *The Papers of Lewis Morris*, 3 vols. (Newark, N.J., 1991), 1:317–18.

14. For an example of publishers' sensitivity to readers' preferences, see Godbeer, *The Devil's Dominion: Magic and Religion in Early New England* (New York, 1992), 231.

15. See Nathaniel Shurtleff, ed., *Records of the Governor and Company of Massachusetts Bay, in New England*, 5 vols. (Boston, 1853–54), 4 (pt. 2): 62, 73, 141. There did appear one notable exception. Emboldened by the less restrictive atmosphere that prevailed under Edmund Andros's brief regime, John Tulley produced an almanac for 1688 that included lewd material discussing, among other things, the rise in sexual activity during cold weather and the dangers of intimacy with diseased prostitutes (John Tulley, *An Almanack for the Year of Our Lord 1688* [Boston, 1688]).

16. James Franklin Jr. was writing as "Poor Job" in the preface to *Poor Job's Country and Townsman's Almanack for the Year 1758* (Newport, R.I., 1757). It was not until after Ames died in 1764 that his series began to adopt a more light-hearted and saucy tone, under the direction of his son and namesake. The astronomical chart for May 1765 noted, for example, that a particular conjunction "promise[d] much fruit of licentious love next winter" (Nathaniel Ames Jr., *An Astronomical Diary, or, Almanack for the Year of Our Lord Christ 1765* [Boston, 1764]). See also Marion Stowell, *Early American Almanacs: The Colonial Weekday Bible* (New York, 1977), 28.

17. Richard Saunders, *Poor Richard: An Almanack for the Year of Christ 1734* (Philadelphia, 1733); Richard Saunders, *Poor Richard: An Almanack for the Year of Christ 1736* (Philadelphia, 1735); Titan Leeds, *The American Almanack for the Year of Christian Account 1721* (Philadelphia, 1720); Titan Leeds, *The American Almanack for the Year of Christian Account 1728* (Philadelphia, 1727); Titan Leeds, *The American Almanack for the Year of Christian Account 1729* (Philadelphia, 1728); and Titan Leeds, *The American Almanack for the Year of Christian Account 1739* (Philadelphia, 1738).

18. Thomas More, *The American Country Almanack for the Year of Christian Account 1754* (Philadelphia, 1753); Andrew Aguecheek, *The Universal American Almanack . . . for the Year of Our Lord 1761* (Philadelphia, 1760); Andrew Aguecheek, *The Universal American Almanack . . . for the Year of Our Lord 1767* (Philadelphia, 1766); Abraham Weatherwise, *Father Abraham's Almanack . . . for the Year of Our Lord 1762* (Philadelphia, 1761).

19. Theophilus Grew, *Virginia Almanack for the Year of Our Lord God 1764* (Williamsburg, Va., 1763); "The Batchelor's Soliloquy," in Philo Copernicus, *The American Calendar, or, An Almanack for the Year of Our Lord 1768* (Philadelphia, 1767).

20. *Pennsylvania Gazette* (Philadelphia), 24/6/1731; *Boston Gazette*, 3/8/1772; *South Carolina Gazette* (Charleston), 3/12/1772.

21. See Charles E. Clark, "The Newspapers of Provincial America," *American Antiquarian Society Proceedings* 100 (1990): 386; and Timothy H. Breen, "An Empire of Goods: The Anglicization of Colonial America, 1690-1776," *Journal of British Studies* 25 (1986): 467-99. My thinking on this subject owes much to Cornelia Hughes Dayton's suggestion that the increasingly bawdy and misogynist tone of New England publications may have constituted "another twist in the cultural process we call anglicization" ("Satire and Sensationalism: The Emergence of Misogyny in Mid-Eighteenth-Century New England Newspapers and Almanacs," paper presented to the New England Seminar at the American Antiquarian Society, Worcester, Mass., 15/11/1991, 21).

22. For examples, see items in the *South Carolina Gazette* for 8/2/1739, 22/5/1762, and 27/5/1768. The latter recounted Lord Baltimore's sensational trial for rape, which was also described in nine installments by the *Connecticut Courant* (Hartford), beginning 21/3/1768, and in four installments by the *Connecticut Journal* (New Haven), beginning 25/3/1768. Salacious material was, of course,

multivalent. For those who disapproved of sexual license and infidelity, it testified to a degenerate climate that threatened to destroy individuals and also to undermine the collective moral fabric on both sides of the Atlantic. Many items could be read as affirmative or condemnatory, depending upon the reader's perspective, but a letter printed in the *Pennsylvania Gazette* for 3/5/1770 condemned quite explicitly the adultery of an English nobleman as "a stain" and "disgrace" that "demeaned" him and his family, "render[ing] his name contemptible."

23. This rehabilitation of women was facilitated by changing assumptions about gender among religious thinkers and moral philosophers. Late-eighteenth-century thinkers saw women as more inclined to piety because of their basic temperament, reflecting a growing tendency to perceive male and female personalities as distinct (Cotton Mather, by contrast, had assumed that experience rather than nature led women to become religious in larger numbers). Meanwhile, psychological theories put forward by influential moral philosophers argued that morality was based in emotional instinct (associated primarily with women) rather than reason (associated primarily with men). Ruth Bloch examines these changes in "The Gendered Meanings of Virtue in Revolutionary America," *Signs* 13 (1987): esp. 47–50.

24. For detailed discussion of the transformation in English depictions of women, see Nussbaum, *Brink of All We Hate.*

25. Richard Saunders, *Poor Richard Improved: Being An Almanack and Ephemeris for the Year of Our Lord 1761* (Philadelphia, 1760); Richard Saunders, *Poor Richard Improved: Being An Almanack and Ephemeris for the Year of Our Lord 1763* (Philadelphia, 1762). Items of this kind had appeared very occasionally in early-eighteenth-century newspapers, for examples of which, see *Boston Gazette,* 13/7/1724 (a "tragical story" of seduction and abandonment); *South Carolina Gazette,* 29/6/1734 (a "virgin's prayer" for "virtue's aid" against "saucy love, or nicer art, which most our sex beguiles"); *Pennsylvania Gazette,* 14/6/1753 (an attack on rakes) and 29/1/1754 (another tragic tale of seduction and abandonment).

26. Richard Saunders, *Poor Richard Improved: Being An Almanack and Ephemeris for the Year of Our Lord 1774* (Philadelphia, 1773); William Andrews, *Poor Will's Almanack for the Year of Our Lord 1774* (Philadelphia, 1773).

27. As with the inclusion of bawdy material in early-eighteenth-century publications, the frequency with which examples of this genre appeared in particular series depended partly on the tastes of individual editors and partly on their sense of public demand. Detailed content analysis of ephemeral print series yields an extremely complex, potentially bewildering, pattern. But the overall shift is clear, earnest discussion of seduction and desertion becoming a significant component in ephemeral print from the 1760s through the 1780s and then mushrooming in the 1790s.

28. "The Flirt: A Morality Tale," *The Universal Asylum and Columbian Magazine* (Philadelphia), June 1791, 390.

29. "Melancholy Tale of Seduction," *Massachusetts Magazine,* April 1795, 41.

See also Davidson, *Revolution and the Word,* 113; and Carroll Smith-Rosenberg, "Domesticating 'Virtue': Coquettes and Revolutionaries in Young America," in Elaine Scarry, ed., *Literature and the Body: Essays on Populations and Persons* (Baltimore, 1988), 167.

30. "A Hint to Young Ladies," *Boston Gazette,* 22/5/1786; "Further Reflections on Celibacy and Marriage," *South Carolina Gazette,* 24/5/1773; "The History of Almeria," *Massachusetts Magazine,* September 1791, 562.

31. "The Instantaneous Impression," *Massachusetts Magazine,* August 1794, 452, 454.

32. "The Vision of Cleanthe," ibid., September 1791, 540-42. See also "The Temple of Pleasure: A Vision," *Gentlemen and Ladies' Town and Country Magazine,* July 1784, 89-90.

33. "An Affecting Letter," *American Magazine and Historical Chronicle,* July 1746, 299-302; see also "The History of Auretta, or, The Fatal Effects of Impatience," *Gentlemen and Ladies' Town and Country Magazine,* May 1784, 17-20; and "Marius and Monimia," *Universal Asylum and Columbian Magazine,* April 1790, 222-25.

34. "The History of Narcissa," *Massachusetts Magazine,* March 1792, 179-81.

35. "Anna, or, The Seduction—An Elegy," *The Boston Magazine,* April 1786, 176; "The Dying Prostitute—An Elegy," *American Museum, or, Repository of Ancient and Modern Fugitive Pieces, Prose and Poetical* (Philadelphia), August 1787, 206.

36. See "The Prostitute," *Philadelphia Minerva,* 18/7/1795; "A Pathetic Story," *Universal Asylum and Columbian Magazine,* September 1792, 170; and "Beauty in Distress: A Pathetic Narrative," *Philadelphia Minerva,* 31/10/1795. Other narratives emphasized the sympathetic grief of parents unable to save their daughters from perfidious suitors, as in "The History of Mira," *Massachusetts Magazine,* August 1790, 464-67; September 1790, 534-37.

37. "The Dying Prostitute—An Elegy," *American Museum, or, Repository of Ancient and Modern Fugitive Pieces,* August 1787, 206; "Reflections at Midnight," *Massachusetts Magazine,* May 1793, 299. See also "A Pathetic Story," 169-73.

38. "Seduction," *The Weekly Magazine of Original Essays* (Philadelphia), 16/3/1799; Abraham Weatherwise, *Father Abraham's Almanack for the Year of Our Lord 1771* (Philadelphia, 1770); "Melancholy Tale of Seduction," *Massachusetts Magazine,* April 1795, 42; "Thoughts Occasioned by a Late Melancholy Event," *Massachusetts Magazine,* June 1793, 371-72.

39. "An Instructing Adventure between a Young Gentleman and a Young Lady," *American Magazine and Historical Chronicle,* September 1744, 546-48; "The Successful Female Angler, or, The History of Dorcas and Olivia," *Gentlemen and Ladies' Town and Country Magazine,* October 1789, 451-53; *South Carolina Gazette,* 14/9/1767.

40. "The Story of Louisa Venoni," *The Literary Miscellany* (Philadelphia),

no. 6, 1795, 3–14. Wronged heroines occasionally moved villains to repentance through more assertive displays of goodness, as in "The History of Adrastus and Camilla," *Massachusetts Magazine,* January 1792, 22–23; and "Claudine: A Swiss Tale," ibid., July 1794, 429–33; August 1794, 472–78.

41. "Marriage Ceremonies of Different Countries Compared," *Columbian Magazine, or, Monthly Miscellany,* June 1787, 497; "The Libertine Reclaimed: A Tale," *Philadelphia Minerva,* 4/6/1796. See also "The Way to Reclaim Him—A Moral Tale," *Gentlemen and Ladies' Town and Country Magazine,* November 1784, 299–302.

42. "Louisa—A Novel," *Massachusetts Magazine,* February 1790, 78–82; March 1790, 147–51. Jan Lewis highlights this reversal in "The Republican Wife: Virtue and Seduction in the Early Republic," *William and Mary Quarterly* 44 (1987): 701–2.

43. Nancy F. Cott, "Passionlessness: An Interpretation of Victorian Sexual Ideology, 1790–1850," *Signs* 4 (1978): 219–36; "Account of the Amazons," *Massachusetts Magazine,* February 1796, 108–9.

44. "A Secret: How to Keep a Husband True," *Philadelphia Minerva,* 27/2/1796 (see also "On Sluttishness in Married Ladies," *South Carolina Weekly Museum,* 4/3/1797); "The School for Husbands and Wives," *The American Museum, or, Universal Magazine* (Philadelphia), October 1789, 312–14; November 1789, 368–70.

45. "Hints for Young Married Women," *The American Museum, or, Universal Magazine,* September 1789, 199; "On the Dangerous Inattention which Ladies Testify to the Morals of their Lovers," *Massachusetts Magazine,* October 1790, 618.

46. "On the Seduction of Young Women," *Boston Magazine,* October 1783, 19. See also "A Pathetic Letter from a Deserted Wife to a Faithless Husband," *American Museum, or Universal Magazine,* May 1792, 221, in which the wronged woman explained her husband's "mistaken conduct" in terms of "frailty" that led him to err.

47. "The Sentimental Libertine," *Massachusetts Magazine,* March 1790, 173; "Letter of a Reformed Libertine," *American Museum, or Universal Magazine,* October 1790, 163; *Poor Robin's Spare Hours, Employed in Calculating A Diary or Almanack for the Year of Christian Account 1758* (Philadelphia, 1757).

48. "A Caution to Young Gentlemen, in the Character and Behaviour of Eugenio," *American Magazine and Historical Chronicle,* November 1743, 111–12; *South Carolina Gazette,* 26/4/1773; "The Sentimental Libertine," 173; "Reflections on the Dangers attending a Propensity to Illiberal Intrigue, With Some Stanzas, and a Letter," *Massachusetts Magazine,* July 1790, 388; "Thoughts on Gallantry, Love, and Marriage," *South Carolina Gazette,* 28/5/1772. See also "Sentiments on Libertinism," *Boston Magazine,* August 1784, 419; and "The Acquisition of a Husband," *Philadelphia Minerva,* 5/12/1795.

49. "Remarks on Female Honour," *American Museum, or Universal Magazine,* December 1790, 281. See also Rodney Hessinger, "'Insidious Murderers

of Female Innocence': Representations of Masculinity in the Seduction Tales of the Late Eighteenth Century," in Merril D. Smith, ed., *Sex and Sexuality in Early America* (New York, 1998), 262-82.

50. "Almira and Alonzo, An Affecting Story Founded on Fact," *Massachusetts Magazine,* June 1789, 363; "Thoughts on a Young Lady's Elopement," ibid., June 1790, 875; "Letter to a Young Lady with Directions concerning her Future Conduct," *American Magazine and Historical Chronicle,* April 1745, 156-57; "The History of Henrietta," *Gentlemen and Ladies' Town and Country Magazine,* September 1789, 431; "Remarks on Female Honour," *American Museum, or Universal Magazine,* December 1790, 281.

51. C. Dallett Hemphill, *Bowing to Necessities: A History of Manners in America, 1620-1860* (New York, 1999), 110; "Letter to a Young Lady with Directions concerning her Future Conduct," *American Magazine and Historical Chronicle,* April 1745, 157; "On the Conduct of a Young Lady during Courtship," *Massachusetts Magazine,* July 1794, 409. See also "Advice to a Young Unmarried Lady From One of Her Own Sex," *South Carolina Gazette,* 27/8/1772; and "Copy of a Letter from a Young Gentleman to his Sister," *The United States Magazine* (Philadelphia), April 1779, 174-80.

52. Hemphill, *Bowing to Necessities,* 112, 121. On 4/5/1789, the *Boston Gazette* printed a short and exceptional essay entitled "An Admonition to Those who Glory in Seducing the Affections of the Fair and Then Desert Them," urging men not to woo unless "assured" that their "conduct" toward the young lady in question was "fixed upon a lasting principle."

53. "Ladies, by Adolescens," *Philadelphia Minerva,* 5/12/1795; "To Mr. Adolescens, by Dorothy Glibtongue," ibid., 12/12/1795. Several dissident voices did question the logic and justice of holding seduced women responsible for their own plight; see "Sentiments on Libertinism," *Boston Magazine,* August 1784, 420; "Infelicia: A Character," *Massachusetts Magazine,* August 1790, 480-81; "Copy of a Letter from a Young Lady to her Seducer," ibid., November 1791, 678; and "On Seduction," ibid., May 1792, 308.

54. Joseph Shippen, "Ladies of Philadelphia," 1766, Shippen Family Papers, 1733-1878, American Philosophical Society, Philadelphia; Andrew Aguecheek, *The Universal American Almanack . . . for the Year of Our Lord 1768* (Philadelphia, 1767); "Remarks on Female Honour," *American Museum, or Universal Magazine,* December 1790, 282; "On the Conduct of a Young Lady during Courtship," *Massachusetts Magazine,* July 1794, 409.

55. For examples, see Don Higginbotham, ed., *The Papers of James Iredell,* 2 vols. (Raleigh, N.C., 1976), 1:138, 149, 173, 211, 213; and Eliza Lucas to Miss Bartlett, May 1742, in *South Carolina Historical Magazine* 72 (1971): 207. Martha Ballard, a midwife and healer in Hallowell, Maine, had two nieces who were named after the heroines of *Pamela* and *Clarissa* (Laurel Thatcher Ulrich, *A Midwife's Tale: The Life of Martha Ballard, Based on Her Diary, 1785-1812* [New York, 1990], 10).

56. Quoted in Carla Mumford, ed., *The Power of Sympathy* and *The Coquette*

(New York, 1996), xxvi. For further discussion of *Pamela*'s readership in New England, see Laurel Thatcher Ulrich, *Good Wives: Image and Reality in the Lives of Women in Northern New England, 1650-1750* (New York, 1982), 256 n. 39.

57. "Character of Sir C. Grandison and Clarissa," *Gentlemen and Ladies' Town and Country Magazine*, July 1784, 90-92; Enos Hitchcock, *Memoirs of the Bloomsgrove Family, in a Series of Letters to a Respectable Citizen of Philadelphia*, 2 vols. (Boston, 1790), 2:86-87.

58. *American Monthly Review, or, Literary Journal* (Philadelphia), May 1795, 88; "On Modern Novels and their Effects," 662; Hitchcock, *Memoirs of the Bloomsgrove Family*, 2:88; "Novel Reading, A Cause of Female Depravity," *New England Quarterly* 1 (1802): 173; "Phebe Smith: A Moral Tale," *Philadelphia Minerva*, 27/2/1796.

59. "Novel Reading, A Cause of Female Depravity," 172, 173; "On Modern Novels and their Effects," 663; "Character and Effects of Modern Novels," *Weekly Magazine of Original Essays*, 10/3/1798, 185.

60. William Hill Brown, *The Power of Sympathy, or, The Triumph of Nature* (Boston, 1789), letter 11.

61. Ibid., letters 21, 40, 45. Jan Lewis addresses the implications of describing seduction as a reenactment of the Fall in "Republican Wife," 718-19.

62. Hannah Webster Foster, *The Coquette, or, The History of Eliza Wharton* (Boston, 1797), letters 1, 5, 41, 49, 68.

63. Carroll Smith-Rosenberg also points out that "Foster dramatizes the new impotence of family and community against the autonomy of youth and the power of the individual" ("Domesticating 'Virtue,'" 178).

64. Foster, *Coquette*, letter 73.

65. For examples, see "Papers and Affidavits Relating to the Plunderings, Burnings, and Ravages Committed by the British, 1775-1784," in *Papers of the Continental Congress, 1774-89*, microfilm copy of original at National Archives, Washington, D.C., reel 66; Varnum Lansing Collins, ed., *A Brief Narrative of the Ravages of the British and Hessians at Princeton in 1776-1777* (New York, 1968); William S. Stryker, ed., *Documents Relating to the Revolutionary History of the State of New Jersey* (Trenton, N.J., 1901), esp. 245-46, 351; *Boston Gazette*, 6/11/1769, 6/1/1777, and 2/6/1777; Julian P. Boyd, ed., *The Papers of Thomas Jefferson*, vol. 1 (Princeton, N.J., 1950), 659; Henry Steele Commager and Richard S. Morris, eds., *The Spirit of Seventy-Six* (New York, 1967), 424; and Charles Wilson Peale, "Diaries, 1765-1826," 20/6/1777, American Philosophical Society, Philadelphia.

66. *Boston Gazette*, 6/11/1769.

67. Thomas Paine, *Common Sense*, ed. Isaac Kramnick (New York, 1986), 99 (emphasis in original), 113; *Correspondence between the Hon. John Adams and the Late William Cunningham, Esq.* (Boston, 1823), 19.

68. See especially Gordon S. Wood, *The Creation of the American Republic, 1776-1787* (Chapel Hill, N.C., 1969).

69. Benjamin Rush, for example, warned that "uncleanness" and other forms

of licentious behavior had "a pernicious influence upon morals, and thereby pre-pare[d] our country for misery and slavery" (Benjamin Rush, *Essays Literary, Moral, and Philosophical* [Philadelphia, 1798], 115, 116).

70. See especially Lewis, "Republican Wife." During the crises that preceded the Declaration of Independence and throughout the war that followed, patriots had emphasized women's role as exemplars of virtue; see Laurel Thatcher Ulrich, "Daughters of Liberty: Religious Women in Revolutionary New England," in Ronald Hoffman and Peter J. Albert, eds., *Women in the Age of the American Revolution* (Richmond, Va., 1989), esp. 227; and Mary Beth Norton, *Liberty's Daughters: The Revolutionary Experience of American Women, 1750-1800* (Boston, 1980), esp. 177-88.

71. "Female Influence," *New York Magazine,* May 1795, 299, 300; "Remarks on Female Honour," *American Museum, or, Universal Magazine,* December 1790, 281; "The Power of Beauty, and the Influence the Fair Sex Might Have in Reforming the Manners of the World," *Boston Weekly Magazine,* 3/3/1804, 74.

72. For discussion of late-eighteenth-century debates concerning female education, see Linda K. Kerber, *Women of the Republic: Intellect and Ideology in Revolutionary America* (Chapel Hill, N.C., 1980), chap. 7; and Norton, *Liberty's Daughters,* chap. 9. See also Rosemary Zagarri, "Morals, Manners, and the Republican Mother," *American Quarterly* 44 (1992): 199.

73. Magazines committed themselves quite explicitly to informing and educating as well as entertaining their female readers. For examples, see *The Lady's Magazine and Repository of Entertaining Knowledge* (Philadelphia), June 1792, i-v; and *Lady and Gentleman's Pocket Magazine of Literature and Polite Amusement* 1 (1796): iii-iv. Davidson discusses self-education through reading in *Revolution and the Word,* chap. 4.

74. Carroll Smith-Rosenberg argues that characters such as Eliza Wharton functioned for readers as "Every*man* as well as Everywoman," highlighting the dangers that "liberty and freedom" posed to both "the individual and society" ("Domesticating 'Virtue,'" 178).

75. "The Happy Pair," in Abraham Weatherwise, *Father Abraham's Almanack ... for the Year of Our Lord 1763* (Philadelphia, 1762); "The Happy Pair," in Isaac Briggs, *Virginia Almanack, or, Ephemeris for the Year of Our Lord 1799* (Richmond, Va., 1798). As with other trends within ephemeral print, there was no simple linear progression; but the overarching trend was clear.

76. Lois K. Stabler, ed., *'Very Poor and of a Lo Make': The Journal of Abner Sanger* (Portsmouth, N.H., 1986), 45, 285, 314, 452. The vituperative barrage of aphorisms included in *Female Policy Detected* did not target any one segment of the female population but was aimed at women in every stage of life, ranging in social rank from the "lofty mistress" to the "whore." Longer versions appended a section bestowing effusive praise upon women who did prove themselves virtuous, loyal, and dutiful wives, but misogynist generalizations were privileged in the book's title and also the text itself.

77. "The Bachelor," *Philadelphia Minerva,* 28/11/1795.

9. "Martyrdom to Venus"

1. Elaine Forman Crane, ed., *The Diary of Elizabeth Drinker*, 3 vols. (Boston, 1991), 3:1633 (12/3/1803); Vagrancy Docket, 16/6/1792, City and County Archives of Philadelphia (henceforth CCAP); Prisoners for Trial Docket, Richard Hart, 6/3/1799, CCAP; Robert C. Smith, ed., "A Portuguese Naturalist in Philadelphia, 1799," *Pennsylvania Magazine of History and Biography* 78 (1954): 80.

2. Benjamin Rush, *Essays Literary, Moral, and Philosophical* (Philadelphia, 1798), 121; Crane, *Diary of Elizabeth Drinker*, 1:337 (18/12/1778). Debra O'Neal discusses these changes in "Mistresses and Maids: The Transformation of Women's Domestic Labor and Household Relations in Late Eighteenth-Century Philadelphia" (Ph.D. diss., University of California, Riverside, 1994).

3. See especially Steven Rosswurm, *Arms, Country, and Class: The Philadelphia Militia and the 'Lower Sort' during the American Revolution* (New Brunswick, N.J., 1987).

4. Kenneth Roberts and Anna M. Roberts, eds. and trans., *Moreau de St. Mery's American Journey* (Garden City, N.Y., 1947), 285.

5. Billy G. Smith examines the lives of poorer Philadelphians in *The 'Lower Sort': Philadelphia's Laboring People, 1750-1800* (Ithaca, N.Y., 1990); see esp. 177.

6. *Pennsylvania Packet* (Philadelphia), 30/12/1785; *Pennsylvania Gazette* (Philadelphia), 8/8/1787; Francois Alexandre Frederic, duc de La Rochefoucault-Liancourt, *Travels Through the United States of North America, the Country of the Iroquois, and Upper Canada*, 2 vols. (London, 1799), 2:677. For brothel locations, see O'Neal, "Mistresses and Maids," 299-300; and Clare Anna Lyons, "Sex among the 'Rabble': Gender Transitions in the Age of Revolution, Philadelphia, 1750-1830" (Ph.D. diss., Yale University, 1996), 157-58, 304-5. Though Philadelphia was well provided with brothels and taverns, it had no equivalent of the "molly houses" that had caused so much controversy across the Atlantic or the homoerotic subculture that London and other major European cities offered. See Randolph Trumbach, "London's Sodomites: Homosexual Behavior and Western Culture in the Eighteenth Century," *Journal of Social History* 11 (1977-78): 1-33; Alan Bray, *Homosexuality in Renaissance England* (London, 1982), chap. 4; and Rictor Norton, *Mother Clap's Molly House: The Gay Subculture in England, 1700-1830* (London, 1992).

7. Roberts and Roberts, *Moreau de St. Mery's American Journey*, 177-78; Lyons, "Sex among the 'Rabble,' " 20. Lyons shows that bastardy was not limited to any one ethnic group; many out-of-wedlock births resulted from relationships that crossed ethnic or racial lines.

8. For examples of pregnant Pennsylvania women in smaller communities outside Philadelphia who prosecuted their lovers with the active support of family members well aware of these sexual relationships and the expectation of marriage on which they had been based, see *Elizabeth Cassner of Mifflin County vs. John Patterson*, 24/5/1797; and *Elizabeth Heddicks of York County vs. Joseph*

Dobbins, 19/4/1799, Pennsylvania Court Papers, Historical Society of Pennsylvania, Philadelphia.

9. Roberts and Roberts, *Moreau de St. Mery's American Journey*, 311, 177–78, 312–13; *The Philadelphiad, or, New Pictures of the City* (Philadelphia, 1784), 2:58–59; George W. Corner, ed., *The Autobiography of Benjamin Rush: His "Travels Through Life" together with his "Commonplace Book" for 1789-1813* (Princeton, N.J., 1948), 225.

10. Corner, *Autobiography of Benjamin Rush*, 190, 311, 317.

11. Account Book and Diary, 14 March, 6 May, 17 May, 2 December, James Wilson Papers, American Philosophical Society, Philadelphia. Wilson bought several sawmills in the late 1780s, including one at the Schuylkill Falls mentioned by the diarist, suggesting that he was in Wilson's employ; an entry written in the same hand and using the same cheap ink recorded some sawing instructions. Internal evidence puts the accounts in the early 1790s. I am much indebted to Susan Klepp for sharing these clues and her transcription of the diary, which helped to fill in some of the gaps in my own (the diary is extremely difficult to read because the author often used a blunt quill).

12. Ibid., 7 January, 23 March.

13. Ibid., 1, 7, 13 January; 12 May; 4 July; 24 November.

14. Ibid., 7 June, 4 July, 24 November, 22 December.

15. *Margaret Erben vs. Adam Erben* (filed 1790) and *Catherine Pemble vs. David Pemble* (filed 1803), Pennsylvania Divorce Papers (henceforth PDP), Pennsylvania State Archives, Harrisburg; Charles Wilson Peale, "Diaries, 1765–1826," 11/12/1778, American Philosophical Society, Philadelphia.

16. *John Mulloway vs. Catharine Mulloway* (filed 1793), *Reuben Bennett vs. Charlotte Bennett* (filed 1796), and *William Britton vs. Catharine Britton* (filed 1797), PDP.

17. *Universal Asylum and Columbian Magazine* (Philadelphia), June 1790, 345; *A Report of the Trial of Henry Bedlow for Committing a Rape on Lanah Sawyer* (New York, 1793), 19, 36–37, 40–41, 44.

18. "The Longing Maid," in *William Crotty, To Which Are Added Five Other New Songs* (Philadelphia, 1767); *The Amorous Sailor's Letter to his Sweetheart, and, The Jolly Orange Woman* (Worcester, Mass., 1781).

19. *John Lovinger vs. Louisa Lovinger* (filed 1800) and *Jacob Lightwood vs. Eleanor Lightwood* (filed 1805), PDP. See also Nancy F. Cott, "Eighteenth-Century Family and Social Life Revealed in Massachusetts Divorce Records," in Nancy F. Cott and Elizabeth H. Pleck, eds., *A Heritage of Her Own: Toward a New Social History of American Women* (New York, 1979), 126. Eleven of fourteen women cited for bastardy by the Philadelphia Quaker meeting between 1760 and 1780 were expelled because they refused to acknowledge that they had sinned (Lyons, "Sex among the 'Rabble,'" 65).

20. Johann David Schoepf, *Travels in the Confederation, 1783-1784*, trans. Alfred J. Morrison, 2 vols. (New York, 1968), 1:394. For examples of "giving notice in the public prints," see *Pennsylvania Gazette*, 10/8/1769, 5/8/1772.

21. For examples, see Susan E. Klepp, *Philadelphia in Transition: A Demographic History of the City and Its Occupational Groups, 1720-1830* (New York, 1989), 116-17. During the colonial period, Pennsylvanians could divorce only by act of assembly; see Merril D. Smith, *Breaking the Bonds: Marital Discord in Pennsylvania, 1730-1830* (New York, 1991), 16-20.

22. *John Jones vs. Catharine Jones* (filed 1787), *John Dicks vs. Mary Dicks* (filed 1789; see also Joseph Kelley, *Life and Times in Colonial Philadelphia* [Harrisburg, Pa., 1973], 189), and *Susanna Evans vs. William Evans* (filed 1793), PDP.

23. See also *Jane Harris vs. James Harris* (filed 1791) and *Mary Side vs. William Side* (filed 1801), PDP.

24. *Catharine Conrad vs. Matthias Conrad* (filed 1788) and *Joanna Brown vs. William Brown* (filed 1800), PDP.

25. Mayor's Court Docket, Philadelphia, 1789-1802, June 1791, CCAP; *Mary Lloyd vs. John Lloyd* (filed 1795), PDP; Philadelphia Quarter Sessions Docket, 1790-95, June 1795, CCAP.

26. J. A. Leo Lemay and P. M. Zall, eds., *The Autobiography of Benjamin Franklin: A Genetic Text* (Knoxville, Tenn., 1981), 52, 71.

27. "Remarkable Occurrences Concerning Marriage," December 1794, July 1797, in "The Records of Gloria Dei Church," Historical Society of Pennsylvania, Philadelphia. Extracts from "Remarkable Occurrences," edited by Susan E. Klepp and Billy G. Smith, are printed in Billy G. Smith, ed., *Life in Early Philadelphia: Documents from the Revolutionary and Early National Periods* (University Park, Pa., 1995), 185-200.

28. "Remarkable Occurrences Concerning Marriage," 10/1/1794, 13/1/1795, July 1797.

29. For examples, see ibid., 3/4/1795, 15/4/1795.

30. Ibid., 12/1/1794, 24/4/1794, 6/9/1794; 6/1/1795; 25/1/1800. From the applicants' point of view, a clerical demand for written verification of their circumstances was often unrealistic. In 1796 Collin refused to marry a young man "late from Ireland, who had brought a girl from that country with intent of marriage," until the applicant "could produce certificates." The Irishman "pleaded in vain his coming from New York and having no acquaintances in this place" (ibid., 5/7/1796). The sister of a would-be bride whose husband could not produce freedom papers railed upon Collin "for this hardship to the poor," to which the pastor responded that "similar precaution" was "taken with people of all conditions" (ibid., 3/4/1795).

31. Ibid., 29/7/1797, 15/7/1805, 8/11/1806.

32. Ibid., 29/5/1797, May 1805.

33. Ibid., 13/4/1800, October 1800. For premarital pregnancy rates in late-eighteenth-century Philadelphia, see Klepp, *Philadelphia in Transition*, 87-88; and Stephanie Grauman Wolf, *Urban Village: Population, Community, and Family Structure in Germantown, Pennsylvania, 1683-1800* (Princeton, N.J., 1976), 259. For examples of marriage certificates that were falsified, see ibid., 260. As Klepp points out, the antedating of marriage certificates should alert us to the under-

representation of premarital pregnancy in official records (*Philadelphia in Transition*, 90).

34. "Remarkable Occurrences Concerning Marriage," 5/3/1794, 2/7/1800, 11/5/1801, 8/11/1806.

35. Lemay and Zall, *Autobiography of Benjamin Franklin*, 70; Claude-Anne Lopez and Eugenia W. Herbert, *The Private Franklin: The Man and His Family* (New York, 1975), 22-23.

36. Smith, "Portuguese Naturalist in Philadelphia," 83. An apparent decline in premarital pregnancy at the end of the century among more affluent city-dwellers (for which see Klepp, *Philadelphia in Transition*, 92-94) may well have been due in large part to this new moral code, which not only discouraged sex during courtship but also would have encouraged concealment of unmarried pregnancy.

37. Drinker had first suspected that Brant was pregnant on 8/8/1794 (Crane, *Diary of Elizabeth Drinker*, 1:580). For Gibbs's dismissal, see 1:584 (19/8/1794).

38. Ibid., 1:623 (2/12/1794), 700 (5/7/1795), 704-5 (13/7/1795, 14/7/1795). They also had the right to lengthen Brant's period of servitude as recompense but did not do so, perhaps because they wanted to be rid of her. See 2:808 (2/6/1796).

39. Ibid., 1:705 (14/7/1795). Brant left the Drinkers in 1796 (2:808) and married "a young barber" in the fall of 1797 (2:995).

40. Ibid., 1:393 (24/11/1781), 396 (21/2/1782).

41. Ibid., 1:632 (23/12/1794), 649 (14/2/1795), 652 (21/2/1795), 705 (14/7/1795).

42. Ibid., 1:584 (20/8/1794), 600 (30/9/1794), 667 (8/4/1795), 672-73 (19/4/1795); Rush, *Essays*, 122.

43. Roberts and Roberts, *Moreau de St. Mery's American Journey*, 134. If the father proved uncooperative, women could seek reinforcement of their claims in court. That involved confessing to a crime, but in most cases of this kind the Mayor's Court focused on extracting support from fathers and declined to fine mothers. See Mayor's Court Docket, CCAP, passim. Pennsylvania county courts were more inclined to punish women for "fornication and bastardy," though during the course of the eighteenth century their focus had shifted as elsewhere away from moral regulation and toward the allocation of economic responsibility; see G. S. Rowe, "Women's Crime and Criminal Administration in Pennsylvania, 1763-1790," *Pennsylvania Magazine of History and Biography* 109 (1985): esp. 348, table 2; and Lyons, "Sex among the 'Rabble,'" 46.

44. Account Book and Diary, 15 February; Records of the Guardians of the Poor, Daily Occurrence Docket, CCAP. Subsequent references to this source are given in a note only if the month and year of the entry do not appear in the text.

45. Crane, *Diary of Elizabeth Drinker*, 1:373 (26/8/1780); Smith, "Portuguese Naturalist in Philadelphia," 83, 88. For more detailed discussion of infanticide in late-eighteenth-century Philadelphia, see Lyons, "Sex among the 'Rabble,'" 73-83.

46. Claude Quétel, *The History of Syphilis*, trans. Judith Braddock and Brian Pike (1986; Baltimore, 1992), 82-83; Smith, "Portuguese Naturalist in Philadelphia," 95-96; Smith, *Life in Early Philadelphia*, 33. The admission register is not always a reliable gauge, since some cases were not diagnosed until after admittance; the clerks were also inconsistent in the amount of information that they entered for each individual. There was, for example, no mention of infection in the admissions entry for Eleanor Leap in March 1790, yet her discharge record in June of that year described her as a "venereal" patient who was "now cured."

47. Account Book and Diary, 22 December.

48. Those prostitutes who had been weakened by repeated exposure to venereal infections were also unable to resist other diseases that were circulating in the city. The "malignant fever" that struck Philadelphia in 1793 was particularly "fatal" to "filles de joie" since "the wretched debilitated state of their constitutions rendered them an easy prey to this dreadful disorder, which very soon terminated their miserable career" (Mathew Carey, *A Short Account of the Malignant Fever Lately Prevalent in Philadelphia*, 4th ed. [Philadelphia, 1794], 61).

49. John Hunter, *A Treatise on the Venereal Disease*, abridged by William Currie (Philadelphia, 1787), 39, 52, 54-55, 89. An author writing in 1793 claimed that almost two thousand works about the disease had appeared thus far. See Quétel, *History of Venereal Disease*, 81, 289 n. 32.

50. Quotations taken from entries recording Mary Carlisle's elopement in August 1794, Sarah Evans's elopement in March 1796, James Thomson's discharge in April 1796, and Eleanor O'Bryan's discharge in July 1796, Records of the Guardians of the Poor, Daily Occurrence Docket.

51. Hunter, *Treatise*, 46, 49.

52. "The Itinerarium of Dr. Alexander Hamilton," in Wendy Martin, ed., *Colonial American Travel Narratives* (New York, 1994), 210. Smaller coastal towns were also affected, for which see Roberts and Roberts, *Moreau de St. Mery's American Journey*, 67. Even passengers on stagecoaches crisscrossing the countryside could find themselves in the company of "courtesans who figure[d] that a stage can be made to serve purposes quite foreign to modesty" (122).

53. Roberts and Roberts, *Moreau de St. Mery's American Journey*, 156. The Holy Ground was also located right next to King's College, later renamed Columbia University; as one visitor to the city observed, this was "certainly a temptation to the youth that have occasion to pass so often that way" (Patrick M'Robert, "A Tour through Part of the Northern Provinces of America," quoted in I. N. Phelps Stokes, *The Iconography of Manhattan Island, 1498-1910* [New York, 1912], 4:862).

54. Edward Bangs, ed., *Journal of Lieutenant Isaac Bangs* (Cambridge, 1890), 29. The troops stationed in New York were not unusual in having been stricken by sexually transmitted disease; see Holly A. Mayer, *Belonging to the Army: Camp Followers and Community during the American Revolution* (Columbia, S.C., 1996), 111. Sexually transmitted disease afflicted both sides in the revolutionary war: according to a physician working with the British army, "many men were in-

NOTES TO PAGES 324–328

fected two or three times a quarter," and so serious was the loss of manpower that some regiments deducted "venereal money" from the pay of incapacitated soldiers so as to discourage the "promiscuous embraces" that led to infection (Sylvia R. Frey, *The British Soldier in America: A Social History of Military Life in the Revolutionary Period* [Austin, Tex., 1981], 44).

55. *Hilliad Magna, Being the Life and Adventures of Moll Placket-Hole* (Philadelphia, 1765), 3–7.

56. Ibid., 7; Carl Bridenbaugh, *Cities in Revolt: Urban Life in America, 1743–1776* (New York, 1955), 316; Peale, "Diaries," 11/12/1778.

57. For examples, see *Pennsylvania Gazette*, 30/10/1766; Bangs, *Journal of Lieutenant Isaac Bangs*, 30; and *Pennsylvania Chronicle and Universal Advertiser* (Philadelphia), 5/6/1769.

58. *Federal Gazette* (Philadelphia), 16/11/1790; *Aurora* (Philadelphia), 24/8/1795. The mayor's speech was published as *An Address to the Citizens of Philadelphia, Respecting the Better Government of Youth* (Philadelphia, 1795). Concerned citizens in Philadelphia itself soon followed suit, for which see *Porcupine's Gazette* (Philadelphia), 16/1/1798. Their Society for the Suppression of Vice and Immorality petitioned the state congress in December 1798, urging representatives to pass an act "for the suppression of vice and immorality," presented in draft to former sessions but not as yet passed (Petition to the Senate and House of Representatives of the Commonwealth of Pennsylvania, December 1798, Historical Society of Pennsylvania).

59. *Claypoole's American Daily Advertiser* (Philadelphia), 23/8/1800; Crane, *Diary of Elizabeth Drinker*, 2:1334 (25/8/1800).

60. Margaret Britton, 16/1/1794; Catherine Cornish, 28/2/1794, Vagrancy Docket, CCAP.

61. Philadelphia County Court of Quarter Sessions, CCAP; Rochefoucault, *Travels Through the United States*, 2:678.

62. Admission record for Christiana Nelson, December 1796, Records of the Guardians of the Poor, Daily Occurrence Docket.

63. Rochefoucault, *Travels Through the United States*, 2:677; Sharon V. Salinger, " 'Send No More Women': Female Servants in Eighteenth-Century Philadelphia," *Pennsylvania Magazine of History and Biography* 107 (1983): 34; O'Neal, "Mistresses and Maids," esp. chaps. 3, 4.

64. Roberts and Roberts, *Moreau de St. Mery's American Journey*, 297; *Pennsylvania Gazette*, 18/9/1760; *Reuben Bennett vs. Charlotte Bennett* (filed 1796), PDP. Although there were male pimps operating in the city, prostitution seems to have been organized for the most part by women. Lyons points out that not all unattached women living in bawdy houses were necessarily working as prostitutes to support themselves ("Sex among the 'Rabble,' " 314). Judith Walkowitz argues that nineteenth-century women turned to prostitution for similar reasons in *Prostitution and Victorian Society* (New York, 1980), 9, 14; see also Timothy J. Gilfoyle, *City of Eros: New York City, Prostitution, and the Commercialization of Sex, 1790–1920* (New York, 1992), 59.

65. Rochefoucault, *Travels Through the United States*, 2:678.

66. See also Frances Finnegan, *Poverty and Prostitution: A Study of Victorian Prostitutes in New York* (New York, 1979).

67. Magdalen Society Manual Book, Historical Society of Pennsylvania; *The Constitution of the Magdalen Society* (Philadelphia, 1800).

68. Magdalen Society Manual Book; see especially reports for 1811 and 1837. The ultimate objective was to place reformed Magdalens as domestic servants, preferably "in the country," far away from "corrupting associates." That would provide them with material support, at least temporarily, but the primary goal of such placements was continued moral reformation. For detailed discussion of the shift toward reformative incarceration in which the Magdalen Society played a part, see Michael Meranze, *Laboratories of Virtue: Punishment, Revolution, and Authority in Philadelphia, 1760-1835* (Chapel Hill, N.C., 1996); Michael Ignatieff, *A Just Measure of Pain: The Penitentiary in the Industrial Revolution, 1750-1850* (New York, 1978); and David J. Rothman, *The Discovery of the Asylum: Social Order and Disorder in the New Republic* (Boston, 1971).

69. *Hilliad Magna*, 5-7; *Philadelphiad*, 1:22-23. According to St. Mery, the matrons of such establishments also had agents combing the streets on their behalf. These "purveyors" would "seduce" women and then "sell them to houses" in the city (Roberts and Roberts, *Moreau de St. Mery's American Journey*, 302).

70. "Reflections at Midnight," *Massachusetts Magazine*, May 1793, 298; *A New Song About Miss Ketty* (Philadelphia, 1765); *Philadelphiad*, 1:21-22.

71. *Philadelphiad*, 1:20-21; 2:30, 31, 33.

72. *The Diary, or Loudon's Register* (New York), 23/10/1793, 24/10/1793. See also *Columbian Gazetteer* (New York), 17/10/1793; *Daily Advertiser* (New York), 16/10/1793; and *New York Journal and Patriotic Register*, 16/10/1793, 19/10/1793. In a remarkable twist of logic, the defense attorneys had played on Bedlow's reputation as "a man of gallantry" to assert his innocence: his skill in seducing women "would probably open sufficient avanues to the gratification of his pleasures and prevent the necessity of force from ever occurring to his mind." He may well have seduced her, they conceded, but that did not make him a rapist (*Report of the Trial of Henry Bedlow*, 20).

73. *Hilliad Magna*, 2.

Afterword

1. Franklin Dexter, ed., *New Haven Town Records*, 2 vols. (New Haven, Conn., 1917-19), 2:160-61.

2. The cases against Kenelm Cheseldyne and Mary Phippard, William Mitchell and Joan Toast, and Edward Coppedge and Elizabeth Risby, discussed in chap. 4, exemplify such differences in perspective.

3. See esp. Barbara Welter, "The Cult of True Womanhood, 1820-1860," *American Quarterly* 18 (1966): 151-74; Kathryn Kish Sklar, *Catharine Beecher: A Study in American Domesticity* (New Haven, Conn., 1973); Nancy F. Cott, *The Bonds of Womanhood: "Woman's Sphere" in New England, 1780-1835* (New

Haven, Conn., 1977); Ruth H. Bloch, "American Feminine Ideals in Transition: The Rise of the Moral Mother, 1785–1815," *Feminist Studies* 4 (1978): 101–26; Gerda Lerner, "The Lady and the Mill Girl: Changes in the Status of Women in the Age of Jackson, 1800–1840," in Nancy F. Cott and Elizabeth H. Pleck, eds., *A Heritage of Her Own: Toward a New Social History of American Women* (New York, 1979), 182–96; Linda K. Kerber, "Separate Spheres, Female Worlds, Woman's Place: The Rhetoric of Women's History," *Journal of American History* 75 (1988): 9–39; and Jeanne Boydston, "To Earn Her Daily Bread: Housework and Antebellum Working Class Subsistence," in Vicki L. Ruiz and Ellen Carol DuBois, eds., *Unequal Sisters* (New York, 1994), 44–56.

4. Journals of William Ormond, 1791–1803, transcript in 2 vols., 2:39, Special Collections Library, Duke University; *The Trial and Conviction of John Clary* (n.p., 1810).

Index

abandonment, of infants, 317. *See also* seduction and abandonment
Abba (slave), 216
Abbot, Isaac, 231
Abbot, John, 104
abortion: among African Americans, 218; among European Americans, 238; among Native Americans, 177
Accerly, Henry, 111
Adair, James, 186–87
Adam (biblical), 55, 60–61, 68, 72–73, 85, 127, 151, 268
Adams, Abigail, 247
Adams, John, 247, 261, 294, 296
Adams, William, 82
adultery, 8; and Native Americans, 157, 163, 166, 183, 187; in 17th-century New England, 20, 26, 27, 35, 39, 41–44, 61, 64, 66–67, 68, 88, 89–90, 91–92, 93, 99, 101, 102–3, 113, 353n34; in 18th-century New England, 243, 245; in Philadelphia, 300–301, 303–10; and print culture, 270, 273, 277, 284–85, 297; in the South, 119, 125, 131–32, 134–35, 136, 138–39, 143, 144, 149, 150, 195, 197, 221–22, 381n15. *See also* informal marriage; Puritans; separation; serial monogamy
Africans and African Americans: abortion among, 218; attraction of Europeans and European Americans toward, 4–5, 193, 211–13, 222; interracial relationships involving, 4–6, 14, 193–94, 200–24, 308, 315, 336–37; —, in the lower South, 208–13; —, in the upper South, 202–8; —, in West Indies, 213–22;

marital customs of, 151–52; seen as licentious, 5, 151–52, 201; sexual coercion of, 5, 152, 193, 200–1, 204, 213–15, 218, 223. *See also* abortion; informal marriage; interracial sex; marriage
Air, Adam, 228
Alden, John, 165
Alford, Joseph, 132
Alice (slave), 204
Allexander, John, 108, 113–14
almanacs, 12, 265, 271–75, 277–88, 297
almshouse (Phil.), 302, 316–21, 326, 328–29, 333–34
American Revolution, 13, 15, 149, 193, 224, 229, 237, 260–61, 267, 279, 293–94, 300, 312–13, 322, 334, 335, 406n70
Ames, Nathaniel, Sr. and Jr., 272, 400n16
Amsden, Isaac (1676), 112
Amsden, Isaac and wife, (1754), 234
Anburey, Thomas, 249
Anderton, Thomas, 318
Andros, Edmund, 165, 399n15
Ann (Native American), 167
Annie (servant), 199–200, 382n27
Archer, Gabriel, 157
Armstrong, Christopher, 309
Arrington, Abraham, 31
Ashley, Edward, 165
Ashley, Elihu, 251
assault. *See* sexual coercion
Atherton, Mary, 32
Atwood, Ann, 140
Atwood, Thomas, 215–16
Aurelia (slave), 219

Frier, Elizabeth, 42
frontier, 158–59, 172–86. *See also*
  backcountry
Frost, John, 36–37
Fulmer, John, 308

Gaines, Lucy, 398n3
Gale, Abijah, 234
Gallagher, Ann, 329
"gallantry" (as colloquialism for sex),
  192–93, 205, 381n15, 413n72
Galphin, George, 183–84, 186
Garden, Alexander, 145
Gardiner, George, 39–40
Gardner, Samuel, 167
Garret, William, 125
Garzia, John, 141, 143
gender: flexibility of, in early New
  England, 55, 79–82; and racial ide-
  ology in the South, 6, 14, 202–3,
  208, 210, 221–22, 337; and repub-
  lican virtue, 15, 267, 279, 294–97,
  302, 306, 314, 321, 333, 337–38; and
  sexual virtue, changing perceptions
  of, 15, 263, 266–98, 305, 331, 337.
  See also double standard, sexual
gentility, 14, 32–33, 190–97, 202,
  205–8, 209, 223
Gibbs, Joe, 315
Gilbert, Benjamin, 260–61, 262–63
Gilbert, Esther, 263
Gilbert, Mary, 263
Giles, Hannah, 321
Gill, Abigail, 101
Gilliard, Philip, 180
Gilligan, Alexander and Elizabeth, 42
Glen, James, 120–21, 151
Goad, Benjamin, 65, 68, 364n56
Goffe, Hannah, 99
Goodell, Elizabeth, 93–94, 95
Gorton, Stephen, 235, 244, 390n18
gossip, 27, 59, 91, 92–93, 163–64, 272.
  See also defamation
Gouge, William, 58, 60, 61
Gowen, Sara, 101
Graffenfried, Baron of, 151
Grant, Christopher, 37, 347n50

Graves, Benjamin, 35, 92, 336
Gray, Hanah, 89
Great Awakening, the, 230, 239, 240–
  45
Greaves, John, 126
Green, Hannah, 30
Green, Joseph, 61, 84–85
Greenfield, Samuel, 28
Greenland, Henry, 94–95
Greensted, William, 203
Griffin, Edward, 317–18
Grosvenor, Sarah, 391n23
Guardians of the Poor (Phil.), 301, 316,
  326. *See also* almshouse
gynecological manuals, 28, 239–40

Hackett, William, 111
Hadly, John, 92
Hall, Samuel, 30
Hamilton, Alexander, 268, 321–22
Hammon, Mary, 105
Hammond, John, 155, 366n8
Harding, William, 30
Hardy, Samuel and wife, 232
Harkins, John, 318
Harriot, Thomas, 155, 156, 207
Harris, Mary, 23
Harris, Rebecca, 38–39
Harrower, John, 398n3
Harvard College, 31, 70, 84, 88, 238,
  259, 272
Harwood, John and Mary, 276
Hassell, John, 134–35
Hatch, Lydia, 365n61
Hatch, Thomas, 124
Hauntine, Elizabeth, 138
Haven, Jason, 396n54
Hawley, Elisha, 257–59
Hawley, Joseph, 258
Hawthorne, Nathaniel, 54, 100
Hay, John, 303
Hazard, Ebenezer, 201, 209–10
Hemings, Elizabeth, 205
Hemings, Mary, 205
Hemings, Sally, 205, 213
Hendly (f), 140
Henley, Elizabeth, 140

Long, Horod, 39–40, 347n56
Long, Sarah, 102
Long, William, 40–41
love, 52–58, 60, 61, 62, 64, 70–83,
196–97, 221, 269, 289–90
Lovell, Weybro, 99
Lovinger, Louisa, 307–8
Lowell, Samuel, 37–38
Lowman, Samuel, 139
Luddington, John, 35
Lumbrozo, Jacob, 382n26
Lutherans, 310
Luxford, James, 42
Lyford, John and wife, 93, 351n12
Lyons, Thomas, 305

Macay, Spruce, 149
MacSparren, James, 151
magazines, 12, 265, 278–88, 293, 329
Magdalen Society, 329–30
manhood. *See* gender
Manigault, Peter, 194
Maria (slave), 216
marriage: and Africans, attitudes toward, 151–52; with Africans and
African Americans, 203; with
Native Americans, 158–89, 385n47;
and Native Americans, attitudes toward, 155–57, 166, 181, 187; official
requirements for, 7, 38, 40, 124–
26, 128, 132–34, 149, 308–13; —,
popular disregard for, 7–9, 38–44,
120–21, 125–32, 308–13, 336; in
print culture, 272–75, 276–77, 279,
283–85, 289–91, 295–98, 307, 308;
Puritan approval of sex within, 14,
54–61, 72–73, 83, 113, 115; sex licit
only within, 7–9, 33–34, 39, 40,
44, 124–25, 132, 200, 300; sexual
access of husbands to wives within,
196–97; sexual duties of husbands
within, 59–60, 69; in the South,
access to, 121, 122–25, 128–30, 133,
148; William Byrd and sex within,
190–91, 196–97, 269–70. *See also*
civil marriage; informal marriage;
Jesus Christ; serial monogamy
marriage manuals, 58–60, 267–68

Marsh, wife of Hugh, 92
Martin, Elizabeth, 23
Martin, Josiah, 137, 141
Martin, Robert, 127
Mary (Native American), 167
Mary ("negro woman"), 383n31
masters and mistresses: sexual coercion by, 45–49, 123–24, 193, 199,
200–1, 204, 213–15, 218, 223, 289,
351n17; sexual regulation by, 29–
30, 32, 96–97, 124–25, 299–300,
314–16, 327. *See also* slaveowners
masturbation, 11, 25, 64, 66, 68–70,
83, 88, 106, 110, 113, 381n21
Mather, Cotton, 61, 62, 63, 67, 68,
69–70, 71, 73, 74, 76, 78–79,
81, 88, 89, 98–99, 164, 169, 227,
346n38, 401n23
Mather, Increase, 32–33, 71, 83, 169,
345n22
Mathew, Walter, 367n10
Matticks, Richard, 30
Mattock, James, 59
Maule, Robert, 179
Maynard, Zechariah, 37
maypoles, 2, 23
McAllen, Mary, 316–17
McCormick, Mary, 328
McCue, Con, 333
McCullock, Mary, 328
Melville, David, 351n17
Melyen, Cornelis, 92
Melyen, Isaac, 30
Melyen, Jacob, 32, 35–36, 92
Melyen, Mariah, 32, 92–93
Mendame, Mary, 167
Merry Mount, 164–65
Mery, Moreau de St., 301, 303, 322
Metacomet's War, 110, 168–69
Methodists, 147, 149–50, 338. *See also*
dissent
Michell, Edward, 109, 365n61
Michelson, Thomas, 112
Middleton, Elizabeth and William, 100
midwives, 232–33, 239, 257. *See also*
gynecological manuals
Mifflin, Thomas, 303
Mighill, John, 38